W9-BVQ-262

International Acclaim for Donald Spoto's

THE DECLINE AND FALL OF THE HOUSE OF WINDSOR

"Donald Spoto has found the perfect tone. He's gentle, forgiving, and delightful. He surveys the matter of the monarchy all over again, with charity and loving attention to wacky detail. Everything is set forth in such a charming fashion—and in some funny way it tells us about ourselves."

—*The Washington Post*

"What a pleasant surprise *THE DECLINE AND FALL OF THE HOUSE OF WINDSOR* is! Here we have a thoroughly literate history of the British royal family from Queen Victoria to the present. This is probably the best book on the subject to date. Spoto writes unhysterically, in a detached yet affectionate vein, and he gives us no unnecessary, salacious scandal."

—*The Literary Review* (London)

"Donald Spoto avoids sensationalism and offers new insights into a family's turbulent history."

—*Today* (UK)

"A fast-paced, completely absorbing account of the lives behind an institution that looks curiouser and curiouser with each passing year."

—*The Boston Sunday Globe*

"In Spoto's extremely readable look at the British royal family, the author has clearly done his research. This is a fascinating read, sure to be talked about—and will undoubtedly be requested!"

—*Library Journal*

"Spoto shows his usual astute judgment in this marvelously incisive book. He views the monarchy piece by piece as a melodrama of celebrity. He does not attempt to scandalize, nor does he roll out the red carpet. He chronicles the fading glory of a once-revered empire, and foremost among his tools of interpretation is his devastatingly sharp wit. He brings to life the dusty leaves of English history."

—*Newsday* (New York)

"Memorable portraits abound. *THE DECLINE AND FALL OF THE HOUSE OF WINDSOR* is a book that's bound to be popular."

—*Booklist*

"This sweeping biography—Donald Spoto's persuasive and entertaining new book—shows how the monarchy controlled its image from Victoria to Elizabeth."

—*People*

"A gracefully fleshed-out timeline of the Windsor family history, packed with just as much information about famous royal nannies as about who was sleeping with whom. . . . Calmly and without sensationalism, Spoto puts their affairs, both sexual and otherwise, in chronological order. . . ."

—*Kirkus Reviews*

"A feast for royal watchers."

—*Manchester News* (UK)

"Di and Chuck, Fergie [and Andrew], are only the last in a long line of marital miscreants in the royal family. . . . Even the current Queen Mother isn't the saint we think she is. Don't ask. Just read."

—*Daily News* (New York)

Books by Donald Spoto

A Passion for Life: The Biography of Elizabeth Taylor
Marilyn Monroe: The Biography
Blue Angel: The Life of Marlene Dietrich
Laurence Olivier: A Biography
Madcap: The Life of Preston Sturges
Lenya: A Life
The Kindness of Strangers: The Life of Tennessee Williams
Falling in Love Again: Marlene Dietrich (photo essay)
The Dark Side of Genius: The Life of Alfred Hitchcock
Stanley Kramer Film Maker
Camerado: Hollywood and the American Man
The Art of Alfred Hitchcock
The Decline and Fall of the House of Windsor

For orders other than by individual consumers, Pocket Books grants a discount on the purchase of **10 or more** copies of single titles for special markets or premium use. For further details, please write to the Vice-President of Special Markets, Pocket Books, 1230 Avenue of the Americas, New York, NY 10020.

For information on how individual consumers can place orders, please write to Mail Order Department, Paramount Publishing, 200 Old Tappan Road, Old Tappan, NJ 07675.

THE DECLINE AND FALL OF THE
HOUSE OF WINDSOR

DONALD SPOTO

POCKET BOOKS

New York London Toronto Sydney Tokyo Singapore

The sale of this book without its cover is unauthorized. If you purchased
this book without a cover, you should be aware that it was reported to
the publisher as "unsold and destroyed." Neither the author nor the
publisher has received payment for the sale of this "stripped book."

 POCKET BOOKS, a division of Simon & Schuster Inc.
1230 Avenue of the Americas, New York, NY 10020

Copyright © 1995 by Donald Spoto

All rights reserved, including the right to reproduce
this book or portions thereof in any form whatsoever.
For information address Simon & Schuster Inc.,
1230 Avenue of the Americas, New York, NY 10020

ISBN: 0-671-00230-9

First Pocket Books printing September 1996

10   9   8   7   6   5   4

POCKET and colophon are registered trademarks of
Simon & Schuster Inc.

Picture research by Natalie Goldstein

Cover photo courtesy of Globe Photos

Printed in the U.S.A.

Acknowledgments

During three years of research and writing, I was blessed with the generosity, kindness and cooperation of many people.

The staffs at the following libraries were unfailingly helpful, and I salute them and the public and private institutions that support them: the London Library; the British Library; the British Library Newspaper Division at Colindale; the Library at the University of Reading (England); the Research Libraries at the University of California at Los Angeles; and the Beverly Hills Public Library.

At the Imperial War Museum, London, Alan Williams was singularly helpful to me and to my London research assistant, Erica Wagner.

At Buckingham Palace, St. James's Palace and Clarence House, I must thank the following gentlemen for their various courtesies: Commander Richard Aylard, R.N., Private Secretary to HRH The Prince of Wales; Brigadier Miles Hunt-Davis, for HRH The Duke of Edinburgh; Kenneth Scott, Press Officer for Her Majesty The Queen; and the late Sir Martin Gilliat, Private Secretary to Her Majesty Queen Elizabeth The Queen Mother.

When I set to work, I consulted at once my good friend and colleague, the author Robert Lacey, who has published (among other important books) several volumes on members of the Royal Family. He very kindly directed me to people and places I might otherwise have ignored.

Especially relevant interviews were of course crucial, and I am indebted to the following for their patience, insights, helpfulness and guidance. As is clear from the text, each has a unique connection to the story; each, too, has a claim on my admiration as much as my gratitude: Cleveland Amory, Michael Bloch, Sarah Bradford, Lady Colin Campbell, David Emanuel, Elizabeth Emanuel, Angela Fox, John Grigg, Nicholas Haslam, Kenneth Rose and Philip Ziegler.

At Hulton Deutsch, Sandra Greatorex worked tirelessly to help locate important photographs, as did Ian Blackwell at Popperfoto.

At Simon & Schuster, New York, Michael Korda—a friend for many years—came to me with the idea for this book, and I am deeply thankful for his guidance, encouragement and constancy (not to say innumerable lunches and dinners) along the journey to publication. His colleague Chuck Adams has been equivalently involved in the life of the book, and so at every stage I was fortunate to have their attention, insights and camaraderie. Maggie Lichota applied the line editor's special skills; her keen eye and judicious comments much improved the text. No writer anywhere can have more reason to be glad and grateful for his editorial team. Also at Simon & Schuster, I must thank Rebecca Head and Cheryl Weinstein for their help in dispatching important daily details.

In the London offices of Simon & Schuster, Nick Webb and Carol O'Brien first believed in the book and engaged its author; later, Helen Gummer came aboard and guided the British publication to term. Her courtesy—as well as her editorial contributions—were always on the mark.

I am equally appreciative for the enthusiastic and friendly support of my French publisher, Renaud Bombard, at Presses de la Cité, Paris. Likewise in Munich, Hans-Peter Übleis at Wilhelm Heyne Verlag has always been the most cordial and careful presenter of my work to readers in Germany.

My literary representatives in Great Britain, Abner Stein and Octavia Wiseman, were supportive from day one; they are prudent, calm and thoughtful people, and they were always a steadying influence on me and the project.

Closer to home are the offices of the Elaine Markson Literary Agency, for seventeen years my secure base in more ways than I can count. It is difficult to find a new way to honor in words my dear friend Elaine: her vigilance on behalf of me and my career, her faith and abiding affection are valued beyond telling. I offer a simple, loving thank-you, hoping that she knows the depth of my gratitude. And Elaine's associates —Tasha Blaine, Sara DeNobrega, Elizabeth Stevens, Geri Thoma and Sally Wofford-Girand—are always there for me, quick to offer warm encouragement, minute attention to detail and endless patience. What a life-support system for a writer!

Just so, I am fortunate in the daily collaboration of my research assistant Greg Dietrich, who somehow manages to balance everything.

From the start ("O lucky man!"), I was fortunate in having the partnership of Erica Wagner, my London research assistant and "in-house editor." She traversed London, virtually lived in libraries and archives, tracked down obscure documents and photographs, read constantly, drafted précis, pointed out serious matters for consideration—and to all of these she added the crowning benefit of her friendship. It is no exaggeration to say that without Erica's lively intelligence, sharp perceptions and alacrity, this book simply would not exist. Everything good in it owes something to her sharpness and enterprise.

For the enduring support of their friendship, I wish also to record my thanks to John Darretta, Lewis Falb, Ed Finegan, Fred McCashland, Irene Mahoney, Gerald Pinciss, Charles Rappleye, Kirtley Thiesmeyer and Graham Waring, M.D. Life would be much the poorer without them.

On the dedication page appear the names of Mary and Laurence Evans. When I first met them six years ago, I had just begun work on a biography of their great friend Laurence Olivier. The concrete help and daily guidance they offered me were invaluable, and their presence and benevolent influence —to Olivier and to me—can be seen and appreciated throughout that book. From that day to this, my life has been enriched by the warmth of their counsel, their humor, their empathy and unfailing good cheer. Never mind what the history books or tourist brochures tell you: it is Laurie and Mary Evans who are the best that England has to offer. They are my generous and true friends, and so it is to them, with very grateful devotion, that this book is dedicated.

D.S.
26 March 1995

for Mary and Laurence Evans,
with affection deep and true

Contents

Contents

Kings are like stars—they rise and set, they have
The worship of the world, but no repose.

SHELLEY, *Hellas*

When people no longer venerate the monarchy,
they will see us as their equals—and then the
illusion is over.

LOUIS XIV

No monarchy should expect to be free from
scrutiny.

QUEEN ELIZABETH II

Clockwise from top: Charles and Diana, Prince and Princess of Wales; Andrew and Sarah, Duke and Duchess of York; Prince Edward.

Preface
The Royals and Other Stars
1994 to 1995

A family on the throne is an interesting idea.
WALTER BAGEHOT, *The English Constitution* (1867)

On a mild November night in 1994, a thousand celebrities, fans and media hawks crowded outside a theater in Century City, that upscale parcel of Los Angeles real estate that was once the back lot of Twentieth Century-Fox, one of Hollywood's legendary dream factories. The occasion was the world premiere of a film, *Mary Shelley's Frankenstein*.

Jack Nicholson showed his engraved invitation and slipped into the theater foyer. As usual, his trademark broad smile was somehow both amiable and threatening, his dark glasses a defense against the blaze of flashbulbs and klieg lights. He was then whisked through a security cordon to meet the real star of the evening—an Englishman who had nothing to do with *Frankenstein* but who had a very significant role offscreen, in the world's longest-running soap opera. Jack shook the guest's hand and offered him a hearty welcome to California.

"I love a good horror movie," replied the man, who was the heir to the British throne—His Royal Highness The Prince Charles Philip Arthur George, Knight of the Garter, Knight of the Thistle, Knight Grand Cross Order of the Bath, Privy Councillor, Prince of Wales, Earl of Chester, Duke of Cornwall, Duke of Rothesay, Earl of Carrick, Baron of Renfrew, Lord of the Isles, and Great Steward of Scotland. According to custom, he was usually referred to simply as Prince Charles or the Prince of Wales.

Jack said yeah, he loved a good horror movie, too, and that he had appeared in a few. Then the two men slowly made their way into the theater, guided by police and bodyguards past the crush of celebrity watchers, photographers and television reporters with microphones and videotape.

Earlier, Prince Charles had sipped tea with the princess of pop, Barbra Streisand. He told her that he was her greatest fan. She replied that it was nice of him to say that. They were very happy chatting together, these two megastars who so admired each other.

One evening while the Prince was in Los Angeles, his estranged wife Diana, Her Royal Highness The Princess of Wales, dined at a country house in Berkshire, England. Elton John was the host, and among the others present were Sylvester Stallone, Richard Gere and George Michael. "Sly and Gere had Diana in fits of giggles," according to another guest. "She clearly loved every minute of it."

Two weeks after his return from Los Angeles in late November, Charles attended a charity benefit in London. Shirley Bassey sang "I Want to Know What Love Is" and tossed the Prince a red rose. He kissed it and stuck it in his buttonhole, and the crowd went wild. A few days after that, Charles showed his own way of identifying with critical issues. He toured a market in rural Surrey, met Marvin the Banana King, listened to John the Singing Fishmonger, pulled a pint of Young's at Ye Dog & Bull, and sampled eels at the seafood stall. This is much easier than playing polo, which, at forty-seven, he has had to abandon after several painful falls from his horse.

Like recent forebears who were Princes of Wales before succeeding to the throne (his great-uncle King Edward VIII, his great-grandfather King George V, and his great-great-grandfather King Edward VII), Charles's sole occupation in life is marking time until the death of his parent, the Sovereign—a situation fraught with all sorts of dark psychological baggage. He is prevented by custom and constitution from direct political action or statement, so he has little to do other than cultivate harmless hobbies, utter banalities, and conduct more or less clandestine love affairs.

Sadly, this idleness was inevitable, for the Queen, in an excess of zeal for her own duty, has treated him just the way Queen Victoria treated her eldest son, who became by default a playboy Prince. By disallowing them any practical on-the-job training for the future and forbidding them the dignity of a regular career, both mothers condemned their sons to polite uselessness. The result was identical in both cases: the Princes aged but did not mature. "I don't mind praying to the Eternal Father," said Victoria's son (later the King) at the time of her Diamond Jubilee in 1897. "But I must be the only man in the country afflicted with an eternal mother."

Charles might have thought similarly. Denied anything like professional responsibilities, he became a rather forlorn, isolated wanderer through life, playing polo, tugging at his sleeves and necktie, and—like many men in such circumstances—turning from a loveless marriage and an idle life to the reliable comfort of his married mistress. "Women adore him," said Lord Charteris, a close friend of the Queen and one of her secretaries for twenty-five years. "Charles is such a charming man—when he isn't being whiny."

The whining, as it happened, was astonishingly public. On June 29, 1994, he said during a television interview that he had been unfaithful to his wife because his marriage had "irretrievably broken down.'' He wanted the world to know about his miserable past and confused present. Of his job, Charles had said in 1983, ''All the time, I feel I must justify my existence'' —to which one might reply, ''Well, then, get another job.'' His deepest feelings had not changed over the years, but whereas once he had shared them only with his one true love, Camilla Parker Bowles, now—what the hell—he told the world.

And so a very long biography of the Prince was published late in 1994, authorized by him and full of lengthy excerpts from his letters and diaries that he doubtless intended to justify his existence and improve his popularity rating. Charles poured out the story of his lonely childhood under remote and detached parents, and a marriage that was wretchedly unhappy from day one. He had never loved his wife and now he said so, humiliating both her as well as their unfortunate children, Prince William and Prince Harry: ''How *could* I have got it all so wrong?'' he asked plaintively. Easy if you know how, his ancestors might have said across the frontiers of time and history.

And then, as if on cue, it was announced that Mr. and Mrs. Parker Bowles were divorcing, an action for which the people of Britain ''will and do hold [Charles] responsible,'' said no less a person than the venerable Harold Brooks-Baker, director of *Burke's Peerage;* and this single action alone ''hurts the chances of the monarchy continuing.'' Now at last, the newly unpredictable Prince of Wales was in a position to hop off with his mistress or to renounce his inheritance and birthright or to do God only knows what. ''My dear firstborn is the greatest ass in the whole world,'' said Queen Caroline, wife of King George II, about her son, the Prince of Wales. ''I heartily wish he was out of it.'' Such may have been the sentiment of Elizabeth II in early 1995.

''Of course [Camilla] is the love of [Charles's] life,'' continued Lord Charteris calmly, and the Prince's divorce from Diana ''will clear the air. It will happen sooner rather than later.'' So, apparently, will the divorce of Prince (''Randy Andy'') Andrew, the Duke of York, one of Charles's younger brothers, whose marriage to the lusty Sarah Ferguson collapsed in scandal. (''Quite simply,'' said Lord Charteris, ''the Duchess of York is a vulgarian. She is vulgar, vulgar, vulgar, and that is that.'' Indeed.)

Would Charles's and Camilla's divorces mean their eventual marriage? Committed to the Church's traditional prohibition against divorce and remarriage, would the Archbishop of Canterbury approve? Would he eventually lower the crown onto the head of such a king—and a moment later, on the head of Camilla Shand Parker Bowles Windsor? The same week as the Parker Bowleses' divorce was announced, the Church of England's House of Bishops discussed the thorny matter of divorce and remarriage. Was it not time for a change in the traditional proscription? Did not marriages indeed collapse—had they not in fact dissolved even before third parties so determined?

In this regard, something had to be said for Edward VIII, who in 1936 put his own desires before his inherited kingship and abdicated before his coronation in order to marry the American divorcée Wallis Simpson. The swiftness of his decision (however complex the motivation) at least averted a constitutional crisis. The present Prince of Wales, however, seems content to temporize.

News of the Prince and Princess of Wales and their intimates was no different from tabloid stories about Mick and Bianca Jagger (or Mick and Jerry Hall), or about Richard Gere and Cindy Crawford, or Lyle Lovett and Julia Roberts—all of them stars of another kind besieged by publicity.

Diana had her own nervy moments at the end of 1994 when a man named James Hewitt claimed to have been her lover. A captain in a regiment of the Queen's Household Division, he had mostly equestrian duties, and for five years (from 1986 to 1991) Hewitt and the Princess of Wales cavorted like characters out of a D. H. Lawrence novel. An account of their affair, published with his cooperation, evoked disapproval, but no denial from Diana or Buckingham Palace. ''I don't see how this can go on,'' said one of the Queen's Privy Councillors, referring to Hewitt, Parker Bowles and company. ''It is making the Royal Family a worldwide laughingstock.''

That same night, Diana was dazzling Paris. Wearing a shimmering, barebacked and sequined gown with a thigh-high slit, the world's favorite cover girl had the international press jostling for photos. The dinner afterward was held, with ironic aptness, in the Hall of Battles. "She draws interest wherever she goes, whatever she does," said the hostess, Anne Giscard d'Estaing, France's former first lady.

Diana is apparently a woman of good will, but her life has lacked focus, and when she is not attending a charity benefit, she gives the impression of being a woman alarmingly adrift and purposeless. She visits her personal astrologer, goes to her gym, drives to her masseur, summons her acupuncturist, submits to her hypnotherapist, calls her aromatherapist. She fondles crystals and pores over zodiacal charts. She has her hair done each day, then she buys clothes. In her sitting room is an embroidered cushion: "If You Think Money Can't Buy Love, You Don't Know Where to Shop." But she is also, by every account, a devoted mother. She takes her children on ski holidays and to Walt Disney World (but only after obtaining the required permission of the Queen). There, she pleads with the press to leave her alone. But then she returns to London and poses, for example, for the July 1994 cover of *Vogue,* for which she engaged Patrick Demarchelier, one of the top fashion photographers. Thus the Princess of Wales simultaneously maintains a high profile and reaches out to a public she needs and courts.

The Prince and Princess of Wales invariably eclipse every other person present wherever they go. Everyone wants to see them, to be near them, to touch them, to shake their hands. Charles and Diana are the most constantly public and visible members of the Windsor dynasty, England's Royal Family, headed by the world's last powerful monarch. And the rituals and privileges attending royal status reach back over a thousand years.

Like the other members of the family, the Prince and Princess, both publicly and privately, play glamorous roles in an extraordinary pageant, and their lives have all the trappings of players in an ongoing drama. They bear ancient titles, and people treat them with almost idolatrous reverence. Their schedules are meticulously controlled by a platoon of public relations directors. Often they have to wear funny costumes and hats, and their wardrobes are carefully prepared, then scrutinized and described by the press for the waiting public. Every journey is documented, every step—around the corner or across the world—followed and photographed, just in case they make a false move to delight the media and thrill the public. The Royals are the century's most photographed stars, the ultimate celebrities. They are part of an unending fable, their deeds and misdeeds sometimes melodramatic, occasionally ridiculous, often pathetic.

The current cast of characters is led by Charles's mother, Her Majesty Queen Elizabeth II. She is the great-great-granddaughter of Queen Victoria.

In the early months of 1995, the Queen was in her counting house with financial advisors and lawyers, preparing a public statement explaining how she spends £20 million of taxpayers' money annually for expenses at three palaces (Buckingham, Kensington and St. James's) and other royal residences (Windsor and Balmoral castles and Sandringham House). This is especially troublesome to many beleaguered, unemployed British citizens precisely because the Queen's personal fortune is estimated at something over £6 billion ($9 billion), which produces about £2 million a day in interest.

Her Majesty's schedule includes such tasks as christening ships, visiting hospitals, conferring awards, opening Parliament sessions, and smiling and waving a lot at strangers. This she has done with admirable skill and patience for over forty years. The Queen's largely ceremonial duties have led many people to believe she has no power at all, that she is simply a figurehead. In fact, she is much more than that, and the notion that she is powerless has become a very convenient and potent myth that helps to sustain her considerable influence.

To be sure, the British constitution has guaranteed that the Sovereign has no direct *political* power. But her authority is formidable. She has, for example, the right to demand consultation with any and all of the government's ministers and to advise and caution them as she desires. She has the right to invite any Member of Parliament to form a government, and to convene and dissolve Parliament itself. In certain circumstances, she can invoke the royal prerogative and declare a state of emergency. She can also mobilize a militia or command existing armed forces since all serving members swear allegiance to the Queen personally, not to the country.

But there is much more to her power, and it is of a kind that is exercised merely by the fact of her birthright. Elizabeth Alexandra Mary Windsor *is* Her Majesty. It is the kind of power that derives from social influence. Her position at the apex of society underscores and endorses the aristocracy and perpetuates class distinctions in Great Britain. The Queen is, therefore, the living embodiment of a system that is fundamentally undemocratic. In light of this monarchic tradition, the nation continues to have inherited, unmerited prerogatives and privileges, all of them extended to her and her family simply because they sprouted from a certain genetic tree. This is further reflected in the inheritance of certain titles, dukedoms, baronetcies and peerages that include seats in Parliament.

More to the point, the Queen's continued usefulness to the nation is now seriously questioned. She is wonderful for the tourist trade, and on state occasions she treats the public to a good show. But life returns to normal very swiftly indeed. In January 1995 a massive poll of the English people revealed that a majority believed the monarchy was doomed, that it would not survive the death of Elizabeth II.

Trained for her job since the age of ten, when her father was pitchforked unwillingly onto the throne and her eventual succession seemed inevitable, she has become fixed in a role that she otherwise would not have chosen. "I wish I could be more like you, but unfortunately my life is such that I can't," she once said to the wife of an aide, and she has often said that given her choice she would have been very happy as a simple country gentlewoman, living with her horses and dogs. Some of her most critical and republican citizens would encourage her to just such a life today. Of her personal probity, her devotion to duty and her sense of honor there is no doubt, but one can say the same of many people who serve in other public and private institutions.

The Queen turned sixty-nine on April 21, 1995, and she has been married for forty-eight years to a man five years her senior. Prince Philip bears the title Duke of Edinburgh, but there is nothing Scottish about him. He is the son of a Danish-German prince who, by a fluke of international political expediency, became a Greek Royal. Through his mother, Philip is a great-great-grandson of Queen Victoria—and his wife's distant cousin.

He has had to walk four paces behind her since the day she became Queen in 1952 at the age of twenty-five. At his wife's coronation, Philip had to vow lifelong submission to her as his sovereign, and this (among other things) helped turn him gradually into a scratchy old curmudgeon who, according to his son Charles, has been an unloving bully to his children. Since then, their homes have always been Elizabeth's homes, their family her family, and their dynastic house bears her name, that of Windsor—despite Philip's fierce attempts to have it called Mountbatten, the anglicized form of his own German name, Battenberg. Unlike Queen Victoria and her beloved husband Prince Albert, Elizabeth never made her husband her official consort. "I'm a bloody amoeba, that's all!" he once bellowed—a man with neither shape nor form to his life. But not, it has been rumored for years, a man without significance for his many mistresses.

What ought to be emphasized in any assessment of a royal person or family is the drift and meaning of their activities outside the bedroom, their concern for others, their integrity—their inner lives, in other words, and the force of moral suasion (not merely sexual persuasion) that invariably accompanies the prestige of being a Royal Highness. What, in other words, is the *meaning* of a dynasty—first for the Royals themselves and then for those they are called to serve? At its most basic, is not honor to be earned?

Adultery ought not to be the critical issue in considering the value of Prince Charles and his family; dalliances and intrigues, after all, are the diversion of very many people other than Princes of Wales, and they are an area of human experience much glamorized by movies and television.

But seriousness of purpose in life *does* matter, as does sensitivity to the feelings of Diana and their two young Princes—not to say simple decency. To a man who told the Prince that he had once met Diana, Charles replied in public, "You lived to tell the tale, did you?" Meantime, his sons' schoolmates were taunting the two young Princes about their mother's boyfriend. Indeed, it seemed the Princess of Wales had one. Her husband was not the first Prince of Wales to stray, but Diana was the first Princess to complain about it and to assert herself similarly.

Even before her husband went public, Diana told people how disconsolate she was, how trapped she felt in her married life with Charles: "He makes my life real, real torture," she said to an intimate in December 1989. "Bloody hell, after all I've done for this fucking family!" Then, to the horror of her in-laws, she went further, taking her plight before the people by cooperating (however indirectly) with a writer who had access to a few of her friends. Thus in 1992 an astonishingly frank account of her troubles was published worldwide, full of details about anorexia, bulimia and crude suicide attempts. What a sad person am I, the book said—how badly treated, how abused, how lonely.

And so the story has taken a dark turn: the Princess seems locked in an ivory tower, emotionally isolated by the palace guards. There is, however, a problem. As mother of the heir presumptive, she has to be treated—managed, even—very carefully indeed. The intrigue is worthy of the twelfth-century court of Henry II and his estranged wife, Eleanor of Aquitaine, with all the attendant plots and schemes, stratagems and wiles, whispering campaigns and vendettas. The family's ups and downs appeared to be extracts from a series of banal confessions—but of the sort heard on television shows.

In January 1995, for the first time in British history, almost forty percent of British citizens said that Prince Charles ought never to be King, that the monarchy ought to be abolished, and that the monarchy must be replaced by a democratically elected head of state. This cry for a British republic was the loudest heard since the seventeenth, eighteenth and nineteenth centuries.

No one today is calling for the scaffold, but some members of Parliament, the press and the public at large are suggesting that the Royal Family ought simply to be shipped out to the countryside, there to tend their beloved horses and dogs; to fish for salmon; and to conduct their love affairs to their hearts' content. More British citizens than ever—fully seventy percent, according to one survey—said yes, the monarchy itself was outdated, outmoded and utterly useless unless you considered the financial value of tourism, of ceremony, flag-waving and all that.

"The nation has turned as never before on the Prince of Wales," ran a typical news story, "blaming him for a series of catastrophic blunders that could bring about the fall of the House of Windsor within the next century."

"A family on the throne is an interesting idea," wrote the nineteenth-century political theorist Walter Bagehot. "A royal family sweetens politics by the seasonable addition of nice and pretty events." Such a family, Bagehot continued, attracts the attention of the world because it reflects "the level of petty life."

Little did he know just how petty the royal lives could become, and how less nice and pretty the events. The players became not merely eccentric and expensive to support but downright irrelevant, even (according to some in the British government) a threat to the survival of Great Britain itself. The only way to help the Windsors get over their past would be to guarantee that they had neither power nor influence in the future.

As these words of introduction are written, new rumors abound and will doubtless pass from idle chatter into newly minted truths. According to these stories, the Queen's second son, Prince Andrew, is not really Prince Philip's son but Elizabeth's secret "love child" by her great friend and horse manager Lord Porchester. Equally fresh "news" is the tale that Prince Edward is the Queen's son by her favorite servant and cherished confidant, the late Patrick Plunket. As such stories are concocted and circulated, what will weigh in as fiction and what as fact?

In the final analysis, nothing has to be fabricated when the truth is far more dramatic, as it has been for two centuries. Tabloids need not destroy reputations when the facts of history shed clear light on these ordinary people with an extraordinary family history—a saga that repeats itself in astonishing patterns.

This book is an attempt to examine the hazards of sovereignty in our time, the dangers of idolatry, the ubiquity of moral hypocrisy, and the inexorable march of the media. It is an attempt to chronicle a dynasty, its antecedents and its founding, its rise and its decline as it bears the mantle of celebrity, which is far heavier than monarchic responsibility. It is the story of a family that has become the world's greatest media stars.

King George III, Queen Charlotte and six of their children.

Introduction

The Family Tree 1670 to 1837

I am nearer to the throne than I thought!
PRINCESS (later Queen) VICTORIA, at age eleven

"I beg you to open your dear heart. Hide nothing, but tell me even the least thing that gives you any hard thoughts of me, that I may justify myself, which I am sure I can do, never having done anything willingly to deserve your displeasure."

So wrote Queen Anne to her close friend Sarah, Duchess of Marlborough.

The two women had met in 1670 when Anne was an awkward, coarse five-year-old Princess and Sarah a remarkably lovely and poised ten-year-old. For years their intimacy flourished, and by 1702, when she came to the throne, Anne was so enamored of her powerful, beautiful companion that she made no large or small decision without Sarah's counsel. Even Anne's marriage, necessitated by dynastic considerations, had to be approved by Sarah. To signify the equality of their intimacy, the Queen devised pet names. She was ''Mrs. Morley,'' Sarah ''Mrs. Freeman,'' and some historians have concluded that they were a pair of passionate lovers. The two husbands, meanwhile, were busy reaping the fruits of Sarah's political manipulation of the Queen.

In her thirties, Anne endured wretched health, and despite many pregnancies, she remained childless. To ensure that the English crown would never rest on a Roman Catholic head—for if she died without an heir there were papist claimants lurking everywhere—the Act of Settlement was passed in 1701. This guaranteed that the royal succession would henceforth pass only to Protestant relations.

When Anne died at forty-nine in 1714, there was a flurry of confusion before the surprising news was spread. The new King of England was a distant relation but the only Protestant available: a fifty-four-year-old German Prince named George Louis of Hanover, the great-grandson of King James I. George found himself in the curious position of being called to the throne of a people whose language he did not know and to whose culture he was completely indifferent. With George, German stock came to the monarchy, where it has remained ever since, disproving any royalist's claim of pure English blood on the English throne.

King George I was resented by the British for his reliance on his old Hanoverian cronies, for his many rapacious mistresses, and for his appalling treatment of his estranged wife. But there was an advantage to his dreadful conduct, for he unwittingly spurred the growth of a constitutional monarchy. In addition, because George spoke no English and could not preside at Cabinet meetings, he had to depend on the canny Robert Walpole, First Lord of the Treasury. Walpole was so effective at his job that he became the first to hold the title of Prime Minister.

George's son, styled George II (and also born in Hanover), succeeded on his father's death in 1727, and three years later Sarah, Duchess of Marlborough, again stepped into the royal picture. Her favorite granddaughter was a lithe and lovely blonde named Lady Diana Spencer, whom Sarah believed would make a perfect bride for the King's son Frederick, the Prince of Wales (the traditional title bestowed on the monarch's eldest son). But for political reasons Walpole scotched the idea. Lady Diana Spencer subsequently married the Duke of Bedford and died of tuberculosis at twenty-six.

With this untimely death, Sarah was almost crazed with grief, but her strength saw her through the ordeal and she remained the most powerful woman in London. From Marlborough House, her London residence, she dominated social life in general and the Spencer family in particular, just as she had controlled Queen Anne. Sarah's great regret when she died in 1744 was that she had failed to form an alliance between the throne and her family. Only much later was Sarah's wish at last realized. In 1981 her descendant, another Lady Diana Spencer, married another Prince of Wales: Charles, eldest son of Queen Elizabeth II and heir to the throne.

King George II was much aided by his formidably intelligent wife, Caroline, who turned a tolerant eye to his rampant infidelity. Literate and artistic, she was also politically astute, recognizing Walpole's brilliance and preventing his dismissal by her less able husband. The period saw major manufacturing and agricultural advances heralding the great revolutions of the nineteenth century, and by the time of George II's death Britain had the world's greatest navy. Thus began the enterprise of worldwide colonization and economic domination.

As it happened, the Prince of Wales who might have married Lady Diana passed away before his father the King died, and so George II was succeeded by his grandson, who was known as King George III. The first Hanoverian monarch to be born and raised in England, he reigned from 1760 to 1820. "Farmer George," as he was affectionately termed by the English, was a careful constitutional monarch, deeply religious and faithful to his wife, Queen Charlotte. George married her six hours after their first meeting and kept her busy as the mother of fifteen children. But from 1811 his sanity was so frail that his son was created Prince Regent, acting in his father's stead for the balance of George III's life. Papa seems to have suffered from the rare neurological ailment known as porphyria, which causes delirium and delusions. Some later scholars read his illness as the effects of lead poisoning while others accepted the view of that time, that the King was quite simply insane.

Whatever the cause, George III took a historic and decisive step to suppress certain stories then rampant in the press—that he was indeed demented. In 1806 he appointed a man named Joseph Doan as Court Newsman. His task was to visit the King when commanded and, after a thorough briefing, to circulate edifying accounts of the monarch's health among the London newspapers. To Doan and his descendants would fall, for the next century, the unenviable task of exerting what would later be called "damage control." In this case the task was singularly challenging, for the monarch became ever more ill.

Farmer George's son finally succeeded as George IV and reigned for a decade, from 1820 until 1830. He had secretly married a young Catholic in 1785, but because the 1701 Act of Settlement prevented the monarch's marriage to a papist, this illegal union was annulled. To pay off his debts, George was forced to marry a rich but despised cousin whom he barred from his coronation; to his great relief she died a few weeks later. The King went on his merry way, taking his pleasure with a legion of mistresses.

George IV took little interest in government, and so Parliament went its own way, too, enacting significant reforms that reinforced criminal law, advanced trade and widened religious tolerance. His lazy, mendacious, intemperate and often decadent conduct alienated many, although some found him harmless and genial. Liver disease ended his life at the age of sixty-seven.

George's only child died at birth, and so the crown passed to his brother, who reigned as William IV from 1830 to 1837. Although he could be earnest, "Silly Billy" mostly comported himself like a sailor on shore leave. He was the father of ten illegitimate children by his mistress, the actress Dorothea Jordan. Then, two years after her death, he married the German Princess Adelaide of Saxe-Meiningen.

Although William's personality was not much more interesting than that of his Hanoverian forebears, his short reign was marked by major changes. He reluctantly helped to push through the 1832 Reform Bill, which extended the vote to more than half a million citizens, reassigned parliamentary seats on a fairer basis, and greatly shifted even more power from the Crown and the aristocracy to the industrialized citizenry.

With no legitimate heir at the time of his death, the crown

passed to one who seemed just as unremarkable and without promise: William's eighteen-year-old niece, Alexandrina Victoria. Just weeks before her eleventh birthday she had seen a chart of the family tree. "I am nearer to the throne than I thought," she remarked to her German governess, and then, pointing to her place in the royal line, she added solemnly, "I will be good." And so she would—but not immediately.

THE DECLINE AND FALL OF THE

HOUSE OF
WINDSOR

Queen Victoria, Prince Albert and five of their children.

1

One Big Happy Family 1837 to 1861

I will show them that I am Queen of England!
QUEEN VICTORIA

Alexandrina Victoria never used her first name in childhood, and as Queen the omission became official. Born in Kensington Palace, London, on May 24, 1819, she was eight months old when her father, Edward, Duke of Kent, fell ill with a heavy cold that turned to pneumonia. After twelve days under the care of his doctors, who applied the popular remedy of incisions, leeches and cupping, the fifty-two-year-old Duke bled to death on January 23, 1820. "English physicians kill you," grumbled Lord Melbourne, Victoria's first Prime Minister, years later. "The French let you die." The Duke's death was followed six days later by that of his father, King George III, and so Victoria was yet closer to the throne.

The child's tutelage was managed by four people: her

mother, the German-born Duchess of Kent, who for years spoke no English; her uncle, Prince Leopold of Belgium; Captain Sir John Conroy, her father's equerry (or royal attendant) and later her mother's lover; and a tutor, Baroness Lehzen. Three of these four were Germans who had not much concern for British history or constitutional theory. "Up to my 5th year," Victoria later recalled, "I had been very much indulged by everyone . . . *all* worshipped the poor little fatherless child." Her only connection to other youngsters was her half-sister Feodora (one of her mother's two children by a former marriage); she married when Victoria was nine and went off to Germany. From then on, the child was left quite solitary in a world of adults.

Life at Kensington Palace was duly quiet, ordered and deferential, with that peculiar combination of English gentility, Hanoverian briskness and Coburg blandness. Trained to be regally courteous, young Victoria nevertheless insisted on her preferences. She had an intense dislike of bishops, for example, and tried to avoid their company ("on account of their wigs and *aprons*")—an aversion that endured to the end of her life. Nor would she suffer scolding easily. "When you are naughty you make me and yourself very unhappy," said her mother. "No, Mama," replied the child, "not *me,* not myself, but *you!*" When a tutor arrived and asked Mama if the child had behaved, the cautious response was, "Yes, she has been good this morning, but yesterday there was a little storm." Victoria sprang to correct her mother: "Two storms—one at dressing and one at washing." Admonished by her music teacher— "There is no royal road to music, Princess. You must practice like everybody else"—the student slammed her piano shut. "There! You see, there is no *must* about it." All that remained, her household may have thought, was the coronation itself.

But her youthful arrogance knew its limits. "How old!" she wrote in her journal on May 24, 1837, her eighteenth birthday, "and yet how far am I from being what I should be."

Four weeks later, in the small hours of June 20, King William IV died of liver failure. The Archbishop of Canterbury and the Lord Chamberlain (head of the royal household) hastened to Kensington Palace, where at six in the morning the Duchess of Kent roused her daughter and told her of the gentle-

2

men's presence. The girl hurriedly put a dressing gown over her night clothes and went downstairs alone to meet them. Seeing the group of men in the great parlor bowing respectfully in her direction, Victoria knew that her ailing uncle had died and that she was now Queen of England. Later that day she wrote in the journal she religiously kept for almost sixty years:

> Since it has pleased Providence to place me in this station, I shall do my utmost to fulfil my duty towards my country. I am very young, and perhaps in many, though not in all things, inexperienced, but I am sure that very few have more real good will and more real desire to do what is fit and right than I have.

The Privy Council confirmed her accession that same day, several members noting with pleasure that the moment forever separated the crowns of Britain and Hanover, for that German kingdom's so-called Salic law would not allow a woman to succeed. Although a tiny figure at her full adult height of four feet eleven inches, Victoria was a commanding presence before the Council. Her ostrich-egg blue eyes, porcelain skin and perfectly coiffed light brown hair were features appealing enough to disarm the skeptics. "She not only filled her chair," remarked the Duke of Wellington. "She filled the room!" Almost immediately Victoria barred her mother, Conroy and their cronies from intimacy in her new life; she rightly distrusted their intrigues and unbridled lust for power.

The new Queen soon manifested to her people and government an odd mixture of girlish high spirits, reticence and imperious pride. There were signs, as her early biographers Sidney Lee and Lytton Strachey noted, of a fierce temper and a hard egotism, and soon the staff at Buckingham Palace (to which Victoria relocated) was overwhelmed with byzantine rules of etiquette. Venial infractions merited sharp glances and haughty corrections from the diminutive Queen.

Her firmness became fixed after her coronation in June 1838. "The self-will depicted in those small projecting teeth and that small receding chin was of a more dismaying kind than that which a powerful jaw betokens," wrote Strachey; "it was a self-will imperturbable, impenetrable . . . dangerously akin to obstinacy.'' And the obstinacy of monarchs is not like that of others.

But within weeks of her coronation Victoria found her life dull and unfulfilled. Although she enjoyed the formalities of Court and rapidly developed a strong sense of herself and her role, she was bored with the endless approbation routinely tendered the Sovereign. The nation adored her, mostly because of the contrast she offered to her immediate predecessors. But adoration from afar was cold comfort to a hot-blooded young woman. Her family and even her Prime Minister thought she should marry as soon as possible.

It was with her Prime Minister, Viscount Melbourne, that Victoria formed the first rewarding adult bond of her life. A handsome, benevolent widower of fifty-eight, he was a political and paternal mentor to the young Queen and also roused what was perhaps her first romantic response to a man. Ignorant of a father's love, separated from normal human friendships and limited in her social contacts, Victoria needed a consort as much as she required a guide through the thickets of monarchical responsibility. Melbourne was not to be the former, but he admirably fulfilled the functions of the latter. That invaluable diarist Charles Greville knew (as did Victoria's mother) that the Queen's feelings were "sexual though she does not know it.'' As for the Prime Minister, his social life was full (mostly with the worldly and well-bred Elizabeth, Lady Holland), and in fact his warm sentiments for a woman forty years his junior were nothing more than those of a surrogate father whose eager, adoring child happened to be Queen of the realm. In any case, she shone in Melbourne's company as in no other.

But to Victoria's dismay a general election meant that Melbourne would soon be replaced by a new Prime Minister, Sir Robert Peel, and a new government—a political shift that was entirely out of the monarch's hands. Unable to face the prospect of a reign without Melbourne, the Queen for the first time behaved unconstitutionally, manifesting her independent spirit in the notorious crisis of the Ladies of the Bedchamber in May 1839.

These Ladies, traditionally the wives of Lords chosen by the Queen for personal qualities of dignity, decorum and loyalty, attended her at important public functions. Because it was thought entirely appropriate in the early nineteenth century for the Prime Minister to surround the Queen with Ladies sympathetic to his political views, Lord Melbourne and his government nominated Ladies of the Bedchamber from his own Whig Party, those vocal predecessors of the Liberal Party who were associated with industrial interests, religious nonconformity and political reform. Indeed, Victoria's household was so resoundingly partisan that a saying went the rounds of London in 1838 and 1839 that "a conservative cat was not so much as permitted to mew within the precincts of the Queen's Palace." With Melbourne's defeat in 1839, Victoria was obliged to summon Peel, the opposition leader, to form a new government.

But Victoria disliked this chilly intellectual, and when Peel's first request was that Ladies of the Bedchamber represent his views rather than his predecessor's, Victoria stood firmly opposed. She could not, she insisted, consent to act in a manner repugnant to her feelings. "The Queen of England will not submit to such trickery," she wrote to Lord Melbourne, adding that Peel's men "wish to treat me like a girl, but I will show them that I am Queen of England." Sensing quite correctly that he did not have the monarch's support, Peel declined to form a government. Melbourne returned to office, and it was clear that Victoria was to be very much a vocal and decisive Queen. Her personal triumph, however, dispelled the last mist of enchantment surrounding a youthful Queen in the year following her coronation, for her action deepened public resentment against the Crown. London crowds rudely shouted at "Mrs. Melbourne" as Victoria rode through the streets of London. "I was very young then," she wrote years later, "and perhaps I should act differently if it was all to be done again."

By the summer of 1839, Victoria demonstrated a snappish irritability that burst forth in Hanoverian fits of temper, increasing impatience with ministers, a kind of desperate clinging to Melbourne or whichever kindly, earnest, older counselors he introduced—and a sudden and alarming increase in her weight. Melbourne and her uncle Leopold (by now King of Belgium) urged Victoria to perform a simple exercise program of daily walks lest her squat figure become downright obese. But when she walked, Victoria objected, stones slipped into her shoes.

"Have them made tighter," Melbourne rejoined.

"My feet swell!" Victoria complained.

"Do more walking, then!" urged Melbourne, who alone could get away with this sort of exchange.

"No!" cried the Queen.

"Yes!" trumpeted Melbourne. Then her voice dropped almost to a whisper, and there was the hint of a smile: "Donna Maria [the Queen of Spain] is so fat and yet she took such exercise." To this Lord Melbourne had no reply. The argument was over, and so were all objections to the Queen's weight; like Topsy, she grew and grew until her final illness. By the time of her marriage, she weighed 12 stone 13—181 pounds —which, because she stood under five feet tall, was "an incredible weight for my size," as she confided to her journal.

Help was on the way—not for Victoria's dietary indiscretions and sedentary disposition, but for the weightier matter of love. Before she was Queen, she had briefly met her first cousin, Prince Franz August Karl Albert Emanuel of Saxe-Coburg-Gotha, always called Albert, who was three months younger than she. She had liked him at once when she was seventeen, but on reaching the throne and being reminded of his eligibility by Leopold (the original marriage broker), she was reluctant to abandon her independence for any man. In addition, Victoria was now pursuing a merry social life—frequent attendance at the theater, opera and circus, and dinners with courtiers (accompanied by the strains of weary musicians) at Buckingham Palace as late as one in the morning. From this round of pleasant activities she initially hesitated to yield to what she considered the demands of matrimony and the intrusive pains of motherhood, vocations she saw as restrictive on a life that was essentially whimsical.

But when she and Albert were reintroduced in October 1839, Victoria was at once hopelessly, passionately in love. "I found [Albert] grown and changed," she wrote in her journal, "and embellished. It was with some emotion that I beheld Albert—who is *beautiful*." He was indeed a striking man—at five feet seven inches tall, Albert towered above Victoria— and contemporary paintings, early gravures and other written witnesses confirm her diary entry:

Albert really is quite charming, and so excessively handsome, with such beautiful eyes, an exquisite nose, and such

6

a pretty mouth with delicate moustachios and slight but very slight whiskers; a beautiful figure, broad in the shoulders and a fine waist.

Clearly, nothing of him escaped her keen eye.

Albert's attractions to the Queen were not merely corporal. Unlike Victoria, he had a rich formal education (from tutors and at the University of Bonn) that embraced the arts, science, languages and music. A proficient pianist, organist, singer and composer, he was also learned in art and architecture. He was, in other words, nothing like the Hanoverian kings, and he represented to Victoria everything she longed for in a teacher, guide and companion. Five days after their reunion that October, she proposed marriage, he accepted, and (according to the smitten Queen) they "embraced each other and he was *so* kind, *so* affectionate . . . and seemed so happy, that I really felt it was the happiest brightest moment of my life."

Of Albert's love for Victoria and their subsequent life together there is no equivalent written commentary, but if fidelity as a husband, constancy as a father and dedication as an assiduous consort are emblems, then his devotion matched hers. On November 23 their engagement was announced, and on February 10, 1840, the marriage was held in the Chapel Royal of St. James's Palace, London. Bride and groom were both twenty. That morning, full of anticipation, she wrote that the previous evening was "the last time I slept alone."

Theirs was clearly a union of two passionate souls, and any image of the Queen as a movie-cliché Victorian—all muddy repressions and sexual revulsion—is a complete distortion of her character. "I & Albert alone, which was SO delightful," Victoria wrote of her "most gratifying and bewildering" wedding night at Windsor Castle; "I NEVER NEVER spent such an evening." She never imagined she "could be so loved. . . . His love and affection gave me feelings of heavenly love & happiness. . . . He clasped me in his arms, and we kissed each other again and again! His beauty, his sweetness and gentleness —really, how can I ever be thankful enough to have such a *Husband!* Oh! this was the happiest day of my life!" She added significantly that she and Albert "did not sleep much."

Before the end of March, the Queen was pregnant, "the ONLY thing I *dread,*" as she had confided to her journal three

7

months earlier. And dread pregnancy she did forever after—a fear that did not deter her, however, from bearing nine children, all of whom survived to adulthood. The passionate young woman who abandoned herself full throttle to the marriage bed spent twenty-one years alternating between "the sufferings and miseries and plagues" of pregnancy and the "enjoyments to give up" during that time.

"Without that [pregnancy]," she wrote to her first child—Princess Victoria ("Vicky")—eighteen years later, "certainly it is unbounded happiness if one has a husband one worships! But I had 9 times to bear with real misery . . . and it tried me sorely. One feels so pinned down—one's wings clipped—in fact, only half oneself. This I call the 'shadow side [of marriage].' " Sounding very much like a campaigner of the late twentieth century, Victoria wrote again after the birth of Vicky's first son, the future Kaiser Wilhelm II of Germany: "It is indeed too hard and dreadful what we have to go through and men ought to have an adoration for one, and indeed do everything to make up for what after all they alone are the cause of!"

And so a Germanic dynasty in England was reinforced when Victoria married her cousin; the House of Hanover was officially replaced by the House of Saxe-Coburg-Gotha, and Albert's descendants would bear his family name, Wettin. He learned fluent English, which he and Victoria spoke together as much as German; that, after all, was her first language, and its accents forever lightly shaded her speech.

At first Victoria was slow to share any power or responsibility with her husband. "In my home life I am very happy," Albert wrote to his old friend Prince William of Löwenstein three months after his marriage, "but the difficulty of filling my place with proper dignity is that I am only the husband, and not the master in the house." In other words, he had nothing to do.

Finally, on November 21—at Melbourne's urging and just as Victoria went into labor with her first child—Albert was officially given access to government boxes and represented the Queen at the Privy Council; he was also appointed Regent should she die in childbirth. From that autumn Albert was Victoria's unofficial private secretary, and by the time she formally named him Prince Consort in 1857, he had been virtu-

ally a co-sovereign for seventeen years. This expansion of his
influence certainly sprang from her respect and devotion; it
also derived from Albert's assumption of duties during and
after her nine pregnancies when, according to custom, she was
entirely removed from public life and restricted mostly to her
bedroom for more than a year each time. Thus many referred
to an ''Albertine Monarchy.''

Much of their early life and work together occurred at Buckingham Palace. Bought by George III from the Duke of Buckingham, it was refurbished by George IV; Victoria was its first
royal occupant when she and her entourage moved there within
weeks of her coronation. She did not like it, but at least it was
convenient to her ministers and to London entertainments. But
with its endless narrow, cold corridors linking more than six
hundred rooms, there was nothing about it to invite a cozy
family life—especially after an assassination attempt on the
Queen and the ''Boy Jones'' incident.

On June 10, 1840, with the Queen's first pregnancy well
advanced, she decided to take the air with Albert. ''We had
hardly proceeded a hundred yards from the Palace,'' he wrote
in a graphic memorandum,

> when I noticed on the footpath on my side a little mean-
> looking man holding something towards us, and before I
> could distinguish what it was, a shot was fired, which almost
> stunned us both, it was so loud and fired barely six paces
> from us. Victoria had just turned to the left to look at a
> horse, and could not therefore understand why her ears were
> ringing. . . . I seized Victoria's hands and asked if the fright
> had not shaken her, but she laughed at the thing. I then
> looked again at the man, who was still standing in the same
> place, his arms crossed, and a pistol in each hand. . . . Sud-
> denly he again pointed his pistol and fired a second time.
> This time Victoria also saw the shot, and stooped quickly,
> drawn down by me.

The culprit turned out to be an unbalanced eighteen-year-old
who was remanded to an asylum; at least six other attacks on
the Queen occurred over the next several years in London—
from firearms loaded and unloaded, from sticks, from objects
rudely hurled. Although in each case the Queen gamely contin-

ued on her journey through the city, the incidents certainly encouraged the family to vacate London. Albert, susceptible to bouts of exhaustion and depression in the best of times, rarely found solace in urban life, and it was he who pressed Victoria to transfer the family to one of the royal residences—Windsor Castle, Balmoral Castle or Osborne House—whenever possible.

In another incident, during the night of December 2, 1840, a seventeen-year-old named Edmund Jones blithely leaped over the palace wall, crept through one of the windows, sat on the throne, and then toured several apartments before one of the infant Princess Victoria's nursemaids heard him and summoned a page. As it happened, this was Jones's second visit to Buckingham Palace, his first having ended quickly before he could reach the inner sanctum. "I wanted to know how they lived at the palace," declared "Boy" Jones, as he was called in the annals of minor palace lore. "I thought a description would look very well in a book." His research earned him a brief term in the House of Correction, and after yet another uninvited visit to the royal residence a year later, Jones was shipped out to sea. There was a lesson here for Prince Albert, who set himself the unenviable task of improving security, at which he had little success. (One hundred forty-two years later, as Queen Elizabeth II was to learn, things had scarcely improved.)

Eventually, Victoria, Albert and their children spent as little time at Buckingham Palace as possible, although the Court was officially centered there from January 1841. Parliament allotted more than £175,000 for improvements to the palace, and many members, as thrifty as Victoria, were none too pleased that the Royals were so often absent. The family favored Windsor, the largest inhabited castle in the world, occupied uninterruptedly since it was built by William the Conqueror in the eleventh century; here Albert modernized the farms and supervised major exterior and interior improvements. But they were most comfortable at Balmoral Castle in Scotland, which was completed in 1856. The surrounding valley and forests reminded Albert of the German landscapes he loved, and Victoria much preferred the Scottish Highlanders to any company save that of her family. Equally remote was Osborne House on the Isle of Wight in the English Channel, where Victoria eventually died. On an estate of nearly a thousand acres, the Prince Consort worked with the renowned London architect Thomas Cubbitt, supervising between 1845 and 1851 the construction of this grand Italian villa. The design and construction of Balmoral and Osborne were entirely under the supervision of the Consort.

In a way, Albert's management of the royal residences was an emblem of his leverage. Indeed, it is no exaggeration to say that the entire reign of Queen Victoria was directed by her husband's spirit, as much after his death as before. Cultivated and sensitive, he had a wide streak of German melancholy, and with this he tempered her impetuous, passionate nature; taught her the virtues of order, discipline and hard work; confirmed her in a stern morality, and undertook her education in the arts, history and government. Because of Albert, the brittle prerogatives of a mostly discredited English throne were replaced by a potent political influence. Active in the national social crusades against slavery, child labor and dueling, he was, thanks to his European background, just as valuable to the Queen in international affairs. Disputes with Prussia in 1856 and with America in 1861, for example, were settled largely because of Albert's skillful negotiations: Foreign Office dispatches were recast so as not to bear the timbre of saber rattling.

His major contribution to British political history, however, may have been his insistence that the monarch remain detached from party ties in order to be *"necessarily* a politician''—to exert a proper political influence that would be all the more effective precisely because it was nonpartisan. In this way Albert developed the constitutional role of the monarch, since he believed that only she could understand the true needs of her people and advance a disinterested view of the common good.*

---

* Albert did not come to his political theories on his own. He was much influenced by Baron Friedrich Christian von Stockmar, an *éminence grise* at Coburg and at Windsor who had been a counselor to Leopold and to Victoria. He envisioned a constitutional monarchy raised by Albert "to a height of power, stability and symmetry which has never been attained . . . [a monarch who would be] not a mandarin figure which has to nod its head in assent . . . but who will take part in the initiation and maturing of government measures.''

Culturally and intellectually, his contributions were no less significant. Albert raised the standards of the nation's art appreciation and education through a proliferation of free museums, and he supervised the enhancement of the royal collection of paintings. In 1841 he was appointed chairman of a commission on the arts, and his first task was to oversee the decoration of the rebuilt Houses of Parliament. As a gifted musician, he was an active and influential patron of composers: Mendelssohn, among others, was a frequent visitor to the Royal Family. Until her marriage, Victoria's aesthetic tastes were solidly bourgeois, but Albert altered that, and she was soon applauding performances of Mozart's *Magic Flute* more heartily than the trifling entertainments to which she had been accustomed. And as chancellor of Cambridge University, Albert was directly involved in updating and broadening both its curricula and the number of valuable foreign visiting scholars. Poorly educated herself, Victoria was awestruck by her husband's various competences.

Earnest, intelligent and dutiful, Albert eventually won the respect of British statesmen and citizens, if not their affection; there was still a wide band of the population suspicious of a foreign consort. His German accent and manner, his austerities, his preference for the intellectual over the sporting life all conspired toward his unpopularity—until Albert successfully sponsored and personally managed the six-month-long Great Exhibition of 1851, the world's first international fair and an unprecedented celebration of more than one hundred thousand products of the Industrial Revolution. And even after several years of conflict with the palace in the 1850s, Lord Palmerston, Prime Minister and no warm friend of Albert, had to acknowledge his "extraordinary abilities and wisdom."

Of a total national population of twenty million, six million came to the Great Exhibition in the Hyde Park exhibition hall, nicknamed the Crystal Palace for its three hundred thousand panes of glass supported by a cast-iron frame.* This event alone was a personal triumph for Victoria and Albert as it was a national one for Britain. Not long after, the word "Victorian" was first used in print and conversation to express the nation's

---

* When the exhibition closed, the Crystal Palace was dismantled pane by pane, and the whole was rebuilt in Sydenham, south London.

new sense of both achievement and destiny—as well as of a dutiful family life as the foundation of society.

And so Victorian society prospered from the 1850s. Wages, incomes and profits soared, and there was a golden era for agriculture as well as for industry; nevertheless, there were vast pockets of poverty and unemployment and a wide disparity in the privileges enjoyed by the various ranks in society.

Victoria was the first monarch to be solidly middle class in social attitudes; she distrusted aristocratic smugness, believed in the proprieties of life and heralded the sanctity of duty. Free all her life from racial prejudices and no guarantor of class distinctions, she was at the same time not a crusader for democracy, and under Albert's custody she was learning the godly necessity of her position and the quasi-divine mission entrusted to the Empire. In her education she was always the most docile pupil of her adored husband.

That Empire was spreading broadly across the world. British sea power was at its strongest, British pluck at its most daring, and the economy at its most adventurous in, for example, the rapid growth of railroads, factories and canals. And the Queen herself embodied the nation as had no monarch before. Her cozy tastes and her preference for a quiet family life and a simple, ordered existence harmonized perfectly with the aspirations and imaginations of precisely the people who had made possible Britain's rise to supremacy: the working middle class. It was, after all, at the beginning of the nineteenth century that commerce at last was considered respectable and that a gentleman might work without shame. Those who toiled in a factory could for the first time ascend to be titled tycoons, enjoying as much influence (if not as much social prestige) as the landed gentry who for centuries had ruled the nation. Thus the economic power base of England experienced a radical overhaul just as the monarchy—and people's attitude toward it—was changing, too. The respect for the Crown which Victoria and Albert had regained was, in this regard, perhaps the primary element that kept Britain from revolution in 1848 when the political structures of all Europe shook and toppled.

Nor was the Queen herself, however authoritarian and parochial, uninterested in the Continent. In 1843 she was the first monarch to make a state visit to France, where a statesman was impressed by her "air of dignity, and she had a sweet expression which gave one confidence''—this despite a ''dreadful toilette. . . . She wore geranium flowers placed here, there, and everywhere. She had plump hands with rings on each finger and even on her thumbs; one of them held a ruby of prodigious size [and so] she found difficulty in using her knife and fork . . . and even more difficulty to remove and replace her gloves.''* Victorian excess extended beyond home furnishings.

But Victorianism (perhaps the only ''ism'' to draw its name from a monarch) also began to signify a host of restraining moral characteristics: well-mannered, respectable behavior, a sense of duty and thrift, and an uncomplaining approach to hard work. To borrow from the era's great playwright Oscar Wilde, the important thing was to be earnest, although Wilde himself (among others) criticized and satirized the artifices of the upper classes who too often raised social standards to a ridiculous level.† But no such objection was leveled against the Royal Family, whose domestic life was quickly restoring luster to a Crown darkly tainted by the last century's monarchical antics.

Upright and severe in the way of the German court, Albert took in hand the moral education of his highly sexed, whimsical young bride, and it was he who really formed her personality into the woman of legend. In many ways Albert was the sterner and more persuasive character, and before long his philosophy (based on an ethic of decency without any specifically religious substructure) was hailed by the Church of England and put before the entire nation as a tone-setting element of Victorian style. From him the Queen learned to prefer only the company of those considered to be of immaculate character, a social standard for which she herself had previously cared

---

* Victoria mistakenly believed the rings would detract from what she considered her stumpy, unattractive fingers. Melbourne pointed out that the jewels simply called attention to them.

† Besides Wilde, John Stuart Mill, Matthew Arnold, John Ruskin and Charles Dickens mocked Victorian smugness and the ignoring of unpleasant realities in society. A good example is Dickens's Mr. Podsnap (in *Our Mutual Friend*), a complacent businessman who ''felt conscious that he set a brilliant social example in being particularly well satisfied with most things, and, above all other things, with himself.''

"not a straw," according to the Duke of Wellington. And yet her rigor had a balancing distinction, for she loathed aristocratic snobbery and pretensions, hated class divisions, and was genuinely concerned for the poor and disenfranchised.* Victoria had scant patience and little time for "the society of fashionable and fast people," and the mere hint of pomposity in her own family roused her ire: if her grandson, the Kaiser of Germany, whom she much loved, continued to adopt "imperial airs in private as well as in public, he better not come here," she said late in life.

Albert's intense moralism, inculcated by tutors in his youth and fortified by his own gravity in adolescence, had an even earlier origin. Like Victoria, he had been deprived of a parent in childhood. When he was five, his mother was banished from the house because of her love affair with a military man she eventually married. Victoria and her Consort devoted themselves with undiluted solemnity to the creation of a family life impenetrable to scandal, and at least until the maturity of their eldest son they were successful. The respect they earned can be amusingly summarized by the often-cited comment of a Victorian lady who at the end of a performance of Shakespeare's *Antony and Cleopatra* remarked that it was "so very unlike the home life of our own dear Queen!"

In fact, the royal home teemed with new occupants, for Victoria bore nine children between 1840 and 1857. Although she hated childbearing and had not much interest in her offspring until they were well out of toddlerhood, she gladly risked pregnancy for the pleasures of Albert's bed. This ample progeny was not planned, and in this regard it is important to recall that the Church of England forbade any form of birth control except abstinence—just as nineteenth-century secular society thought abstinence the only respectable option to parenthood. (Such a perspective contributed to the great new ranks of prostitutes catering to the middle class.) As for Victoria and

---

* At thirteen, Victoria visited the industrial towns of Wales and the Midlands and returned to London horrified by what she saw: "the houses all black [from] smoking and burning coal heaps . . . wretched huts and little ragged children." The journey marked the beginning of a social conscience.

Albert, they were not much educated in reproductive matters and followed the orders of physicians, who recommended against intercourse on the days just after menstruation and, as safest, the time of a woman's mid-cycle. In light of such counsel, the population explosion—at Buckingham Palace and nationwide—is not surprising.

Thus it happened that shortly after the birth of their first child, Princess Victoria (on November 21, 1840), the Queen was dismayed to learn that she was pregnant again. A boy was born on November 9, 1841, and christened Albert Edward; throughout his life, his family called him Bertie. His mother created him Prince of Wales that December, and at the age of fifty-nine he became King Edward VII. Before releasing the official announcement of the birth, Albert read it to his wife: "Her Majesty and the Prince are perfectly well." The Queen threw back her head and laughed heartily: "My dear," she said, "this will never do!"

"And why not?" asked Albert.

"Because it conveys the idea that *you* were confined [with childbirth] also!" At the Queen's suggestion the bulletin was modified: "Her Majesty and the infant Prince are perfectly well."

But following the child's birth, all was not to the Queen's amusement. Victoria fell into a severe postpartum depression, convinced she was useless and unnecessary—a feeling she may have at least partly brought on herself by having a wet nurse breast-feed the infant. She then fought bitterly with Albert when he insisted that her own childhood governess and confidante, Baroness Louise Lehzen, be dismissed in favor of a new English nanny for their children, a woman who had no ties to Victoria's mother and an earlier Court. The conflict over this matter was, as it happened, a noisy and bitter one, with Albert storming off to his quarters, pursued by a screaming Victoria. She rapped on his door, shouting, "I am the Queen!" but was met only with the scorn of silence. But she grew frightened at such uncharacteristic *froideur* from her husband and collapsed outside his suite, sobbing, "Please, listen—I am your wife." With that, the door opened, and Albert bent down to lift his wife into his arms. "That is better," he said, "and that is the truth—I am your husband." Lehzen soon departed, and from that day, Albert was indisputably master of the royal household.

At least one other commotion occurred in 1853, after their fourth son, Leopold, was diagnosed as a hemophiliac. Victoria's anguish was manifest in a sullen silence, followed by a series of petty but violently loud arguments she incited with Albert—and then more reticence. Albert then wrote his wife a long letter, urging her to speak openly of her pain and anguish, not to harbor everything secretly. It was a lesson she would take to heart.

Their third child, Princess Alice, arrived in 1843; she was to marry Louis IV of Hesse-Darmstadt and was the mother of Alexandra, who married Czar Nicholas II.* The fourth child, Prince Alfred, born in 1844, married Grand Duchess Marie, daughter of Czar Alexander II; their descendants included kings and queens of Romania, Yugoslavia and Greece. In 1846 came Princess Helena, who wed Prince Christian of Schleswig-Holstein; in 1848, Princess Louise, who married the ninth Duke of Argyll; in 1850, Prince Arthur, who wed Princess Louise of Prussia; in 1853, Prince Leopold, whose wife was Princess Helena of Waldeck-Pyrmont; and finally, in 1857, came Princess Beatrice, who married Prince Henry of Battenberg (their daughter married the King of Spain). Thus, with descendants in almost every country on the Continent, Victoria merited the nickname given even in her lifetime—"Grandmother of Europe."†

The Grandmother of Europe had a very definite resentment of some aspects of her station, however. A woman, she once complained, "is bodily and morally the husband's slave. That always sticks in my throat. When I think of a merry, happy, free young girl—and look at the ailing, aching state a young wife is generally doomed to . . . you can't deny [this] is the penalty of marriage!" Queen Victoria was no campaigner for

---

* Princess Alice was also the great-grandmother of Prince Philip of Greece, who as Lieutenant Philip Mountbatten married Princess Elizabeth (later Queen Elizabeth II) in 1947 and was subsequently titled Duke of Edinburgh.

† At the time of her death, she was survived by six of her nine children, forty grandchildren, and thirty-seven great-grandchildren. In this number were four future sovereigns: her son Edward VII, her grandson George V, and her great-grandsons Edward VIII and George VI.

women's suffrage (which she saw as a "mad, wicked folly"), but neither was she blind to certain raw facts of nineteenth-century family life. Whereas the confinement of pregnancy was the "shadow side," wifely subservience was a "penalty." Yet by all accounts and despite the depressions that accompanied her pregnancies, Victoria, Albert and their children were for several years a remarkably happy and close family.

There were, of course, the usual problems of childhood discipline, and in January 1847, Victoria and Albert devised a plan for the training of their children. Until six, their education (French, English, German and religious instruction) was entrusted to a governess; afterward, there were classes in more advanced subjects with special tutors.

Particular care was taken with Bertie, the heir to the throne. At her husband's recommendation, Victoria deliberately distanced herself emotionally from the Prince of Wales, apparently in the belief that he would mature more independently and develop leadership qualities if he were not tied to maternal affections. But by the age of seven, Bertie showed a marked preference for sport over study. Intimidated by his father, he developed an embarrassing stammer that would take several years to overcome; this handicap would be virtually a family trait, inherited by several of his sons and grandsons, and surmounted with varying degrees of success.

The Queen and her Consort wished Bertie to be the perfect heir to the throne, and an intense curriculum was drawn up. A strict timetable and daily reports were instituted, but these led to a monotonous round of boyish failures and parental scenes. Alternate methods were then briefly attempted. At the age of twelve, Bertie was under the mentorship of an indulgent teacher named Henry Birch, who believed that long walks through the countryside were more effective in inculcating good study habits than actual extra sessions of mathematics or history. This failed miserably.

Then, as was often the custom of the time, a phrenologist was summoned to assess the bumps on the boy's head; it was believed that the discovery of a dramatic map of his scalp would reveal where the Prince's best talents lay. This examination proved ineffective, alas, as did an experimental diet ordered by a doctor who hoped to improve Bertie's intellect and temperament by a complicated nutritional scheme.

18

The girls were similarly free-spirited but not so intractable and far more intelligent. Yet they were not to be dealt with easily. When a certain Dr. Brown entered the household staff, six-year-old Vicky (named Princess Royal at birth) heard her father address him simply as "Brown" and took to the same familiarity. The Queen, to no avail, corrected her daughter time and again, impressing on her the necessity of the more courteous "Dr. Brown." Finally, Vicky was threatened with "bed!" if she disobeyed one more time. When next the doctor arrived, the Princess looked at him and in a loud voice said, "Good morning, Brown!" Then, seeing her mother's angry face, Vicky rose and curtsied, adding, "And good night, Brown, for I am going to bed."

Similarly willful was Princess Beatrice. Once, at the age of two, she wanted a particularly rich dessert at lunch. "Baby mustn't have that," said her mother quietly, "because it's not good for Baby." Taking a large helping, the child calmly continued the third-person allusion: "But she likes it, my dear."

Her younger sister Louise, who married the Marquess of Lorne (later the ninth Duke of Argyll), shocked the family at a later age by separating from her husband in 1884. He had been governor-general of Canada until the previous year, and the couple had been admirable pioneers in the rough Northwest Territories. Following a serious sleigh accident, Louise convalesced in Europe, where she came to the conclusion that her husband bored her to distraction. For the rest of her long, regained single life, she dedicated herself to art and education.

Vicky and Beatrice, especially, grew up to develop significant intellectual and artistic gifts. Vicky spoke fluent French and German by the time she was six and later excelled in a variety of disciplines. Even after she married Prince Friedrich Wilhelm of Prussia, becoming Crown Princess and eventually Empress, she pursued her cultural interests and became an accomplished painter and sculptor. Benefactor of liberal causes, opposed to all kinds of authoritarianism, founder of schools for the higher education of women and the training of nurses, Vicky was a sensitive and devoted daughter and herself the mother of eight. More than eight thousand letters passed between the two Victorias, a correspondence providing rich insight into the family and their times.

As for Beatrice, she, too, shone in studies and distinguished herself as a pianist and composer; several of her works were published to some critical acclaim. But her enduring achievement was her role as her mother's private secretary, a function she filled before and after her marriage to Prince Henry of Battenberg and the birth of her four children. Widowed at thirty-eight, she devoted herself, after her mother's death, to the transcription and editing of 111 volumes of the Queen's journals. This turned out to be a compromised project, however, for Beatrice—more Victorian than Victoria—considered her mother's frank and even racy diction most unqueenly and deleted what she thought were inappropriate comments. Queen Elizabeth II, decades later, often shows visitors to Windsor Castle sample pages of the expurgated diaries, noting her personal regret that Beatrice had too freely altered Victoria's style and even, in an excess of zeal, consigned the originals to the fire.

The delight of the parents in their daughters was more than counterpoised by their disappointment with the young Prince of Wales. No heir had been born to a reigning monarch since the first child of George III eighty years earlier, and so the birth of Albert Edward in 1841 led many to hope for the continuation of the monarchy to which Victoria and Albert so dedicated themselves. But this was rash optimism. Despite the parents' ambitions for the future King and their attempt at strict disciplinary control of his life, he failed to develop intellectually and morally to any degree remotely approximating their standards.

Because the Queen regarded the aristocracy as appallingly depraved, it was unthinkable that Bertie attend school just like any other gentleman's lad. Egalitarian fraternization would, she reasoned, drag him down even further from his royal estate. And so he was kept at home with private tutors, where his slowness and indifference had little real correction apart from the ponderous lectures his father regularly offered. By the age of twenty, Bertie was a pleasant, carefree, congenial layabout with, it seemed, little to recommend him except his pedigree. Because of his frivolity, the Queen refused to entrust him with any civic, social or ceremonial responsibilities. And because he was given no duties, he grew more and more irresponsible.

Could Victoria and Albert have recognized them, there were signs of some real abilities in their son. He did reasonably well in brief enrollments at Oxford and Cambridge, although his father disallowed him residence with other students and set him up privately with equerries and servants to guard against bad conduct. Only when the Prince of Wales was sent on a royal visit to Canada and America in the summer and early autumn of 1860 had he any degree of freedom. He saw grain elevators in Chicago, bid at a country fair in St. Louis, and danced past midnight at a ball in Cincinnati.

Photography was all the rage worldwide that year—Queen Victoria had sent an official photographer to document the Crimean War in 1856—and it is no exaggeration to say that the Prince of Wales became the world's first celebrity precisely because of photographers. All over the world people knew how the heir to the throne of England grew, what he looked like with each passing year, how he dressed. His family sat immobile for the long sessions then necessary, but Victoria was naturally shy and avoided the camera when she could. Bertie had no such reticence. All over America he was besieged by photographers so that the press could have their answers to questions people asked: How did he dress? Was he handsome? What was the style of his hair? In Pittsburgh and Baltimore he walked with citizens along the cobblestoned streets; the newspapers had done their job, and he was mobbed. For the first time there was some consideration given to his safety, and in Washington and New York, Bertie was restricted to carriages. After three hundred thousand turned out to cheer and accompany him in Manhattan, it took several hours for him to travel the few miles from the pier to the Fifth Avenue Hotel. There he was warmly received by politicians and the public, and news of this pleased his parents—until he returned to them with a casual American wardrobe and an American cigar in his mouth.

In January 1861, Bertie arrived at Cambridge, where no less a lecturer than Charles Kingsley, Regius Professor of Modern History, found that he asked "very intelligent questions." Bertie's father sent him that summer to spend ten weeks attached to the Grenadier Guards near Dublin. There, Prince Albert set his son an impossible training regimen at camp: to rise through the ranks a week at a time, which was of course beyond his

21

ability. He did manage, however, to keep up with the demands of an aspiring actress and soldiers' camp follower named Nellie Clifden, a local of easy virtue who was so familiar with the army barracks that from routine she could find her way to any particular man's bed in the dark. Letters from Albert urging Bertie to think about marrying a Continental Princess were politely ignored; he would marry, replied the Prince, for love only. Nevertheless, he agreed to meet the Danish-born Princess Alexandra, then not quite seventeen. Perhaps because Bertie was besotted with the fiery Nellie, he failed to be impressed by the stunningly beautiful Alix (as she was called by intimates); in any case, he returned to Cambridge and to occasional meetings with Nellie in London.

That autumn of 1861, news of the young Prince's affair was kept from Victoria but not from his father, who was predictably outraged and drafted a letter to Bertie. Nellie was already smirkingly termed the Princess of Wales, Albert wrote. Doubtless she would soon have Bertie's child, and Bertie would be summoned to court to present "disgusting details of your profligacy!" Albert's anger was directed not only at what he considered his son's immorality but also at the potential damage to the image of the monarchy at a time when memories of the Hanoverians were still fresh and democratic voices were being heard more and more stridently in the land.

Albert himself was ill and exhausted from overwork and a chain of concerns both familial and national; he had also been in considerable gastric distress since October 1860, and abdominal pain had taxed him to the point of nervous collapse that December. Weary, too, from fighting the unfair allegations registered against him during the Crimean War (specifically, that he had tried to influence Parliament in favor of the Russians), Albert now had to cope with a doubled burden of work, for Victoria had withdrawn into months of mourning after the death of her mother that March.

Additionally, eight-year-old Prince Leopold's worsening hemophilia was a torment to him; there was a threat of war in Europe over several German duchies; and the American Civil War threatened to involve Britain, whose mills needed the South's cotton. At the same time, Bertie was trying his patience, and at the end of November he forced himself to visit his son, then back at Cambridge, in the vain hope of putting an end to the boy's scandalous conduct.

Albert returned to Windsor Castle shaking with chills and fever, unable to take any food or water. More alarming still, by early December his lucidity was often affected. With his beloved eighteen-year-old daughter Alice attending him as best she could, he wandered about Windsor, moving from one bedroom to another, addressing Victoria irrationally, then sleeping, only to awake fully reasonable and coherent. The alternation of moods, of bright optimism with dire talk of death, panicked the Queen and her children.

At last the Prince's doctors diagnosed typhoid fever, which they said would soon pass, but by Tuesday, December 10, everyone knew the situation was grave. (Historians later suggested that his terminal illness was either a perforated ulcer or, more likely, stomach cancer.)

Victoria was almost paralyzed with fright, but she sat with her husband and cradled his head against her shoulder. On Thursday the twelfth, Albert said he heard the birds chirping at Rosenau, his family's country home near Coburg; he then inquired of Victoria about cousins he had not seen for years. Then, as Alice was ministering to him, he asked if Vicky, in Berlin with her own new family, knew he was ill.

"Yes," replied Alice. "I told her you were very ill."

"You should have told her that I am dying. Yes, I am dying."

And so he was. On Friday the thirteenth, at Alice's summons, Bertie rejoined the family. "The breathing was the alarming thing," wrote Victoria, "it was so rapid. There was what they call a dusky hue about the face and hands, which I knew was not good." By five o'clock that afternoon, a bulletin was issued to a hitherto ignorant public, and the Queen was told her Prince was swiftly losing ground. Between fits of hysterical weeping, she sat calmly at her husband's bedside. But all his mental confusion seemed to vanish as he became weaker. He kissed his wife, clasped her hand and whispered over and over, *"Gutes Fraüchen . . . Gutes Fraüchen . . . Good little wife . . ."*

On December 14, Bertie, Helena, Louise and Arthur gathered quietly around their father's bed. His beloved Vicky was still in Germany, Alfred at sea, Leopold on the Riviera for his health and Beatrice—only four years old—was kept far distant. When the Queen noticed how rapid her husband's breathing had again become—short, desperate gasps—she leaned over him. "Es ist Fraüchen. It's your dear wife," and she begged for a kiss. Remarkably, he stirred, kissed her and then sank back. Victoria left the room sobbing. Just before eleven, the forty-two-year-old Prince drew his last breath, and Alice calmly and wordlessly went to bring her mother back.

"Oh, yes, this is death!" the Queen cried, her voice rising in a terrible wail as she entered the room. "I know it, I have seen it before!"

She collapsed onto Albert's lifeless form, calling his name and nicknames in English and German. For the next several months the Queen was almost mad with grief, and her family and ministers feared a permanent descent into madness. That, as it happened, was unwarranted pessimism. But it is true that Victoria was pitched into a dour widowhood from which she never really recovered and into a seclusion from which she did not emerge for years. She wore full mourning dress for the rest of her life.

Four monarchs: Queen Victoria with (from left) her grandson George, her son Bertie and her great-grandson David.

2

Bertie 1861 to 1871

I never can look at him without a shudder.
QUEEN VICTORIA, on her eldest son, Albert Edward ("Bertie")

"This German prince," wrote Benjamin Disraeli at the time of Albert's death, "governed England for twenty-one years with a wisdom and energy such as none of our Kings has ever shown."

As Queen Victoria herself admitted, the passing of her beloved Albert seemed to mark the beginning of a new reign. It was to be a forty-year widowhood, an enduring bereavement

25

of perpetual twilight, virtually a shadow-reign without the Consort on whom she so relied.

The Victorian Age as we think of it owes more to the influence of Albert than to that of his wife, for it was he who established the determining tone of the last sixty years of the century. Albert knew that the survival of the monarchy after the Hanoverians depended on its identification with middle-class virtues. It was his political judgment that saved Victoria from unpopularity by overruling her often violent temper, by demonstrating the prudence of duty and the duty to be prudent. Indeed, the prevailing virtues of every respected monarch since Albert—the earnestness of George V, the courage of George VI, the dignified responsibility of Elizabeth II—demonstrate that the pattern established by Albert was well learned by his descendants.

The Queen refused to open Parliament from 1862 to 1865, by which time both the press and the public deeply resented this willful isolation. "Her Majesty's loyal subjects will be very well pleased to hear that their Sovereign is about to break her protracted seclusion," wrote *The Times,* eager to believe a false report that the Queen was to reenter public life in 1864. "Before long, the whole Court will recover from its suspended animation. . . . We are not a people to take much on trust or to conceive that to be real which does not meet the eye. . . . They who would isolate themselves from the world and its duties must cease to know and to care." Six days later Her Majesty published her reply: "The Queen heartily appreciates the desire of her subjects to see her, and whatever she *can* do to gratify them in this loyal and affectionate wish she *will* do." But she would not, she insisted, engage in public ceremonies unseemly for a widow—not even for one over two years bereaved. It was, then, no mere joke when it was reported that someone had posted a notice on the exterior gates of Buckingham Palace: THESE EXTENSIVE PREMISES TO BE LET OR SOLD, THE LATE OCCUPANT HAVING RETIRED FROM BUSINESS.

Henceforth avoiding London whenever possible, Victoria preferred the isolation of Osborne House, Balmoral and Windsor castles; in fact, she spent no more than one week a year in London over the next fifteen years. She gave as a reason for her retreat the absence of her "dear husband whose presence alone seemed a tower of strength." In September 1865 the satirical magazine *Punch* published a cartoon of the Queen as Hermione in Shakespeare's *The Winter's Tale,* begged by Perdita-as-Britannia to "descend—be stone no more." By 1869 her ministers realized that her eight years of virtual isolation were damaging the image of the monarchy.

Although the Queen did come forth from time to time in the 1860s and 1870s (usually to unveil a memorial to her husband), she seemed to have abdicated her formal monarchical and thus her constitutional duty, and there were repeated calls for her to abdicate in favor of the Prince of Wales; there were even cries for the abolition of a do-nothing monarchy and its replacement by a republic. Her official biographer, Sir Sidney Lee, said of her refusal to hold a state opening of Parliament most years before 1874 and permanently after 1886, "Her defiance of this practice tended to weaken her semblance of hold on the central force of government."

The seclusion—which in time became somewhat self-consciously melodramatic—was often simply a cover for lethargy. Her inactivity persisted despite repeated pleas from her children and from her uncle Leopold, the King of Belgium, that "the English are very personal; to continue to love people they must see them, and even in part touch them." The Prince of Wales also urged ceremonial duties on her, and his secretary noted that if the Queen could dance with her sons and with a select cadre of ministers from ten at night until two in the morning at a Balmoral ball—which she did as early as 1863— she might find time for an occasional meeting at Buckingham Palace. Her eldest daughter, Vicky, then Crown Princess of Prussia, wrote a letter signed by her brothers and sisters, urging "our adored Mama and our Sovereign" not to be oblivious to the threats to the monarchy itself that her apparent inactivity invited. But then a collective skittishness afflicted them, and the note was never sent.

The letter would have been inefficacious in any case. As a lady without a husband, Victoria insisted, she could not be expected to entertain foreign dignitaries or undertake formal engagements. But in saying this she had apparently chosen to ignore her life as Queen before she married Albert, when she certainly was active officially and socially.

There was, in other words, something neurotically selective and obdurate in her retirement. Albert himself, who had ordered the architectural addition of the ceremonial balcony to Buckingham Palace, would have been appalled at the idea that Victoria was honoring his memory by isolating herself in perpetual mourning. It was he who virtually established the concept of a sovereign above party politics, a monarch who had to represent all the people and who must use pageantry as a symbol of that.

But her widow's weeds and disappearance from public ceremonial and social life did not betoken indifference to the life of the Empire, nor were her activities restricted to family outings, weddings, funerals, picnics and christenings. She never ignored either her routine duties or those social and political matters that called for her consultation. Indeed, her ministers were bombarded with letters from the Queen aimed at forestalling British intervention in the Danish-German conflict over the future of Schleswig-Holstein. She wrote to directors of public works reminding them of their duty, she kept in constant communication with the Foreign Office, and she perused all the dispatch boxes, studying ministerial reports and news items on parliamentary debates. On many days she read, signed, and annotated as many as three hundred documents. Her aim, she said, was "to follow the Prince's plan, which was to *sign nothing* until he had read and made notes upon what he had signed."

Furthermore, Victoria insisted on her constitutional right to be consulted regarding every important and even trivial diplomatic, political and ecclesiastical matter and appointment. During the crisis of 1877, when Russia declared war on the Ottoman Empire, she badgered the War Department with seventeen notes and wires in one day. In her widowhood Queen Victoria regarded political responsibilities as far more important than ceremony.

When it came to her prime ministers, the Queen certainly exceeded her constitutional rights. She made life insufferable for Prime Minister William Gladstone, who had four terms over fifteen years and whose policies she resented, including an extension of the right to vote and home rule for Ireland. Victoria found Gladstone's manner condescending, and she tried to avoid summoning him to create a government. "The Queen does not the least care," she pronounced blithely, "but rather wishes it should be known that she has the greatest

28

possible disinclination to take [seriously] this half-crazy & really in many ways ridiculous old man.'' When he came to his last term in 1892, she was even more forthright, writing to her private secretary that ''the idea of a deluded excited man of 82 trying to govern England and her vast Empire with the miserable democrats under him is quite ludicrous. It is like a bad joke!''

Politicians were not much amused at this attitude, however, as they were not when she ignored her Prime Minister's advice and in 1868 made her own choice for a new Archbishop of Canterbury; when she ignored the War Office and sent letters directly to generals in 1885; and when, in 1894, defying the advice of the Liberal Party then in majority in the Commons, she made Lord Rosebery prime minister because he was ''the only person in the Government I consider suitable to the post.''

This was worse than discourteous; it was a rank transgression of the constitutional limitations placed on the Sovereign, as was her habit of privately informing the opposition leader of Gladstone's intentions. Victoria wrote to her prime ministers about anything she disliked and insisted on delays in administrative actions so that she could be consulted. ''In matters of war and diplomacy,'' as one scholar has noted, ''she regarded her ministers as the amateurs and herself as the professional.''

Nor was the Queen above using the threat of abdication to have her voice heard. In 1877, Disraeli hoped to negotiate a diplomatic conclusion to the conflict between Russia and Turkey. Because she had been violently anti-Russian since the Crimean War twenty years earlier, Victoria would not (she wrote to Disraeli) ''kiss Russia's feet [nor] be a party to the humiliation of England . . . and would lay down her crown.''

When one judges such actions dangerously unconstitutional, it must be borne in mind that the British constitution is unwritten; it is one of precedent and custom rather than codified expression. The standard articulation of that constitution of tradition, and of where both the real and the formal power centers are located, remains the 1867 work *The English Constitution* by Victoria's contemporary, Walter Bagehot, a versatile writer and editor fluent in sociology, economics and banking.

As Bagehot explained, the British monarch has three essential rights: the right to be consulted, the right to encourage and the right to warn. Whereas the monarch no longer leads armies or presides over state councils, it still remains a highly significant "dignified" component of the nation's government, and this dignity excites and preserves the "reverence of the population." The use of the Queen in a dignified capacity was incalculable, he insisted, for she focused national loyalty and obedience and strengthened government with the force of religion behind her. Moreover, her existence removes the Prime Minister from the dazzling social function that might otherwise threaten his office in making it tempting to parvenus and courtiers. As head of society, the monarch—especially in the case of Victoria, Bagehot insisted—is the prototype of morality, representing what is "mystic in the claims of [government]; that which is occult in its mode of action; that which is brilliant to the eye." Ceremony was important, therefore, because "the attention of the nation is concentrated on one person doing interesting actions." Even more significant, the monarchy is also a kind of disguise: in its stability, real rulers may change without public upheaval.

Taking his cue from the example of Victoria and Albert and their children, Bagehot observed that "a family on the throne is an interesting idea also. It brings down the pride of sovereignty to the level of petty life. . . . A princely marriage is the brilliant edition of a universal fact, and as such it rivets mankind. . . . A royal family sweetens politics by the seasonable addition of nice and pretty events."

But above all things, Bagehot wrote, "our royalty is to be reverenced, and if you begin to poke about it you cannot reverence it. When there is a Select Committee on the Queen, the charm of royalty will be gone. Its mystery is its life. We must not let daylight in upon magic."

Bagehot's dedication to the ideal of monarchy did not blind him to the dangers in Victoria's self-imposed isolation. "The Queen has done almost as much injury to the popularity of the monarchy by her long retirement from public life as the most unworthy of her predecessors did by his profligacy and frivolity." The public cared little how dutiful she might be reading state papers delivered in the famous red dispatch boxes; they sought the ceremonial grandeur of a visible sovereign.

Society was much transformed during Victoria's sixty-four-year reign, and although she had little real power except in the often *pro forma* choice of Cabinet members on the advice of prime ministers, she nevertheless influenced public policy. The Queen was appalled, for example, to see the living conditions of the poor whenever she traveled and complained about such situations to anyone who would listen. Similarly, she had strongly supported the Mines Act of 1842, which forbade the enlistment of women and children workers underground, and since then she had been vocal in her endorsement of various industrial laws proscribing workdays of more than ten hours. In 1867, employed urban men were granted the right to vote. Three years later, competitive examinations were made the standard for entry into the civil service, and free primary education was extended to all. Victoria also looked proudly on favorite causes such as the opening of free public libraries, and in 1871, Oxford and Cambridge were opened to all, regardless of religious beliefs (they had hitherto been restricted to members of the Established Church).

But it was Prime Minister Benjamin Disraeli who succeeded in luring the Queen back into active life. Borrowing a comic line from *As You Like It,* the Prime Minister observed that "when it comes to royalty, you should lay it [flattery] on with a trowel." This psychological masonry he accomplished with great skill, forming the mortar with equal parts of blandishment and sympathy; while convincing her that she was as powerful as ever, Disraeli removed the last traces of that power. Brilliantly, he turned a reclusive widow into a worshiped icon; few seemed to notice the paradox of a staunchly middle-class Queen-Empress.

The major moment in Victoria's return to the world was certainly her acceptance of the Disraeli government's designation of her as Empress of India in 1876; thereafter, she was far more amenable to public activity than at any time since 1861. Disraeli did not design this new title because he was such a devout royalist; he transformed the Queen into a symbol of the Empire so that people would be loyal to the Crown and not concern themselves with the business of statecraft. Fidelity to the Sovereign, in other words, effected another kind of elitism. Led from retirement by Disraeli, Queen Victoria became the living embodiment of personal probity and imperial grandeur. But devotion to an idealized personality could only happen when it was clear that the monarchy played no part in government and yet deserved personal respect. That was the double achievement of her favorite Prime Minister.

A monarch's personal and public character can be seen as incarnating qualities most hallowed in a given society. In the sixteenth century, the absolutism of the Tudors enriched the emerging middle class, but in the two centuries following, a constitutional monarchy was required to end religious conflict and to support the ever-widening influence of commercial wealth. But in the nineteenth century, royal authority was at last and forever checked by the democratic ideal—a reality certainly helped by the unpopularity of the Hanoverian Georges and William IV.

By the time of Victoria's death, the British Empire had doubled in size from what it had been at the time of her accession, to include twenty-three percent of the land surface and twenty percent of the world's population. At home there was astonishing urbanization: in 1837, there were five British cities with over one hundred thousand inhabitants; in 1891, there were twenty-three. And apart from a three-year involvement in the Crimean War, England participated in no significant European conflict from 1815 until the Great War of 1914.

Imperialism was the dominant creed and goal of the nation, and it made the mystical aspect of the monarchy even more important. In this Victoria believed with all her heart, and there was a close parallel between the rise of the Empire and the renewed popularity of the Queen. The crown was, after all, a symbol, and that crown rested on Victoria's head. Thus there occurred the conundrum that by the end of her reign the actual power of the Sovereign had diminished, but her prestige had grown. Her grandmotherliness, her sense of duty and morality, the standards of virtue she held before others—these were impressive only because she first lived them herself. Hence she earned the allegiance of the middle class and prevented them from drifting along with the tide of republicanism, as was happening elsewhere in Europe.

But it would be gilding the Victorian lily to credit to the Queen an understanding of constitutional subtleties. Not only would she readily make her will known, she was also for the most part passive in the changes that occurred, for she had neither the intellectual stamina nor the patience to understand them. Thanks to Albert, the prerogatives of the Crown had increased from 1840 to 1861, but after his death they were rigorously monitored, the result of a stern constitutional vigilance exercised by Prime Ministers Disraeli, Gladstone and Salisbury.

Perhaps the single greatest error of Queen Victoria's judgment following her husband's death concerned her oldest son, Bertie—Albert Edward, the Prince of Wales and heir to the throne. Because of her conviction that this playboy Prince was incapable of serious achievement for Crown and country, she refused to share any royal responsibilities with him except minor ceremonial state duties; he never had access to any dispatch boxes or papers, much less was he invited to ministerial audiences. "Her Majesty," she wrote to the Home Secretary,

> thinks it would be most undesirable to constitute the Heir to the Crown a general representative of Herself, and particularly to bring Him forward too frequently before the people. This would unnecessarily place the Prince of Wales in a position of competing as it were, for popularity with the Queen. Nothing . . . should be more carefully avoided.

But in so acting, the Queen provided her heir with no effective preparation for the job that must one day be his. Part of the reason for her intransigence was an irrational resentment, for when she finally learned about Bertie's licentiousness, she held him directly responsible for his father's death. Had his immoral conduct not required Albert's presence at Cambridge, she reasoned, Prince Albert would never have fallen ill and died. This seems to have been little more than additional support for her own long distrust of her son and dismay over his life; in any case, it was certainly unjust, and it did little to bridge a distance between mother and son that had been widening since childhood. "I never can or shall look at him without a shudder," she said. There were occasional pleasant meetings, but they were always wary in each other's presence. And because she virtually locked Bertie out of her royal life, he had to find an occupation for his time and an outlet for his energies, so the Prince of Wales became precisely what she feared, a libertine, and his frank entry into a life of pleasure-seeking made him even more cautious in his mother's presence.

With her profound reverence for her own station, Queen Victoria did, of course, inspire awe. Additionally, she was naturally quite shy of others—"girlishly shy," according to one who married into the family. In conversation the Queen had a habit of hesitantly shrugging her shoulders and nervously smiling, which revealed prominent gums and small teeth. Except for her girth, everything about her was doll-like: short and plump, dressed in black silk and wearing a lace cap on her graying hair, she had both an imposing dignity and a homely simplicity. As she gained even more weight in her fifties and later, Victoria came to resemble a rather overstuffed fieldmouse—but this belied a real benevolence and kindliness that were, as she aged, more and more evident to her family, and especially to her grandchildren, whom she adored.

The family grew rapidly. Just over a year after Albert's death, there occurred the arranged marriage between Bertie and Princess Alexandra, daughter of the future King of Denmark and a woman with royal connections all over Europe—a fact that in Victoria's mind made her the ideal bride for the future expansion of the Empire.

But the Prince of Wales was not entirely indifferent. Now that the Nellie Clifden affair was history, he recognized Alexandra's beauty and charm. Not long after their reunion in 1862, Bertie, encouraged by his mother and her ministers, duly proposed marriage.

Alexandra was not only one of the eligible belles of Europe, she was also an eighteen-year-old of great warmth and modesty. Raised in genteel but straitened circumstances, she was a girl whose polished manner appealed to Bertie. Gracious, compassionate and concerned for the poor and suffering, Alexandra bewitched everyone she met. Tall and slender, with chestnut hair, ivory skin and blue eyes that seemed to turn violet at dusk and in candlelight, she retained a timeless radiance and dignity well into her seventies.

Bertie and Alexandra, twenty-one and eighteen, were married at St. George's Chapel, Windsor, on March 10, 1863, an event celebrated by the Poet Laureate, Alfred, Lord Tennyson:

Sea King's daughter from over the sea,
                         Alexandra!
Saxon and Norman and Dane are we,
But all of us Danes in our welcome of thee,
                         Alexandra!

Jenny Lind, the famous soprano known as the "Swedish Nightingale," sang at the wedding. Her rendition of the late Prince Albert's chorale, "This Day with Joyful Heart and Voice," was interrupted only by a momentary wail from Vicky's unmanageable four-year-old son, William. Prevented from further noise by his uncles, the child bit them on the legs, threw a purloined jewel into the choir and generally made himself a nuisance. Decades later, as the Kaiser of Germany, William would cause his uncle Bertie further anxiety.

Alexandra was pregnant within the month, and in her protracted mourning the Queen hoped that progeny would mean the end of Bertie's intemperate youth and the beginning of a quietly stable domestic life. Such was not to be.

After the newlyweds moved into the renovated Marlborough House, Pall Mall, London, their first child was born prematurely on January 8, 1864, and (at Victoria's insistence) named, like his father, for his grandfather. Second in line to the throne, three-pound Prince Albert Victor Christian Edward (nicknamed Eddy at home) was sickly and apathetic even after several months, and Queen Victoria, so ardent a supporter of the marriage, began to wonder if she had chosen a daughter-in-law wisely. Whereas earlier she had thought Alexandra "a dear, excellent, right-minded soul," the Queen now occasionally vacillated and wondered if she might be not "worth the price we paid for her." Meantime, father or no, Bertie resumed a playboy's madcap life of gambling, late-night dining, endless indiscriminate socializing, and cavorting with mistresses in England and on the Continent, where he frequently repaired—perhaps as much to defy his mother as to pursue his own pleasures. "Sad stories have indeed reached our ears of scandals in high life," wrote the Queen to her son, "which is, indeed, much to be deplored; and still more so in the way in which (to use a common proverb) they 'wash their dirty linen in public.' " But Victorian London needed a master of the revels, and none was a more willing candidate than the Prince of Wales.

For a time Alix tried desperately to keep up with her husband's whirlwind of social activities. They seemed at first to have been well paired; neither cared for anything remotely highbrow—they much preferred clothes and entertainment to culture and aesthetics. But whereas Bertie loved to carouse nightly until dawn, Alix lived for the warmth and security of home and children. Increasingly intemperate and corpulent, he was a jolly roué and an indefatigable philanderer; she, virtuous and abstemious, was a simple and straightforward soul. "I often think her lot is not an easy one," Queen Victoria noted accurately, "but she is very fond of Bertie—though not blind!"

Indeed, Alix was entirely aware of her husband's misdemeanors, but she remained long-suffering, patient and conscientious. She was also vague, scatterbrained, uncurious about the world and wildly disorganized—venial faults, to be sure, but irritating nonetheless. She was a spontaneous, elegant, empathetic and devoted woman, but to a mercurial gadfly like Bertie, who knew his educational deficiencies and appreciated the company of bright people, his wife must have been maddening to live with. Her idea of a spirited evening was parlor games at home, pastimes much less exciting for him than his expensive nights at the Midnight, Garrick and Savage clubs. He frequently darted off to Paris for a week at liberty. As a couple they could not have been more different from Victoria and Albert.

Their differences and his infidelity notwithstanding, Bertie and Alix were deeply fond of and always respectful toward each other. Had divorce been an option for them (it was unimaginable for Royals and rare enough in polite society), they almost certainly would not have pursued it.

As for public opinion of the Prince of Wales, the press was astonishingly mercurial. At times Bertie was reviled as worthless and irresponsible (not by name, of course, but as one of "those at Court"); at other times he was viewed with affection precisely because of his all too human weaknesses. In any case, in the 1860s he was regarded as mostly irrelevant; the march of progress would continue perfectly well without him.

But Victoria set a precedent. In 1864, she engaged the palace's first full-time salaried Royal Press Secretary. Thomas

Septimus Beard, the thirty-seven-year-old grandson of Joseph Doan (Court Newsman to the hapless George III), was henceforth required to attend Queen Victoria every day she was in London and, at her direction, to deliver approved memoranda concerning royal matters to the editors of the city's nine daily newspapers. With Beard's appointment began the tradition that in the late twentieth century has evolved into the Office of the Press Secretary to Her Majesty the Queen—a staff charged with the delicate task of representing the royal image before a press with an increasingly insatiable appetite for the tiniest morsel of royal news, and especially royal scandal.

Bertie was not the only occasion for Beard's employment. There were whispers of impropriety about Victoria herself, and although never substantiated, she apparently thought them potentially damaging. The talk had to do with Victoria's favorite servant, the Scotsman John Brown, who had attended her and Albert as early as 1849. Seven years younger than the Queen, he began as a "gillie," or huntsman's guide, when the royal couple visited the Highlands; by 1859, Brown was, she thought, "really the perfection of a servant." Handsome and plainspoken, he won a special place in the affections of the monarch after her husband's death—a position so widely known that the Queen was for a time thought to have been his lover or even to have secretly married; she was often referred to as "Mrs. Brown."

Those closer to the palace knew better. Sir Henry Ponsonby, Victoria's private secretary, understood Brown's value and why the Queen put up with his unusually brusque and familiar manner: he was a first-class servant, and his refusal to bow to protocol was a refreshing counterpoise to the archness and awe that prevented the Queen from having any other close male friend. With hindsight, Victoria's warm attachment to Brown —and his to her—suggests that they may have been in love, but there is not a shred of evidence that they were ever lovers. Any expression of intimacy other than noncarnal words or gestures would have been entirely out of character for both. Ponsonby wrote to his brother Arthur what everyone close to the Queen knew: that Brown was "certainly a favourite—but he is only a Servant and nothing more—and what I suppose began as a joke about his constant attendance has been perverted into a libel that the Queen has married him."

To be sure, Brown enjoyed an unprecedented direct access to the Queen that enabled him to enter her rooms without knocking, to address her in his thick burr as "wumman," and, when she asked if he thought she had grown fat, to reply plainly, "Well, I think you are." His injunctions to her to sit still while he tucked in her carriage rug or pinned her cape seemed sure signs of familiarity. "Hoots, then, wumman," he said loudly one day after pricking her chin with a hat pin, "can ye no hold yer head up?"

His honesty and bluntness extended to her children and her ministers. "Ye'll no see your royal mother till five o'clock!" he shouted at the Prince of Wales, who arrived an hour earlier for a visit. This was as typical as his remark to General Henry Gardiner, who arrived for an appointment and, en route to the Queen's rooms, asked Brown how she was and what she was saying. "Well," replied Brown airily, "she just said, 'Here's that damned fellow Gardiner come, and he'll be poking his nose into everything.' " Everyone else, after all—even her family—treated Victoria as the Queen; Brown endeared himself to her because only he (after Albert) looked upon her as a "wumman."

Brown was also a heavy drinker whose eventual death was hastened by a lifetime of excessive alcohol intake. But even this habit failed to anger Victoria, for Brown worked long hours in her service without complaint and, for her, without error, much less disgrace. He could pass out cold drunk in a palace corridor after leaving her rooms, but the Queen dismissed the report with a wave of her chubby hand, for John Brown was beyond criticism. In fact, with him the Queen felt free to indulge her own occasional liking for a sip in late afternoon, for she loathed both the taste and the ubiquitous ritual of tea. Once, when she had a cold and drank a cup of tea that Brown had prepared, she congratulated him: it was the best brew she had ever tasted. "Well, it should be, ma'am," he replied matter-of-factly. "I put a grand nip o' whiskey in it."

Four years after Albert's death, the Queen brought Brown from the Highlands to be her personal attendant at London, Windsor and Osborne, a gesture that roused the jealous ire of courtiers and of her family. His familiarity was misunderstood and his constant proximity was unappreciated, even when he courageously leaped to save her from several assassination attempts. Thus it may well have occurred to the Queen that in addition to managing the press reports about Bertie, Septimus Beard would be useful in diluting those about Brown. He remained close to her—indeed, her closest friend—until his death eighteen years before hers.

Bertie and Alexandra's second son, christened George Frederick Ernest Albert, was born June 3, 1865; in due course he would be Duke of York and King George V. From the start he was healthier and more alert than his older brother, the indifferent and neurasthenic Eddy. As the boys approached adolescence, they became close friends, Georgie assuming protective leadership and setting a good example of diligence and obedience. Eddy was second in line to the throne after his father, but no one wished to allude to this eventuality when looking into the vacant eyes of a boy who was growing up but not maturing, who stared but seemed not to see, who took an interest in nothing but himself (and had by adolescence an almost consuming interest in sex), and who utterly lacked personality. As for Georgie, his childhood attracted little public attention.

However much people condoled Alix and admired her patience, the family she shepherded was generally regarded as *infra dignitatem*—there was by now enough bad talk about her hedonistic husband to taint the entire Royal Family. Bertie seemed to be the useless prince of a distant mother.

The gossip was not stemmed by the circumstances attending a tragic development just before Alix gave birth to her third child, Princess Louise, on February 20, 1867. Confined during the last six weeks with a serious case of rheumatic fever, she bore a healthy daughter but was not comforted by her husband, who was at the Windsor Races. The fever left Alix with a permanent limp and exacerbated her congenital (but until now quiescent) otosclerosis—a progressive ear disease that was untreatable at the time and soon resulted in total deafness. This rapidly deteriorating condition alienated her even more from the companionship of her husband and his social circle, and it led her to depend ever more heavily, as a substitute, on the love she gave and received from her children.

As with all such relations by default, her devotion, for all its depth and sincerity, was not without problems. When Alix wrote to George and ended "with a great big kiss for your lovely little face," he was a bearded twenty-five-year-old navy gunboat commander, well accustomed to other female attentions. Still, he addressed his replies as ever to his "own darling sweet little beloved Motherdear" and signed them from "Your loving little Georgie." Perhaps no letters surviving from the Victorian era were more overripe with endearments. Perhaps, too, only the essential goodness of Alix and the rugged navy life she allowed Georgie prevented the attachment of dangerously neurotic bonds between them.

Alix's next child, Princess Victoria (born July 6, 1868), was kept at home so long as her mother's confidante, companion and secretary that she never acquired the normal give-and-take of social life. A plain girl with heavy-lidded eyes and widely spaced teeth, she was socially repressed by her mother, who unwittingly stifled the child and stymied the progress of suitors. Even after Alix's death, "Toria" had been so immured in her ways that she remained single, much loved by her brother George and her nieces and nephews, but lonely and enclosed behind emotional walls not of her own making. Her sister Maud, a year younger, fared better: her marriage made her Queen of Norway. The last of the Waleses' six children, Prince Alexander, died the day after his birth in 1871.

Little Georgie's father, meanwhile, continued to be the talk of the town. By now very fat but meticulous in the cut of his wardrobe, the King was helped by his tailor, who disguised his plumpness with style. Particular about the slightest element of finery, Bertie popularized a number of sartorial innovations: the homburg hat, the Norfolk jacket, the black dinner jacket and the practice of leaving unfastened the bottom button of a gentleman's vest—the latter more a concession to corpulence than to elegance.

With their purchase of Sandringham House in Norfolk, the Waleses had a more private residence than Marlborough House. Previously an unsightly and neglected country mansion, Sandringham (bought cheaply by Prince Albert not long before his death) was set on remarkably fecund game territory, and soon Bertie enthusiastically expanded the estate and supervised the complete reconstruction of the house. Still, it remained a gloomy, forbidding place, drenched in dark colors, overlaid with imitation Tudor beams, fumed oak and stained glass, surrounded by heavy shrubbery, and dotted with forlorn statues and unimaginative gardens.

Much as Bertie loved Sandringham, no place could hold him for long. His annual schedule took him there for sports at Christmas and through January, but then he was off to Paris and the European capitals in March, to London in June, and to the races at Goodwood, yachting at Cowes and the German spas in July (where he took the cure after months of culinary overindulgence). He spent August grouse-shooting at Balmoral before returning to Sandringham. There, guests were gaily entertained, dragooned into raucous parlor games and, in the tradition of rude English amusement among the upper classes, regularly subjected to the most outrageous practical jokes. More than once, for example, Bertie put a live lobster in a guest's bed; Christmas mince pies were stuffed with hot mustard; a visitor climbing the carpeted staircase had to mind his step or be knocked senseless by Alix and the children, careening down on silver trays and crying "Hoy!" and "Whee!" as they enjoyed a substitute for a winter toboggan. None of this was considered unroyal deportment.

And so went the routine, virtually unchanged, through Bertie's years as Prince of Wales and as King. Endless travel, ceaseless philandering, indiscriminate hunting and shooting, the patronage of expensive restaurants and cheap entertainments—these defined the life of the man who seemed in no way suitable for the role of king.

Were it not for Alix, who on the contrary had many of the traits required to make her the ideal Queen Consort, the whispers of public disaffection with her husband would have swelled to shouts after the Mordaunt scandal. Harriet Mordaunt, a somewhat highly strung and unstable society lady, was known to the Royal Family for years. She was a Moncrieffe, daughter of a family living near the Queen at Balmoral. In 1866, at eighteen, Harriet married Sir Charles Mordaunt and two years later bore him a blind child. "Charlie, you are not the father of that child," Harriet soon announced tearfully. As it happened, she could not be entirely sure who had sired the hapless infant, for Harriet added that she had been quite busy during the first year of her marriage, keeping company with a number of the Prince of Wales's social set—in fact, with the Prince himself.

To render the situation still more soap-operatic, Sir Charles broke into his wife's writing desk and found letters to her from Bertie. Although these were boringly innocent notes such as might have come from an old schoolmate, Mordaunt chose to play the dishonored husband and to believe the ravings of an obviously demented wife who spoke of herself as if she were the greatest courtesan since Madame de Pompadour. For once wrongly accused of precisely the illicit activity at which he had become proficient, the Prince of Wales was summoned to court during the Mordaunt divorce case, where he acquitted himself with great dignity. Poor Lady Harriet could not give testimony from her cell in a lunatic asylum, and the case was dismissed. With that, Bertie was off to relax at a Prussian gambling casino, sans Alix. But the public delivered an independent judgment, and after the Prince returned, ugly remarks were hurled at the Waleses when they appeared at Ascot and at the theater; contrariwise, there were only cheers for Alix when she ventured out alone.

Identical reactions from London crowds followed the charges (also in 1871) quietly brought by the aptly named Lady Vane Tempest, one of Bertie's mistresses. Her alcoholic and insane husband left her penniless, and she was not above threatening to reveal publicly the "sad secret" of her affair with the Prince of Wales unless he was forthcoming with "funds to meet necessary expenses and to buy the discretion of servants." Her Ladyship was given a cottage in Ramsgate, but soon, like the fisherman's wife, she turned up again in London, petitioning the Prince's secretary for money to meet "the expenses of two houses and extra servants." Eventually she settled down quietly and vanished into a well-deserved obscurity.

A small sum also had to be sent to the family of the late Giulia Barucci, who had openly styled her career as that of "the greatest whore in the world" and whose clients included several crowned heads of Europe. Unlike the bland missives he had addressed to Harriet Mordaunt, the Prince had written letters his own representative described as "of a delicate nature." The letters were bought back for a reasonable sum.

These tawdry matters, yoked with Queen Victoria's persistent absence from public life, led even Conservative members of Parliament to rise in chambers, condemning an indolent and irresponsible Royal Family. Similarly, crowds gathered more and more frequently in Hyde Park, shouting for an end to the monarchy and the establishment of a Republic of Great Britain.

Victoria, unmoved and unfrightened, rightly believed her son innocent of Harriet Mordaunt's charges and lamented the public's imputation of guilt against him. Nevertheless, the Queen saw the slurs in the first case as reasonable in light of the second and third. Prime Minister William Gladstone then suggested that Bertie might be gainfully employed as some kind of administrator in Dublin—"an admirable opportunity," Gladstone wrote, "for giving the Prince the advantage of a political training which, from no fault of his own, he can have hardly be said hitherto to have enjoyed." For the Queen, however, Ireland was "in no fit state to be experimented upon." Furthermore, in a letter to her Lord Chancellor she mourned Bertie's

> imprudence which cannot but damage him in the eyes of the middle and lower classes, which is most deeply lamented in these days when the higher classes, in their frivolous, selfish and pleasure-seeking lives, do more to increase the spirit of democracy than anything else.

For Queen Victoria the only thing worse than the spirit of democracy would be a Prussian army in Kensington Gardens. No tyrant or absolutist, she nevertheless attached to the word "democracy" her own connotation of a dreaded rule by unruly masses. None was more threatening to her than the dissolute aristocracy; considering her Hanoverian ancestors, it is hard to disagree.

As if to remind the public of her beloved Albert, who had no patience with reprobates or aristocrats, many of the Queen's public forays were excuses to memorialize her late Consort. The Queen opened the Royal Albert Hall in 1871 and, nearby, the ornate Albert Memorial five years later. A lavish confection, the memorial rose almost two hundred feet and was studded with crystal, jasper, onyx and marble.

With its own increasingly democratic spirit, the London press was turning up the heat too. "Even the staunchest supporters of monarchy," ran a typical newspaper editorial, shake their heads and express anxiety as to whether the Queen's successor will have the tact and talent to keep royalty upon its legs and out of the gutter. When, therefore, the people of England read one year in their journals of the future King appearing prominently in the divorce court and in another of his being the centre of attention at a German gaming table, or public hall, it is not at all surprising that rumours concerning the Queen's health have occasioned anxiety and apprehension.

Amid this cauldron of public and private complaints, destiny intervened—very nearly tragically but at last auspiciously. Exactly ten years after his father fell ill with (as it was thought) a fatal case of typhoid fever, his son went down with the same illness in November and December 1871. Delirious, shaking with seizures and struggling to breathe, thirty-year-old Bertie lay for weeks very near death. Bell ringers in London's churches and cathedrals were at the ready, black bunting was hauled out of camphor in shops and government offices, and the Queen alternated with Alix in keeping a loving, attentive and terrified vigil at the bedside.

But to everyone's astonishment the Prince recovered—an event celebrated by a thanksgiving service at St. Paul's. For several months the earlier cries for a republic were drowned out by repeated choruses of "God Save the Queen."

Clockwise, from left: King Edward VII, Alice Keppel, Lillie
Langtry, Edward VII at play.

3

Maidens and Mistresses 1871 to 1901

The trials of life *begin* with marriage!
QUEEN VICTORIA

It was not until 1886, when his friend Archibald Rosebery
became Foreign Secretary, that the Prince of Wales, then near-
ing forty-five years of age, received copies of various secret
dispatches making him privy to the workings of government.
This was done without the knowledge of the Queen, who con-

tinued to disallow her son any participation in official duties and therefore any practical preparation for the throne.

Bertie had won his mother's approval for the way he comported himself on a two-month visit to India in 1876 when he condemned the racial prejudice of British officials who treated the Indians (as he wrote to his mother) "with brutality and contempt." In addition, he showed promise in dealing with that country's leaders. But another unpleasant bit of calumny attended the voyage, and this quickly diluted his mother's admiration.

Lord Randolph Churchill (father of young Winston) threatened both Alix and Bertie with public humiliation after Lady Aylesford, who once had an innocent flirtation with Bertie, became the lover of Churchill's brother while Lord Aylesford was on the royal tour of India. Attempting to charge the Prince of Wales with having been the broker for the affair after he pressured Aylesford to join the tour (thus deliberately leaving the field clear for the seduction), Churchill went as far as to confront poor Alix in her own drawing room. All this finally came to naught, and the Waleses emerged more popular than ever—but not before the issue directly involved Her Majesty, who saw her son vindicated only after considerable anguish.

Bertie was, then, almost invariably connected with some unpleasantness or other, an association justified in Victoria's mind when the Prince openly and flagrantly took his first long-term mistress, the comely and ambitious Lillie Langtry. Unhappily married, an actress of no great talent but beguiling charm, she was for more than a dozen years acknowledged as the favorite of the smitten Prince of Wales. Together Bertie and Lillie traveled, accepted invitations for weekends at country houses and dined in public; Alexandra patiently sustained all this, partly because she knew objection would have availed her nothing, partly because she would not disgrace her husband or herself. With an understanding that must have come from real devotion, the Princess of Wales disallowed any ill word against either Bertie or Lillie. She spoke of him only in the most loving terms to their children, and with typical magnanimity she invited Lillie to dine with her family at Marlborough House.

In an important way, both Court and public countenanced the Prince's mistresses more readily than they did his wider social circle. Actors, Americans, Jewish bankers, self-made millionaires—all those considered to inhabit the fringes of polite society he found fascinating, although aristocrats and some politicians thought this kind of company disreputable. But the Prince kept his own counsel, believing it foolish snobbery to prefer the upper classes over charm, talent or money. In this regard he was contributing to the modern idea that people ought to be respected for what they do, not for what they inherit.

Bertie's connections to all classes of people evoked a real compassion for the condition of the poor. On February 22, 1884, he gave his first speech in the House of Lords. On surveying some of the worst slums in London, he was appalled at the sight of hungry urchins in rags, shivering in doorways and unheated buildings, many of them ill or moribund from starvation and cold. "The condition of the poor," he told Parliament, "was disgraceful." He could not introduce legislation, of course, but he could chide and encourage, and this the Prince of Wales, now in his forties and trying to find his place in history as well as society, was determined to do.

Meantime, his mother, however much she preferred to isolate herself from the public, could not insulate herself from "the changes and chances of this mortal life"—one of many phrases that stayed with her from the Book of Common Prayer. In 1878, at fifty-nine, the Queen became a great-grandmother when Vicky's daughter Charlotte had a child. But from that year onward there seemed to be more tragedies than joys for the House of Saxe-Coburg-Gotha. Princess Alice, the Queen's second daughter, who had lovingly attended Bertie during his typhoid, lost her three-year-old son in a dreadful accident and then succumbed to diphtheria at thirty-five. Depression enshrouded the Queen again on the deaths of her hemophiliac son Leopold and of her great friend and counselor Disraeli. Frail and often restricted to the sidelines of life because of hemophilia, Leopold went to the Riviera for a rest in 1884. There he fell on a hotel staircase and died after a hemorrhage at the age of thirty; after Alice, Leopold was the second of Victoria's children to predecease her. And then Vicky's husband, the Emperor of Germany, died of throat cancer.

But it was the passing of John Brown, after thirty-four years in her service, that most devastated the Queen after the death of her husband.

In March 1883, Brown collapsed with a severe infection and died in a coma; his immune system had been compromised by years of seven-day-a-week duties and heavy drinking. "My good, faithful Brown passed away early this morning," Victoria wrote in her journal on the twenty-ninth of March. "Am terribly upset by this loss, which removes one who was so devoted and attached to my service and who did so much for my personal comfort. It is the loss not only of a servant, but of a real friend." To a wreath she sent for his coffin, Victoria had a dedication affixed: "A tribute of loving, grateful, and everlasting friendship and affection from his truest, best, and most faithful friend Victoria R. & I." *

As one of Victoria's biographers observed, Brown "seduced no women, accepted no bribes, lived for no one but the Queen." And referring to her family's jealousy of John Brown's devoted familiarity toward their mother, Bertie's aide, Sir William Knollys, wrote, "I presume all the Family will rejoice at his death, but I think very probably they are shortsighted." The Queen, he might have added, was not. Scorning the contempt and mockery of the small-minded, she had allowed herself a rich and true friendship, and when she wrote his obituary for *The Times*, she clearly wished the world to know that the heart of the Queen was not sealed against love.

By the time of her Golden Jubilee at the age of sixty-eight, in the summer of 1887, Victoria had the respect and affection of the entire nation. Tens of thousands lined a parade route, cheering the Queen and holding up banners embossed with "Fifty years runs not out!" and "Good sovereign—no change required!" The tiny, plump figure disdained ermine, a state coach, and an imperial crown, preferring her white bonnet, a plain black dress, and a ride in an open landau. To the crowds she was not, at last, a grieving, reclusive, and aloof widow neglecting her public duties as monarch; quite the contrary, Victoria was the mother of them all. She was familiar and cozy, but at the same time she was the corporate personality

---

* The letter *I* was added after the *R* when the Queen accepted the designation Empress of India in 1876; thus she was *Victoria, Regina [et] Imperatrix,* Queen and Empress. Just so, male descendants on the throne would be *Rex* and *Imperator* until the independence of India in 1947. Queen Elizabeth II has always therefore signed herself "Elizabeth R."

who represented a nation's achievements, its cherished ideal of domestic virtue, its wish to be at once grand and homely. She herself was Imperial England.

However much that Empire depended on its navy, Victoria did not think much of it as a preparation for the throne. It was too narrow a life, she felt, and led to a crude, jingoistic chauvinism. "The very rough sort of life to which boys are exposed on board ship is the very thing not calculated to make a refined and amiable Prince," she wrote perceptively, displaying a canny sense of men and monarchs.

Victoria was not pleased, therefore, when Bertie enrolled his two sons in that branch of the Queen's service. When Eddy and George were sixteen and fifteen, they shipped out for a three-year stint aboard H.M.S. *Bacchante,* accompanied by their tutor, the Reverend John Neale Dalton. At Bertie's explicit direction, Dalton was no academic martinet; his children, the Prince insisted, would not be subjected to the fierce rigors of his own childhood. Thus Eddy and George had only the most casual private education; indeed, their grounding in all formal subjects was inferior to that of the dullest country schoolboy. They learned much more about things like tattooing. In Japan the brothers acquired on their arms impressively fearsome dragon designs, much elaborated later in Jerusalem.

In the navy Eddy was such an incompetent that in 1883 his father transferred him to Trinity College, Cambridge, where he failed just as miserably—doubtless because he could barely read. Coarse of speech and manner, Eddy was also dyslexic, partially deaf, listless and lethargic. He spent two fruitless years at college where the only impression he made seems to have been on a cadre of handsome young men who attached themselves romantically to him. Thus with an ironic twist of fate, his father found himself repeating *his* father's journey and with the same purpose: just as Albert had swept down to reprimand Bertie at Cambridge, so now Bertie moved in fury and snatched Eddy from school.

The hapless simpleton was then sent off to the army, of all places, where he was incapable of following the most basic commands, much less of leading his fellows. In 1890, twenty-six and back in civilian life, Eddy was created Duke of Clarence and Avondale by his grandmother. Still, his avid pastimes were sex and, less seriously, polo. He seemed to have a languid, seductive charm with young ladies—and not only with ladies, for he was at least once involved in a raid on a notorious homosexual brothel in Cleveland Street. The charm may have had more to do with his royal status and prerogatives, however, than any genuine appeal as a Lothario, although that forte would surely not have required any special mental talent or social grace. In any case, by 1890 his health was already deteriorating. French brandy and Turkish cigarettes were taking their toll; he suffered severe attacks of gout, and he seems to have contracted every venereal disease known to doctors.

"He frankly preferred pleasure to any form of work," wrote one historian; in that regard he was his father's son. He also inherited a mythic sense of indiscretion. His grandmother wanted him to marry a German Princess, and so Eddy dutifully fell in love with his first cousin, Princess Alice's daughter, also called Alix. She wisely refused him, married the Crown Prince of Russia, later the Czar, and with her husband and children met a dreadful fate in 1918. Within weeks of Alix's refusal, Eddy was courting Princess Hélène of Orléans, daughter of the Comte de Paris (pretender to the French throne), who offered to renounce her Roman Catholicism to be his bride; her parents and the Pope put a stop to that romance.

Meanwhile, George fared better—in character if not intelligence. At his maturity he was only five feet six, with fair brown hair, crystalline blue eyes and a shy smile. His manner lacked confidence and his speech conviction, but he was candid and had a keen, unsophisticated sense of fun that was mostly manifest in teasing mates. To his credit he always took as good as he gave.

George was punctual, tidy, reliable and dutiful, which is often the best that can be said for Victoria's male progeny. The inspiration for these respectable habits was owed to his tutor's constantly setting before him the model of his grandmother, in whose presence George felt both warmth and awe; he recognized that the monarch was both separate from ordinary life and somehow a participant in it. Much of this reverence George also felt for his father, the man who would one day be his liege Lord and Sovereign. And Bertie's punctilious attention to the details of official wardrobe and ceremony underscored for George the grand nature of Papa's destiny.

For cozier matters, there was his mother, for whom his affection always remained deep and floridly expressed, as hers was for him. In the tone of their overripe letters, George took his cue from Alix, whose devotion became ever more benevolently possessive and stifling with each year.

But maternal devotion did not prevent George from explorations other than seafaring. Although his sexual life was never so louche as Eddy's, his diary entries for 1892 reveal that by that time he had kept a mistress in a flat at Southsea. And in St. John's Wood, London, there lived another, who shared her bed alternately with both brothers. "She is a ripper," George wrote enthusiastically in his diary. But his true love was elsewhere, and it seems never to have been consummated. Julie Stonor, daughter of a lady-in-waiting to Alix, adored the Prince, and he was smitten with her. But she was a commoner and a Catholic, two insurmountable impediments at the time. "There it is," wrote Alix sympathetically to her son, "and, alas, rather a sad case for you both, my two poor children. I only wish you could marry and be happy, but, alas, I fear that cannot be."

George at twenty-five had a stolid, serious character determined by his years in the navy; ten years later that was still his occupation. "His temperament, his prejudices and affections, his habits of thought and conduct, his whole outlook on life," wrote his biographer, Harold Nicolson, "were formed and molded" during his years aboard the *Britannia* and the *Bacchante.* In other words, he was a loyal, sober young royal, but at the same time he lacked his grandfather's intellect and his father's charm. Like the King, however, he had a fierce temper, and after months of placid affability, he might explode in a terrifying tirade over some minor matter. "Life at sea," as another chronicler noted, "had given him set opinions, a mania for order and punctuality and a stiff social manner which hid an inner diffidence and narrowness. It had also developed a deep devotion to duty and the sturdy faith in British superiority that Queen Victoria so abhorred in a prince."

To put the matter bluntly, George's mind was as small as the rooms he preferred—not crowded but tidy, neat, and reminiscent of the shipboard bunks always so fondly remembered. Throughout his life his only diversions were stamp collecting and an occasional game of polo and billiards. Like

51

most Royals (although not always those who married them), he avoided books as if they were contaminated with a deadly germ. As late as 1891, when he was twenty-six, his letters and journals contain not a single reference to domestic or international political events. But this was not considered much of a handicap. At the end of the nineteenth century the Royal Family was not summoned nearly as often to civic functions and ceremonies as they were later. Even so, there was general public satisfaction even if one not in the direct line of succession to the throne pursued an unimaginative career without distinction. After the Prince of Wales, the dreary Eddy was heir, but such considerations preoccupied no one, for Victoria at seventy-two was quite hale, and Bertie at fifty seemed indefatigable.

At the end of November 1891, however, George fell gravely ill with typhoid fever. Victoria and Alexandra responded to this news with almost deranged panic. It was thirty years exactly since Prince Albert had died, and twenty since Bertie's near-fatal illness. There was not a moment of ease for anyone at Sandringham until Prince George was out of danger at Christmas. In fact, that holiday season and into the new year there was a series of dramatic events which by turns affected and afflicted the family—an engagement, a sudden death, and a shifting of the line of succession. Within five weeks the future of the British monarchy was forever altered.

On December 7, 1891, *The Times* announced the engagement of His Royal Highness Prince Albert Victor, Duke of Clarence and Avondale, eldest son of the Prince of Wales, to Princess Victoria Mary of Teck, a girl he had known since childhood. The union, arranged by the mothers of the young couple and enthusiastically approved by Queen Victoria, was not forced on anyone—in fact, Bertie (like Alix) made it clear to all his children that he wanted their choice of marriage partners to be their own.

For all his weakness of character, Eddy recognized the opposite in others and felt the stirring of love for Mary. She felt the call of duty. ''To my great surprise Eddy proposed to me,'' she wrote in her diary, adding with typical *sang froid,* ''Of course I said yes. We are both very happy.'' As were both families, for the girl was the Queen's second cousin.

Princess Victoria Mary was considered the ideal mate for a royal heir and a suitable future Queen Consort. She was an elegantly attractive, graceful young woman with alert, china-blue eyes, a porcelain complexion, a slim waist and a shy smile that simultaneously gave the impression that at any moment she might be wonderfully amused and that she had a kind of modest nobility. Most important, she was of sterling character.

Never vulgar, she loved to laugh, and when amused she did so without either affectation or false dignity. She had an astonishing memory and acute powers of observation, and so she rarely forgot the details of anything she saw or heard. This instilled a trait that grew with age: she was invariably right, which was a far more attractive virtue in a Royal than in someone less august. Her erect carriage, stately comportment and golden brown coiffure made her seem taller than her adult height of five feet five, an illusion that was abetted by toques, tiaras and high heels. Even in her twenties she wore the trademark stacked-up hairstyle that would be hers to the grave: pulled back tightly at the temples, with a braid in the back and a curled fringe over the forehead.

Princess Victoria Mary was successively Duchess of York, Princess of Wales, Queen of England and Empress of India, and finally the Dowager Queen. Her life spanned the reigns of six monarchs, and in this saga she was perhaps the single most important influence on the family into which she married. Thus the personal history of Victoria Mary Augusta Louise Olga Pauline Claudine Agnes of Teck—always called May by her family—should be briefly considered.*

She was born on May 26, 1867, in the same room of Kensington Palace as Queen Victoria, her second cousin: May's great-grandfather was King George III, her grandfather the brother of Victoria's father. May was the daughter of poor German parents who can only be called minor royalty. Her father, born in Vienna, was the gloomy, nervous and peevish Prince Francis of Teck, impoverished son of the Duke of Würt-

---

* When she became Queen, Princess Victoria Mary dropped her first name forever since "Queen Victoria" was obviously unsuitable. "May" was only a family nickname, and so she styled herself Queen Mary. To avoid the confusion of so many Victorias at this point in the narrative, "May" will be used here until her accession and "Mary" thereafter.

temberg and an emotionally unstable wraith after a stroke in his forties; her mother, born in Hanover, was the jolly, imperious, extravagant and enormously obese Princess Mary Adelaide of Cambridge ("Fat Mary," as she was called with apparently genuine affection by those who knew her), and her grandfather was George III. Despite the burden of an infirm and difficult husband and a purse that was always near to empty, Mary Adelaide had a congenitally sunny disposition.

The only girl among five children, May learned early on to comport herself with tact and diplomacy in a boy's world. In her mother she saw how a strong and determined woman could manage a mercurial and troublesome man; thus Mary Adelaide's example was before her as she contemplated marriage to an intemperate roué.

"Do you think I can really take this on, Mama?" she asked her mother plaintively after the engagement to Eddy, as she gradually heard more and more about her fiancé's dissolute life. Of course she could, replied her mother. See how Mama herself had managed a weak man? May certainly was dutiful in accepting the summons to bring her talents and life to the service of the Royal Family. She had, after all, been raised to revere and support the throne, which was itself the lynchpin for the aristocracy. At the same time there was much of the Cinderella story in her case. She was a nobleman's daughter consigned to genteel poverty whose station was now to be altered; one day she would be the Queen. The marriage to Eddy may have seemed daunting, but as Mama said, it was both manageable and teeming with advantages. May would move at once from obscurity.

She continued to develop intellectually and culturally throughout her life although her education proceeded haphazardly. At four she made her first visit to the Continent and began lessons in German. By sixteen she was also fluent in French, and she learned Italian when financial ill fortune forced her family out of England and they settled in a Florentine *pensione*. During this time May acquired her lifelong interest in art and antique collecting, a hobby that did not require great sums at that time. She also became a passionate reader, although of mostly middle-brow fiction. (She first saw *Hamlet* and read the great Russian novelists only a few years before her death.)

"I have spent all my afternoons lately going to *Museums,*" she wrote. "How much one learns & picks up, & how much nicer than going out to tea & gossip." Yet it must be said that her primary interest in art was royal iconography—miniatures, portraits and bibelots depicting the English royal families of the eighteenth and nineteenth centuries. "She could usually identify the better-known marks on English china," according to her biographer, "and could recognise, in furniture, the works of Hepplewhite or Chippendale; but she never bought a good painting in her life."

May disliked analytical discussions and was generally very much a woman of her time—that is, uninterested in the social causes of the widespread misery in England that made her family's straitened circumstances seem like sybaritic luxury. Yet from her mother's active involvement in charitable causes (a trait Mary Adelaide shared with her friend Princess Alexandra), May learned the emptiness of mere verbal sympathy for the disadvantaged, and in later life her concern for the poor suggests that she never forgot the modest condition of her own early years. As a child she assisted her mother in volunteer work with soldiers' widows and children who had neither pensions nor property and were farmed out in wretched public housing. This work and her visits to homeless children were the basis of her later, well-documented concern for housing, hospitals and effective charities. She could tell bogus sentiment from genuine concern as readily as she noted the difference between a Regency fauteuil and a Jacobean armchair.

Sensible, self-confident and industrious, May found herself in young adulthood a lonely companion to her extravagant, good-natured mother, a lovable eccentric from whom May wished to be as different as possible. Because Mary Adelaide was an incessant chatterer, her daughter remained taciturn and developed the habit of reading; because Mary Adelaide was a woman of astonishing girth, strident high spirits and casual crudeness, her daughter cultivated the opposite presence, maintaining a rigid diet and, at first, approaching her dancing and voice lessons timorously, afraid that she, too, might seem indelicate, ungainly and unattractive. But she liked to dance, and eventually she could do so freely; she also sang heartily at the proper group occasions. May was also meticulous, orderly and disciplined, kept a detailed diary and carefully listed appointments, tasks and catalogues of her possessions.

In the fashion of the time, May was dressed in intractable clothing, all starch and stays and whalebone. These constrictions reinforced her sense of awkwardness and made her seem formidable when she was really shy and rather gentle; they also gave her posture a veritable royal dignity.

Her reticence, May said years later, was due to her mother's garrulity, "and then of course in our day children were brought up to be seen and not heard. There's something in it: we learned a lot by listening to our elders—only when we went out into company, it was supposed that—hey! presto—we should at once scintillate in sparkling conversation."

Back in London after the European jaunt when she was eighteen, May was put under the tutelage of an Alsatian lady who drilled her in literature, history and economics—in all of which the girl excelled. She had a particular love for English monarchical lore and could recite the royal lineage from Egbert to his remotest descendant in the time of Victoria. She was, as Queen Victoria described her, "a particularly nice girl, so quiet & yet cheerful & so v[er]y carefully brought up & so sensibly. She is grown very pretty." She also had the requisite demeanor of a Royal—stately, cool and unemotional.

This, then, was the desirable young lady who had been dragooned into the Royal Family and affianced to Prince Eddy in December 1891, in the hope that she would set him on the right path. But she was ever more hesitant, and as the wedding date of February 1892 drew near, her suspicions grew that because of Eddy there were skeletons rattling in the royal closets.

She need not have worried. At Christmastime, an influenza epidemic swept across England. May was invited to join the Royal Family at Sandringham for the holidays, which extended to a celebration of Eddy's birthday on January 8. But by that time the Prince was morbidly ill with a raging fever, dehydration, anorexia and dementia. For decades this was reported as influenza, but all the signs point to the ravages of syphilis. On January 12 the unfortunate young man could recognize no one and was raving hysterically about his romances. Alexandra sat bravely at his bedside for hours, holding his hand, wiping his brow and watching in terror as his lips and fingernails turned ashen. She whom everyone thought would collapse at the illness of a loved one was the strongest of all, never leaving her son in his agony and infusing strength into all the others.

Eddy's system collapsed: his kidneys failed, fluid filled his lungs, and in the small hours of January 14 he began slowly to expire of pneumonia. Gasping in terror for each breath, he was somehow briefly restored to a poignant lucidity, recognizing the family and professing, perhaps for the first time, his love for them. Indeed, as he called for his mother and sobbed apologies for everything he had done to hurt her, it seemed as if a kind of childhood innocence was restored to this benighted sufferer. At 9:35 that morning poor Prince Albert Victor, Duke of Clarence and Avondale and heir presumptive to the throne, died after seven hours of appalling agony. He was twenty-eight.

In March 1892 the Tecks—Francis, Mary Adelaide, May and the boys—repaired to friends at Cannes, hoping to recuperate fully from their bouts of influenza and from the sadness of Eddy's funeral. As it happened, the Wales family was at nearby Cap Martin for the same purpose, and on the twenty-ninth Prince George, now catapulted into the direct line of succession, sent a note to May that he and his father would come to visit. The young pair politely condoled each other, and when this was reported to Queen Victoria, an idea occurred to her. At twenty-seven it was time for the new heir presumptive to find a suitable bride. After a respectable interval of mourning, why should George and May not continue where Eddy had so abruptly and inconveniently left off?

This notion became even more fixed in the Queen's mind after an alternative candidate removed herself—George's seventeen-year-old cousin, Princess Marie of Romania (daughter of his uncle Alfred and his wife, who was Czar Nicholas II's daughter). Marie instead chose to marry the Hohenzollern Prince Ferdinand, and eventually this couple became King and Queen of Romania. As it happened, the match of George and Marie would not have been auspicious. "Missy," as she was called, was a voluptuous and sensual blonde whom many men found irresistible; before long she became a melodramatic fantasist, self-absorbed to the point of comedy. Among her curious habits was a predilection for leaving notes in various rooms of her palace declaring "Marie of Romania—one of the most wonderful women in the world. A woman like that is born once in a century.''

Marrying the beloved of one's brother had a precedent in the case of Henry VIII's marriage to Catherine of Aragon, who was briefly married to his brother Arthur. Notwithstanding the unhappy finale to that union, the pairing of George and May could properly be encouraged. And so Victoria, now an expert in such matters, began by creating George Duke of York that spring, just days after suggesting to him that May was a suitable bride. Not oblivious to the girl's charm, he quite readily accepted the idea; it was thought indelicate, however, to proceed hastily or to make too precipitous a public announcement. As for May, she was at first insulted and embarrassed by the idea, for she must have felt like a porcelain at an auction. But during the summer and autumn of 1892 she grew to like her cousin, and she warmed to her duty. Her mother was discreetly addressed; Mary Adelaide summoned her daughter, and a favorable reply was reported to the Queen. The bereaved fiancée quickly and rightly deemed George a better prospect than his late brother.

If this entire enterprise seems to have been undertaken reasonably, without much emotion, that is because such was the way. In 1892—not only in royal English circles but also among polite American families as well—love (much less passion) was scarcely considered a critical requirement for espousals. If a couple eventually developed a mutual tender affection, that was a pleasant accident. But the fortunes of a clan and the extension of its influence by healthy progeny were the dominant factors in grafting appropriate branches onto family trees and arranging favorable unions. And so an unofficial courtship ensued in 1892 and early 1893.

Apart from his sudden eruptions of a fierce temper with his servants or counselors (a family trait as old as his Hanoverian ancestors), George was not given to displays of emotional outbursts. As for May, she was not apathetic, but her shyness made her seem detached. ''Yet,'' wrote her biographer, ''she was consumed by one single abstract passion, which ruled her life, and dictated her whole conduct. . . . This was her passion for the British Monarchy.'' The fact that she would marry a future king filled her not so much with personal ambition as with a sense of reverential duty and the expectation of a life of sacrifice. For one like May, there could be no richer blessing, but this conviction was manifest in quiet, discreet action, with impeccable manners.

She knew the dangers of exaggerated protocol. "I am very sorry that I am still so shy with you," she wrote to George not long before the wedding.

> I tried not to be so the other day, but alas failed, I was angry with myself! It is so stupid to be so stiff together and really there is nothing I would not tell you, except that I *love* you more than anybody in the world, and this I cannot tell you myself so I write it to relieve my feelings.

"Thank God," replied George the same day, with breathless disregard for a never mastered sense of punctuation,

> we both understand each other, and I think it really unnecessary for me to tell you how deep my love for you my darling is and I feel it growing stronger and stronger every time I see you; although I may appear shy and cold.

Forever after, they would prefer writing to speaking their feelings. From all accounts these were two people incapable of revealing themselves face-to-face to just about anybody. "He hid his true feelings behind a quarter-deck bluster," according to one chronicler; "she hers behind an almost unnatural imperturbability."

For later eras, which place so high a premium on uninhibited (and public) expression of every shade of emotion and opinion, this couple may seem wooden and wearying. Unlike their parents, they were certainly repressed, and this would cause unwitting problems when they, too, became parents. Partly, their reticence derived from the formalities of Victorian society and the concomitant requirements of polite discourse. It was bred partly, too, in the ordinary English bone. One simply did not openly express any feeling with much enthusiasm. (Queen Victoria, sick with grief when Eddy fell ill, noted simply in her journal that his absence from Christmas festivities was "tiresome.") Fervent words or spirited gestures might offend the sensibilities of others; the naked expression of sentiment was the way of the ill-bred commoner.

* * *

It might erroneously be assumed that the press of that time was uniformly respectful and adulatory of the Royal Family and especially deferential toward the heir presumptive and his chosen lady. But such was hardly the case. The very day the engagement was announced (May 3, 1893), the *Star* gleefully reported the fiction that George, on duty in Malta three years earlier, had secretly contracted a marriage to the daughter of a British naval officer. "I say, May," George said, handing over the newspaper at tea that afternoon. "We can't get married after all. I hear I have got a wife and three children." By simply ignoring the groundless rumor and proceeding with their plans, the couple effectively dispelled the story. It would come back to haunt them, however; although Victoria's press secretaries courted the favor of journalists, the proliferation of newspapers was igniting a battle for readers. The boundaries of respect and good taste—not to say truth—were already being blurred.

The wedding of George and May was held amid clamorous public rejoicing on a fiercely hot July 6, 1893, in the Chapel Royal of St. James's Palace. Vast crowds poured into London to see the newlyweds—now the Duke and Duchess of York—and to cheer Queen Victoria, who smiled and waved shyly from her open coach. The Prince and Princess of Wales were loudly hailed, too: Bertie, barrel-chested and courtly in his regimental regalia, and Alexandra, as melancholically beautiful as a Chekhov heroine. Mary Adelaide was a vast, earthy counterpart, her frail husband almost vanishing amid so much pomp and character. George, handsome and unaffected, with his beard neatly trimmed and his blue eyes avoiding the gaze of his bride, wore the blue uniform of a navy captain. May shone in white silk, with a train of silvery brocade. Among the bride's attendants was an eight-year-old flower girl, George's second cousin, little Alice of Battenberg. She would one day be the mother of Philip, husband of Queen Elizabeth II.

The wedding gifts were assessed at £300,000—more than £4 million ($6 million) by the standards of a century later. But to George nothing was more precious than the fifteen hundred valuable stamps he received for his beloved collection. May, unaccustomed to incalculable personal splendor, now had a different kind of catalogue to supervise—an extravagant wardrobe and a teeming cornucopia of precious jewels. When in London, their apartments were the recently refurbished but still dreary and sunless rooms at York House, St. James's Palace. George, who always loved anything that reminded him of navy cabins, had no complaints.

At first, more time was spent on the grounds of Sandringham, in the ugly villa known as York Cottage. This choice of residence was made by Prince George, who loved the estate; and it was duly prepared by Alexandra, who loved the thought of having her son remain close to her. This arrangement was a sore disappointment to May, who found her first home prepared for her *tout court* and tried to bear the situation with her usual grace. Furnished on instruction from Alix by servants on a quick assignment to large, characterless shops, the rooms were cluttered with dark, heavy furniture and bibelots chosen by the Princess of Wales. None of this much interested George, who was content to pore over his stamp collection.*

His father Bertie, the Prince of Wales, distracted himself from indolence by a social whirl, a sequence of more or less discreet liaisons and reckless gambling. This was not the nature of George, however, who took a dim view of his father's amours and seems to have resolved on a life of unimpaired fidelity. His idea of diversion was stamps and shooting waterfowl—the life, in other words, of a somewhat unimaginative and unadventurous country gentleman. As for their official capacities as heirs to the throne, not much came to their secretary's attention. A royal wedding in Copenhagen, a function in Liverpool, a state visit to Ireland—little more was required of them during their time as the Yorks. Except for the births of her three eldest children, there was little to occupy May; until her responsibilities broadened later with other titles, she felt thwarted and sometimes useless.

And so May, who had far more leisure time than she would have liked, set herself the task of rearranging the furniture and lightening the atmosphere of the gloomy, cramped rooms, a job she saw not as a burden but as a challenge. Always fervent

---

* At his death King George V owned the most comprehensive British stamp collection in the world—a quarter-million items contained in more than 325 volumes. Of incalculable value, it eventually became part of the national heritage.

to improve her mind as well as her surroundings, May accurately described herself: "I like energy & doing & seeing things, but the way people fritter away their time & their vitality doing *absolutely* useless things makes me furious." When she sat for her portrait, someone read to her; if her hair was being dressed, she wrote or dictated a letter; if she had an hour's leisure, she snatched up a volume of British history.

Alix's intentions in preparing York Cottage were doubtless good, and her affections sincere. "I pray God to give you both a long and happy life together," she wrote to George, "and that you will be a mutual happiness to each other, a comfort to us, and a blessing to the nation." But already there were the signs of classic mother-in-law interference, in this case based on her (surely unconscious) terror of losing her only surviving son, of being even more isolated by abandonment than she was by deafness. "There is a bond of love between us," Alix added, "that of mother and child, which nothing can ever diminish or render less binding—and nobody can, or ever shall, come between me and my darling Georgie boy." Her daughter-in-law, had she read this, might have felt a shiver. "The trials of life *begin* with marriage," Queen Victoria had written cheerlessly but perhaps with deliberate caution to May at the time of her engagement to Eddy. So the young Duchess of York was now learning.

"I sometimes think," May wrote to George one year into the marriage,

> that just after we were married we were not left alone enough & had not the opportunity of learning to understand each other as quickly as we might otherwise have done, & this led to many little rubs which might have been avoided. You see we are both terribly sensitive & the slightest sharp word said by one to the other immediately gave offence & I fear that neither you nor I forget these things in a hurry.

As for the decorating tips, May was restrained but clear. George wrote—they exchanged notes almost daily—that "Motherdear lunched with me today . . . and afterwards moved the furniture in the drawing room, which certainly gives ever so much more room, & I think looks much prettier." May's reply: "I am so glad 'Motherdear' tried to arrange our drawing room, she has so much taste ... [but] it was scarcely worth while to waste a lot of time arranging it when [it will] have to be changed.''

In those more reserved times, the specifics of the "little rubs" and "sharp words" to which May referred were left undescribed, but they can hardly have concerned the placement of chairs and tables. She may well have had in mind her mother-in-law's endless disruptions. Scatterbrained but admirably cheerful, Alix annoyed May with her incessant suggestions and involvements in the life of what Alix regarded as her enlarged family. Alix thought little of sweeping in with a band of relatives or a daughter or two and some puppies. What some took for May's aloofness and social ineptness, therefore, was more often a tight-lipped patience against the invasion by her in-laws. Before Christmas 1893, May learned she was pregnant, and Alix was on the scene with the advice of a platoon of nurses. An assault of such good intentions could drive even hardy souls to madness.

The Queen was no such meddler. "Each time I see you," she wrote to May, "I love & respect you more & am so truly thankful that Georgie has such a partner—to help & encourage him in his difficult position." Indeed, a deep rapport was formed between the two women, especially as Victoria began to suffer the infirmities of her late seventies—crippling rheumatism and incipient cataracts, which finally left her virtually blind. May always consoled Victoria, and the old lady responded with frank affection as if she were her own daughter. "She was always so kind to me & ever a good friend and counselor," the Duchess of York wrote later. Perhaps it was Victoria's ability to befriend without intrusion that evoked May's affection.

As 1893 drew to a close and George was told of May's pregnancy, he discovered deeper feelings for his wife than he had hitherto believed. At the time of his proposal of marriage, he wrote,

> I was very fond of you, but not very much in love with you, but I saw in *you* the person I was capable of loving most deeply, if you only returned that love ... I have tried to

understand you & to know you, & with the happy result
that I know now that I do *Love* you darling girl with all my
heart, & am simply *devoted* to you. . . . *I adore you sweet
May*.

Such feelings were as usual confined to paper—as they were
with his children later.

The first of these was born June 23, 1894, at White Lodge,
Richmond Park, a royal residence and the Tecks' temporary
home at May's birth; later it was the address of the Royal
Ballet School. Ten miles from Kensington and convenient to
Windsor Castle, the Lodge was a Victorian nightmare: its
rooms were crammed with heavy, undistinguished furniture
draped with shawls; the floors were dotted with an excess of
occasional tables covered with Turkish rugs; the walls were
festooned with dark family portraits and dour landscapes; the
spaces were crowded with inlaid chairs and obstructed with
elaborate footstools and lamps. Any vacant spot was filled with
potted palms. Small wonder, perhaps, that the Yorks' first child
seemed nervous and depressed from the day he opened his
eyes.

Victoria's congratulations to the Yorks were accompanied
by the request that the boy be named after her late Consort—
just as *her* firstborn was named Albert and *his* firstborn was
named Albert. But just as Bertie and Eddy never styled themselves Albert, so George and May decided that the infant would
be christened Edward after the late lamented Eddy. Nonsense,
Victoria replied, the *real* first name of George's brother was
Albert. She protested to no avail, although the young parents
acceded with the next child.

And so, with the presence of Prince Edward Albert Christian George Andrew Patrick David of York—always called
David by his family—there were now three living Heirs Presumptive to the throne of Britain: after Victoria would come
Bertie, George and Edward. Unlike his father, brother and
niece, this boy was Heir Apparent at birth. "At 10 o'clock this
evening, May gave birth to a sweet little boy," the Duke of
York wrote in his diary. "I imagine," said the subject of these
words at seventy, "that this was the first and last time my
father was inspired to think of me in exactly those terms."
Edward would in time be Duke of Cornwall, Prince of Wales,
King Edward VIII and finally Duke of Windsor.

The child was prematurely praised by the press and the government, but not universally. Keir Hardie, the first Labour member of the House of Commons and a tireless fighter for peace, social change, women's suffrage, national insurance and housing reform to aid the poor, stood up in Commons and uttered an eerily accurate prophecy reflecting his resentment of royal privilege.

> The assumption is that the newly born child will be called upon some day to reign over this Empire, but up to the present we certainly have no means of knowing his qualifications of fitness for this position. From childhood onward, this boy will be surrounded by sycophants and flatterers by the score and will be taught to believe himself as of a superior creation. A line will be drawn between him and the people he is to be called upon some day to reign over. In due course, following the precedent which has already been set, he will be sent on a tour round the world, and probably rumours of a morganatic alliance will follow and the end of it all will be [that] the country will be called upon to pay the bill.

His speech was attended by loud cries of "Shame!" and "Order!" But later some would remember and hail him as a seer, and even the subject of his remarks had to admit, after the fact, that "Keir Hardie's prophecies were uncomfortably accurate."

Before Edward was two, he had a brother: at York Cottage on December 14, 1895, the anniversary of the Prince Consort's death, May bore a second son. This time the parents yielded to Victoria's desire, and the infant was christened Albert Frederick Arthur George. He would eventually receive from his father the King his own former title, Duke of York; May had now given the Royal Family two heirs in two years, an admirable achievement by any standard, it was widely felt.

With Prince Albert's birth there were now living at one time a monarch and four future kings of England who would account for the throne until 1952: Victoria still reigned, to be succeeded by her son Bertie (as Edward VII, 1901–10), her grandson George (as the fifth of that name, 1910–36), her great-grandson Edward (as Edward VIII, 1936), and her great-grandson Albert (as George VI, 1936–52). George and May's family was augmented further still in 1897 with the birth of Princess Mary (later styled Princess Royal); Prince Henry, later Duke of Gloucester, in 1900; Prince George, later Duke of Kent, in 1902; and Prince John, who was born in 1905 and died in 1919.

The Duke of York was a professional navy man to the core, a simple man of simple tastes, disciplined, meticulous, and something of a martinet. Unfortunately, for all his essential good will toward his children, he was no more psychologically or emotionally suited to be a father than May was to be a mother. On this issue all accounts are unanimous, from their children's memoirs, to biographers authorized and unauthorized, to anecdotes recalled by relatives and eyewitnesses. George was raised with an exalted sense of his place in a special family; no one was permitted, in manner or speech, to trespass into untoward familiarity, not even his own children. His wife certainly had a fond place in his heart, but even she was outside the magic circle of his destiny.

For her part, May quite willingly saw herself as first servant to the future king, blessed to do his will and privileged to make him happy. He was her world, and even the children were subordinate within it. "I always have to remember," May said later, "that their father is also their King." The children grew up with such awe for their parents—and virtual terror of their father—as to sabotage the flowering of any warm affection.

For one thing, they would always have to keep their distance. "Despite his undoubted affection for all of us," wrote Edward years later, "my father preferred children in the abstract, and his notion of a small boy's place in a grown-up world was summed up in the phrase, 'Children should be seen, not heard.' " Little ones, their father reckoned, were nosy and noisy midshipmen, while he was captain. The concomitant discipline was meted out in much the same naval tradition, usually in their father's library. If the boys were late for a teatime meeting with their parents, they were scolded; if they spoke too loudly or did not speak up, they were sent to bed without supper; if their shoes were lightly scuffed, they would forfeit playtime privileges; if a nanny or tutor reported a slip of decorum or a dip in achievement, there were privileges lost and a cane applied. Papa's library, lined with guns rather than books, became the "place of admonition and reproof," Edward recalled.

Occasionally the Duke of York took his sons fishing, and he taught them to hunt and to play cricket, but he was always the superior, always the stern taskmaster, rigid in his outlook, firm in his expectations of immediate obedience, inflexible in his rules of proper conduct, dress and order. Perhaps most disconcerting of all for a youngster, his generally cheerful expression or a rare afternoon of laughter and games could alter at any moment to fierce rage over a minor infraction—and then a moment later their father would reach out to tousle their hair and play a joke. The children were always on the alert, ever insecure, and never knew where they stood in Papa's affections.

Mother's boudoir, however, was different from father's library. Here they were not scolded but taught. Each evening before supper the children were brought to her, and while they sat on little chairs at her feet, she read to them, showed them picture books, explained bits of English history, told stories of her years in Europe, and taught them to crochet and to do tapestry needlework, a pastime Edward developed into a real skill and took with him into adulthood. This was casual culture, and from it the little ones learned much.

These afternoon periods with Mama were doubtless pleasant for the youngsters, amusing and, in May's haphazard and uncritical way, intellectually stimulating. But the job could have been done by any genial nanny, for it was accomplished without a scintilla of personal warmth or involvement in the children's lives. May was not much different with her children than with her husband: warm words were consigned to the occasional handwritten note. Like George, her tongue failed when praise or terms of endearment were appropriate with them. Never an emotionally demonstrative woman, she made no attempt to understand a child's mind, and none of them could remember embraces, kind words or kisses. According to the Queen's oldest daughter Vicky, May lacked "the passionate tenderness for her little ones which seems so natural to me." Where her husband was impatient and unimaginative, May was merely remote. To be sure, there was no overt cruelty in the York home, but neither was there manifest warmth.

Much of this, it must be recalled, was simply the way of the Victorian upper class everywhere in the Empire. Parents and children led separate lives (this was thought healthier for all concerned), and the children were routinely consigned to the care of servants and footmen, scheduled on the fringes of their parents' timetables for an hour in late afternoon, then whisked off for supper and bed. For the York children there was even more distance: Papa was always accompanied by a manservant, Mama by a lady-in-waiting. Everything about the parent-child bond, then, was tactful, proper, artificial, emotionless. In this regard George and May were unlike their own parents: Bertie and Alix had loved to romp with their children and surprise them with treats, and Mary Adelaide (if not the infirm Francis) regularly laughed and frolicked with her grave daughter. "I asked her," said a confidante of May, "did she never go and sit on [Edward's] bed and have a chat with him as mother and boy, and she said she could not do it."

So detached were George and May from the daily realities of their children's lives that it took years before they learned that Edward and Albert's nanny, a Mrs. Green, was quite literally a sadist. Unable to bear children herself, she had suffered a breakdown when her husband left her. Mrs. Green simultaneously resented the royal children and wanted them for herself, becoming pathologically jealous of their parents. Intent on turning the boys against their mother by associating her with pain, Mrs. Green twisted and pinched Edward's arms before sending him into his mother's boudoir each evening. Thus he entered whimpering in pain, which was unacceptable to his father, who expected a composed little navy subaltern, and to his mother, who was embarrassed by any display of emotion. And with that the child was of course dismissed as unpresentable and sent back at once to the arms of the redoubtable Mrs. Green, who covered him with welcoming kisses. Edward was growing up thoroughly confused about the nature of parental affection and what to expect from their surrogates. The royal librarian, Owen Morshead, was on the mark when he said, "The House of Hanover, like ducks, produce bad parents. They trample on their young." He was echoed by Alec Hardinge, a royal secretary, who thought it "a mystery why George . . . who was such a kind man, was such a brute to his children."

Nor were things any better for his younger brother Albert (who, like his grandfather, was always called Bertie). Where the bright and active Edward suffered from the excessive attention of servants, Albert—painfully shy and alarmingly slow-witted—was systematically ignored in his early years. The wretched Mrs. Green irregularly fed him poorly prepared meals, and before adolescence Albert was already suffering from chronic dyspepsia that would soon worsen to peptic ulcers. "Am at my wit's end to know what to do," read an entry in the diary of the under-nurse, Charlotte Bill. "Today Mrs. Green snatched from my hands Prince Albert's bowl containing his lunch, remarking that 'he has had quite enough for one day.' Which indeed he has not. The poor little thing will waste quite away." Finally, Charlotte—subsequently called "Lala" by the children—broke her frightened silence and reported her superior to the Yorks, who dismissed Mrs. Green forthwith. Next day Lala Bill began her reform of the royal nursery.

It is no surprise that, with no playmates, emotionally distant parents and this early experience of a psychotic nanny, both boys suffered from constant nervous tension. Poor Albert developed a serious stammer that prevented him from engaging in even a simple conversation without heroic effort and humiliating embarrassment. Terrified of rejection, Albert as late as his teen years would often sit alone in a dark room rather than ask a servant to light the gas. He gave no one any indication of remarkable traits.

The great relief in the lives of these two boys came during visits to or from the Prince and Princess of Wales, who were doting grandparents. Bertie "could be quite as bad-tempered and as much a stickler for protocol as his son," wrote Edward's biographer, "but to his grandchildren he was almost as indulgent as he was to himself." As for Alexandra, she provided the laughter and games, the romps and hugs for which the children were starved. They adored her and hated her departures.

The Prince of Wales had never indulged himself so much as during the twilight of Victoria's reign. His affairs with Lillie Langtry and others were history, but in 1898, almost fifty-six, Bertie was as randy as a schoolboy. That year he began a romance with Alice Keppel that lasted until his death. Only twenty-nine, she had the beauty and sophistication of Bertie's lifelong *belle idéale*. She soothed his short temper, entertained him lavishly but appropriately (her husband was a patient bystander, but in fact there was little he could do), joined him for short holidays, and was often deliberately placed next to important statesmen at dinner, to ascertain their views or even (she was that charming) to pry confidential information crucial for the Prince to know. The details of the affair are unknown to historians, and even Edward's biographers have been stone-walled by an absence of specific scenes and anecdotes. After all, the liaison was carried on with complete discretion, and the press would never have mentioned it. Nevertheless, much of London's aristocratic society knew of the intrigue. But it was impossible to dislike or resent Alice Keppel. She was nothing but beneficial for the Prince, as even Alix had to admit.

Although his affairs were not noted, Bertie's position as heir to the English throne was. Prince of Wales, debonair so-cialite, lover of theater and denizen of London and Paris boîtes, he continued to dictate men's fashions. Men of all classes strove to imitate, as best they could, one or another of his outfits: a black silk jacket, light-colored or patterned trousers, silver gray spats, shiny boots, a hat invariably worn at a rakish tilt, suede gloves and an ivory walking stick. As a fashion plate he was a prime target for music hall performers such as Vesta Tilley (later Lady de Frece), the famous male impersonator. Strutting the London stages in smart men's evening dress, she sang,

> I'm Burlington Bertie
> I rise at ten-thirty
> And toddle along to the Strand

and brought the house down with good-natured laughter and applause. Everyone knew to whom she referred.

Bertie's fame had grown over the years with the interna-tional proliferation of photographs, which not only documented but now, accompanied by essays, also interpreted and mythi-cized. Family sittings were staged like pageants, with artificial (sometimes exotic) backgrounds, elaborate costumes, plants, trees, flowers and melodramatic poses, and weekend parties at country houses concluded with a group sitting on the lawn. From the time of his accession, Bertie cannily supervised a cadre of officially approved court photographers and claimed the copyright to every photo of himself and his family. He was always his own best publicity manager.

As for the other women in his life, a different but equally

deep connection was formed with Agnes Keyser, a formidable forty-seven-year-old nurse who used her inherited fortune to found and personally manage a nursing home for military officers in her Grosvenor Crescent mansion. A handsome, generous and prudent maiden lady, she became (thus Bertie's most recent biographer) his "part-nanny, part-mother and intimate confidante." To the end of his life, Agnes Keyser was a great comfort to Bertie, full of sound advice on matters medical and personal. But she could not prevail on the Prince to curtail his excessive smoking, which even then she saw as lethal. Their friendship, uncomplicated by sex (which seems to have been of absolutely no interest to Agnes), was the closest nonromantic intimacy of Bertie's life and certainly the most edifying.

By 1897, no one in the Empire was admired more than Queen Victoria, the longest-reigning monarch in English history. She was at the height of her popularity, as celebrations of her sixtieth year on the throne clarified for all the world. On June 22 a stunning pageant acclaimed her, and by inference the British Empire. A procession in an open carriage took her from Westminster to St. Paul's Cathedral, then to poorer districts south of the Thames. Everywhere there were deafening cheers; to everyone the plump, dark-cloaked figure shyly waved and smiled. "How kind they are to me!" she exclaimed over and over. "How kind they are!"

With her children and grandchildren around her, she was indeed the Mother of the Realm, the living symbol of the Mother Country to whom colonial prime ministers and their citizens gave homage. Fireworks, parties, parades and church services filled local calendars around the world for weeks. "From my heart I thank my beloved people," Victoria wrote in a telegram to every British territory in the world. "May God bless them!"

Touched by such an outpouring of affection, the Queen detailed her feelings about June 22 in her journal:

A never to be forgotten day! No one ever, I believe, has met with such an ovation as was given me, passing through those six miles of streets. The crowds were quite indescribable, and their enthusiasm truly marvelous and deeply touching. The cheering was quite deafening, and every face seemed to be filled with real joy.

The era to which the Queen gave her name saw more changes than any preceding in the fabric of everyday life. There were now bicycles and motor cars, electricity, phonograph records, photography, the cinema, machine guns, railways and steamships, telephones, the telegraph, an efficient post office bureau and anesthesia.

Through sixty revolutionary years and despite the inexorable waning of her power and influence as monarch, Victoria had been a living totem of national stability perhaps unknown in the history of the world. Victoria alone filled and satisfied the imaginations of her people; she had made the monarchy respectable in more than six decades of loyalty and decency—the monarchy not as a political power but as a family institution. She had single-handedly restored the luster to a tarnished crown and laid down the standards of royal deportment according to which her descendants would be judged. If honesty and sincerity, duty and dignity are among the hallmarks of good character, Queen Victoria was indeed an admirable human being and raised the monarchy to a deserved respect. In the absence of those virtues, it is easy to understand how her progeny, a century later, effected the collapse of that institution.

Most emphasized on her Diamond Jubilee, however, was the fact of the British Empire—the largest and richest the world had ever seen, and it was continuing to expand. In addition, England ruled the seas, a fact that seemed to ensure, for the present, the invulnerability of the Empire. In 1897 no one could have foreseen that within two years this Empire would be so vast that it became almost impossible to defend and administer. Still, Britain led the scramble for power in Africa, eager for what Otto von Bismarck, the German chancellor, called "a place in the sun." *

---

* Excluding England, Scotland, Wales and Ireland, the British Empire at the end of the nineteenth century encompassed nineteen territories in Africa; Antarctica; Australia and New Zealand; Canada; eighteen islands or chains in the Caribbean; India and Ceylon; eight groups of islands in the Indian Ocean; Cyprus, Gibraltar, Malta and the Ionian Islands; Kuwait and Qatar; the Falklands and other islands in the South Atlantic; six protectorates in the South China Sea; and eighteen territories and groups of islands in the South Pacific.

Despite Jubilee Week's free milk, the parades and the sense of Imperial pride, there was little real concern for the details of the Empire in the streets of London. There could not be. It was the world's largest city, with almost six million residents, but over two million were living in appalling poverty. Beggars flocked the streets, squalid huts had no fuel and little food, children covered themselves with rags and newspapers, drunken fathers abandoned their families, half a million men had no regular wages, and the average laborer earned (in the value of a century later) less than seven dollars a week. Britannia may have ruled the waves abroad, but too many British citizens were foundering at home.

In the 1880s and 1890s—up to her early seventies, in fact —Victoria was well enough to enjoy traveling. She went regularly to Biarritz for the spring, to Switzerland or Spain for part of the summer, and entertained at Windsor, Balmoral, Cowes and Osborne. The widow was well out of her weeds by 1889 when she invited the great actors Henry Irving and Ellen Terry to perform scenes from *The Merchant of Venice* at Sandringham and then, to the shock of her courtiers, invited them to her table for dinner. With Albert gone, she cultivated theatrical dramatic taste, too, enjoying the ribaldry of George Grossmith's comedy *How Ladies of the Future Will Make Love,* which drew from her gales of laughter when it was performed at her command.

This was indeed no austere and frightening old lady. Her children, grandchildren and servants often staged impromptu theatricals for her at Balmoral and Osborne House, and to these she responded with as much unfeigned delight as the youngest child. "It is extraordinary," wrote her grandson, "how pleased Grandmama is with such small things. . . . She takes such interest and pleasure in these performances."

Amid all the grandeur of Victoria and her vast Empire, she was no mere passive observer: she visited hospitals, made troop inspections at home during the Boer War, and bestowed medals at more award ceremonies than ever. Where earlier she had been taught by Lord Melbourne to interpret dissent as radical mania, she now had an ear for those who championed the poor and the sick. Similarly, Disraeli had taken for himself her Imperial duties, blandished her with flattery and convinced her of the rightness of England's shouldering "the white man's burden." His views perfectly coincided with her own. Yet, unable to understand those against Disraeli who called for a restructuring of the class system and a new socialism, she nevertheless had a natural compassion that edged her growing confusion with pity and softened her last years with new depths of humanity never seen in the shallow young Queen or the withdrawn matriarch.

By 1900, Victoria was, in the final analysis, a paradox. Obsessed with awe for the monarchy but personally humble, she preferred a lace cap to a crown and a donkey cart to a state coach. Stern at Court, where she would not be ignored, she was to her staff and visitors in the Highlands and at Osborne a lovable doyenne who imposed herself on no one, rewarded the slightest kindness and never forgot the birthday of the humblest. In her last years, the Queen and Empress was by all accounts large-hearted and sympathetic. Much of this occurred, as ever, in the annealing fire of heartache: on July 30, 1900, just before his fifty-sixth birthday, her son Alfred, Duke of Edinburgh and Saxe-Coburg-Gotha, died of throat cancer. A few months earlier Alfred's estranged son had killed himself. After the untimely deaths of Alice and Leopold, the sudden passing of her third child threw Victoria into a deep depression: "It has come as such an awful shock," she wrote in her journal. "I pray to God to help me to be patient and to trust Him."

Albert's pupil to the end, Victoria devoted her usual meticulous attention to the details of state papers and dispatch boxes, demanding her right to be consulted, the right to encourage and the right to warn—in fact, she often assumed the right to heckle and hinder her ministers. With her family she was more patient and less imperious: "Sharp answers and remarks only irritate and do harm," she wrote to Bertie who wanted to give Kaiser William II (her grandson and his nephew) a stern lecture. "In Sovereigns and Princes such tactics should be most carefully guarded against. William's faults come from impetuousness (as well as conceit); calmness and firmness are the most powerful weapons in such cases."

By her eighty-first birthday, in June 1900, she was lame

enough to require a wheelchair, and cataracts restricted her vision so that even eyeglasses availed little. Ladies-in-waiting went hoarse reading aloud to her the mountains of state papers and letters from relatives, and secretaries were exhausted from drafting the Queen's lengthy, pointed, dictated replies. Duty, dignity, simplicity and vitality were hers to the end.

Every night at Windsor Castle the clothes of her beloved Prince Albert were laid out, freshly cleaned and pressed for the next day, as if she expected him to return on an excursion from Paradise, hoped to meet him in the corridors and go back with him to blessedness—a future in which she believed with all her being. And every morning fresh water was poured into Albert's bedside basin as if she could trick time into reverse. At Osborne, too, the presence of Albert was felt everywhere; there were photographs and mementos of him in every room. Wherever she slept, the Queen had a photograph of her husband over her bed—an image of his head and shoulders, calm and composed in death, waiting silently, lovingly for her.

Finally the long separation drew to a close.

From February 1900, at the age of eighty, Victoria began to fail, and by that summer even she had to admit in her journal, "I now rest daily, which is thought good for me but loses time." By October, Lord James, Chancellor of the Duchy of Lancaster, observed that the Queen "had lost much flesh and had shrunk so as to appear about one-half the person she had been. Her spirits, too, had apparently left her." His Lordship was correct, for the normally plump Queen, triple-chinned from her mid-thirties until her Diamond Jubilee in 1897, now weighed less than a hundred pounds and seemed to have the body of a sickly adolescent. To her beloved daughter Princess Vicky she asked forgiveness for being "a poor old thing not almost myself."

She was exhausted, and sometimes her memory was confused, but with the weariness came the concomitant inability of the aged to sleep. By late 1900, Victoria was dependent on a generous intake of chloral at bedtime, but to this she unfortunately developed a tolerance. "Had a shocking night," she noted in her journal on November 11, "and no draught could make me sleep, as pain kept me awake. Felt very tired and unwell when I got up. . . . Could do nothing for the whole morning. Rested and slept a little.''

"Did not feel well," she wrote in her journal on December 9, "though they say I am getting better." Yet until the last week of her life, despite worsening rheumatism, rapidly failing eyesight and chronic indigestion that made her virtually anorexic, she forced herself to the usual round of duties. By mid-December these were a torment, for by then her inability to eat anything robbed her of virtually all energy and took a toll on her circulatory system. Victoria's health also suffered from anxiety over the Boer War and its casualty lists.

Christmas 1900 at Osborne was cold, dark and cheerless despite the servants' attempts to bedeck the Queen's private quarters. "I felt very melancholy as I see so very badly," she wrote, now almost totally blind from cataracts. Her depression was all the more acute when she was told of the death of her close friend Lady Jane Churchill, who succumbed to a heart attack on Christmas Eve. She was also greatly saddened at the news of the death of her soldier grandson Prince Christian Victor, a victim of fever in South Africa. Worse still, her beloved daughter Vicky, Empress Frederick of Prussia, had been diagnosed with terminal cancer of the spine.

By New Year's Eve, the Isle of Wight was battered with a round of fierce winter storms, and Victoria was denied her afternoon rides in a carriage or even in a wheelchair. "Another year begun," she wrote in her journal the next day, "and I am feeling so weak and unwell that I enter upon it sadly." Yet on Saturday the twelfth she impressed one of her ministers, who found her voice "distinct as usual, and she showed not the slightest sign of failing intelligence." The following day, she dictated the last entry in a daily journal she had begun at the age of thirteen; by Tuesday, January 15, it was clear to her physician, Sir James Reid, who observed a partial right-side facial paralysis and impaired speech, that the Queen was suffering a series of small strokes.

Kaiser William II, Victoria's eldest grandson, arrived from Berlin just as her children were gathering, a congress she would have much resented, in even a moment's lucidity. To have relatives surrounding her deathbed, she had said, would be "very dreadful. . . . I shall insist [that] is never the case if I am dying. It is awful.'' Always referring to herself in the third person when she spoke or wrote as Queen, she had explained a quarter century earlier that ''The Queen wishes never to be deceived as to her real state'' when she became too ill to issue instructions. This her physician agreed never to do, but on Saturday the nineteenth she told him she wished ''to live a little longer,'' as she still had ''things to settle.''

That weekend more ferocious storms swept the isle, the wind howled around the Flag Tower and the Clock Tower of Osborne, rain struck against the great windows, and the fire could not forestall a damp chill in Victoria's small bedroom. On Sunday, January 20, she was only intermittently conscious, but on Monday she seemed to rally and asked for her beloved Pomeranian dog Turi to be brought onto her bed, where she patted and stroked him. Just before noon the Prince of Wales and the Kaiser arrived, and when Victoria awoke that evening, she had a warm conversation with Bertie. When he departed, her physician returned, only to be surprised when the Queen took his hand and repeatedly kissed it; he then realized that in her blindness she confused him with her son.

On Tuesday, January 22, it was clear that Victoria was near death. Reid issued a public statement—''The Queen is sinking''—which inspired the Queen's son-in-law, the Duke of Argyll, to the unintentionally irreverent allusion that ''the last moments were like a great three-decker ship sinking. She kept on rallying and then sinking.''

The large family—even grandchildren whisked down from London and across the Channel—came in and out of the small room, but the Kaiser stayed the entire time, as did Bertie's wife, Alexandra, Princess of Wales. Alix was the most attentive, along with the Queen's own children, Bertie, Arthur, Helena, Louise and Beatrice. Far away in Prussia, Vicky, who could no longer walk, wept quietly and refused narcotics, the better to keep vigil for her dying mother.

From four o'clock in the afternoon, when her breathing began to be labored, the Kaiser and James Reid supported her, one on each side. The storm had blown away from Wight, and gray light streamed in through the narrow windows. At one point her dressers had been trying to make her more comfortable, and she stirred, saying with great tenderness for the trying work they had to do, ''My poor girls.'' Her daughter Louise heard her whisper, "I don't want to die yet. There are several things I want to arrange."

Toward the end, Victoria's face was quite beautiful in its way. There was little pain, and her expression was for the most part calm. She liked her hand to be held and knew when it was not. For the last hour this comfort was lovingly tendered by Alexandra and Louise. A few minutes before she died, Reid recalled, the Queen's eyes turned fixedly to the right and, though blind, she seemed to gaze on a painting of the entombment of Christ over the fireplace. Randall Davidson, bishop of Winchester (and later Archbishop of Canterbury), drew near to lead a few prayers and to read one of Victoria's favorite hymns, John Henry Newman's "Lead, Kindly Light."

> Lead, kindly Light, amid the encircling gloom,
> > Lead thou me on;
> The night is dark, and I am far from home;
> > Lead thou me on . . .
> I was not ever thus, nor prayed that thou
> > Shouldst lead me on;
> I loved to choose and see my path; but now
> > Lead thou me on . . .

When Davidson came to the words

> And with the morn those angel faces smile
> Which I have loved long since, and lost awhile

Victoria's changed expression showed she understood their meaning at last.

The Queen's final words were uttered as she opened her arms to her son and heir: "Bertie," she whispered gently, taking his hand and kissing it, as if all the old rancor and the decades of mistrust had melted with the weekend snow, as if she would be the first to do proper homage to the son who would presently be England's new monarch. He kissed her cheek and lowered his face next to hers on the pillow.

At 6:20, angular winter daylight was fading and a few candles and a lamp were lit in the darkening room. That afternoon, the weather had turned mild, and now, after the storms, the cedars in Prince Albert's carefully designed gardens were as luxuriant as in high summer, the lawns glistening a vivid green. In the twilight, there was no trace of midwinter gloom. The gentle splash of a fountain could be heard below the Queen's bedroom. At precisely 6:30, Victoria's face, which had been strained by paralysis, relaxed and became calm.

King Edward VII (seated) with his son George and grandson David.

4

The Edwardian Decade 1901 to 1910

> My good man, I am not a strawberry!
> EDWARD VII, when a servant spilled cream
> on the royal trousers

Queen Victoria's daughter Louise, Duchess of Argyll, had a sly humor that her mother would certainly have appreciated. While she was kneeling with her sisters Beatrice and Helena in the Frogmore mausoleum on the anniversary of the Queen's death, a dove flew into the chapel.

"Dear Mama's spirit," Beatrice murmured piously. "We are sure of it."

"No, I am sure it is not," replied Princess Louise.

"It must be dear Mama's spirit," Helena insisted.

"No," Louise said quietly. "Dear Mama's spirit would never have ruined Beatrice's hat."

The Prince of Wales—the new King Edward VII—had a good sense of humor, and he appreciated the anecdote when he was told it. But early in his reign he had not much to smile at. After waiting so long in the wings, Albert Edward finally heard his cue: at fifty-nine he acceded to the throne of the Empire.

His mother had reigned almost sixty-four years, and the vast majority of Britain's forty-one million citizens in 1901 had known no other monarch. As a constitutional ruler with no executive or judicial authority, she had been legally powerless, but her influence was enormous. The Empire had propagated its values by referring to the staid simplicities of its virtuous Queen and Empress, and had expanded its economic and military might behind her capacious, mythic image. Victoria had given the stamp of her personality to a time that bore her name, and the cliché resounded with truth: an era died with her.

And another was ushered in with her son. At first, life for ordinary people seemed impossible to imagine without the dutiful and dour, generous and kindly old lady. But things were moving quickly. Victorian sober frugality was within weeks a quaint memory as the new monarch gave the English Court a spirit of gleeful luxury. Some suspected the merriment might not last, and the sense of brevity added to its piquancy; that it was soon followed by a great war augmented, at least in retrospect, its poignancy.

The day after the Queen's death, a cascade of lengthy and sanctimonious articles in *The Times* was accompanied by a cautionary essay. Acknowledging pro forma that as Prince of Wales the new King had "never failed in his duty to the throne and the nation," the editor then adopted the tone of a prim, cautionary rhetorician: "We shall not pretend that there is nothing in his long career which those who respect and admire him would wish otherwise." The allusion was not unclear. One thought of the scandals involving Bertie in bedrooms and Bertie at baccarat tables, the roué who embarrassed his mother precisely because she gave him nothing better to do than perfect the role of Playboy Prince Charming.

One thing was immediately certain. In Paris and Vienna

those who could afford it were dancing to the heady, intoxicating measures of *la belle époque*. Bertie, who much appreciated Continental luxury and sophistication, brought that "lovely time" to England. The royal style, almost overnight it seemed, went from sedate to sensational, from Victorian black to Bertie's vermilion. The monarchy would now be a social institution, not a morally persuasive one. Pageantry returned, and with it a spirit completely different from Victoria's.

The late Queen had shunned society, condemned horse racing as an undignified interest, kept faith with her dead husband and avoided the encroachments of modernity. Of the latter, automobiles were a good example; "Horrible machines," she dubbed them, which "smell exceedingly nasty." In this judgment she was not alone, for most respectable people disdained the newfangled mode of transport as fit only for the profligate.

The new King, on the other hand, ran from boredom, required constant amusement and stimulating company, loved the races, was unashamedly adulterous, and embraced everything new—especially the motor car. Edward and Alix were often seen being driven in an open Daimler, he puffing a cigar, squeezing the four-note bugle he attached to a door, and waving his homburg at startled villagers in Norfolk or Sussex. Speed was of the essence: "Faster! Faster!" he urged his driver, while his wife clutched one of her small dogs in her lap and prayed for a safe arrival. To the King alone was due the social acceptability of the automobile, for by 1903 he also owned a Mercedes-Benz and a Renault, all of them painted a deep burgundy and with the royal coat of arms emblazoned on a door.

He lost no time in announcing that things would have a new and independent style. The day after Victoria's death, Bertie hastened to London for the formalities of the accession meeting with the Privy Council; the last had been so long ago that rubrics had to be consulted for lack of a living courtier to act as eyewitness. The coronation would have to await a decent period of public bereavement, of course, but that morning— January 23, 1901—Frederick Temple, Archbishop of Canterbury, administered the oath of sovereignty. And then, to everyone's astonishment, the new King announced that notwithstanding his late father's many virtues, he wished to be known by his second name and would not, as his mother had hoped in naming him for his father, be called King Albert I. To London and to the world was then presented His Majesty, the Liege Lord Edward, by the Grace of God the Seventh of that name, King and Emperor. Not for him the German name, nor the association with a stern Teutonic dynasty.

"The German element," Victoria once said, must be "cherished and kept up in our beloved home." In this regard she had been thrilled with Vicky's marriage to the Crown Prince of Prussia and with the many unions of her children and grandchildren with Teutonic heirs (George to May, among them). But despite the fact that Edward VII had scarcely a drop of English blood in his veins—both his parents were of completely German stock—he quickly established himself as the most English of monarchs. The House of Hanover officially was no more; the new dynastic name was Saxe-Coburg-Gotha, that of the new King's father. Rarely has a simple change in designation so clearly marked a revision of national style and purpose. Yet despite the Englishness that would henceforth mark the monarchy, "Saxe-Coburg-Gotha" was obviously Teutonic, and it would take a war to banish it from the shores.

Although Edward was only five feet six, he somehow towered over all those around him.* Noble in bearing, always perfectly dressed and groomed, he exuded authority whether he was wearing a lounge suit, a military uniform or a royal robe of state. A warmhearted host who loved laughter and a good cigar, he spoke flawless German and French, put princes and commoners at ease, and—however rigid in his observance of protocol and the rules of proper dress and comportment—was both awesome in manner and comforting in the impression of indolence his corpulence conveyed. His charm, according to a contemporary,

> amounted to genius. . . . It *made* him. With a dignified presence, a fine profile, and a courtly manner, he never missed saying a word to the humblest visitor, attendant or obscure official—no one was left out. The appropriate remark, the telling serious phrase and the amusing joke, accompanied by a gurgling laugh to a close friend, made all delighted even to watch him.

---

* In this narrative he will be designated not as Bertie but by his kingly name. His grandson, Prince Albert of York, George's second son, was also nicknamed Bertie by his family.

These qualities, added to what one chronicler called "a genuine goodness of heart . . . [and] loyalty and generosity towards his friends," gained Edward VII much admiration and, in short order, the love of a people who saw his faults as egregiously all too human. He was also patient with the faults of others. When a servant accidentally spilled cream over him at breakfast, Edward looked up and said, "My good man, I am not a strawberry." And those fortunate to meet him under any circumstances came to understand at least some of the reasons that his Queen, the magnificent Alexandra, never ceased to adore him, at whatever cost. But his influence in political affairs was at most a carefully maintained illusion, encouraged by the pressman at Buckingham Palace whose duties now included positive reinforcement of the King's image as well as the deflection of attention away from his mistresses.

On February 14, 1901, the King and Queen braved bitter cold to travel a long and slow parade, for Edward intended to demonstrate his brand of monarchy. Victoria had not presided over the opening of Parliament for the last fifteen years of her life, but Edward insisted that this was the right moment to demonstrate the difference in their styles. Henceforth, there was to be pageantry, and so he ordered the gold coach of state, locked away since his father's death forty years earlier, and the most lavish ceremonial robes for himself and Alix. Majestically self-assured in crimson, his barrel of a chest heavily brocaded with medals and ribbons, the King appeared; the stunning Alexandra was at his side, glistening in diamonds, pearls and satin. He looked his age; Alix might have been taken for his daughter. She had aged not at all; even at close range, her skin was smooth as alabaster, her eyes bright, her composure eminent but benign. No one thought she looked a day over thirty-five.

The Lords, King Edward decreed, were to wear their gold coronets to this initial ceremony and their finest ermine, silks and velvets. Exactly two weeks later the King traveled simply and without fanfare to Berlin, to comfort his dying sister Vicky. There was to be no state welcome, nothing to distract; he was a man who happened to be King visiting a beloved sister who happened to be a Dowager Empress. Never mind that politicians in England and Germany were eyeing one another with increasing hostility and suspicion; this was strictly a family visit. Of it we have no record, but of their lifelong devotion there is no doubt. King Edward returned to England quietly, without stopping for a gay weekend in Paris or Deauville.

However grand his public appearances in London, Edward seemed never to forget in private that his luxuriant self-presentation was just that. He did not have his mother's mystic reverence for the monarchy, nor did he dissociate the crown from its wearer; indeed, he had a ruthlessly honest assessment of himself as a man, whatever his responsibilities. Just as Victoria's mouth always turned down in shy gravity, so Edward seemed always on the verge of smiling, his blue eyes invariably curious, merry, seductive, attentive. Tolerant, unprejudiced, accepting people of all ranks and stations into his confidence (as women into his love life), Edward had no time for the hypocrisies of courtiers. When one of them praised him for sending a warm message to a difficult, radical member of Parliament, the King bolted into a rage: "You don't understand me! I am the King of *all* the people!" And so he was, although he gloried even more in being the epitome of the English country gentleman, nowhere more relaxed than at Sandringham, with his rifles and dogs and livestock. There, he romped with his grandchildren, who tugged at his beard and rode on his back; there, too, Mrs. Keppel's children were welcomed and were never scolded when they called him "Mr. Kingy." Victoria had always meant well, but her natural shyness and sense of being queen discouraged the sticky embraces of children.

As for his royal duties and prerogatives, it was true that Edward, having been denied any training, lacked the habit and hence the ability to concentrate on papers at his desk. This did not, however, lead him to neglect; he simply developed his own style, preferring to meet ministers en masse, or one of them over a drink or for a stroll through the palace gardens. Lord Esher, one of Edward's closest confidants, recalled that

> the scene at Marlborough House during the first weeks of King Edward's reign was in sharp contrast to everything to which we were accustomed. He himself was accessible, friendly, almost familiar, frank, suggestive, receptive, discarding ceremony, with no loss of dignity, decisive but neither obstinate nor imperious. . . . He permitted those who had access to him to smoke in his presence. . . . You were

told to enter the room unannounced, and if you desired to do so, you left the room with a bow to the King and returned when you wished. He was still questioning, dictating, deciding. His memory never seemed to betray him. . . . The impression he gave me was that of a man who, after long years of pent-up inaction, had suddenly been freed from restraint and revelled in his liberty.

As his prime ministers (Salisbury, Balfour, Campbell-Bannerman and Asquith) quickly learned, the King's decades as royal understudy had not left him a shallow dissolute ignorant of the throne. He had a natural gift for statecraft, his travels had familiarized him with important diplomats, his linguistic gifts facilitated his communication with international politicians, and his charm accomplished what the stiff and blustery formality of many a Cabinet member could not. (Unlike his four successors, Edward could speak engagingly and clearly in public without resorting to a prepared script.) Herbert Asquith, no friend of the King and often an adversary, admitted that Edward's

> duty to the State always came first. There was no better man of business. . . . Wherever he was, whatever may have been his preoccupations, in the transactions of the State there were never any arrears, never any trace of confusion, and never a moment of avoidable delay.

Perhaps precisely because Victoria had denied him any participation at all in the affairs of state, Edward was extremely sensitive about being ignored by his ministers. This King would not be, in his words, "a mere 'signing machine.' " He knew well that his tasks were mostly ceremonial—laying foundation stones, awarding medals to old soldiers, speaking at city functions, encouraging charities. But these he executed with such cheerful panache that they somehow seemed activities fit for a king rather than a privileged goodwill ambassador, which he was becoming.

As for England's relationship with the rest of the world, events made clear that Britain could no longer bask unselfcritically in its splendid isolation, especially after the treaty forced on South Africa by London at the end of the Boer War in 1902. European sympathy had been mostly against the Empire in that three-year-long conflict. Detaining white South Africans (mostly of Dutch descent) in concentration camps won the British no allies, nor did a fantastic display of Imperial military might as half a million British soldiers poured into South Africa. "There is far too much talk of Empire nowadays," the King said a few years later to Richard Haldane, his War Minister, who may well have imagined Victoria writhing in her tomb. Far more catholic in temperament and outlook, Edward was at heart a citizen of the world. Paris was a second home, and the King prided himself on feeling at ease anywhere in Europe. At least three months of every year he spent on the Continent.

This time was not devoted to idle holiday but to promoting, at his Cabinet's insistence, British commercial interests and to meetings with statesmen, sovereigns and ministers—meetings during which he could not initiate any action (much less speak publicly on any political matter) but at which he could, like a diplomatic John the Baptist, prepare the way for one more important to come after, a minister or a Cabinet member. As Prime Minister Balfour wrote, "His Majesty did what no minister, no cabinet, no ambassadors . . . were able to perform. He by his personality, and by his personality alone, brought home to the minds of millions on the Continent the friendly feeling of the country [England]."

Since William IV signed the Reform Bill of 1832, there had been a progressive decline in the English monarch's power, engineered by the rise of democracy and by acts of Parliament, and emphasized by one Prime Minister after another. But whereas Victoria had occasionally acted outside her constitutional privileges, her son was far more circumspect. Invariably behaving according to ministerial advice, he maintained friendships with ministers of all parties and set the pattern for a more rigorous modern constitutional monarchy; in a phrase, he managed to broaden the social base of royalty without cheapening it, which is very different from being an ambassador. The phrase arose much later than the Edwardian era, but it was Edward himself who in effect made the monarchy an instrument of what would later be called "public relations." And in this regard he was a skillful manipulator of the press, ensuring that newsmen attended public ceremonies; smiling endlessly for the photographs which then required long, motionless sittings; instructing his equerries to summon a news editor to hear a royal statement and a kingly laugh.

Edward's reputation, as if he were an effective minister with portfolio, is certainly overrated, and it is based mostly on a wildly successful and much publicized visit to France in 1903, a journey followed by the efforts of the two countries to form a historic alliance. But other political abilities served him well at home, primarily as the master of glamorous domestic ceremonies. Alix, who loved the intimacy of Marlborough House, dreaded moving into the cavernous and gloomy apartments of Buckingham Palace. The King, who saw himself at the center of the nation's social life, insisted that the palace was the only proper venue for the Royal Family. He prowled the corridors and ordered paints; he poked into unused rooms, saw that there were only three toilets for six hundred rooms, and gave orders for the installation of new pipes, electrical wiring, heating and plumbing. New curtains and carpets were installed, chandeliers suspended, paintings brought out of storage. If there was to be a revised scenario for the monarchy, the leading player required colorful and refurbished sets. When she saw that all this was inevitable, Alix involved herself with typical grace in this department, too. She ordered floral designs where once there had been dark wool, and cheerful wall coverings to brighten musty rooms.

But there were, alas, certain perhaps inevitable alterations to the marriage, too. After almost forty years, a passionate romance between Edward and Alix could hardly have been expected, royal mistresses or no. But there is no doubt that Edward's insistent infidelity, carried unchanged into his reign, saddened and angered Alix, all the more so because she was by 1901 virtually excluded from everything in his life. The King traveled abroad five or six or ten times a year for several weeks, on vaguely ambassadorial missions or on holiday, with a small entourage or with two assistants, and Alice Keppel as his companion. In his absence Alix withdrew to Sandringham or to Denmark for a visit with her family.

Besides devotion to her grandchildren and house pets, the Queen continued to work on behalf of important charitable causes. Anxious for the plight of the unemployed, she instituted a fund to help them that provided financial assistance and job training. Nor was her kindness merely impersonal and institutional. At Christmas her first year as Queen, Alix was preparing for the customary servants' party at Sandringham when the Royal Family presented a small gift to each member of the household staff. Amid the bustle of activity she noticed a footman gazing sadly out a window; she soon learned he had lost his parents, was unmarried and was now quite alone in the world. "I cannot bear anyone to be lonely in my house at Christmastime," Alix said, and she spent the afternoon with the man, sipping hot cider and banishing that particularly poignant holiday solitude with her direct warmth and easy camaraderie. Later that evening she sought out the man again and without any bountiful affectation presented him with a gift of gold cuff links in a leather case. "These are my personal present to you," she said. "But of course you will also receive your ordinary present at the tree tonight."

The Queen was in an important way the ideal Edwardian Consort. Lovely to behold, she inspired the fantasies of artists and young poets and bedazzled those invited to Buckingham Palace or to a royal ceremony. Yet everyone knew she much preferred the quiet anonymity of Sandringham where she could fuss endlessly over her grandchildren and her dogs. But when called on to assume her public duty, she sparkled. Even her husband's nephew, the arrogant and problematic Kaiser, could not ruffle her. "Willy, dear," she said to him when he at last fell silent after delivering a lengthy harangue against England, "I am afraid I have not heard a single word you were saying."

Alix would never have spoken this way to her grandchildren, of whom, by 1901, there were seven. Those she saw most often and pampered were the four born thus far to May and George: Edward, seven; Albert, six; Mary, four; and Henry, one.*

When King Edward saw his beloved grandchildren, he

---

* Of Edward and Alexandra's three daughters, the Princesses Louise and Maud had two daughters and a son, respectively; Princess Victoria never married.

could not imagine them wearing coronets and ermine, for he had an unshakable belief that the monarchy would not survive his son George—"the future last King of England," he said cheerlessly. This judgment was delivered not because of any contempt for his son's abilities but because he considered kingship an increasingly obsolete reality that would not withstand the inevitable spread of democracy. In this regard, he doubtless underestimated the fundamental conservatism of the British people, not to say of Parliament, whose members (like their constituents) regarded the monarch not only as the bearer of certain colorful national traditions and quaint customs but also as a focus for a kind of Imperial pride of race.

Whatever his suspicions about the outlook for the throne, however, Edward insisted on training George for it; there would be no repetition of Victoria's disregard. From the first week of his reign, the King shared state papers with his son, who at thirty-five much needed encouragement and assistance in finding his own place in life. Awed by his father's apparently effortless performance of duties, George was equally shy of the King because he so disapproved of his infidelity to Alix. Edward sensed this and to elaborate on what he wished George to learn, he wisely appointed Sir Arthur Bigge (later Lord Stamfordham) as his son's private secretary.

A chronicle of George and May from the time of their marriage to his father's accession does not provide the stuff of compelling reading. Essentially the life of a country squire was ordered, calm, undisturbed by responsibilities other than those of child-rearing, and, by all accounts, monumentally dull. "He constantly blessed his good fortune in marriage," wrote an early biographer, "and asked nothing better than to enjoy it and the simple pleasures of domestic life" at York Cottage, Sandringham, where one day was very like the next. In the mornings he tended to his gardens or to sport or to financial affairs; he lunched with his wife; worked at his stamp collection in the afternoon and (in season) shot pheasant; visited with the children before dinner, read with his wife afterward, and then retired early—perhaps after a billiard game with an equerry, which provided the day's major excitement.

But whereas this schedule was congenial for George, May found it dull. Her intellectual life went unnourished, her energies untapped, and from her in-laws she received neither warmth nor encouragement. "Now do try to talk to May at dinner," said George's sister, Princess Victoria, to a guest, with peculiar malice—and then added with a sneer, "though one knows she is deadly dull." May was of course nothing of the sort, but the speaker, like other members of her family, was suspicious of May's shyness, which was often interpreted as arrogance or dullness. Even Alix, usually a model of courtesy, often ignored May, though doubtless this had to do with her unacknowledged (and hardly rare) maternal conviction that no one was as good for her dear Georgie as herself.

After the deaths of her parents, May felt more than ever disconnected from her past, and her husband's lifelong reserve pushed her further into a hard and distant shell that many took for a regal attitude. "As a girl she had been shy and reserved," wrote her oldest friend, Mabell, Countess of Airlie, "but now her shyness had so crystallized . . . [that] the hard crust of inhibition which gradually closed over her, hiding the warmth and tenderness of her own personality, was already starting to form."

Far more acutely than Alix, May suffered from the royal tendency to alienate those who marry into the family. A candidate for espousal to a member of that family must, according to the Royal Marriages Act of 1772, obtain the sovereign's consent—usually (but not always) a formality, but one that establishes from the start a kind of subtle subjugation, a royal scrutiny of the candidate to determine suitability. And precisely because the very nature of royalty presumes their difference from ordinary mortals, those who pass through the gate of marriage find the subsequent journey often strewn with obstacles to full acceptance. Certainly that was so for Princess May, descendant of George III though she was; even more obviously, it would be true for wives a century later. In her mid-thirties, then, May found herself unoccupied, bored and depressed. The Boer War had only temporarily given her some purpose: she visited hospital ships and assumed some of Alix's duties, but then her pregnancy (with Prince Henry) foreshortened any semblance of public life.

It may well have been a quiet, unacknowledged resentment, therefore, that made the artistic and naturally generous May seem somewhat forbidding. "She has something very cold and stiff & distant in her manner,'' said Queen Victoria's eldest daughter Vicky. ''Each time one sees her one has to break the ice afresh.''

There is some evidence, though not at all conclusive, that precisely at this time May's need for a spiritual life led her regularly to prayer and services at Roman Catholic churches in the West End whenever she was in London; that she gave regular contributions for beautiful and lavish altar flowers; and even that she was secretly but formally received into the Church. That final step is highly unlikely, for it would have placed in jeopardy the very family acceptance she so desperately sought. More to the point, conversion would later have robbed her children of their right of succession when (as was the customary Roman requirement) she raised them as Catholics. Finally, a conversion to Rome would have alienated her husband and effectively tarnished the Royal Family, and May's duty to the Crown was too deeply rooted. Even if there had been ways to escape these impasses, it would have been impossible for history not to record it; her allegiances would simply have been transferred, and with no loss of intensity or integrity.

Yet of her attraction to the Church of Rome there is no doubt. After all, she had spent impressionable adolescent years in Florence and felt comfortable in both the towering grandeur of vast cathedrals and the prayerful quiet of small chapels. May was such a frequent visitor to one London church that she became known as ''The Lady of the Roses,'' after her custom of giving coins to the sacristan for altar flowers. The traditions, the great ancient liturgies, the discipline and restraint of Rome would have appealed greatly to May's personality, and the emphasis on the redemptive power of suffering, focused in the centrality of the Cross, would have struck a chord in her own experience of feeling rejected and outcast.

In light of her discomfort with her in-laws, it was not surprising that within weeks of Edward's accession, George and May undertook a long journey—with her hearty enthusiasm. This she infused into her husband, who was not at all certain he could manage the role of deputy for the King. Despite his misgivings, the Cabinet was firm, and so George and May visited several of the dominions. On March 16 the Yorks left for what was essentially a public relations tour, representing the Crown as symbols of a united empire.*

"Her smile is commented on in every paper," wrote Lady Lygon, who was in attendance; "she is having a *succès fou,* winning golden opinions." And this she accomplished despite seasickness, intense heat and cold, and handshaking with as many as three thousand people in one afternoon. Like Alix, her natural preference would have been for a more interesting life, but she was sacrificing for her husband, playing a destined role, and her sense of responsibility evoked strengths even she could not have predicted. "Only give me the chance," May said, turning her love of sightseeing into an advantage for the throne, "and I will do things as well as anybody. After all, why shouldn't I?" In a way she, her mother-in-law and Queen Victoria were far more courageous and resourceful than the men of the Royal Family. They were also allowed far fewer compensations. For her, one was collecting: May returned home with valises crammed with bibelots, artifacts, picture frames, household items and hundreds of mementos provided by governors and their wives. Little of this booty was ever abandoned over the years.

For George, the eight-month tour provided both testing and training grounds. He acquitted himself admirably in ceremonies and grew considerably in self-confidence, all this simply by opening schools and hospitals, laying foundation stones, attending receptions and reviewing troops, routine royal duties that have changed little since his time. For all that, George's quaintly outdated sense of his role—to encourage, as he said, a "loyalty to the Crown that did not exist even a few years ago"—was hardly shared by his various hosts who were too far along the path to democratic independence to be swayed by London's last Imperial pretensions. But like his father, George saw the House of Saxe-Coburg-Gotha as a kind of exalted family business that had to perpetuate itself as the primary agent for Great Britain.

* * *

---

* Their route took them to (among other stops) Gibraltar, Malta, Ceylon, Singapore, Melbourne, Brisbane, Sydney, Auckland, Adelaide, Perth, Mauritius, Durban, Cape Town, Quebec, Montreal, Ottawa, Vancouver, Toronto, Niagara and Halifax.

During this long journey the York children were left at Sandringham in the care of their grandparents, who spoiled them shamelessly, doubtless a welcome change after the dreaded Mrs. Green. King Edward allowed them to push pats of butter, like racing horses, along the seams of his trousers and bellowed with delight when they called the winner; Queen Alexandra fed them anything they liked and allowed them to stay up late, in full control of the house, until the children (and the servants) collapsed from exhaustion. Edward, now second in line to the throne after his father, was a lively, dominating child, the fearless captain of military and naval games in the nursery. Short family films survive in which he commands his little band of subordinates carrying toy rifles: Albert, highly strung, avoids the camera whenever possible; Mary, also timid, follows placidly in his footsteps. Only the infant Prince Henry was exempt from conscription. The bits of silent celluloid do not reveal perhaps the most worrisome element—Albert's worsening, disabling stammer that embarrassed him and everyone in his presence, and his tendency to sudden rages and fits of weeping.

Thus passed the summer of 1901, a prolonged children's hour that was very likely the most contented time of Alix's life since she had nurtured her own babies. But for King Edward there was a dark interval. After a bitter struggle that concluded with months of agonizing paraplegia from spinal cancer, his sister Vicky, Dowager Empress of Prussia and Queen Victoria's eldest child, died on August 5 at the age of sixty. Over the years Vicky had remained close to her brother without interruption, much preferring his liberal politics to the puffery and saber rattling of her son the Kaiser. She also retained her intimacy with the most sophisticated literary and scientific circles in Berlin and never resigned from the fight for women's rights to the vote and to higher education. Alert and courageous to the end, Vicky had continued her avocation as a sculptress and had recently completed her last piece: a terra-cotta head of Christ, gazing with infinite benignity, soon to be placed over her parents' tombs at Frogmore.

But there was little time for the King to mourn. He returned from the funeral in Potsdam to a mountain of reports from the colonies, and he dictated replies to each governor-general and lengthy letters of gratitude and congratulations to his son and daughter-in-law on their evident success. He also prepared to enhance George's way of life and to expand his duties as Heir Apparent to the throne. First, the King ordered three residences to be prepared for George and May: Marlborough House in London; Abergeldie, a small and gloomy castle near Balmoral; and Frogmore, a far more cheerful Georgian house near Windsor Castle.

Then, on Edward's sixtieth birthday (just a week after the Yorks' return on November 1), he named his thirty-six-year-old son Prince of Wales. "In making you today 'Prince of Wales and Earl of Chester,' " he wrote,

> I am not only conferring on you ancient titles which I have borne upwards of 59 years, but I wish to mark my appreciation of the admirable manner in which you carried out the arduous duties in the Colonies which I entrusted you with. . . . God bless you, my dear boy, & I know I can always count on your support and assistance in the heavy duties and responsible position I now occupy. Ever your devoted Papa, Edward R. I.

With the designation came added tasks for George. King Edward, rupturing once and for all any similarity with his mother's monarchical style, opened the ritual dispatch boxes for the Prince's scrutiny. On long winter afternoons, father and son discussed the latest debates in Commons; the gossip from the House of Lords; the ambassadorial reports from the Continent; the growing nationalist movement in South Africa despite the British victory in the Boer War; and an imminent treaty with Japan that protected the countries' mutual interests in China and Korea. Drawing his son into his confidence was, the King knew, the best preparation for his succession. The monarch was utterly powerless, but he was not without influence, and the strength of that influence came, as Edward knew, from being informed. For himself, the King suddenly had to compensate for years of enforced idleness as Prince of Wales; he would neither allow nor subject his son to the same languorous disengagement.

The coronation of King Edward VII and Queen Alexandra was finally held on August 9, 1902, following the King's recovery from an appendectomy that required a six-week postponement from the original date. Edward sent for young Edward and Albert before he departed Buckingham Palace for Westminster Abbey. Splendid in his royal regalia, he saw their awe-stricken faces, smiled and said, "Good morning, children! Am I not a funny-looking old man?" And with that there was nothing for any of them to do but laugh together.

But as the footmen arrived to escort the King and his Consort to the golden state coach, Alix was nowhere to be found. Edward at last found her before her dressing table, rearranging the last strands of pearls and putting a final touch to her hair. He extended a watch and tapped it: "My dear Alix, if you don't come immediately, you won't be crowned Queen!" He whisked her downstairs, and they were off.

England's first coronation in sixty-three years was certainly sublime, laced with medieval character and dazzling in its solemnity. The Duchess of Marlborough, the American Consuelo Vanderbilt, was one of Alix's canopy-bearers, and she recalled how

> the trumpets were blaring, the organ pealing, and the choir singing the triumphant hosannas. . . . [There were] the Court officials with their white wands, the Church dignitaries with their magnificent vestments, the bearers of the royal insignia . . . the lovely Queen, and then the King, solemn and regal.

The congregation was as still as a lake when the proclamation was made of "The Most High, Most Mighty and Most Excellent Monarch, Edward The Seventh, by the Grace of God, of the United Kingdom of Great Britain and Ireland and of the British Dominions beyond the Seas, King, Defender of the Faith, Emperor of India."

It sounded very grand indeed. Edward was the corporate personality on whom was focused England's past traditions and present identity. Despite the new tone he brought to the palace, he stood for continuity, for stability amid the shifting winds of politics. Not required to be a military tactician, a skilled diplomat or a beguiling leader of society, he simply had to *be*—the heir to a family's succession widely (and wrongly) thought unbroken for a thousand years. The paradox was that the man so solemnly hailed that August day—this short, heavy figure, bald and bearded, surrounded by bishops, peers, a radiant wife and a vast throng of loyal subjects—was in many important ways subject to his own Parliament.

However splendid, the occasion also demonstrated that the Victorian era had certainly yielded to the Edwardian. At the King's command a section close to the high altar had been reserved for Lillie Langtry, Sarah Bernhardt, Jennie Churchill (Winston's mother), Alice Keppel and a few other royal favorites. Less controversially, back at the palace five hours later, Alix as usual summed up the day's conjunction of hallowed splendor and human simplicity: she refused to wipe the oil of anointing from her brow and then gaily allowed the children to wear her crown.

Apart from Alice Keppel's, perhaps no relationship with the King so typified the new era than that enjoyed by the great Sarah Bernhardt. The actress had performed scenes before Queen Victoria and was thereafter invited to meet Edward when he was Prince of Wales; an ardent (if sporadic) affair ensued. "I have just returned from a visit with the Prince of Wales," she wrote one afternoon to the manager when she returned from his private rooms and was late for a rehearsal with a dramatic troupe. "It is 1:20 and I cannot rehearse at this hour. The Prince kept me from eleven o'clock on." In fact, London society knew of the affair: "It is an outrageous scandal," Lady Cavendish wrote in her diary.

The King and the actress regularly exchanged gifts (puppies among them), and whenever Bernhardt was in England, she gave command performances at Windsor, Sandringham or in London, where the two spent intimate hours together. When she staged *La Sorcière* while he happened to be in Paris, he telephoned to arrange a meeting and to inquire about the time of the performance. Not recognizing his voice, she asked, "Who is it?" and when he announced himself, she said— knowing his fondness for prolonged pre-theater dinners— "Oh, for you, Sir, nine o'clock."

But Edward was not always confined to the audience; in fact, he greatly enjoyed performing cameo roles in her plays. His favorite was that of the corpse in the first act of Sardou's *Fedora*, in which Bernhardt entered to learn of her husband's assassination. Parting the heavy brocade curtains of an onstage alcove, she saw the "body," cried, "My Vladimir, my husband!'' and threw herself sobbing on the dead man. In 1883 the ''corpse'' was none other than the Prince of Wales, who naughtily changed positions from one night to the next so that Bernhardt found his feet where she expected to see his head and vice versa. Once he stuffed some musical toys under his costume, and when she laid her head on his body in the scene's final moments, Bernhardt heard some disconcertingly amusing squeaks.

A public holiday was proclaimed that Coronation Day, and there were park festivals, free milk and fireworks. But this soon passed, and the harsher realities of everyday life were once again rudely visible. Now more than a million people in England and Wales were on the dole, and a third of the population was designated as living below the poverty level. One indicator of this was poor housing and wretched sanitary conditions; another was the low level of public health. Parliament in 1902 had not the remotest idea of how to approach these problems.

There were also international threats to the nation, and the worst came from none other than Edward's nephew, Kaiser William II. Relations with Germany had never been easy. Vicky herself loathed Prussian militarism and was humiliated by her son's chauvinistic bombast. The Hanoverians had lost in the Austro-Prussian War of 1866, and following that, Edward's sympathies for France in the Franco-Prussian War further poisoned Germany's attitude toward England. On a personal level, too, the differences between nephew and uncle were vast: where Edward was always polite, genial, gregarious and entirely devoted to international concord, William was rude, smug and bellicose. Nor, as it happened, was good sport much help. George had lost the Queen's yachting cup to William at the Cowes race of 1893—which was bad enough, but William also exploited the event as a showcase for the burgeoning German navy.

Throughout 1902 and 1903 the King and the Prince of Wales, with the approval of the Prime Minister's Cabinet, tried to deal with insults and intimidation from the Kaiser. In official papers from Germany, British ministers were called ''unmitigated noodles''; and the King, said the Kaiser at a Berlin dinner, was ''a devil—you cannot believe what a devil he is.'' This was merely rhetoric, but what it portended was not. The

unchecked growth of the German navy was alarming to all of
Europe, and an attempt to form an alliance and a pact regarding
the high seas failed. By 1904, Admiral John Fisher, First Sea
Lord, frankly told the King that Germany was Britain's chief
threat. In the face of possible conflict there would be a fleet of
new battleships, called Dreadnoughts, equipped with guns so
powerful as to render previous warships obsolete.

Otherwise, Edward enjoyed good relations with Continental
powers. In April 1903 he became the first English King to visit
Rome in over a thousand years (since Aethelwulf, father of
Alfred the Great), and while there he became the first titular
head of the Church of England to visit the Pope—in this case
the ninety-three-year-old Leo XIII, then in the last months of
his tenure. Prime Minister Arthur Balfour, fearful of Protestant
anti-Catholic bigotry, had counseled the King against this
meeting. Nonsense, said Edward. As Prince of Wales he had
thrice met the previous Pope, Pius IX; he refused to yield to
prejudice and, in the bargain, to offend his Catholic subjects.
When they met, Edward charmed the frail but wary Pope Leo,
who in turn praised the monarch's tolerance of Catholics (who
had enjoyed civil rights in England only since the time of
Victoria).

Rome was the last of several triumphant visits that year: the
King was equally well received in Portugal, Italy and France.
In Paris, his social skills were never more successful, and after
his visit the basis was firmly set in place for the so-called
Entente Cordiale of 1904, a French phrase coined by Edward
himself.

Among other problems, two especially critical ones were
resolved, due at least partly to Edward's badgering of his government simply to get the job done because it was beginning
to bore him: France's rights in Morocco were recognized, as
were Britain's in Egypt. (Not incidentally, this further soured
Kaiser William, who had also staked claims in Morocco.) The
King, who spoke flawless French and in France signed himself
"Edouard," departed Paris to loud cheers of *"Vive le Roi!"*
and *"Vive l'Angleterre!"* From March to September 1903, he
had traveled more than eight thousand miles in five countries.
This made him one of the world's first celebrities.

With the fame came an outpouring of general good will
toward Edward. He was the first head of state to receive a

wireless message from inventor Guglielmo Marconi, who addressed the King from South Wellfleet, on Cape Cod, Massachusetts. After offering "on behalf of the American people most cordial greetings and wishes to you," Marconi received an immediate reply. "I thank you most sincerely," said Edward. "I sincerely reciprocate the cordial greetings and friendly sentiment expressed by you ... and I heartily wish you and your country every prosperity."

On home turf the King's life was equally peripatetic. By this time he had a fixed annual schedule. At Christmas and the New Year he was at Sandringham, and in January and February at Buckingham Palace for the state opening of Parliament and social events. March and April found him in France or cruising the Mediterranean. In May and June he shuttled between London and Windsor where there was virtually a nightly round of evening courts, state balls and dinners formal and informal. Every summer weekend he was at one house party or another, with time out for the Goodwood and Cowes races. After this he very much needed to take the cure at Marienbad, only to return for hunting and riding at Balmoral before the cycle began again. Except for the visits to Europe (and the endless and unhealthy nightly banquets), this is much the same routine as that followed by Edward's four successors, up to the end of the twentieth century.

Meanwhile, life for George's sons was as remote and detached from public life as their grandfather's was totally immersed in it. When they were eight and seven, Edward and Albert were transferred from the ministrations of nannies to the care of a manservant, Frederick Finch, who acted as valet and nurse *in loco parentis*. Then a tutor arrived who would see to their studies and be a constant companion until their maturity, a somewhat uninspiring thirty-nine-year-old Oxford graduate named Henry Peter Hansell. Devoted to the welfare of his two young charges, tactful and benevolent, Hansell lacked two qualities essential for a teacher: humor and imagination. He was, Edward wrote years later, "melancholy and incompetent." That Edward and Albert were forever after bored with the things of the mind can be traced to their tutelage under Hansell; had their mother herself taken their education in hand or known how arid was Hansell's classroom, the boys may have fared better. As it was, their education was doomed by a triple conspiracy: a fatal lack of stimulation and healthy competition, the hermetically sealed atmosphere of privilege and the absence of any incentive to excel. Doubtless the tutor had appealed to their father because he was an ardent yachtsman.

In Hansell's defense it must be said that he objected to the home-study course, recommending instead to George and May that the boys be sent to a normal preparatory school. George would not hear of it; just as he and Eddy had been taught by a private tutor, so would Edward and Albert. Hansell's accomplishments with the boys were so unremarkable that George—who could not imagine he had chosen badly in the tutor or the system—was in due course convinced that his sons were irredeemably stupid.

The atmosphere was grim. A makeshift classroom was arranged on the top floor of York House: small, uncomfortable wooden desks, a freestanding blackboard, a few books on history, Latin and mathematics. Finch woke the two princes at seven and led them to the classroom for forty-five minutes of quiet study. Only then would they be led downstairs for breakfast, after which it was back to the dark and cramped room from nine to one (with an hour's sport on fine days). After lunch there was a walk or perhaps some more recreation, another hour of work, and then jam and milk at teatime, which was also their last meal of the day. Washed and dressed, they were ushered into their parents' presence for an hour before being sent to bed. Except for the isolation from boys their own age, Edward and Albert were subjected to much the same family atmosphere as most boys in Victorian and Edwardian upper classes.

The Countess of Airlie considered the King and Queen as "more conscientious and more truly devoted to their children than the majority of parents in that era," which must evoke a chill for the nameless millions of other wretched youngsters. "The tragedy," continued Mabell Airlie, "was that neither had any understanding of a child's mind . . . they did not succeed in making their children happy." Much of this must be put down to George's unpredictable anger, which was aggravated by chronic indigestion for which the only palliative in those days was patience and large glasses of milk. The Prince was short of the first and detested the second.

"My father had a most horrible temper," Edward confided years later. "He was foully rude to my mother. Why, I've seen her leave the table because he was so rude to her, and we children would all follow her out; not when the staff were present of course, but when we were alone." When mother and children were truly alone (when George trotted off to shoot in the Midlands, for example), things were different. "We used to have the most lovely time with her alone—always laughing and joking—she was a different human being away from him."

George believed it was his duty to dominate manfully. And in this style, as his wife realized, he had been confirmed by virtue of the 1901 journey to the colonies. There was, he had long believed, an almost mystical association between the sovereign and his people; and so George developed an equivalently mystical idea of his own vocation. "Loyalty" for George meant fidelity to the place of the Crown, as if it were the primary pipeline to God. Henceforth, as one of his biographers wrote, he looked upon the monarchy "as something distinct from ordinary life, as something more ancient and durable than any political or family institution, as something sacramental, mystic and ordained."

As for Princess Mary (who was five that autumn of 1902), she had her own German nursemaid and French tutor, although in after-class hours and evenings she joined her brothers. The only girl (her fourth brother, George, was born that December), she was pampered and indulged by her father and never felt his wrath or rejection, as did Edward and Albert. The first was the star, the golden-haired eventual heir to the throne; the youngest was the favorite; between them was the inarticulate, bowlegged, spindly Albert. Countess Airlie recalled, "He was more in conflict with authority than the rest of his brothers." By 1904, Albert had more reason to complain of unhappiness and isolation: from the age of eight he was forced to wear heavy, painful splints on his legs for several hours daily and every night in an attempt to correct the contours of his knock-kneed legs.

"Practically all Prince Albert's work with me has been combined with the splints," Hansell wrote to the Prince of Wales in June 1904. "It is now quite certain that such a combination is impossible." The results were soon obvious: Albert's reports were dismal, and these, too, provoked his sudden, ungovernable fits of temper followed by tears. Ironically, the splints had the desired physical effect, and Albert's knees were finally "rectified." Free of the splints at last by the time he was twelve and growing into a slender and naturally athletic boy, Albert almost at once took to riding; from that time he formed a lifelong, almost emotional bond with horses, a diversion to which his sister Mary was even more passionately attracted. Of this sport Grandpa the King heartily approved, for he was the keenest royal horse-fancier since Charles II. Edward's horse won the Derby and the Grand National, and his patronage made betting, like riding, the sport of kings and commoners alike.

The repressed, isolated childhood of the Wales offspring had, of course, serious consequences. Mary, by her teens, had an iciness that forestalled her emotional maturity and, perhaps unsurprisingly, led her to marry a much older man. Edward became a lifelong fidget and a fearfully dependent and obsessive lover. Albert could carry on a conversation only with Herculean effort and subjugated his personality to a bride who dominated him and their children. Henry, who chose perhaps the quietest woman to join the family, had a habit of barking both commands and strange outbursts of laughter. George was not notably nervous but later was, for a time, rather dangerously given to drugs and supplemented his marriage with numerous gay liaisons. The family was indeed as ordinary as their descendants have insisted.

By a sad irony the sixth and last of George and May's children—Prince John, born July 12, 1905—was both the least and the most problematic. Pale, neurasthenic and unusually quiet all through infancy, he also suffered from a series of seizures that were terrifying to his parents and nannies. Epilepsy was diagnosed at the age of four, and he was quietly shipped off to the country, to be cared for by Charlotte Bill, the older boys' former nanny. At that time epilepsy was still considered an unacceptable embarrassment to polite families, a shameful sign of mental deficiency and genetic failure, something to be grimly excluded from recognition.

When John was three months old, George and May departed for an official tour of southeast Asia and India as representatives of the King-Emperor. Traveling more than ten thousand miles in six months, the couple impressed millions with their political astuteness, their unhaughty dignity and their lack of prejudice.

Typically, the Princess prepared by reading every book she could acquire. "You know what trouble I took to get the right books," May wrote to her childhood tutor, adding that she was flattered to be told by Sir Walter Lawrence, chief of staff for the tour, that she had "a very good grasp on Indian affairs." She took special pains to learn something of Indian religious history, too: "All this knowledge helps one to take a keen interest in all one sees & I therefore hope to enjoy to the utmost every detail of the wonderful sights."

As Prince of Wales, George insisted on performing his duty and living up to his public image to the fullest. He arrived in every city in an open carriage, notwithstanding the frequent displays of hostility caused by conflict between Indian civilians and the British military. He met British and native officers; he shot tigers, pinned medals, presided at parades and acted as the visible agent of the Empire. No champion of a nascent movement for Indian independence, George was nevertheless outraged when he saw how badly most British treated Indians— "like schoolboys," he complained. Equally, the Prince was offended by the treatment of wives and daughters: "I cannot see how there can be real self-respect while the Indians treat their women as they do now."

It is impossible to overstate the effect this journey had on George. More than ever convinced of the Crown's value and the role of a democratic sovereign, his sense of destiny was fixed by the time he returned to England. "He saw," according to John Gore, who wrote a memoir of his association with George, "the extent to which the whole Empire might stand or fall by the personal example set by the Throne." To this Gore might have added that the Prince was more than matched by his wife.

However gravely they took their roles as the future King and Queen, neither George nor May believed that the significance of the Empire lay in permanent British rule in India. He wrote to Lord Esher after his return,

> Personally, I think we have now come to the parting of the ways. . . . We must either trust the Natives more and give them a greater share in government or anyhow allow them

to express their views; or else we must double our Civil Service, [which has] got out of touch with the villages on account of the great increase in their work.

In their parents' absence, the Wales children were once again deposited with the King and Queen. As usual, if a governess or teacher attempted to end playtime with the grandparents, Alix drew Edward, Albert, Mary and Henry to herself, to prevent separation. "It's all right," said King Edward, "let the children stay with us a little longer. We shall send them upstairs presently." The youngsters were, by every account, far more in awe of their parents than of the King and Queen. "It was," recalled Edward years later, "like being given an open-sesame to a totally different world." He remembered peering down grand staircases to see Grandpapa and Grandmama receiving guests at Sandringham, "a brilliantly varied company—statesmen, diplomats, bankers, luminaries of the arts and international society, *bons vivants.*"

Young Edward did not know it, but Grandpapa had weightier matters to deal with than romping with his grandchildren or playing host at Sandringham. While the Waleses were in India, a general election swept the Liberal Party into Parliament. This shift did not mean the House of Commons would be packed with mad-eyed Bolsheviks; in fact, many powerful Liberals were staunch Imperialists—men such as Herbert Asquith, Edward Grey and Richard B. Haldane. The victory was more prosaic and owed to the problems of Balfour's government, especially in the areas of social and tariff reforms, education and the reduction of Chinese laborers in South Africa to the level of slaves. With these problems the Liberals won the election. Among the party leaders were Asquith (who succeeded as Prime Minister in 1908 when Henry Campbell-Bannerman fell ill), David Lloyd George (Chancellor of the Exchequer and paymaster of social welfare programs) and Winston Churchill who, like Lloyd George, was frankly committed to an extension of social welfare programs. None of these would be easily achieved. King Edward, although suspicious of what he called "a radical wave," strictly followed his duty to remain above politics and acted as a conciliator between the new Commons and the still Conservative House of Lords.

* * *

By 1906, Queen Alexandra was deeply concerned about the state of the King's health. Edward, never abstemious at table, now had the habit of indulging in the comfort of rich foods, which he ate with the voracity of a giant. A typical breakfast began with two platters of bacon and eggs, followed by smoked fish, roast chicken and perhaps half a loaf of bread. A bowl of soup was served mid-morning, and a few hours later a four-course lunch with more meat, fish and potatoes. At teatime a servant rolled in a trolley of more eggs, cakes, shortbread and scones topped with clotted cream and preserves. Dinners, in mid-evening, normally meant twelve courses. And although earlier his intake of alcohol was restricted to a glass of champagne at dinner or a brandy after, the King soon became (though nothing like an alcoholic) an intemperate tippler.

He also smoked heavily: more than a dozen large cigars and two dozen strong Egyptian cigarettes daily. Alix, who shared Victoria's conviction that smoking was not only unseemly but perilous, tried to alter her husband's excesses, but her remonstrances were to no avail. Attacks of bronchitis became frequent, and there were the first signs of emphysema, the condition that eventually killed the King (and was not revealed to the public until after his death).

The Queen's anxiety was shared by Alice Keppel, about whom aristocrats smiled; as for Alix, she resented that her husband's relationship with the lady continued uninterrupted by the duties or dignity of kingship. A little public embarrassment or a light scolding from an editor might have done Edward no harm, Alix thought, but of course in those days the press kept its discreet silence.

By early 1907, when he was sixty-five, photographs showed a smiling monarch with a jauntily tipped hat, almost invariably holding a large cigar. He looked very much like a benevolent grandfather or a prosperous board chairman. But his diet and smoking were taking a grave toll on his health, and in February 1907 he was so weak with bronchial congestion that he spoke to Alix of abdicating in favor of George. This was an uncharacteristically grim threat, and in April they were in Malta, combining minor business with a rest holiday.

Edward spent that summer (without Alix) at his favorite Bohemian spa in Marienbad, where he met with the Russian and French prime ministers, effectively sealing a new Anglo-Russian pact and a new triple Entente Cordiale with Russia and France. The Kaiser, displeased by all this English alliance-making, visited, too, and observed that his uncle was taking the waters but had failed to modify his gargantuan appetite. Nor did Edward keep only to his own suite of rooms, for there were many new attractive ladies to meet that season.

In April 1908, the King could not endure the protracted London winter, and he repaired to Biarritz, where the new Prime Minister, Herbert Asquith, traveled to present himself. Yet two months later the King insisted on visiting Czar Nicholas II to mark the new entente and to seek tacit support against the Kaiser. The sojourn was also a family visit: the Czar's wife was, after all, Edward's niece (daughter of his sister Princess Alice), and the Czar himself was Queen Alexandra's nephew (son of Czar Alexander III, who married Alexandra's sister Dagmar).

The popularity of his uncle in Russia and France only aggravated the jealousy of Kaiser William, intent on demonstrating world supremacy by building a bigger navy than England's. In this mad scramble for power by the eccentric Kaiser (born with the handicap of a useless undersized arm that humiliated him), he acted unchecked by Otto von Bismarck, the Iron Chancellor, who had effectively accomplished the unification of Germany but failed to keep William under constitutional control; since Bismarck's death in 1898, the Kaiser was his own law.

After Edward's return to England, William summoned interviewers from the London *Daily Telegraph*. Oh, he loved Britain, he said unconvincingly—a hollow protestation repeated ever since he received an honorary degree from Oxford in November 1907. But he also admitted that during the Boer War he had gladly sought ways to "humiliate England to the dust." And then he gave away his true feelings: "You English are mad, mad as March hares. What has come over you that you are so completely given over to suspicion quite unworthy of a great nation?" British suspicions were, of course, quite well founded; indeed, all Europe looked uncertainly at the unpredictable, militaristic Kaiser, simultaneously recognizing that Edward was the genial, honest peacemaker. Before long, Lord Northcliffe, owner of *The Times*, was warning in editorials that any perceptive citizen could see that Germany was preparing for war. Few people agreed with that likelihood, however.

Meantime, the conservative House of Lords was continually obstructing the social reform and tax bills of the Liberal government in Commons. The prime conflict concerned Lloyd George's frontal attack on aristocratic privilege by means of his "People's Budget." The stage was set for a fierce battle that would involve and potentially embarrass the Crown. Urged by the ruling Liberal Party to create more Liberal peers in the House of Lords to override any opposition there, King Edward declined to compromise the monarch's political impartiality. The general election of 1910 temporarily defused the matter, but by this time the King was mortally ill with emphysema.

As for George's children, the education of Edward and Albert now focused on naval careers, the direct and deliberate inheritance of their father's experience. At thirteen, Edward entered the Naval College at Osborne as a cadet; Victoria had willed the royal residence to the nation, and Edward VII had given it over to the navy. The King had excelled in his own preparation for such a career years earlier, and so with his arrival at Osborne, the young Prince's education in history, constitutional theory and languages was effectively aborted.

That summer Edward stood at five feet three inches; in three years he would reach his full adult height of five feet six. He appeared younger than thirteen, too pretty and too vulnerable. Because he was no specimen of hardy youth and was the son of the Prince of Wales, Edward was soon nicknamed "Little Sardine" by his mates—slight of build and offspring of the "whales"—and this designation was later passed on to his brother Albert. Perhaps to appear more mature, but also because he was introduced to it at home, Edward was by this time a habitual smoker.*

---

* His grandfather would soon die from the effects of smoking, as would his father, his brother and, finally, Edward himself. The tendency to suffer smoking's worst effects began with his uncle, Prince Alfred, and even perhaps with his aunt Vicky. Nor is it true to say that the dangers were unknown at the time: Queen Victoria's ardent crusades against smoking set the pattern, and in every reign thereafter Court physicians (especially homeopathic specialists) were never more stern than in urging their royal patients to decrease the number of daily cigars and cigarettes. They were speaking to the wind. Obedience to Prime Ministers and Cabinet members is required by the constitution; acquiescence to doctors is exempted.

"Just as we found out who this new termer was," recalled a contemporary, "we seniors ensured that he had a bad time. Looking back on it now, I do see that we seniors were nothing better than a pack of hounds. But it had long been a tradition to give all new termers a miserable time to show them their place."

The miserable time started when Edward had red ink poured over his head. What was his name? mates asked. "Just Edward," he replied, unwilling to identify himself as Prince Edward and so risk further exclusion.

"At first it seemed especially hard," Edward wrote later,

> because I was caught up, without the previous experience of school, in the unfamiliar community life of small boys, with all its fierce and subtle relationships. Formerly I had had Finch [the valet] to take care of my clothes and pick up after me; I now had to look out for myself. And from the comfortable rooms of our different homes I found myself thrust, in company with some thirty other boys, into a long, bare dormitory. The orbit of my living shrank to a hard, iron bed and a black-and-white sea chest.

Some of this toughening was harmless and even beneficial to a future monarch in a modern world. But there were serious disadvantages, among them the disapproval of all questioning of authority. Said a classmate who became an admiral,

> We were taught that there were only two ways of doing anything, the Navy way, which was consistently right, and the non-Navy way, which was as invariably wrong. No deviation was countenanced. We were being made into stereotypes, just as our predecessors . . . had been rigidly trained not to think. All experimentation was damned. . . . Mathematics, science, navigation and engineering—that was all. No Latin, no logic, no geography and no history, not even naval history.

In early 1909, Albert (then thirteen) joined his brother as an Osborne cadet, and at once he faced similar problems, all of them exacerbated by his speech defect. "He looks terribly young and fragile to be thrown out into the real world," noted

Lala Bill in her journal. "But funnily enough I feel more confidence in Bertie overcoming his difficulties and handicaps than I did his elder brother."

Albert had never been to school with boys his own age or attended a class with more than three, and his entire social life had been abnormally reclusive and sheltered. His arrival at Osborne—a pale-faced, insecure and inarticulate lad—was not made easier when he was told that contact with his brother, a senior, was forbidden. But in the boy's favor was his inheritance of his father's blazing temper. Essentially he was angry at himself and at what he might have considered his fate—a stammerer too often taken for an idiot. This he was not, although he certainly never distinguished himself in the classroom. But his sudden rages kept his mates on the alert, and soon it was taken for granted that young Prince Albert was not to be taken for a fool, however disappointing his report card. At the end of his second year it could not have been worse: Albert ranked sixty-eighth in a class of sixty-eight.

Life at Osborne was that of a typical military school. In their spartan, cold and cheerless dormitory the boys were awakened at six by a bugler. A cadet captain's gong meant prayers at their bedside, another gong toothbrushing, a third a group plunge in the cold-water pool. Life was regimented at double time: everyone ran everywhere, and at day's end the boys had three minutes to undress, lay out the next day's clothes, wash and hop under the bedclothes. The food was schoolboy English edible, which meant not very.

While the boys were in rugged training for seafaring, Grandpa had naval trials of a more ominous kind. The King's several visits to the Kaiser, to discuss the rapid buildup of German warships, ended in a public display of camaraderie, but privately there was an edgy hostility.

At the last of these missions, King Edward was often racked with coughing and intermittent bronchitis, and by the end of 1909 both Queen Alexandra and Alice Keppel were much the worse for worry. The King could not be persuaded to lighten his duties, however, for he sensed more than ever the looming constitutional crisis. Since the Liberal victory in 1906, welfare legislation originating in Commons had been systematically blocked by the House of Lords, where the Conservatives had a considerable majority. In light of this, the growing Labour Party joined sides with the Liberals, decrying a hereditary aristocracy (Lords) stymieing the will of the elected representatives (Commons).

The matter of Lloyd George's "People's Budget" now reached a crisis. The Chancellor of the Exchequer sought to levy a small supertax on annual incomes over £5,000 (then $24,000) and to tax unearned income (that is, hereditary wealth and land) more heavily than wages. The Tories denounced this as a socialist evil. Prime Minister Asquith then dissolved Parliament in December 1909, calling for a general election and asking the question, "Shall peers or people rule?" King Edward was much distressed. "The monarchy," he said grimly, "will not last much longer. I believe my son will stay on the throne, as the people are fond of him, but certainly not my grandson."

Fearing that the Prime Minister might eventually move to curtail (or even to end forever) the Lords' power to defeat legislation, Edward urged both Tories and Lords to accept the budget and thus defuse the crisis. The alternative would be that Asquith might force the King to create more Liberal peers so that the House of Lords would be "stacked" with political cronies. This would threaten the hereditary system of the House of Lords and was thus an implicit attack on the monarchy itself. If Asquith had required him to create Liberal peers, the King would have had to comply. As it happened, the budget proposals passed in the House of Lords, but attention would henceforth be focused on the Parliament Bill, which was designed to restrict the power of the Lords themselves.

That winter Edward's health worsened, his emphysema now a chronic and often crippling illness. He was not an old man (he turned sixty-eight on November 9, 1909), but he seemed so. Nevertheless, the King forced himself to open Parliament on February 22, 1910, in the thick of arguments over money and the power of Lords. Unlike his mother, he had never once failed in this duty. Besides, notwithstanding his own love of luxury, Edward learned from Alix a sympathy for the poor; his feelings were paternalistic, however, and never found focus in counsel to his government. He never had the remotest liking for socialists or radicals, much less for suffragettes. None of this entered his speech, for of course he could read only what the Cabinet prepared for him.

* * *

More than four hundred million people were allied to the British Empire in 1910, and they inhabited 11.5 million square miles, over one-fifth of the world's land. It was true to say that the sun never set on the British Empire—perhaps because, as someone insisted, God would never trust an Englishman in the dark.

The travels of Edward VII and of his oldest son George, Prince of Wales, much augmented the Crown's popularity. But the monarch was admired and loved mostly for a chain of personal characteristics: his apparent accessibility and his delight in the theater, in good food and wine, in all sorts of company; his public geniality; his all too human faults of the kind so easy to forgive and never hurtful to anyone (save his wife, who discreetly hid every reaction); his charm and unfailing polish; his love of a romp with his grandchildren; and his loyal Alix. Not since the days of young Victoria and Albert had the Royal Family been so much a family.

Additionally, Edward VII dispatched his responsibilities with dignity and great vigor, leaving behind him an impression of a concerned and benevolent monarchy. In nine years the throne had gone swiftly from a hidden, mysterious artifact of history to a prop of civilized society. Just when a burgeoning popular press and the arrival of "flickers" began to capture the imagination of the public, this jovial, modern King had a genius for humanizing his royal status. Courting the press, engaging photographers, calling on his consummate charm, he was what he seemed. When his reign came to an end, it could only be assessed as a triumph of illusion: the role had little substance, but he played it to perfection—or, to shift the emphasis, he showed that the monarchy was no longer engaged in the creation of high drama. By his warmth and sincerity, his generosity and lack of pomposity, Edward VII saved it from becoming a Middle European farce. His descendants throughout the twentieth century owed him a crucial debt.

After the opening of Parliament, doctors were at last to prevail on the King to rest at Biarritz. Because no one knew the King was in the first throes of a life-threatening illness, Alix was encouraged to visit her Danish-Greek royal relatives on Corfu, which she gladly undertook. Edward stopped in Paris on March 7, short of breath and with a dull, continuous chest pain, but this did not prevent him from going to the theater, where he caught a cold. By the next afternoon, en route to Biarritz, he had influenza and bronchitis. Among the attending party were Alice Keppel and her daughters, who were quietly available to divert and comfort the ailing monarch. "I am sorry to leave Biarritz," he said hoarsely on the eve of his departure. "Perhaps it will be forever." The townspeople lit fireworks, set out marching bands and hailed the King who had done so much to make the place fashionable. "I hope everyone was thanked," he said to his secretary—adding, ever aware of public image, "especially the press." He was assured that the media had been alerted.

On April 27, he returned to London and headed straight for Covent Garden and one of his favorite operas, *Rigoletto*. Lord Redesdale, who saw him there, found the King "very tired and worn, with a very sad expression on his face."

On Saturday, April 30, the King went to Sandringham. The staff, who ordinarily found him "quick-tempered, insisting on things being done at once, ever kind but accustomed to being obeyed," now noticed that he was "so quiet, so gentle, so unlike his impulsive nature." He returned to Buckingham Palace on May 2, coughing constantly and with a terrifying dark color. But he refused to curtail his activities. "No—I shall not give in. I shall work to the end," he said, lighting a cigar. "Of what use is it to be alive if one cannot work?" So long denied any usefulness, he was not to abandon it easily. That night he made a supreme effort and dined with his old friend, the nurse Agnes Keyser.

The next day, despite his doctor's warnings, King Edward insisted on meeting the American Ambassador Whitelaw Reid, who recalled that their conversation was interrupted by

> spasms of coughing, and I found that he was suffering from a good many symptoms [of] bronchial asthma. . . . It seems to me that these attacks are coming on more frequently . . . and are harder to shake off. Still, he is a man of tremendous vigor of constitution, and of extraordinary energetic habits.

That evening Alice Keppel joined the King for dinner and an early card game. After she departed, he slept badly and was much worse in the morning.

On May 4, Alix—alerted for the first time the day before by Prince George—arrived in London. By this time the King was ashen, his features sunken, his breathing so labored as to terrify the bystanders. Alix comforted her husband and then joined George and May, with whom she collapsed in tears. The family vigil continued for the next two days.

By the morning of May 6, it was clear the King could not survive much longer.

Then Queen Alexandra did a remarkable thing, a gesture for her dying husband that has entered the history books as an act of extraordinary grace and selflessness. Thinking of the comfort the King would derive from Alice Keppel's presence, she ordered the royal favorite to be brought to the palace, where she was led by Alix herself to Edward's bedside. "I am sure you always had a good influence over him," Alix said, and she left Alice alone with the King for several minutes.

In the early afternoon the King, with superhuman effort, pulled himself out of bed and walked over to his two caged canaries, to whom he muttered a friendly greeting and encouraged them to twitter along with him. Then he lost consciousness and fell to the floor. He was suffering a series of small but lethal heart attacks, and the doctors administered morphine for the pain and attached an oxygen mask to ease his breathing. At a quarter past four that afternoon, he awoke briefly to see George at his bedside. His son told him that the King's horse, Witch of the Air, had won a race. "Yes, I have heard of it," Edward replied. "I am very glad."

At eleven that evening the Archbishop of Canterbury arrived and led the family in bedside prayers. Just as the chimes of Westminster struck the quarter hour before midnight, King Edward VII died quietly and without struggle.

"I have lost my best friend and the best of fathers," George, soon to be proclaimed the new king, scribbled in his journal that night. "I never had a [harsh] word with him in my life. I am heartbroken & overwhelmed with grief but God will help me in my great responsibilities & darling May will be my comfort as she always has been."

As for Alix, she was bereft. No matter the complexities of their marriage and the certain wounds she had felt for years, she was as devoted to her husband the King as she had been when he was Prince of Wales. He could be called a cad by his enemies, but whenever Alix sensed a whisper of criticism against her Bertie, she dismissed the speaker forever from her presence. He had given her life a purpose, a focus and field for her religiously motivated works of charity; he had appreciated her more than anyone in her life. And he had given Alix her adored children.

"The Queen," wrote Sir Arthur Ponsonby after she summoned him to the bedside of the dead King, "spoke quite naturally and said how peaceful he looked and that it was a comfort to think he had suffered no pain." Then her newly deepened isolation overcame her. "She said she felt as if she had been turned into stone, unable to cry, unable to grasp the meaning of it all, and incapable of doing anything." Such visits continued for eleven days of vigil. "They want to take him away," she said, her voice shaking, "but I can't bear to part with him. Once they hide his face from me, everything is gone forever." Finally yielding to reason, Alix pressed a rose into her husband's folded hands and allowed his body to be removed on May 17. For three days and nights before the public funeral, Edward VII lay in state at Westminster Hall, while tens of thousands paid reverential and loving respect, forming a long and quiet queue far down the Embankment.

Prince (later King) George, his wife Mary and
their children.

5

The Mumps 1910 to 1917

I don't intend to move for any bombs!
KING GEORGE V, at the front during World War I

Early on the afternoon of Saturday, May 7, 1910—just twelve
hours after the death of King Edward VII—vast crowds of
Londoners poured into the streets near St. James's Palace and
around Friary Court. The late monarch's eldest surviving son
was to be proclaimed King, his accession having followed
automatically at the moment of his father's passing. Precisely
at four o'clock the heir arrived from Marlborough House and

was escorted into the chamber of the Privy Council at St. James's Palace. There the proclamation was read by Sir Alfred Scott-Gatty, who bore the arcane title of Garter King of Arms.

The Councillors, led by the Archbishop of Canterbury and the Lord Chancellor, then approached King George V, each bowing and kissing his hand. These formalities concluded, the new monarch, who was known to have an even deeper dislike for ceremony than he had for social life, read a short speech prepared by his secretary, Sir Arthur Bigge, but given final form by himself. His words had a touch of personal and heartfelt sentiment, establishing at once the tone of direct simplicity that would characterize his tenure.

The King then departed the chamber and returned to his wife, who was waiting at Marlborough House and facing her first royal dilemma: how would she be called as Queen Consort? "May" was a nickname and so quite out of consideration; her first given name was Victoria, but that was also, for obvious reasons, inappropriate; and George disdained double names, thus Victoria Mary would not do, either. That evening the decision was made, and Queen Mary she would be. "It strikes me as curious to be rechristened at the age of forty-three," she wrote on May 15 to her aunt Augusta.

The King arrived at his task a month before his forty-fifth birthday, fifteen years younger and in many ways better prepared than his predecessor. He had been introduced by his father to ceremonial duties, had been shown samplings of state papers, had been initiated in matters of parliamentary policy, and had been sent on official visits to Australia and India.

But King Edward, determined not to make his sons' education as severe as his own, had also been indulgent, and Queen Alexandra had loved him to the point of infantilism, still referring in 1910 to her "darling Georgie boy." In addition, Georgie's tutor, Reverend Dalton, had been lackadaisical, often substituting sport and games for studies, and Georgie's handwriting was that of a schoolboy. His intellectual life was so shallow, in fact, that it was routinely said he never got through an entire volume of literature. "People who write books ought to be shut up," the King said without a trace of irony; any whisper of a literary discussion embarrassed and annoyed him.

As Prince and as King, George's only real adult cultural

mentor was his wife, but he was not a man to submit easily to tutelage. "There you go again, May," he would say with benign exasperation when his wife mentioned her latest acquisition. "It's always furniture, furniture, furniture!" One item in the Queen's collection struck his fancy, however: a silver and gilt statuette of Lady Godiva. The reason for his fondness was that he had heard the nearsighted Queen Olga of the Hellenes, as she peered at the figurine, whispering with a contented sigh, "Ah, dear Queen Victoria."

In his natural conservatism, his lack of education, his obsession with orderliness, neatness and punctuality, the King was very much the quintessence of a middle-class burgher whose simple values and homely virtues he seemed to embody, although sometimes with a touch of the fanatic. When a housekeeper accidentally rearranged items after cleaning, George was so enraged at the disruption of his regime that his rooms were photographed for future reference, to ensure against a repetition of this unwelcome alteration. Senior courtiers and humble footmen were loudly and angrily rebuked for the slightest infraction against hoary protocol (trousers instead of knee breeches at a formal dinner party or a bad job of sealing wax on an envelope). The halls of Windsor Castle and York Cottage routinely echoed with the King's temper, leveled as often against house staff as against his sons. But no servant was dismissed for an obviously human error. Five minutes after a reprimand a footman might be summoned to the King's side, to be told the latest risqué story making the rounds of the palace. "I fear I was somewhat irritable," was a typical way of apologizing for a sudden outburst, "but you know it means nothing."

To be sure, George could be a kindly and considerate man, careful to see that gentlemen who attended him were not (as had been the custom) long separated from their wives and families, a situation he would not have liked for himself. If he learned that a palace scullery maid or carriage driver was ill or burdened with family misfortune, cash gifts quietly found their way to the one in need. On the return from Kenya of Sir Edward Grigg, after a difficult term as governor of that colony, the King told him, "I know what you are feeling. You have been away a long time, trying very hard to get things done. You have not succeeded as you hoped, but no one seems to realize that you have even tried, or that you have been having a hard time, or bothered to say thank you. Well, *I* say thank you.''

Thus while aspects of his naval background gave him strength and courage, bonhomie and lack of pomposity, some elements made him narrow: he insisted, for example, that at sea he had learned all the important things a man needed to know, and to this idea he kept a lively attachment by sending both Edward and Albert to continue for him as surrogate seamen. Nothing so pleased him as to discuss the sailor's life: it had spiced his speech, for he routinely used salty language, to which Queen Mary was suddenly and conveniently deaf. When Sir Samuel Hoare resigned as Foreign Secretary, the King tossed off an unwelcome joke: ''No more coals to Newcastle, no more Hoares to Paris.'' The first question he put to transatlantic pilot Charles Lindbergh was equally unexpected: ''What do you do about peeing?'' But he was the King, after all, and some may have thought that he was simply saying what many wondered and wanted to know. He could also appreciate the rare hilarious palace gaffe and roared with laughter when his sister relayed an incident on the palace telephone. ''Is that you, you old fool?'' Princess Victoria asked, after requesting that the telephone operator put her through to the King. ''No, Your Royal Highness,'' replied a voice. ''His Majesty is not yet on the line.''

But George had neither mental astuteness nor political instincts, and despite his best intentions, his reign added to the confusion surrounding the links between the throne, the government and the people of Britain. With neither the interest nor the sharpness to deal with partisan intrigues, he could not appreciate the conflicting demands that kingship made on him. ''The King is a very jolly chap,'' wrote David Lloyd George to his wife a few months after the accession, ''but thank God there's not much in his head.'' The words were not meant to be insulting: the Chancellor of the Exchequer was simply expressing the view of many that a king with an inquiring mind might be a hindrance to a duly elected representative government.

If George V was not empty-headed, neither was he given to reflections on the march of time. Unlike his father, he judged by the standards of the past and deplored the encroachments of modern life. Edward VII had dabbled in European diplomacy, had made the Crown less German and more cosmopolitan. But George's interests were British to the core; indeed, he had no interest in foreigners. Additionally, from the start everything about the new reign seemed less social and more domestic. There were no mistresses and no matrimonial intrigues, nor were there capricious weekends in Paris or Biarritz. The new King's idea of diversion was not an evening at the opera or a formal dinner with witty companions; a weekend at York Cottage, Sandringham (which continued to be his family's main residence), suited him fine. There, as one chronicler wrote,

> the King and Queen, their six children, their equerries, ladies, secretaries, their children's tutor, governess and their servants, were all crammed into something hardly bigger than a suburban villa. . . . Ill at ease in grandiose surroundings and disliking entertaining, he had every reason to be satisfied with the tiny rooms and inconvenient layout of York Cottage.

In a way the household was itself a metaphor, for George was, as it happened, perfectly cast in a role that was devolving swiftly and inevitably to the status of a respectable homey ornament. Whereas Prince Albert had established in Victoria the ideal of a constitutional monarch, his death and her widowhood had diminished its power, which was ceded more and more to the prime ministers. By the end of her long reign, Victoria was little more than a much loved symbol—a development confirmed by the short tenure of her son, however much he seemed to incarnate the more humane aspects of that symbol. The march of progress, in other words, was continuing both because of and despite the aura of the monarchy.

To this task George now turned with his straightforward, decent and uncomplicated view of life—a life in which so far, as his biographer wrote, he had done almost "nothing at all but kill animals and stick in stamps." He would continue to shoot and to paste, but he would also serve, advise and be a model of probity in difficult situations for more than a quarter century. Like his grandmother he had a profound sense of duty; unlike his father he was a model of domestic honor.

As for Queen Mary, King George was her life, and her perpetual devotion to the British monarchy was entirely focused in this cousin she had known since childhood, the Georgie she had wed, the man for whom she bore royal children. Alexandra had had a very clear sense of her husband's frail humanity and managed to carve for herself something of an independent life with her Danish relatives, her charities and her family. But for the new Queen there was only the King. Everything was done for him and his equanimity; everything served him. She never openly contradicted him before the family, and only in private or in letters would she protest if he lost his temper or unfairly treated one son or another. Mabell Airlie, the Queen's lady-in-waiting and closest friend, recalled that Mary's tact and quiet home life "sometimes earned her the reputation of being dull—which she was not." In the presence of others she simply subjugated her personality to her husband's.

To the King's every day, Mary brought a power of single-minded dedication. "She believed," wrote her biographer, James Pope-Hennessy, "that all should defer to the King's slightest wish, and she made herself into a living example of her creed. Outwardly this was not a spectacular part to play. Inwardly it required a constant and dramatic exercise of imagination, foresight and self-control."

And, it must be added, a virtual obliteration of her own tastes. Queen Mary's wardrobe, which for the rest of her long life never advanced beyond the fashion of the turn of the century, was frozen in time at the express command of the King, who in everything—clothing styles included—had an absolute horror of change. She outlived him by seventeen years, but by then she was in every way, as she would write to her oldest son, too old to change. Pastel, ankle-length dresses with matching coats, a toque and a parasol: these became Queen Mary's trademark for public appearances, while at York Cottage the simplest square-necked, muslin shift would do. Like her husband, Mary had not the slightest interest in anything that recalled fashionable Edwardian society, which she rightly considered vulgar and flamboyant. This was especially true of a splendid Court life, which she considered nothing but "a surfeit of gold plate and orchids." There was, in other words, a majestic simplicity about the Queen: she was the King's

Consort, she must proudly dedicate herself to him and to his people, but there was no need for her to adopt excessive props, wardrobe or sets to clarify the role.

In one domestic sphere the King permitted the Queen some stylistic freedom, but even in this she elected to follow his taste and interests. When Mary undertook to redecorate the private apartments of Buckingham Palace in 1911, there were no bold strokes of renovation. She simply brought down from Sandringham a tiger-skin rug, swords, spears, tusks, barometers, navy charts, maps and a ship commander's desk. In this matter her attention to the details of "furniture, furniture, furniture" suited him admirably.

It would be wrong to suppose that George did not respect his wife's taste or value her opinions in weightier issues. Everything relevant to matters of state which his father had confided in George, George shared with his wife; and as King he regularly discussed with her the contents of the dispatch boxes. Their conversations on such matters seem to have differed little from an ordinary couple's discussion of daily news. The King, after all, was simply being informed of the government's actions, and most of the Cabinet papers made for tedious reading. According to Mabell Airlie, among others, Mary's was a sharper, more original mind than her husband's, and their views on issues of the day often diverged remarkably. George trusted Mary's common sense and her grasp of ministers' personalities, but the Queen would no sooner press her point than she would wear a color the King disliked.

George had no such fundamental trust of his sons. Vowed to duty, he saw them as similarly bound from birth, and he constantly feared that the merest hint of scandal would revive the improprieties of his father in his sons. Thus a severe scolding was the routine when a mild reproof would have worked. When Prince Edward arrived in his father's presence wearing new-fashioned trousers with turned-up cuffs, the King berated him: "Is it raining in *here?*"—implying that his son had rolled up his trousers to cross puddles in the street. Similarly, the monarch loudly mocked their slightest mistakes or boyish clumsiness and demanded of them a perfection (in dress, speech and social form) to which no mortal could aspire. Countess Airlie put the matter frankly: the King "was fond of his sons, but his manner to them alternated between an awkward jocularity which makes a sensitive child squirm from self-consciousness, and a severity bordering on harshness.'' The harshness did not extend to his beloved parrot Charlotte, however, who strutted freely over the breakfast table at Sandringham and pecked into the boiled eggs of anyone she chose. When the bird soiled the table, her master calmly placed a plate or jam pot over the mess. His indulgence toward Charlotte— when the bird squawked out a repetition of the scolding for a tardy son—could not have endeared her to anyone but the King.

The Queen was still as problematic a mother as ever, devoted but undemonstrative, a woman of her time and station, ''very buttoned up and very unbending,'' as the Earl of Harewood, her grandson, said years later. ''She didn't find it easy to discuss vital things, crucial things—to show warmth to people.'' Of this personality trait Mary often seemed to be quite poignantly aware: ''David dined with me in the evening,'' she wrote typically of her meetings with her eldest son. ''We talked a lot but of nothing very intimate.''

The eldest was then, and would ever be, the least happy of all her children. On the death of King Edward, his grandson Edward automatically inherited the title Duke of Cornwall, which placed at his future disposal a vast income from estate lands in that county as well as a goodly share of London property. Then, on his sixteenth birthday that June, his father created him Prince of Wales, for he was now, of course, heir to the throne. Edward was still at the Royal Naval College, Dartmouth (and would be until May 1911), where he did respectably in his studies save for mathematics and science. Eager to please, Edward had an undisciplined mind and poor powers of concentration, his boyish curiosity dulled by both a haphazard education and social convention. He was also embarrassed that his status prevented him from being completely accepted by his companions. Edward was, in addition, completely disenchanted with the idea that the throne would one day pass to him in the ordinary course of things. Years later his nanny, Charlotte Bill, wrote to Queen Mary, reminding her that even in his teens the Prince ''never wanted to become King.''

Neither did his brother Albert, who wrongly presumed he

never would be. Albert was at Dartmouth during Edward's last term in 1911; the younger brother's academic performance was markedly poorer, as it had been at Osborne. His stammer was worse, his temper shorter. By contrast, Prince Henry at first got on well in his studies at St. Peter's Court Preparatory School in Kent, where he arrived in 1910—the first son of a British sovereign to be sent away to school (rather than being entrusted solely to tutors or being enrolled at a military or naval academy). Prince George joined Henry there in 1912; Princess Mary continued to be tutored at home; and poor Prince John was quietly tucked away with a small staff at Sandringham.

As for Alexandra, Queen Dowager, the earliest days of her widowhood required a difficult readjustment. According to the terms of her husband's will, she could occupy Sandringham as her country residence for the rest of her life; Marlborough House would be her London home. But she was slow to quit Buckingham Palace, and this caused considerable difficulty for Queen Mary, who during the summer of 1910 had arranged the transfer of her own household from York Cottage. The movers were virtually at the palace gates, but Alix remained in apartments destined for her successors.

Her intransigence was not due to simple nostalgia or a hesitation to change. The fact is, as Lady Cynthia Colville* and others knew, Alix "could never quite bring herself to look on her son and daughter-in-law as King and Queen." This sprang not from a tenacious will to retain her own queenly status; rather, true to her character, she regarded herself more as a mother than a royal personage, and she would not be removed from her own house. She had acted the part of Queen but was still alive, so why should someone else usurp the role in her home—especially the wife of her Georgieboy?

Finally, by the end of 1910, Alix was gently eased out of the palace. A witness remembered her departure day.

> Every servant to the last scullery maid stood in the hall as her Majesty slowly descended the great staircase, looking so beautiful in her widow's weeds. . . . The only sound was the weeping of the servants—she herself was in tears. She shook hands with each one in turn. She wanted to say a few

---

* She was later one of Queen Mary's ladies-in-waiting.

words of regret at leaving them, but her voice was too choked with sobs. When she had shaken the last hand, the front doors slowly opened—and bowing her head [she] made the lovely gesture of farewell which was so graceful and in a way her very own.

She found Marlborough House "sad and desolate without my beloved," as she wrote to her husband's niece. "I miss him more and more." During the next few years, Alix became increasingly retiring. She occasionally visited her daughter, now Queen Maud of Norway, but her life seemed rudderless and lonely. "It is very sad, seeing her like this so hopeless and helpless & one feels so sorry for her," wrote Queen Mary to her aunt in May 1911.

There were additional sorrows for Alix in 1912 when her son-in-law and her brother died; and the following year her beloved brother George, King of Greece, was assassinated. Solitude and grief thus made her dependent on her daughter-in-law. "Having made my arrangements for the day," Queen Mary noted at Buckingham Palace, "dear Mama suddenly announces herself to lunch or tea & everything has to be altered." Shuttered by the solitude occasioned by deafness and death, Alix became a figure of affectionate sadness. Mary was invariably kind to her, and Alix was notably grateful in expressing her thanks—especially that she was still welcome as the perennial grandmotherly baby-sitter.

Before the end of 1910, King George was pitched into a prolonged and thorny political crisis, during which his advisors convinced him that the monarchy itself was threatened.

The House of Lords had yielded on the matter of Asquith's budget, but there remained the problem of passing the Parliament Bill, designed to limit forever the financial and veto powers of Lords. Asquith, threatening to resign and to dissolve Parliament, extracted from the King a confidential promise that he would create new Liberal peers if the Parliament Bill were first rejected in the House of Lords. To this the King reluctantly and resentfully agreed, accurately sensing that Asquith was unethically exploiting both his inexperience and his obligation to accept counsel. "I have never in my life done anything I was ashamed to confess," George complained. "And I have never been accustomed to concealing things." Forced to accept his Prime Minister's instruction, the King therefore had to betray his own conscience; indeed, he was not at all certain that what was asked of him was the wish of the nation. His promise, therefore, could be pronounced unconstitutional precisely because he would be acting out of partisanship.

The dilemma was peculiarly sharp for George because from the beginning he and Mary had tried to identify the monarchy with the needs and desires of ordinary people. In the first three years of their reign they made special efforts to visit poor industrial sections of England and Wales; they attended sporting events, they greeted London's most indigent, and—this was an important symbol—they were photographed wearing clothes typical of any respectable (solvent) family. King Edward's desire to place the Royal Family at the center of smart society, a goal that had been a reaction to Victoria's dour retreat and the drabness of Court life, was fast fading. Georgian England was becoming an idealized image of dignified middle-class domesticity.

The image was only briefly questioned when an article appeared in the November 1910 issue of *The Liberator*, an English-language newspaper published in Paris and sent to all members of Parliament. The author, E. F. Mylius, revived the groundless old rumor that George had once secretly married a naval officer's daughter in Malta and that he had then abandoned her when Eddy died and he was in direct line for the throne. When it was easily proven that the article was a hoax and that George had never been in Malta during the entire time of the supposed romance and marriage, Mylius was convicted of libeling the King and sentenced to a year in prison. The predictable result of the Mylius affair was an increase of sympathy and affection for George and Mary.

But even this restoration of his good name was endangered when the Parliament Bill came to a head during the summer of 1911. An open constitutional crisis was averted only because a second election had made possible the bill's passage in the House of Lords. This occurred because the election produced a slightly Liberal majority and because enough non-Liberal peers absented themselves from the debate; they were motivated by the dual desire not to embarrass the King and not to be overwhelmed by a sudden influx of Liberal peers when the

King kept to his word—his pledge by this time having been made public after the election.

The matter settled, the King was predictably relieved. "I am afraid it is impossible to pat the Opposition on the back," the King wrote to Sir Arthur Bigge (one of his two private secretaries, by this time ennobled as Lord Stamfordham), "but I am indeed grateful for what they have done & saved me from a humiliation which I should never have survived. If the creation [of the new Liberal peers] had taken place, I should never have been the same person again." Nor would Parliament have been the same. The result, however, was that the powers of the House of Lords were permanently and profoundly restricted. Thus King George, by an embarrassing political moment he never fully understood, furthered the cause of democracy in Britain and unwittingly acted to curtail the power of the aristocracy. This he effected not because he was a Liberal, which he was not (much less a radical), but because the only issue clear to him was his obligation to represent all that was honest in the national character. Collusion, subterfuge, mendacity, egotism—these were the grave sins in the catechism of King George.

As preparations began for two great events—the coronation of the King and Queen in June 1911 and the formal investiture of Edward as Prince of Wales the following month—no one outside the Royal Family knew that the life of the latter was being forever changed and that a childhood illness would eventually affect the succession to the throne.

In February 1911, Edward and Albert were still submitting to the untaxing round of sea-training studies at Dartmouth. An epidemic of both mumps and measles tore through the dormitories, leaving two young men dead, most cadets severely ill and Edward and Albert felled with bad cases of both diseases. The situation was so grave that *The Lancet*, Britain's leading medical journal, issued an unconvincing (and uncharacteristically inaccurate) statement: "The Princes are at the age of least danger, and the important measure of confinement to bed, to the lack of which so many complications and *sequelae* are frequently due, is being enforced."

But the age of the royal brothers was crucial; at sixteen and fifteen, they were thin, short and still physically immature, their voices had not settled, they scarcely needed to shave and they had hardly any bodily hair—all of which indicate a delayed onset of sexual maturity. The fever and rashes of measles had weakened their immune systems, and when mumps followed, it was in Edward's case particularly virulent; he was desperately ill for two weeks. Far from being "at the age of least danger," he was singularly susceptible to the worst effects of mumps especially. In 1911 there were no vaccines against either infection.

Mumps is an acute contagious viral disease that causes painful enlargement of the salivary glands, most often the parotids (thus its formal medical name, parotitis). It is most common in children between the ages of five and fifteen, occurs easily in epidemics when those susceptible live in crowded conditions, and for reasons unknown peaks in late winter. Young children who contract it do not ordinarily have their future fertility affected, nor do adult males. But the vast majority of adolescent males who fall ill suffer unilateral or bilateral testicular atrophy, and this inevitably causes occasional or permanent sterility.

In addition, a significant number of patients (especially in situations where sanitation and nutrition are compromised, as in Britain circa 1911) can contract forms of the disease that leave other permanent neurological effects—a tendency to sudden rages, to acute depressions, and to what psychologists would call a loss of affect, all due to the interference by certain forms of the virus with key chemical neurotransmitters.

These details must be set forth in order to understand much that occurred later in the lives of both Princes but especially Prince Edward. At this point it may be sufficient to record that in 1911 something changed forever in Edward—or, more accurately, something happened to *prevent* some very important changes later. Photographs and films of him at close range in July 1911, at his investiture as Prince of Wales, do not show anything like a typical seventeen-year-old but rather the face and figure of a boy of nine or ten, somehow stunted in growth as a preadolescent; nothing of him suggests a normally maturing young man.

In medical terms, Prince Edward had all the symptoms of hypogonadism, an underdevelopment of both primary and secondary sexual characteristics. This explains the unnaturally youthful appearance of the Prince as late as his twentieth birthday. Alan Lascelles, who was to be Edward's assistant private secretary for nine years, observed that "for some hereditary or physiological reason, his mental and spiritual growth stopped dead in his adolescence, thereby affecting his whole consequent behavior." Prime Minister Stanley Baldwin agreed: "He is an abnormal being, half child. . . . It is almost as though two or three cells in his brain had remained entirely undeveloped." Edward's discerning biographer, Philip Ziegler, summarized the matter:

> To be child-like is in many ways attractive. The Prince never lost his enthusiasm, his curiosity, his freshness of outlook, his open-mindedness. But the word also carries with it connotations of volatility, irresponsibility, self-indulgence, an inability to establish a mature relationship with another adult. With all these the Prince can fairly be charged.

As for Edward's sexual maturity, his father's biographer, Sir Harold Nicolson, wrote in an unpublished diary entry, employing the euphemism of that time, that "something went wrong with his gland on reaching puberty." The meaning was clear: the Prince of Wales was left sterile in adolescence.* While "something wrong with the gland" can be traced to other causes, all of them are consistent with the effects of mumps orchitis; indeed, no alternative etiology has ever been adduced in the case of Prince Edward. Most telling of all was the permanent evidence of this episode from his adolescence. Frank Giles, aide-de-camp to the Governor of Bermuda in 1940 (and later editor of the *Sunday Times*), recalled seeing the naked Edward emerge from a shower after a game of golf, "with absolutely no hair on his body, even in the place where one would most expect it to be."

On Thursday morning, June 22, 1911, King George and Queen Mary went to Westminster Abbey for their coronation. George was anointed first, approaching the high altar in his

---

* Later, his wife would tell people quite openly that her husband was "not heir-conditioned."

crimson state robe, his train borne by eight pages. The Archbishop of Canterbury advanced toward the four sides of the sanctuary, proclaiming to each section of the congregation: "Sirs, I present unto you King George, the undoubted King of this Realm: wherefore, all you who are come this day to do your homage and service—are you willing to do the same?" To which the trumpets blared, the choir cried "Vivat Rex!" and the congregation shouted "God save the King!"

George knelt, placed his hand on the Bible and took the coronation oath, swearing "to cause law and justice in mercy to be executed" in all his judgments; to maintain the Protestant religion and the Established Church; and to govern "the people of this United Kingdom of Great Britain and Ireland, and the Dominions thereto belonging, according to the statutes in Parliament agreed on and the respective laws and customs of the same."

The promise to maintain Protestantism was, as it happened, a bold alternative chosen by the King, for it was a much weakened version of an earlier denunciation of Roman Catholicism. This the King was unwilling to make, not because he had any particular sympathy for the Roman Church but because he feared offending Catholics all over Great Britain, especially at a time when Irish home rule was so delicate a matter. The so-called Protestant Declaration had required the sovereign, since the seventeenth century, to open Parliament and to take his oath of coronation condemning certain specifics of Catholic doctrine as "superstitious and idolatrous."

Even before he opened his first Parliament that February, George had objected to this blanket condemnation. After considerable turmoil and outspoken fears of "popish infiltration," a simpler phrase was devised by Prime Minister Asquith that managed to pass both houses, was approved by the King, and used by him in February and June 1911: "I declare that I am a faithful Protestant and will uphold the Protestant succession," he said, and that was that.

There was, however, a very good reason for the King to take so tolerant and sensitive an attitude. The bishops of the Church of England—indeed, the Archbishop of Canterbury himself—knew quite well that the tendencies in their Church were toward rather than away from precisely the forms of worship and creed that were once condemned as "Roman."

Throughout England both practice and doctrine were becoming more like the ancient apostolic faith of Rome, without its most fanciful (post-medieval) devotional and doctrinal accretions. As liturgical formality had been staunchly revived in England, local parishes such as All Saints Margaret Street openly designated themselves Anglo-Catholic, and the appellation of its ministers as "Father" rather than "Mister" or "Reverend" was more and more prevalent. There was an increasing preference for sung liturgies; for the use of incense, gold brocade vestments, wearing black cassocks in public; and for leading pious weekday devotions.

All these elements, once savaged and outlawed in the Church of England, had become popular again since the Oxford Movement in the nineteenth century. Led by John Henry Newman, John Keble and Edward Pusey, this cause had encouraged the adoption of considerable Roman ceremonial—and, more important, a quest for doctrinal orthodoxy—as they sought the renewal and revival of Anglicanism as it was practiced by Henry VIII and his daughter Elizabeth. The Oxford scholars called for a renewed Anglo-Catholic Church set over against "Low Church" Protestant tendencies. (Newman eventually became a Roman Catholic.) When King George V refused to offend Roman Catholics by denouncing Catholic faith and practice, he was therefore as sensible as he was tolerant: how could he condemn the very practices that the Established Church was so warmly embracing?

His coronation oath concluded, the choir began Handel's anthem "Zadok the Priest," and the Archbishop anointed George's brow, breast and hands. He then sat on King Edward's chair, the throne beneath which is the so-called Stone of Destiny (or Stone of Scone), which Edward I brought from Scotland to Westminster in 1296. Since that time all English sovereigns have been crowned seated above this stone. (Even that old rebel Oliver Cromwell used it at his installment as Protector.) George received the ruby ring and the two scepters, and then St. Edward's crown was placed on his head. Peers donned their coronets, trumpets blared, drums rolled, guns in the Tower and in the parks were fired, and all in the abbey cried again, "God save the King!"

Moments later the Prince of Wales knelt before his father, whose eyes glistened with tears as the boy, in his high, thin voice, recited his oath: "I, Edward Prince of Wales, do become your liege man of life and limb and of earthly worship; and faith and truth I will bear unto you, to live and die against all manner of folks. So help me God." The boy then rose, touched his father's crown and kissed him on the left cheek. The senior peers of each degree then followed, and only then was Queen Mary anointed, crowned and enthroned. A short communion service and a few final prayers concluded the coronation.

By all accounts of both his contemporaries and later biographers, George was a religious man to whom the event was sacred, not merely magnificent. He saw himself as hallowed by a covenant with God, bound by a vow to serve his people. But since he was not an expressive or articulate man, his journal entry for that day, which began with his usual nautical observations, was typically restrained. Nevertheless, shafts of emotion pierce his staid language:

It was overcast & cloudy with some showers & a strongish cool breeze, but better for the people than great heat. Today was indeed a great & memorable day in our lives & one we can never forget, but it brought back to me many sad memories of 9 years ago, when the beloved Parents were crowned. May & I left B.P. in the Coronation coach. . . . There were over 50,000 troops lining the streets under the command of Lord Kitchener. There were hundreds of thousands of persons who gave us a magnificent reception. The Service in the Abbey was most beautiful, but it was a terrible ordeal. It was grand, yet simple & most dignified and went without a hitch. I nearly broke down when dear David came to do homage to me, as it reminded me so much of when I did the same thing to beloved Papa. . . . Darling May looked lovely & it was indeed a comfort to me to have her by my side, as she has been ever to me during these last eighteen years. We left Westminster Abbey at 2.15 (having arrived there before 11.0) with our Crowns on and sceptres in our hands. This time we drove by the Mall, St. James's Street & Piccadilly, crowds enormous & decorations very pretty. On reaching B.P. just before 3.0 May & I went out on the balcony to show ourselves to the people. Had some lunch with our guests here. Worked all the afternoon with Bigge & others answering telegrams & letters of which I have had hundreds. Such a large crowd collected in front of the Palace that I went out on the balcony again. Our guests dined with us at 8.30. May & I showed ourselves again to the people. Wrote & read. Rather tired. Bed at 11.45. Beautiful illuminations everywhere.

A pageant almost as glorious followed exactly three weeks later when Edward traveled with his family to be formally invested as Prince of Wales at Caernarvon Castle. Here there was more inspired, theatrical improvisation than precedent, for although the title had been worn by predecessors there had been no ceremony; it had been more than three hundred years since a monarch had presented his son to the Welsh as their prince. But Chancellor of the Exchequer David Lloyd George, himself a Welshman and Constable of Caernarvon Castle, recognized a golden political opportunity to curry Welsh favor, and so ancient rituals were hastily ''discovered.''

As it happened, this was fine with King George, who saw that pomp, if connected to probity and a fulfillment of national duty, was purposeful. Ceremony had underscored his awe of his own father, and now as crowned King he saw his own Royal Family as heirs of ancient traditions that must be revived and enlivened. In turn, the King expected obedient reverence from his children as heirs of those titles and traditions. Thus an unpleasant family row erupted over Edward's preparation for the ceremony on July 13. He looked nothing like seventeen, and he knew it. A nervous, frail, underdeveloped schoolboy, he felt foolish as he tried on a fancy costume, white breeches, an ermine cape, and a gold coronet. ''What would my Navy friends say if they see me in this preposterous rig?'' This brought a loud scolding from his father and another in the unending series of criticisms. Only his mother's gentle encouragement and persuasion got him through the day, for Edward hated anything redolent of separation from his classmates. He was trying so hard to be one of them and already had so much against him physically, socially and educationally that the investiture would, he felt, further ostracize him, further postpone his entrance into an ordinary world of his fellows.

Edward wrote later,

When all this commotion was over, I made a painful discovery about myself. It was that, while I was prepared to fulfill my role in all this pomp and ritual, I recoiled from anything

133

that tended to set me up as a person requiring homage. Even if my father was now beginning to remind me of the obligations of my position, had he not been at pains to give me a strict and unaffected upbringing? And if my association with the village boys at Sandringham and the cadets of the Naval Colleges had done anything for me, it was to make me desperately anxious to be treated exactly like any other boy of my age.

There was, in other words, a disturbing set of mixed signals given to the young Prince. Kept at a distance from his parents, he had known an artificial, sequestered childhood in the care of a sadistic and then a loving nanny. Then came an indulgent but ineffectual tutor before he was abruptly pitchforked into Osborne, where he was commanded to live unpretentiously, to stoke the ship's fires with his fellows, to accept mockery and hazing like any fresh recruit. At the same time he was moving along in his route to the throne, and at sixteen was first in line. He was at school to be an ordinary fellow, but he was anything but that.

Most poignant, he could never please his father, whose intent was to prepare him for the throne but whose method was that of a martinet.

"You must be able to find time to write to me once a week," the King scolded when Edward had failed in this duty for a fortnight.

"I must say I am disappointed" was a constant refrain in his letters.

"Do smoke less," the King urged. This was good counsel as far as it went, but it was unfortunately counterpoised by what followed: "Take less exercise. Eat more and rest more ... [otherwise you will] remain a sort of puny, half-grown boy." To read at eighteen that one is thought by one's father a "puny, half-grown boy" must have added to Edward's already fragile self-image. Only rarely did his father have no corrections to make: "No faults have been found," Edward wrote triumphantly in his diary one day in 1913. "Such a change!" As for Queen Mary, she never interfered in these father-son exchanges; deference to her husband increased an already established distance from her children.

That distance was underscored geographically when the

King and Queen traveled to India five months after their coronation, there to hold a durbar, or homage, to themselves as Emperor and Empress. Believing that his presence would revive and even consolidate the loyalty of Indians, George encouraged a ceremony held in Delhi on December 12, 1911—a ceremony that was every bit as splendid as that at Westminster. One hundred thousand Indians attended, fifty thousand troops lined the streets, brass bands and scarlet-and-gold-clothed attendants glistened in the morning sun. Wearing the new imperial crowns especially made for the occasion, George and Mary were enthroned on high beneath a golden dome, remote but magnificent, entirely consistent with the Oriental image of Imperial potentates. Everything was stage-managed for the silent motion picture cameras to document, just as such events were rehearsed and presented all over Europe by royal families of the time. All the great monarchies devised rituals promoting an almost religious fidelity based on adoration and awe. This primitive form of hype can be traced, of course, all the way back to ancient societies.

The Delhi durbar had double significance. First of all, for England it was a grand reaffirmation of the Empire and of the apparently unswerving loyalty to them by millions of Asians. Britannia, it seemed, ruled not only the waves but the deserts as well, and no one could have imagined that in less than forty years George's son Albert would witness the independence of India. And second, the King was convinced of the sublimity of his office and its responsibilities. From this extravagant ceremony, impressive to him and Mary precisely because it was so exotic and placed them at the center of a foreign culture, they drew new confidence and a heightened sense of their vocation—that in a sense they were Emperor and Empress of a universal people, not merely inheritors of an island destiny. That no monarchy in the world was so prestigious as theirs simply added to their sense of superiority. In light of this, it is remarkable that they retained (indeed, deepened) any empathy or compassion for others at all.

Yet it stood to reason that with this sublime sense of self came a certain arrogance. Advised that his passion for hunting wild animals in profusion was not appropriate, George waved away objections and on this journey brought down thirty-nine tigers, eighteen rhinos, and four bears. "The fact is," said

Lord Crewe (Secretary of State for India) with scarcely veiled contempt, ''that it is a misfortune for a public personage to have any taste so strongly developed as the craze for shooting is in our beloved Ruler. His perspective of what is proper is almost destroyed.'' Lord Durham (a horse-racing peer and Garter Knight) agreed: the tigers, increasingly rare, had been slaughtered wholesale, rounded up for sheer sport with no chance of escape. At home, most Englishmen had to be content with shooting ducks.

Quite a different atmosphere awaited their return to London in February 1912. There were massive civil unrest, railway, dock and coal strikes, street riots for minimum wages and the growing crisis over Irish home rule. That year more than forty million working days were lost due to strikes, and economists pointed out that the purchasing power of the pound sterling had dropped (since 1901) by twenty-five percent, while weekly wages over a decade rose but a few pence.

To such widespread economic disaster and equally loud complaints, George and Mary were not indifferent. As before, they lost no time scheduling visits to docks, iron and steel works and coal mines, and so again an English King and Queen were seen by ordinary people in ordinary environments. Edward and Alexandra had been willing to be hailed at public functions and cheered in the streets of London, but Alix could indulge her desire actually to help others, to comfort them, only on her own. George and Mary, on the other hand, knew that despite their political powerlessness their presence counted for something. Insisting that their financial contributions remain secret, they gave several thousand pounds to help the most distressed families, those out of work and those affected by strikes.

The constitution enjoined partisan political activity, of course, and so the royal couple's concerns could have no official effects in social legislation. But the support of charities—even the establishment of them and the attachment of their names to them—surely counted for something. Monarchical interference in any political or legal issue, as the Sovereign knew from the Parliament Bill, was not only ill advised but also downright dangerous. But the realm of moral suasion—perhaps the best that could be asked of the Royal Family—was a way of involvement open to them and a path gladly taken by the best of the dynasty from Alexandra, Princess of Wales, to Diana, her titular scion in the next century.

George and Mary were not at ease in such situations as a miner's foul cottage or a docker's airless tenement. How could they be, arriving as they did in fancy cars and escorted back to pleasant surroundings while their hosts lived so wretchedly? To their credit, George and Mary dismissed the complaints of those aristocrats who saw their sojourns among the poor as inappropriate or merely condescending.

"These visits," according to an enthusiastic eyewitness, "were no mere sightseeing. They were expressions of homely friendliness for the simple folk on whose daily work the triumphs of industry depended. If the politicians were out of touch with the things that really mattered, were not the King and Queen doing what they could to redress the balance?" And so Queen Mary drank cups of tea with the wives of railwaymen and coal miners, and King George asked the children's names as he cheerfully invited them to come and shake his hand. More than once Mary found herself meeting a weeping mother who had insufficient food for her family; when she could, she arranged for hampers of provisions to be sent to this or that household before sunset.

There were unexpected light moments in these visits, too. "Is his father very dark?" Queen Mary asked a fair-haired woman whose dark-haired baby she was admiring one afternoon in a maternity ward.

"Sure, Ma'am, I don't know," replied the mother artlessly. "He never took his hat off."

But these brief visits to the poor in critical times, however sincerely undertaken, were few and had an unmistakable air of noblesse oblige; the King and Queen were close to their people only occasionally. Their mystical self-awareness and their religious zeal for the royal vocation may at first have discouraged them from moving too close to ordinary people. But paradoxically it was precisely their majestic self-awareness that allowed them to offer to an impoverished, passing stranger the kind of affection they could never give their own children. There is an inevitable circle here: greeted with reverential awe, bows and curtsies, George and Mary were confirmed in the conviction of their uniqueness.

But Queen Mary's pragmatic sensibilities were especially

aroused. "If only one could act," Queen Mary wrote to her aunt during the coal strike of 1912, "but one feels so impotent, & all this time our blessed and beloved country is in a state of stagnation & misery. Most people seem to go on as if everything were in a normal state, but we feel the whole thing too much to take it lightly." Yet the Royal Family could not, by definition, be ordinary members of society.

The restriction to uniqueness was imposed on their children, too. When George enrolled Edward in Magdalen College, Oxford, in the autumn of 1912—the first royal offspring to live in rooms in college—it may have seemed to some that the monarchy was becoming more ordinary. Such was not the case. Edward was attended by a tutor, a secretary, a valet and an equerry; his apartment was furnished by his mother with Sheraton antiques; he had the first private bathroom ever installed for any student; he was not required to sit for any examinations; and he could decree his own daily and weekly schedule. This, for a lad so slow to mature mentally and physically, was disastrous.

Sent to Oxford to study languages, history, economics and political science, Edward was completely impervious to books and lectures. By the time he left in 1914 (without earning a degree), he knew little more than before, and at twenty he was still writing "colision" and "dammaged" and "explaned." Sir Herbert Warren, Master of Magdalen, summarized the Prince's educational status with discreet understatement shortly after Edward left Oxford: "Bookish he will never be." His parents wished him to learn French, but this he never mastered. Edward was much more attracted to German, especially after he spent term holidays with relatives in Prussia; by the time the war began he found himself in the awkward position of being rather too fond of everything German—as he would be later as King and then Duke of Windsor.

At Oxford, Edward was as genial as his status and his stunted physical and emotional growth permitted. He resented the restrictions his position imposed on him and tried mightily to avoid assuming a patronizing attitude with students. He rode to hounds and played polo, took to copious drinking and, like his grandfather Edward VII, became a Prince of Wales for whom the most avid study was that of fashion. Wide flannel trousers, a checked sport coat, trousers with cuffs: to these he gave considerable attention, wishing to make himself seem more mature and attractive, to be accepted by his peers for his sportiness and not his position. He also cultivated a kind of boyish charm, an open and friendly manner that won him friends. He inspired camaraderie, and although most fellow students kept to addressing him as "Sir," the formal address did not preclude sharing a risqué story or a glass of sherry. Nevertheless, his grandfather's confidant, Lord Esher, who frequently visited, found him a "strange boy—sad with the sadness of the world's burdens."

Part of this gloomy demeanor derived from the princely role he hated and could not escape because he saw it as socially isolating, and of it he was constantly reminded by frequent summonses to Court. "What rot & a waste of time, money and energy all these State visits are," he confided to his diary after one such, complaining of "this unreal show and ceremony!" Such republican sentiments, which his parents saw in his dress, manner and general attitude, did not endear him to them one bit, although for the more fashionably radical mates at Oxford it was one of his appealingly shocking traits. George and Mary took cool comfort only in the reports from his guardians that, yes, as he approached twenty, Edward's virginity was still intact; in fact, he seemed to show not the remotest interest in forming attachments to young ladies. A disaffected confusion, manifest in sudden withdrawals from everyone, also partly explains the sadness that so struck Lord Esher.

Seventeen-year-old Albert, meanwhile, finished (very near the bottom of his class) at Dartmouth in December 1912, and for the final part of his naval training he joined the cruiser *Cumberland* the following month. He had none of the easy affability Edward had learned to cultivate, and although he was maturing physically, his speech impediment made every meeting painful. When asked to speak publicly, he engaged another cadet to stand in for him; when required to attend a party or ball, he broke out in a cold sweat at the prospect of asking a girl to dance. For these reasons (and also perhaps the Saxe-Coburg temper he inherited from his father and grandfather), Albert was still prone to embarrassing outbursts of rage —and for his father's son and a marine student, an even more embarrassing susceptibility to seasickness. Yet there was a wide streak of empathy in Prince Albert, who fraternized comfortably with enlisted commoners often ignored by class-conscious officers.

In the autumn of 1913, Albert joined the battleship *Collingwood* as a midshipman. Known for practical reasons as "Mr. Johnson," he never loved the sailor's life and would rather have been at Oxford with Edward, but he acceded to his father's wishes and acquitted himself admirably on Mediterranean maneuvers, in Egypt and in Greece. Always reliable and utterly lacking in guile or pomposity, Albert endured chronic stomach trouble (exacerbated by wretched seasickness) without complaint. Only later was a serious ulcer diagnosed, a condition aggravated by the strong Turkish cigarettes to which he had become addicted by the spring of 1914. That summer Albert fell gravely ill with acute appendicitis and was transferred back to Aberdeen for surgery. His recovery was delayed by severe gastritis and the flare-up of the ulcer, which Albert found as humiliating as it was painful. By this time Edward was in the Grenadier Guards and in November was posted to France, where he worked at the general headquarters of the British Expeditionary Force.

Most Britons cheered when war was proclaimed that summer of 1914. There was at once a groundless optimism in the land and a litany of jingoistic oaths about an early, guaranteed victory. But a month after Archduke Ferdinand was assassinated in Sarajevo by a Serbian nationalist (on June 28), the Austro-Hungarian government sent Serbia an impossible ultimatum. Russia immediately took the side of the Slavs, thus pitting the Czar against his cousin the Kaiser; Germany backed Austria; France could not allow German mobilization to proceed unchecked; and on August 4, Britain declared war on Germany for failing to respect Belgian neutrality. Thus the Kaiser became an enemy of his cousin the King. "I held a Council at 10.45 to declare war with Germany," George wrote in his diary that August day.

It is a terrible catastrophe, but it is not our fault. An enormous crowd collected outside the Palace; we went on the balcony both before and after dinner. When they heard that war had been declared, the excitement increased & May & I with David went on to the balcony; the cheering was terrific. Please God it may soon be over & that he will protect dear Bertie's life.

By the end of September more than a million Englishmen had volunteered and been shipped off to Europe. It was assumed this would be a glorious combat easily ended once the Royal Navy destroyed the German fleet and the British Expeditionary Force cleaned things up in France. With the help of the French and the Russians, victory would be theirs within a few months. Young men, bidding good-bye to Piccadilly and farewell to Leicester Square, were confident of returning in time for cozy Christmas dinners of goose and plum pudding, and that would be that: the latest triumph of the Empire.

Concurrent with this exhilaration there emerged a hysterical anti-German sentiment in England. Everything that even sounded vaguely Teutonic was the target of savage indictment. German literature was expunged from school curricula, works by Beethoven and Mozart were removed from concert programs, and shopkeepers with German names had their businesses destroyed by overzealous hooligans calling themselves patriots and acting under the banner of a group called the Anti-German League. To aggravate the situation, not many among the general populace objected, fearing a charge of collaboration with the enemy or even of treason. "People insulted German governesses," recalled Lord Louis Mountbatten (Victoria's great-grandson) years later. "They'd even kick dachshunds in the street. They saw spies under every bed. And the press played up this hysteria and made it worse. They attacked my father because of our German name."

His father, one of the earliest casualties of this pitiful chauvinism, was a man of unswerving loyalty to the Crown who happened to have been born in Austria. He was Prince Louis of Battenberg, eldest son of Prince Alexander of Hesse-Darmstadt. After becoming a British citizen and a Royal Navy recruit at fourteen, Louis had married Queen Victoria's granddaughter, the Princess Victoria (daughter of Alice); he was thus a cousin by marriage to King George. His naval skills then accelerated a stunning career, for Louis rose from director of Naval Intelligence to Rear Admiral to Commander-in-Chief of the Atlantic Fleet to Vice Admiral to First Sea Lord, which made him, at sixty, the leader of the entire British Navy as it entered the war. But his German name and Prussian-tinted speech were too much for the public, who clamored for his resignation. "I have lately been driven to the painful conclusion,'' he wrote to Winston Churchill, First Lord of the Admiralty, on October 28,

> that at this juncture my birth and parentage have the effect
> of impairing in some respects my usefulness on the Board
> of Admiralty. In these circumstances I feel it to be my duty,
> as a loyal subject of His Majesty, to resign the office of
> First Sea Lord, hoping thereby to facilitate the task of the
> administration of the great Service to which I have devoted
> my life, and to ease the burden laid on His Majesty's ministers.

This news very much grieved the King, who could not resist
his ministers and had to appoint a successor. In his formal
acceptance of the resignation, Churchill acknowledged that the
war was raising, between men of various heritages, ''passions
of the most terrible kind''—words of little comfort to Prince
Louis, who withdrew into undeserved obscurity. He died in
1921, three months after the birth of a grandson named Philip,
whose wife became Queen Elizabeth II.

The cavalier booting of Louis was only the beginning.
Within the year, the King was forced by his Prime Minister
and a self-righteous London press to remove the banners of
eight Knights of the Garter from St. George's Chapel, Windsor
—including those that many years earlier honored Queen Victoria's family: George's cousin the Kaiser, the Kaiser's son,
and, perhaps most significant, the Duke of Saxe-Coburg-Gotha,
Victoria's grandson and the bearer of the dynastic name. This
matter the King rightly considered a silly and empty gesture
that defied history and was not within the government's mandate; logic suggested the synchronous striking of honors earlier
accorded to English royal scoundrels as well.

''The *Daily Express* has been to the forefront in demanding
that these banners be removed,'' trumpeted that newspaper on
the front page of its May 14, 1915, edition. ''The banners are
besmirched with those responsible for the murders of women
and children.'' One overly ardent cleric even asked that a flag
commemorating the marriage of the Kaiser's mother, the beloved Princess Vicky, be burned, at which point King George
firmly stomped his navy boot and cried hell, no. Of German

lineage himself, the King never shared the witless wartime rejection of everything German, nor would he consent to an absurd demand regarding the brass name plates of the dishonored Garter knights. "They are historical records," wrote Stamfordham at the King's request, "and His Majesty does not intend to have any of them removed [from the chapel stalls]."

Besides, the King rightly claimed, there were more important tokens of patriotism, and he gave several examples of these by his visits to the front. Devout sailor though he was, George saw no glory in war and was the soul of compassion for fighting men on both sides. At one hospital near Le Havre hundreds of soldiers, their faces bluish gray after they had been gassed, were struggling for breath. Stopping at the bedside of wounded Germans as well as Englishmen, King George rebuked Frederick Ponsonby (a Privy Councillor and close aide), who regretted the pity wasted on a wounded German. "But the King said that after all this was only a poor dying human being, in no way responsible for the German horrors."

George returned from France that autumn of 1914 sorely depressed by the casualty lists and determined to repeat his visits to the troops whenever possible. After one of them, George himself required some compassion. On October 18, 1915, while in France to inspect a detachment of the Royal Flying Corps, his horse reared in fright at the soldiers' cheers. The King was thrown, the horse fell on top of him, and by the time he was extricated, his pelvis was fractured in two places, ribs were cracked and the poor man was in appalling agony.

Edward, who was dispatched to the First Army Corps and had accompanied his father on this particular expedition, ran to his aid and went with the ambulance to a nearby château serving as headquarters, where George, hurling pungent curses, was put to bed. During the night General Sir Douglas Haig, fearing a German bombardment of the château, suggested that the King be transferred—an idea relayed by a doctor who was asked to bring back George's reply: "You can tell him to go to hell and stay there. I don't intend to move for any bombs." His tone changed dramatically a moment later when he expressed his worry that the offending horse might have been injured, too; assured that the animal was fine, the King smiled and relaxed.

A week later George confided to his diary that he had endured "agonies. . . . During October 29, 30 and 31, I suffered great pain and hardly slept at all." Never especially robust, he was in his fiftieth year and had been a heavy smoker for decades, a habit which of course weakened his lung capacity, hindered the healing of his bones and generally inhibited his recuperation. The broken pelvis mended very slowly, but not a day of his life thereafter would he be entirely pain-free; his temper was quicker to flare, his impatience with others and himself more obvious to secretaries, counselors and companions. But the King was equally demanding of himself and made several more visits to France during the war. In July 1917 the Queen insisted on accompanying him, and for two weeks she toured hospitals, casualty clearing stations, ammunition dumps, airfields and nurses' hostels. Like her husband, Mary never spared herself the worst of the war.

George's eldest sons were still involved, although as heir to the throne the Prince of Wales was kept far from danger. "I do hate being a prince and not allowed to fight!!" he wrote in 1915, resentful that his work was largely limited to visiting hospitals. His father assented to a few forays to the trenches, where according to one witness Edward "loved danger" and another recalled that he "did take risks." Yet forever after he complained that protocol prevented him from serving at the Battle of the Somme, where almost five hundred thousand British soldiers died in six months. "What does it matter if I am killed?" he asked Lord Kitchener, Secretary of State for War. "I have four brothers." But no one else was quite that phlegmatic about his future, and Edward had to be content with serving as an aide to the army commander in France and then as a staff officer in the Mediterranean.

During this time he was much admired for his friendliness, modesty and zeal, and for his refusal to seek any special privilege. More to the point, he was acutely embarrassed when the President of France pinned on him the Croix de Guerre. "At first he flatly refused [to wear it], as he said he had not earned it," recalled Frederick Ponsonby; "but I pointed out to him that his refusal to wear it would hurt the feelings of the French, so reluctantly he pinned it on."

By this time, at age twenty-one in 1915, Edward was subjecting himself to a curious regime that sometimes endangered his health. Moody about his lot in life, he became obsessed with the idea that he was becoming fat. Although he never weighed more than 140 pounds and was actually somewhat scrawny, the Prince allowed himself the barest minimum of food and sleep. He also took long walks and was generally inclined to a monastic style of mortification that suggested a real contempt for his own body. This may have derived from feelings of physical inadequacy, for he still looked about fifteen years old. It may also have owed to embarrassment over his total lack of sexual experience, for his comrades were not, typically, chaste young men. Edward's celibacy was not altered until one night in 1916 when, at twenty-two, several army buddies turned him over to a French prostitute. Thereafter he was as randy as a teenager and just as indiscreet, crowing to whoever was near that he had at last found what he considered life's greatest pleasure.

Ordered home from the Continent to tour armament factories at the end of 1917, the Prince of Wales was now far from being the social wallflower he had been a few years before. He swiftly became a staple of London social life, dancing until dawn, dashing for a swim in a friend's pool, hopping off for a game of squash, and then charming young ladies at a dinner party. Edward at twenty-three was very different from the callow youth who had complained at nineteen, "I had to dance, a thing I hate. The whole thing was a great strain." He now led every quadrille.

By this time there were also the first rumors of a romantic affair—with a married woman twelve years his senior. Lady Marion Coke, wife of a viscount, was a lively, dark-haired little dancing partner with a fondness for champagne and giggling. He was also linked to Lady Sybil Cadogan, who was quite the opposite of Marion: his own age, tall and awkward, she was a powerful personality and a passionate companion who gave the Prince (so he noted in his diary) "the best nights I have ever had. I'm madly in love with her!!" It may be that Lady Sybil wearied of sharing Prince Edward's attention with Lady Marion, not to say with a team of other London ladies; it may be that she found him tiresomely self-absorbed with his royal routine and disliked his moods; it also may be that one of Edward's schoolmates, Edward Stanley, was simply more to her liking. Whatever the reason, her Ladyship suddenly announced her engagement to Stanley in June 1917, sending a telegram to her parents—"Engaged to Edward"—that briefly caused them to believe their daughter would one day be Queen of England.

Albert, meanwhile, spent most of the war being shuttled from hospital ward to ship's sick bay or to less demanding shore duty—anything to avoid life at Buckingham Palace, which (like Edward) he found "an awful prison" where their parents had "funny ideas about us, thinking we are still boys at school or something of that sort, instead of what we are." (Princess Mary was similarly bored with palace life and became a volunteer nurse on the home front during the war.) Although confined belowdecks with gastric distress and a black depression when he was back aboard the *Collingwood* during the Battle of Jutland in May 1916, Albert nonetheless showed an astonishing resilience. An officer recorded,

> A signal was received that the German High Seas Fleet was out and engaging our battle cruisers only forty miles away and that the battle was coming in our direction. Huge excitement. Out at last. Full speed ahead. Sound of "Action"— can you imagine the scene! Out of his bunk leaps "Johnson." Ill? Never felt better! Strong enough to go to his turret and fight a prolonged action? Of course he was, why ever not?

"I never felt fear of shells or anything else," Albert told Edward later about the battle. "It seems curious, but all sense of danger goes except the one longing of dealing death in every way possible to the enemy." Further naval service was forestalled by illness, however, and at last Albert had to submit to ulcer surgery in 1917; later he transferred to the newly formed Royal Air Force.

Of the younger Royals' lives there was nothing remarkable to document. At the outbreak of war, Princess Mary was a blond-haired, blue-eyed, seventeen-year-old English rose and, in her penchant for gymnastics and fishing, something of a tomboy. But in studies she was also the quickest of George's children, with a natural flair for languages, history and geography that was recognized by a gifted governess. "What a pity it's not Mary," Edward said one day when the subject of his future kingship was introduced, "for she is far cleverer than I am." It could also not have escaped Edward's notice that Mary was by far her father's most adored child, compared constantly and favorably to her brothers.

After a reasonably successful start at St. Peter's Court preparatory school, Prince Henry, at fourteen, was enrolled at Eton, where he was not much interested in anything except sports. "Do for goodness sake wake up and use the brains God has given you," scolded Queen Mary. "All you write about is your everlasting football, of which I am heartily sick."

As for Prince George, he was by far the most promising of the children. Darkly handsome, with alert blue eyes and a quick smile, he was articulate, witty even at twelve, and inclined to appreciate things cultural that left his father and brothers bored. George shone at St. Peter's Court and at home was an enthusiastic companion to his mother's interests in antiques, bibelots and the art of knitting. Whenever he could, he spent time with Edward: "We became more than brothers," the Prince of Wales wrote, "we became close friends." In each was a streak of rebellion that would bind them even closer in the future.

Of Prince John there was never any news. Consigned to the care of Lala Bill in a cottage on the Sandringham estate, he suffered increasingly from epileptic seizures and fits of violence and shrieking that perhaps indicated brain disease. Alone of his family, his grandmother visited regularly. Alexandra cheerfully and lovingly ministered to John, brought him playthings, read to him and relieved Lala Bill from her endless vigils. Drawn to the hapless child as to a fellow outcast, the Queen Dowager—oblivious to the unfortunate social stigma still attached to a family epileptic—lavished constant loving attention on her grandson.

Alix's kindness was also evoked by the horrors of the war, and she gave herself with equal alacrity and generosity to the relief of its victims. Visiting a hospital crowded with wounded soldiers, she noticed one particularly depressed young man whose injuries left him with a severe limp. Not to worry, Queen Mother Alexandra said; she had been lame in one leg for over forty years, since the bout of rheumatic fever that had also left her deaf. "But look what I can do with it," she announced, pointing to her bad leg—which, with a gymnastic sweep, she then swung gaily over a chair. The soldier smiled for the first time in months.

There was little Alix's son the King could do during the war except mobilize the national sentiment and advise, encourage and warn, which he did in his lengthy and often spirited replies to the war documents that came daily to his desk. He was neither required nor permitted to make any military decisions, of course; constitutionally, George was prevented from anything like the direct involvement exercised on their sides by his cousins the Czar and the Kaiser. But he found a way of being more than a symbol. During the war, according to the most conservative counts, George visited seven British naval bases and three hundred hospitals, held almost five hundred military inspections, toured bombed areas, met tens of thousands of citizens and traveled five times to visit soldiers in France. According to David Lloyd George, who became Prime Minister in 1916 and who was always ruthlessly honest in assessing the King's limited intellectual capacity, ''the high level of loyalty and patriotic effort which the people of this country maintained was [due to] the attitude and conduct of King George . . . [and] to the affection [he] inspired.''

But the King thought it was important to provide more than good example, and he lost no time in imposing on Buckingham Palace the austerities felt by all working people. Food was rationed, meals streamlined, delicacies banned. According to Ponsonby, there was so little food put out for breakfast at the palace that those courtiers who were late went hungry; when one staff member asked for a boiled egg, ''he could not have made a bigger stir . . . if he had ordered a dozen turkeys. The King accused him of being a slave to his inside, of unpatriotic behaviour, and even went so far as to hint that we should lose the war on account of his gluttony.''

Matters went further. At the suggestion of Lloyd George (then minister of munitions), the King with great reluctance forbade alcohol in all royal residences and at Court: ''I have done it as an example,'' he wrote in his diary, ''as there is a lot of drinking going on in the country. I hate doing it but hope it will do good.'' Predictably, this had no effect on the nation's tippling and made the King and Queen look quaintly foolish, thanks to Lloyd George. But other measures were more successful. Horses from the royal stables were trotted out for ambulance work, and the carriages themselves were turned over to convey wounded soldiers from railway stations to hospitals. The King wanted to turn most of the palace into a convalescent hospital, but doctors and officers who surveyed the rooms found them badly heated, badly lighted and altogether unusable for the purpose.

Nevertheless, George insisted that in fine weather the palace gardens, at least, be given over to the wounded, with whom he sometimes visited. Such forays with the sick were brief, however, for the King was never at ease and could not summon the geniality he showed friends and guests privately. "We sailors never smile on duty," he said flatly when Stamfordham (his private secretary) suggested he soften his manner a bit. When Edward once tried to compliment his father by claiming that something the King had done was "good propaganda," George replied stiffly, "I do things because they are my duty, not as propaganda." The remark could have been a motto for his life.

For her part, Queen Mary frequented hospital wards and organized relief efforts within days of the war's outbreak. At the beginning, she inquired about everything, inspected operating rooms, talked with doctors and nurses, sat with the blind and the limbless, tasted hospital food and discreetly suggested how it might be made more palatable. "If she notices anything that is amiss or might be improved, she does not hesitate to say so," wrote an eyewitness. "Everyone knows that Her Majesty's knowledge of hospital equipment and requirements is very thorough." Part of the personal hardship for Mary in all this was the fact that while she was a compassionate soul, her personality did not radiate warmth, and like many people with the sick, she did not know what to say in their presence.

As for relief work, the Queen had her ladies of the Needlework Guild providing blankets for wounded soldiers, supervised a Relief Clothing Fund at St. James's Palace and brought some society friends to labor without pay at the Red Cross. But their good intentions produced some discomfiture in Parliament, for these aristocratic volunteers were putting poor women out of work. Undaunted and efficient, the Queen suggested a "Work for Women" fund that sponsored businesses employing women. It is absurd to claim (as some have) that the cool Queen Mary was only nominally or for appearance's sake involved in war relief efforts. She confronted the most demanding issues of the war with the same swift, quiet strength she had shown thirty years before when she toiled on behalf of veterans' widows and children.

In fact, Mary's dedication to alleviating wartime suffering led to a deep, lasting and in many ways an astonishing friendship with the formidable Mary Macarthur. Then thirty-four years old, Macarthur was a political radical, the champion of Britain's exploited working women and an outstanding person in the most progressive movements of the nation. "She improved the conditions of hundreds of thousands of the most helpless and pitiable women in the country, and not in a material sense only," as one social historian wrote. "Her action, her example, her achievement, won for all women a new status. The world looked at them differently and they looked differently at themselves." Specifically, Macarthur organized strikes against companies that paid women but a few pence a day for twelve hours of sewing or metal work; she mobilized training corps for women to enter the ranks of better office jobs; and she helped abolish the atrocious working conditions to which women were everywhere subject in England.

A gifted and tireless revolutionary, Mary Macarthur seems an unlikely candidate for collaboration (much less friendship) with Queen Mary, whose background, breeding and staunch conservatism had prevented contact with such women. But the Queen judged people on their merits, and her fair-mindedness created a far more humble and generous disposition than her outward manner might at first have suggested. In addition, her sincere religious sensibility, never paraded for the admiration of others, propelled her to do on her own what her position as the King's wife might not have otherwise encouraged. In this regard, she knew what she could learn from Mary Macarthur; in this regard, too, she was her own person.

So it was that this controversial proto-feminist was invited to tea with the Queen at Buckingham Palace, an appointment that raised eyebrows along those long, winding corridors. No respecter of monarchy, which was in many ways at the apex of a social hierarchy responsible for precisely the conditions she battled, Macarthur was at first suspicious of the Queen's interest. Was this royal tokenism? Was she to be defused by a regal smile?

Before the day was out, she had her answer, which she quickly reported to her colleagues. "The Queen does understand and grasp the whole situation from a trade union point of view," she said. "I positively lectured the Queen on the inequality of the classes, the injustice of it. Here is someone who *can* help and who *means* to help!" And so she did, reading books and tracts Macarthur gave her on modern social problems and traveling to training centers throughout the country. "These visits gave me the opportunity of meeting workers with whom I do not often come in contact," the Queen wrote to a friend, "& I was glad that this was so." When Macarthur fell ill with a disease that took her life in 1921, at only forty-one, she had no more attentive friend than the Queen, who subsequently became an active patroness of the Mary Macarthur Holiday Homes for Working Women.

As the war dragged on in 1917, whatever popularity was enjoyed by one or another member of the Royal Family was more than outweighed by several threats to the Crown itself—as grave, it seemed, as those that were toppling kings and emperors throughout Europe. Afrikaner generals in South Africa rebelled against the Imperial presence; there were continued bloody uprisings in Ireland and threats of the same in India and Egypt; and in Westminster and on the edges of Hyde Park there were huge rallies calling for a Bolshevik revolution and a war between classes—demonstrations in which thousands sang in praise of Lenin and Trotsky. The former social certitudes were questioned, and the great Victorian-Edwardian Empire itself was beginning to crumble—and with it the confidence of the King himself. "He is clearly asking himself," recalled the Earl of Crawford, "what the future has in store for the Royal Family." He was right to ask. Republican sentiment and leftist anti-monarchist cries were increasing so alarmingly that George had to make a particularly poignant decision that revealed the greater obligation he felt to the preservation of the throne than to any considerations of family loyalty or friendship.

Perhaps more than any British monarch, King George V sacrificed every personal preference—and, as it happened, even some relatives—to serve what he thought were the needs of the Crown. In March 1917 his cousins Czar Nicholas and

Empress Alexandra were forced to abdicate by the Russian revolutionaries. When they sought refuge for themselves and their children in England, His Majesty's government was prepared to take them in. But George advised against this humane action; his secretary Stamfordham was instructed to write to the Foreign Office that they would be "strongly resented by the public and would undoubtedly compromise the position of the King and Queen." George urged that Nicky and Alix, as he affectionately knew them within the family, be turned away so that the monarchy could avoid any association with unpopular, pro-royalist sentiments.

In other words, he did not want to appear a champion of a deposed monarch at a time when the very future of his own crown was at stake. A gesture of asylum, the King believed, would rouse the ire of the socialist wing in the House of Commons, would cast doubt on his own patriotism, would encourage every extreme of republicanism and might even be the catalyst for a violent revolution in London. He could not, of course, have foreseen the ultimate fate of the Romanovs. On the other hand, George could not have been ignorant of the danger to which the Czar's family was exposed in light of the revolution—so much was evident from the assembled masses right in Kensington Gardens. One can perhaps admire the King's fidelity to his sense of vocation and his commitment to the Crown's stability; at the same time, it is hard not to criticize a stubborn, single-minded idealism that cannot reflect on the very real danger to the lives of loved ones. King George V's profound sense of duty to the ideal of sovereignty explains but does not excuse his decision. With tragic irony, it was his developed familiarity with political subtleties and sinewy machinations that eventually stained the King's hands with the blood of the Romanovs, relations he had long claimed to love.

Precisely in the middle of these international and family crises, the anti-royalist force reached critical mass. "We shall be lucky," declared the normally unruffled Lord Esher, "if we escape a revolution in which the Monarchy, the Church and all our Victorian institutions will founder. I have met no one who, speaking his inmost mind, differs from this conclusion." The collapse of the Czar's Empire evoked a sense of imminent and dramatic global change as workers of the world, invited to throw off their shackles and unite, were roused to a vision of new opportunity. Powerful left-wing socialists invited delegates to the Trades Union Convention that June, announcing that the meeting "would do for this country what the Russian Revolution had accomplished in Russia." No less a famous voice than that of H. G. Wells was raised that season when —referring to the "alien and uninspiring Court"—he asked Britons to rid themselves of "the ancient trappings of throne and sceptre" and support those who would replace the monarchy with a republic. "I may be uninspiring," the King told a visitor, "but I'll be damned if I'm alien."

And yet, as an epidemic of anti-German sentiment reached the point of lunacy, that was exactly what more and more people were encouraged to believe: that the Royal Family's German dynastic name, Saxe-Coburg-Gotha, implied a pro-German bias. Even Lloyd George himself fell into the trap. "I wonder what my little German friend has got to say," he whispered once when summoned to the King's presence at Buckingham Palace. Letters poured into 10 Downing Street asking how Lloyd George expected to win the war if the King himself was German. When the Prime Minister reported these complaints to the King, as he was bound to do, George "started and grew pale."

Hence in May 1917 the King discussed the matter with Stamfordham, who had to admit that, yes, Teutonic names drawn from territories were sprinkled over all branches of the Royal Family, although no one was quite sure just what the *family* name was. The director of the Royal College of Heralds was consulted: what indeed was George's surname? Well, he wasn't quite certain, to tell the truth. Saxe-Coburg-Gotha was a geographic designation. The name was not Stuart, either— and not Guelph, which was the ancient family name of the Hanoverians and which (by common law) was lost when Victoria married. Perhaps if one then looked at Prince Consort Albert's pedigree, it was Wipper or Wettin? There was much furrowing of brows and shrugging of shoulders.

As the academics rambled on, George announced that a great public gesture of solidarity with English history was necessary to show the British nation that their First Family was indeed one of them. The Duke of Connaught said the new family name ought to be Tudor-Stuart; you could not get more

British than that, after all. No, there were unsavory implications with this idea, replied Lord Rosebery and Herbert Asquith. Well, chimed in others of the Cabinet and Court, what about Plantagenet? Or York? Or Lancaster? No, someone cried; be plain about it—"George England."

As the meetings took on the character of a parlor game—something along the lines of "Can You Top This?"—clever Lord Stamfordham serenely interrupted. King Edward III, he said, had often been known as Edward of Windsor. That brought the meeting to silence. The King nodded. The resonances were so solid, so assuring: the castle, the town—a dynasty. Windsor would be the family name.

And so a tradition was devised. On July 17, 1917, the announcement was approved by the Privy Council, and every newspaper in the nation carried it the next day.

Whereas We, having taken into consideration the Name and Title of Our Royal House and Family, have determined that henceforth Our House and Family shall be styled and known as the House and Family of Windsor;

And whereas We have further determined for Ourselves and for and on behalf of Our descendants and all other descendants of Our Grandmother Queen Victoria of blessed and glorious memory to relinquish and discontinue the use of all German Titles and Dignities;

And whereas We have declared these Our determinations in Our Privy Council: Now, therefore, We, out of Our Royal Will and Authority, do hereby declare and announce that as from the date of this Our Royal Proclamation Our House and Family shall be styled and known as the House and Family of Windsor, and that all descendants in the male line of Our said Grandmother Queen Victoria who are subjects of these Realms, other than female descendants who may marry or may have married, shall bear the said Name of Windsor:

And do hereby further declare and announce that We for Ourselves and for and on behalf of Our descendants and all other descendants of Our said Grandmother Queen Victoria who are subjects of these Realms, relinquish and enjoin the discontinuance of the use of the degrees, styles, dignities, titles and honours of Dukes and Duchesses of Saxony and

Princes and Princesses of Saxe-Coburg and Gotha, and all other German degrees, styles, dignitaries, titles, honours and appellations to Us or to them heretofore belonging or appertaining.

There were more rechristenings, among them those of Queen Mary's brothers, the Duke of Teck and Prince Alexander of Teck, who became the Marquis of Cambridge and the Earl of Athlone; their family name would henceforth be Cambridge. The unemployed Louis of Battenberg had his surname translated, and he became Louis Mountbatten, first Marquess of Milford Haven.

Grandmother Victoria, who had once reminded her family that "the German element in our home must be cherished and kept up," surely would not have been sympathetic to so capricious a change of name, decreed under pressure and inspired by mere public relations propaganda. She might indeed have appreciated the bemused cynicism of the Kaiser when told about the new name for his English relatives that July. Cousin Willy smiled indulgently, then rose from his chair and excused himself. He was off, he said, to the theater—to see Shakespeare's play, *The Merry Wives of Saxe-Coburg-Gotha*.

King George V and Queen Mary with Princes Edward, Henry, Albert and George, and Princess Mary.

6

A Doll's House 1918 to 1925

The press is a powerful weapon in the twentieth century!
CLIVE WIGRAM, Press Secretary to King George V

At the height of the Great War, a mere change of dynastic name was certainly not enough to justify the British monarchy when the rest of the world was dismantling thrones, melting crowns and shipping into exile those who had worn them. It was all very well to rechristen the family "Windsor," to let the people know how English their Royals were (when in fact they were not), but it was also—thus the Lord Chamberlain—"imperative that in the critical times with which the country is now faced, no stone should be left unturned in the endeavour to consolidate the position of the Crown."

That canny old courtier Lord Esher, who had served Victoria and Edward VII with distinction before he was relegated to dispatch minor errands for George and Mary, agreed. Buckingham Palace, he complained, "remains unchanged. The same routine. A life made up of nothings—yet a busy scene. Constant telephone messages about trivialities." Esher went further in a letter to Stamfordham, pointing out that "a war-torn and hungry proletariat, endowed with a huge preponderance of voting power," would demand some justification for paying in tax the enormous expenses of the monarchy. It was a time, Esher advised, for considerable imagination—risks, even, and the abandonment of "old theories of constitutional kingship." Esher had in mind the situation of the United States, whose power was clear in the last two years of the war and whose president, Woodrow Wilson, made democracy seem romantically prophetic to very many politicians the world over. "The strength of republicanism," said Esher, "lies in the *personality* of Wilson. . . . He has made the 'fashion' of a Republic. We can 'go one better' if we try."

One of the first to try for new ideas on keeping an old institution was Clive Wigram, an enthusiastic grouse hunter and an avid cricketer who had become assistant private secretary to King George V on his accession. In 1918 he was an idiosyncratic forty-five-year-old courtier who termed general elections "test matches," referred to the Prime Minister without disrespect as "the Skipper," described political disputes in old-boy sporting terms and had (according to the other assistant private secretary, Sir Frederick Ponsonby) a "true British contempt for all foreigners." Wigram thought conscientious objectors and pacifists during the Great War were cowards and union leaders traitors, and he agonized over petty details of protocol: should women working in munitions factories remove their gloves when introduced to Queen Mary? All these conservative traits and middle-class quirks endeared him to his King. Wigram cited the list of thrones toppling in Austria, Germany and Russia; the exile of Constantine of Greece; every German aristocrat stripped of his rank and title. He pointed out the growing tide of republicanism in England, and he counseled a tactic that could only be called revolutionary. To all this George V listened attentively.

Wigram was among the most formidable of royal press

secretaries; indeed, he was something of a publicist and damage-controller. In the days of George I and of Queen Victoria, there had been court-based journalists to provide pleasant little essays to newsmen and to offset potential scandals with edifying tidbits from the royal working schedule. But by 1918 the men who had been charged with the job (mostly descendants of Joseph Doan and Thomas Septimus Beard and their friends) visited the palace only occasionally and had not kept pace with the increasing freedoms assumed by a more democratic, critical and exacting press and demanded by the public; these journalists were little more than ineffective diary-keepers.

For all his staunch conservatism, Wigram saw the Royal Family as a great public relations organization for Great Britain; the company lacked only effective sponsors and spokesmen. And so he urged that the press be skillfully enlisted to promote the image of the King and thus to publicize the value of the monarchy. As the primary agent in this task, Wigram suggested that the palace employ "a well-paid press representative, with an office and sufficient sums for propaganda purposes." A few years earlier the King would have booted Wigram down the grand staircase, for George V regarded newspapers as "filthy rags." But now he knew Wigram was right. The monarchy simply had to work harder to ensure its permanence, and more work meant greater visibility, more accessibility. The press would be invited to document their endeavors as never before.

But as it happened, the man appointed to the post of press secretary in 1918 was largely ineffective: Samuel Pryor lacked the requisite polish, imagination and tact. So Wigram himself stepped into the breach, issuing advance reports to newspapers about when the King might turn up at this hospital or that factory and reminding journalists that convalescing soldiers were enjoying the palace gardens and a chat with Queen Mary. He ensured, too, that newsmen were present in impressive numbers at the silver wedding anniversary thanksgiving service at St. Paul's in July 1918.

Wigram wrote to a friend,

> I think that in the past there has been a tendency to despise and ignore, if not insult, the Press, which is a powerful weapon in the twentieth century. I have been working very

hard to try to get Their Majesties a good press, and have been to the Press Bureau and other places. I hope you may have noticed that the movements of the King have been better chronicled lately.

In his task Wigram was remarkably competent, using the Royals' best qualities to best advantage. He arranged for reporters to be present when George and Mary attended a peace celebration in December 1918, although an officer in the Brigade of Guards remembered that men with pads and cameras were so zealous they almost caused disaster. Newsmen crowded the stand from which the King and Queen were waving to the people, and suddenly it seemed the platform might collapse. The police were helpless, and the King made several futile gestures to urge the crowd back.

Just then the alert Wigram signaled to the fearless Queen Mary, who pulled herself up to full height, flashed a royal glance of disapproval and raised her hand, as if ordering a class of unruly schoolchildren to behave and be seated. "It worked like magic," recalled the eyewitness who saw the awe of reporters. Ashamed of its bad manners, the mob retreated. Wigram struck up a chorus of "God Save the King," and thus an early photo opportunity on behalf of the monarchy was documented forever. Henceforth, newsmen were invited to attend every royal visit to industrial areas, to see the King or one of his sons mingling with the working classes. Admiring stories began to appear and flattering photographs to be circulated about a hardworking Royal Family.

Wigram also suggested that receptions at Buckingham Palace imitate those of Washington's White House, and so a wider range of professions began to be represented at Court functions and garden parties. Now mingling among the aristocrats could be found schoolteachers and civil servants, labor leaders and political commentators; they all went away predictably dazzled at finding themselves within royal precincts. It was a brilliant ploy. The monarchy was being marketed to the people who had to pay for it as a symbol of themselves; loyalty to the Crown was thus a logical extension of self-love. Until King George's death, Clive Wigram (who received a peerage for his efforts) was a tireless promoter of royal media hype. Had he lived to the end of the twentieth century, he would certainly have regretted the voracious appetite of press and public for every morsel of "life with the Royal Family"; he would just as surely have despised the public's pronounced taste for scandal.

As photographs multiplied, it was clear that Queen Mary was no longer only His Majesty's Consort; she was also one of the world's instantly recognizable celebrities, but this was a role she neither welcomed nor encouraged. "The sense of being constantly watched haunted her," wrote her biographer, "and she felt as self-conscious and shy in public as she had in childhood." Only in private could she be herself—"laughing over the jokes in [the satirical magazine] *Punch*," as Mabell Airlie recalled,

> sending me comic postcards; learning the words of "Yes, We Have No Bananas" and singing it with me at the top of our voices for the joy of shocking a particularly staid member of the Household; hopping in a green and white brocade dress round one of the drawing rooms at Windsor to represent a grasshopper in a game of [charades] after dinner. She was not always the dignified Queen Consort known to the world.

But such high spirits were restricted to private gatherings with a few trusted confidantes or family members.

Her reticence and apprehension were not for herself, however; as ever, Mary thought only and constantly of the King. Because his devotion and reliance on her support could be expressed only in writing, she was often uncertain as to whether she pleased him. George was so high-strung and exacting of their sons, how could the Queen know that she, too, was not a disappointment? "Somehow I always find it difficult to express what I feel except in a letter," the King wrote, "especially to the person I love & am always with like you darling. . . . I feel lost when you are not there & everything seems out of gear." Mary had to content herself with these shy notes. "What a pity it is you cannot *tell* me what you write for I should appreciate it so enormously."

She would also have appreciated some diversion after a day's appointments, but her husband rarely granted it. By all accounts the King's desire for secluded simplicity meant they dined alone, and afterward he read the newspapers while she picked up her knitting needles. Perhaps five or six times a season someone was invited to join them for dinner; otherwise their evenings were completely inconsistent with the revived social life of the Jazz Age. All the more reason, then, why Princes Edward, Albert, Henry and George avoided quiet evenings with their parents; if they were not quizzed or scolded, they were majestically bored. So was their mother: "I would have turned cartwheels for sixpence," she once murmured, never entirely accustomed to the quiet evenings her husband preferred. Stable and staid, the King drew a curtain of respectability around everyone in his circle.

An important preoccupation for the Queen, however—indeed, an obsession—was her enthusiasm for an intricate and fantastic doll's house, commissioned to enable future generations "to see how a King and Queen of England lived in the twentieth century and what authors, artists and craftsmen of note there were during their reign." Among her collections she had always had a fondness for miniatures, and so the famous architect Sir Edwin Lutyens was engaged to design and execute a four-story Georgian doll's house. It eventually contained literally tens of thousands of tiny pictures and pieces of furniture, made to scale by sixty well-known artists and three hundred craftsmen.

The doll's house, three years in preparation and nine feet long when completed, could have accommodated a family of six if none was taller than six inches. They would have arrived at their luxurious residence in any of six miniature, expensive reproductions of the royal Daimlers. Then they would have gone to dinner and eaten minute portions of real foodstuffs and drunk from tiny bottles of expensive wine, served on small gold or Royal Doulton plates. After dinner they would have chosen their favorite music on the gramophone, which played thumb-size recordings, or they might have chosen to select a book from the two hundred postage-stamp-size volumes in the dainty library, which was festooned with hundreds of infinitesimal watercolors and drawings. They could have ridden in tiny mechanical elevators to their little bedrooms, washed in real water that spouted from miniature taps, and then climbed into beds covered in the finest minute swatches of linen and silk. Here, Lutyens had his little joke. Aptly ordering the initials

MG and GM to be embroidered on the little pillows, he confided to cronies that, yes, they stood for the royal initials—and more: "May George?" on his pillow and "George May" on hers. It is doubtful the King and Queen ever had a clue.

But despite all this effort to achieve the quintessence of accurate and adorable daintiness, there was one significant and eerie omission: there were actually no dolls to represent the royal inhabitants—no stand-ins for humans, just real little *things*. In a way this project, the closest enterprise to Queen Mary's heart in her entire life, was a perfect miniature representation of her own existence. There were very grand living quarters and meticulous attention to the details of elegant props and supports. But at the heart of it, there was nothing human.

Almost fifty-seven when the doll's house was completed, Queen Mary's life lacked emotional fulfillment, and her doll's house spoke loudly of her isolation. On it she lavished all the loving attention that might otherwise have gone to and been reciprocated by her real family, of which there was no representation because there was, alas, no actual counterpart. Her relations with her husband were defined by formality and raised to the level of reverence, and she was never on anything like warmly intimate terms with any of her children. Victimized perhaps more than any royal person of her time by the role she had chosen, Mary put all her repressed love into her doll's house. But no one was at home.

When it was completed, the doll's house won Queen Mary enormous admiration as its sponsor, and Wigram used it as part of his public relations campaign, inviting noteworthy ladies from all over the realm to join the press for a private viewing. At the same time many important tasks were also assumed by the Prince of Wales. The failure of the postwar anti-monarchist spirit to reach crisis proportions in England can be credited to Prince Edward's popularity, which derived directly from his being seen and hailed by the press everywhere. It helped that he had an understanding of the national mood of discontent over massive unemployment (two million by 1921), a severe industrial slump after the boom of wartime manufacturing, and a depressed standard of living. "I shall have to work to keep my job, too," the Prince of Wales told Mabell Airlie. "I don't mind that, but the trouble is, they won't let me have a free hand." By "they" the Prince meant the King.

As the heir to the throne reached his twenties, the gap separating father and son widened. Harsh and demanding as ever, George found something to criticize in every aspect of his eldest son's life. The Prince was "the worst dressed man in London," his father complained. "I hear you were not wearing gloves at the ball last night," the King complained. "Please see that this does not occur again." His manner was too perfunctory for his father ("Why doesn't my son ride like a gentleman?"); his public appearances were sometimes vulgar ("You and Dick [Mountbatten] in a swimming pool together is hardly dignified, though comfortable in a hot climate"). Prince Edward seemed, at twenty-five, to cultivate only a playboy's image, to be in no hurry to marry, which the King saw as a talisman against decadence (and an absolute requirement for the Heir Apparent). "If you are one day to be a constitutional King, you must first be a constitutional Prince of Wales." Henceforth, they were never friends. "I do envy you, being able to weep for your father," said Prince Edward to his bereaved cousin Louis Mountbatten. "If my father died, I'd be glad."

The late Prince Eddy had been adversely influenced by his father's openly scandalous conduct, but George, although he loved and admired Papa's majesty, frankly disapproved of his scandalous private life. Fearing a repetition of Edwardian license, the King was suspicious of his son's increasing popularity and resented his wholesale embrace of modernity. He also thought it ungentlemanly that Prince Edward complained about his inadequate education. Schooling fitted commoners for jobs, George thought with typical aristocratic prejudice, but Royals were exempt from this, and he held intellectuals in gravest suspicion. The navy was good enough for any man.

There was more to annoy the King. Prince Edward had climbed into a biplane and flown solo—for amusement—on the very day the dynasty's new name was proclaimed. The boy liked jazz, went to private house parties, dined with women who wore their hair bobbed, their skirts short and their makeup vivid! This was not appropriate princely behavior, and George made his displeasure clear. Edward's younger brother Prince George agreed that their father was "impossible. I will have no more of being told off without answering back. I'm sure it's the only way."

163

Prince Edward sought a measure of freedom and independence from the constraints of a hermetically sealed, polite upbringing—which is why in 1919 he moved out of Buckingham Palace and into his own apartment in York House. Impossibly, he longed to be a nonroyal peer, not distanced from his fellows by rank or accident of birth, although in time he would abandon this apparently egalitarian sentiment. For now, his actions—like prolonging a visit that year among Welsh miners forming trade unions—fully endorsed Queen Victoria's statement: "Danger lies not in the power given to the Lower Orders, who are becoming more well-informed and more intelligent, and who will *deservedly* work themselves to the top by their own merits, labour and good conduct, but in the conduct of the *Higher Classes* and of the *Aristocracy*."

Predictably, Edward's affinity with commoners did not go down any better with some senior courtiers than with his father. "If I may say so, Sir," offered Frederick Ponsonby when the Prince of Wales asked for an honest assessment of his conduct, "I think there is risk in your making yourself too accessible."

"What do you mean?" the Prince retorted.

"The monarchy must always retain an element of mystery. A Prince should not show himself too much. The monarchy must remain on a pedestal." His words could not have been framed better by Walter Bagehot himself.

The Prince maintained otherwise, arguing that in the aftermath of war one of his tasks was to bring the monarchy closer to the people, not remove it further.

"If you bring it down to the people," Ponsonby continued, "it will lose its mystery and influence."

"I do not agree," Edward said flatly. "Times are changing."

"I am older than you are, Sir," Ponsonby said crisply. "I have been with your father, your grandfather and your great-grandmother. They all understood. You are mistaken."

So also thought the King—who could be unexpectedly indulgent with his other sons. Why could Edward not be more like his brothers? "You have always been so sensible & easy to work with," the King wrote to Albert a few years later. "You have always been ready to listen to any advice & to agree with my opinions about people & things"—the crucial test of affection was obedience, after all—"that I feel we have always got on very well together. Very different to dear David.''

When David arrived late for a meal at a royal residence, he was barred from the table or at least severely reprimanded; punctuality was the politeness of princes as well as kings. Henry, on the other hand, would be forgiven with a joke. After several months abroad, he arrived home just after his father had sat down for dinner. The King looked up. ''Late as usual, Harry,'' he said, and that was that.

King George could be quite relaxed with the children of others, perhaps because he felt no personal responsibility for their future. ''What is your name?'' he asked the young grand-daughter of a Balmoral neighbor.

''I am Ann Peace Arabella Mackintosh of Mackintosh,'' the child replied scrupulously.

''Ah,'' said the King with a smile and a pat on her head, ''I'm just plain George.''

That kindly manner in public was no affectation, although at home just plain George was never really as relaxed as his wife. When someone told her of a certain woman whose seven marriages had given her as many name changes, she said, ''Well, I have had to change mine quite a lot: Princess May, Duchess of York, Duchess of Cornwall, Princess of Wales, Queen. But whereas mine have been by accident, hers have been by enterprise.''

A different sort of accident in February 1918 resulted in an enterprise embarrassing for the King and Queen but sensational for the Prince of Wales: the first great passion of his life.

Sent back from France to boost the morale of English factory workers, the Prince of Wales was invited to a ball at the Belgravia mansion of Maud Kerr-Smiley, wife of an officer fighting with the Royal Irish Rifles.* Just before midnight the air-raid sirens wailed—a terribly destructive bombing was indeed about to occur—and all the guests hurried to take shelter in Maud's basement. A young woman outside, huddling for refuge with her escort in the doorway, was spotted by the hostess, who brought her in and rushed her downstairs for

---

* Maud's brother was an Anglo-American businessman named Ernest Simpson, who would later play a crucial supporting role in this story.

safety with her guests. By the time the bombing stopped, the spontaneous refugee had spent two hours chattering merrily with the Prince of Wales, who was instantly besotted with her.

She was Winifred Dudley Ward, always Freda to friends and Fredie to Prince Edward. Daughter of a wealthy Nottingham lacemaker, she was exactly his age and had been married for five years to a Member of Parliament sixteen years her senior. But the bloom had faded from this union, and Freda and William Dudley Ward effectively lived separate lives with independent interests and companions; they were nevertheless united in their devotion to their daughters, Angela and Penelope, and they resided at the same address. At the time she met the Prince of Wales, Freda had another admirer she did not soon give up despite the jealous imprecations of her royal suitor.

Just over five feet tall (and thus a good dancing partner for the diminutive Prince), with a high aristocratic forehead and a wide, warm smile, Freda was cultivated, pretty rather than beautiful, and utterly lacked the shallow affectations common to her wealthy class. Gifted with a sprightly sense of humor and keen athletic prowess, she was as proficient on the golf course and tennis court as on the dance floor or supervising her household staff at a dinner party—which was something she did in so direct, friendly and uncondescending a manner that her servants felt quite like her friends, which often they were. "To a butler or secretary," recalled a woman who knew her, "she made the same jokes and observations she would have made to the master of the house."

By all accounts Freda was a woman who had no enemies, much less anyone who could claim to have been the object of her envy or ill will. "She was truly a remarkable woman," recalled Angela Fox (whose son, the actor Edward Fox, married Freda's granddaughter). "Freda was very elegant, not at all self-centered or pushy, but really quite generous and always interested in others." This amalgam of traits, plus a strong personality that her delicacy could not mask, attracted the Prince's ardor. The affair blazed intensely for over a year, and although occasionally cooler and more complex, it endured until the arrival of Maud Kerr-Smiley's sister-in-law fifteen years later.

It is not difficult to see why the Prince found Freda irresistible; for her part, she found his playfulness agreeable, his deferential charm flattering, his generosity with gifts impressive. His family connections could not have diminished those assets. But Freda was neither a gold digger nor an adventuress. "It wasn't as if I were trying to marry [him]," she said years later.

> Or even wanted to! He asked me often enough, ardently, too. But just as often I said, "No!" The whole idea was ridiculous. I was already married, of course, so there would have to be a divorce, and his parents and friends and the Church would never have allowed it. I kept telling him, "I'm not going to let you do such a stupid thing!" and finally I persuaded him. He was very suggestible. Someone once said of him, "He reset his watch by every clock he passed." It was true.

From the first two years of their relationship, no letters survive. But those that follow clearly reveal that the heir to the throne not only loved her, he was completely dependent on her constant encouragement, consolation and reassurance—perhaps what he felt he had missed from his own mother. His boyish face and figure, his sad eyes and anxious half-smile appealed to Freda, as they did to very many women who longed to comfort and nurture the sad Little Prince. In Edward of Wales, Freda was the first to find an eternal Prince Charming who never seemed to age but, alas, who also never seemed to mature very much at all.

This complete reliance on her strength and superintendence may at first have flattered her vanity, but very soon she must have found that it wore a bit thin. At twenty-four, Edward still regarded himself as a pathetic specimen, which his whining self-absorption did nothing to disprove. His letters to Freda are filled with puerile references to himself as an incompetent "little boy." They are also remarkable for what was perhaps intended as cute but became cloying: his reliance on hackneyed upper-class affectations such as the use of the French *moi* and *toi*.

November 18, 1920: "Fredie darling, beloved *à moi*, I feel *ever, ever* so much better since our little talk on the phone this evening, sweetheart; you just can't think what a huge comfort it was to *your* little David just to hear your divine little voice

167

again. . . . I'm terribly lonely tonight my Fredie darling and it maddens me to be away from *TOI.* . . .''

February 3, 1921: ''I love you, love you now beyond all understanding and all I can say is bless you, bless you, for being so sweet and divine and tender and *sympathique* to your David last night and for saving him, *mon amour.* . . .''

May 7, 1922, from Kyoto, Japan: ''I've pined for *TOI* my precious beloved, and I'm always wanting *TOI.*''

And so it went throughout the 1920s.

Did she love him? ''Oh, no,'' she said in a frank moment late in her life, ''he was much too abject.'' Her retrospective insight into his character was both accurate and profound, for the Prince of Wales had to be dominated the way a naughty child wants to be reprimanded, corrected—however formally or with whatever sort of sophistication. Freda, who was no dominatrix but had a strong sense of herself and of propriety, got him through his depressions when he was sour at the prospect of a lifetime as a Royal; and she encouraged him to his duty even when it took him away from her. She discouraged him from smoking and drinking to excess and sometimes succeeded—as she could not when it came to his intellectual and cultural life.

''Who is this woman Bront?'' David asked querulously, ignorant of the author's name when she handed him a copy of *Wuthering Heights.* And she opened the warmth of her home to him when her husband was absent, which was often. Her two small girls loved their ''Darling Little Prince,'' as they called him, treating him like an indulgent uncle. And his sister Mary (like Albert) loved Freda and only encouraged the romance. But the Prince of Wales could be only a part-time companion when in 1919 his father (who derided the affair as unseemly and referred to Freda as a whore) sent him on the first of a series of world tours—journeys similar to those he and Mary had undertaken earlier, meant to restore solidarity and prestige with the colonies and dominions after the war.

Not surprisingly, the King's resistance only confirmed Edward in his pursuit of Fredie. ''Papa seems to think that anything you do which he doesn't like has been influenced by Fredie,'' wrote Albert to Edward. ''This of course is due to the great popularity which you have everywhere, and Papa is merely jealous." In this regard Albert was perhaps quite close to the mark. And to further underscore the irony, Edward's four tours between 1919 and 1924 (covering fifty-five countries and 150,000 miles) made him increasingly impatient for total freedom.

In the United States and Canada, in Australia and the West Indies, Fiji and India, there was nothing like the formality of Court. The Prince returned more casual and free-spirited than ever, but he was miserable on the job itself. He wore a head-dress and smoked a peace pipe with the Stony Creek Indians in Canada; he spent his energies personally greeting three hundred thousand Americans (and for compensation suffered a swollen right hand); he hunted kangaroos and quaffed ale with Australian miners. But these were not holidays. For months the Prince had to feign fascination with every detail of colonial governments and protocols; had to find every conversation riveting; had to act as if every indigenous tree was the first he saw, every textile factory a marvel of progress. He was excruciatingly bored, he wrote to Freda; his attendants saw only his exhaustion and depression.

In this regard an important letter survives—from the Prince on Christmas Day 1919 to his private secretary Godfrey Thomas, to whom David confided

> a sort of hopelessly lost feeling, and I think I'm going kind of mad!! I feel faint at the thought of next year's trip— Christ, how I loathe my job now, and all this press-puffed empty success. I think I'm through with it, and long and long to die. I tell you as my greatest friend and the one man I can trust and who really understands me. I do feel such a bloody little shit.

As usual, the merry press reports of a happy touring Prince were completely at odds with the grim reality.

"He really is a marvel, in spite of his 'fads,' " Queen Mary wrote to King George after the Prince of Wales's tumultuous reception in New York in 1919, "& I confess I feel very proud of him, don't you?" Her husband had to admit the Prince was impressive to the public.

The "fad" Queen Mary found most distressing was her son's anxious restlessness that sought outlets in a colorful and sometimes embarrassing social life both away and at home. According to Edward's official biographer, Philip Ziegler, "from the early evening onwards his intake [of alcohol] was considerable. He had a strong head, but not strong enough. Many sightings of a noticeably intoxicated Prince of Wales were recorded. . . ." More than once, in fact, Edward became drunk in public and had to be carted home by his staff, and an Englishman abroad reported that Edward gave the impression "of a desperately unhappy, wilful, dissipated boy without much brain, who could be very charming when he chose, but who was always seeking to avoid the duties of his position."

That—and news reports of the Prince's superb skill at the tango—obliterated the King's begrudging admiration. "I see David continues to dance every night," he wrote to his wife. "What a pity they should telegraph it every day. People who don't know will begin to think that he is either mad or the biggest rake in Europe!" The fact is that Queen Mary herself was not nearly so censorious about this particular aspect of modern life, and she had asked one or another courtier to teach her some of the new Jazz Age dance steps. When her husband walked in on a lesson, he barked his disapproval so violently that she never again attempted this innocent diversion.

While on his public relations tours, the Prince of Wales grew fonder of Freda, who tried, when he returned from the second journey in 1922, to place their relationship on a more platonic level. But when she did so, he became petulant, drank heavily, and without a care for discretion flamboyantly squired women he scarcely knew; these were not artful stratagems to regain the ardor of someone like Freda. But Prince Edward would accept nothing less than his lover's complete absorption and attention, which Freda was not prepared to offer. And so he brooded, all those fifteen years beginning in 1918, in a kind of Gothic-Romantic gloom. This did not mean he was faithful to her, however; there were numerous other passing fancies. Freda refused to act the jealous mistress, whatever his dour laments about his outcast fate.

Yet the Prince's dark and somber moods and his constant complaining about his future may well have had the most obvious basis, one that explains why he chose lovers who would be inaccessible as legitimate spouses: it all had to do with the fact of his sterility. Freda Dudley Ward was the ideal

occasional partner and full-time confidante because she was
unavailable for anything more permanent—like all those with
whom he took up. He had to pick women who were unacceptable, for should his favor fall on a maiden eligible to become
Princess of Wales and then Queen, she would only precipitate
the revelation of his infertility, a condition in a Prince of Wales
that was even more undesirable than promiscuity. From his
twenties, then, the Prince of Wales was living in such a way as
to make inevitable the drama that eventually occurred; thus, a
fact of biology explains the nature of his choices. It was not a
restless, childlike quest for withheld maternal warmth that
drove the Prince of Wales to the loving arms of married mothers; he chose unattainable ladies precisely because they were
unattainable, and he rejected the eligible because they were so.

For most Englishmen the end of the war brought nothing
like prosperity. In 1919 there was a major strike somewhere
every day; prices soared as wartime controls were discon-
tinued; race riots led to dozens of deaths in Cardiff and Liverpool; communist flags were briefly flown over the city halls
of Glasgow and Edinburgh; veterans shouted their discontent
at George and Edward during a military review in Hyde Park;
and the influenza epidemic, circling the globe and killing more
people than the Great War, took 150,000 lives in England and
Wales alone.

It was not the Spanish influenza that dispatched young
Prince John, however. On January 18, 1919, at the age of
thirteen, he suffered a fatal epileptic seizure. His mother the
Queen noted in her diary,

> At 5.30 Lalla [*sic*] Bill telephoned me from Wood Farm,
> Wolferton [on the Sandringham estate], that our poor dar-
> ling little Johnnie had passed away suddenly after one of
> his attacks. The news gave me a great shock, tho' for the
> poor little boy's restless soul, death came as a great release.
> I broke the news to George and we motored down to Wood
> Farm. Found poor Lalla very resigned but heartbroken. Lit-
> tle Johnnie looked very peaceful lying there.

On January 21, Prince John was buried at Sandringham next
to the infant Prince Alexander John, the last child of King

Edward VII and Queen Alexandra, who had lived for only one day in 1871. "Now our two Johnnies lie side by side," Alix wrote to the Queen.

Except for Lala Bill, Alexandra had been the person most attentive to Prince John. The pitiable child had been for several years her main reason for living, and when he was gone, Alix —now seventy-five—felt lonelier and more purposeless than ever, despite the companionship of her daughter Victoria. "But she retains her old grace and charm," wrote a visitor, "and her wonderful smile. She never complains and keeps her slim pretty figure."

Despite their frequent meetings with the masses, the Windsors lived a sheltered life. In March 1919, Albert began flying lessons (which he disliked as much as seafaring, yet accepted on assignment from his father). But at the end of a course of study, his trainers found him physically too frail and psychologically too nervous for flying, although he earned his wings as a pilot. In an airplane he would have invited disaster. And so the King took him off duty and sent him, with Henry, for a year's study at Trinity College, Cambridge, beginning that October.*

Lethargic and diffident, Henry was also unsuited to university. He passed a few unremarkable terms there with Albert, the pair studying economics, history and constitutional theory. Fearing they might fall into bad company, the King insisted his sons live not in college housing but rather in private accommodations, surrounded by a protecting and vigilant entourage. Albert tackled Bagehot's *English Constitution* and excelled at golf and tennis; Harry, when not sleeping in lecture halls, caught field mice. Of "poor Harry," as his mother called him, there is little else to say during the immediate postwar years. He was certainly not at all as witty, polished or bright as the youngest surviving brother, Prince George, who took an interest in things cultural and by 1920 was a dashingly handsome eighteen-year-old primed for social success.

At the end of this term of study, on June 3, 1920, King George created Prince Albert Duke of York, the most ancient

---

* Prince Albert was the first Royal to become a qualified pilot, a tradition continued by the next Duke of York, his grandson Prince Andrew.

dukedom in the realm. "I feel that this splendid old title will be safe in your hands," George wrote to Albert as the new Duke of York, sounding every bit like a venerable business executive, "& that you will never do anything which could in any way tarnish it. I hope you will always look upon me as yr. best friend & always tell me everything & you will find me ever ready to help you & give you good advice."

While at Cambridge, Albert first used the word "firm" to describe the Royal Family in business terms. He understood the Court's intentions, that the postwar business of the monarch and his family was their own self-perpetuation and that this could only be accomplished by much the same means with which modern businessmen promoted their companies—by a distinctive program of advertising, by being agreeably conspicuous. But the term he coined came from a moment of some bitterness. Reprimanded by a house master for smoking while wearing his academic robe and told that as a Prince of the Blood he must set a better example, Albert muttered, "We are not a family, we are a firm." The larger implication of his remark was that members of the Royal Family did not and should not go their own separate ways but were united like officers in a boardroom: the King was chairman, the children subordinate partners. It was a profession, a specialized kind of job in which the family was invited to achieve excellence.

To this pursuit Albert applied himself with a diligence worthy of his namesake and great-grandfather, Queen Victoria's Prince Albert. The new Duke of York accepted the position of patron and president of the Industrial Welfare Association, an organization founded to improve the lot of manual workers. In 1920 this was a daunting task, for little had changed since the time of Dickens: in factories and mines, workmen's compensation and pensions were not yet even imagined; one lavatory had to do for hundreds of men and women; working conditions bred disease and depression; and no consideration was given to the education of poor boys, who from the age of five or six worked alongside their elders. Public opinion had to be roused, and for this the association's advisors looked hopefully to the Duke.

They were not disappointed. Without a formal entourage and insisting there be no ceremonies accompanying his tours, Albert visited factories, listened to workers and apprentices, descended the dankest coal mines, endorsed charity campaigns —and thus was soon affectionately known as the Industrial Prince or the Foreman in many distressed areas. He developed a real rapport with workers, remembering names and appearing (perhaps because of his speech defect) to be a fellow-sufferer.

With a generous grant from a concerned layman, the Duke of York's Camp was also instituted—an annual summer one-week holiday shared by privileged boys and working-class youngsters. Knowledge and experience would later prove that if the idea of such a camp was benevolent, its reality was naive and condescending (not to say essentially fruitless); this was, however, the first postwar attempt to introduce a degree of organized democratization into the social lives of the young, and the Duke's prestige and his direct meeting with all classes of workers and youths gave it a cachet it would not otherwise have had.

Just as he was jealous of Prince Edward's popularity, so was King George unenthusiastic about the Duke's success in these endeavors. Resentful at the collapse of Europe's monarchies and fearful of anything modern, the King was something of a dyspeptic tyrant after the war, continuing to alienate himself further from his family by a relentless carping criticism. Now everyone was fair game for his wrath, and no son was immune from his disapproval. Harry was an idler, the monarch complained (although after Cambridge the young man began a respectable military career); Albert's shyness and stammering were maddening; Edward was an immoral roustabout. Only Princess Mary won his approval—and sometimes George, although regal smiles at him would also soon change to scowls. The King would brook opposition on nothing. While he loathed flattery and insincerity, he was (thus Frederick Ponsonby, who was as much in his presence as anyone at Court or in government, Queen Mary excepted) "so accustomed to people agreeing with him that he resented the candid-friend business."

Among the Windsors' major problems was a distressing lack of peer friendships. Like their father, the Princes were always treated with deference, surrounded as if by a mystic nimbus. The Prince of Wales had no male friends except Captain Edward "Fruity" Metcalfe, a charming, irresponsible Irish cavalry officer who joined his staff in 1921 and endeared himself to the Prince by a raucous informality. "People were sometimes shocked by the familiarity of his attitude towards me," said Metcalfe. As for Prince Albert, his older brother was his closest friend.

But the Princes might have mistresses, and in 1919, at twenty-three, the Duke of York had what was apparently his first brief romantic affair, with the robust and good-natured dancer and actress Phyllis Monkman, four years older than he. On a summons from Albert's equerry, Monkman met the Prince for an evening in private quarters in Mayfair. How carnal, how serious, or how protracted the relationship was cannot be determined, for despite show-business rumors of gifts and assignations, neither the Prince nor the showgirl seems to have confided a single detail to anyone. A similar mystery hangs over Albert's brief flirtation, also in 1919 and early 1920, with Lady Maureen Vane-Tempest-Stewart, the lovely and aggressive daughter of a millionaire aristocrat. In any case Albert did not have his brother's zealous and passionate nature, nor was he one to fall quickly in and out of love—which was the only occupation that interested the Prince of Wales at all.

And so the two Princes seemed to reflect their respective namesakes: Albert Duke of York manifested the conscientious temperament (if not the keen intelligence) of their great-grandfather Prince Albert; Edward Prince of Wales, on the other hand, recalled their sybaritic grandfather Edward VII, even to open affairs with married women.

But there were complications that their forebears did not have to endure. Whereas the symptom of young Albert's neurotic anxiety and tension was an almost crippling stutter, Edward suffered periods of paralyzing depression; both conditions were owed, at least partly, to the unfortunate combination of imposed duty without emotional supports. In July 1920 he was very near a complete breakdown after visiting more than two hundred places and traveling fifty thousand miles: the Prince's speech was erratic, he wandered from topic to topic even in casual conversation, he appeared pale and shaking. There were, reported foreign correspondents, "renewed signs of nerve strain [that were] very disturbing," and "the situation at any moment may become serious."

* * *

At the time, the public saw only the boyish heir to the world's most prestigious throne, the eligible Prince Charming who dazzled both crowds and the press merely by his presence. He was society's great Jazz Age celebrity who seemed to embody both the kingly and the common touches. But there were, in point of fact, no compelling reasons for his enormous popularity. He lacked an intellectual or aesthetic sensibility. He was whimsical, frivolous and inconsiderate. His rejection of reverence owed more to self-resentment and revolt against his father than to any reasoned stance toward the modern world. And although for the most part Prince Edward rose to the demands of his tour schedule, these journeys were not without constant perquisites—women were available to him whenever he desired, and he had a staff of aides to gratify less intimate requests. To sum up, the future King was hailed for very little other than the coincidence of his role with the rise of twentieth-century media notoriety.

More than anything the insistently libertine conduct of the Prince of Wales effectively marked the wide gap separating the conservative older generation from the younger generation of postwar rebels. Even the King's favorite, the Duke of York, grew weary of some royal routines, especially social events such as the opening of the racing season at Ascot. Of that rite of spring Prince Albert complained to Mabell Airlie: "No new blood is ever introduced . . . and no originality in the talk—nothing but a dreary acquiescence in the order of the day. Traditionalism is all very well, but too much of it leads to dry rot."

As ever, the King loathed change in any degree regarding anything at all, and he barely tolerated the photographic journals, the press and the radio: they were vulgar, they were American-inspired intrusions destroying forever the sedate dignity of the Victorian era. "All his life," according to an official chronicler, "he regarded the exclusive family life created by his father and mother in his youth as an ideal towards which every succeeding generation should strive."

But George did not have his father's easy manner and tolerance, much less his sartorial sophistication. Just as he required Mary to adhere to Victorian fashion, so he kept unchanged his Victorian wardrobe of gloves, frock coats, side-pressed trousers and bowler hats. The King resolutely maintained that he had nothing to learn from the younger generation. His eldest son summed him up: "My father resisted change, and to the day he died he still looked back to the pre-World War I days and used to say, 'Oh, for the good times, the good old times.' "

To calm his fears for their futures (and the realm's), the King looked forward to his children's marriages to suitable partners and the raising of their own families. In 1920 the eldest was twenty-six, the youngest eighteen; no one had spoken of marriage or introduced a prospective mate at Buckingham Palace. Three years earlier, responding to Parliament's counsel, the King had relaxed the unwritten rules about brides for his progeny: the Royal Family no longer needed to marry only other Royals; after all, there were few enough left on the Continent, and in any case only Prince Edward had any experience of European social life. In fact, there was considerable pressure for them to pick British spouses. "If our monarchy is to endure," as essayist Cecil Battine wrote (expressing the sentiments of a vast majority), "our princes must find consorts among their own countrywomen . . . must marry British subjects or lose their rights." *

Earlier, English kings had married foreign Royals to acquire territory. Queen Victoria and her eldest daughter and son had married foreign Royals, but "times have changed," as Victoria herself conceded in 1869, "and great foreign alliances are looked on as causes of trouble and anxiety, and are of no good. . . . I feel sure that *new* blood will strengthen the Throne *morally* as well as physically." In the aftermath of the war and of the Royal Family's rejection of its own German heritage, a marriage to any German was of course impossible, and although the Greek and Danish Royals remained (however weakened and intermarried), George and Mary were now willing to consider an English or Scottish aristocrat suitable.

To this the King agreed with Battine and his colleagues

---

* In the same essay, Battine asked that "princes nearest the succession, and in particular the heir to the Crown, must be entrusted with duties which will test his ability and train his judgment. He must, like other officials, be allowed to act on his own initiative and to make mistakes. The king must be permitted sometimes to do wrong [or he will cease] to be king, or anything else but a fifth wheel to the coach of State."

that even members of the British nobility, though commoners, would be acceptable as partners for his children. Two such alliances would occur within the next three years.

Just one week after he was named Duke of York, Albert met an aristocratic gentlewoman—a commoner but well born —who took his fancy. On June 10, 1920, he, his sister and Prince Henry accompanied the Queen to a soiree in Grosvenor Square, at the home of Lady Farquhar, whose husband was dining that night with the King. Among the guests was a five-foot-four-inch, nineteen-year-old girl with alabaster skin, sparkling blue eyes and dark brown hair. She was, recalled Mabell Airlie, who knew her and her family, "very unlike the cocktail-drinking, chain-smoking girls who came to be regarded as typical of the nineteen-twenties." She radiated a kind of confident charm, she had (thus another friend) "a sense of fun and a certain roguish quality," and she gloried in the considerable male attention she invariably won, despite her rather dowdy dress and coiffure.

The lady was in some ways very like Queen Mary, who for some reason did not much like her but had no reason to say so. That maternal diffidence counted for nothing with Albert, who soon asked to meet the young woman again. Her name was Lady Elizabeth Bowes-Lyon, and like Queen Mary she would eventually be Duchess of York, Queen and Queen Mother. In the saga of the Windsors, hers may accurately be called the most authoritative voice in the family for most of the twentieth century; her influence endures uninterrupted into her nineties.

Born August 4, 1900, in her grandfather's London residence, Elizabeth Angela Marguerite Bowes-Lyon was the ninth of ten children of the Earl of Strathmore and Kinghorne, a Scottish aristocrat whose wealth derived from coal mines and ironworks.* Since the fourteenth century, the Bowes-Lyon family had occupied Glamis Castle in Scotland; to this property the family added ownership, over the centuries, of another castle in northeast England, a mansion in Hertfordshire and an impressive house in St. James's Square, London.

---

* There has been some doubt about the actual birthplace of Elizabeth Bowes-Lyon, and this is one of the questions she herself has never resolved. For the most recent summary of the matter, see Michael De-la-Noy, *The Queen Behind the Throne* (London: Hutchinson, 1994), pages 49–50.

Elizabeth's mother, Lady Strathmore, daughter of an Anglican priest, was devout but not fanatical, a devoted parent, an amusing hostess and a woman who took her material possessions lightly. When a guest pointed out that rainwater was seeping through a wall of a sitting room, she replied airily, "Oh, dear, we'll have to move the sofa again." Little Elizabeth, not at all a shy child and sometimes quite perverse, knew what she could test in this regard. When a nanny scolded her for taking a new pair of scissors to a set of bedsheets—"What will your Mother say?"—the child replied without concern, "She will say, 'Oh, Elizabeth.' " Lady Strathmore loved gardens, music and painting as much as English history, and she was by all accounts the greater parental influence on her daughter than her melancholy husband, a handsome, conscientious and somewhat dull landlord whose personality much resembled the King's.

Lighthearted and amusing, interested in people and current events, Lady Strathmore passed on these qualities to little Elizabeth, who from her earliest years was poised and clever. "How do you do, Mr. Ralston," the four-year-old said to a servant one day. "I haven't seen you look so well for years and years, but I am sure you will be sorry to know that Lord Strathmore has got the toothache." To a new governess in Hertfordshire, a year later, she expressed politely, "I do hope you will be happy here." Indeed, her family so doted on her and endorsed her charm—calling her "the little Princess" in the bargain—that by the time she was six the girl took the nickname seriously: "I call myself The Princess Elizabeth," she announced—thus proving herself, according to one tutor, "a child far more mature and understanding, even prophetic, than her age warranted." And perhaps more opinionated than most: "Some governesses are nice, some are not," she claimed, and of course no one corrected her. The nicest of the lot, as it happened, was one Clara Knight, called Alah by the child Elizabeth (and Alah she remained to Elizabeth's daughter years later).

The Bowes-Lyon children were raised in considerable comfort in several residences, with house pets and horses, servants, conveniences, toys aplenty and precisely the parental warmth and indulgence denied to Albert. Like the Royals and most aristocrats, little importance was attached to education, which was a casual business handled by governesses at home. Dancing, music and the social arts were the important things; books were for shelves, leisure time for fishing and riding. The Strathmores created an atmosphere "filled with human beings whose purpose in life was to serve this family," as Lady Donaldson has written; that they were also a better family than any other was part of the air the children breathed.

But circumstances precluded Elizabeth from being merely a spoiled rich girl. The Great War broke out on her fourteenth birthday, and of her four brothers who volunteered, one was killed and another gravely wounded. Glamis Castle became a hospital for returning soldiers, and Elizabeth assumed practical domestic and nursing duties for the duration of the conflict—a commendable way for the youngest girl in a family of nine to be acknowledged, to prove her mettle. "During the first few months we were so busy knitting, knitting, knitting and making shirts for the local battalion," she recalled. "My chief occupation was crumpling up tissue paper for the linings of [soldiers'] sleeping bags." She also comforted the returning casualties, chatting with them, playing cards and piano and writing letters for them. And when her mother fell ill in 1918, Elizabeth managed the entire place. "She had," recalled one young man in 1915, "the loveliest eyes, expressive and eloquent eyes [and a] sweet, quiet voice, that hesitant yet open way of talking. For all her fifteen years, she was very womanly, kind-hearted and sympathetic." Lady Elizabeth, from adolescence, made herself both necessary and appreciated, and simultaneously she enjoyed the attention, respect and gratitude of wounded young men—an appealing situation for many women.

It was not surprising, therefore, that Albert, who himself had considerable physical and emotional handicaps, would be attracted to so poised, charming, generous and direct a young lady, or that he would arrange to be invited to Glamis later that summer of 1920 and arrange for her to be formally presented to the King and Queen. Elizabeth, for her part, was pleased to have been noticed by the Duke and flirted coyly, but she was not at all interested in anything like a serious courtship with him. "Her radiant vitality and a blending of gaiety, kindness and sincerity made her irresistible to men," recalled Mabell Airlie. Among the many were Lord Gorell ("I fell *madly* in love with her—they all did''), the millionaire Christopher Glenconner, the diplomat Archie Clark-Kerr, and the Duke of York's own equerry, James Stuart. But Albert, whose speech and manner were so painfully awkward, did not for the present make much of an impression, and this disappointed and depressed him. ''I have discovered that he is very much attracted to Lady Elizabeth Bowes-Lyon,'' Queen Mary confided to Lady Airlie. ''He's always talking about her.''

By early 1921, Albert was so smitten that he proposed to Lady Elizabeth, only to be gently denied but not deterred, even after three more proposals and three more rejections in 1922. ''The Duke looked so disconsolate,'' Mabell Airlie wrote to Lady Strathmore; ''I do hope he will find a nice wife who will make him happy.'' The reply was perceptive: ''I like him so much, and he is a man who will be made or marred by his wife.'' And with that, Prince Albert temporarily withdrew, only to marshal his forces for the next approach. His parents watched the strategy quietly, for although Queen Mary was no ardent supporter of the match, dynastic hopes were rather limited: the Prince of Wales was attached to Freda Dudley Ward and showed no interest in marrying. The royal gaze, therefore, settled on Albert, who turned twenty-six in December 1921, and his was firmly fixed on Elizabeth. Even Queen Mary had to admit that this was ''the one girl who could make Albert happy.'' Prudently, she resolved to ''say nothing to either of them. Mothers should never meddle in their children's love affairs.''

Both the Duke's ardor and his awkwardness touched Elizabeth, however: the same nurturing instincts that made her a comfort to wounded soldiers gradually warmed her toward Albert who was so needy of precisely the feminine qualities she had in abundance. For all his decency and sense of responsibility, the Prince was also a dependent and nervous man who had not hitherto known any womanly warmth but that of his nannies.

And so, as they visited occasionally throughout 1921 and 1922, a matrimonial campaign was brilliantly maneuvered at tea and dinner by Lady Airlie, who cast herself in the role of matchmaker; other chaste rendezvous were scheduled at the Strathmores' new London address, 17 Bruton Street, Mayfair. Gradually, Elizabeth saw Prince Albert as someone she could please and encourage. Handsome and kindly, he was different from the consciously clever, bright young things and dashing cavaliers who pressed their intentions.

Perhaps, too, with the most benevolent of feminine wiles, she saw that her own poise and confidence might be the perfect antidote to Albert's crippling reticence, that her own gifts of personality could shape and improve a man who had disturbing inadequacies. The egos of few people, after all, are impervious to the subtle amalgam of another's need, dependence and love. Nevertheless, Elizabeth was, according to her mother, "torn between her longing to make Albert happy and her reluctance" to take on such a responsibility. Especially, she might have added, since it was clear that Elizabeth shared neither Albert's passion nor his essential loneliness. "He had few friends and was almost entirely dependent on her, whom he worshipped," wrote the diarist and royal confidant Henry Channon (aptly called "Chips" because of his close friendship with a man nicknamed "Fish").* "She was his willpower, his all." And as Frances Donaldson cannily observed, Lady Elizabeth Bowes-Lyon "cannot have been cold to her opportunity."

As it happened, the first of George V's children to wed was Princess Mary, who married Henry, Viscount Lascelles, at Westminster Abbey on February 28, 1922; it was the first royal wedding there since 1352. In Queen Victoria's time such marriages were privately solemnized, but they had become increasingly splendid events to rally the loyalty of the public. This was also the first great state occasion since the armistice. Prince Edward, although fond of his sister, hated weddings (which he considered both a reproof and a summons) and was glad to be on tour in India at the time.

A war veteran and the wealthy heir of the Earl of Hare-

---

* Channon was born in Chicago, and after attending Oxford University, settled in London and became the most ardent American anglophile and naturalized British citizen since Henry James. He made royal and aristo-cratic connections the way George V collected stamps, lovingly and avari-ciously. Channon took Prince Paul of Serbia for a lover and an Earl's daughter for a wife. He was elected to Parliament, eventually given a knighthood, and quietly, over several decades, wrote remarkable diaries; published after his death, they contain some of the most important and illuminating comments on twentieth-century English society.

wood,* Lascelles was forty, fifteen years Mary's senior, and looked and acted even older; he had neither good looks nor charm (he was rather accurately described as a "dismal bloodhound"), but he shared with Princess Mary a fondness for horses and racing. Perhaps the most memorable moment of their very grand wedding and reception occurred when the nearsighted novelist E. M. Forster bowed deeply to the cake, taking it for Queen Mary. The two Harewood children, George and Gerald—the King and Queen's first grandchildren—were born in 1923 and 1924.

By the time of Mary's wedding, her brother Prince Albert was, as a confidant revealed after his death, "desperately in love" with Elizabeth Bowes-Lyon but feared that he had lost her forever. Encouraged to continue his pursuit, Albert swept down on his intended all during 1922—at Glamis, in Hertfordshire, in London, at Ascot and Henley.

But right up to January 1923, she was not to be easily persuaded.

For one thing, Lady Elizabeth had grave doubts about such a transition in her life. As a royal duchess she would have little materially that she did not already have: to her own customary comfortable life there would be added only restrictions and isolation—and unwelcome publicity attending even the most casual outing. Yet she had grown quite fond of the Prince, drawn as much to his kindness and decency as by the desire to help with his difficulties and to evoke those deeper qualities (thus his biographer) "she thought, rightly, that she could bring out."

The matter came to a crisis with the January 5 issue of the London *Daily News*, which trumpeted that Elizabeth was to marry not the Duke of York but his older brother: SCOTTISH BRIDE FOR PRINCE OF WALES. "Heir to the throne to wed Peer's daughter: an Official Announcement imminent." Friends at a house party that weekend "bowed and bobbed and teased her, calling her 'Ma'am,' " recalled Chips Channon. "I am not sure that she enjoyed it." † Her anxiety at this announcement,

---

* The Earl of Harewood was a cousin to Alan "Tommy" Lascelles, the assistant private secretary to Prince Edward (and later private secretary to King George VI).

† "Ma'am" is the proper form by which the Queen is personally addressed after the first salutation, "Your Majesty."

it was long rumored, owed to the fact that Lady Elizabeth found herself in the awkward position of hoping to wed an older brother while being wooed by the younger. But there is no evidence for an Edward-Elizabeth connection; he was, after all, with Freda when he was not on tour. On the contrary, Elizabeth did not enjoy the speculation that she might be another passing fancy in the life of the Prince of Wales.

Elizabeth knew she would have to make a decision or suffer even more speculation and prying in the press. Finally, she yielded. "It was my duty to marry him," she said years later, "and I fell in love with Bertie afterwards." The sentiments were worthy of Queen Mary, who found herself transferred from an engagement with Eddy to one with George.

Thus on January 13, 1923, Lady Elizabeth accepted the Duke's proposal. "We gladly gave our consent," the King noted in his diary two days later. "I trust they will be very happy." As for Queen Mary: "We are delighted and he looks beaming." To the helpful Mabell Airlie, Prince Albert wrote:

How can I thank you enough for your charming letter to me about the wonderful happening in my life which has come to pass, and my dream which has at last been realized.

It seems so marvellous to me to know that my darling Elizabeth will one day be my wife. We are both very, very happy and I am sure always will be. I owe so much to you and can only bless you for what you did.

The wedding took place on April 26, 1923, at Westminster Abbey. At first the couple was pleased at the suggestion that the ceremony be radio-transmitted, but they were disappointed when the Dean of the abbey disagreed: people might hear it in pubs, people might listen without doffing their hats. And so the wedding was not broadcast.

There was no visible sunrise that morning, for a spring rain washed the city, and clouds threatened to overhang it all day. Then, as if nature herself conjoined to give the magic touch required for a good story, the sun peeked through just as Lady Elizabeth entered the abbey, and by the time vows were exchanged and the new Duchess of York departed on the arm of her Duke, there was bright sunshine.

Before heading toward Glamis Castle, the Yorks spent a few days golfing at Polesden Lacey, Surrey, at a house lent to them by Mrs. Ronald Greville, a short, plump, social-climbing hostess. Her taste in furniture was vulgar and her standards insufferably snobbish, but Royals like people who are wealthy enough to provide free and comfortable lodging. Mrs. Greville's guest lists for soirees the Yorks attended over the years included European Royals, sheiks and maharajahs, barons, wealthy old earls and (if Americans) only the most venerable names, such as Vanderbilt and Astor. "It was," wrote the Duke's biographer, "a setting in which Prince Albert felt at home, with people whom he met at Court or in the great London houses."

At twenty-seven, Prince Albert was the first of four royal sons to marry, and none of his brothers would follow for over a decade. This was also the first marriage of a royal Prince to be held at Westminster in over five hundred years. More to the point, Lady Elizabeth was the first woman who was a commoner to marry legitimately into the Royal Family. Thus the occasion was also a sign of democratic progress. From a public relations standpoint, it was a stroke of great luck, for here were two upright young noble folk whose names were untouched by scandal and whose marriage affirmed the monarchy's status as carriers of traditional family values. The wedding was a glittering affair, Elizabeth was most enthusiastically hailed by the public and the press, and the earnest, dutiful Duke would soon return to his work on behalf of the Industrial Welfare Society and the boys' camps.

Everything about the Yorks, in other words, reinforced King George's desired impression that Royals be above reproach, and that the family belonged to all the people. "The better I know and the more I see of your dear little wife," he wrote to Prince Albert soon after the wedding, "the more charming I think she is." As proof, he sustained Elizabeth's chronic unpunctuality. When she arrived late for a meal at Windsor, he waved away her apology by saying calmly, "You are not late, my dear, I think we must have sat down two minutes too early." Anyone else would have heard a royal mutter or been transfixed with an icy stare. He insisted on only one alteration in her style: she must give no more interviews to journalists; and she did not, neither during the King's lifetime nor afterward. "Unlike his own children," Elizabeth said after his death, "I was never afraid of him, and in all the twelve years of having me as a daughter-in-law, he never spoke one unkind or abrupt word to me."

Perhaps because she had instantly won over the King, Elizabeth made no effort to ingratiate herself with the Queen, from whom she was always distant. The Duchess of York did not need the protection of Queen Mary; in fact, she did not much like the Queen and never spoke of her with affection.

They were, after all, very different women from very different backgrounds: Mary's poor Anglo-German stock versus wealthy British aristocracy. From the start, the new Duchess's relationship with her mother-in-law was cool, and the Queen always kept a cordial distance from the Duchess—not because she was jealous of her prerogatives or possessive of her son but because Elizabeth had precisely the qualities of personality Mary envied. The Queen was shy; she had not enjoyed an undilutedly happy life; she considered herself unpretty and awkward (especially as successor to the beautiful Queen Alexandra); she had to force herself to seem comfortable in the presence of strangers; she was not emotionally demonstrative; and she subjugated her style to the quaint tastes of her husband. In every way she represented another age, even to the slightly guttural German tint to her accent, which she never lost.

Elizabeth, on the other hand, shone like the proverbial English rose. She had never known the uncertainties of Mary's early years; she was invariably the life of any social gathering, not by extraordinary beauty or dazzling fashion but by a warm personality and a sense of fun that, unlike her mother-in-law, she had no reason to suppress. Most of all, she showed her feelings quite openly: she and Prince Albert would be as frankly affectionate with their children as the King and Queen were aloof. The thirty-three years separating the two women comprised a century's cultural gap, and both women seem to have sensed this at once. In addition, Elizabeth always had to curtsy to Queen Mary, and this was a constant reminder that her mother-in-law was her superior.

But there were other reasons for a keener coolness among certain members of the Royal Family in 1923, just when the

Lascelles and York marriages threw into sharper relief the protracted bachelorhood of the Prince of Wales. "There is but one wedding to which [the public] look forward with still deeper interest—the wedding which will give a wife to the heir to the throne." So ran a somewhat ungracious (if accurate) article in *The Times* the day after the Duke of York married.

There was more behind this admonition than the Freda affair: Prince Edward was becoming an ornery, often difficult character. When he found an official program tedious or was unexcited at a social event, he made no secret of his boredom, and he had less and less regard for time and manners. "I was like a man caught in a revolving door," he wrote later of this time. His sadness often turned to anger (a family trait in any case), and too often the Prince appeared to support rumors that when he appeared in public he was suffering from a hangover or was still frankly inebriated. All the same, when he appeared he never failed to draw cheering crowds. People saw what they had come to see, and in this celebrity they saw only charm. But to those closer to the reality—men such as Fruity Metcalfe and Alexander Hardinge (assistant private secretary to George V and in time secretary to Edward)—the Prince of Wales was increasingly difficult to manage and awkward to apologize for. His parents, too, did not know what to do, and the King was faced with an awkward dilemma. He kept trying to fit for sovereignty a son who, he was becoming more convinced, would be a failure at the job. "The Prince of Wales," noted Chips Channon, "would not raise his finger to raise his future sceptre. In fact, many of his intimate friends think he would be only too happy to renounce it."

Just as the eldest Windsor was increasingly problematic for the King and Queen, so was the youngest. At twenty-one, Prince George was the handsomest, most cultured, most socially adept of all the royal offspring. He dressed even more nattily than Edward, his dark hair was impeccably groomed, he smiled readily, he was witty and articulate. He kept a commission in the Royal Navy until 1929, and although he enjoyed frequent leaves, his father rewarded him for naval duty by appointing him Knight of the Garter. George also had a disarming way of defusing the King's explosions of anger and even of offering a sharp riposte. George was always the Queen's favorite. He shared her love of collecting and her interest in historic paintings and antiques, and she frequently confided in him. George felt none of the pressure applied to his older brothers; he was, after all, so far down the line of succession as to be virtually out of consideration.

But both parents must have been dismayed when they learned about some aspects of George's private life, although their reactions to the issue remain predictably undocumented. Contrary to some chronicles, it is unlikely that they would not have known of George's love affair with Noël Coward (certainly not the last and perhaps not the first of his male lovers), who was only three years older than the Prince. George was doubtless aware of the King's belief that "men like that shot themselves," but never mind.

In 1923, George and Noël were the open secret of London society, although of course the relationship "remained concealed from the general public and suppressed among [George's] intimates, so that his reputation remained intact," as one royal biographer has written. George was often seen alone, entering Coward's home in Gerald Road, Belgravia; together they were spotted in gay nightclubs in full makeup, a common affectation among a certain louche set at the time. The "little dalliance" (as Coward masterfully understated it) lasted for two years, until late 1925. Because the press would never allude to such a liaison, the two attractive bachelors could attend dinner parties, the theater, and concerts together without fear of exposure. A curtain of discretion even covered the Prince's occasional forays to Bond Street's Embassy Club, where he sought out those handsome young blond continentals that struck his fancy.*

With Freda Dudley Ward and Noël Coward hovering at the palace gates, as it were, the quiet propriety of the Duke and Duchess of York was all the more precious to Their Majesties. George and Mary chose White Lodge in Richmond Park

---

* Noël Coward claimed that there was also some homosexual dabbling by the Prince of Wales, who sometimes accompanied George to gay gathering places: "He pretends not to hate me," said Coward, "but he does, and it's because I'm queer and he's queer but, unlike him, I don't pretend not to be." Coward's remark is provocative; it is also not easy to corroborate.

(where Queen Mary had lived as a girl and where Prince Edward had been born) for the Yorks' first home. But the newlyweds found this primitive residence quite inhospitable with its antique plumbing, lack of central heat and array of uncomfortable outhouses. Life was so crude that the Yorks seemed to suffer an unending series of colds, influenzas and attacks of rheumatism, and it is perhaps noteworthy that the Duchess did not (perhaps could not) become pregnant during the two years at the Lodge.

Their life was quiet and undemanding. The Yorks were not seen in nightclubs, dance halls or fashionable restaurants, or at ski resorts, Riviera beaches or gambling casinos. Their social life was populated with respectable country folk who played cards and tennis, sipped gin and tonic, shot birds and deer and fished for salmon.

King George might have cheered loudly: such activities continued the tradition of bourgeois Windsorism. For her part, the Duchess took as her vocation the care and guidance of the Duke, presenting herself as a charming affiliate and guiding him with maternal warmth through the rigors of public events, which he loathed because of the stammer that so often made him incomprehensible. At such times the Duchess whispered, "Wave, Bertie, wave!" and in a few seconds things ran more smoothly. So went their first round of travels—mostly extended holidays, with a few official appointments interwoven —to the Balkans in the autumn of 1923, to Northern Ireland in the summer of 1924, and to Africa from December 1924 to April 1925. "Elizabeth has been marvelous as usual," Albert wrote to his father, "& the people simply love her already. I am very lucky indeed to have her to help me as she knows exactly what to do & say to all the people we meet."

To Princes George and Edward, a social schedule like the Yorks' would have been very dull indeed. George always preferred exotic private venues for racier entertainment, and Edward (who rated Mrs. Greville and her crowd as sycophantic bores) reveled in the more glistening society attracted to Mrs. Greville's archrival, Lady Cunard, a birdlike socialite with a chirpy voice, yellow hair and the ability to dazzle her guests with apparent ease.

Born Maud Burke in San Francisco, she had married the shipping magnate Sir Bache Cunard and subsequently took the conductor Sir Thomas Beecham for a lover. Assessing Maud a rather inert name, she rechristened herself the more sparkling Emerald and became in London society (thus Chips Channon) someone "beloved, dazzling, bright, fantastic." She also had a keen and quick wit that made her pretensions endurable. When Somerset Maugham, who had a predilection for country boys, declined an invitation to one of her late supper parties on the pretext "I have to keep my youth," Emerald replied briskly, "Then bring him with you!" On another occasion just after World War II, Chips Channon gazed at an assembly of well-dressed Londoners and whispered to Emerald, "This is what we have been fighting for." To which the irrepressible Lady Cunard replied, "What? Are they all Poles?"

Her Ladyship remained Edward's ally throughout his thorny years to come; she was also an attentive and amusing comfort to him after the several dangerous falls he took during polo matches, for "with alarming regularity" during the 1920s (as the Prince's biographer wrote), Edward fell, breaking collar-bones, spraining limbs, blackening his eyes, suffering concussions. Eager to return to the sport when he could, Edward seemed obsessed with proving his mettle, his manhood, his abilities in something, for he was so badly educated and informed—and showed so little inclination to supplement the intellectual and cultural gaps—that even his intimates found him singularly ignorant.

"I don't want to be King," Edward said more than once. "I wouldn't be a very good one." That may have been among the most perceptive remarks of his lifetime and one with which his father would have ruefully concurred. In fact, the Prince's choice of friends, his disreputable private life (so the King considered it), his cavalier dismissal of protocol, proper dress and court ritual convinced George V that he was trying in vain to prepare as heir to the throne a son who would inevitably disgrace it.

This was not merely the King's opinion. On the eve of Edward's return from a tour of South America, *The Spectator* published an unprecedented critique of his character. After noting the Prince's "charm, modesty and friendliness," the editorial expressed "a good deal of anxiety about the future of the Prince of Wales" after a notorious lapse in courtesy that had been widely printed in the Argentine press.

One day the Prince was due to visit a school. The building had been specially decorated and the children had arranged to sing in English "God Bless the Prince of Wales" and another English song. One of the children was also to make a short speech in English. All this had meant a good deal of preparation. . . . The whole company waited for some time, but the guests did not come, and were told that the engagement had been cancelled. . . . Our correspondent then goes on to say that of course you cannot prevent people talking and that comparisons were, perhaps inevitably, drawn between the Prince of Wales's willingness to dance or attend supper parties in the small hours of the morning, but not to keep an engagement a few hours later.

And at this point the essay sharpened its tone to an edge worthy of Jonathan Swift:

We suggest the Prince of Wales [take] the rest which he has earned and richly deserves [and then] attach himself to some public cause. Being associated with a great purpose, he would be bound to some regular application of his energies which once and for all would put an end to any false notion that it is his desire to live a butterfly existence. . . .

The Monarchy is now safer even than it was in the days of Queen Victoria. Amid the tumbling monarchies of Europe ours has become more firmly based. . . . The nation desires to see the Prince of Wales, by a process of stabilization, qualifying himself for that great office with the consent and good will of all classes.

As far as the King was concerned, some of the blame for Edward's increasing laxity had to do not with the tour but with the former colonies. Americans and the New York style were the undoing of the Prince of Wales—such was the King's belief. Americanization had modernized and democratized him to the point of anarchy, and here he was, showing no interest at all in marrying a decent British aristocrat. Emerald Cunard was typical of the new breed of imported socialites; others included Elsa Maxwell, Laura Corrigan, Chips Channon and Nancy Astor, who brought with them American cocktails and American slang, American fashions and the full bag of American vulgarities—everything, in other words, that King George V opposed with all his conservative being. The aristocracy, he and his circle felt, had been sufficiently undermined by the war and social decay; it did not require the antics of the Prince of Wales and his American friends to complete the task of its dissolution. Foreign parvenus comprised virtually a syndicate that seemed to be a powerful element in London society, but ironically the old aristocracy held them to be merely snobs whose social climbing tactics indicated their desire to infiltrate polite English ranks. It was perhaps never clear just which camp cornered the market on snobbery.

One way to counter the trend of Americanization was the British Empire Exhibition, held in 1924 and 1925 at the Wembley Stadium, the country's largest arena. Like the Great Exhibition of 1851, it was designed to celebrate Imperial aspirations and Commonwealth achievements in industry, the arts, and technology—a profusion of pavilions boasting British products. On April 23, 1924, the exhibition was opened by the King himself, who at the Queen's urging agreed to read a short welcoming speech on the radio. This was the first important national event transmitted by the BBC, and the King's words were heard by millions. There was, however, an awkward catch to it all, for it could not be said that the monarch was the first member of the Royal Family to make a public broadcast. In this he had been preempted by his eldest son, who on October 7, 1922, had addressed a greeting from St. James's Palace to the Boy Scouts.

To those who were gently but insistently guiding the palace along the paths of modern public relations—to Clive Wigram and his allies—the broadcast was a great moment indeed. Royalty became a bit less remote as the King's voice, a rich, surprisingly warm yet formal baritone, filled great drawing rooms and grimy pubs. It was not what he said (a few words about the genius of his people) but the fact of the sudden proximity that struck everyone; it was the first time that more than a few dozen citizens had ever heard a sovereign's voice at one time.

This success was not repeated during the exhibition's second season, when the unfortunate Duke of York was put to the microphone; this time the audience was more than ten million worldwide. Alas, this choice of host was disastrous, for Prince

192

Albert's stammer was worse than ever, and despite repeated
rehearsals, his anxiety overwhelmed him. Several times no
sound at all issued from his mouth while his jaws opened and
shut, his hands shook, his tongue clicked. Only a few choked
words could finally be painfully strung together. The impression at home and abroad was that whereas the Prince of Wales
was an increasingly feckless playboy, the Duke of York was
completely unsuited to any kind of public life. They had been
widely admired, but now the general estimation about the
Princes was subject not only to the ubiquitous camera but also
to the uncompromising microphone. Wigram and company
were perhaps surprised that their promotional ideas might have
unforeseen, detrimental repercussions, that the tools might take
over the trade.

No such danger of exposure threatened the senior members
of the Royal Family—especially beloved old Queen Alexandra, who by 1925 had outlived her husband by fifteen years.
Since the death of Prince John in 1919, she had felt more and
more useless and became increasingly reclusive, the isolation
of her deafness compounded by failing eyesight. "It is so hard
to see that beautiful woman come to this," remarked Queen
Mary sympathetically.

From 1921, Alexandra was immured at Sandringham, still
lovingly attended by her spinster daughter Princess Victoria
and two devoted servants. She tried to keep up with the news
of her family and turned ever more frequently to the simple
pieties and prayers of her youth. By all accounts, she seemed
to grow more serene with age and frailty, as if all the quiet
grace and patience that had animated her over the years had
come to reward her with a profound inner confidence. Her sole
surviving son, the King, was most attentive, and her grandchildren visited regularly, often accompanying her to the nearby
church for worship, which became ever more important. She
was in a real sense the first modern mother among British
Royals, involved with and present to her children as were few
other mothers of the upper or middle classes of her time. The
result was plain: King George V grew up without remarkable
neuroses, an uncomplicated fellow without dark angles or
agendas. He may have been limited, but he was not notably
wounded, and much of the credit for this goes to his mother.

In December 1924, Alexandra marked her eightieth birthday. "I never realised what the beauty of old age could mean," wrote a reporter who visited her,

> until I saw Queen Alexandra in the late autumn of her days. A vision of exquisite fragility, her face still that perfect oval that captivated London long ago, her figure slender and willowy. . . . But it was her smile of greeting that I shall always remember, that wonderful smile which ravished all in the days when she came a girl-bride, and remained with her in its undying beauty.

In the autumn of 1925, Alexandra suffered a heart attack at Sandringham. With Princess Victoria and the King and Queen at her bedside, she lingered for a day before dying on November 20. Five days later, after a service in the local church, Alix's body was carried—amid a windless, early snowfall—to Wolferton Station and thence to Westminster Abbey and her final resting place, Windsor Memorial Chapel. The dark and chilly streets of London were thronged for the farewell route. Men stood hatless, shivering for hours in the cold, while women wept openly, as if for their own mothers.

Perhaps no member of the Royal House, before or since, was more loved than the Sea-King's daughter from over the sea, as Tennyson had called her. For in the final analysis it was not Alix's beauty or even her queenly dignity that endeared her to millions. It was her mildness, her identification with those who felt themselves outcast, her spontaneous, unrestrained gestures of good cheer to all who suffered. "Look what I can do with it!" she had cried gaily to that depressed, wounded soldier as she swung her lame leg and so brought encouragement where there had been only despair. With those same words, Queen Alexandra could have spoken of her long life, and of the radiant smile that had been a benediction on all who knew her.

Four brothers: Prince George, King Edward VIII, Prince Albert (later King George VI) and Prince Henry.

7

Of Fathers, Sons and Lovers

1926 to 1932

> Anything except the damned Mouse!
> KING GEORGE V, when asked which movie
> he might like to see

During the evening of April 20, 1926, there was a lively exchange of telephone calls between Mayfair 5250, the number at the London town house of the Earl and Countess of Strathmore, and Western 0823, the private line of the Home Secretary, Sir William Joynson-Hicks.

Finally, early in the morning of Wednesday, April 21, the last and most important call came, and Sir William was bun-

dled into a car and driven to the Strathmore residence, 17
Bruton Street. He was led to an upper suite where the Duchess
of York, after a difficult labor and emergency surgery, had just
given birth to a girl.* Prince Albert stood proudly by his wife's
bedside, beaming down at the red-faced infant who gave Sir
William the same treatment he got in the Commons: she
yawned in his face. The Home Secretary then bowed, departed,
and set to his task of telegraphing the news to the Lord Mayor
of London and to the governors of all the Dominions and
Colonies. At dawn the bells of St. Paul's Cathedral pealed, and
gun salutes were fired in Hyde Park and at the Tower of London. The King and Queen were informed at Windsor Castle,
and before the day was over they hastened to Bruton Street
with gifts and good wishes. But before that visit, Queen Mary
kept her luncheon engagement, welcoming Princess Alice
(wife of Prince Andrew of Greece) and Alice's mother-in-law,
the Dowager Marchioness of Milford Haven. By an odd coincidence, these two guests were the mother and grandmother of a
five-year-old boy named Prince Philip of Greece. One day he
would be the newborn baby's husband.

The girl was not the first grandchild born to George and
Mary, of course: Princess Mary and the Earl of Harewood had
two boys. But the Yorks' daughter, by virtue of being born to
a male heir of the King, took precedence and was third in line
to the throne. For this reason and because she was such a
pretty, alert, blue-eyed little charmer, and because their cameras, tripods, microphones and jotting pads were now ordinary
props within a mile of any Royal, the press swept down to
record every detail of the child's infancy.

The commotion began outside Buckingham Palace, where,
on May 29, the baby was baptized Elizabeth Alexandra Mary,
after her mother, great-grandmother and grandmother. Her
christening dress, then her first tooth, her first step and her
first word were described with breathless urgency. Still, few
assumed that Princess Elizabeth might one day be Queen;
surely her uncle the Prince of Wales would soon do his duty
and produce offspring to take precedence over her. Besides,

---

* The particular dangers of the last days of the Duchess's pregnancy
and the likely need for a medical team required her to leave the inconve-
nient White Lodge.

there were grave problems facing the country; it had much more on its collective mind than celebrating a royal birth.

In fact, all of England was in a wretched economic and social plight. Just one week after the birth of Princess Elizabeth, a general strike was called—the worst of more than three hundred labor disputes afflicting Britain that year. In support of the coal miners' rejection of pay cuts and longer working hours, every union stopped work on May 4. Trams, buses, gas, electricity, the underground and other essential services halted, and a national state of emergency was declared. But there was little violence, volunteers pitched in by the thousands, and a week later the strike by four million workers was called off. Only the miners refused to return to work—until near-starvation forced them back six months later.

Life did not improve for workingmen, however, as the King clearly saw. He urged his Prime Minister, the unobtrusive, avuncular, pipe-smoking Stanley Baldwin, to continue his usual wait-and-see attitude, to maintain a conciliatory tone toward workers and not to prohibit banks from making loans to unions. When the wealthy Lord Durham condemned his mine workers as "a damned lot of revolutionaries," the King spoke to the point: "Try living on their wages before you judge them." He also contributed privately to the miners' relief fund. In the continuing matter of the economic hardships that racked Britain after World War I and into the worldwide Depression, the monarch felt with considerable poignancy his inability to effect significant change.

Indeed, political expediency and parliamentary languor irritated him; never before, as Queen Mary noted in her journal, had he felt so frustrated in his duty to be King of all the people. Nonetheless, maintaining his impartial, nonpartisan stance, in 1926 the King made unannounced visits to the humblest of homes in London's East End, in Liverpool, Manchester and Cardiff. Legally he could do little more than sympathize, but this he did with genuine affection and admiration.

When the old Empire became the new Commonwealth of Nations after the Imperial Conference that November, Canada, Australia, New Zealand and South Africa became self-governing dominions equal in status to Britain yet united in allegiance to the Crown. The frequent recurrence of chronic respiratory infections, exacerbated by years of heavy smoking, prevented King George from following his ministers' recommendation that he make a foreign tour in 1927, and in his place the Duke and Duchess of York were groomed for a six-month journey instead of the overworked and increasingly unreliable Prince of Wales. As preparations began, the Duchess's own childhood nurse Clara "Alah" Knight was invited to assume care of Princess Elizabeth. A plain, no-nonsense matron, kindly but unsmiling, patient but not indulgent, she was the first important influence on the child after her mother.

The King and the Duchess realized, however, that the Yorks' visit abroad would be a fiasco unless something was done to correct Prince Albert's stammer. After discussing the matter with a woman who helped found the Society of Speech Therapists, Elizabeth was convinced that her husband's problem was rooted in his father's intimidation and could best be treated by a man. She was sent to a gifted speech therapist named Lionel Logue, who had emigrated from Australia and successfully treated many patients. Although he found it difficult to believe he could be helped, Prince Albert agreed to meet Logue on condition that his wife—for whom (thus one royal chronicler) he had "a total, almost slavish adoration"—accompany him on his first visit, on October 19.

As it happened, Logue had heard the Duke's halting speech at the closing of the Empire Exhibition at Wembley the previous year. "He was too old for me to manage a complete cure," the therapist told his son. "But I could very nearly do it. I'm sure of that." After intense effort he succeeded to a remarkable if not total extent.

"He entered my consulting room at three o'clock in the afternoon," recalled Logue, "a slim, quiet man with tired eyes and all the outward symptoms of the man upon whom habitual speech defect had begun to set the sign. When he left at five o'clock, you could see that there was once more hope in his heart." The hope was reinforced by weekly therapy sessions, aimed at convincing Prince Albert that he was not an incurable case. By specific breathing and relaxation exercises and by reviewing speeches to alter long or difficult sentences, the stammer was slowly ameliorated but never entirely cured. His terror of public speaking dogged him for the rest of his life, but instead of the dreaded repetition of initial consonants, there was only the occasional awkward pause. Whenever the Duke had a momentary hesitation, he looked to his wife, who nodded and smiled—and thus he proceeded—''the pluckiest and most determined patient I ever had,'' said Logue. Those same qualities were evident in the Duchess. Lady Donaldson wrote,

> Onlookers have described how [the Duke] would sometimes turn and look at [the Duchess] across a room and how, when he did this, she left what she was doing and went immediately to his side; he then seemed enabled to carry on. . . . When she sat on a platform beside him, no trace of anxiety or doubt ever disturbed the smiling serenity of her bearing; by no flicker of her features did she betray concern if he stumbled or hesitated.

For Albert as for his brothers, the presence of strong, confident women was absolutely essential at home and abroad. And so on January 6, 1927, the Prince and his resolute wife set off on HMS *Renown* for their first Imperial tour, bound for Australia and New Zealand by way of the Caribbean and the Pacific. They returned on June 27. Prince Albert's confidence was much improved after the warm welcome they had received everywhere and because of the comparative steadiness with which he had read his various speeches. The King and Queen met them at Victoria Station and whisked them back to Buckingham Palace, where Princess Elizabeth awaited in Alah's arms. She had passed her first birthday during her parents' absence, and some inevitable reacquaintance was necessary. But whereas Queen Mary had not been inclined to offer maternal hugs or to extend her time with her children, the Duchess was by nature a more modern mother. Her attachment to her daughter was real and expressed.

When the Yorks gave up White Lodge and moved that year to a mansion at 145 Piccadilly, everything seemed to center around the nursery. By all accounts this was a happy and affectionate family household, and the parents of the world's most celebrated Princess were intent on giving the child a normal life. To that end there were no barriers between the nursery and the formal rooms. Toys were everywhere, and little Elizabeth—and eventually her sister—had free rein over the entire house. ''We used to be so shy!'' exclaimed the Duke, amazed that his own children were so relaxed and unafraid of adults. It would be, his wife insisted, an ordinary English family.

In this she was singularly naive, for Princess Elizabeth's life was nothing like that of a typical girl. For one thing, she was a regular visitor at Buckingham Palace and Windsor Castle, where she was the darling of the day. For another, the Princess never attended school and had hardly any contact with children her own age. Moreover, at the center of her social circle were her royal parents (often absent on official duties), her formidable mentor Queen Mary, and the King of England —hardly a folksy British clan. Servants prepared and served Elizabeth's meals with appropriate bows and curtsies, they cleaned and set out her clothes and managed her parents' large and comfortable home. She was, in other words, the child of enormous privilege, raised in an insulated world that shared none of the harsh realities of her countrymen's lives. The mansion on Piccadilly overlooked Green Park and commanded a clear view of what was her second home, Buckingham Palace; from her nursery window Princess Elizabeth waved serenely, imitating the gesture of her family toward the crowds below the palace balcony. "She is a character," noted Winston Churchill. "She has an air of authority and reflectiveness astonishing in an infant."

That summer of 1927, the Prince of Wales departed on yet another foreign itinerary, this time a month-long tour of Canada and the official opening of a bridge to America at Niagara Falls. With Prince Edward were his brother Prince George (whom his parents wished disengaged from his fast London friends) and Prime Minister Stanley Baldwin and his wife. "One feels somehow that people are so much more genuine out of England," Edward wrote to Freda Dudley Ward on August 12. This would be a deepened sentiment in the coming years, for England meant so much that was painful—his parents and the constant reminder of the impossible duty that lay ahead.

That the Prince of Wales was happier with foreigners (particularly casual Americans) was "always the case," according to his equerry John Aird. "He seems much more at ease with them than with the British." But the nonchalance that increasingly characterized Edward was too much for his high-principled assistant private secretary Alan Lascelles. After several of his master's late-night forays with various local beauties, Lascelles wrote to Godfrey Thomas (the Prince's private secretary and thus Lascelles' immediate superior), stating his belief that "it would be a real disaster if, by any ill chance, he was called on to accede to the throne now." That event was some years distant, but Lascelles' resignation was imminent. The immediate cause of it was a series of royal revelries that had far-reaching consequences.

In 1928 the King created Prince Henry Duke of Gloucester, Earl of Ulster and Baron Culloden, and it was decided that he would be the next brother to accompany the Prince of Wales on a journey, this one mostly an African holiday. A professional soldier and sportsman, Henry at twenty-eight was neither brighter nor wittier than he was at school—that is to say, not at all. Lanky and slightly arrogant, he was genial enough with army buddies, but in other situations he was remarkable only for a certain elegant lethargy and an equine laugh perhaps inspired by too frequent visits to his own stables. Then as later, he cheerlessly accepted the royal duties assigned him. "I am thinking of writing my memoirs," he said years afterward. "And do you know what I shall call them? *Forty Years of Boredom.*" That title could also have described the feelings of anyone (apart from his family) forced to spend an hour in his company. Even the woman he eventually married and who was devoted to him for forty years described him as "a very vague sort of person." He had also inherited a Hanoverian philistinism. At a performance of *Tosca* he sat unmoved and indifferent even in the final dramatic moments when the heroine threw herself over the ramparts of Castel Sant'Angelo. His voice was then heard above the orchestra's final notes: "Well, if she's really dead, we can all go home!"

And so in the summer of 1928, Henry and Edward left England for their East African shooting safari. There all romantic hell broke loose when both brothers became involved with the notorious Beryl Markham, a racehorse breeder and one of the first women to hold a commercial flying license; in 1936 she became the first pilot to fly solo, east to west, across the Atlantic—an achievement detailed in her memoir *West with the Night.*

Born in England as Beryl Clutterbuck in 1902, this courageous, amusing, funny but cold-hearted trailblazer was raised on her father's farm in Kenya. Hurling spears before she could read and hunting before she could write, Beryl matured, insouciant about sex, into an almost savage adventuress. Alarmingly aggressive by any standard and not easily (if ever) denied her amatory whims, she gave new meaning to the word voracious. Her biographers, attempting to detail her love affairs, have been forced to offer simple inventories of the many she bedded. Beryl's great passion in the 1920s seems to have been for the pioneer and flier Denys Finch Hatton, for whose attention she competed with the writer Karen Blixen (Isak Dinesen) and who took the Prince of Wales on safari.

Tall, lithe and golden-skinned, with almond-shaped eyes, long, expressive hands and thick blond hair that fell wantonly about her shoulders, Beryl was later described as resembling both Greta Garbo and Vanessa Redgrave, but she lacked the wistful melancholy of the former and the dazzling intensity of the latter. In that fall of 1928 she had been married for a year to her second husband, the industrial magnate Mansfield Markham, and was five months pregnant; neither of these conditions prevented her from taking both the royal Princes for lovers.

Henry was the first to succumb. He met her on October 2 when they danced at a ball marking the opening of Kenya's royal season. The following morning they were reunited at a racetrack, where instead of the traditional curtsy the nontraditional Beryl threw her arms over her head, palms open, in a typical African *salaam* of defenselessness: "Hello, there!" she called to the Duke. From that moment, according to one of her friends, he was "besotted." The affair endured almost four years on two continents; the lovers met regularly in London throughout 1929, in rooms he booked for her at the Grosvenor Hotel, Victoria.*

---

* For years it was whispered that Beryl's son Gervase was sired by Prince Henry, a rumor she never took pains to discourage, perhaps because the marriage to Mansfield Markham quickly went sour and was eventually terminated by divorce. But Gervase was born after a full-term pregnancy on February 25, 1929, and so was conceived months before the Prince met Beryl.

At the same time, Beryl's fancy extended to Edward. "Beryl knew how to treat men," said a woman who knew her. "She treated them, on the whole, badly." This would not have deflected the Prince of Wales, who often pitched himself into brief, unemotional liaisons with commanding women—as if he could recreate and then correct his unfortunate relationship with Queen Mary. According to Markham's biographer, Errol Trzebinski (and those who knew her—Sir Derek Erskine, among others), bungalows were rented for the Edward-Beryl tryst the same season in Kenya and Uganda; and in London the following year, they met in rooms at the Royal Aero Club, Piccadilly. What each brother knew about the other's relationship is unclear, although given Beryl's frankness, the close quarters of all concerned, and the warm alliance between the Princes, it seems unlikely there were many secrets. The matter is no less complicated if Henry and Edward suspected but did not discuss the matter of this odd triangle; if they did, then their spirited dalliances with the same woman from the autumn of 1928 through 1929 may be more psychologically disordered than just carnally libidinous.

As it happened, Henry's intrigue with Beryl became the more potentially embarrassing and publicly inflammatory. After he began to cavort openly with her in London, Mansfield Markham found their love letters. He and his brother Charles at once threatened to cite Henry as corespondent in a divorce case—"unless the Duke took care of Beryl," as Sir Charles Markham put it years later. A divorce lawyer was dispatched to Buckingham Palace with the news that the Royal Family had two days to negotiate. An agreement was hastily made, and the Duke placed £15,000 in a trust fund for Beryl. His signature on the document guaranteed the income on bonds with a fixed-rate annuity, providing her with a yearly income of £500 from December 1929 to her death in August 1986. But the affair withstood Mansfield's threats despite an interval when Prince Henry was dispatched to Japan to confer the Order of the Garter on the young Emperor Hirohito.

Meantime, Prince George was more than ever a worry to his parents. The Canadian sojourn had not tempered what his brother Edward called his "unusual charm," which he soon exploited to win from his father release from his hated navy career. There followed various minor positions as a civil servant and a factory inspector, jobs George undertook with good will but only fair results. "There has been no regularity about the Prince's visits," complained one of the Home Office supervisors at the time. "Social and other functions have been allowed to take precedence over his inspection work, with the result that in some weeks [his duties were] entirely or almost entirely crowded out."

The reason for the uneven service is easily explained. "Being somewhat Bohemian by nature"—thus the Prince of Wales in a hilarious understatement—George often slipped away to the Riviera, romped on beaches by day and in casinos and clubs by night. An expert on the dance floor, he registered under an assumed name in a tango contest at Cannes and won first prize; that dance was also Edward's special expertise.

After the Noël Coward affair, George had various tempestuous intrigues with a roster of foreigners, including (among other talented black women then working in London) the American entertainer Florence Mills, whom he had seen onstage and quickly rushed to bed. But the most enduring, passionate and potentially the most perilous of George's liaisons from the standpoint of international relations was with José Evaristo Uriburu, the son of the Argentine ambassador to Great Britain. Uriburu, then in his twenties, had arrived in London with his parents and sisters and was studying at Cambridge when he met George at a diplomatic reception. The Prince and the ambassador's son were subsequently seen at the most fashionable soirees in Mayfair and Belgravia, and as a couple they spent many weekends at the country homes of several encouraging and sympathetic friends.

With his chiseled features, dark hair, provocative smile and seductive, heavy-lidded gaze, Uriburu could have been a Latin film star. But he was also highly intelligent, trilingual and groomed to follow in his father's ambassadorial footsteps. Señor Uriburu was therefore predictably concerned about his son, and although he considered Prince George a desirable guest at the consulate dining table, he did not feel quite so welcoming when the Prince emerged from José's bedroom at dawn. An altercation of operatic grandeur ensued between the older and younger Uriburus, resulting in two broken lamps, one bruised ego, a shattered relationship and the restoration of paternal primacy.

José, who tried unsuccessfully to settle the matter, was disconsolate when George told him their love affair was becoming politically embarrassing. The unhappy Uriburu was then sent back to Argentina, ostensibly to visit his grandmother for two months. But Princes fare better amid such melodrama, and George found comfort with an Italian aristocrat from the defunct royal house of Urbino and then with a Parisian architect. (George wrote passionate love letters to both Uriburu and the Frenchman, letters purchased years later, for obvious reasons, by the Royal Family.) As if these incidents were not enough to worry Buckingham Palace, George was then arrested for dancing rather too amorously at The Nut House, a gay nightclub, whence he and a boyfriend were spirited away by the police. Only when his identity was confirmed did the cell door at Bow Street discreetly swing open next morning on its well-oiled political hinges and the unembarrassed George stepped out, still luminous in full nighttime makeup.

Less innocently, the youngest Prince fell into a precarious habit during 1928 and 1929. An attractive, irresponsible American socialite named Kiki Whitney Preston introduced him to cocaine and morphine, to which he quickly became addicted; it was not a rare habit among the fast set but "a terrible and terrifying thing," as the Prince of Wales wrote to his father, adding in a letter to his mother that George "seems to lack all sense of knowing what is so obviously the wrong thing to do." To his credit, Edward attended George through a long and painful drug rehabilitation in 1929, and this won him even the King's praise: "Looking after him all those months must have been a great strain on you, and I think it was wonderful all you did for him."

The Duke of York, decent but dull like his father, was respectably married; otherwise, the King and Queen had good cause for anxiety about their sons. Even in the character of Prince Albert (thirty-three in 1928) there was much that was fearfully boyish and incompetent. More obviously, Edward (thirty-four), Henry (twenty-eight) and George (twenty-six) all seemed mired in a condition of protracted adolescence.

The core of the problem was that they had no real responsibilities, held no jobs and were accountable to no employer. Their father could only fume and scold, and to diminishing effect.

*   *   *

Additional evidence for this sad state of affairs occurred at the time of their father's grave illness in late 1928. On November 21, while Edward and Henry were still on safari, the King fell ill with a lung infection that was even worse than the bronchitis that had attacked him three years earlier. His smoking habit, never modified, was by now taking a graver toll, as it had on his father. The next day a streptococcal infection was diagnosed; pleurisy then set in, and soon the King was struggling for breath. By the twenty-sixth, the doctors feared the worst. Prime Minister Baldwin, aware of the bad history between father and son, sent a wire to the Prince of Wales in Africa: "We hope that all may go well, but if not, and you have made no attempt to return, it will profoundly shock public opinion." Prince Edward's reaction eventually led Tommy Lascelles to resign from his service: "I don't believe a word of it," said the Prince, tossing aside the telegram. "It's just some election dodge of old Baldwin's."

Lascelles was furious. "Sir, the King of England is dying, and if that means nothing to you, it means a great deal to us." And with that, as Lascelles recalled, "he looked at me, went out without a word, and spent the remainder of the evening in the successful seduction of a Mrs. Barnes, wife of the local Commissioner. He told me so himself next morning."

Finally, the Prince of Wales was persuaded, and he arrived in London on December 11, fearful that he might inherit the throne. He found his father barely conscious and near death from a rampant infection that was placing a dreadful strain on the heart. Lord Dawson, the physician who had cared for Edward VII, supervised a team of doctors who frantically tried to locate the source of an abscess in the King's chest cavity. On December 12, as the monarch began to fail, Dawson took a brilliantly calculated risk: plunging a syringe into what he reckoned was the precise spot of disease, he extracted a pint of gross fluid and thus saved his life. Two weeks passed, however, before an announcement of recovery was issued, and it was three months into the new year 1929 before King George was able to receive Baldwin in a regular audience. On February 9 the King was blithely allowed to resume smoking: thus two serious relapses, requiring additional procedures, occurred in May and July.

He was sixty-four but looked a decade older; in the years

remaining, he grew ever frailer, a man aging too speedily, often bent and breathless from the effort of a short walk. At the service of thanksgiving for his recovery on July 7, no one knew from his cheerful bravado that King George was suffering the pain of an open chest wound and would suffer a second relapse two days later.

During the King's convalescences in 1929—mostly at Bognor, on the south coast—he took comfort from the quiet devotion of Queen Mary who relayed neither her fears nor the doctor's reports to her children. They had to learn of their father's progress from doctors, nurses or Cabinet ministers. "Through all the anxiety," wrote the Duke of York to the Prince of Wales about their mother, "she has never once revealed her feelings to any of us. She is really far too reserved; she keeps too much locked up inside herself."

The King was also buoyed by the visits of the granddaughter on whom he doted shamelessly and whom the Queen, even at this stage, was taking under her tutelage. Three-year-old Princess Elizabeth (who was on the cover of *Time* magazine the week of April 21, 1929) could not easily manage her name: it came out "Lilibet," and so she was called forever after by her family. The King was (thus Queen Mary in her diary) "delighted to see her. . . . I played with Lilibet in the garden making sand pies!" This was perhaps a first for the sixty-two-year-old Queen, and it is amusing to picture her kneeling in a sandbox, her toque perfectly in place, ropes of pearls dangling over a little girl's toys, white-gloved hands shaping inedible pastries. Any similar scene had been unknown with Mary's own children.

Lilibet brought her grandfather to heel, too. When the Archbishop of Canterbury called on the King, he found him on all fours, the Princess riding his back, crying "Giddyap!" and pulling his beard to spur him on. Not long after, Grandpa substituted the real thing for himself: it was he who inspired her lifelong love of horses when he bought her a Shetland pony. Princess Elizabeth was a feisty little solo rider by the time she was four, obeying the injunctions of Henry Owen, the Duke of York's groom. When he urged her to "Curl in underneath" or "Keep on your guard," the Princess replied, "Yes, of course, Owen." Throughout her childhood he became something of a heroic oracle to her: "Owen says this" was a constant refrain or "Owen said to do that." This annoyed her father, who, when consulted on some household detail, told his daughter with some annoyance (and perhaps a bit of jealousy), "Don't ask me. Ask Owen. Who am I to make suggestions?"

According to Mabell Airlie, King George was fond of his two Lascelles grandsons, George and Gerald, "but Lilibet always came first in his affections. He used to play with her—a thing I never saw him do with his own children—and loved to have her by him. . . . She made his convalescence at Bognor bearable to him." And because his affection for her was so evident, she took some unprecedented liberties. It is impossible, for example, to imagine any of the King's sons calling after him, as did the child Elizabeth when he had left the room, "Grandfather, you forgot to close the door!" Invariably patient and jovial with Lilibet, the King was still the King: he adored her but not her taste in entertainment. A few years later, having been asked what film he would like to see when she left the palace after a visit of several days, George muttered, "Anything except that damned Mouse!"

His humor could be saltier, too. Sir Owen Morshead, the King's librarian, recalled when the people of Bognor asked if they might add "Regis" to the name of their town (thus making the municipality "royal" in honor of their patient). "Bugger Bognor!" grumbled the old sailor in reply; he would sooner forget the place. Ah, yes, the King's secretary reported to the waiting delegation, His Majesty would be pleased to grant their request.

During the King's prolonged convalescence that summer of 1929, he was prudently denied one bit of family news. The Prince of Wales had wearied of the reliable and steadying Freda Dudley Ward, to whom in any case he had been unfaithful for years. Now, following his preference for Americans, he had fallen for the twenty-four-year-old society belle Thelma (pronounced Telma) Furness, who became even more critical a player in the Prince's life than Freda.

Thelma was one of three girls born to the American diplomat Harry Hays Morgan and his wife Laura Kilpatrick, a general's daughter. Her twin was Gloria (Mrs. Reginald) Vanderbilt; their older sister was Consuelo, then married to Benjamin Thaw, Jr., First Secretary at the American embassy in London. Small and slim, with penetrating eyes and fair skin, Thelma wore her dark hair in a tight, fashionable wave. Her angular features and a tendency to purse her lips sometimes made her look rather severe, and the Prince of Wales might first have been struck by this deceptively sharp, chic appearance. In fact, as he soon learned, she was an aggressive but sprightly creature, frivolous, amusing but not very bright, independent and a trifle bossy—a woman who had managed a great deal of life in her twenty-four years.

Born August 23, 1905, she was married at sixteen to a man twice her age whom she divorced three years later. She then settled briefly in California, where she had a romance with the much older actor Richard Bennett (father of Constance, Barbara and Joan). In the midst of this affair she swept off to Paris where she met the steamship magnate Marmaduke "Duke" Viscount Furness, a sporty, cigar-chomping lummox she married in 1926. He was twenty-two years her senior, and by 1929 the wedding bonds had slipped considerably: the Viscount pursued quick foxes and fast women, and Lady Furness was available for romance. Into the breach stepped Edward, Prince of Wales, who was only eleven years her senior. They met at the Marquess of Londonderry's summer ball, not long after Lady Furness had given birth to a son.

"The Prince seemed to me to be winsomely handsome," Thelma recalled years later.

> He was the quintessence of charm. And after the swaggering earthiness of Duke, the Prince's natural shyness and reserve had a distinct appeal. We sat by the fireplace and had cocktails, while the Prince chatted pleasantly about the small things one can discuss without strain or effort. In time he asked me where I would like to go for dinner. We decided on the Hotel Splendide, which was famous for its cuisine and its Viennese orchestra.

Had Lady Furness pondered more deeply, she might have realized what many saw in the Prince of Wales: that his charm was not in fact natural but was rather like an effect he could summon when he wished to be liked. It also had more to do with his lightning shifts of mood than with any spellbinding force of character. A man of the moment, he was often quickly transported from boredom to winsomeness to intense concern to tiresome frivolity.

Edward and Thelma dined and danced thrice more within the next week and were soon seen dancing at the Embassy and the Kit Kat clubs. Lord and Lady Furness even invited the Prince to dinner parties at their home. Such was the solid front of appearance that characterized many typical upper-class marriages at a time when the legal requirements for divorce were still messily undesirable. And so once again the Prince was attracted to a married woman, maternal yet domineering; once again he seemed to have a ready-made family to adopt him. Just as he had loved to frolic with Freda's two young daughters, so he grinned over Thelma's infant son. In fact, Edward himself was something of a boy with her: he bought two teddy bears, one for each of them to take along as talismans whenever they were separated. He called her Toodles; to her, he was the Little Man. It was all terribly cute—and dangerous, for irresponsible Thelma encouraged the worst of Edward's bad habits: tardiness, self-indulgence and subordination of others' comfort to one's own.

In the spring of 1930, Lord and Lady Furness were on safari in Africa; so, as it happened, was Prince Edward. He was joined by Thelma, who was, as she wrote, "inexorably swept from the accustomed moorings of caution. Each night I felt more completely possessed by our love, carried ever more swiftly into uncharted seas of feeling, content to let the Prince chart the course, heedless of where the voyage would end." But hindsight gave her memory a rosy glow: for most of the safari the Prince was gravely ill with malaria.

King George, who knew of the romance by this time, might have appreciated Thelma's preference for nautical metaphors, but he did not countenance the affair. But for once he tried to comprehend Edward's melancholy, and he yielded to his son's desire to move into Fort Belvedere, a neglected eighteenth-century property in Windsor Great Park. "What could you possibly want that queer old place for?" the King asked. "Those damn weekends, I suppose. Well, if you want it, you can have it." By the summer of 1930, Toodles and the Little Man were at the dour, castellated Fort every weekend.

The place was no castle; it was actually rather a small

house, and the few guest bedrooms were more cramped than cozy. But there Prince Edward worked tirelessly on repairs and improvements, toiling in the gardens, clearing undergrowth, planning and planting. He added a swimming pool and tennis courts, and he supervised the redesign and modernization of various rooms to create the atmosphere of a lodge. Fort Belvedere would be, for the next six years, Edward's favorite residence. He loved it, he wrote, "as I loved no other material thing—perhaps because it was so much of my own creation. More and more it became for me a peaceful, almost enchanted anchorage."

As for Thelma, she was a jolly hostess with others and an attentive companion when alone with the Prince, enduring his bagpipe-playing and childish games (tossing gramophone records like boomerangs, for example, to the great risk of lamps and statuary). She tried to curb his excessive late-night tippling, supplementing the knitting he had learned from Queen Mary with an introduction to the art of needlepoint ("The hand that holds the needle cannot hold the brandy snifter!"). Her father, who often visited, read aloud to them from Dickens or Sir Walter Scott, and the Duke and Duchess of York were among the frequent friendly visitors, ice-skating or swimming as the season allowed and driving over from nearby Royal Lodge, a country retreat they took over and began to refurbish in 1931.

But life was not so merry for the King. In January 1931, his eldest sister Louise, the Princess Royal, died—a shock followed two weeks later by the death of Sir Charles Cust, whom he had known since their navy days together. Cust was one of the very few who could speak boldly to the King. Shortly after the accession of George V, Cust was seated in the billiard room at Balmoral, poring over books he had drawn from the shelves and piling them hither and thither on the floor.

"I say, Charles," said the newly anointed King, "is that the way you treat my books?"

"*Your* books!" replied his friend with a laugh. "Why, you haven't in the whole of this house got a book that's worth reading. Your so-called library is nothing but beautifully bound piffle!" Which was true of the King's library forever after, although he tried to improve the selection by asking that interesting books be added and the worthless removed—a project in which he took no more interest than he did in reading any of them.

Cust's death was followed in March 1931 by that of Lord Stamfordham, the King's trusted confidant and private secretary. "I shall miss him terribly," the King admitted. "His loss is irreparable. . . . He was the most loyal friend I ever had. . . . He taught me to be a King." It was, he wrote in his diary, "a bad beginning for a new year. I feel very depressed."

But his sorrow was brightened by the presence of another grandchild. On August 21, 1930, the Duchess of York gave Princess Elizabeth a sister, born amid a terrifying thunderstorm at Glamis Castle, the Strathmores' ancestral home. That autumn she was christened Margaret Rose. "I shall call her Bud," said Lilibet. "She's not a Rose yet." The two sisters were taken from the house in Piccadilly by Clara Knight for strolls in Green and Hyde parks, but they rarely met those their own age. "Other children always had an enormous fascination," recalled their nanny, "and the little girls used to smile shyly at those they liked the look of. They would have loved to speak to them and make friends, but this was never encouraged. I often have thought it a pity."

And so it was. The little princesses had a cozy but unnaturally isolated home life; life-size toys and wooden animals were their only companions except for each other. They did not know the normal interchanges of children with other children, the need for patience and unselfishness, the pleasure of gaining new friends, the need to deal with sacrifice and challenge, the necessity of coping with others' feelings and antipathies. In this regard their childhood was no different from that of any monarch.

But there was one critical nonroyal influence on Princess Elizabeth. In 1930, when her baby sister was still in the cradle, there came into Lilibet's life another Margaret, one Miss MacDonald, always called Bobo. She was twenty-one, redheaded, trim and bespectacled, the spinster daughter of a Scottish railwayman. Engaged by the Duchess of York as a nursery maid for Princess Elizabeth, Bobo recommended her married sister Ruby for the same job with Princess Margaret. These sisters transferred with their charges from the nursery to the boudoir, becoming dressers and confidantes to the royal pair; Ruby remained in her job for thirty-one years, Bobo for sixty-three. "Teach that child not to fidget!" Queen Mary commanded Bobo. Thus from the age of four, Elizabeth was instructed to curtsy to her grandparents, the King and Queen, to keep still in church and in the presence of adults, to wave with dignity, to smile on command for cameras and even to suppress her need to go to the lavatory.

On another occasion the Queen delivered a sharp reprimand to Lilibet when she commanded a visitor her own age to treat her like a Royal ("Curtsy, girl!"). Another scolding followed the day she felt she was being ignored; Lilibet tugged at the sleeve of an adult and piped up, "Royalty speaking!" Her grandmother was quick with a reprimand: "Royalty has never been an excuse for bad manners." These displays of childish self-importance Queen Mary would not sustain, nor was she slow to point them out to the Duchess. There was, then, a real danger that the articulate, self-assured little Princess, taking a cue from the gravity of her parents, might take herself rather too seriously too soon.

But help was on the way in the person of a bright and perceptive Scotswoman named Marion Crawford, who in May 1932 (after a one-month trial period the previous year) was engaged as the governess to Princesses Elizabeth and Margaret. This meant a total of three servants for Elizabeth alone—a nanny, a dresser and a tutor.

Then twenty-two, Crawford had worked briefly as tutor to the Duchess of York's niece, and she so impressed the family that she was asked to come to London—but only for a month, it was agreed. Crawford intended to return to Edinburgh where she hoped to teach poor and underprivileged children. That aspiration would never be realized. She remained in the service of Princesses Elizabeth and Margaret for seventeen years.

Arriving at Royal Lodge, Crawford noticed at once a highly ordered, even regimented household. First she was interviewed by the Duchess in her white and yellow boudoir, then the Duke in his dark, wood-paneled bedroom, decorated with all the furnishings of a ship's cabin. Princess Elizabeth, Crawford was told, adhered to a strict schedule—a virtue the Duke had inherited from his father. She was awakened promptly at 7:30, had breakfast in the nursery, and then for fifteen minutes saw her parents before being turned over to nanny Knight for a morning of quiet games and stories. At 11:00 she was given a glass of orangeade and a cookie. Lunch followed at precisely 1:15, sometimes with her parents. Afternoons were spent outdoors, with sedate sojourns in a park (where Lilibet waved graciously when Alah so commanded) or proper ladylike games in a garden; if the weather was inclement, there was instruction in drawing or dancing. The Duchess arrived for an hour's play with Lilibet and Margaret at 5:30, supper followed, and promptly at 7:15 the Princess was put to bed. This unvarying routine prevailed at 145 Piccadilly and at Royal Lodge.

Crawford had arrived late in the afternoon, and it was the children's bedtime when she was at last introduced to Alah in the nursery. The nanny at once imagined that a competitor for the children's affection had stepped over the threshold. Sensing the old retainer's reserve and apprehension, the governess was, as she recalled, "very careful not to tread on her toes." She then met Princess Elizabeth. "A small figure with a mop of curls sat up in bed," Crawford remembered. "She had tied the cords of her dressing gown to the knobs of the old-fashioned bed and was busy driving her team" of imaginary horses.

"This is Miss Crawford," said Alah coldly.

"How do you do," said the Princess with precocious formality. Then, Crawford recalled, "she gave me a long, comprehensive look I had seen once before on the face of the Duke, and she went on, 'Why have you no hair?' " Crawford pulled off her hat to reveal a short, neat cut of red hair: "It's an Eton crop," she said, and with that Lilibet picked up her reins again. "Do you usually drive in bed?" asked the governess.

"I mostly go once or twice round the park before I go to sleep, you know. It exercises my horses. Are you going to stay with us?"

"For a little while, anyway."

Alah unhitched the team and pulled up the child's bedclothes. "If ever I am queen," Lilibet said, rather as if that were not in doubt, "I shall make a law that there must be no riding on Sundays. Horses should have a rest, too." There was a slight pause. "Good night," said the child. So ended Crawford's first audience. The next morning she saw Margaret, who was not yet two and not nearly so formal as her sister.

The first minor skirmish occurred within days of Crawford's

relocation. Little Elizabeth routinely called the various servants by their first names, and so she addressed her governess as Marion. But the tutor thought this imprudent for the sake of discipline and corrected the child. The matter was solved only when they were playing ball, and the Princess dropped catch after catch. "Oh, Crawfie!" she cried in exasperation and then looked up with a pleased expression. "There! That's what I'll call you."

Within two weeks of her arrival, the grandparents came to inspect the new recruit. King George prodded the ground with his walking stick and then muttered, "For goodness' sake, teach Margaret and Lilibet to write a decent hand, that's all I ask you. Not one of my children can write properly. I like a hand with some character in it." Due attention was thenceforth given to penmanship.

While the royal grandparents liked and attended the young Princesses, Margaret seems never to have had the same warm attachment to them that Elizabeth enjoyed, perhaps because she was once more removed from the succession; perhaps, too, because she was always rather more frisky and irrepressible than her older sister. Asked years later about the legend that King George V was known to the Princesses as "Grandpa England," Princess Margaret replied it was nonsense: "We were much too frightened of him to call him anything but Grandfather." As for Queen Mary, Margaret said later that a visit with her brought "a hollow, empty feeling to the pit of the stomach." There was good reason for her discomfiture, for her grandmother had often said to her as a child, "How small you are! Why don't you grow up?"

As she did in all her assignments, Princess Elizabeth from childhood approached everything with the utmost gravity. When Crawfie told her to put the next day's clothes at her bedside and her shoes under the bed, the child arranged everything with military tidiness. She lined up her toys as if for inspection, folded her hair ribbons neatly, put lessons and books in the proper places. She was invariably well behaved —sometimes unnaturally so, Crawfie thought; there was an exaggerated seriousness in the child's manner. Princess Elizabeth sat upright in an open carriage, her back not touching the cushions, in imitation of Queen Mary.

Not so Margaret, who was careless, casual, often "charmingly naughty," as Crawfie wrote in a memoir. Both children were memorably pretty, with crystal blue eyes, the purest complexions and brown hair flecked with red and gold. But there was a vivacity about the younger sister, a puckishness Lilibet never manifested; small wonder, then, that she created more mischief—and sometimes got Lilibet into it, too. "Neither was above taking a whack at her adversary if roused," according to Crawford, "and Lilibet was quick with her left hook! Margaret was more of a close-in fighter, known to bite on occasions. More than once have I been shown a hand bearing the royal teeth marks." Sent to her room for some impishness, Margaret was once recalled by her mother: "Come along, dear, you need not stay there any longer. I'm sure you're going to be good now, aren't you?" To which the child replied, "No, I'm naughty still. And I'm going to go on being naughty." It was a promise she fulfilled, some would say, for decades.

By her teen years Margaret also showed a keen appreciation for colorful, fashionable clothes, doubtless because until then her wardrobe was identical to her sister's. The Yorks clothed their daughters like twins, perhaps to minimize the age difference and create a kind of parity between them. "The Duke was very proud of Lilibet," according to Crawfie, "but in Margaret he took great delight." He was (thus Lady Donaldson) "bewitched" by this little pixie, by her precocious gift for mimicry and her lack of shyness in singing and dancing on command. His pleasure had to be inferred, however, for while the Duchess was a loving mother, the Duke did not show affection easily. When Margaret ran to embrace him or asked to be held in his arms, Crawfie remembered, he was inept. Perhaps because he had so little experience of affection as a child, Prince Albert was, as Crawfie saw, "not a demonstrative man."

Their governess was quite serious about the girls' lessons, but in this she received little support from her employers. "I had the feeling that the Duke and Duchess were not overconcerned with the education of their daughters. They wanted most for them a happy childhood, with lots of pleasant memories stored up against the days that might come—and later, happy marriages." Otherwise, it was thought, dancing, drawing, music appreciation and etiquette would be enough. But the

Yorks gave the governess a free hand. Six days weekly, mornings were devoted to the usual grade school subjects, but special tutors were brought in for lessons in French and constitutional history; afternoons were alternately given to music and art. On Queen Mary's advice, history, Bible study and royal genealogy were later added to the program.

Crawfie also felt that the girls needed more of "the outside world, of which they knew so little," but the Duke and Duchess, perhaps in reaction to the ceaseless socializing of the girls' uncles, stressed the virtues of home life and kept their daughters well sheltered. The Prince of Wales loved to visit his nieces, and he often arrived with a cache of toys from Woolworth's, their favorite store. But although Elizabeth and Margaret were frequently escorted to the palace, they were rarely brought to York House for a visit. Perhaps their parents hesitated because they were aware that the little girls might encounter a small platoon of guests behaving rather too gaily. Such fears were well founded, for the girls' uncles led a merry social life.

One such event eventually found its way into history books. For a weekend of hunting on January 10 and 11, 1931, Thelma Furness invited a half-dozen friends—including her sister and brother-in-law, Consuelo and Benjamin Thaw, and the Prince of Wales—to her country home, Burrough Court, Melton Mowbray, Leicestershire. But earlier that week Consuelo's mother-in-law fell ill, and she went to Paris to nurse her. Thelma therefore recruited as replacements an American couple she had met some time before.

Ernest Simpson was born in Chicago to an American mother and an English father, worked in the family shipping business, and eventually took British citizenship and moved to London with his wife Wallis, whom he had married in 1928. He was a formidably proper, somewhat dull fellow, much less jovial than his sister, Maud Kerr-Smiley, who had given shelter to Freda Dudley Ward that frightening night in war-torn London when she accidentally met the Prince of Wales. People did not have very vivid impressions of Ernest Simpson; he was variously described by those who knew him as "very polite, very correct, but an absolute jackass . . . a feeble boor [who] made no impact . . . a puppet" who worried over losing any royal social connections. Such were not the judgments made of his wife.

Mrs. Simpson's mother, Alice Montague, was a well-born beauty from a prominent old Virginia family. But the Montagues had fallen on hard times, and only a good pedigree, refined speech, proper etiquette and a few pieces of family silver survived by the time Alice married Teackle Warfield in June 1895. He was the penniless scion of a respectable family from Baltimore, a city as rigid as New York in its social liturgies and its idolatry of the right connections. Bessiewallis War-field, called Wallis from childhood, was born on June 19, 1896, high in the hills of Blue Ridge Summit, Pennsylvania, where her parents had gone because of Teackle's ill health. Alice's fortunes became even more unstable five months later when her husband died of virulent tuberculosis.

The widow Warfield worked hard to support herself and her daughter, and for a decade they further economized by sharing the modest quarters of Teackle's family. Lacking the means to enter the polite society of which they believed themselves worthy and to which the family names would have admitted her, Wallis was raised by her mother in an atmosphere of deprived propriety, dependent on the occasional handout from relatives and surrounded by neighbors and schoolmates who were more solvent but less polished. Her friends were better dressed, lived in larger homes, had luxuries and servants. And here was the basis for Wallis's lifelong ambition to improve her status: from childhood she needed to prove that she was just as deserving of privilege, that she belonged in a class from which she had been, by a trick of fate, unfairly excluded.

In 1908, Alice remarried and moved, and with help from her grandparents Wallis was sent to boarding school. By 1914 she was eighteen, a senior at the Oldfields School in Glencoe, Maryland, where she was admired by teachers and classmates alike—not for her academic achievement, which was unremarkable, but for her vibrant personality. Clever rather than profound, she had a quick sense of humor, a sharp memory, an irrepressible vitality, unerring poise and all the right social skills. She also had a certain fearlessness and did not suffer fools gladly. At the school cotillion in her last year, she knew how a canny choice of color in wardrobe, makeup and costume jewelry could compensate for her essentially plain features; she therefore emphasized her slender, slim-hipped figure, softened with powder, pencil and lip rouge the line of her angular jaw, highlighted her expressive eyes and splendid complexion and alternately arranged her raven hair in an elegant bob or a tight wave. She also had the give-and-take of bright conversation, and she knew better than many prettier girls how to attract and keep the attention of boys she wanted to meet.

After graduation, Wallis was determined to improve her lot, and she seized her first opportunity—a handsome naval officer named Earl Winfield Spencer, Jr., whom she married in November 1916 when she was twenty. But soon "Win" Spencer began to drink heavily, and by the time he was transferred to Hong Kong in 1921, the marriage was effectively over. Wallis remained in Washington, where there followed a close friendship (and perhaps more) with Felipe Espil, the First Secretary of the Argentine Embassy and, as it happened, a friend of the Uriburu family. Wallis and Felipe spoke of marriage, but he was frank: he needed a wife with money to fulfill his ambition of being Argentine ambassador to Washington. Espil found such a woman, and in 1924 he married her.

Wallis, distraught, sailed to Hong Kong, hoping for a reconciliation with "Win" Spencer. This proved hopeless—he was by now a confirmed alcoholic—but she remained in China, living and traveling with her new and eventually lifelong friends, Herman and Katherine Rogers. Her life was essentially peripatetic, crowded with undemanding social patter, recreations and dinner parties among American and English businessmen, diplomats and their families. By 1926 she was back in Washington where she won an uncontested divorce from Spencer and met the respectable but married Ernest Aldridge Simpson, who was about to obtain British citizenship. Wallis, recalled the first Mrs. Simpson, "was really a very helpful woman. First she helped herself to my clothes and my apartment, and then she helped herself to my husband." The Simpsons were divorced in 1927, and by the spring of 1928, Wallis and Ernest were courting in New York and London, where he had business.

Her attraction to him is easy to understand, for he was a stable, reasonably handsome man who offered money, respectability and security, just the combination of qualities to place her higher on the international social ladder. "I can't go wandering on the rest of my life,'' she wrote to her mother after Ernest proposed marriage, ''and I really feel so tired of fighting the world all alone and with no money. Also 32 doesn't seem so young when you see all the really fresh youthful faces one has to compete against. So I shall just settle down to a fairly comfortable old age.'' They were married in London in July 1928.

Wallis was the ideal companion for the ambitious Simpson. Although not beautiful, she was strong-willed and conspicuous in company, a perfect hostess and an excellent conversationalist whose brittle banter appealed to the rich and influential socialites Ernest believed were good for his business. She made certain she was up to date and could talk a little about everything; thus she read the newspaper headlines, flipped through the pages of the latest best-sellers, and strained to hear every bit of society gossip. Prudently, she made no effort to affect an English accent, and most found her aristocratic Baltimore/Hunt Country diction rather quaint.

Willing to state opinions but just as quick to learn, she was assertive but not uncharming. Chips Channon, always glad to identify and puncture pomposity, could not do so when he met Wallis at Emerald Cunard's home. Channon found Mrs. Simpson ''jolly, plain, intelligent, quiet, unpretentious and unprepossessing,'' which from him was high praise. Her husband soon found other qualities besides those that appealed to him: ''She had a terrible temper,'' Simpson said many years later, after he had taken a third wife. He believed that all her husbands were afraid of her and added, ''I know most of the time I was.''

There is every reason to believe that Ernest and Wallis were genuinely fond of each other, as their subsequent conduct during difficult times suggests. Wallis may have had a temper in private, but there is no evidence from anyone that she was violent, much less psychoneurotic. But according to Herman Rogers there was one aspect of her life that goes far in explaining her temper, her need to control and the nature of her first two marriages—and even, as will be seen, the third. In 1955 when Wallis engaged the American writer Cleveland Amory to assist with her memoirs, Amory felt he had to supplement her memories with those of longtime friends, and so he spent weeks with her oldest confidant, Herman Rogers, at his homes in London and Cannes.

Although he and Amory knew that the information had to remain privileged, Rogers confided what Wallis herself had told him: "No man is *ever* allowed to touch me below the Mason-Dixon line," by which she obviously meant the restricted geography of her own body. On another occasion she also told Rogers, "You know, Herman, I was married twice before I met [the Prince of Wales], but I never slept with either of my husbands."

To many people Wallis's statements to Rogers might sound incredible, but there would have been no reason for her to invent such intimate, provocative and somewhat compromising details about herself. Over the years there was some speculation (and some have made the speculation a settled conclusion) that Wallis was born a hermaphrodite—that to some degree she had the sex organs and hormonal chemistry of both a woman and a man, a rare conundrum that is sometimes corrected at birth, frequently later. If true, this condition would certainly explain her insistent rejection of conventional heterosexual intercourse and the presence of those masculine features that many noticed throughout her lifetime. James Pope-Hennessy, the scholarly biographer of Queen Mary, was not alone in his estimation of Wallis Simpson as "an American woman *par excellence* [except for] the suspicion that she is not a woman at all." But perhaps he went too far. Various psychological or hormonal conditions may account for a woman's "manly" characteristics. There is no evidence to support the provocative thesis of hermaphroditism, nor can the details of Wallis Simpson's medical history be ascertained. Yet with all that caution, her own statements on her unusual sexual and marital history remain.

As for Spencer and Simpson, the question naturally arises why these two men would marry a woman who apparently established specific regulations about the severe limitations of marital intimacy. In the case of Earl Spencer, the revelation may have come as a shock; this would certainly help explain the decline of the marriage and his rapid descent into excessive drinking.

The matter is somewhat more complicated in the case of Ernest Simpson. Wallis was a socially desirable woman of consummate charm and perfect skills as hostess, and it was of great importance to him to have such a companion in London, where he hoped to rise in the best professional and social circles. By his own admission, he feared her and her temper; he may indeed have contracted something of a marriage of convenience and intended, like many Englishmen he admired, to go his own way in the matter of a passional life. Or he may not have required more than whatever was meted out to him. Finally, there remains the fact that the means of personal (not to say sexual) satisfaction are of course various and that many people sustain restrictions and demands placed on them by partners because the marriage or liaison has other compensations and because they secretly harbor the expectation or hope that in time a partner's preferences may change.

It is also crucial to recall that until the end of the twentieth century, there was an enormous amount of ignorance about sex and very little in print or discussion about it. People did not marry primarily for sex but for other emotional, professional and social reasons, and premarital cohabitation and sexual experimentation were not the commonplace they later became.

As it happened, Wallis Simpson was not at all eager to accept Lady Furness's invitation: she had a frightful cold, and she resented the condescending tutelage offered by her sister-in-law, Maud Kerr-Smiley, on how to behave in the Prince's presence. But Ernest insisted, and off the Simpsons went for a weekend in the country. In a letter to her aunt Bessie Merryman the following week, her introduction to the Prince is mentioned only casually, between comments on her indisposition and the difficulty of finding good servants in London.

That she was not unduly impressed with him is indicated by her reply to his first conversation with her. Was it true, he asked, that every American home enjoyed the benefit of central heating? "I am sorry, Sir," she replied, "but you have disappointed me. Every American woman who comes to your country is always asked that same question. I had hoped for something more original from the Prince of Wales." There was a deafening silence in the room until everyone saw the blush and then the smile on Edward's face. To a man rebuffed by his father and distanced by his mother, a man who relished the company of strong, resolute, original (and married) women, she was magnificent.*

"Wallis and I became great friends," recalled Thelma Furness years later, offering a description of her in 1931:

> She was not beautiful; in fact she was not even pretty. But she had a distinct charm and a sharp sense of humour. Her dark hair was parted in the middle. Her eyes, alert and eloquent, were her best feature. . . . Her hands were large; they did not move gracefully, and I thought she used them too much when she attempted to emphasize a point.

Nevertheless, Thelma and Wallis, who had already met at parties given by other Americans in London, had much in common (they might have passed for sisters, there was so close a resemblance). Their friendship flourished for almost three more years, during which time Thelma was still first in the Prince's affections and his relationship with Wallis Simpson was uncomplicated and cordial. For the remainder of 1931 the Simpsons and the Prince of Wales met only three more times at other gatherings, and their conversations were brief, casual and unextraordinary. Reciprocal dinner parties at the Simpson flat in Bryanston Court were limited by their budget and by Wallis's recurring ulcer attacks in 1931. Prince Edward was not a guest there until January 1932, after which he invited them to Fort Belvedere for a weekend.

In any case, the Prince of Wales was off on a three-month trade-boosting tour of South America from mid-January to late April 1931. His brother George accompanied him in order to visit his old flame José Uriburu in Buenos Aires. On June 10, Wallis was presented to the King and Queen at a Buckingham Palace garden party; her momentary, distant introduction, one on a long line of Americans, owed to the advocacy of Thelma Furness.

*   *   *

---

* Actually, Wallis and her first husband had been introduced to the Prince of Wales years before. Returning from his Australian tour, Edward had been honored at an American navy reception on April 7, 1920, in San Diego. Lieutenant and Mrs. Spencer were two on a long receiving line. She recalled the event; the Prince did not.

The Prince's continuing affair with Thelma prompted a confrontation with his father in March 1932. Informing Edward that "the whole of London" was talking about the relationship, the King warned him that "the conscience of England" would not sustain such a scandalous life—even of so popular a figure as the Prince of Wales. When Edward replied that people were more tolerant in 1932, the King denied this was so, insisting, as the memorandum of his secretary Lord Wigram detailed,

> that the days when royal princes kept well-known mistresses and had families by them were gone forever, and that the people of England looked for a decent home life in their Royal House. Young men sowed their wild oats, but was not the Prince of Wales at 38 rather beyond that age? His liaison with Lady Furness was a well-known fact. The Prince did not attempt to deny that Lady Furness was his mistress.

The King's main concern was the Prince of Wales as heir to the throne, on which he believed the people wished a married man to sit. Well, replied Edward, the only woman he wanted to marry was Freda Dudley Ward, "but the King said that he did not think this would do," as Wigram noted.

And so the matter stood. King George got nowhere, and when he turned to the business of the country, he faced even more trouble. Since 1931, Britain had been in the throes of the terrible worldwide Depression, and every town seemed affected—the industrial areas were particularly hit. Confidence in British exports and shipping failed, and the pound continued to be devalued. Almost three million people (twenty-five percent of the total labor force) were unemployed, and in London many great private residences were sold and turned into hotels. Yet the class system was still triumphant. One percent of the population owned sixty-two percent of the nation's wealth, and ten percent of the people owned ninety-one percent. Both fascist and communist rallies were held in parks and squares; five thousand jobless workers staged a demonstration south of the Thames at Battersea Town Hall; angry postal workers stopped traffic in the West End; and civil servants joined massive protest marches. Nowhere was there any visible sign of stability.

In August 1931, the Labour government of Prime Minister

Ramsay MacDonald collapsed after a split in his Cabinet, which proposed tax increases, unemployment cuts and wage reductions for civil servants, police, teachers and the military. Twice, MacDonald went to Buckingham Palace to tender his resignation, but the King prevailed on him—with the approval of Conservative and Liberal party leaders Stanley Baldwin and Herbert Samuel—to head a coalition National Government (which was actually almost wholly Conservative). In September the gold standard was abandoned in favor of sterling, and the value of the pound dropped by twenty-five percent.

During this turmoil the King was widely and wrongly accused of partisanship. Why, many complained, did he not consult the majority of the Labour Party instead of summarily backing MacDonald and proceeding with plans for a coalition? The truth was that the King acted constitutionally: as long as MacDonald was a duly elected Prime Minister, the King was neither obliged nor able to consult others without an expressed mandate from MacDonald himself, who was willing to stay on.

As George's biographers have detailed, there was a crisis caused by the necessity of hasty action. The nation's fiscal reserves were ebbing away, foreign investors lost confidence by the hour, and the governor of the Bank of England openly warned that national bankruptcy was imminent. The King did not have the luxury of time on his side, and so he could not pursue the prescribed course of action—to accept MacDonald's resignation and call for a general election. As it happened, the National Government had an impressive collection of talent, and the nation, while still in the grip of a general Depression, avoided anarchy and chaos.

That the British Empire was in decline had long been evident. In October, Mahatma Gandhi, barefoot and dressed in his familiar loincloth and simple drape, was led along the carpeted corridors of Buckingham Palace to take tea with the King and Emperor. With his consummate politeness but admirable firmness, Gandhi informed King George that India must be independent and that membership in a commonwealth was acceptable but not in an Empire. "Remember, Mr. Gandhi," said the King, his Hanoverian blood rising, "I won't have any attacks on my Empire!" With a smile, Gandhi replied, "I must not be drawn into a political argument in Your Majesty's palace after receiving Your Majesty's hospitality." On one important matter, however, the King and the pacifist were united: they both condemned the racism that characterized the British in India.

Just thirty years after Queen Victoria's death, the Empire that had touched every part of the world was now in swift decline. That December 1932, the Statute of Westminster formalized the end of the old Imperial mission and enacted laws based on the spirit of the Imperial Conference of 1926. Hitherto, colonial policy was established by Downing Street. Acting on ministerial advice, the monarch appointed viceroys and governors-general. Henceforth, the parliaments of the dominions would elect their own leaders and legislate without reference to the United Kingdom; contrariwise, the British Parliament could not legislate for any dominion without its consent. However grandly some colonial Prime Ministers spoke of their loyal ties to the monarchy, the Crown was now little more than a vague symbol within a free Commonwealth whose connections were for economic, not patriotic, reasons.

But there was one moment of national sentiment in that chaotic year 1932, and, as so increasingly often, it depended on confirming the King as a public figure.

Alert more than ever to the power of radio, Clive Wigram (who had succeeded Lord Stamfordham as His Majesty's Private Secretary) urged the King to accept an invitation from the BBC to deliver a Christmas message. Ever since he had stood before a microphone at the British Exhibition at Wembley, the King had staunchly resisted efforts to bring him back for a return engagement on the wireless. He scarcely recognized the existence even of newspapers, the King said in 1932 when the topic of a holiday speech was again set before him. Why should he ruin his Christmas dinner at Sandringham for the sake of modernity?* His protest was not quite ingenuous, as it happened. The King and Sir Clive regularly supplied *The Times* with advance copies of the monarch's speeches and enlisted the help of its editorial staff in making revisions so that he might communicate more effectively.

Now Wigram had a ready reply to the King's hesitation.

---

* It was almost impossible to prerecord for the radio with any quality in 1932; only live transmissions were audible, and these were not invariably clear.

Rudyard Kipling had drafted a few sentences for His Majesty to read as a Christmas address. Would he not just have a look at them? There was a clear allusion to the Statute of Westminster, to the needs of the Empire or the Commonwealth, whatever it was; no one was quite sure. In any case, would Christmas not be the proper moment for the King to reassert his primacy?

For a week before the holiday, King George read the speech aloud over and over until even Queen Mary and the Prince of Wales were gazing heavenward in bored exasperation, mouthing the words they, too, knew by heart.

Then, at 3:50 on Christmas afternoon, the King's country-gentleman voice—modest, clear and avuncular—was heard, broadcast from a cramped and ugly little room underneath the staircase at Sandringham.

Through one of the marvels of modern science, I am enabled this Christmas Day to speak to all my peoples throughout the Empire. I take it as a good omen that the wireless should have reached its present perfection at a time when the Empire has been linked in closer union, for it offers us immense possibilities to make that union closer still.

It may be that our future will lay upon us more than one stern test. Our past will have taught us how to meet it unshaken. For the present, the work to which we are all equally bound is to arrive at a reasoned tranquillity within our borders, to regain prosperity without self-seeking, and to carry with us those whom the burdens of past years have disheartened or overborne.

My life's aim has been to serve as I might toward those ends. Your loyalty, your confidence in me, has been my abundant reward. I speak now from my home and from my heart to you all: to men and women so cut off by the snows, the desert or the sea that only voices out of the air can reach them; to those cut off from fuller life by blindness, sickness or infirmity, and to those who are celebrating this day with their children and their grandchildren—to all, to each, I wish a happy Christmas. God bless you.

Twenty million Britons heard the Kipling speech read that day by King George, and perhaps ten times that number listened when the BBC later relayed it worldwide; within three days more than two thousand newspapers and twenty-five thousand columns of newsprint were devoted to it. Thus was born a new monarchical tradition, the Christmas Day address.

The *Daily Express* was certainly a trifle hysterical with its headline two days later—WORLD'S GREATEST BROADCAST— but there was no doubt that for the moment the King was a triumphant celebrity, eclipsing even the Prince of Wales. Why, the King seemed in everyone's home, gushed newspapers: His Majesty was in the humblest parlor as well as the grandest mansion. He was no longer such a remote figure, glimpsed only in the distance from photographs and the rare newsreels, no longer the distant man on the balcony of Buckingham Palace. He seemed closer than Greta Garbo or Ronald Colman.

Only with the passing of many years would it seem that the King had been quite right in recognizing that the "marvel of modern science" was not an unmixed blessing. Indeed, Walter Bagehot might have said that the blessing had a blight: he might have warned that once the public had heard the King's voice, they would want more, and more often. And that the media, as the instruments of mass communication were not yet called, would certainly give the public what was demanded. Television was far from the commonplace it later became, but it did exist in laboratories and on factory drawing boards in 1932, and within five years there would be a "visual broadcast" in London, the machine itself unmarketed only because of the subsequent World War II.

King George rose from the makeshift studio that afternoon and joined Queen Mary for the traditional dinner. He asked after Prince Edward, who had perversely chosen the moment before his father's speech to demonstrate his independence: Edward had blithely left the room and strolled into the chilly garden, deliberately distancing himself from his father's influence. Four years later Edward would also sit before a radio microphone and address the people, announcing once and for all his distance from kingship itself.

King Edward VIII and Mrs. Simpson on
holiday.

8

Wallis *January 1933 to April 1936*

> Christ! What's going to happen next?
> KING EDWARD VIII, at the funeral of his
> father, King George V

During the first three months of 1933, Wallis Simpson cheerfully accepted four invitations to join other guests at Fort Belvedere with the Prince of Wales and Thelma Furness.
Wretchedly sick for much of the previous year with chronic
ulcers, she was glad for the comfortable distraction of presti-

gious company. Her husband Ernest, for most of these week-ends, was abroad, attempting to enliven prospects for his shipping business, which was much affected by the worldwide economic depression.

For her part, Lady Furness's primacy in Prince Edward's life was soon to be threatened, not because he had as yet chosen a successor to her but because he was often withdrawn, more melancholy and emotionally adrift than ever, and she saw his gloominess as a danger signal. At the same time, he and his brothers Henry and George were under ever greater pressure from their parents and palace courtiers to select suitable brides. Of the King's four sons, only the Duke of York had married, but that event was ten years past and was unimitated. Prince Albert alone had provided progeny, two little girls for the next royal generation, and gossips wondered if Prince Edward would ever find an unmarried woman or if Prince George would ever find any woman at all. There was even talk of stage-managing royal nuptials: appropriate brides would be found for the Princes unless they came to timely decisions.

During her weekends at the Fort, Wallis cheered the Prince of Wales without sycophancy. She made him laugh, she asked questions, she challenged him and even scolded him for a breach of etiquette or a misspoken sentence. If he reached for a sandwich before tea was poured, Wallis did not hesitate to reprimand him; if he used an incorrect word or lapsed into poor grammar, she was quick to amend; if she thought he was talk-ing too much, she kicked him under the table; if he was too taciturn, it was a gentler prod. Shades of Nanny Green's pinch-ing when Edward was a child. To such corrections Edward responded as if he had been shuttled to Paradise. Wallis made him forget that he was heir to the throne. He was a young man again with her—in fact, he was almost a boy. Encircled by protocol, he relished her American breeziness, her vivacity and her genuine interest in what he had to say. He was fascinated by her assertiveness and touched by her friendly direction, and that is what made up the relationship during its first three years —an amalgam of support and endorsement. For the present, however, there was nothing apparently romantic: "If the Prince was in any way drawn to me," she wrote later, "I was unaware of his interest."

But that interest became clearer during the summer of 1933.

On June 19, to mark Wallis's thirty-seventh birthday, Prince Edward gave a dinner at Quaglino's (a fashionable West End restaurant not far from his residence, York House). He presented her with a large orchid plant and then, in his champagne salute, remarked how fortunate Ernest was; burnished by the radiance of his royal host, Ernest could only smile and mumble his agreement.

When Ernest was again away that autumn and Wallis was a firmly established member of the Prince's set, she was invited to meet the Greek-Danish-German Princess who would soon be engaged to Prince George—a lady who, ever since she had appeared as a slender teenager at Princess Mary's wedding in 1922, routinely reduced men to nervous adoration and women to wistful admiration or grudging jealousy. And she was a foreign Royal.

Princess Marina, who might have sprung straight from the pages of a romantic novel, was the daughter of Prince and Princess Nicholas of Greece. A dark-haired, porcelain-skinned, twenty-seven-year-old, Marina was by common consent one of the great beauties of Europe. Her grandfather was Queen Alexandra's brother (the Danish Prince who became King George I of Greece); the other grandfather had been Grand Duke Vladimir, Czar Nicholas II's brother.

Once a friend of Freda Dudley Ward, Marina had also been, during her 1927 summer sojourn in England, one of Prince Edward's girlfriends. She was, according to her brother-in-law, Prince Paul of Yugoslavia, "completely overwhelmed by [Edward's] unusual interest in her [and by] his attentions, which were more than passing and went far beyond the call of duty and politeness." Marina's mother and sister, meanwhile, held their breath and hoped. As it happened, they were all disappointed. The affair between Marina and the Prince of Wales (thus Chips Channon) "might well have led to marriage and was progressing very well, but Freda Dudley Ward, at the last moment, interfered and stopped it."

Radiant, indomitable Marina was born with a crooked left foot that remained weaker and shorter than the other; throughout her life she wore specially fitted shoes to correct the slight imbalance. She also had a slightly angular, lopsided smile that somehow made her all the more mysteriously attractive, as if she were a femme fatale with astonishing secrets, a woman bemused by everyone she met. Although her most appealing quality was a consummate, unstudied elegance, Marina was skillful in both domestic and fine arts, adept at languages and altogether right for George, as no less than Queen Mary felt. "No bread-and-butter miss would be of any help to my son," she told Mabell Airlie significantly, "but this girl is sophisticated as well as charming." The Queen chose to overlook the fact that Marina was also penniless.

George was, perhaps to the surprise of no one who knew him well, less than besotted by Marina despite whatever he may have learned from his brother Edward about her passionate nature. George found her "bossy," and it took a year of quiet family encouragement for him to see the social and personal advantages of marriage to this confident beauty. Beneath Marina's quiet sensuality there was strength, independence and cosmopolitan refinement, qualities fortified by her years in Paris when she and her family were forced into exile from Greece. She was a woman who, the Queen must have perceived, would take wayward George in hand, although perhaps George thought that marriage alone would please the family and that he might be able to maintain his own independent intimacies. This would be, the family believed, marriage as reformation: two handsome people each impressed by the smooth charm of the other and both of them benefitting from an alliance maneuvered by the Crown.

"She is the one woman with whom I could be happy to spend the rest of my life," George said somewhat equivocally at the time, prepared to yield to pressure. "We laugh at the same thing. She beats me at most games and doesn't give a damn how fast I drive when I take her out in the car." For Wallis Simpson, as for many who knew her, Princess Marina was both emblem and model of what a woman could become by virtue of innate energy and intense purpose, and despite deprivations and a peripatetic background. Wallis returned from Emerald Cunard's dinner party for Marina, in September 1933, bedazzled by the guest of honor, as who did not.

The pace of life for the Royal Family in 1933 was slow, routine, unadventurous and unimaginative. But in 1934 things began to happen quickly.

In January, Thelma Furness departed for America to visit her sister, Gloria Vanderbilt, who was involved in a legal contest for custody of her eight-year-old daughter, also named Gloria.

> Three or four days before I was to sail, I had lunch with Wallis at the Ritz. I told her of my plans ... and she said suddenly, "Oh, Thelma, the little man is going to be so lonely."
>
> "Well, dear," I answered, "you look after him while I'm away. See that he does not get into any mischief."

It was later evident that Wallis took my advice all too literally. Whether or not she kept him out of mischief is a question whose answer hinges on the fine points of semantics.

According to Wallis, the dialogue was somewhat different: "The day before she sailed she asked me for cocktails," she wrote in her memoirs. "We rattled along in our fashion; as we said good-bye she said laughingly, 'I'm afraid the Prince is going to be lonely. Wallis, won't you look after him?' I promised that I would." Her account implies that Wallis's attention to Edward was inspired by Thelma, whereas in Thelma's version she says something quite innocent in reply to *Wallis's* fantasy that the Prince would be lonely.

In any case, the following weekend the Simpsons were at Fort Belvedere, Ernest still apparently just as pleased with the royal social connection as Wallis. Four days later the Prince was at Bryanston Court for dinner, where (as she recalled) he spoke of "the creative role he thought the Monarchy could play in this new age, and also dropped a hint of the frustrations he was experiencing." She sensed, as he spoke, "a deep loneliness, an overtone of spiritual isolation." This she acknowledged by the simple expedient of attentive and respectful listening, thus providing precisely what Edward had been denied by the coolness and criticisms of the King and Queen.

A week later Edward and Wallis danced at the Dorchester Hotel while Ernest tried to talk about his business with influential Americans. "Wallis," the Prince said, "you're the only woman who's ever been interested in my job." And a week after this he was at Bryanston Court again, where he now began to appear without announcement, asking for a drink or, rather like a lost child, hoping for an invitation to supper.

"She was really the perfect hostess," recalled Angela Fox,*
who was present. "Wallis Simpson was a thoughtful and generous lady, and this needs to be said. She was never ostenta-
tious but quite lavish—even though, as we all knew, the
Simpsons were on a budget." Lady Dudley agreed: Mrs. Simpson was "a Southerner with very good manners" and not to be
thought of as a vulgarian, much less a common adventuress.
And Walter Monckton, Edward's friend and attorney, was not
alone in observing that, as host or guest, Wallis "immediately
found out what one's interests were, and they were immediately hers for the next ten minutes." As for elegance, the
Prince of Wales (thus his biographer Philip Ziegler) "had no
taste at all, but she had a very evolved sense of taste, quite her
own and reflective of her own personality—which was of
course very powerful."

In addition, Wallis had a positive influence on Edward,
tempering his occasionally boorish and inconsiderate manners,
urging him to greater sensitivity to the feelings of others and
deflating some of his arrogance by her lack of flattery. She
also insisted that he reduce his alcoholic intake. Besides being
bejeweled and eyebrow-plucked, she was, wrote no less an
observer than Harold Nicolson,

> virtuous and wise. I was impressed by the fact that she
> forbade the Prince to smoke during the *entr'acte* in the
> theatre itself. She is clearly out to help him . . . [but] I have
> an uneasy feeling that Mrs. Simpson, in spite of her good
> intentions, is getting him out of touch with the type of
> person with whom he ought to associate.

—by which, presumably, Nicolson meant serious people with
concerns greater than social. At any rate, he judged her "a nice
woman who has flaunted suddenly into this absurd position"
of confidante to a man who needed expert tutoring. To those
who might have insisted that Wallis was like a mother taking a
child in hand, one could have replied that in some ways this
was what he required and that in any case he delighted in such
treatment.

---

* Wife of the noted agent Robin Fox and mother of actors James,
Edward and Robert.

By early spring the first rumors made the rounds of London society that Mrs. Simpson was replacing Lady Furness in the affections of the Prince of Wales. Wallis wrote to Aunt Bessie that it was all idle gossip, that she was not the sort to steal her friends' beaux, that her task was to amuse the Prince, and that after all Ernest was "hanging around [her] neck so all is safe." Compared to Emerald Cunard, Princess Marina and those Wallis met at events to which she was invited by the Prince, Ernest and his business cronies must have seemed like dull potatoes; still, there was no reason for anyone to presume that the friendship between Edward and Wallis had moved to another level.

Yet some observers noticed subtle differences in the Prince's manner as Thelma's absence lengthened to months. George Kilensky, an American friend of the Simpsons, recalled that Edward's eyes "lingered on her face for a moment after she had finished talking and someone else had taken up the general conversation" and that he experienced "a feeling of unease, as if trouble lay ahead for Ernest and Wallis, two of my dearest friends. It was the new sense of intimacy in the conversation and exchanged looks" the Prince of Wales offered Mrs. Simpson.

Kilensky could not have known there was more than affectionate glances: Edward gave Wallis a signed photograph of himself and then—ever more extravagantly over the next several years—jewelry, brooches, bracelets and earrings, most of which had belonged to his grandmother, Queen Alexandra, and some of which he had put in smart new Cartier settings. On several occasions the Prince withdrew money from his private accounts to finance jewelry purchases totaling more than £10,000 ($50,000 at that time). Queen Mary was shocked to learn later that Queen Alexandra's heirlooms were being transferred out of the family.

But while some noted Edward's fascination and others knew the source of the jewelry, almost no one reported that Edward's loving glances and gestures were returned by Wallis. She was by far the more controlled, more discreet in her conduct and, it must be said, sensible enough to know that this little foolishness was unlikely to have a fairy tale ending.

On March 22, Lady Furness returned from America, and at Fort Belvedere the following weekend she noticed a distinctly cool attitude from His Royal Highness. Several days later Wallis told Thelma that the "little man" was lost without her—and then she left the room to take a telephone call from the Prince. "The door was left open," according to Thelma.

> I heard Wallis in the next room saying to the Prince, "Thelma is here," and I half rose from my chair, expecting to be called to the telephone. There was no summons, however, and when Wallis returned, she made no reference to the conversation. This omission would have been surprising at any time; it was all the more surprising at a moment when the Prince was the point of our conversation.

The surprises continued the following month when Wallis joined Thelma and Edward at Fort Belvedere. At luncheon he picked up a lettuce leaf with his fingers, a breach of manners that immediately invited a slap on his wrist from Wallis and an almost audible gasp of shock from the other guests, who never saw such a proprietary liberty taken with the Prince. The chastisement drew from him a blush of embarrassment, as if he regretted disappointing an adored mother. Later, Thelma retired to her room with a bad cold, and the Prince came to inquire if she needed any remedy. "The cold was by now a negligible issue," Thelma wrote later. "I searched his face for an answer to the central question. Would *his* expression be as outspoken as Wallis's?"

"Darling," she asked bluntly, "is it Wallis?"

"Don't be silly," the Prince replied curtly, and without another word he left the room.

"I knew better," Thelma concluded. "I left the Fort the following morning." Before the end of that April 1934, Thelma Furness was out of the Prince's life forever. They never communicated again. Nor did Freda Dudley Ward, who, on telephoning the Fort to inquire of the Prince, was told there were orders not to put through her calls. Now it was clear that, whatever the extent of their intimacy, Edward had placed only Wallis at the center of his attention.

There was, however, a coda: when Thelma saw Wallis later, she asked if the Prince was "keen" on her. "Thelma," replied Mrs. Simpson, "I think he likes me. He may be fond of me. But if you mean by keen that he is in love with me, the answer is definitely no." And so, it seems, Wallis really believed. "Searching my mind," she wrote later with admirable frankness,

> I could find no good reason why this most glamorous of men should be seriously attracted to me. I certainly was no beauty, and he had the pick of the beautiful women of the world. I was certainly no longer very young. In fact, in my own country I would have been considered securely on the shelf.

As for her attraction to him:

> He was the open sesame to a new and glittering world that excited me as nothing in my life had ever done before. . . . Trains were held [for him]; yachts materialised; the best suites in the finest hotels were flung open; aeroplanes stood waiting. . . . It seemed unbelievable that I, Wallis Warfield of Baltimore, Maryland, could be part of this enchanted world. . . . It was like being Wallis in Wonderland.

The Prince of Wales desperately needed more from Wallis than mere carnal pleasures: her control, direction and approval were the sealing elements to the attraction. For her part, she was genuinely drawn by his charm, his gentleness and his dependence on her. Loyal and committed to his happiness, Mrs. Simpson believed only she could please him, which is just what the Prince said. In his relationship with her, the primitive truth of the cliché was clear: denied paternal support and maternal nurturing, the Prince of Wales had for fifteen years sought in his affairs with assertive married women the idealization of parental affection.

In Wallis he found it. Raised in the Southern tradition of a mannered matriarchy, she was ready to tend, cherish, protect and even, if necessary, chasten her man. "Sometimes," she wrote to the Prince with laudable insight, "I think you haven't grown up where love is concerned and perhaps it's only a boyish passion. . . . You can't go through life stepping on other people. I know that you aren't really selfish or thoughtless at heart, but your life has been such that you have been the one considered. . . . [You] may always remain Peter Pan." As he later said, she was his "severest critic, and hers is always the last word."

That spring there was no doubt about the identity of Freda's and Thelma's successor. In public the Prince of Wales was seen opening doors for Mrs. Simpson, seating her at a table and lighting her cigarettes, even in the presence of her husband. Contrariwise, she interrupted and corrected him before others and assumed a somewhat domineering attitude that he accepted as if it were his vocation to do so. The Prince, according to his equerry John Aird, had "lost all confidence in himself and followed W[allis] around like a dog." Yet Aird, too, believed her influence was positive and that she did not have "any illusions about the situation and definitely does not want to do anything that will lose her husband."

In fact, of course, she was doing just that: there were limits to the patience even of the snobbishly complaisant Ernest Simpson, and although Wallis wrote to Aunt Bessie that "life goes on the same here quite peacefully with Ernest in spite of HRH on [the] doorstep," the marriage was swiftly deteriorating. Simpson began to complain to friends that he never had his wife to himself anymore and that the heir to the throne could not, after all, be addressed like any other competition. Sometimes he found excuses to work late when the Prince came to supper, and he even invented business trips to avoid embarrassment.

The Prince, Chips Channon wrote in his diary, was "obviously madly infatuated . . . and she has completely subjugated him." Among others, Channon saw the couple at the Royal Opera, where large, aromatic cigars peeped up out of the Prince of Wales's breast pocket. "That doesn't look very pretty," Wallis whispered to him. At once they were tucked elsewhere, out of sight.

Others spoke more to the point of Prince Edward's emotions. "He delighted in her company," Winston Churchill wrote of Edward and Wallis,

and found in her qualities as necessary to his happiness as the air he breathed. Those who knew him well and watched him closely noticed that many little tricks and fidgetings of nervousness fell away from him. He was a completed human being instead of a sick and harassed soul. This expe-

rience which happens to a great many people in the flower
of youth came late in life to him, and was all the more
precious and compulsive for that fact.

For Chips Channon, Wallis

> enormously improved the Prince . . . and she [is] a jolly,
> unprepossessing American, witty, a mimic, an excellent
> cook. Never has [Edward] been so in love. She is madly
> anxious to storm society while she is still his favourite, so
> that when he leaves her (as he leaves everyone in time) she
> will be secure.

The diarist was partly correct. On April 25, 1934, Wallis
wrote to Aunt Bessie that she was "trying to meet English
people through [Prince Edward] and he has had different ones
every week-end lately. I'm afraid I'll have to give up soon as
it naturally takes more money" to be in the Prince's society.
She was, she added, "dying to be asked for Ascot week." But
she suspected that Edward would "find another girl or return
to Thelma" and that eventually she would have to keep Ernest
—still the security of her life—"in good humour."

Channon and others echoed the Duke of York's belief—
and, it seems, Wallis's—that this romance would surely be
short-lived. They apparently did not know, as Helen Hardinge
(the wife of King George V's secretary, Alec Hardinge) wrote
later, that Edward "had decided to try to marry her before he
came to the throne." That this was a fantastic idea evidently
meant little to the Prince. As Wallis wrote to Aunt Bessie on
April 15, she was trying to keep a balance, an "even keel" to
their relationship, and to avoid seeing the Prince alone, although she was flattered by his constant attention.

But in his presence something in her, too, had blossomed,
something she had never known with Spencer or Simpson. At
least from 1932 to 1936, "her gaiety," according to photographer and designer Cecil Beaton, was "contagious. . . . She is
all that is elegant. . . . I am certain that she has more glamour
and is of more interest than any public figure." As for more
substantial qualities, Beaton thought her "intelligent within her
vast limitations. Politically she may be ignorant, aesthetically
she is so, but about life she knows a great deal."

In August, Edward invited Wallis to join a few others as his guest of honor at a holiday villa in Biarritz. Aunt Bessie accompanied her niece as chaperone, for Ernest was again elsewhere on business. Angela Fox, her husband and father-in-law were in the party. "I spent a considerable amount of time with Wallis while the men went off to play golf," Angela recalled.

> She taught me to play gin rummy and backgammon, and she was always pleasant to be with. It was clear that in her youth she was well raised, from a good family. She was like Freda and Thelma—not a showoff. Some of us envied her way with cosmetics and a limited wardrobe, for she could work wonders. And she was very natural and unpretentious in sharing her advice on these things with us. I wasn't the only one who really liked Wallis. She had that wonderfully casual, American way about her—a wonderful antidote to a lot of the stuffiness in royal entourages.

From Biarritz they traveled to Cannes, where one evening after dinner the Prince took from his pocket a small velvet case and pressed it into Wallis's hand. She opened it to find a diamond and emerald charm for her bracelet, to which he would make regular additions. And from Cannes came the first news story to mention her by name: "The Prince of Wales danced the rhumba with an American woman identified as Mrs. Simpson," but editorial blue pencils removed the last eight words.

Wallis could not, however, "work wonders" with the Royal Family. At a Court ball before the wedding of George and Marina that autumn, the Prince of Wales formally presented Mrs. Simpson to his parents—an introduction freighted with far more significance than the mere garden party encounter of 1932. The King and Queen, who by this time knew of the affair, merely stared at Wallis unsmilingly when Edward brought her to them (without Ernest, who was left unescorted on the dance floor). Wallis curtsied, there was an almost imperceptible nod from Queen Mary, and the Prince guided Wallis away for a waltz. "That woman in my house!" raged the King later. It was the only time Mrs. Simpson met the King and his Consort.

There were other introductions that evening, among them to Prince Christopher of Greece, who recalled that Edward "laid a hand on my arm in his impulsive way: 'Christo, come with me. I want you to meet Mrs. Simpson.'

" 'Mrs. Simpson—who is she?'

" 'An American. She's wonderful.' " Those last two words, Prince Christopher felt, "told me everything. It was as though he had said, 'She is the only woman in the world.' "

That the lady in question was "wonderful" was not an assessment shared by the Prince's family. The Duke of York believed Wallis simply would not last long in his brother's affections. No woman had. The Duchess of York disliked everything about Wallis: her boldness, her democratic attitude, her violet lamé dress with a green sash. According to Helen Hardinge, Wallis was deeply resented by the Duchess, who was never discourteous to her but who nevertheless made it "very apparent that she did not care for Mrs. Simpson at all." This was not surprising, for these two ladies could not have been more different. One preferred fly-fishing and quiet weekends with her daughters; the other liked society's latest gossip and fashions.

The antipathy would only deepen in the following year—first of all in February 1935 when the Prince of Wales took Wallis (but not Ernest, who pleaded business affairs) and a small party for a ski holiday in Kitzbühel and thence on a shopping jaunt to Vienna and Budapest. When they returned, Edward ordered two rooms at the Fort to be permanently turned over for the use of Mr. and Mrs. Simpson as regular guests. But the furnishings, decor and provision for a lady's maid indicated that this was a woman's suite and that no thought was given to anything relative to a gentleman or his valet.

When this arrangement became clear to the Yorks on a visit to the Fort, the Duchess said she would never meet Mrs. Simpson again. Some weeks later when Albert and Elizabeth saw Wallis join the Prince for a dinner at the Dorchester Hotel, the Duchess left within minutes, taking along the compliant Duke and a number of others. (Prince George never expressed his disapproval, and Prince Henry, typically, seemed unaware of what was happening.) But such snubbings, prejudices and resentments are often the stuff of ordinary family life, and the Windsors and their extended family were not immune to them.

* * *

In October 1934 the King revived a title unused for over a century; thus it was that his youngest son was named Prince George, Duke of Kent, when he married Princess Marina (thenceforth Duchess of Kent) at Westminster Abbey on November 29. They settled into 3 Belgrave Square and soon after, as well, into a country house in Buckinghamshire where George planned the meals and supervised the decorating of the rooms. When Lady Airlie complimented Marina on a fine dinner, the Duchess replied, "I must confess that I didn't know what we were going to eat until the food appeared. My husband chose the dinner and the wine—and the flowers and everything else. He enjoys doing it, and so I always leave the household affairs to him. I let him make all the decisions over furniture and decorations."

But Marina left her mark in other areas. Society women began smoking in ever greater numbers because the Duchess of Kent did. Her coiffeurs were copied by stylists, and she initiated the fad for turbans and pillbox hats. She made trousers respectable for Englishwomen, and, even more boldly, she revived interest in cotton. Until Marina did so, no fashionable woman in London wore cotton frocks in public. But when her husband told her of the Depression's effects on Lancashire industry—that the cotton factories were virtually idle—she asked her dressmaker to design cotton dresses, and she wore them until they were widely accepted as stylish.

As Queen Mary soon learned, Marina's intrepidity went all the way to Buckingham Palace. On seeing her new daughter-in-law with fingernails painted bright red, the Queen said, "I'm afraid the King doesn't like painted nails. Can you do something about it?" Marina was unfazed. "Your George may not like them," she said unblinkingly, "but mine does." Thus did the Queen learn that the Duchess was indeed "no bread-and-butter miss." Such directness with the Royal Family characterized Marina throughout her lifetime; she regarded herself as the inheritor of true Imperial Royalty, of far more ancient and genuine blue blood than the Teutonic Windsors. She considered her sisters-in-law, the Duchess of York and the Duchess of Gloucester, for example, "those common little Scottish girls." And Marina was even quite sure of God Himself. Telling her sister Olga that she now prayed in English instead of Greek, she explained, "I have arranged it with God. I told Him

I liked to talk to Him in English, and He said, 'Please yourself, Marina.' " And so she always did, and not only at prayer.

Queen Mary always regarded Marina with some xenophobic suspicion and resented that the new Duchess of Kent seemed to ignore her. But Mary had her own good reason to be gratified that autumn when there was a sudden change of plans for the christening of a new ocean liner, originally to be called *Queen Victoria.* Told by a Cunard executive that the ship was to be named for "the greatest of all English Queens," King George exclaimed with delight, "Oh, my wife will be *so* pleased!" And so, on September 26, the *Queen Mary* was launched.

At the end of 1934, sixty-nine-year-old King George caught a bad cold; with his history of respiratory infections and his continued heavy smoking, he soon caught influenza. To avoid the winter fogs in London and the cold of Sandringham, the King took his doctor's advice early in the new year and accepted the loan of the Duke of Devonshire's country home near the Channel. A movie theater was installed in the house for his amusement; there, he particularly enjoyed *Lives of a Bengal Lancer* and invited the servants to join him for screenings and a glass of sherry.

The King's recovery was protracted throughout 1935 when he and the Queen moved up to Windsor, but during the remaining year of his life he was not really recovering at all. With his lung capacity diminished, his heart was steadily weakening and his vascular system seriously impaired. This prompted Lord Wigram to approach Prince Edward at Fort Belvedere on April 11. The King, Wigram said, was a frail man and thus there was the possibility of the Prince's early accession. The press "would not remain silent," Wigram said, in the matter of the Prince's open friendship with Mrs. Simpson; nor would the nation tolerate "a Sovereign keeping company with another man's wife, however innocent their relations might be." The Prince replied that his private life was his own business and that he was really rather surprised that anyone would be scandalized about a friendship with so charming a woman. The King, when hearing how his son had blithely dismissed the importance of a growing scandal, was enraged.

With this matter constantly on the King's mind, the great

plans for his Silver Jubilee on May 6, 1935, were carried out in a triumph of British pomp and ceremony, notwithstanding (indeed, perhaps partly because of) the general economic woes that beleaguered the nation. London was festooned with decorations, merrymakers in the hundreds of thousands poured into London for the festivities, and the entire extended Royal Family piled into open carriages for the parade route toward St. Paul's Cathedral, where a solemn Thanksgiving Service was offered. At Buckingham Palace that afternoon and evening, the King and Queen had to return time and again to acknowledge the roaring cheers from crowds, and at eight o'clock he sat before a hastily installed microphone to speak to the nation words written neither by Kipling (who had drafted the first Christmas broadcast in 1932) nor by Archbishop of Canterbury Cosmo Lang (who had prepared those subsequent), but by himself:

> At the close of this memorable day, I must speak to my people everywhere. How can I express what is in my heart? . . . I can only say to you, my very, very dear people, that the Queen and I thank you from the depths of our hearts for all the loyalty and—may I say so?—the love, with which this day and always you have surrounded us. I dedicate myself anew to your service for all the years that may still be given me. . . .
>
> My people and I have come through great trials and difficulties together. They are not over. In the midst of this day's rejoicing, I grieve to think of the numbers of my people who are still without work. We owe to them, and not least to those who are suffering from any form of disablement, all the sympathy and help that we can give, to find them work and bring them hope. . . .

Still later that evening the King and Queen had to return to the balcony to acknowledge the one hundred thousand shouting, "We want King George!" He waved with both arms, and Queen Mary could be seen in a most uncharacteristic gesture: she extended both arms forward as if to embrace all the people. It was an action more typical of Queen Alexandra, but there it was, along with Mary's shy smile.

In Hyde Park thousands sang throughout the warm night.

Piccadilly, from the Circus to Park Lane, was filled with more than eighty thousand dancers and merrymakers, and someone had stuck a Union Jack in the hand of Eros. Confetti was inches deep in the road and traffic was snarled for days, but there was little ill temper. Dance bands came from West End restaurants and amused those stalled. Underground and overground stations were jammed, and corner houses were quickly out of sandwiches and ale. People shared spontaneously; the police blotters were virtually free of crime reports.

For His Majesty, the loud adulation of the people that day was, as he wrote in his diary, "most touching." Masses of people gathered outside the palace every night for a week, hailing the King and singing "For he's a jolly good fellow," and during a wildly enthusiastic reception as they drove through the poor East End of London, George and Mary were moved almost to tears. Overwhelmed at the outpouring of affection, the monarch said to the Archbishop of Canterbury, "I cannot understand it! I am quite an ordinary sort of fellow"— to which His Grace replied dubiously, "Yes, Sir, that is just it." As the celebrations continued through Queen Mary's sixty-eighth birthday on May 26 and his seventieth on June 3, the King was stunned. "I am beginning to think they must really like me for myself."

Did they indeed? Could the King evoke from the general population a response of warm affection that even his own sons did not feel? Or was he hailed because his image was a fixture of common life, because so many people had known no other monarch? Was he cheered because he had touched millions of hearts with his words and deeds, or because his picture had become commonplace in newspapers and newsreels, and his voice had reached their ears in annual Christmas broadcasts? Was the success of the Jubilee due to the government's savvy efforts to make people happy in a grim time and thus reinforce its own political clout? Was the cheering stage-managed? Was it, in other words, an idealized image of a man that was adored or the man himself who was loved?

Perhaps some of the applause was simply for a handsome and dignified national grandfather, a man in whom people wished to believe—a husband and father who inspired stability in the country. Perhaps, too, some of the adulation derived from that English national pride in a monarchy that had survived while crowns fell worldwide. In this regard, George was (like Victoria) a corporate personality, an emblem of the decent, plucky simplicity the English consider their great national virtue. We got through the Great War, we will survive the Great Depression. We are English. We endure.

There to guarantee continuity were reliable King George and steadfast Queen Mary, dignified and without affectation. They were what the English believed themselves to be. The Jubilee was, then, an act in the theater of monarchy. But people applaud the theater only when it is a focusing and concentration of a parcel of reality. The liturgy of celebration did not correspond to falsehood but to truth; its pageant honored something more permanent than flags and free milk. Amid all the ceremony there was a plain and unpretentious man. Never mind that in private with his family he was a very different creature.

That, in fact, may be the clue to the popularity of this man. He put on no airs, adopted no attitudes or false graces, and this, most of all, may be what people want from their sovereign. In the final analysis it was her honest simplicity that endeared Victoria to people; it was the frail folly of Edward VII that made him a recognizably human monarch; it was the unfussy directness and responsibility of George V that appealed to millions.

King George was always reluctant to accept change, preferring the traditional ways of doing just about everything—that is in the very nature of monarchy, after all—but he understood how inevitable were transition and transformation. He had a sense of rectitude without self-righteousness. Amid the turmoil of a modern world he resented, George did not try to transform personal prejudice into national policy. But he had no trouble correcting ministers who ignored the plight of the poor, and he utterly lacked racial or class prejudice—no small virtue at any time—and was always uncomfortable with the smugness of the rich and the empty honorifics tendered by sycophants. "Too many parsons getting in the way," he muttered when a gaggle of ministers lunged forward and prevented him from greeting a crowd in Trafalgar Square. "I didn't know there were so many damned parsons in England!" Sympathetic with striking workers and the disenfranchised, King George never condescended to ordinary people, yet his respect for the Crown gave the monarchy a certain cachet.

In this he embodied an idea as old as English history: the notion that the monarch and the common people are allied against the upper classes. POOR BUT LOYAL read the signs in the London slums during Jubilee Week, and LONG LIVE THE KING, BUT DOWN WITH THE LANDLORD! When he saw these placards, King George himself applauded in the direction of the people, smiling broadly and supporting them as they did him. They knew he had no real power, but in a way that was a bond between them. They were all anxious for the future, nervy about the status quo, deceived by politicians. The King radiated a kind of moral suasion. He was more than a mere media celebrity, more than a phony concoction manipulated by publicists.

George V had never courted popularity. He was a conventional old man who had no patience with highbrows (he thought the word was "eyebrows" and so never understood the source of all the fuss), a brusque old sailor who hardly ever smiled in public. The image of him and his wife was that of a quiet elderly couple with their needlepoint and stamp collection, and the comforting, comfortable image perfectly reflected the reality. Yet the King worked constantly, walking that maddening line between the constitutional requirements of the day and his own longing for an earlier order.

The government might have been able to produce a few hours of bread and circuses that May, but it could not have managed to extend the celebration to weeks of honor. "I'd no idea they felt like that about me," he said, amazed at the waves of affection that washed over him that last springtide of his life. They did feel that way. The people respected him because he stood for tradition, for an England that preceded and would outlive him. But they also liked him, as he hoped, for himself.

And yet even this is too simple a reading of the Jubilee hysteria.

The cheers and tears for a man no ordinary person knew are instructive. Earlier, when the monarch was an executive, a powerful leader who could raise an army, order an execution, proclaim or withhold benefits with a writ or a barked command, he was subject to attack from every element in society. Only since the death of Prince Albert did the British people no longer fear royal interference: Victoria's Consort had firmly established a constitutional monarchy—a Sovereign above politics—and it was no longer necessary to attack the individual Sovereign. Gradually, people sought a figure they could adore without reserve.

In addition, when the King was anointed, he was Head of the Church and Defender of the Faith. This doctrine alone and the anointing of the monarch in the context of a religious service endorsed the King as a divine surrogate. It was, then, easier and more necessary to adore a man one did not know. Bagehot had insisted on maintaining the magic of monarchy, but this is precisely the source of its danger. Once it is believed that the King is not a partisan, it is all too easy to replace respect with adoration, to substitute homage for acceptance of a symbol. With that, an irrational feeling about the monarch and his family substitutes for a rational respect for its chief civil servants. Everything is done to diminish the Sovereign's place as a human in the national order and to cover him in magic and adoration, yet it was precisely the homey aspects of Victoria, Edward VII and George V that endeared them to the people. And herein lies precisely the paradox that is the key to the British people's love-hate relationship with their Royal Family. They are—sometimes, at any rate—recognizably human, one of us. Yet lest they shatter their own mystique, they dare not appear too human.

The Jubilee Year turned Queen Mary's attention to family matters—primarily the marriages remaining to be contracted by her sons. "I hope now you, my darling boy, will think about marrying," she wrote in September 1934 to Prince Henry, Duke of Gloucester, adding the names of two eligible foreign princesses and the sprightly observation, "Marriage is in the air!" On November 6, 1935, Henry finally breathed that air at the age of thirty-five, marrying Lady Alice Montagu-Douglas-Scott, daughter of the Duke of Buccleuch. Henry's proposal to Alice was much in character—without style, barely audible and somewhat doltish. "There was no formal declaration on his part," Alice recalled. "I think he just muttered it as an aside during one of our walks; nor was there any doubt of my acceptance. Apart from my great happiness in getting married, I felt too that it was time I did something useful with my life."

Over many years this practical, plain couple shared their interests in African travel and gardening; like Henry, Alice utterly lacked any interest in the arts or intellectual society and was happiest on horseback.

As with the Duchess of York, the King had a better relationship with his new daughter-in-law than he had with his sons. Alice's father had died shortly before her wedding, and she wrote to King George to express loyal feelings. He replied,

> Thank you for your charming letter. How touched I was by yr kind words, especially those about finding a new father to take the place of the one that you have lost. I should love to try and take his place & I shall always do everything to try & help you. Wishing you every possible happiness,
>
> > Ever yr devoted father-in-law,
> > G.R.I.*

The Duke and Duchess of Gloucester appear but rarely in this chronicle of the monarchy for the simple reason that they played no part in any of its drama.

''Now all the children are married but David,'' wrote the King succinctly in his diary that autumn. That was his real worry—and the gravity of the relationship between the heir to the throne and Mrs. Simpson, of whom he naturally disapproved and about whom only a small circle in London society knew anything at all. But the secrecy could not last long, as the King appreciated. Prince Edward had told his father at the time of the Jubilee Ball that Wallis was not his mistress; indeed, people such as Emerald Cunard firmly believed they were not lovers before they married. In this case sex was almost a minor detail, for Wallis sported enormous diamond clips at the ball —a Jubilee present from Edward, rather as if she were a Queen-in-waiting. His parents were further annoyed when (without Ernest) Wallis also attended Ascot in June. Whatever the precise nature of the liaison at the time, Edward and Wallis were most certainly, to the Royal Family, a ''WE,'' as they called themselves in a coy conjunction of their initials.

There were additional reasons for concern about the Prince

---

* For informal letters to family and friends, the fully written conclusion was abbreviated, but the titles of the monarch always remained, thus here to Alice: G[eorgius]. R[ex]. I[mperator]—George, King-Emperor.

of Wales, not least of them his expressed esteem for things German, which he kept into his reign. Like many in his time, Edward made no secret of his admiration for the accomplishments of National Socialism (reduced unemployment and improved housing conditions) as compared to the inertia of a weakened France, a country for which Edward had no love (despite his cloying use of quaint French phrases with his lovers). At the same time he was blind to the most outrageous fantasies of the Third Reich. Prince Edward also felt there was a ''great danger from the Communists,'' whom he saw as a far greater threat to the West than fascism. Despite Hitler's rearmament of the Rhineland (which had been specifically forbidden by the Treaty of Versailles), Edward—in an address to the British Legion in June 1935—urged war veterans to visit Germany, ''to stretch forth the hand of friendship'' and seal a spiritual alliance with that country. This statement embarrassed the government, fearful of offending French allies, and it infuriated the King, who ordered his son never again to speak on such controversial matters without consulting the Foreign Office.

But by this time George V had lost all confidence in the Prince of Wales. ''He went as far as to say that he was beginning to think it would almost be better if the [Prince of Wales] abdicated,'' wrote Edward's chief of staff, Sir Lionel Halsey, ''but of course that was a course which would be bound to cause trouble.'' But so would another plan of action: by October 1935, marriage to Mrs. Simpson had become Prince Edward's obsession; and the more she dismissed the idea as ridiculous, the more insistent he became.

''He does not see any decent society, and he is forty-one,'' the King complained to his cousin, Count Albert Mensdorff-Pouilly, the former Austrian ambassador. But Prince Edward had many fine qualities, his charm not the least of them, replied the Count. ''Yes, certainly,'' said the King. ''That is the pity. If he were a fool, we would not mind. I hardly ever see him and I don't know what he is doing.''

At the end of 1935, depressed by illness, the King was speaking plainly and frequently of his worst fears. ''My eldest son will never succeed me. He will abdicate,'' he said to a courtier. To Stanley Baldwin, the calm and diplomatic Prime Minister who was on friendly terms with Prince Edward, King

George confided a dark prophecy: "After I am dead the boy will ruin himself within twelve months." When the Archbishop of Canterbury congratulated the King on the high status of the monarchy, George gazed sadly away: "What use is it, when I know my son is going to let it down?" And most famously and painfully, the King said, "I pray to God my eldest son will never marry and have children, and that nothing will come between Bertie and Lilibet and the throne." *

On December 3 the King was told that his sister, Princess Victoria, had died at her home in Buckinghamshire. She had been her mother's faithful companion, secretary and nurse, a somewhat vague and mysterious figure who never married and, after Alexandra's death in 1925, lived quietly, tending her garden, listening to music and strolling to town where she greeted shopkeepers and villagers. There had always been a spontaneous affection and candid humor between Toria and George, who were only three years apart. "How I shall miss her," he wrote in his diary, "& our daily talks on the telephone." The morning of her death the King declared an official mourning and canceled the state opening of Parliament, at which he was to speak that afternoon. As it happened, Toria's funeral was to be his last public appearance.

Ill and feverish though he was, King George was not about to depart from the tradition of Christmas at Sandringham. Concerned for his shortness of breath and evident exhaustion, the family gathered to cheer the King and Queen: the Yorks, with their two girls dancing around the decorated Scottish fir tree; the newlywed Gloucesters; and the Kents, with their infant son Edward, born that October. The Prince of Wales was present, too, but he was, as he wrote later, "caught up in an inner conflict and would have no peace of mind until I had resolved it." His moodiness notwithstanding, the family enjoyed a gay Christmas dinner, after which they assembled to hear the King's broadcast message.

But he was not well enough for his usual winter hunting parties or for a soiree planned to ring in 1936. By January 7

---

* King George V would never have confided to anyone outside the Royal Family the fact of Edward's sterility—if in fact he believed it was an irremediable condition.

his periods of breathlessness were alarming, although he slept peacefully. On Monday, January 13, the King felt wretched. He tried to help the Queen catalogue the collection of Alexandra's Fabergé eggs, just inherited from his sister, but he was too ill and had to be helped to his room, which he never again left. On Friday the seventeenth, the King made the last entry in a diary he had scrupulously kept since 1880: "Dawson [his physician] arrived this evening. I saw him and feel rotten."

Indeed, his heart, worn out by fighting years of pulmonary weakness, was failing. The Prince of Wales was summoned by Queen Mary from a Windsor shooting party. Realistic but calm, she also sent for Lord Wigram, confiding to them both her belief that the King had not long to live. When they visited the King after dinner, he apologized for being so tired and unable to focus on a conversation. That same Friday evening the first bulletin was issued from Sandringham by Lord Dawson; no death certificate for the King was ever recorded, and this overly cautious release remains the only clinical report:

> The bronchial catarrh [inflammation of the mucous membranes] from which His Majesty the King is suffering is not severe, but there have appeared signs of cardiac weakness which must be regarded with some disquiet.

While the King rested somewhat more easily on Saturday morning, the Queen, the Duke of York and the Prince of Wales talked about the future of the family's homes. Like many in such a situation, they sought refuge from their anxieties in a discussion of purely material matters. When Prince Edward said that Sandringham had no special appeal for him and that as King he could not foresee supporting it financially, his mother was "horrified"—thus Wigram, who when told of the conversation suggested a joint stock company, with Princes Albert and Edward contributing equally toward the upkeep of Sandringham. Well, said Queen Mary, that was a possibility. She also told Wigram that she was giving much of Princess Victoria's jewelry to Princess Mary and to the Duchesses of York, Gloucester and Kent. There would be no bequest of these items to the Prince of Wales, however, "who might pass them on to Mrs. Simpson." That same day Chips Channon was scribbling in his diary.

My heart goes out to the Prince of Wales tonight, as he will mind so terribly being King. His loneliness, his seclusion, his isolation will be almost more than his highly-strung and unimaginative nature can bear. Never has a man been so in love. . . . How will [he and Wallis] re-arrange their lives?

By Monday morning, January 20, the King's doctors were anxious; clearly the Sovereign's heart was failing, and he could not long survive. Wigram found King George with the pages of *The Times* spread out on his bed. Wigram noted soon after,

He murmured something about the Empire and I replied that "all is well, Sir, with the Empire." H.M.'s mind then faded away. When the blood circulated in his brain again the King said "I feel very tired. Go and carry on with your work. I will see you later."

The Cabinet had decided that it was constitutionally necessary for the King to initial his approval of a Council of State to act for him in his illness, and for this purpose the Privy Council had been summoned. At noon the King tried to participate in this moment. He greeted his ministers, and with great difficulty he tried to put his initials to the legal document. "On taking leave," Wigram wrote, "the Members received a delightful smile and nod from H.M."

The Prince of Wales and the Duke of York, having gone to London to discuss an imminent council of accession, returned to Sandringham that afternoon. Meantime, Lord Dawson, asked to issue another report, took up a blank menu card and, writing on his knee, drafted an announcement that in its final form would become legendary: "The King's life is moving peacefully towards its close." After obtaining the consent of the Royal Family, this statement was then telephoned to the BBC for evening broadcast. One of the King's physicians, Stanley Hewett, administered morphine when the patient began his last struggle. Roused by the injection, the old sailor mumbled, "Goddamn you," before subsiding into a gentle sleep. At this, Queen Mary had to laugh.

At about ten o'clock the King seemed to slip into a coma. Except for the Duke of Gloucester (who was confined with a winter cold), all his children had gathered round with their mother. (At one point the Queen inquired about her neighbor and friend Ruth, Lady Fermoy, who was in labor nearby. That night Lady Fermoy gave birth to a girl, Frances, who would one day have a daughter named Lady Diana Spencer.)

Prince Edward had told Lord Dawson of the Queen's wish, endorsed by himself, that the King's life should not be prolonged when his illness was terminal. More than this they would not say, but, they added significantly, they would support whatever decision Dawson wished to take. And so it was that the life of King George V indeed moved peacefully toward its close—but with a little push from his physician.

For fifty years the full account of the King's death was suppressed, until Dawson's complete notebooks became available. The euthanasia was timed and carried out not to alleviate the King's pain, for he was unconscious, but for the sake of his family—and (thus Dawson) because of "the importance of the death receiving its first announcement in the morning papers rather than the less appropriate evening journals." Dawson also telephoned his wife in London, asking her to advise *The Times* to hold its first printing because an announcement was expected.

Wigram, who had no part in the decision and apparently none in the timing, was in a way vindicated. He knew the power of press and radio and must have been pleased to learn that the judicious exploitation of the appropriate newspaper was relevant to so awesome an event. Indeed, the timing of the death of King George was determined according to the demands of proper publicity.

"At about 11 o'clock," Dawson wrote later,

it was evident that the last stage might endure for many hours, unknown to the Patient but little comporting with that dignity and serenity which he so richly merited and which demanded a brief final scene. Hours of waiting just for the mechanical end when all that is really life has departed only exhausts the onlookers & keeps them so strained that they cannot avail themselves of the solace of thought, communion or prayer. I therefore decided to determine the end and injected (myself) morphia gr.3/4 & shortly afterwards cocaine gr.1 into the distended jugular vein: "myself" because it was obvious that [the nurse] was disturbed

by this procedure. In about ¼ an hour: breathing quieter,
appearance more placid, physical struggle gone. . . . Then
the Queen and family returned and stood round the bedside,
the Queen dignified and controlled—others with tears, gentle but not noisy. . . . Intervals between respirations lengthened, and life passed so quietly and gently that it was
difficult to determine the actual moment.

The moment chosen for the sake of both the news broadcast
and the historic record was 11:55 on the evening of January
20, 1936. When Dawson had determined that death had occurred, he nodded at Queen Mary. She kissed her husband's
forehead and then, in a gesture of consummate regal propriety,
went to her oldest son, bowed, took his hand and kissed it. The
King who had been her husband was dead; the King who was
her son lived on. And with that, King Edward VIII collapsed
into a spectacle of grief, crying loudly and embracing his
mother frantically.

His emotional display cannot be simply explained by a
sense of filial loss, for there was little love between father and
son. Rather, Edward seems to have suddenly seen, as his
mother bowed before him, that the future he dreaded had suddenly arrived. And there was another reason for the outburst:
his plan to flee the country with Wallis was now sabotaged.
Soon after, Alan Lascelles confided to Harold Nicolson that
this was indeed the case: "Edward and Mrs. Simpson had laid
plans to run away together in February, and only King George
V's death prevented it." That this was his expectation was also
indicated by a note from the Prince to Wallis only three weeks
earlier, on New Year's Day: "Oh! my Wallis I know we'll
have Viel Gluck [German for "much luck"] to make us *one*
this year." For years he had owned a ranch in Canada: he was
keeping it, he told Alan Lascelles, for a refuge. "You mean for
a holiday, Sir?" Lascelles asked. "No, I mean for good,"
replied Edward.

"In its outward manifestation," wrote Helen Hardinge,
"[his sorrow] far exceeded that of his mother and his three
brothers, although they had loved King George V at least as
much as he had. . . . While he demanded attention for his own
feelings, he seemed completely unaware of those of others."
As the new King composed himself, Queen Mary went with

great dignity from one person to the other in the room, to her children first, then to the physicians, nurses and servants, comforting and thanking each.

A telephone call was put through to London, and fifteen minutes later the BBC announced the news to the world. By this time Edward had recovered himself sufficiently to order that the clocks at Sandringham be set back a half-hour to the correct time. Thus the new King's first action was to reverse his father's hallowed tradition of gaining more shooting time in the short winter daylight. "I wonder what other customs will be put back," muttered Cosmo Lang, Archbishop of Canterbury; he would not have long to wonder. The order seemed to some callous and offensive, to others childishly rebellious, but it was typical of Edward to act impulsively on a thought, however ill the timing. He also knew that his entire family, his mother first among them, hated the queer system of timekeeping at Sandringham. That night courtiers, Georgian loyalists and those who had already decided they disliked the new King at once seized the clock command as ominous: trouble lay ahead. They were right, but for the wrong reasons.

The Duke of York and his older brother departed Tuesday morning, the twenty-first, for the Accession Council in London —by airplane, Edward thus becoming the first King to fly, as he had been the first Royal to make a public radio broadcast. In the banquet hall of St. James's Palace, the forty-one-year-old monarch—the first bachelor King to ascend the throne since George III in 1760—addressed more than a hundred councillors promising to uphold the constitutional government and to labor on behalf of the welfare and happiness of his subjects.

That day the front pages of London's newspapers were emblazoned with the details. His Royal Highness Edward Albert Christian George Andrew Patrick David, Prince of Wales and Earl of Chester, became King Edward The Eighth. Ignoring the Duke of York entirely, the papers ran column-wide photographs of nine-year-old Princess Elizabeth, perched smilingly above the headline: LITTLE PRINCESS IS NOW SECOND IN LINE TO THRONE.

Next day, Wednesday, January 22, King Edward VIII was officially proclaimed King from a balcony at St. James's Palace where he invited a few friends to watch with him from a nearby palace room. As the trumpets blared, Edward broke with tradition yet again, moving to the window to watch his own proclamation—and there by his side, clear in the newsreels and photographs that have survived, was Wallis Simpson. Later that day Parliament also took its oath of allegiance and did official homage in chambers. Mrs. Simpson did not attend, but if she had, her presence would perhaps have gone unremarked. Very few people outside her own social circle and the King's intimate society knew her, and the press and the general public had not the remotest idea of her identity, much less of her relationship with the King.

George V's body remained in the cold stillness of the little church at Sandringham until Thursday, the twenty-third, when the coffin was transferred to London by train. The route of procession took the cortege from King's Cross Station by way of Euston Road, Southampton Row, Kingsway, the Strand and Whitehall to Westminster Hall for the lying-in-state. Only one inauspicious note was struck. The Imperial crown was secured to the lid of the King's coffin, but the heavy jolting of the caisson loosened its moorings, and the Maltese cross atop the crown—set with a sapphire and two hundred diamonds—came loose and fell to the pavement. "Christ!" muttered King Edward VIII. "What's going to happen next?" And those words, suggested Walter Elliott, the Parliamentarian who overheard the outburst, might well become "the motto of the new reign." For Godfrey Thomas, the accident was a metaphor: "I am not superstitious, but it confirms me in my conviction that he is not fitted to be King and that his reign will end in disaster. . . . I don't think he will last very long."

Dense masses of people stood along the route. At Westminster nearly eight hundred thousand people filed past the coffin over four days, the queues outside stretching over a mile. On the last night a guard of vigil was kept for a quarter-hour, the late King's four sons standing at attention at the four corners of the catafalque. The King's body was buried at St. George's Chapel, Windsor, on January 28.

Amid all the state and family business, one person was remarkable for strength of character and dignity of purpose. "The sons were painfully upset," wrote the Archbishop of Canterbury, "and it was the Queen, still marvellously self-controlled, who supported and strengthened them. . . . I had a long talk with her [and found] her fortitude still unbroken. Let it not be supposed that this unfailing self-control was due to any sort of hardness. On the contrary, her emotions were always ready to break through; only her courage restrained them.'' Amid the bell-tolling, the great impersonal rituals and the symbols of transcendence and eternity, the Windsors were still a family—united in their loss but anxious, divided, frightened of the future, envious and suspicious of one another.

The new King returned to Sandringham on Wednesday, January 22, when his father's will was read for the family, and thus occurred Edward's first great shock, for his father had left him no money. After the bequests to the others were announced, Edward blurted out in a high-pitched whine, ''Where do I come in?'' Well, explained the solicitor, Sir Halsey Bircham, King George V believed that after twenty-five years as Prince of Wales his son must have amassed a considerable fortune from his income and investments from the Duchy of Cornwall, and there would be no need for further provision. With precisely the same reasoning, King Edward VII never left George V any money. ''But my brothers and sister have got large sums and I have been left out!'' said Edward VIII. And so he continued to pace and complain. On only one matter could all agree: the coronation must await a respectable period of mourning; it would be best held in fine weather and would in any case require complex preparations. May 12, 1937, was the date fixed.

Regarding finances, the King was ''not reasonable,'' according to Lord Wigram, who was later the first to learn that in fact King Edward had squirreled away more than a million pounds sterling. ''I tried to assure His Majesty that he would be very well off, but [he] continued to be obsessed about money.'' The battle lines about the late King's wishes continued to be redrawn during the entire year; as late as December 1936, Edward VIII asked for the will of George V to be altered in his favor. ''King George would turn in his grave,'' replied Wigram to King Edward's face, ''if he thought that his eldest son was not willing to give effect to his wishes.'' But by then Wigram had retired from service and was merely a temporary advisor helping to settle his late master's will; his duties as secretary were assumed by Alec Hardinge.

* * *

In 1936 the growing disapproval of those close to the new King had to do with more than the issue of Mrs. Simpson; in fact, she finally became the best excuse to judge him as incompetent and undesirable.

Even as Prince of Wales, Edward had a frivolous attitude toward protocol, a cavalier disregard for the traditions of palace dress and manner and a scratchy impatience with the rigors of an antiquated Court life. In addition, he seemed to embrace everything that displeased his father: the social company of married women who smoked in public and painted their fingernails, cocktail gatherings, American jazz and slang and weekend house parties.

Most of all, Edward resented what he called "the relentless formality of their lives," which he saw as a hindrance to some of the best they could achieve in a new world. In this regard and despite all his eccentricities, the King accurately judged that the monarchy was hopelessly strangled by tradition and by the antiquated system of courtiers, whose deference and pride of place did few people much good besides the courtiers themselves. "I was soon to find," he wrote later, "that any tampering with tradition is fraught with trouble." There were, for example, endless protocols to be observed, footmen for this task, aides for that one, gestures of empty ritual and prescriptions for the running of a household that caused only expense and in no way furthered the needs of the nation.

For his smiling, breezy nonchalance and his outgoing manner—but most of all because of the celebrity he had earned from being the most photographed person in English history thus far—the Prince of Wales ascended the throne with a popular support perhaps unrivaled in world history. From the Orkney Islands to Australia, from Canada to Fiji, everyone in the Commonwealth approved of him, though with very little reason to do so. And in America, where the desire to adopt or create a Royal Family has always been part of the unspoken national longing, the new King was proclaimed as a man even for the democracies.

But behind the movie-star popularity there was, as so often, very little substance. Although it is true that royalty (like film stars) do not have to be bright or imaginative—they simply have *to be*—it is equally true that King Edward VIII took no

259

steps to improve himself in any way and was interested almost exclusively in what affected him alone. He spent his life in a state of edgy resentment and barely concealed revolt, neglecting his kingly desk work from the first week that winter ("I have never had much zeal for paperwork") and depending only on Wallis's encouragement and emotional stamina to get him through the early period of kingship.

Alec Hardinge, who had once very much liked the Prince of Wales, found his new King an embarrassment, for as the months passed he stopped reading state papers almost completely. The reason was clear: "Every decision, big or small, was subordinated to [Wallis Simpson's] will. It was she who filled his thoughts at all times, she alone who mattered. Before her the affairs of state shrank into insignificance." But there was another reason for the private secretary's concern: "The King hardly ever attended meetings without his brother, the Duke of York . . . [whose] presence was by no means always essential."

Hardinge therefore believed that "there must have been another, less obvious reason for insisting that his brother accompany him on such occasions"—to prepare Prince Albert for the succession when Edward abdicated. Similarly, Edward's insistence that Albert learn the precise details for the coronation service suggested to the Archbishop of Canterbury, among others, that the event would finally be held for the Duke of York. His impression was reinforced when he learned that, against all tradition and without permission of any liturgical commission, the King ordered that the names of the Duke and Duchess of York be added to those for whom special prayers were offered in churches each Sunday. "I think his motive was to get out of being King, to pass on the responsibilities," said Edward's biographer, Frances Donaldson, years later. "That's why he misled [Wallis] into believing that they might reach safe ground. The great attraction was that she enabled him to give up the monarchy."

Regarding both his duties and the implications for his family and the nation of his relationship with Mrs. Simpson, the King was "not a thinker," said his Prime Minister, Stanley Baldwin. "He takes his ideas from the daily press instead of thinking things out for himself. No serious reading: none at all." The consequences were grave. Eventually Baldwin sorted and sifted through documents that should have gone to the King's desk; sensitive papers were withheld, for Edward routinely left them lying openly about for any and all to see. The Prime Minister held firmly to this custom when he learned that the King usually handed state papers and confidential telegrams over to the Duke of York.

Baldwin was not alone in his evaluation: many in the government knew that King Edward's character was so unformed, so untested in the waters of deprivation, so unmoored to a concept of sacrifice that he was unsuited to any responsible occupation. Of this, of course, no one spoke openly as they did not of the King's rank immaturity. "He was just like a little schoolboy," said Edward's old and close friend Lord Brownlow later. "His bed was surrounded by chairs, and on each was a picture of his beloved Wallis. It was an obsession." Just so the King's life at Fort Belvedere, which he made his headquarters, refusing to work regularly at Buckingham Palace.

Few at Court believed the truth: that Wallis was much the cleverer, the stronger and more courageous of the two, and a woman evidently willing to focus her abilities on the support of the man whose deficiencies and frank dependence were so appealing to her. "I love you more and more and need you so to be with me," Edward wrote to Wallis two days before his father's death. "I do long long [*sic*] to see you even for a few minutes my Wallis it would help so much. You are all and everything I have in life." This she entirely appreciated: "God bless you and above all make you strong where you have been weak." This sentiment may have a tincture of emotional exploitation; it is also dead right.

And what of her love for him? Her letters mention this but rarely, although that is not necessarily a sign of anything other than epistolary reticence about such things. Cecil Beaton, whose eye was as sharp for characters as for the lights and shadows surrounding his photographic subjects, believed she was "determined to love him though I feel she is not in love with him. She has a great responsibility in looking after someone who, so essentially different [from herself], entirely relies upon her."

Wallis Simpson certainly lacked any sophisticated knowledge of British history (much less of constitutional theory and practice). But she knew more of life in general, as Harold Nicolson and others admitted. Like Edward, she had been through the mill of various liaisons, but she had also lived in cultures very different from her own and benefitted from a variety of acquaintances. Unlike Edward, she had no resentment against her family or background; she was never merely insubordinate; and she was not dependent on anyone for an endorsement of her worth. She radiated confidence, even to the point of not needing the man who so desperately needed her. With that self-assurance and poise (among other qualities), Wallis became more necessary to King Edward VIII than anyone or anything. For the rest of his life he contended that his kingship failed because he was not permitted to be his own master. The truth was that such mastery was beyond him.

With his accession, everything changed and nothing changed, for it is no exaggeration to say that during the 325-day reign of King Edward VIII, only one substantial issue confronted his ministers and, finally, the people: the King's private life. Such a narrowed focus of attention on one single aspect of a head of state had never occurred before anywhere. As for the press, a frank reporting of compromising details was still out of the question. There had been gossip about King Edward VII's marital indiscretions and even allusions to his less than perfect character in the press, but specifics were religiously avoided, and no journal would ever have published a compromising photograph.

Yet in 1936 the press was poised for change. Newspapers from many countries found their way to England—London and New York were particularly eager and swift about such daily exchanges—and the American press felt no need to censor royal news from its pages. As Prince of Wales, Edward had known worldwide the celebrity of Douglas Fairbanks and Charles Chaplin; attached to him was the glamour of Ramon Navarro and Rudolph Valentino. From the moment of his accession he was regarded as Prince Charming, the Smiling Prince who would now be the perfect King, although there was one gnawing problem in the collective British mind: they liked a family at Court, and he was still, at forty-one, a bachelor.

Certainly the desires and decisions of a few people determined the eventual outcome of the reign of Edward VIII. But for the first time in history, things were hastened—and therefore the possibilities for a different result were narrowly limited —by a British press that would no longer be contained after the Americans ended their silence later in 1936. The sequence of events which we call the course of history was therefore quickened by two realities: the speed of modern communications and the desire of the public to know more about those they believed they knew. Movies perhaps had a lot to do with this desire to be intimate with the famous and the glamorous, and movie newsreels were more and more presented along with, and very like, the "trailers" for coming attractions. Next at this theater: Robert Donat and Madeleine Carroll . . . Marlene Dietrich and Gary Cooper . . . Edward VIII and Mrs. Simpson. All of them were gods and goddesses, up on the screen and in the pages of journals and fan magazines, smiling and waving, blessing the crowds simply by their beautiful, bountiful presence among them.

Although the British press at first maintained its usual ban on reporting anything relative to the King's private life, the name of Wallis Simpson was now heard in every fashionable set and before long would be routinely touted in the American press, which of course reached the shores of England daily. At the start, there was much hasty excision of unseemly pages from the foreign journals, but such editing could not long endure.

It was known in London society, for example, that the King visited Wallis every evening at her flat in Bryanston Court and that they spent every weekend together at Fort Belvedere, more and more often without Ernest, who by this time seems to have found diversion elsewhere. The King and his inamorata "sometimes invited us over to dinner," recalled Princess Alice, Duchess of Gloucester, years later. "This was awkward, as we were as unhappy with the liaison as the rest of the family, but as a brother Prince Henry felt obliged to go. Mrs. Simpson was always charming and friendly and, being American, a wonderful hostess. After dinner we would play *vingt-et-un* or rummy or watch a film."

As for the King's relationship with the Yorks, it was strained from the accession. Prince Albert was now Heir Presumptive, Princess Elizabeth was second in line to the throne, and his Duchess was the second lady of the land, superseding

Princess Mary, the Princess Royal.* Marion Crawford recalled one visit of Wallis and the King to the Yorks' country residence, Royal Lodge. Mrs. Simpson had, she recalled, "a distinctly proprietary way of speaking to the new King. I remember she drew him to the window and suggested how certain trees might be moved and a part of the hill taken away to improve the view." This, recalled Crawford, was astonishing—that Mrs. Simpson could even dictate to the King how the Yorks' gardens should appear. On two subsequent evenings when the King and Wallis dined with the Yorks and others, the Duchess was (thus Diana Cooper, the actress, royal confidante and wife of Cabinet member Duff Cooper) "cool and remote from first to last."

There was a concomitant complexity: even among the doyennes of London society (Sibyl Colefax, Margot Oxford, Diana Cooper and Emerald Cunard), Wallis was genuinely liked for her style and admired for her good influence on the playboy Prince, despite the fact that this was a society virtually defined by its antipathy toward Americans. But there was a notable exception to the favorable response, from no less than the influential American Nancy Astor, who had married a British aristocrat. "London is seething with gossip about the new King and his blatant exploiting of his Mistress Mrs. Ernest Simpson & her 8th rate husband always in tow," she wrote in her diary on March 22, 1936.

> Everyone seems to have a new disease "Simpsonitis" & "sucking up" to dear Wally is the thing to do. . . . It really strikes me as being ludicrous, all this toadying it is all so temporary, one never knows when Mrs. S. will be "out" & some new horror "in"—the King is selfish & slip-shod . . .

As the months of 1936 passed, more and more people agreed with Nancy Astor. Whether Wallis was actually the King's mistress or (as the principals and their friends always claimed) the relationship remained chaste until their marriage

---

* The Duke of York was Heir Presumptive (not Heir Apparent) because his right to succeed his brother could be defeated by the birth of someone with a superior right—in this case any son yet to be born (so it was hoped) to Edward VIII.

is quite beside the point (and, one might add, no one's business). It was beyond question, however, that she constantly
appeared in public at his side, usually wearing an array of
jewels he gave her. Thus she proclaimed herself *maîtresse en
titre* to the world. It was the vulgar display rather than private
conduct that offended members of polite society.

To make matters more complicated still: whereas the King
was preoccupied with the mechanism by which he could marry
Wallis, she believed this was a hopeless (even an undesirable)
fantasy, not only because she knew well enough the difficulties
of marrying a King but also because, as her letters to her aunt
early that year indicate, she was beginning to find the King
exasperating and demanding, and therefore a trifle boring.
"That little King insists I return [from Paris] and I might as
well, with [him calling me on] the telephone about 4 times
daily—not much rest." At the same time she was starting to
address the King in terms suggesting that he lower his sights
somewhat, which would of course enable her eventually to end
the relationship: "Perhaps both of us will cease to want what
is hardest to have and be content with the simple way," she
wrote to him in February 1936: a love affair, she implied—
whatever it meant for them—would be wiser and more realistic
than marriage.

But common sense would not prevail against the King or
her husband, neither of whom was pleased with the situation.
In March, Ernest Simpson asked his close friend Bernard Rickatson-Hatt to accompany him to a meeting with the King, still
residing at York House and postponing as long as possible the
inevitable move to Buckingham Palace. "I didn't like Buckingham Palace," Edward said later. "It was very drafty. Somehow, I had a feeling I might not be there very long. I never got
over the feeling of not quite belonging there. I felt lost [that
word again!] in its regal immensity."

Wallis's hope, according to Rickatson-Hatt, was that she
could

> have her cake and eat it. She was flattered by the advances
> of the Prince of Wales and King and enjoyed his generous
> gifts to her to the full. She thought she could have them
> and at the same time keep her home with Simpson. . . .
> She enjoyed the attention she received [from the King] and
> [thought] there was no harm in it.

And, Rickatson-Hatt added significantly, "but for the King's obstinacy and jealousy, the affair would have run its course without breaking up the Simpson marriage."

At this meeting with the King, the matter reached a crisis point. Bluntly, Ernest asked the King if he intended to marry Wallis. "Do you really think," replied Edward as if the matter were already settled, "that I would be crowned without Wallis at my side?" This was the first time the issue was mentioned by anyone: the Wallis-Edward correspondence and their later published memoirs indicate their silence on the question hitherto. At that moment, however, as Wallis was in Paris on a shopping trip, Ernest agreed to end his marriage and the King promised to do the proper thing and provide for her forever after as her husband. According to Rickatson-Hatt, no mention was made of Simpson's own private life; this gave Ernest the apparent moral advantage, for he could appear the sacrificing party in a situation that was effectively giving him precisely the freedom he wanted.

As for the King's freedom, it was presumed for decades that the idea of abdication came to him only days before the reality occurred—indeed, that it was forced on an unwilling monarch by a hostile government. But quite apart from the fact that everything in his life as Prince of Wales (including many explicit statements) attest to Edward's loathing the idea of being King, there is evidence that he spoke openly of it with his family. David Lindsay, the Earl of Crawford and a man at the center of London's social and political life, wrote in his diary on February 2, 1936: "Criticism [of the King and Mrs. Simpson] may become insistent, bitter; then he may do something fatuous by talking of abdication: he has done so *en famille* before now."

At the same time, Edward's mother (now Queen Dowager, although she was always known as Queen Mary until the day she died) first confided her anxiety about the King to Countess Airlie, her oldest friend and lady-in-waiting. "Your sons are about the age of mine, Mabell," she said one afternoon. "Tell me, have they ever disappointed you?"

Lady Airlie replied that she thought all sons and daughters disappointed their parents at some time, that when this had happened in her own case she had tried not to be possessive and to recall that her children's lives were their own.

"Yes," continued the Queen, "one can apply that to individuals but not to a sovereign. He is not responsible to himself alone." There was a long pause while Queen Mary picked up her embroidery and stitched for some time. "I have not liked to talk to David about his affair with Mrs. Simpson," she said quietly, speaking with astonishing familiarity to her friend,

> in the first place because I don't want to give the impression of interfering in his private life, and also because he is the most obstinate of all my sons. To oppose him over doing anything is only to make him more determined to do it. At present, he is utterly infatuated, but my great hope is that violent infatuations usually wear off.

It was of course impossible, Queen Mary added, that she should ever become acquainted with Mrs. Simpson, for Her Majesty would not—even for her son—alter her regal interdiction. No divorced (much less remarried) woman could ever be admitted to conversation with the Queen.

King Edward VIII before the microphones.

9

Abdication

May to December 1936

Well, Prime Minister, here's a pretty
kettle of fish!
QUEEN MARY to Stanley Baldwin during
the abdication crisis

In a constitutional monarchy, nothing is so resistant as an entrenched Establishment confronting a headstrong King or Queen. Nothing, too, is so uncompromising as the Court of a sovereign whose life it finds reprehensible. King Edward VIII, in the spring of 1936, was both shortsighted in his estimation of that double resentment and determined to surmount it by the simple expedient of pursuing his own will. As a result, the Windsors that year were a family riddled by tensions and suspicions, for it was clear that Edward's relationship to Mrs. Simpson posed a real threat to the prestige of the throne.

Indeed, much of the family's anxieties in the twentieth century have focused on the love lives of the three men with the title Prince of Wales.

The fast life of Victoria's eldest son, the man who became King Edward VII, caused the Queen constant anxiety and embarrassment, but at least there was never any fear that he would divorce Princess Alexandra—even for his great love, Alice Keppel.

For his grandson, King Edward VIII, nothing mattered so much as a public acknowledgment that the unacceptable, twice-divorced American, Mrs. Simpson, was the love of his life. That acknowledgment became the obsession of his brief reign. "The King," noted Chips Channon with his usual succinct accuracy, "is insane about Wallis, insane."

The object of the royal delirium was very much calmer than the man besotted with her. Of her husband and the King, Wallis wrote to her aunt as if she were coping with obstreperous children: "It is not easy to please, amuse, placate two men. . . . Ernest and HM [His Majesty] have often talked the situation out so everything has been on a most friendly and arranged basis . . . though things *might* go on this way forever." In England, she added, "they consider me important and my position at the moment is a good and dignified one . . . [but] should HM fall in love with someone else I would cease to be as powerful or have all I have today. . . . I expect nothing." On the matter of divorce and remarriage Wallis was quite clear-eyed: "Whether I would allow such a drastic action depends on many things and events," but in any case she was trying "to prevent a rather stubborn character [from doing] anything that would hurt the country and help the socialists"—by which she clearly meant abdication.

In negotiating the terms of her future, Wallis valued material security, for she had risen from genteel poverty to an intoxicating social circle and had become the recipient of money and jewels from the Prince of Wales, now the King of England. Edward, she told her aunt, had settled "the financial side for my lifetime. . . . I am 40 and . . . I know I can only control the financial side of the future . . . but if the worst happens I shall fold my tent and steal silently away. . . . I can only hope that HM will remain fond of me for some time—but I don't plan my future relying on that in any way."

The actions of Wallis and the subsequent events of 1936 indicate that she expected little more from this affair than a period of intensely flattering attention. The idea that she was a calculating woman out to snag a King and ascend a throne as Queen Consort is absurd. She was, on the contrary, someone out for a good time, someone who liked to create an atmosphere of pleasure for herself and for others. Beyond those goals, she seems rarely to have considered the long-range consequences of her wishes or actions. She often looked rather like a playing card—the Queen of Clubs, perhaps, or even the Jack. Nothing like the dangerous reprobate English royalists have loved to portray, she was a rather ordinary middle-class woman. Her aloofness (like that of Marlene Dietrich or Greta Garbo) aroused many, attracted some and fascinated just about everyone, and she was often assumed to be mysterious. She was, one might say, a transplanted American who had sprung straight from the pages of a Henry James novel.

Edward, on the other hand—from the day he approached Ernest while Wallis was shopping in Paris—did everything to effect her divorce and to maneuver his marriage to her, despite her assessment of the situation and even against her desires. The King insisted, for example, that she retain a lawyer and that she consult his own attorneys as well, to ascertain the most expeditious plan for divorce. Up to early autumn Wallis tried to avoid this eventuality, but the King was relentless. She was, in the final analysis, his excuse to give up the throne.

"I think the King had always had a claustrophobic repugnance for the throne," said Sir Donald Somervell, who as Attorney General in 1936 was intimately connected to the crisis.

> He is a man, I imagine, with few spiritual resources in religion or imagination. He is happy if the passing moment is fair—otherwise and therefore he is generally very unhappy. Such a character would be more than most at the mercy of an infatuation such as he had for Mrs. Simpson. . . . To surrender a kingdom because it's a bore is unimpressive, to surrender it for love seems on a bigger scale.

The King's relations found the situation increasingly unmanageable during the spring and summer of 1936 and finally tried to impress Edward with the gravity of their feelings by avoiding Wallis altogether. The Duchess of York flatly refused to visit Fort Belvedere, for the King's presence there meant Mrs. Simpson's, too. (Family gatherings had to be at the Fort for the simple reason that King Edward VIII spent not a single night at Windsor Castle.) Elizabeth's intransigence in this matter saddened Albert perhaps as much as his own silent compliance humiliated him, for the once close relationship between the brothers was now not merely threatened, it was inexorably deteriorating.

The Gloucesters, not quite so resolute in their conduct, motored down to the Fort for lunch two or three times, but these occasions were notoriously difficult even though the guests had to do little other than sip tea or cocktails and chat with the King as he puttered in his rose garden or hacked through the gorse. Wallis considered Henry's broad humor and forced laughter crude, while Alice simply smiled politely, trying to find an appropriately neutral subject for conversation.

No one was laughing when, of all people, who should appear in London but Beryl Markham. Her affair with the Duke of Gloucester was certainly history by this time, but he was still paying her a handsome annuity. With typical impertinence she rang Henry to ask if she might use rooms in Kensington Palace (his and Alice's London address) for her hotel. Alice was perhaps more frightened concerning the stability of her marriage than the impropriety of housing so unconventional and profligate a woman. She was, therefore, greatly relieved when assured by courtiers and advisors that—precisely because of Mrs. Simpson—she must not allow Beryl to become her guest, for then the gossip over Markham and the Duke would be revived with a vengeance.

The Kents also accepted several invitations, but their natural tact enabled them to finesse the awkwardness of the situation in a way the Yorks could not. George found Edward distant, absorbed only with pleasing Mrs. Simpson, while Marina (her dignity ever unruffled) went so far as to invite the King and Wallis to tea in return for their hospitality. This was not, as many thought, the Duchess of Kent's benediction on the King's behavior; it was her way of demonstrating her independence from her husband's family and especially from the strictures laid down by Queen Mary.

* * *

But the coolness did not have to do only with the King's romantic fixation. There was also the matter of the monarch's continuing friendly overtures to Germany and the threat this posed to national security. No less than the Third Reich's ambassador to London, Leopold von Hoesch, believed that Edward was warmly disposed to accommodate Hitler among the great heads of state. The King's "friendly attitude toward Germany," wrote von Hoesch in a dispatch to Berlin as early as January 21, 1936, "might in time come to exercise a certain amount of influence on the shaping of British foreign policy." Edward was, he concluded, "a ruler who is not lacking in understanding for Germany and a desire to see good relations established between Germany and Britain." When Hitler broke the Versailles Treaty and took the left bank of the Rhine in March 1936, the King saw this dangerous occupation as a mere "breach of law" that had to be conciliated so that England might "get on to the practical discussion of the Führer and Chancellor's proposals." In a masterpiece of understatement, Joachim von Ribbentrop, German ambassador to London from August 1936, told Hitler that German supremacy in Britain would be extremely difficult to achieve after the reign of Edward VIII since he alone "would not cooperate in an anti-German policy."* The public knew nothing of the King's ill-considered politics until many years later.

On May 28, 1936, Edward hosted his first official dinner, an event specifically intended to enable him to introduce Wallis Simpson to Stanley Baldwin: "Sooner or later," in the King's words, "my Prime Minister must meet my future wife." This designation of her was an idea Wallis found "ridiculous and impossible [because] they'd never let you." For the time being, Baldwin and the other dinner guests chose not to panic when the King's beloved was thus pitchforked into the royal circle, a group who seemed convinced that the affair would pass into history. After all, Ernest Simpson was on hand that evening, escorting his wife.

---

* In his evident indifference to what the Third Reich stood for, the King was not alone in Britain, although he was certainly temperate (indeed, almost liberal) compared with the ravings of Sir Oswald Mosley, the ardent Nazi who was calling for a fascist dictatorship in England.

But by early July the King was more insistent, and from this time he brought in his old college friend, the attorney Walter Monckton, to be his confidant and legal advisor on the developing crisis. Things then happened with astonishing swiftness. First, Monckton met quietly with Winston Churchill who although out of office at the time was singularly influential in Court and Cabinet circles.*

Monckton wanted to know from Churchill what the reaction of the British people would be if Ernest Simpson were to divorce his wife, a step that the King was urging. Churchill wrote later,

> I said that such a divorce would be most dangerous; that people were free to believe or ignore gossip as they chose; but that court proceedings were in another sphere. If any judgment was given in court against Mr. Simpson it would be open to any Minister of Religion to say from the pulpit that an innocent man had allowed himself to be divorced on account of the King's intimacies with his wife. I urged most strongly that every effort should be made to prevent such a suit.

Churchill's advice was unheeded by the King, who proceeded headlong in his rush to have his way. Two days after Monckton sat with Churchill, Edward again invited Mrs. Simpson to a small private dinner party, this time without her husband. Wallis's name appeared alone on the Court Circular detailing that evening (July 9), and from this date the whispering in London's higher social circles gathered to a constant tremulous rumble. "The people of this country do not mind fornication," said Ramsay MacDonald, former Prime Minister and then a Member of Parliament, "but they loathe adultery."

Churchill was not, then or ever, either censorious or disapproving of Edward's choice of Mrs. Simpson. The issue of paramount importance to him (as to Baldwin and company) was the stability of the throne. Had the King been more discreet about Wallis during the official mourning period for his father,

---

* In 1936, Churchill was sixty-two and had been a Member of Parliament, president of the Board of Trade, Home Secretary, First Lord of the Admiralty, Minister of Munitions and Chancellor of the Exchequer.

maintained Churchill and others, he would have won himself more friends. Had the King not rushed ahead so precipitously with his project, had he waited perhaps a year or two, Wallis might have been quietly divorced, perhaps become something of a welcome social figure, and then the King might have been able to marry her. Such was the feeling of Duff and Diana Cooper, among others. And despite the Established Church's firm opposition to divorce and remarriage, it might have been proven that Wallis had been the wronged and innocent party in both cases, and annulments may have been granted her. But of course the subjunctives never prevailed, for haste virtually predetermined the outcome.*

Known only to those present at the dinner were the details of an awkward exchange between Churchill and the Duchess of York. Churchill somehow fixed on the topic of King George IV and his secret, illicit wife, the charming Catholic widow Maria Fitzherbert. "Well, that was a *long* time ago," said the Duchess, attempting to kill the topic. In this she succeeded, only to have Churchill turn the conversation to the fifteenth-century civil wars between the Houses of York and Lancaster, a subject taken at once as a reference to the increasing chilliness between the Duke of York and the King, who was also Duke of Lancaster (which was the pseudonym he used when traveling). "*That*," said the Duchess, her voice rising even more insistently, "was a very, *very* long time ago!" And so the evening went.

For weeks some of the press and public wrongly thought that there was a link between the rumors of royal impropriety and the unpleasant surprise the King had on July 16. Riding toward Constitution Hill after presenting honors to three battalions of guards in Hyde Park, he saw a metal object fly in his direction. A loaded gun had been hurled by a deranged Irish

---

* The Church of England permitted a wronged party in a divorce to remarry in the Church's good graces; other cases were individually determined, but in no instance could the Church contravene the civil law, which allowed (however much it condemned) divorce and remarriage. Until 1937, however, the divorce laws were tortuous and hypocritical, as Ernest Simpson's subsequent actions attest. In this regard it is interesting to recall that the Church of England originated when a monarch (Henry VIII) wished to divorce and remarry.

journalist with a grudge against the Home Secretary. A policeman leaped to the King's defense, and the revolver landed (undischarged) beneath the monarch's horse. The King continued his journey without so much as an expression of concern.

But the detachment that so impressed the crowds that morning had the opposite effect a few days later when the distracted and disaffected King refused to stay the course of meeting a bevy of debutantes at a palace garden party. He wanted only to rush off to Wallis. This casual misdemeanor unfortunately coincided with a royal request then before the House of Lords: King Edward wanted a provision of £50,000 a year for his (unnamed) future wife. The peers of the realm, many of them aware who that might be, were not to be swayed. They disapproved of his choice as much as they did of his refusal to attend church; as head of the established religion, he was setting a wretched tone for his reign.

As for Ernest Simpson, he proceeded just as his Sovereign desired and as he himself wished, for his favor, too, had fallen on another. On July 21, after another secret meeting with the King, Simpson booked a room at the Hotel de Paris in Bray, not far from London; there he arranged to be seen by the staff —seen, in fact, in bed with his friend Mary Raffray, the woman he would eventually marry. Following the eccentric British legal rite, this was necessary in order to establish adultery, thus enabling Mrs. Simpson to sue for divorce as a wronged party. And so Simpson and Raffray simply left their door unlocked, and along came an unsuspecting chambermaid who believed the room had been vacated. The added touch of a Feydeau farce was achieved when the hotel register was consulted: Mary Raffray, soon to be Mrs. Simpson, had booked under the name ''Buttercup Kennedy.''

Wallis, who was understandably suffering a painful recurrence of ulcer pain, spent much of June and July in a haze of confusion, disbelieving that she could ever become the King's wife—indeed, counting on the fact that she would never be— and hoping that the matter would simply resolve itself.

If it was the King's desire to win favor for himself and his mistress, he could not have done worse than to arrange a summer cruise with Wallis and a few friends. From August 10 to September 14, aboard the steam yacht *Nahlin,* they made their way along the Yugoslav, Turkish and Greek coasts. The boat's library was ordered removed and a new bedroom adjacent to the King's installed in its place. "We all knew it was a love affair," said Lady Diana Cooper, who was aboard the *Nahlin.* "But we didn't expect a divorce or marriage or abdication. She was still married to Ernest Simpson, and he would write to her quite often. She would throw an envelope across the table [to the King] and say, 'Ernest has sent you these stamps.' 'Oh, how good of Ernest,' he would say. He was a stamp collector, you see."

> The news angle of American coverage was definitely romantic; that of the English press only emphasized the omissions. In every possible way, journalistic subjects of the King avoided mention of Mrs. Ernest Simpson, auburn-haired, maturely lovely former Baltimore belle who had for two years been one of the King's closest friends and who was cruising with the King's party.

So ran a story in the American journal *The Literary Digest* on September 26, 1936, without adding that the King had asked for a polite silence from Canadian-born Lord Beaverbrook, the newspaper tycoon who controlled London's widely circulated *Daily Express* and *Evening Standard,* and from Esmond Harmsworth of the *Daily Mail.* America's *Time* magazine, though circulating worldwide, had no reason to demonstrate such loyalty: it picked up a photo of the King and Wallis from the more independent *London Illustrated News* that summer and ran a caption identifying her. The foreign press were led everywhere by American journalists who documented the crowds greeting the party at every stop.

By mid-September delicate but pointed questions were being raised in London about the growing scandal, thanks to the first provocative story in any newspaper—published under the headline EDWARD'S FRIENDS ARE BRITISH ISSUE in *The New York Times* on October 4. "The spotlight has been thrown on Mrs. Simpson, while her husband, who is also a personal friend of King Edward, rarely gets more than a bare mention." The friendship, ran the article, has "caused a good deal of raising of eyebrows among the older members of King George's court circle. . . . But Edward considers his private life a thing apart from his kingship. This attitude [is] unusual in a King."

As Baldwin later said, he was receiving

a vast volume of correspondence, mainly at that time from British subjects and American citizens of British origin in the United States of America, from some of the Dominions, and from this country, all expressing perturbation and uneasiness at what was then appearing in the American Press.

Other international newspapers swamped the kiosks with shocking images: the King dressed casually, often shirtless, wearing only bathing trunks or walking shorts, hiking, swimming, smoking, drinking—and Wallis invariably nearby, standing with dignity, always impeccably coiffed and attired. The entourage, led by the royal pair (for so they had to be considered), wandered through white-washed alleys, jumped from the yacht into the sparkling waters of the Adriatic and strolled through obscure Slavic and Turkish villages. Wallis danced to Greek melodies and gypsy airs while Edward assumed bartending duties; one boozy evening at the Ritz Hotel in Budapest he stepped onto the balcony of his suite, cocked a gun and showing off his skill, shot out a row of street lamps along the embankment of the Danube. By comparison, Wallis's behavior was more regal. She never appeared in bathing attire except when swimming, she always took the greatest care of her appearance and she never thrust herself into the camera's eye.

John Aird, the King's equerry, found his monarch's conduct embarrassingly undignified throughout the cruise and told him so, in terms that earlier would have led to his death on Tower Hill. "I told [the King] that much as I liked him as a man I could not despise him more as a King." Edward then summoned Wallis, who to the surprise of both men agreed with Aird that, yes, the King's deportment left much to be desired. Was she, as many have claimed, a sadist intent on humiliating her masochistic partner? Or, more likely, was Wallis Simpson attempting to end the relationship by distancing herself from the King? That was the opinion of Diana Cooper at the time: "The truth is, Wallis is bored stiff with the King." Herman and Katherine Rogers, also aboard the *Nahlin* that summer, agreed.

This seems not to have been merely a vague impression Wallis left, for on September 16 she wrote to the King, who had returned to London two days earlier while she went on to

Paris. ''I must really return to Ernest for a great many reasons,'' she announced—the major one being that they were a compatible couple and that she was ''better with him than with you.'' Yes, Wallis admitted, she loved beautiful things and the glamorous life, ''but weighed against a calm and congenial life I choose the latter, for I know . . . I shall be a happier calmer old lady.''

''I am sure dear David,'' she concluded,

> that in a few months your life will run again as it did before and without my nagging. Also you have been independent of affection all your life. We have had lovely beautiful times together and I thank God for them and know that you will go on with your job doing it better and in a more dignified manner each year. . . . I am sure you and I would only create disaster together. . . . I want you to be happy. I feel sure I can't make you so and I honestly don't think you can me. I shall have [George Allen, the King's lawyer, who had arranged the financial settlement on Wallis] return everything. I am sure that after this letter you will realize that no human being could assume this responsibility and it would be most unfair to make things harder for me by seeing me.

According to Alan Lascelles, the King at once telephoned Wallis and threatened to kill himself. That old melodramatic ploy worked (perhaps because Wallis had seen for herself how high-strung and unpredictable the King could become), and on September 24 the Court Circular—again at the King's request —announced that Mrs. Simpson had arrived alone at Balmoral to visit His Majesty. Two nights later when Edward and Wallis invited the Yorks to dinner, Elizabeth breezed past her hostess: ''I came to dine with the King,'' she said to no one in particular.* But to her mother-in-law she confided that the growing ''sadness and sense of loss'' was due to ''a certain person,'' and Queen Mary knew exactly whom the Duchess meant. It

---

* The Duchess had good reason to be annoyed, for she and the Duke had substituted for the King in an official duty he had declined, pleading the Court mourning for his father. While the Yorks were opening the new Aberdeen Infirmary, the King was photographed after motoring sixty miles from Balmoral to meet Wallis's arriving train.

was a family gathering full of the kind of tensions that would not be so acute again until the awkward Christmas holidays at Sandringham in 1992 and 1993.

Two weeks before her divorce hearing, Wallis wrote to the King, suggesting that it would be "best for me to steal quietly away." The King would not hear of this and forced the judicial hearing, and so on October 27, Wallis Simpson was granted a temporary decree of divorce from her husband Ernest, an event minutely detailed in *The New York Times,* with almost daily references (that month and after) to her special friendship with the King. The "decree *nisi*" required by law meant that a "decree absolute" to terminate the marriage would be forthcoming in six months unless (*nisi*) either party could be found consorting with a member of the opposite sex or unless it were determined that the initial proceedings were undertaken under false pretense (that is, with the collusion of the married couple). That evening Wallis dined with the King at the furnished house she had taken in Cumberland Terrace, Regent's Park, where he gave her an enormous emerald engagement ring (later valued at $500,000) inscribed: "WE [Wallis and Edward] are ours now, 27 .X. 36." This present she accepted. King Edward VIII had won his greatest victory. As for Wallis, she had now effectively demolished the bridges behind her.*

Whether she believed the marriage would ever occur and that she would one day be Queen can never be known. She still took several steps indicating that she *hoped* to avoid the marriage and indicating, too, that she was indeed "bored stiff" with the King. But over the next six weeks a vortex out of her control dictated her future. "I don't think she was scheming from the start," said Diana Cooper (no admirer or friend of Wallis). "She was enjoying all the attention [from the King], and then it all got beyond her."

She was now convinced that Edward would be a devoted husband and provider for the rest of her life. In any case by early November she read the mood of the Court and ministers

---

* At the time, King Edward's personal fortune could be conservatively estimated at more than £1 million, about $5 million then, or about a billion dollars in 1994 valuation. Most of it came from the substantial annual revenues due him as Duke of Cornwall and Lancaster.

accurately enough to repeat her conviction that she had no real chance of being crowned Queen of England. All along Wallis had done nothing to force his hand in her favor; now she encouraged the King to pursue Esmond Harmsworth's suggestion to Parliament of a morganatic marriage, one between a man of exalted rank and a woman of lower station who despite the marriage would subsequently be denied his dignities, title and royal position, as would their children. But unlike European royal houses, England had no precedent for a morganatic marriage, and special legislation would be required; it has always been common law in Britain that a woman automatically takes the "style and title" of her husband.

In addition, the King was lukewarm to this idea, for he was now openly intent on abdicating if he could not gain approval for making Wallis Simpson his Queen Consort. As for Wallis, she was increasingly in an impossible situation. Urged by society friends and politicians to leave the country, she knew this would be futile: "They do not understand," she told Sibyl Colefax, "that if I did so, the King would come after me. They would then get their scandal in a far worse form than they are getting it now."

Wallis was now clearly seeking a way out of the King's life, but his obsession had made her a world-renowned figure. Either way, she felt a dreadful burden of opprobrium. By a terrible irony, what she saw as an honest and honorable way out was the most likely to earn her the scorn of everyone: if she abandoned the King, she would be a heartless woman responsible for his misery—so warned the international press and many in her London social circle, among them Emerald Cunard, Harold Nicolson, Chips Channon and even Winston Churchill. They and others felt (thus Channon) that such a judgment would be passed on her precisely because the English did not appreciate "how charming, how wise and sympathetic she is, [and] what an edifying influence [on the King]."

With the decree *nisi* granted on October 27, Beaverbrook and Harmsworth agreed to the King's request to limit their news story to a simple statement of the fact of Mrs. Simpson's divorce, without linking the item to the King's future. There was nothing abject or servile in this gentleman's agreement of silence. It had to do with the tradition of respecting the institution of monarchy. But this deference could not long withstand the major daily articles from the North American press. On October 25 a headline in *The New York Times* ran, NO LAW RESTRAINS EDWARD VIII FROM WEDDING MRS. SIMPSON IF SHE GETS DIVORCE. Four days later the same newspaper continued: "There is no further mention of the Simpson divorce case in British newspapers, but that does not prevent its being almost the sole topic of private conversation everywhere in the social world of London."

The *New York Mirror* went further: KING TO MARRY 'WALLY,' ran a two-inch headline: WEDDING NEXT JUNE. Beneath it was a story from the paper's London correspondent:

> Within a few days, Mrs. Ernest Simpson of Baltimore, Maryland, USA, will obtain her divorce decree in England and some eight months thereafter she will be married to Edward VIII, King of England.
>
> King Edward's most intimate friends state with utmost positiveness that he is very deeply and sincerely enamoured of Mrs. Simpson, that his love is a righteous affection, and that immediately after the Coronation he will take her as his consort.
>
> His brother, the Duke of York, has been extremely happy and fortunate in his marriage to a lady of the people, a commoner, so-called.
>
> King Edward believes that the marriage he contemplates would be equally happy and that it would help him to do what he wants to do—namely, reign in the interests of the people.
>
> Finally, he believes that the most important thing for the peace and welfare of the world is an intimate understanding and relationship between England and America and that his marriage with this very gifted lady may help to bring about that beneficial cooperation between English-speaking nations.
>
> Primarily, however, the King's transcendent reason for marrying Mrs. Simpson is that he ardently loves her and he does not see why a King should be denied the privilege of marrying the lady he loves.

But for Parliament and the Dominions, a twice-divorced American—after more than a century of the likes of the faithful

Victoria, Alexandra and Mary—was not acceptable and a morganatic marriage impossible. And, it was warned, if the King would not yield to the counsel of his ministers in this regard, his intransigence would force a constitutional crisis.

"Your association with Mrs. Simpson should be terminated forthwith," ran a letter from the government destined for the King's attention. "Should this advice be refused by Your Majesty, only one result could follow in accordance with the requirements of constitutional monarchy"—that is, the resignation of the government. Baldwin rightly realized that such a written (and eventually published) ultimatum would rally public support for a beleaguered monarch who certainly seemed to be blackmailed by his own government. The letter never reached the palace, much less the King's attention.

But Chips Channon recorded a dinner party at the home of Emerald Cunard at which Leslie Hore-Belisha (Minister of War) drank rather too much whiskey. Baldwin, he said, had protested directly to the King about Mrs. Simpson "and declared that unless the King promised never to marry her, his Government would resign." That, of course, would precipitate an unprecedented dilemma, for both Labour and Liberal leaders had told Baldwin they would not form an alternative government under those circumstances. If this exchange between Baldwin and the King occurred (and there is no reason to postulate otherwise), then Baldwin was cleverer than the King realized. The ultimatum would have had to be given verbally if it was to have any possibility of success.

On November 10 the name of Wallis Simpson was heard in Parliament for the first time. During a discussion of the coming coronation, a representative for Glasgow stood to declare that there might very well be no coronation. "Shame!" cried many in the hall. "Yes!" retorted the speaker, his voice rising above the din. "Yes, shame! Mrs. Simpson!" This was not a universal sentiment. Winston Churchill disliked Baldwin and urged the King to withstand the Prime Minister's pressure and insist on a conjunction of his private and public lives. In support, Churchill himself was briefly willing to help form a royalist party against the possibility (indeed, the growing likelihood) that the Duke of York would inherit the crown. This was the last thing Edward wanted; Wallis was, after all, his passport to freedom.

"Perhaps he really never wanted to be King," Freda Dudley Ward had said earlier that year. To Walter Monckton, Edward confided: "I am beginning to wonder whether I really am the kind of king they want. Am I not a bit too independent? As you know, my make-up is very different from that of my father. I believe they would prefer someone more like him." With his brother George, he was even blunter. "The King told him," wrote Chips Channon after a visit to the Kents, "that, over two years ago, while he knew he was an excellent Prince of Wales and liked his job, he nevertheless felt that he could never 'stick' being King. He could never tolerate the restrictions, the etiquette, the loneliness; so perhaps if this issue had not arisen, something else would have."

On Monday, November 16, Edward and Baldwin met again. The King refused to yield to his Prime Minister's request that he ask Wallis to delay or cancel her final decree of divorce. With almost hilarious disingenuousness (since he was the architect of the divorce in the first place), Edward told Baldwin that he could not interfere in the private lives of his subjects. "It was," Baldwin wrote later, "the one lie" the King had ever told him. As to the prospect of marriage, Baldwin reminded the King that "the position of the King's wife was different from the position of the wife of any other citizen in the country; it was part of the price which the King has to pay. His wife becomes Queen; the Queen becomes the Queen of the country; and therefore in the choice of a Queen the voice of the people must be heard."

Then Edward dropped all pretense of fence-sitting. "I want you to be the first to know," he whispered to Baldwin, "that I have made up my mind and nothing will alter it. I have looked at it from all sides, and I mean to abdicate to marry Mrs. Simpson."

But to give the world the impression that he was being forced to depart against his will, the King's brilliant final step was to ask Baldwin to canvass the opinions of the Dominions of the Empire. Constitutionally, of course, the King was entitled to consult the governors-general himself, as Baldwin made clear. But Edward deliberately ignored the opportunity to plead his own case. "I realised," he wrote later, "that with that simple request I had gone a long way towards sealing my own fate. For in asking the Prime Minister to find out the sentiments of the British and Dominion Governments, I had automatically bound myself to submit unquestioningly to their 'advice' "—which he could certainly foresee. Thus a multiple-choice question was set before the premiers: should His Majesty marry Mrs. Simpson, thus making her his Queen? Ought Parliament to draft a law permitting an unprecedented morganatic marriage so that the King might make Mrs. Simpson his wife but not his Queen? Or should the King abdicate? The replies were unanimous. The King must either give up Mrs. Simpson or the King must go. For Canada, South Africa, New Zealand and the rest, anything else was "unthinkable."

When that reply came back, it seemed to the world that Edward was indeed being booted out; in fact, abandonment of the throne was what he desired from the first. "He would *never* listen to reason," Baldwin said later of the King at this time.

> He had *no* spiritual conflict *at all*. There was no battle in his will. He is extraordinary in the way he has no spiritual sense, no idea of sacrifice for duty. That point of view never came before his mind. . . . It was like talking to a child of ten years old. He has no religious sense. I have never in my life met anyone so completely lacking in any sense of the —the—well, what is *beyond*. There was simply no moral struggle. It appalled me.

Baldwin's sad recital (phrased in much the same terms as those of Lascelles, Thomas and others who had spoken of their Sovereign) focuses the character of the King. The tragic nature of the man was not, in the final analysis, that he wished to marry a divorced woman. Rather, it is that from the start he felt "no spiritual conflict." He was like a child of selfish whim and utterly egocentric fancy who saw no problem save those who opposed him. Had he agonized over the decision, had he given to anyone, for a single moment, the impression that his decision to quit the throne was arrived at only after anguish and soul-searching, then he would be less vulnerable to criticism. As it was, however, he considered no one's happiness but his own—not even Wallis's. The next three weeks were, in light of the King's settled intention, a false drama, an over-rehearsed tableau—merely the formalities and not at all the tortured tragedy of a love-smitten King denied his beloved as a helpmate.

The evening of November 16 the King dined with his mother and sister.

"I am going to marry Mrs. Simpson," he said, "and when I do, you will have to receive her."

"Oh, I shall, shall I?" replied Queen Mary, who of course shared the prevailing etiquette that divorced people are socially unacceptable. "Well, we shall see about that." She was shocked and horrified at the prospect that her son could put personal happiness before public duty; when Edward asked her to meet Wallis, the Queen said that was quite impossible. "She is," said Queen Mary, "an adventuress." And with that single remark, the breach between mother and son was widened. "I don't think we could ever imagine a more terrible tragedy," she wrote later, "and the agony of it all has been beyond words." By an additional irony, the old Queen's obduracy sealed precisely the step she deplored: had Mary agreed to receive Mrs. Simpson, she would very likely have heard that Wallis herself wanted the King to stay on the throne, and she would have gladly fled in order to prevent the marriage. Doubtless Queen Mary, in this regard, would have been able to prevail on Baldwin to find a political solution to a temporary embarrassment.

It is interesting to note, then, that Mary and Wallis, such dominant influences in the life of Edward VIII, could not succeed in changing his mind. The King was not, as some have portrayed him, a weak and passive instrument in the hands of his political or personal torturers; in fact, a case can be made that the situation was exactly the reverse. The King knew precisely what buttons to press so that Wallis would remain enthralled with him: her desire for security, her terror of poverty, her fear of social rejection and international shame—all these he used to push his case to marry her. "The easy view is that she should have made him give her up," said Walter Monckton. "But I never knew any man whom it would have been harder to get rid of. . . . The whole crisis [of the abdication] might have been avoided if Queen Mary had agreed to meet Mrs. Simpson." The day after the King dined with his mother, she received Baldwin. "Well, Prime Minister," said Queen

Mary, taking his hand and holding it tightly, "here's a pretty kettle of fish!"

From that year the relationship between Queen Mary and her eldest son changed forever. "There is something steely and inhuman in the monarchical principle," Wallis wrote years later.

> No form of discipline can be more repressive of the simpler instincts of the heart than that of a monarchy in defense of its institutional self. . . . Even Queen Mary, for all her love of her eldest son, could not make room in her heart for something that had altered the natural order of monarchy. David had put aside what he had been born to fulfill until he died; now in his mother's eyes he had become something different and apart. Her love remained; but his place at the hearth had gone, along with his place on the Throne. As for me, I simply did not exist.

As for Mary herself, in July 1938 she wrote to Edward:

> You will remember how miserable I was when you informed me of your intended marriage and abdication and how I implored you not to do so for our sake and for the sake of the country. You did not seem able to take in any point of view but your own. . . . I do not think you have ever realised the shock which the attitude you took up caused your family and the whole Nation. It seemed inconceivable to those who had made such sacrifices during the war that you, as their King, refused a lesser sacrifice. . . . My feelings for you as your Mother remain the same, and our being parted and the cause of it grieve me beyond words. After all, all my life I have put my Country before everything else, and I simply cannot change now.

That, indeed, was the difference between mother and son. For Queen Mary, England was the prime concern: responsibility to (even *for*) the realm dictated everything in her life. But for her son the King, his personal life took precedence—he knew only responsibility to himself. "He for whom we agonized," said Queen Mary, "is the one person the tragedy has not touched."

* * *

An unfortunate intermission in the London melodrama occurred amid the grinding poverty in South Wales, whose depressed areas the King visited three days later. "You may be sure that all I can do for you I will," he told hundreds of unemployed miners, out of work for years and unable to feed their families. Despite their misery, they believed in their King and stood shivering in the early winter chill outside cold hovels, singing an old Welsh hymn of welcome to their Sovereign. "Something must be done," Edward added. At first these destitute people were elated that the King himself had noticed their circumstances and promised the weight of his influence in aid, as were the people of the great cities of Britain, who read the account of the royal visit the next day. But within weeks he abandoned that promise in order to marry. People then felt a deep sense of desertion, and bitterness toward Edward VIII ran very deep. And not only in South Wales.

Betrayal of duty was the primary judgment passed on the King by his family. For the Duke of York, the matter was compounded by the dreadful fear of an enforced accession. "If the worst happens and I have to take over," he wrote to Godfrey Thomas, "you can be assured that I will do my best to clear up the inevitable mess, if the whole fabric does not crumble under the shock and strain of it all." In private with his wife and mother, his nerves were in a tangle of terror. "David only told me what he had done after it was over, which I might say made me rather sad," the Duke of York wrote to his mother. "He arranged it all with the official people. I never saw him alone for an instant." Prince Albert felt that he had lost a lifelong friend and was rapidly losing a brother; worse, he now seemed to have only a few weeks' advance notice that he might have to be King.

Edward, meantime, was close to losing Wallis. Hounded by the press, she could not step outside her home without being surrounded by staring crowds, reporters and photographers from all over the world, where she also received daily packets of hate mail. On November 27 occurred the first mention of her name on the front page of a London journal: "American newspapers last night reported that a former U.S. society woman now living in London, Mrs. Simpson, has had her life threatened," reported the *Daily Mirror*. "Special guards have been engaged for her, it is said, and detectives assigned to open all postal packages she receives."

Very near to complete physical and nervous collapse, Wallis and her aunt Bessie (who had come from America to offer moral support) departed London for Fort Belvedere. There, a physician ordered a week's bed rest. Precisely at this time she decided to leave the King forever.

"I am very tired with and of it all," Wallis wrote to a close friend on November 30. "I am planning a clever means of escape. After a while my name will be forgotten." She would "fold her tent" in England and steal away. To another confidante she added that she would not return to England until after the coronation. But illness kept her at the Fort three more days, until Thursday, December 3. That morning—after the King's Cabinet formally rejected the idea of a morganatic marriage, the London press at last broke its silence. Queen Mary first saw the printed news on her way to inspect the smoldering ruins of the Crystal Palace, Victoria and Albert's landmark celebration of the British contributions to the Industrial Revolution, which had burned to the ground on November 30.

The immediate catalyst for the newspaper publicity in 1936 was a statement by the Right Reverend A.W.F. Blunt, Bishop of Bradford. At a diocesan conference on Tuesday, December 1, he addressed the religious significance of the coming coronation service, commending the King "to God's grace, which he will so abundantly need . . . if he is to do his duty faithfully. We hope that he is aware of his need. Some of us wish that he gave more positive signs of his awareness."

The effect of the Bishop's remarks—one wag suggested that the King had been struck by a Blunt instrument—was like that of a stroller in the Alps who kicks a stone and precipitates an avalanche. The *Yorkshire Post,* on December 2, was the first to link the Bishop's words to the King's private life: "Certain statements which have appeared in reputable United States journals cannot be treated with indifference. . . . The King may not yet have perceived how complete in our day must be that self-dedication of which Dr. Blunt spoke." The editorial wondered further about "a constitutional issue of the gravest character." That same day the last of the Dominions to reply to the Prime Minister's inquiry reported that the King must give up Mrs. Simpson or abdicate.

At first the London press did not, as many expected, leap to condemn the King personally. Instead the issue was the dignity of the Crown and the prestige of the realm. *The Times* was calm, reminding that "the high office which His Majesty holds is no man's personal possession. It is a sacred trust handed down from generation to generation and maintained for the last century with growing strength by the willing allegiance of the whole people to the sovereigns who were secure because they were respected." The British monarchy must, therefore, "stand as a rock to the world outside, [and] the public needs some definite reassurance if the rock is not to be shaken." Thus Britannia, it was fervently hoped, would ever rule the waves. *The News Chronicle* argued that it was for His Majesty alone to decide who should be his life partner, but the paper's editor argued in favor of a sensible morganatic marriage. *The Daily Telegraph* respectfully whistled in the dark: the King would not, the editors wrote, "choose for himself alone"; they were confident that he would "do nothing which would impair his dignity or harm the realm." *The Catholic Times,* probably to everyone's surprise, argued simply that the King had a right to marry the woman of his choice.

People gathered outside Buckingham Palace in support of Edward, singing "For He's a Jolly Good Fellow." But it was clear that if he were indeed so, it was only by comparison with Baldwin; thus the issue became one of a London population beleaguered by the Great Depression, supporting a monarch they saw as bullied by a Prime Minister who was doing too little for the masses, too.

Soon there were loud voices fanning the fears of civil unrest. How could the King love anything more than England? Was not the monarchy itself in danger of collapse if it came into the hands of the inexperienced Duke of York? That nervous man was beginning a series of frenzied meetings with his mother, his brothers, the Prime Minister and Cabinet members. Accustomed to the constant, supporting presence of his wife, Albert was now pitched into the battle quite alone, for the Duchess of York went down with a feverish cold—"a not uncommon reaction, throughout her life, to moments of great stress," as one of her biographers has noted.

Within days the national verdict became more depressing: the aristocracy and the upper class resented Mrs. Simpson being an American more than they objected to her as a divorcée. Working people, on the other hand, did not care that she was an American but that she had had two husbands. Caught between the jaws of xenophobic snobbism and bourgeois morality, the marriage did not have a chance. The age-old conflict between Crown and Parliament now had a curious twist: Parliament and the press urged royal responsibility on the King, and the King was begging for the same rights as a common man.

Inevitably, newspapers began to take a harder line against the King. *The Times* had altered its stance: without even condescending to mention her name, the paper proclaimed that "the lady whom the King desires to marry is not fitted to be Queen." More to the point, the paper subjoined the dubious observation that "institutions are incomparably more important than the happiness of any single individual" and that there was "something lacking" in his character. Quoting the Earl of Clarendon's remonstrance to Charles I, *The Times* had the temerity to indict the King for "the current, or rather the torrent, of his impetuous passions." Added *The Daily Telegraph,* "There are some concessions which cannot be made to the best beloved, some rules which cannot be broken, some conventions which must be upheld."

The mood of the public, recently so warm to the King, was also quickly becoming colder, for the marriage of Edward to Mrs. Simpson simply did not fit into the pattern expected of a British King. "I do not find people angry with Mrs. Simpson," wrote Harold Nicolson in his diary. "But I do find a deep and enraged fury against the King himself. In eight months he has destroyed the great structure of popularity which he had raised." According to the noted American correspondent Janet Flanner, the prevailing attitude could be summed up in a single phrase: "He's let us down." Years later Princess Margaret said to a friend, "You know, we didn't dislike Wallis—it was *he* we hated so much."

On December 3, Edward suggested to Wallis that she ought to leave the country to escape the press, and so she left for Cannes and her old friends Herman and Katherine Rogers. Before her departure, however, Wallis urged Edward to broadcast to the nation that she had gone forever: "Tell the country

tomorrow I am lost to you." Four days later a statement from
her was released to the British press: "Mrs. Simpson, throughout the last few weeks, has invariably wished to avoid any
action or proposal which would hurt or damage His Majesty or
the Throne. Today, her attitude is unchanged and she is willing,
if such action would solve the problem, to withdraw from a
situation that has been rendered both unhappy and untenable."
In a private note to Edward, Wallis wrote, "Think only of your
own position and duties, and do not consider me." There is no
reason to doubt the sincerity of that sentiment, which hardly
reflects the will of a woman mad for power and status. It
was her final attempt to extricate herself permanently from the
King.

But the King was adamant: "His mind was made up," said
Baldwin a few days later, "and those who know His Majesty
best will know what that means." Edward had no intention of
letting her go free while he was stranded on the throne, there
to wear a tarnished crown, permanently unforgiven for his
unseemly conduct and eyed suspiciously when he vowed a
sacred oath to the nation on his coronation day. "You must
wait for me no matter how long it takes," he had told her
before she departed. "I shall never give you up."

Since his twenties, Edward had defied tradition and craved
attention in so doing. More than anyone or anything, a "forbidden" woman (Thelma, Freda and most of all Wallis) was not
only a surrogate mother, she was also one through whom he
could strike back at his parents by the very nature of his choice
—and effectively impede his path to a throne he dreaded. The
foreign Wallis—divorced, American, without title or inheritance or pedigree—was as far from home and hearth as he
could travel.

"I did not want him to give up the throne," Wallis said
after Edward's death. "But nobody could make David do anything he didn't want to do, or stop him from doing what he
wished. I begged David not to abdicate, begged him not to do
it. I would have gone back to America. But he loved me. He
really loved me." As for herself, having lost Ernest she was
stranded. It seemed to all the world that she had been responsible for the King's imminent departure from his throne. What
could she do but agree to marry him?

And what, in the final analysis, did King Edward VIII and

Wallis Simpson want? From all appearances, from their language, their statements to others and most of all their separate and very different kinds of actions, it is clear that he was madly, obsessively in love—in a way "insane," as Chips Channon had put it—and that she, almost certainly, was not; in fact, she did everything to prevent both the abdication and the marriage. Fond of him, grateful to him, honored by his attention, she was satisfied by the adoration of one of the two or three richest and most famous men in the world. But at the time she was trying desperately to disengage herself from the jaws of a marital vise she now saw as horrifyingly inevitable. She wrote to her friend Sibyl Colefax in December that she had urged Edward and (through her attorney) the government to postpone further discussion of a marriage for a year, by which time "I would have been so very far away." After all, she had "already escaped," as she said, from England to France. By late 1937 she would be safely home in America.

On Monday, December 7, the government and the Royal Family knew that the matter was settled. "The awful & ghastly suspense of waiting was over," wrote the Duke of York in his diary, who at his brother's request went to meet him at Fort Belvedere. "I found him pacing up & down the room, & he told me his decision that he would go." The decision had visibly altered the King's mood. "My brother was the life & soul of the party," said Prince Albert of a family dinner the next evening, noting Edward's relaxed, almost manically cheerful demeanor.

By Wednesday morning the terrifying impact of his own imminent destiny had gripped Albert, who felt entirely unprepared for the task and—his wife being still bedridden—hurried off to his mother for comfort. "I broke down & sobbed like a child," he wrote in his diary and was (thus Queen Mary) "appalled" at the prospect of being King—a reaction identical to that of Edward months earlier. "I'm only a naval officer," he wailed to Louis Mountbatten, his second cousin, "it's the only thing I know about!"

On Thursday morning, December 10, at ten o'clock, Edward VIII performed his penultimate act as King. In the presence of his three brothers, two lawyers and two courtiers, he set his signature on seven copies of the formal Instrument of Abdication:

I, Edward the Eighth, of Great Britain, Ireland and the British Dominions beyond the Seas, King, Emperor of India, do hereby declare my irrevocable determination to renounce the Throne for Myself and My descendants, and My desire that effect should be given to this Instrument of Abdication immediately.

And with that single document there ended the 325-day reign of the only monarch in English history to abdicate.* Albert, Henry and George signed as witnesses, and the papers were locked in the red dispatch boxes. Minutes before noon, the boxes arrived at 10 Downing Street, and that afternoon Prime Minister Stanley Baldwin gave his report to the House of Commons. (Exactly nine years earlier, on December 10, 1927, Wallis received her decree of divorce from Earl Spencer.) By evening the crisis was over, and soon Great Britain would have a new King.

Precisely at 1:52 on the afternoon of Friday, December 11, Edward gave his formal royal assent to the Declaration of Abdication Bill, approved in the Commons the previous afternoon and brought to him at Fort Belvedere. It was his last act as King, and at that moment the Duke of York, Prince Albert Frederick Arthur George, acceded to the throne—as George VI, having decided to abandon his own name in deference to his father whose honorable reign he would strive to replicate. "Does that mean that you will have to be the next Queen?" six-year-old Princess Margaret asked her sister Elizabeth that afternoon. "Yes, someday," replied the future monarch after a word with their mother. Margaret paused. "Poor you," she said with a sigh.

King George VI's first act was to announce that the former King would be known as His Royal Highness The Duke of Windsor, a title suggested by that sharp-eyed old courtier Clive

---

* After his conversion to Roman Catholicism and in the face of the so-called Glorious Revolution, King James II was deposed and fled to France in 1688. Parliament subsequently declared that he had voluntarily abdicated, which could not have been further from the truth. It may be noted that James, like his descendant Edward, departed England on December 11.

Wigram. Abdication did not remove the fact of Edward's royal birth, but the dukedom was not a sudden warm honorific, an embrace of brother by brother. The fact is that several members of Court and the government were afraid that Edward's popularity might lead him to return to England one day. Mr. Edward Windsor could be elected to the House of Commons, and Lord Edward Windsor could sit and vote in the House of Lords. Both possibilities were appalling. The solution was obvious, Wigram said quietly. As a *Royal* Duke—which was only his birthright and no favor—Edward could not speak or vote in the House of Lords, so salutary did proper protocol prove itself.

After dining with his mother, sister, brothers, aunt and uncle at Royal Lodge that evening, Edward was driven to Windsor Castle where the paraphernalia for a radio broadcast had been set up and where he was introduced on the air as "His Royal Highness Prince Edward." He then broadcast a speech heard round the world:

At long last I am able to say a few words of my own.

I have never wanted to withhold anything, but until now it has been not constitutionally possible for me to speak.

A few hours ago I discharged my last duty as King and Emperor, and now that I have been succeeded by my brother, the Duke of York, my first words must be to declare my allegiance to him. This I do with all my heart.

You all know the reasons which have impelled me to renounce the Throne. But I want you to understand that in making up my mind I did not forget the country or the Empire which as Prince of Wales, and lately as King, I have for twenty-five years tried to serve. But you must believe me when I tell you that I have found it impossible to carry the heavy burden of responsibility and to discharge my duties as King as I would wish to do without the help and support of the woman I love.

And I want you to know that the decision I have made has been mine and mine alone. This was a thing I had to judge entirely for myself. The other person most nearly concerned has tried up to the last to persuade me to take a different course. I have made this, the most serious decision of my life, upon a single thought of what would in the end be best for all.

This decision has been made less difficult to me by the sure knowledge that my brother, with his long training in the public affairs of this country and with his fine qualities, will be able to take my place forthwith, without interruption or injury to the life and progress of the Empire. And he has one matchless blessing, enjoyed by so many of you and not bestowed on me—a happy home with his wife and children.

During these hard days I have been comforted by my mother and by my family. The ministers of the Crown and in particular Mr. Baldwin, the Prime Minister, have always treated me with full consideration. There has never been any constitutional difference between me and them and between me and Parliament. Bred in the constitutional tradition by my father, I should never have allowed any such issue to arise.

Ever since I was Prince of Wales, and later on when I occupied the throne, I have been treated with the greatest kindness by all classes, wherever I have lived or journeyed throughout the Empire. For that I am very grateful.

I now quit altogether public affairs, and I lay down my burden. It may be some time before I return to my native land, but I shall always follow the fortunes of the British race and Empire with profound interest, and if at any time in the future I can be found of service to His Majesty in a private station, I shall not fail.

And now we all have a new King. I wish him, and you, his people, happiness and prosperity with all my heart. God bless you all—God save the King!

Returning the short distance to Royal Lodge to bid farewell to his family, Edward saw the cold December mist gathering quickly across the Thames valley. He was to leave that same night by ship from Portsmouth, across the Channel and then on to Austria, there to spend the time at Baron de Rothschild's castle, Schloss Enzesfeld, until Wallis's divorce decree became absolute; during the six months, they were to have no contact.

"Then came the dreadful good-bye," wrote Queen Mary in her diary. "The whole thing was too pathetic for words." And so it was, at least for the Duke of Kent. For the second time that evening he broke down sobbing. "It isn't possible!" he cried. "It isn't happening!"

But indeed it was. Edward embraced his mother, his sister Mary and his brothers, the Dukes of Gloucester and Kent, and then bowed to the new King. Before midnight the former monarch, now the Duke of Windsor, was sitting quietly in the rear seat of a black Daimler, heading swiftly through the thickening fog toward sea transport—aboard the aptly named destroyer *Fury,* which would carry him to what he called "life in the real world."

Princess Margaret, King George VI, Queen Elizabeth,
Princess Elizabeth.

10

The Ivy Climbs   *1937 to 1947*

Can you do a lot afterwards?
QUEEN ELIZABETH to Cecil Beaton
about retouching her photo

For exactly a century, from 1837 to 1936, the British monarchical pendulum had swung in wide arcs, each generation producing a sovereign very different from the preceding. Dutiful Victoria, who followed the oafish hedonist William IV, was succeeded by the carousing Edward VII, who in turn sired the stern, bourgeois George V, father of the sybaritic socialite Edward VIII, brother of the staid, grave George VI. As George and his consort Elizabeth prepared for the coronation that was to have been Edward's, they strove to present to the nation and the world an image completely different from that of their predecessor. For the next fifteen years they succeeded remarkably well.

George's essential decency and courage would be refined in the annealing fire of World War II, and during the fifteen years of his reign, his best allies and most effective public relations aides were not advertising men or palace image-makers but his wife and daughters. The core of the abdication crisis had been that Edward had openly threatened the virtues most precious to the English—the enduring primacy of home, family and duty—and it was precisely this amalgam the Duke and Duchess of York brought to the throne. In fact, they and their daughters became the first Royals to be presented to the world as characters in a family romance.

The new King projected an image of simple, gentlemanly gravity—the devoted paterfamilias consecrating himself to the task of leading the nation back to a sense of honor and purpose. That was an accurate perception but not a complete one, for there were darker aspects of King George VI's personality. He was a nervous, basically inarticulate, mercurial, chain-smoking, hard-drinking man of astonishing intellectual mediocrity on whose unready shoulders fell the heavy mantle of kingship during the most dreadful period of twentieth-century British history.

Even before the coronation in May 1937, the new King and Queen and Princesses Elizabeth and Margaret were much loved, perhaps most of all simply because the people wanted a representative family, a national icon to embrace. Accordingly, the media went into action to gratify the public. "Here's the opportunity you've been waiting for," said Geoffrey Dawson, editor of *The Times,* to a staff member. "Try and spread the loyalty of our readers a little more widely over the Royal Family." And so it was: of 101 newsreels made by Movietone News in 1937, 89 concerned the new inhabitants of Buckingham Palace; two concerned the ex-King and his wife.

The family could be seen in all the media, waving to crowds, taking tea in a garden, feeding the ducks in St. James's Park, taking a picnic lunch at Windsor. And touching, homey little stories were sent forth. "You must ask Mummy," King

George was reported to have said to Princess Elizabeth when she wanted to do something. Princess Margaret could be seen pouting when her mother sent her back to the house for a warmer winter coat. From the beginning, the Windsors were to be seen as the cozy embodiment of homey British middle-class virtues, and so the public, longing for reassurance after the cataclysm of December 1936, rushed eagerly to support the new monarch. Like the Cheerybles in *Nicholas Nickleby*—"simple, warm-hearted and kindly"—the Windsors were soon admired everywhere, heroes (like Dickens's characters) mostly because they were preceded in the story by such louts. Conveniently, not only did the new Sovereign and his immediate family fill the bill, but so did the relatives: the Kents were busy creating an attractive family, and on Christmas Day, Princess Marina gave birth to their second child. She was named Alexandra for her paternal grandmother (just as her one-year-old brother Edward had been named for their paternal grandfather). During the war, the Gloucesters would provide two more Windsor royal cousins.

Occasionally, the adulation was lethal. In 1938, a recruit on leave from the British Army overheard a civilian speak in what he considered an offensive manner about the Royal Family. Furious, the soldier confronted the speaker, beat him to the floor and killed him. The fact that he was defending the name of the Windsors justified his anger, the court decreed, and the soldier was given two years' probation. "Most seemed to believe that justice had been done," as one chronicler wrote, "[and] the soldier was all but praised for his actions." Chauvinism had such extremes even before World War II.

In some ways the image-making was a masterpiece of improvisation, for like his father, George VI was a man of such unpredictable temper and occasional violent outbursts that at least once he was (thus one royal chronicler) "so out of control that he actually struck his own wife." Doubtless there was instant remorse, but it was equally certain that members of the royal household always trod gingerly if there were whispers of the King's ill humor. Such an explosion may also have been a reaction to the fact that, as a friend of the Queen remarked, "she rules the roost, make no mistake about that." Lady Pamela Hicks, daughter of Lord Louis Mountbatten and one of the closest friends of the King's daughter Elizabeth, recalled that

King George "would suddenly get extremely annoyed over some quite trivial thing. There would be a violent explosion, and it would be absolutely terrifying!"

Still, whatever unpleasantness may sometimes have occurred between them in private, George VI was—like his older brother Edward—entirely dependent on his wife: "she was his willpower, his all," as Chips Channon wrote. Strong and determined like Wallis whom she so hated, the new Queen Elizabeth was an impressive person under any circumstances. Endlessly energetic on behalf of the image of the Crown (which endeared her to Queen Mary) and for the sake of her husband (which endeared her to him), she turned tardiness into a virtue, never rushing through an appointment or an audience for the next engagement if those with whom she was speaking were valuable for good publicity.

The restoration of the monarchy's image, after all, could not depend only on the shy, stuttering King, and no one knew this better than his wife. With steely determination that was almost programmatic, she became what she was, raising her presence as a plump young matron in chiffon to truly regal status. And with her two little Princesses, she was the guarantor of the throne's future. The chiffon, it must be noted, was an inspired device to camouflage her prematurely matronly figure —thus her lifelong admiration for photographer Cecil Beaton, who also posed her in profile to conceal her ample features. "Can you do a lot afterwards?" the Queen knowingly asked Beaton just before one photo session. He could, and thus began the system of carefully retouching the Royal portraits in order to magically remove inches from the waist and bosom. The Queen was insistent that an almost unreal aura of loveliness surround the documentation of her family.

Privately there were still enormous family tensions relative to Edward, for the Windsors in England feared the return of the Windsors abroad. Thus it was that the financial settlement made on the former King (a payment of £20,000 per year) required that he never set foot in his native land without Royal permission. Here was an unprecedented move, a punishment entirely outlawed by Magna Carta in 1215. Yet even this appalling act of personal retribution for what the Royal Family saw as Edward's unseemly conduct was exceeded by George's first kingly decree.

On May 27, 1937, the new Sovereign signed papers formally known as Letters Patent. The effect of this document was that the ex-King, Prince Edward, would henceforth bear the "title, style or attribute of Royal Highness"—but that designation would be withheld from his wife and from any children born to the marriage. Wallis would be known simply as the Duchess of Windsor.

The previous December, the new King George VI had instructed (all the brothers had agreed to it, and their advisors concurred) that the abdicating monarch be introduced as His Royal Highness The Prince Edward for the historic radio broadcast of abdication. Far from abdicating a royal status, Edward had abandoned only the throne; more to the point, according to British common law, it is quite impossible to abdicate one's royal status. If one is born a Prince of the blood royal, one is so unto death; thus, as son of the legitimate King George V, Edward was legitimately His Royal Highness. But King George, on a thoroughly absurd pretext, decided that it was necessary to recreate his brother a Royal Highness, and the only reason for this action was to attempt to deny that status to Wallis.

But this was not within the King's competence, power or ability under any provision of the British constitution. Every wife, says common law, automatically enjoys the status of her husband.* Not incidentally, the press office at Buckingham Palace claimed that the Letters Patent was a decree that the government pressed, but in fact the palace—that is, the King and Queen (no subordinate would have dared to assume so historic a prerogative)—insisted that the government draw up the Letters Patent for the King's signature. The King did not consult the Prime Minister; he had instructed him on what to do.

---

* A Royal or a peeress who marries "beneath" her status may retain her own title as a courtesy. Thus, to cite one example, when Princess Alexandra (daughter of His Royal Highness Prince George, Duke of Kent) married Sir Angus Ogilvy, she remained Princess Alexandra. An admirable lady who spurns affectation, she prefers to be known as Mrs. Angus Ogilvy, and she allows the designation "The Princess Alexandra" to be attached (doubtless not to offend the memory of her parents and the dignity of her cousin the Queen).

With this single juridically absurd act, Wallis became the only wife of an Englishman to be disallowed her husband's rank. In marrying Prince Edward, Wallis at once became a Princess and a Royal Highness. Such was the case when George had married Elizabeth in 1923: "It is officially announced that, in accordance with the settled general rule that a wife takes the status of her husband, Lady Elizabeth Bowes-Lyon on her marriage has become Her Royal Highness The Duchess of York, with the status of a Princess." By interfering with common law, the newly anointed King George VI, who had sworn before God and the Empire to serve the people and their constitution, had acted unconstitutionally. This, with royal absolutism (and no little ignorance), he never acknowledged. As late as 1949, George told Edward, "You must remember that I made your wife a Duchess despite what happened in December 1936. You should be grateful to me for this. But you are not." This would be amusing were it not pathetic: Wallis had married His Royal Highness Prince Edward, The Duke of Windsor, and she automatically became Her Royal Highness Princess Wallis, The Duchess of Windsor.

Furthermore, the Letters Patent created precisely the morganatic relationship (the denial of title and status to a man's wife) that in 1936 had been rightly called unconstitutional according to British law. The Letters Patent, which by a cruel stroke Edward received the day before his wedding, was a gesture so vindictive and cut so deeply into the heart of the virtually exiled ex-King that he never recovered from it for the rest of his life. He knew, as did anyone with the remotest familiarity with English common law, that a woman takes the title and style of her husband and that the King had neither the power nor the competence to deny Wallis the royal designation. In this regard, forty years later the youngest son of George, Duke of Kent (Prince Michael, born in 1942) married a divorced Roman Catholic (Mrs. Thomas Troubridge, the Bohemian-born Baroness Marie-Christine von Reibnitz). But despite her first marriage, there was no doubt that she would be known as Her Royal Highness, and so she is.

But in 1937 the perceived wound caused by the abdication was so fresh that nothing stopped the King from inflicting a cruel, senseless (not to say illegal and invalid) blow against his brother. No less an authority than *Burke's Peerage* proclaimed in 1967 that King George VI's gesture was "the last act of triumph of an outraged and hypocritical establishment [and] the most flagrant act of discrimination in the whole history of our dynasty." In 1937 the Duke of Windsor fought the royal decree, placing several angry telephone calls to the King that summer—communications finally halted on orders of the Queen whose will no one (not even the King) contravened. In this she was supported by Alec Hardinge and Alan Lascelles, who of course had been only too happy to see Edward go.

The King's action caused a lifelong estrangement between him and his brother. Privately, the Duke of Windsor insisted on the curtsies and courtesies rightly due his wife. "I know Bertie," cried the Duke when the announcement arrived. "I know he couldn't have written this letter on his own!" Who influenced his brother? "Those closest to him," the Duke said, and no one mistook his meaning: it must have come from the King's wife, then Queen Elizabeth—"the ice-veined bitch," as the Duke now called the sister-in-law of whom he had once been so fond. She had orchestrated the Letters Patent and saw to it that Edward would never consider England a home again. Her main concern, as those who knew her understood, was to shield the King from his brother's overpowering personality and from what she saw as the undignified presence in the Windsor family of a common American.

It is, therefore, not to the credit of a woman with so many admirable qualities that, by sheer force of personality, she saw to the permanent estrangement of two brothers who had once been so close. As long as the Duchess of Windsor was considered a non-Royal, morganatic wife—the law be damned—Queen Elizabeth would never have to receive her. And assessing quite accurately that Edward would not appear publicly in England without Wallis at his side, she could thus count on the permanent absence of the ex-King, too.

"Wallis had been beaten by the Queen, who was in this matter a very clever and devious woman," said Angela Fox, summarizing the eventually widely known fact that it was King George's wife who insisted on the denial of royal prerogatives to Wallis and on a separation from the family that would last their lifetimes. "Here was Wallis, a more real, much more sophisticated woman than most of the Royals, and the palace was creating this myth that she was a power-mad person. Life *did* take on a tragic level for her later, as she and her husband had virtually no life. But they were victimized by a royal vindictiveness that would never have occurred to either of them.'' The result was permanent animosity between the once close brothers; ''that stuttering idiot'' was Edward's typical description of his brother as late as fifteen years after the abdication.

''It was hard for the younger amongst us,'' recalled the King's nephew (Princess Mary's son, later Lord Harewood), ''not to stand in amazement at the moral contradiction between the elevation of code and duty on the one hand, and on the other the denial of central Christian virtues—forgiveness, understanding, family tenderness.''

All over London, encouraged by the palace, Wallis Simpson's name was reviled. ''One hears charming, intelligent people make quite revolting statements about her,'' recalled another observer of the contemporary social scene. ''I should hate to be hated the way she is in London since the abdication.'' According to Chips Channon, Queen Mary and the entire Court ''hate Wallis Simpson to the point of hysteria, and are taking up the wrong attitude: why persecute her now that all is over? Why not let the Duke of Windsor, who has given up so much, be happy?'' Why not, indeed? Kings and Queens can afford to be gracious, after all, but not, apparently, this new Queen. Asked by one of her ladies-in-waiting if the Duchess of Windsor would accompany the Duke on a hypothetical visit to England, the Queen snapped, ''No, certainly not; wouldn't receive her if she did.''

As for Wallis, who at last married Edward on June 3 in France, she admitted that of course she had expected the designation HRH—''but not from a mere desire for social status. Rather, I wanted it [because] I dreaded being condemned to go through the rest of our lives together as the woman who had come between David and his family.'' But Windsor pettiness prevailed. ''The reign of George VI,'' Wallis added, ''is a split-level matriarchy in pants. Queen Mary runs the King's wife [Queen Elizabeth], and the wife runs the King.'' As it happened, she was quite correct. The King wanted to visit his brother the summer after his marriage, but Queen Elizabeth forbade it because Queen Mary had issued ''strong instruction'' to that effect, just as she had tried (unsuccessfully, as it turned out) to sabotage a visit to the Windsors by the Kents. And when Henry and Alice, the Duke and Duchess of Gloucester, dined in Paris with Edward and Wallis, ''the response from the public made it clear,'' according to Alice, ''that a [family] reconciliation with the Windsors would not be popular.'' After that evening in Paris ''[Prime Minister] Neville Chamberlain's idea, not ours,'' Alice added, the Gloucesters received a stack of hate mail.

For all the pomp and glitter of the coronation that spring, there was a definite air of whistling in the dark. A certain gloom had descended on the monarchy, a darkness attended by the gathering storms on the Continent and the alarming rise of fascism. To counter that impending dread, the splendor proceeded without dilution or economy on May 12. At first it was to have been televised, but the Archbishop of Canterbury feared the King would do something embarrassing, and so it was filmed (and later edited) and broadcast on radio. Television transmission was restricted to a single camera perched atop a column at Hyde Park Corner, capturing the royal entourage in transit from Buckingham Palace to Westminster Abbey.*

Precisely because the monarchy had no political power, its almost priestly role had to be emphasized, and there was an array of articles focusing on the religious devotion of the King and Queen—above petty political strife but not, of course, above petty family politics. (*Destiny Called to Them* was the title of a typical book on the Windsors published in 1939.) The people had a profound need to believe in themselves, and on this apparently ordinary family was placed the need for the nation to see itself as exalted, as blessed, as indestructible. The rites for which this family knelt on May 12, 1937, were thus seen as grand projections, as blessings for all the people, to whom the new monarch and his wife made an explicit act of dedication.

Whereas the King was nervous and irritable, his wife was relaxed, warm, an asset to him on any occasion. Her increasing

---

* On August 26, 1936, the BBC had broadcast the world's first live high-definition television transmission to the few households who had sets.

plumpness, as it was interpreted, added to her matronly charm; in a sense it made her at once more appealing (as a mother) and less threatening (as a woman). She seemed always to smile in public, which was certainly breaking with tradition (for Queen Mary rarely did), and she knew how to put people at ease. When film designer Vincent Korda was preparing the sets for the Princesses' Christmas pageants at Windsor Castle during the war, the Queen noticed that Korda seemed physically uncomfortable. Inquiring what was wrong, she was told that his feet hurt. "Mine do, too!" cried Elizabeth, kicking off her shoes so that her guest could do the same. That was the essence of royal decorum: above all, one's visitors were to be comfortable.

Very soon after the coronation, as royal biographer Sarah Bradford wrote, "the Queen had slipped into her new part successfully and with ease; she was a natural actress . . . [and] she was thoroughly enjoying it." There was, as some noted, a rather too studied royal air behind the magnetic charisma. Harold Nicolson, who greatly admired the Queen, had a similar impression after dining with the Windsors and a few friends. "She wears upon her face a faint smile indicative of how she would have liked her dinner party were it not for the fact that she was Queen of England." One of her most appealing characteristics, in fact, was the pose she conveyed that she was forced against her will, by the abdication, into being Queen. This was patent nonsense, for she was by all accounts delighted with her new station in life. (Similarly, years later, she implied that her husband's death at fifty-six was caused by the war effort; she conveniently ignored the fact that he was a chain-smoker and a heavy drinker whose death was caused by lung cancer and cardiovascular collapse.)

Of the ways in which the King differed from his father, the most dramatic was in his relation with his children: by all accounts, King George and Queen Elizabeth were doting parents, and life at home had an affectionate serenity that was, alas, not to be repeated in subsequent generations. However much George bristled under the demands of his new job, no matter how he recoiled from rehearsing speeches and meeting strangers, he could always be certain of the cheerful support of his family at the end of a day. For the first time the children of the King and Queen did not have to curtsy to them. Contrary to their governess's injunction, Lilibet and Margaret were told by their father that this would be unnecessary, although their mother, taking a cue from Queen Mary, was adamantly opposed to this relaxation of royal protocol. The children ought to understand that the monarchy is above all things, even family life. But George would not have his daughters as intimidated by him as he had been by his father. In their presence both parents eventually became more relaxed—admiring of Lilibet's gravity and amused by Margaret's high spirits.

Life at Buckingham Palace was not nearly as pleasant for the family as at Windsor Castle, Balmoral or Sandringham. At "Buck House," the girls loved only the gardens; otherwise, they found the place monumentally uncomfortable, rather like camping out in a cold museum. Margaret asked for a bicycle to negotiate the endless corridors; denied this, she found a pair of skates.

The education of the two young Princesses continued under their governess, Marion Crawford, but since eleven-year-old Lilibet was now Heiress Presumptive to the throne, she was taught an introduction to British constitutional history by Sir Henry Marten, provost of Eton.* Queen Mary stepped in to supplement these private classes with educational sojourns to the Tower of London, Hampton Court, Greenwich Palace and other places of royal importance. And when the King and Queen were abroad on official business—visiting Paris in 1938 and America in 1939 to cement friendships with those countries as the threat of war became clearer—Lilibet and Margaret were left in the care of Queen Mary, who was not one to spoil them the way dear Queen Alexandra had spoiled *her* grandchildren.

With her grandmother, Lilibet learned all the protocols, the manners, the history, the royal demeanor she later exhibited as adult Princess and Queen. At Marlborough House, Mary received her granddaughter formally, and there Lilibet saw that the old Queen refused to use the telephone, for it was beneath the dignity of royalty. One ought to ring if one required some-

---

* Because Princess Elizabeth's place as second in line could theoretically have been superseded if her parents were to have a boy, she was only "Heiress Presumptive"; the new young Prince would then have been "Heir Apparent," for no one could have preceded him.

thing. If she wished a word with the King or Queen, she sent a written note and expected a written reply. As for hats—well, the matter was really quite simple. No lady ever went out without one, regardless of the season. Princess Elizabeth received more hats from her grandmother than counsel or correction, and this directive evidently took as deep a root as any: thus the lifelong habit of the future Queen of England for a variety of hats.

Mary also enjoined on Lilibet a quiet piety. When a priest departed the palace and promised to send Lilibet a book, she thanked him but asked that it be ''not about God, please. I know everything about Him''—presumably from Queen Mary, who claimed to be on intimate terms with the Deity.

Trained by her grandmother to observe the tiniest detail of royal decorum, the child had scant patience for a lack of it in others. Passing a sentry box with one of their beloved corgis on a lead, Elizabeth and Margaret could not prevent the dog from rushing the young guard and tangling the rope in the flustered man's feet. The scene took on the atmosphere of a Keystone Kops routine as the guard tried to salute, tripped and punctured the ceiling of the sentry box with his bayonet. Margaret clapped her hands and laughed. Elizabeth scrutinized the man with a withering glance and, in perfect imitation of Queen Mary, said, ''I'll overlook it this time.''

But she could not overlook her sister's occasional naughtiness. If Margaret hid a gardener's rake or rang a bell for no reason, Lilibet hid, embarrassed. ''I do hope she won't disgrace us all by falling asleep in the middle,'' Lilibet said of her sister as they set out for the coronation at Westminster Abbey. Taught to keep her emotions in check, she encouraged Margaret to do the same. When their parents departed for a journey to America in 1939, the girls were brought to the pier. ''I have my handkerchief, too,'' said Margaret. ''To wave, not to cry,'' announced Lilibet. Tidy as a schoolmistress, the older Princess went so far as to assume her sister's minor chores rather than see them left undispatched. Lilibet's mother was no stern monitor in all this; it was Mary who instilled the domestic virtues and devotion to duty in the future Queen.

''The girl must be taught to be a Queen, but she must not be spoiled,'' her grandmother insisted. One day in 1938 she took Lilibet to a store in Oxford Street, where a curious crowd quickly gathered to see the royal shoppers. "Think of all the people who'll be waiting to see us outside!" the Princess said to Queen Mary, who at once whisked the child out a rear door and deposited her back at the palace. On another occasion Lilibet said that something in the royal kitchen would be prepared very differently "when *I* am Queen." The temperature of the room dropped sharply when Queen Mary's frosty voice was raised: "Before you become a Queen, my dear, you will have to learn to be a lady."

Just how a lady acted—even under the most demanding and dangerous circumstances—was clarified for Lilibet in May 1939 when Queen Mary's automobile was hit broadside by an enormous delivery truck. The seventy-two-year-old matriarch was injured more seriously than her driver or companions, for she sustained painful contusions from head to foot and a sliver of glass in her eye. Queen Mary had to climb down a ladder to leave the wrecked car, and she did so, wrote a witness, joking bravely and retaining her dignity. "She had neither her hat nor one curl out of place. The only outward sign of disorder she showed others was a broken hat pin and her umbrella, broken in half." Taken to a nearby house to rest, she would not do so until assured that her companions were safe.

When Lilibet came to visit her grandmother a few days later, Queen Mary admitted that her back hurt abominably, but she would not remain in bed; in fact, she rose to write a note to the offending truck driver, whom she wished a speedy recovery. The doughty lady never complained about herself, made no change in her motoring schedule that summer, and would ask for no special comforts during the time of her recuperation. Thus she communicated to her granddaughter the necessity of both royal reserve and dignified courage.

As for Margaret, she was at once aware of being relegated to second place. Her grandmother, for example, was puzzled by the girl's feisty independence and easily angered by what she considered girlish, unroyal comportment. To the day she died Queen Mary could not understand Margaret's desire to give and attend parties; worst of all was the girl's fondness for dancing.

That year of 1937, six-year-old Margaret was conscious of a shift in her own destiny, an impression reinforced when she and her sister were given prizes at a Windsor horse show—

"just because we are princesses," she said bluntly. Well, partly that was true, conceded Crawfie. "Oh," said Margaret, visibly saddened. "I see." And with that she lost all interest in riding.

Not so Lilibet, who, as if to adjust to the unfair advantage, at once set herself the task of becoming an expert horsewoman. She had been riding ponies since 1929; Henry Owen, the royal groom, had trained her on a succession of horses: Gem, Snowball and now the full-size Comet. "The Princess was painstaking," reported Horace Smith, her new instructor. By 1938 she was an expert jumper, and even greater proficiency as an equestrienne would follow with each year. As Queen she rode regularly and often until her mid-sixties.

"I used to be Margaret of York," the younger daughter once complained, "but now that Papa is King, I am nothing." As it happened, there would be a sad truth to this childish self-dramatization. To compensate, from an early age Princess Margaret liked deference and often insisted on it, much to her mother's chagrin. In addition, she became willful, often to the point of smugness. "Darling," her mother asked Margaret one evening after she had rescued the child from a paternal scolding, "what would you do without Mummy?" The reply came without hesitation: "I'd do what I like, Mummy." And so she would, for the rest of her life; thus she would try to establish her identity within the daunting confines of the Royal Family.

The triumphant visit of King George and Queen Elizabeth to Paris in 1938 was a stunning public relations coup, a brilliant show of Anglo-French friendship and a personal success for the shy monarch and his gregarious wife as they were hailed everywhere. When Hitler saw a newsreel of the Queen placing a flower at the Arc de Triomphe's tomb of the unknown soldier, he told his aides that she was "the most dangerous woman in Europe"; indeed, insofar as his purposes were concerned, he was scarcely exaggerating, as her conduct during the ensuing war would prove. As the international situation worsened, the King and Queen then had an even greater success. In June 1939 they visited Canada and the United States, becoming the first British sovereigns to visit the New World.

Roosevelt was keen to cement his friendship with King George, for he saw that American neutrality could not long endure and that Great Britain would be his major ally against

European fascism. But the results went deeper. In New York City, Hyde Park and Washington, the King and Queen were cheered as loudly as Charles Lindbergh had been after his transatlantic flight a dozen years earlier. Their combination of dignity and simplicity endeared them to both press and public, and at once a firm friendship was established between the President and the King—a relationship reflected during the war in a lively and important personal correspondence. When the royal party arrived at the presidential home in Hyde Park, on the banks of the Hudson River, Roosevelt offered his guests a drink. "My mother," he said to the King, "thinks you should have a cup of tea; she doesn't approve of cocktails." Gratefully accepting a gin and tonic, the King replied with a wink, "Neither does my mother." The visit was indeed more than political, and George—who by now had so practiced breathing and relaxation techniques that he could speak in public with very little stammering—returned to London at the end of June with deepened faith in himself. With the gracious Elizabeth at his side, he had been very much his own man in the company of the more experienced, self-confident President.

As for the Queen, America began a lifelong love affair with her. "Crisp and bonny, Her Majesty at once became the heroine of the occasion," gushed *Time* magazine. "Elizabeth was the perfect Queen: eyes a snapping blue, chin tilted confidently, fingers raised in greeting, she was as girlish as she was regal. Her long-handled parasol seemed out of a storybook." She frequently caused the police some distress, interrupting a formal procedure or arranged stroll to greet ordinary citizens, to shake hands with workers and schoolchildren—and thus made it possible for the otherwise more reserved King to project a new warmth and ease at just such moments, which were unprecedented in royal protocol. "It is the small unscheduled things that count most," wrote an eyewitness, "and for these they have an infallible instinct. The capacity of Their Majesties for getting in touch with the people amounts to genius." It was indeed a conquest: U.S. WON BY CHARM OF ITS ROYAL BRITISH "COUSINS" trumpeted *Newsweek* in a typical headline. Elizabeth assessed the trip accurately when she said later, "That tour made us! I mean it *made* us, the King and I. It came at just the right time, particularly for us."

There were other congruent, auspicious events that summer

of 1939. To a visit at his alma mater, Dartmouth Naval College, the King brought his wife and children and Lord Louis Mountbatten, son of that unfortunate head of the British Navy who had been forced to resign in 1917 and who had his surname changed from Battenberg. As it happened, Mountbatten's sister Alice had married Prince Andrew of Greece, and their youngest child, Mountbatten's nephew Prince Philip, was then an eighteen-year-old naval cadet at Dartmouth. On the morning of July 22 the sheltered, shy, thirteen-year-old Princess Elizabeth first laid eyes on Prince Philip, a six-foot, blond-haired, blue-eyed, cheeky athlete. She followed him everywhere that day, staring with uninterrupted adoration. When the Royal Family departed late that day, Margaret turned to the Queen. "Look, Mother!" she said. "Lilibet's crying!" The seeds of an adolescent infatuation had been planted, and the fruit of it would eventually be a long marriage.

Philip's life had been as confused as his background. Although he was a Greek Prince and the son of one, his father Andrew was the son of Prince William of Denmark (later King George I of Greece); his mother, Alice of Battenberg (Louis Mountbatten's sister), was English, Queen Victoria's great-granddaughter. Born on the island of Corfu on June 10, 1921, Philip's life had been remarkably peripatetic—rootless, in fact. Political turmoil forced the family out of Greece, and they relocated to France. There, Andrew's gambling and womanizing soured his marriage, and he moved to Monte Carlo when Philip was ten. Alice, who had been deaf since the age of eight but could lip-read in half a dozen languages, endured a series of nervous breakdowns, but from these episodes she emerged strong and devoutly religious. She took to wearing the habit of a Greek Orthodox nun, and in 1949 she founded the Christian Sisterhood of Martha and Mary, a contemplative order devoted both to prayer and the care of the sick poor.

This was no romantic idyll, for Alice's life was one of serious prayer, self-discipline and tireless work on behalf of others. During World War II, at great personal risk, she harbored Greek Jews in her Athens home in the face of daily threats from the Gestapo. When the Nazis interrogated her, she mumbled incoherently, adding feigned madness or stupidity to the affliction of her deafness. The ruse worked, and for two years Alice saved Jewish families from extermination. In recognition of her heroic efforts, Alice was posthumously awarded the title of "Righteous Among the Nations" by Yad Vashem, the Holocaust Remembrance Authority in Jerusalem, where she was at last buried almost twenty years after her death.

Young Philip—virtually a stateless exile despite the fact that he was a great-great-grandson of Queen Victoria—was off to school, bounced from one academy to another, from Greece to France, England, Germany and back to England. After two years at a school outside Paris, where he coped with the problem of his identity by calling himself simply "Philip of Greece," he was brought to England by his uncle George Milford Haven and sent to the Cheam School in Surrey from 1930 to 1933; that was followed by a year at the Salem School in Germany and then three years at Gordonstoun in Scotland, whose headmaster was Salem's founder. "Prince Philip is universally trusted, liked and respected," read his final report.

He has the greatest sense of service of all the boys in the school. He is a born leader, but will need the exacting demands of a great service to do justice to himself. His best is outstanding; his second best is not good enough. Philip will make his mark in any profession where he will have to prove himself in a full trial of strength.

An indifferent student who excelled only in French, he was a crack athlete and a keen oarsman, and after leaving school he was accepted into the Royal Naval Academy at Dartmouth, where he met the smitten Princess Elizabeth. He made friends easily, never tried to capitalize on his royal background (however muddled and minor) and was a matey player and a salty wit. But when the Royal Family came to meet him that day, he was a lad who had long been emotionally neglected.

"When he needed a father," said Michael Parker, who became an Australian wartime friend and was later Philip's first private secretary, "there just wasn't anybody there." The result was a personality that was apparently outgoing and gregarious but also severely reserved. His schooling was based on rigorous discipline and spartan physical challenges, both in sports and in self-denial. In the absence of anything like a home or family life, Philip became the ideal company man—loyal, tough and competitive. "Everyone adored him, he was so good-looking," said Hélène Foufounis, who was a family friend since childhood and was later known as the nightclub doyenne Hélène Cordet. Like Philip's older sisters, she recalled a boy who was a great showoff, sometimes boisterous, lazy in school but not on the playing field, not studious in good manners but conscious of his appeal to women. "He is the type," said an American friend at the time, "who would be considered a good all-around man at an American university and would make the best fraternity on the campus. But some of his frat brothers would undoubtedly find him painfully exuberant at times with his practical jokes. He gives the impression of being a man's man." As for being also a busy ladies' man with a long list of conquests, such would be rumored about Philip from his teens to his seventies.

"She never took her eyes off him the whole time," recalled Marion Crawford of the Princess's attention to Philip that July afternoon. "At the tennis courts I thought he showed off a good deal, but the little girls were much impressed. Lilibet said, 'How good he is, Crawfie! How high he can jump!' He was quite polite to her." Mountbatten, for one, saw the light in Princess Elizabeth's eyes that July day. A man who thrived on emphasizing (and exaggerating) his connections to the Royal Family, Mountbatten at once hatched a plan that, however proleptic, he helped maneuver to its term.

Later in 1939, Philip was posted to H.M.S. *Ramillies*, commanded by an old friend of Mountbatten. To this superior, Captain Baillie-Grohman, Philip confided that he wished to become a British subject and to pursue a career in the Royal Navy. "Then came a surprise," the Captain said later. "Philip went on to say, 'My uncle [Louis Mountbatten] has ideas for me; he thinks I could marry Princess Elizabeth.' I was a bit taken aback and after a hesitation asked him, 'Are you fond of her?' 'Oh, yes, very,' was the reply. 'I write to her every week.' " According to one of Philip's cousins, Mountbatten had this in mind from the start; he had "steadfastly procured his nephew an invitation to lunch on the royal yacht" that day in 1939. (The same cousin recalled Philip's regular correspondence with Lilibet during the war.)

To his cousin, Philip was even more forthright: "I'm going to marry her," he said as early as 1941, after visiting Windsor Castle for one of the Princesses' Christmas pantomimes. At that time Marion Crawford found him "greatly changed. It was a grave and charming young man who sat there, with nothing of the rather bumptious boy I had first known. He looked more than ever, I thought, like a Viking, weather-beaten and strained." Chips Channon, among others, was convinced that Philip was being groomed as the future husband of Princess Elizabeth: "He is to be our Prince Consort, and that is why he is serving in our navy."

His name? Well, officially he was simply "Philip of Greece." If even minor Royals can be said to have a surname, he was Philip Schleswig-Holstein-Sonderburg-Glücksburg, which was the German-Danish family pedigree. Eventually, at the insistence of Uncle Louis, he assumed the revised Anglicized name of the Battenbergs, and when he took British citizenship in 1947, it was as Lieutenant-Commander Philip Mountbatten, Royal Navy. "I suspect," Philip said years later, "that Louis [Mountbatten] tried too hard to make himself a son out of me. . . . I was not madly in favor [of the name Mountbatten], but in the end I was persuaded, and anyway I couldn't think of a reasonable alternative." And, he might have added, Uncle Louis was trying too hard to make himself an intimate of his royal distant cousins. Apparently even the Windsors were not enough for his ambition, for Mountbatten claimed a kingly ancestry all the way back to Charlemagne. "We always took [him] with a pinch of salt," said Queen Elizabeth years later when she was Queen Mother.

Lilibet and Margaret were on holiday at Balmoral when war was declared on September 3, 1939; they remained there with Crawfie until Christmas, when they joined their parents at Sandringham and then went on to Royal Lodge, Windsor. The so-called phony war of inactivity lasted until the spring of 1940 when Germany invaded Norway, Denmark, Belgium and France before beginning the bombing of London. After that there was a real threat to the safety of the Royal Family, each of whose existence carried the burden of national morale.

Children of English aristocrats were shipped off to safety in Canada or America; those related to the few remaining European sovereigns were similarly protected. But when the Queen was asked whether her daughters would leave England, she was surprised, and her reply became the most famous utterance of her life. "The children would not leave without me, I would not leave without the King, and the King will never leave."

This statement of solidarity with the lives of normal Englishmen and -women—in constant peril from the time the London Blitz began in September 1940 until the end of the war five years later—earned for the King and Queen the lasting affection, gratitude and admiration of all citizens. Whereas George V had adopted his people, the people adopted George VI. He and his family became the most loved Royals in British history, and the bond between Crown and people was sealed when Buckingham Palace was bombed. "This war has drawn the Throne and the people more closely together than was ever before recorded," wrote Prime Minister Winston Churchill to the King on January 5, 1941, "and Your Majesties are more beloved by all classes and conditions than any of the princes of the past." The public affection was not at all threatened by the King's darker moods and habits, which were vouchsafed only to his family and a few courtiers.

The children remained at Windsor Castle for the duration of the war, exchanging their German grammars for American history books, while their parents were driven each day to duties at Buckingham Palace and to the sad business of visiting bombed neighborhoods of London—especially in the East End. The King never went out without a pistol in his pocket and a shotgun in his car, and the Queen asked for and received instruction in how to fire a revolver. "I shall not go down like the others," she said, clearly referring to refugee European Royals. "The Queen never showed that she was worried," according to Marion Crawford. "She seemed to drop her cares [when she returned home to the children] and became just Mummy."

From the day war began, the King wore in public only his uniform as Admiral of the Fleet. Although his wife was Commandant-in-Chief of the three women's services, she refused any official dress and stuck to her pastel-colored frocks. She would not be upstaged by the properly aristocratic Queen Mary. "They [ordinary citizens] would wear their best dresses if they were coming to see me" was her justification for appearing in her subdued but elegant civilian wardrobe.*

Their refusal to seek refuge outside the country; their obvious care for the homeless, the wounded, the families of the dead; the quiet strength they communicated by simply being present to the people—all this gained for them and for the Crown a tide of patriotic sentiment that outlasted the end of the war. "I'm glad we've been bombed," said the Queen after Buckingham Palace was hit in September 1940. "It makes me feel I can look the East End in the face." Just such sentiments propelled her and her husband to all the devastated centers of England: to Coventry in November 1940, for example, when 449 German planes inflicted heavy damage on the city and left hundreds dead; and to Bristol, Birmingham, Liverpool and Glasgow, where there was similar destruction.

Elizabeth and George were, by virtue of the horror of the bombing of London, no mere constitutional abstractions; they were, as Churchill wrote, real people, closer to the masses than any sovereigns in history. "If Goering had realized the depths of feeling which his bombing of Buckingham Palace has aroused throughout the Empire & America," wrote Louis Mountbatten to the King days after the first bombs fell on the palace, "he would have been well advised to instruct his assassins to keep off." On many occasions a nervous populace took their cue from a courageous Queen. "When the car stops," Harold Nicolson wrote, describing Elizabeth's tour of troops in Sheffield,

> the Queen nips out into the snow and goes straight into the middle of the crowd and starts talking to them. For a moment or two they just gaze and gape in astonishment. But then they all start talking as one: "Hi! Your Majesty! Look here!" She has that quality of making everybody feel that they and they alone are being spoken to.

---

* As for the King's siblings, the Duke of Gloucester held various liaison posts of no great consequence until he became Governor-General ·of Australia for two years, beginning in 1945. The Duke of Kent toured RAF bases and factories. Their sister Princess Mary was by far the most effective, serving tirelessly as Controller-Commandant of the Auxiliary Territorial Service, which sent her all over Britain on inspection and hands-on working tours of troops and canteen services.

Nor was the royal concern limited to public appearances. At the King's insistence, strict wartime rations were observed at Buckingham Palace. Signs urging various abstentions were posted everywhere. The depth of hot bathwater was limited to five inches, log fires replaced central heating and only one lightbulb was permitted in each bedroom ("no mean sacrifice in view of the size of the rooms," as one chronicler reported).

In a sense, the monarch's task was easier than his father's had been during World War I, for Churchill was a far more powerful and effective leader than Lloyd George. Although he was Head of State and Commander in Chief of the Armed Forces, King George of course had no more influence over the course of the war than he had when he was a young man in World War I. But his relationship with Prime Minister Winston Churchill, one of great mutual respect and finally of close friendship, made the King more than a figurehead. He was provided with every detail of the war's progress and had access to information known to very few others. "I made certain he was kept informed of every secret matter," Churchill said, "and the care and thoroughness with which he mastered the immense daily flow of state papers made a deep mark on my mind."

"Churchill was a tremendous monarchist, and therefore he took his duty to the King very seriously," recalled Lieutenant General Sir Ian Jacob, military assistant to the War Cabinet. "He would not give way on something he thought important, of course, if they were at odds, but he would certainly give full attention to everything the King said." Throughout the war George exercised his constitutional right to advise, to counsel and to warn.

With a certain irony, he had the opportunity to do all of that within days of the declaration of war. On the afternoon of September 14, 1939, the Duke of Windsor met privately with the King at Buckingham Palace for an hour before Queen Elizabeth and the Gloucesters joined them for tea. This was the first time Edward had seen his family since his departure from England on December 11, 1936. Queen Mary did not attend, perhaps because she was unaware that Wallis would not be there; the Duchess had remained with her hosts in Sussex.

The purpose of the meeting was to respond to Edward's desire for a position—something of service to the nation, he insisted, some post abroad. This was a matter of singular delicacy, for intelligence reports indicated (how truthfully would not be known until after the war) that the Third Reich had planned, once England was invaded, to put the Duke and Duchess back on the throne. Following the Windsors' brief visit with Hitler, Goebbels and company in Germany in the autumn of 1937, the Nazis were convinced that Edward and Wallis would be the consummate quislings, ideal representatives of a fascist puppet kingdom. In this estimation they were profoundly wrong, for although the Duke was politically naive, he was also thoroughly English and never gave any indication that he would be a willing traitor. He and his wife may have been locked into an increasingly shallow life of wandering, but they were nothing like the ardent Nazis their detractors would always claim. To be sure, Edward uttered some astonishingly stupid, anti-Semitic remarks, and until war was declared, he spoke of little but appeasement. But it is important to recall that in this regard he was hardly alone among his countrymen, and as for appeasement, Prime Minister Neville Chamberlain himself orchestrated the disastrous Munich Pact of 1938.* In this regard King George VI made perhaps the most appalling constitutional blunder of the century by appearing on the balcony of Buckingham Palace at Chamberlain's side after the Prime Minister returned from his disastrous meeting with Hitler. On one of the most controversial issues of the day, the monarch did what no monarch must do: he identified himself with a party position.

But the former King and his wife were considered the greatest embarrassment of all to the current Sovereign, who had no certainty that the Duke and Duchess would not be manipulated by Nazis. The King, therefore, decided to send his brother back to France as an observer. There the Duke and Duchess remained until 1940 when they left for the Bahamas, where he accepted the post of Governor-General. That, as it happened, was as far as the King and his government could reasonably transfer the wandering couple whom the King, Queen and Court, unreasonably, always saw as a threat.

* * *

---

* On the history of Joachim von Ribbentrop's failed plot to kidnap the Duke of Windsor in Spain and return him to the British throne, see Michael Bloch, *Operation Willi* (London: Weidenfeld and Nicolson, 1984).

George and Elizabeth tried, insofar as they were permitted, to give some indications that normal life could proceed in wartime. On November 13, 1939, they went to the movies to see the British propaganda film *The Lion Has Wings;* cinemas, being entirely enclosed and windowless, were exempt from the blackout. An animated cartoon was hastily added to the program when the management was told the King enjoyed Mickey Mouse (as his father had not). Two weeks later the King and Queen, the Kents and the Gloucesters attended a West End musical revue. The royal party went unnoticed until, just as the houselights dimmed, an officer in the audience saw them entering a box, sprang to attention and precipitated loud applause and cheers.

Like his father before him, George VI was called on to lift the national morale during an international conflict. But now there were no enthusiastic cries of confidence in an early victory, no chauvinistic claims that England must easily prevail. Instead, it was a daily struggle for survival. World War I was an episode in the reign of George V, and his legacy and memory were not bound up with the Allied victory in that war. But for George VI, World War II proved his mettle, evoked his best resources as a dignified leader and national symbol. The war defined him, and his memory—and the Queen's—is inextricably linked to the image of courage and sacrifice they daily set before their people.

The Princesses, meantime, studied at Windsor Castle. On the night of the first air raid over London, the girls took a half-hour to respond to the sirens ordering them to the dungeons for safety. When they finally went for cover, Lilibet and Margaret explained that Clara Knight had insisted on dressing them neatly and precisely, as if they were headed for an official engagement—this much to the angry anxiety of the Master of the Household, who had feared for their lives and his reputation.

In fact, dressers and governesses were not accustomed to lighter duties in wartime. With officers of the Grenadier Guards posted to Windsor Castle and the King and Queen in London most days, Princess Elizabeth was permitted to play hostess. Thanks to Queen Mary, she had exquisite manners and knew what questions to ask the men. Serious-minded and considerate, she cut a very different figure from her sister: "Lilibet developed rapidly," recalled Marion Crawford,

> and those . . . months at Windsor helped a lot. For the first time, she was on her own, away from her parents. At various mealtimes and when we gave parties, it was she who had to do the honours, play hostess and see to the seating of her guests. She who had been a rather shy little girl became a very charming young person, able to cope with any situation without awkwardness.

On her sixteenth birthday in 1942, her father appointed her an honorary colonel in the Grenadier Guards, and she walked past troops and took the salute at castle reviews. The appointment had an amusing origin, for each time she was compelled to accompany the King and Queen on such inspections from 1939 to 1942, she fell into the habit of asking her father, "Papa, shall I have to do this when you're dead?" This finally exasperated King George to such a point that, to give her a task she would not have to wait to inherit, he made her a Guard.

This was a mere ceremonial formality compared to the harder work expected of her: attention to her father's brief but focused periods of instruction in matters of state and her daily lessons with Sir Henry Marten on the role of the monarch. The photographer Lisa Sheridan watched King and Princess during a working session one afternoon. "I noticed," she recalled,

> that he drew the Princess's attention to a document and explained certain matters very earnestly. The Queen and Princess Margaret, meanwhile, sat silently with their books and knitting. . . . There is a particular bond of understanding [between George and Lilibet], and the King makes a point of explaining everything he can to her personally.

The King insisted that his daughter would not ever be so unprepared for duty as he had been. Sometimes, in fact, she was rather too conscientious. Reviewing a passing-out parade of officer candidates, she went down the line, solemn and eagle-eyed, until she stopped before one nervous cadet. Pointing to a brass buckle, she said, "It is not too well polished." The commandant reddened, calling out the wretched cadet's name and number.

Not since Wellington had a guest scolded a man in public. Princess Elizabeth, however, was meticulous to the point of obsession, as in childhood when she perfectly aligned her shoes each night for next morning's wear. Hours after her appearance that day, the barracks were in almost open revolt. "Whoever may come in future," said a spokesman for the offended platoon, "we do *not* want Princess Elizabeth!"

The King also granted his daughter's request that she join the Auxiliary Territorial Service, and in this capacity she donned a mechanic's uniform and learned how to service an automobile engine. "She was a very junior officer," said Marion Crawford of Second Subaltern Elizabeth Windsor, Number 230873, "and had to salute her seniors along with the rest." By 1943 when the King went out to visit troops in Malta and North Africa, Princess Elizabeth was acting as a Counsellor of State, making public appearances on behalf of charitable organizations and even meeting with visiting dignitaries—not for official duties, of course, but merely to reinforce her naturally formal but graceful posture in the company of important others.

Margaret, on the other hand, was more relaxed and casual about everything, and within the family she provided the amusement—calling for songs at the piano and games after dinner—where Lilibet sprang to assume duty after duty. "Isn't it a pity we have to travel with royalty?" she asked straight-faced. The younger Princess also became something of a flirt. She "began to develop into a real personality with the male element about." One of the castle footmen, Margaret reported, was "frightfully handsome"; for another, the Princess wore a gash of red lipstick and heavy face powder. Nor had she lost her impish sense of humor. "Dear Lady Godiva," she wrote when Marion Crawford asked her to practice correspondence by answering an imaginary invitation,

> I am so thrilled with your invitation to your dance, which sounds such fun. I shall do my very best to bring a partner —would Lord Tulip do?
>
> Yours affectionately, Diaphenia

Surrounded by the formal courtesies and blandishments of Court life, the teenage Princess Elizabeth was not unaware of the dangers arising from such privilege. Once when a group of Girl Guides visiting the palace complimented her on a blue headscarf, she took one of them aside and asked anxiously, "Do you really like it?" The other girl was puzzled and replied of course she did, why did the Princess ask again? "Because back at the palace, whatever I do, whatever I wear, however I'm dressed up, everyone always compliments me. There's just no way for me to know if I have any taste at all."

Her official radio debut occurred on October 13, 1940, when she spoke on the BBC "Children's Hour" in a high, steady voice. To children being evacuated she read a speech prepared by a minister, expressing sympathy for those separated from their parents and homes. "My sister Margaret Rose and I know from experience what it means to be away from those we love most of all," she had to say with somewhat synthetic overstatement. "We send a message of true sympathy . . ." Even Prime Minister Chamberlain's assistant private secretary, John Colville (son of Queen Mary's lady-in-waiting and, later, private secretary to King George VI and to Princess Elizabeth), was "embarrassed by the sloppy sentiment she was made to express, but her voice was most impressive, and if the monarchy survives, Queen Elizabeth II should be a most successful radio Queen."

It was clear to regular visitors, however, that despite Princess Elizabeth's dutiful stance toward life, she was something of a moody girl, bright and amusing one moment and sulky and depressed the next—even in the midst of a glittering social occasion. Her parents were alarmed, for example, that during modest wartime parties at the palace she would "play the wallflower and refuse to mingle or converse." Her father may have best understood that this alteration of attitudes occurred when Elizabeth realized the enormous prospects before her. Let her be herself now, he said at such moments. "Look what she has ahead of her, poor thing."

From her father the elder Princess inherited an eye for detail, a profound sense of duty, a frank boredom with chatty folks and a love of the outdoors. But she lacked her mother's even, gracious manner: the Saxe-Coburg/Windsor temper was always below the surface in Princess Elizabeth. At sixteen she had reached her full adult height—just under five feet four inches. She had thick brown hair, brilliant blue-green opalescent eyes, perfect teeth and a creamy complexion. That she tended to a certain Scottish dumpiness was not helped by the tutelage of Queen Mary and that of an unimaginative dresser. "Who could possibly look chic," confided an acquaintance, "being dressed as she was by a provincial Scotswoman [Margaret MacDonald] whose idea of the latest fashion is what they're wearing in wartime Aberdeen?"

Although she often visited her granddaughters and supervised them when George and Elizabeth were gone for more than a day, Queen Mary herself had been evacuated to safety. Considering her London residence at Marlborough House too perilous, the King and his ministers sent her to a country house in Gloucestershire for the six-year span of the war. This absence from London the old Queen resented, for she considered it "not at all the thing" to seem so derelict in her duty, especially in light of her daughter-in-law's constant presence in London. "So *that's* what hay looks like," said Mary to her hostess (her niece, the Duchess of Beaufort) as she was shown round the gardens and fields of Badminton House (later, when the country boundaries were redrawn, it found itself in Avon).

At seventy-two the Queen Mother was not about to slip into an idle retirement. With a zest that shamed many of the servants, she set herself the task of clearing vast patches of ivy from walls and trees, a task in which she joined workmen and which was doubtless her first experience of anything like manual labor, much less rustic husbandry. Her hostility to this energetic clinging vine was a lifelong preoccupation whose basis is hard to fathom; in any case, she took every opportunity to tidy up gardens, walks and fields by attacking any sign of ivy. "She was fundamentally very, very German," said the Duchess of Beaufort years later, "for the two things she likes most are *destruction* and *order*." Throughout the long, dark seasons of wartime, Queen Mary enlisted everyone on her personal staff—ladies-in-waiting, secretary, guard and chauffeur (not to say visitors)—in what became known as her Ivy Squad. The most common sight at Badminton House from 1939 to 1945 was Queen Mary, neatly dressed right down to toque, gloves and pearls, hacking away with a saw or a scythe, urging on her little team, stopping to have a cigarette with them, then cheerfully announcing the end of the break and the return to the task. From all accounts Mary's hard work and good humor evoked only warm admiration.

She was, in other words, becoming in her own way as close to the people in her smaller circle as the King and Queen were in their larger one. Mary's eccentricity merely endeared her to everybody. And they knew she had more on her mind than ridding the world of ivy. She visited bombed areas and hospitals, helped organize first-aid shelters, and often ordered her driver to stop on a country road to give a ride to a serviceman in transit. "Some Australian soldiers and airmen happened to be [at Bath]," she wrote, "and asked me to be photographed with them. I said yes and they crowded round me and I suddenly felt an arm pushed through mine and another placed round my waist—in order to make more room, I suppose. It really was very comical and *unexpected* at my age!"

There was very soon a great grief in Queen Mary's life. On August 25, 1942, her youngest surviving son, George, Duke of Kent—then thirty-nine and only weeks earlier the father of a third child—was flying to Iceland, there to tour air force installations. The seaplane, proceeding low in dense fog and mist, smashed into a hill in the Scottish countryside, and only one of the fifteen aboard survived. The Duke was killed instantly.

Thus the indomitable old lady had now lost her husband and two sons (three, if one counted the ex-King, which she sometimes did). The death of George, Duke of Kent, was singularly poignant, for he often visited his mother at Badminton House, and together they pored over the bibelots at nearby antique shops. Animated, amusing and artistic, he lightened the burdens of his mother's senior years. If she knew about his continuingly peripatetic love life, she never let on; what mattered to her was that she could speak "openly and with ease," while she found the King and Gloucester *"boutonnés"*—tight-lipped, buttoned-up. Told the news, she stiffened, sighed for a moment, and then said that of course she must rush at once to comfort Princess Marina.

Princess Elizabeth and Prince Philip of Greece, meantime, were exchanging occasional letters throughout the war, and at

Christmas 1943 he was invited to stay several days at Windsor Castle after the holiday pageant—that year *Aladdin,* with Elizabeth in the title role. It was the usual soup of feeble jokes, song and dance and a colorful finale. In Philip's presence, Elizabeth sparkled, singing and tap-dancing with surprising verve and matching Margaret's boisterous slapstick humor. For the elder Princess there seemed to be only one person in the audience—the man whose picture now graced her night table. ("I believe Elizabeth fell in love with Philip the first time he went down to Windsor," Queen Mary told her old friend Lady Airlie.) "Philip has a good sense of humor & thinks about things in the right way," the King wrote to his mother about Philip, adding at once that at seventeen Lilibet was much too young to think of marriage to a sailor earning £11 a week, a man who had become a naturalized British citizen in order to join the navy. After all, as the King was the first to admit, she had never met any young men her own age, "so Philip had better not think any more about it for the present." There were other objections: the Queen's brother was adamantly opposed to Philip, considering him un-British, therefore unacceptable, as were old royal favorites such as Lord Salisbury, Lord Eldon and Lord Stanley. Philip was not their idea of a British gentleman. Asked years later if he thought there was more than a tinge of xenophobia at the time, he replied tersely, "Inevitably: *vide* Albert"—remember the case of Victoria's Consort.

But the King's major caution had to do with Lilibet's youth and inexperience. Her Auxiliary Territorial Service experience had not exactly widened her social circle, and the war had necessarily imposed a strict isolation on her. Shy ("to the point of gaucheness," said one of her father's attendants), grave, dutiful, tutored for monarchy by her father and thus ever aware of the destiny that lay ahead, Elizabeth was becoming a somewhat stiff and conventional young woman. Capable of enjoying a joke, a game or a dance, she just as quickly showed an earnest face to those around her, and she was not slow to reprimand anyone—from her sister to a stranger at a court ball—for conduct or speech she thought inappropriate. "Wherever did you learn such slang?" Elizabeth asked her sister. "Oh," Margaret replied, "at my mother's knee—or some other low joint." A stranger was summarily rebuked by the teenage Elizabeth for asking, "What does your father think of that?" The quick, frosty reply: "Are you speaking of the King?" But Margaret could get away with a gentle revenge for her sister's formality. "Lilibet!" she cried in a loud voice one afternoon when her sister took a second cookie, "that's the *fourteenth* chocolate biscuit you've eaten! You're as bad as Mother—you don't know when to stop!"

After the holiday reunion at Christmas 1943, Elizabeth began to knit woolen socks for Philip. When his rumored romance with a wealthy and attractive Canadian girl in 1944 came to nothing, courtiers—who were sufficiently concerned about his growing relationship with Elizabeth to post unofficial spies hither and thither—were convinced this meant he was serious about the Princess.

Meanwhile, the extrovert, fourteen-year-old Margaret (*espiègle,* as Queen Mary called her: "an imp") was demonstrating a barely concealed romantic interest in Group Captain Peter Townsend, a married, thirty-year-old RAF hero of the Battle of Britain assigned as equerry to the King. The Royal Family was very fond of Townsend and his wife Rosemary, and when she bore a second son in 1945, the King was pleased to stand as godfather. He liked his equerry (both suffered from nervous anxiety and a recurrent if usually controlled stammer); at the same time no one took Margaret's adolescent infatuation very seriously. More to the point, few appreciated her perseverance. "When he first appeared," Margaret said, "I had a terrific crush on him, but there was no question of a romance until much later."

Perseverance was a virtue, however unconnected to romance, that Margaret inherited from her grandmother, Queen Mary, who to everyone's astonishment grew to love the country life in Gloucestershire during the war. Not since her youth had she enjoyed such freedom to fix her own schedule, to mingle with the locals, to give rides to wandering servicemen, to saw wood and root ivy and even to plant seedlings and flower beds on the grounds of Badminton House. At small house parties she danced into the small hours as if to make up for all the fun she had missed in bowing to the will of her late husband.

Just before returning to London life at war's end in May 1945, she summoned all the workers on the Beaufort estate. With tears streaming down her face—hardly her typical demeanor—she presented each with a valuable gift she had wrapped herself. "Oh, I *have* been happy here!" she said. "Here I've been anybody to everybody—and back in London I shall have to begin being Queen Mary all over again."

And so she was when she had her first reunion with Edward since he abdicated. Mother and son met at Marlborough House in October and agreed to stand for photographs—he stiff with embarrassment, she ramrod-straight but with a noticeable smile. This was not some kind of triumphant moral victory for her, said one friend; it was the emergence of a simple, long-repressed maternal pride. For a moment it did not matter that he had been, all too briefly, King Edward VIII. He was David, an old widow's firstborn son.

The King and Queen and their daughters were, by 1946, thoroughly English in a way the monarchy had never been. For all George V's protestations and symbolic gestures of abandoning his Saxe-Coburg-Gotha heritage, his domestic life with Mary and the children more closely resembled a late-nineteenth-century Prussian household. But the influence of Lady Elizabeth Bowes-Lyon on her husband cannot be overstated, especially in the department of Anglicization. Family life was not nearly so tense as it had been under George V; the private residences of the Windsors allowed for games and spontaneous evening gatherings. The atmosphere was certainly formal—the Queen saw to that—but it was more like a comfortably aristocratic home than a King's. The family fished for salmon and stalked deer at Balmoral and danced and sang at Sandringham. Much of royal life was what it seemed: comfortable, middle class, somewhat dull, lacking in imagination. No one who realized this could diminish anyone's appreciation of how much the King and Queen had done for national morale during the war.

Unknown to the press and the public, Philip spent three weeks as a houseguest at Buckingham Palace in 1946. The purpose was simple: Princess Elizabeth was being given an opportunity to see how she liked being with him constantly, without the glare of publicity. Margaret MacDonald and Marion Crawford, who saw the Princess at her most natural and relaxed, were convinced that she was utterly bedazzled by him. He knew just how to court her, even while it was clear that he had serious hesitation about eventually inheriting the Albertine mantle of Prince Consort. But the King was only fifty-one years old. Surely Philip and Lilibet would have at least ten or twenty years of private life before she was catapulted onto the throne?

An overwhelmingly positive consideration for Philip, on the other hand, was the domestic stability he saw with the Windsors, a stability he had never known in his life. He saw the encouraging rituals at the palace, the unchanging liturgies of mealtimes, work times, reading times, recreation times, meeting times. Visting Lilibet often, he took acceptable liberties, playing a recording of "People Will Say We're in Love" from the musical *Oklahoma!* on her gramophone. He asked the King if he might dine alone once or twice with the Princess in a small private dining room. Permission was granted.

Despite a palace injunction regarding confidence, with a staff of hundreds it was inevitable that rumors would soon fly around London that an engagement announcement was imminent. To discourage talk, the Palace Press Office was instructed in September 1946 to issue an official denial of any imminent wedding plans. That made the newspapers even hungrier for details.

Weeks after Philip's departure, Princess Elizabeth returned from an official visit to a factory and rang for her governess-companion.

"Crawfie," she said, holding back tears, "it was horrible. They shouted at me, 'Where's Philip?' " From that day the Princess, usually calm and confident on her forays into society, dreaded public appearances; only after years as Queen would she seem sometimes at ease amid the public and comfortable with the press.

But none of her discomfort was evident on February 1, 1947, when she and Margaret, with their parents and a staff headed by equerry Peter Townsend, departed for a holiday in South Africa that was also aimed at countering that Dominion's growing threat of republicanism. Princess Elizabeth, smiling and poised, was hailed everywhere as a relaxed and lovely *diplomate manquée,* which was all the more a triumph of illusion because of her unwillingness to leave Philip for three months. Pleasant diversion came from Townsend's attentiveness to her and Margaret; for example, he arranged for the finest horses to be available for riding and accompanied them in the cool mornings. Both responsibility and romance seem to have affected Elizabeth in a conventional way, for she confided to Townsend that she could not sleep much. Margaret simply gazed at him with adoration.

At the same time, Margaret began to resent her sister's attachment to Philip and the happy outcome that was certain to result from the romance, a resentment that certainly sprang from her suspicion that her own future with Peter was not so guaranteed. In London she had often accompanied Lilibet and Philip on outings and had frequently made a third when the couple would have preferred some privacy. Marion Crawford, for one, observed that "the constant presence of the little sister, who was far from understanding, and liked a good deal of attention herself, was not helping the romance."

The King was exhausted and haggard, and not only from the strain of the war and its economic aftermath in Britain. He had left a new government coping with record unemployment, a dangerous fuel crisis during a harsh winter and worrisome cutbacks in both trade and power. In addition, the Empire itself was in its final decline. The India Independence Act was being prepared, and later that year the monarch would no longer be Emperor of that nation.

But there were other, more personal reasons for his increasingly wretched appearance. James Cameron was one of the pressmen assigned to cover the royal tour, and he recalled the King shaking at each stop of the journey, not with nervous anxiety so much as with the effects of alcohol. More than once, according to Cameron, journalists found the King "experimenting, with some dedication," with bottles of liquor. "We must not f-forget the purpose of this t-tour," said the Sovereign. "Trade, and so on. Empire cooperation. For example, South African b-brandy. I have been trying it. It is of course m-magnificent, except that it is not very nice. But then there is this liqueur called V-Van der Humm. Perhaps a little sweet. But if you mix half of brandy with half of Van der Humm— please try!" The Queen, Cameron recalled, got her husband through the ordeal of the trip by sheer force of will.

A lifetime of intemperate drinking now began to affect King George's circulation, and on this journey he suffered severe leg cramps—the first signs of the debilitating arteriosclerosis that made every official engagement a trial. As it happened, the King was also suffering the first symptoms of chronic obstructive pulmonary disease, the result of a half-century of chain-smoking. He lost seventeen pounds on the trip; only fifty-one, he looked almost seventy.

This would be the last time the Royal Family traveled together. There was already talk of Princess Elizabeth's eventual accession, a fact obliquely acknowledged by her public act of self-consecration to the Commonwealth on April 21, her twenty-first birthday. Sitting before a microphone in an African garden, she said in a high, thin voice:

> There is a motto which has been borne by many of my ancestors, a noble motto, "I serve." These words were an inspiration to many bygone heirs to the throne when they made their knightly dedication as they came to manhood. I cannot do quite as they did . . . but I can make a solemn act of dedication with a whole Empire listening. I should like to make that dedication now. It is very simple: I declare before you that my whole life, whether it be long or short, shall be devoted to your service, and the service of our great Imperial family to which we all belong. But I shall not have the strength to carry out this resolution unless you join in it with me, as I now invite you to do. I know that your support will be unfailingly given. God help me to make good my vow. And God bless all of you who are willing to share in it.

There was another vow Elizabeth longed to make, one she could do only while holding Philip's hand and at an altar. They had secretly pledged to one another in 1946 when the King agreed to the marriage; he had asked that they wait until after Lilibet's twenty-first birthday and the subsequent South African tour. Now, in July 1947, the palace made a formal announcement of the forthcoming marriage. Philip was a British subject at last; he had abandoned his Greek princely title and had formally transferred his allegiance from Greek Orthodox doctrine to that of the Church of England (a "conversion" that is not much of a leap to make since both traditions trace to apostolic tradition). On November 11—"so that she will be senior to Philip,'' as he said—the King bestowed the Order of the Garter on Princess Elizabeth and then conferred the same on Philip eight days later, the day before the wedding in Westminster Abbey.* At the same time Philip was made a Royal Highness and created Baron Greenwich, Earl of Merioneth and Duke of Edinburgh; the last would be the title commonly used. Noble names or not, Philip had been penniless since birth; he had only £6 in his bank account when he proposed to Princess Elizabeth, and he had to ask his mother to draw diamonds from a tiara to make his fiancée a ring.

Deprived postwar Britain was no better off, but the wedding touched off a flash of light and color. It was the first marriage of an immediate heir to the throne in eighty-four years (since Victoria's eldest, the Prince of Wales, married Princess Alexandra in 1863). At the bride's expressed wish, the older form of the marriage vow was preserved, with the Princess promising to ''obey'' and ''serve'' her husband—a decision that caused some stir not because of any enlightened feminist argument but because of her royal precedence over her husband and, it was presumed, her eventual sovereignty over him. But it was consistent with the Princess's belief that a husband was head of the family, a conviction she maintained as Queen throughout the many years of her marriage.

Like any doting father, the King was both proud of his daughter's new life and lonely for her. After the wedding she received a handwritten letter from him:

> I was so proud of you & thrilled at having you so close to me on your long walk in Westminster Abbey, but when I handed your hand to the Archbishop I felt that I had lost something very precious. You were so calm & composed during the Service & said your words with such conviction, that I knew everything was all right.
>
> I am so glad you wrote and told Mummy that you think

---

* The Garter is the senior and most prestigious order of chivalry in the realm. Its origin, much disputed and highly romanticized, was most likely simply a strap or belt used to attach ribbons of knightly fraternity to armor. The order's motto, *Honi soit qui mal y pense* (''Shame on him who thinks this evil''), probably refers to Edward III's claim to the throne of France.

the long wait before your engagement & the long time before the wedding was for the best. I was rather afraid that you had thought I was being hard hearted about it. I was so anxious for you to come to Africa as you knew. Our family, us four, the "Royal Family" must remain together with additions of course at suitable moments!! I have watched you grow up all these years with pride under the skilful direction of Mummy, who as you know is the most marvelous person in the World in my eyes, & can, I know, always count on you, & now Philip, to help us in our work. Your leaving us has left a great blank in our lives but do remember that your old home is still yours & do come back to it as much & as often as possible. I can see that you are sublimely happy with Philip which is right but don't forget us is the wish of

> your ever loving & devoted Papa.

The coronation of Queen Elizabeth II.

11

In the Sight of All the People

1948 to 1955

I want him to be a man's man.
PRINCE PHILIP, on rearing his son Prince Charles

"Philip told me," said Michael Parker, his private secretary, "that his job, first, second and last, was never to let her down."

Philip's father had died in 1944, and his mother led mostly a contemplative religious life; at last he had a home, a wife and family, a country, a passport, and his first sense of stability and security. After a short stay in a suite at Buckingham Palace, on July 4, 1949 (American Independence Day, as Philip wryly observed), the newlyweds moved into Clarence House, used by royal relatives for over a century. Very near the palace and overlooking The Mall, it had sustained major damage during the war and required extensive and expensive renovation, much of it supervised by Philip himself.

Until her accession as Queen in 1952, the lives of Elizabeth and Philip—the Edinburghs, as they were then known in Court and aristocratic circles—combined his shore job at the Admiralty and her royal duties. But marriage did not much mellow the rambunctious sailor. Just as her background and breeding had made Elizabeth a proper, subdued young Royal, so Philip's had given him an independent, outspoken personality and a tendency for rowdiness. She was "sometimes quick-tempered and inclined to be a little overcritical," as Marion Crawford had said, but those occasions were soon mollified by Philip. He had lived his entire life on his own terms, and so he would for the most part continue to do—with a remarkable equanimity and self-confidence.

For one thing, he continued to carouse with his navy buddies after hours, stopping for a pint of beer or a double shot of brandy. He crashed his bicycle into the gates of Buckingham Palace and skidded away, laughing. He kept up the salty sailor's banter, matching a mate's bawdy story with another—which, when told in company, his wife simply ignored just as Queen Mary had ignored the same tales told by King George V. More than once the Prince and Parker returned so late from a night out with the boys that the private entry gate was locked and they were forced to climb over a wall and through a window. "Serves them right," said Princess Elizabeth when told the next morning.

But she could let down her guard just a bit. In response to an invitation from American Ambassador Lewis W. Douglas, the Edinburghs outfitted themselves as a Cockney chambermaid and butler and attended a masquerade ball at the embassy.

As it happened, the surprise hit of that evening was Princess Margaret. Now more confident and conscious of her appeal (she stood just over five feet and had a twenty-two-inch waist, sparkling blue eyes and a glorious complexion), she arrived as a decorously costumed Madame Butterfly and then tossed aside her ankle-length kimono to become Mademoiselle Fifi, the belle of the boulevards. After a diligent rehearsal with the ebullient comic Danny Kaye (who was a good friend to Margaret and a sometime lover to the widowed Duchess of Kent), Margaret and seven friends staged a high-stepping cancan complete with lace panties, black stockings and suspenders—and a bottom-wiggling finale. Three hundred guests shouted their approval and called for an encore, and the next day the *Daily Express* headline announced PRINCESS MARGARET DOES THE CANCAN.

Margaret did more than that. She painted her fingernails shocking pink or bright red and wore lipstick to match (Elizabeth wore only the slightest touch of lip rouge). Margaret reacted to Queen Mary's annoyance at photographs of her granddaughter smoking in public by using ever longer and more bejeweled cigarette holders. She was photographed drinking and dancing with a retinue of friends and social climbers at fashionable and not-so-fashionable London nightclubs. When her mother asked if Margaret might not be drinking just a wee bit too much, she replied that after all her father downed at least four whiskies and water before dinner and several brandies after. At least. After the theater or the ballet, Margaret would be driven with friends to The Society or The Bagatelle restaurant and then later to the Four Hundred Club for dancing until four in the morning. Often she did not return to her small bedroom, sitting room and bath at Buckingham Palace until dawn's early light.*

Finally, on an Italian holiday, Margaret was snapped wearing so brief and pale a swimsuit that the play of light and seawater on the fabric made her appear quite naked. The *Daily Express,* for propriety's sake, retouched the photos, decorously darkening the suit. But this was so obvious that British readers

---

* As for her mother's objections to Margaret's drinking, the Queen was in no position to scold. "She enjoys gin and loves champagne," wrote an admiring biographer. "She has been known to enjoy two glasses of white wine at a midday reception before driving off to a luncheon, where, whilst moving through a suite of rooms, she has sipped at least three separately prepared gin and Dubonnets before enjoying a glass of vintage champagne. At the same luncheon two glasses of white burgundy would seem normal, followed by a glass of claret. When offered a fine Chateau Yquem [*sic*] with the pudding, she exclaimed, 'Oh, no, I mustn't drink any more. I'll just have another glass of champagne, if that's agreeable' " (De-la-Noy, page 177).

were all the more suspicious. "Very undignified," muttered the King, although no one was quite sure whether he meant his daughter or her detractors. Margaret, of ample bust, small waist and shapely legs, apparently relished the fuss, for she sent copies of the photo to many friends.

By 1950 she was the most visible member of the Royal Family and certainly the one quickest to mingle with non-Royals; in other words, she was establishing herself in the spotlight by molding an image very different from her sedate sister. Stylish, highly strung, as flirtatious with the sons of aristocrats as she was with footmen at the palace, she never received anything more than an indulgent tut-tut from her parents: "She could charm the pearl out of an oyster," said the King, tolerating antics he would never have sustained from the lowliest country gardener in his employ. Her sister's attitude was a patient sigh: "You are only young once," although Elizabeth herself had never acted quite so young. "Her feeling was motherly and protective," according to Marion Crawford. But "Margaret's antics made [Elizabeth] uneasy and filled her with foreboding."

Eager to free herself from the constraints of protocol, she was equally quick to get her way with escorts. "Quite a handful for the chaps who qualified" was the estimation of one who briefly did.

A man would know that she wanted to dance with him. Nothing too obvious—a quick, meaningful glance often out of the corner of one eye, an expression. One of her problems was how to shake off her loyal, hard-pressed personal detectives, [and] often one of them was left standing when Margaret roared off in a boyfriend's car.

"I'm Just a Girl Who Can't Say No," Margaret sang gaily as she dashed through the palace corridors. Her sister and brother-in-law had *their* romantic song from *Oklahoma!* and now Margaret had her naughty one. She was, incidentally, not without real musical talent, especially for comic and novelty songs. No less a judge than Noël Coward thought she had "an impeccable ear, her piano playing is simple but has perfect rhythm, and her method of singing is really very funny. The Queen is genuinely proud of her chick."

Lively, fun-loving, mischievous and utterly without purpose or gravity in her life, she seemed to have only one aspiration: "to be ... independent and carefree," as one journalist wrote at the time, "[and] to be the best-dressed woman in the world." When her mother said, "I do not desire to be a leader of fashion," Margaret added at once, "Well, I do."

Part of the apparent shallowness of her conduct derived from the unfortunate fact that as a major Royal she was not permitted to take a job or develop a career. She had only to think of her personal happiness and fulfillment, not of improving herself intellectually or socially.

Thus Margaret sailed toward her twenty-first birthday believing that the married Peter Townsend would somehow, someday be hers. Until then she danced and dined with eligible bachelors such as "Sunny" Blandford (later the Duke of Marlborough); Johnny Dalkeith (later the Duke of Buccleuch); Billy Wallace, a sportsman; Lord Porchester (later the Queen's racing manager) and Mark Bonham-Carter, grandson of Lord Oxford. But Peter—tall, angularly handsome, with a slightly melancholic and needy look that reflected his several nervous collapses during and after the war—was the one who was "entertained" by Princess Margaret, as Michael Parker's wife Eileen delicately phrased the first stages of the affair in 1949.

> Rosemary Townsend and I were both married to men frequently lured from us by the lustre of glittering prizes. But it was slightly easier for me then. At least, to the very best of my knowledge, Mike was not having an affair and creating public humiliation. Rosemary as a wife and mother had to stand to one side while Princess Margaret, hardly out of ankle socks, entertained her husband. Understandably, she had every cause to sound bitter sometimes.

Philip expressed no opinion on the matter of Margaret—for the present. He loathed pomposity, especially of the moralistic sort, as a somewhat stuffy scientist learned when he offered the Prince a tour of the National Physics Laboratory. Droning on endlessly about atom-splitting and industrial electronics, the guide finally stopped for breath. "That's all very well," said Philip, "but you still haven't found out what makes my bathwater gurgle when I take the stopper out."

He never suffered fools or journalists gladly, and for him the latter are mostly to be identified with the former. "Which are the apes and which are the gentlemen from the press?" he once asked while looking into a cage of simians. When he saw an intrusive photographer climb a nearby flagpole to get a better picture, and then crash down atop the crowd below, he muttered, "I hope to God he breaks his bloody neck!" He could be even sterner. One morning a newsman approached him as he was leaving a church service in Sandringham. The man had just published a complimentary account of Philip's role in the navy, and he expected a warm comment or at least a friendly greeting. No such luck. "Fuck off," said Philip to the reporter—a reply learned and also used to great effect by his daughter Anne in similar circumstances.

As for riskier, more embarrassing behavior, there were, almost from the first months of the marriage, rumors of Philip's rampant infidelity.

"The royal collection [of] women in the Duke's life," as the favorites have been called, has included countesses and cabaret singers, duchesses and society doyennes. The Duchess of Abercorn is a tall blond beauty descended from Czar Nicholas I, and the Duke has traveled (with others discreetly present) to the Bahamas to visit her tropical retreat.

Lady Cavendish is a chic artist, much admired by Philip. Henrietta Dunne is a slim, busty, glamorous type who has vast armies of dogs and regular shooting parties; the Prince is "a big fan" of hers, wrote one royal correspondent. The Countess of Westmoreland, at the center of the fashionable horsey set, is particularly close to Philip and feels intimate enough to bestow gifts. Hélène Cordet and Pat Kirkwood—a nightclub patroness and a musical star, respectively—are or were among other close companions.

Not one of these women (or the many others rumored to have been his mistresses) has stepped forward to tell of an intrigue or a past liaison with Prince Philip despite the incentives to fame and fortune offered by publishers and ghostwriters. This egregious lack of witnesses to affairs; the absence of love letters, journals or statements from the women in question or the Duke himself; and the lack of incriminating photographs will doubtless not prevent imaginative writers from coming up with all sorts of half-imagined, scurrilous tales.

Some have explained the dearth of evidence by a journalistic hesitation to embarrass Elizabeth, especially after she became Queen. But that does not take into account the fact that vast sums of cash offered in England and America for a spicy tale—an offer that surely would overcome *someone's* scruples —have always gone unclaimed.

In 1992 a fearless interviewer bluntly confronted Philip about the rumors. "Have you ever stopped to think," the Prince replied, "that for the last forty years I have never moved anywhere without a policeman accompanying me? So how the hell could I ever get away with anything like that?"

He could have got away with it, of course. But whatever is the truth of the Duke's extracurricular life, he has always been in very deep ways loyal to the Queen, and he has enjoyed her uninterrupted confidence and company. Cynics may smile, but the weight of evidence is against the presumption of his unfettered philandering.

In addition, bodyguards, secretaries, an ever watchful press, and even a cadre of people inside and outside the palace who have not liked Philip's abrasive, sometimes undignified personality—all these can come up with no compromise to his marriage. As Parker believed, so it was: the Duke's commitment was not to let his wife down. "I just don't think he's at all sexual in that way," said a courtier who never really liked the Prince. "He gets it all out playing polo or sailing or working. But not that [that is, an affair]. It's just not in him." According to Philip's friend, the American musician Larry Adler, the Duke harbored an amicable envy of Prince Bernhard of the Netherlands. "You can go where you like," he told Bernhard, "see who you like, and even have affairs, and no one knows. I am known everywhere, and I am constantly being trailed by secret service men." Adler recalled that Philip complained throughout the 1950s about his "moral straitjacket, and he felt really bitter about the position in which he found himself, especially walking behind his wife [when she became Queen]. He didn't like that; he just didn't like it at all."

After a difficult labor, Princess Elizabeth delivered a son on November 14, 1948, a birth unique in that her father had decreed an end to the awkward tradition of having the birth eyewitnessed by government ministers. Then, at the infant's christening, there seemed a deliberate gesture of dissociating the child from his German ancestry: the baby Prince Charles Philip Arthur George bore distinctly English and Scottish names. One old professional was present at the baptism in December. Charlotte "Lala" Bill, the King's own nanny a half-century earlier, was so carried away that she kissed the monarch, and to everyone's surprise, he returned the gesture.

The nation had a holiday, for the second generation of future sovereigns had been guaranteed. "Don't you think he is quite adorable?" wrote his mother to a visitor who had seen the baby at four days old. "I still can't believe he is really mine, but perhaps that happens to new parents. Anyway, this particular boy's parents couldn't be more proud of him. It's wonderful to think, isn't it, that his arrival could give a bit of happiness to so many people, besides ourselves, at this time?"

Charles's parents may indeed have been proud of him, but the fact is that neither of them had the opportunity or the personality to be attentive parents. Philip had no firsthand experience of fatherhood—his own had been a remote figure with whom he lived only briefly—and pampering (much less sentimental doting) was not in the Duke's temperament. The baby's mother had certainly enjoyed a cozy childhood in her mother's care. But now she was so close to the throne and was accepting so many appointments for public appearances that she became, in effect, a distant and benignly negligent mother —a typical aristocratic one, that is—and her son was turned over to a pair of nannies (Helen Lightbody and Mabel Anderson) and a governess (Catherine Peebles, always called Mispy, as in "Miss P").

From infancy, then, Charles received the treatment typical of an upper-class boy. He was taken to see his mother for a few minutes each morning at nine, and then Mummy appeared again at teatime or bathtime; Papa popped in for an hour or two each week—little more, for beginning in 1949 he was often away on naval assignments. "To my knowledge," said Eileen Parker, with whom the Princess often discussed the role of motherhood, "she never bathed the children. Nanny did all that." Embraces, loving affection, the normal physical and emotional needs of any infant, these were never second nature to the undemonstrative Elizabeth and so were delegated to dutiful ladies acting as professionals. Just as before. Charles worshiped his mother and saw what deference she received from everyone. But his worship was tendered from afar. He confided to a girlfriend years later that as a child his nanny had given him more emotional support than his mother.

As for Philip, a clerical confidant summed up the relationship between father and son: "I think it has always been unfortunate that the chemistry between Prince Philip and Prince Charles has not been the same as the chemistry that exists between [Philip and his next child, Princess Anne]," according to the Reverend Michael Main, Dean of Windsor. "Prince Charles tends to be intimidated" by his father. The reason was simple: "I want him to be a man's man," said Philip, and to that end no strategy for toughening the boy was considered too severe. From birth, Philip's attitude toward his son was disastrous. "He often seemed intent not merely on correcting the Prince but even mocking him as well," wrote Charles's official biographer years later, after interviewing the heir to the throne. Charles was "frequently brought to tears by the banter to which he was subjected and to which he could find no retort, [and] even his closest friends found the Duke's behaviour inexplicably harsh." He wanted to mold his son for kingship; instead, Philip was simply a bully.

Despite his good cheer about becoming Grandpapa, the King must have suspected that he was seriously ill, and his fifty-third birthday that month passed without even a quiet family celebration. "The King is suffering from an obstruction to the circulation through the arteries of the legs" went the medical bulletin from the Palace Press Office nine days after the birth of the monarch's grandson. "The defective blood supply causes anxiety." The King and Queen's trip to Australia was canceled, and a flurry of alarms ran through the Royal Family as the patient became irritable and moody, unaccustomed and unwilling to be confined to a chair. "He also declined to give up smoking," reported *Newsweek*'s London bureau chief, "although doctors say this has been known to aggravate arterial conditions." By New Year's Day 1949 there was fear of the general population's becoming alarmed, and so the palace dissembled: "Although the King's general health, including the condition of his heart, gives no reason for concern, no doubt the strain of twelve years has appreciably reduced his resistance to physical fatigue." In fact, his condition worsened so significantly that on March 12 doctors operated to correct the obstruction, and the King was confined for a lengthy recuperation.

With that event the Princess was pitched into a more demanding round of activities, interrupting both her married life and the attention she might otherwise have given her baby. Substituting for her ailing father, she demonstrated an appreciation for how her presence might gratify ordinary people, and one incident reveals how poignantly that could occur if another's child was involved. Before a tour of Wales that April, she had received a letter from Mrs. F. M. Allday, welcoming her to the countryside and saying she would be waving a brightly colored rosette as the Princess motored through the village.

"I went to a hill on the road from Barmouth, in Dolgelly," recalled Mrs. Allday, "and when the royal car came along, I waved my rosette and the Princess saw me. The car stopped, and I had a chat with her for three or four minutes. My married daughter was there with my grandson, and the Princess took the baby in her arms and said, 'What a fine baby he is!' " The family had the clear impression that Elizabeth missed her own son and husband.

As it happened, Philip would have his wish and leave his shore job. He took up a post as First Lieutenant and second-in-command on HMS *Chequers,* which was to go on peacetime maneuvers around the Mediterranean in the autumn of 1949. That the Princess would be a "navy widow" for about two years may have influenced her choice of remarks to the Mothers' Union on October 18. Speaking in bitter opposition to the rising incidence of divorce in Great Britain, the Princess caused a storm of criticism for what some Members of Parliament called her meddling in moral issues. The government and the public, however, were put on notice that even at twenty-three their next sovereign had a mind and will of her own. Elizabeth took further steps in her political education in late 1949 and early 1950 when she dined with the Speaker of the House of Commons—the first heir to the throne to do so—and when she entertained the President of France and his wife, thus becoming, as one chronicler noted, "a symbol of the Entente Cordiale."

On November 20, her second wedding anniversary, Elizabeth flew to Malta to meet Philip, who bounded aboard the plane to greet her. Whisked away to Louis and Edwina Mountbatten's estate overlooking the harbor, they celebrated at dinner with champagne and a three-tiered cake. They enjoyed Philip's month-long leave before he had to return to the ship and she to London duties. From this reunion Philip was confirmed in one suspicion: his wife's passion for horses. Offered the choice of watching him play cricket or Louis Mountbatten play polo, she went to the polo match. For her sake, Philip took up the sport. "I made the serious mistake," he said, "of underestimating my wife's interest in horses."

Early in the following spring of 1950, it was announced that Princess Elizabeth would accept no engagements after early May: she was pregnant with her second child. Anne Elizabeth Alice Louise was born at Clarence House on August 15, 1950. Again, Papa was off on naval duties to Malta, this time aboard the *Magpie,* where one of his crew recalled that "he stamped about like a fucking tiger"; another said he would rather die than serve under Philip once more; and a third claimed that "he worked us like hell, but he treated us like gentlemen."

Elizabeth went out to meet her husband, this time for almost four months. The palace reported that she was "in the same position as the wife of any ordinary naval officer: she was joining her husband on his station." This was hardly the case, for Elizabeth arrived with a staff of ten, her own car, forty large pieces of luggage, a new polo pony for her husband, and without the burden of child care, for Charles and Anne had of course been left behind with nannies.

Elizabeth returned to London at the new year of 1951 and was stunned at her father's appearance. Yes, her mother told her, he seemed haggard and listless, easily exhausted and depressed. At fifty-five, the King dragged himself along the palace corridors as if each step were the effort of a very old man. When he opened the Festival of Britain on May 3—a display of artistic and scientific achievement all over London, designed to show the nation's recovery from the war—the press and public were shocked at how ill the monarch looked. Later that month he was confined with influenza. "I am having daily injections of penicillin for about a week," George wrote to his mother. "This condition has only been on the lung for a few days so it should resolve itself with treatment."

By July the King seemed to have recovered, but he still tired easily and was constantly short of breath. His physician, Sir Horace Evans, suspected the real cause of the King's chronic illness was graver than influenza or pneumonitis, and on September 16 a bronchoscopy revealed a malignant lung tumor. Told only that he had a bronchial blockage that necessitated removal of his left lung, the King underwent surgery a week later at Buckingham Palace. By that time Philip was "on indefinite leave" from his beloved command of the *Magpie*. The temporary release, due to the King's illness and Elizabeth's desire to have her husband with her as she assumed more and more state duties, turned out to be permanent.

Besides the serious matter of lung cancer, the King's history of circulatory problems added to the danger of a pulmonary embolism or a coronary thrombosis, and Churchill's physician, Lord Moran, suspected that the King would not live another year. The Queen was told the gravity of the situation, and she confided this to her daughters; the nation, meanwhile, was kept as poorly informed as the patient himself. Elizabeth was not surprised, for she suspected what her father's appearance and her added duties meant. As for Margaret, she turned more and more to Townsend for comfort, but how that love would be fully realized neither of them knew. "I stretched out in the heather to doze," Townsend recalled of one afternoon in Scotland with the Royal Family that summer.

Then vaguely I was aware that someone was covering me with a coat. I opened one eye to see Princess Margaret's lovely face, very close, looking into mine. Then I opened the other eye and saw, behind her, the King, leaning on his stick with a certain look—typical of him: kind, half-amused. I whispered, "You know your father is watching us?" At which she laughed, straightened up and went to his side, took his arm and walked him away, leaving me to my dreams.

From October 8 to November 17, Elizabeth and Philip undertook the strenuous tour of Canada and the United States that had originally been planned for her parents as a repetition of the successful 1939 visit. At the Duke's suggestion (and over the objections of the Cabinet), they became the first Royals to fly over the Atlantic. Welcomed enthusiastically by Canadians and then by President Harry S Truman, the Edinburghs were thrown into a public relations whirlwind. At thirty and twenty-five, they were attractive, genial, photogenic—instant stars for a postwar world famished for glamour, despite the fact that Canada was politically divided about the British monarchy (HOME RULE THE ONLY RULE read some unwelcome placards) and that Truman's mother was a bit confused. "I'm so glad your father has been reelected," she told the Princess in November when Churchill was restored as Prime Minister.

Reporters noticed that Elizabeth did not have her mother's immediacy or warmth with crowds; she was "perfectly trained" but "self-conscious and tense," while her "dashing husband relieved some of the sedate stiffness of the tour [and] his whispered asides helped ease Elizabeth's nervousness." When photographers came too close to the Princess, Philip all but shoved them back. At one luncheon he complained that she could scarcely eat with a thousand people hovering. "This is a waste of everyone's time," he announced, and spirited his wife back to her private suite. With that, the world was put on notice that Philip would be no passive coat-holder to his wife. Despite her exhaustion on their return in November, she at once agreed to substitute for her father on a five-month round-the-world tour beginning early in 1952.

At Christmas, George had hardly recovered. His six-minute radio address, the first to be made in advance, required two days of brief recording sessions, so short was he of breath. Doctors were cautiously optimistic after an uneventful January, and on the thirtieth of that month the King and Queen took Elizabeth and Margaret to see *South Pacific* at the Drury Lane Theatre.

The evening was a kind of gala farewell, for the next afternoon, January 31, 1952, the Edinburghs left for what was planned as a worldwide tour. Despite a chill wind, the King insisted on standing hatless with his wife and Margaret at his side on the airport tarmac. The King and the Queen then went up to Sandringham, taking along Margaret, Charles and Anne. On the evening of Tuesday, February 5, they listened to a BBC report on Elizabeth and Philip, who were at a wild game sanctuary in Kenya. At ten-thirty George and Elizabeth retired to their separate rooms, and around midnight a watchman noticed him fixing his window latch. At seven the next morning a valet went as scheduled to awaken His Majesty, but sometime during the night his weary heart had stopped. He was fifty-six. His wife, summoned from her room nearby, asked that a vigil be kept outside the King's door: "He must not be left alone."

In New York an hour later, the Duke of Windsor was informed by a palace official of his brother's death. It was a double shock, for he was also told that the Duchess would not be welcome to accompany him to the funeral. Angry and heartsick, he sailed alone for London—aboard the *Queen Mary,* as it happened. And when that eponymous lady was approached by a sad-eyed attendant that morning, she anticipated the news: "Is it the King?" she asked quietly. In her eighty-fourth year, she had now lost her husband and three sons. From this death she never recovered, but became frailer and more withdrawn over the next year. "I suppose," she said sadly to her old friend Lady Shaftsbury, "that one must force oneself to go on until the end." And so she did.

Elizabeth and Philip were resting between official engagements at a Kenya lodge. They had spent the previous day with hand-held cameras, filming elephants, rhinos and baboons, and making notes for the amateur documentary they wanted to take home for the family. That morning they went trout fishing, and after lunch they retired for a nap. It had taken Michael Parker and the couple's staff six hours to confirm the news that had been incompletely flashed over the wires. Finally, he tapped at the door of the royal suite and asked Prince Philip to step outside.

"He's not the sort of person to show his emotions," Parker said years later, "but I'll never forget it. He looked as if half the world had fallen on him." Another aide elaborated: "He didn't want it [that is, his new role] at all. It was going to change his whole life, take away the emotional stability he'd finally found." From that day he would be forced to submit every personal need and desire to the demands of his wife's position. A brusque and often cheerless exterior often characterized him, a formal façade only a few intimate friends could ever penetrate.

"It was not my ambition to be president of the Mint Advisory Committee," he said forty years later, referring sarcastically to only one of the legion of organizations he must nominally head. "And I didn't want to be president of the World Wildlife Fund. I was asked to do it. I'd much rather have stayed in the navy, frankly."

His first task, of course, was to break the news to his wife, and one can only imagine what passed between them in those few moments in the hot African afternoon. Then their chief of staff came to Elizabeth, bowed and asked by what name she wished to be known as Queen. "By my own name, of course," she replied, dry-eyed. "What else?"

At that instant she was what she had been raised to become from childhood: an unworldly, composed girl whose conduct was carefully self-controlled yet somehow unaffected. She had always kept her emotions in check, thought always of her duty to her family and dignity in public. It was second nature for her to consider what was expected of her, not what she wished. Order, discipline, a modulated voice, only the subtlest exposure of her emotions: these had become habits of being. As with any suddenly bereaved young family member, there was an avalanche of obligations. She sent cables at once to her mother and sister, to her grandmother and to one of her uncles, the Duke of Gloucester—but not to the Duke of Windsor.

"I remember seeing her moments after she became Queen," said a member of her staff, "moments, not hours. And she seemed almost to reach out for it. There were no tears. She was just there, back braced, her color a little heightened. Just waiting for her destiny."

Eager to please parents she loved, Elizabeth repressed beneath the mantle of duty her grief over her father's death. Next afternoon, February 7, she stepped from the BOAC airplane at London Airport. A petite figure in black, she was greeted by Winston Churchill (her Prime Minister), Clement Attlee (leader of the opposition party), and her uncle, Henry Gloucester. They had been told not to kiss her hand in obeisance. "Her old Grannie and subject must be the first to kiss her hand," said Queen Mary, and so Lilibet sped to Marlborough House that same afternoon.

The Council was held the next day at St. James's Palace. "By the sudden death of my dear father," the Queen said,

I am called to assume the duties and responsibility of Sovereignty. At this time of deep sorrow it is a profound consolation to me to be assured of the sympathy which you and all my peoples feel towards me, to my mother and my sister, and to the other members of my family. My father was our revered and beloved head as he was of the wider family of his subjects: the grief which his loss brings is shared among us all.

My heart is too full for me to say more to you today than that I shall always work, as my father did throughout his reign, to uphold the constitutional government and to advance the happiness and prosperity of my peoples, spread as they are the world over. I know that in my resolve to follow his shining example of service and devotion, I shall be inspired by the loyalty and affection of those whose Queen I have been called to be, and by the counsel of their elected parliaments.

I pray that God will help me to discharge worthily this heavy task that has been laid upon me so early in my life.

She was not yet twenty-six years old.

Those words spoken, the public proclamations of the accession of Her Majesty Queen Elizabeth II were made at Charing Cross and Temple Bar, the Royal Exchange, the Tower of London, and Middlesex Guildhall. Guns then boomed across Hyde Park. Only then did she leave for Sandringham, where the body of her father the King lay. She was the youngest monarch to succeed to the throne since the eighteen-year-old Victoria in 1837.

Until the funeral a week later, Elizabeth was inundated by a tide of official business. She met the High Commissioners of the Commonwealth Countries; she welcomed Foreign Ministers, Ambassadors, Consuls and Ministers of her own state; she sat for portraits for the new stamps and coins; she stood for hundreds of official photographs. By May 31 she had dispatched 140 engagements, and by year's end another 308. She announced that she would be crowned June 2, 1953. What was her attitude toward her new job by the end of the year? "She loves being Queen," said a palace official. "It's like champagne to her. The truth is that the Queen likes being boss."

"I didn't have the apprenticeship," she said years later. "My father died much too young, and so it was all a very sudden kind of taking-on and making the best job you can. Here you are, it's your fate. Continuity is very important. It's a job for life.''

Philip liked nothing about the new arrangement. His eldest sister, Margarita, recalled his severe depression at the time of King George's funeral. ''You can imagine what's going to happen now,'' he said sadly, hardly leaving his rooms for almost a week. As it turned out, the coming coronation was the only event in which Philip had any substantial role; otherwise, he was very much a shadow. Unlike Victoria's Albert, he was not (then or ever) proclaimed Prince Consort, nor was he given any official duties that marked him as anything like the Sovereign's confidant. The Queen's Cabinet, her government and the palace courtiers made it known that his presence as an active, influential figure would not be welcome. ''I do not have a job,'' he said. ''In fact, the more I do, the more it costs me.'' For two months he was ill with hepatitis. No one took this very seriously.

Philip later described the problem succinctly:

Because she's the Sovereign, everybody turns to her. If you have a King and Queen, there are certain things people automatically go to the Queen about. But if the Queen is also the *Queen* [that is, the reigning monarch in her own right rather than the Consort], they go to her about everything . . . [and] it's frightfully difficult to persuade many of the Household not to go to the Queen, but to come to me.

Within days, Elizabeth wrote of her father's death to a family friend, Elizabeth Cecil, the Marchioness of Salisbury. ''The [hand]writing was young,'' recalled one who saw the letter, ''but the style of the first paragraph was as formal and cold as possible. Betty [Cecil] said it was like a letter from Queen Mary. Then suddenly she broke down and the second paragraph read, 'Oh, Betty, this is so awful for Mummy and Margaret. I have Philip and the children and the future, but what are they to do?' Then the third paragraph was Queen Mary style again, and the signature very grand and big, like a child writing to show off—'Elizabeth R.' ''*

* * *

---

* And so she would sign henceforth: Elizabeth R[egina].

The new Queen need not have worried about her strong-willed mother and independent sister. On the death of her husband, the former Queen ceased to exist as one with official rank or status. She had absolutely no constitutional function and might have chosen to style herself the Duchess of York or Queen Dowager (Queen Mary was officially Dowager Queen Mother, but she was never called, nor did she wish to be known as, anything but Queen Mary). In any case, the widowed Queen Elizabeth was owed nothing more than a comfortable retirement and the respect of the nation.

But in what the *News Chronicle* called "a statement without parallel in the history of kingship," she at once chose to call herself Queen Elizabeth The Queen Mother and wrote a "little note" to the people explaining herself. What she never explained was the horrid slight to Queen Mary, whose title of Queen Mother (whether she chose to use it or not) she thus summarily took for herself. Mary had never acted so forcefully on the death of King George V; she had never placed herself near center stage. If the nation wanted her presence here or there, Mary responded. It was not only her shyness but her sense of propriety and of what the constitution required that enabled Queen Mary to have a life within her family without pushing herself forward.

Not so the new Queen Mother. First she made a public statement of allegiance to her "dear daughter" and urged the nation "to give her your loyalty and devotion; in the great and lonely station to which she has been called she will need your protection and love." This sounded full of affectionate support, but there was a subtext of condescension. It was not her place to tell the nation her daughter's needs. She was speaking in a somewhat patronizing manner, as if a child were going off to a first day at school, and Mummy wished to commend her to the kindness of classmates.

Then she turned the spotlight fully on herself: "Now I am left alone, to do what I can to honour that pledge without him. Throughout our married life we have tried, the King and I, to fulfill with all our hearts and all our strength, the great task of service that was laid upon us. My only wish now is that I may be allowed to continue the work we sought to do together." Such a statement anywhere else might have sounded harmless. With the strict requirements of monarchical diction and action,

351

the Queen Mother's words were frightful. She was asking for an active role in the nation's life, for the unprecedented and unconstitutional function of "continuing the work" she and George had done. It would have been impossible to imagine Queen Alexandra, for example, trying to carve out such a position for herself after the death of Edward VII. Confident in the nation's affection, she withdrew a dignified distance. If wanted, she was there. Like her daughter-in-law Mary, she knew her presence meant something; she need not force it on the nation. Not so George VI's Elizabeth: she took the shocking step of implying that her husband's work *would continue*. What, one might have asked, of the new Queen's work?

She was, then, entirely out of order, and her words were not so much a promise as a threat. She would be present, and God help those who were not canny enough to avail themselves of her experience. This speech to the nation (broadcast February 17, 1952, just days after her husband's burial) was a stunningly unconstitutional gesture. Her words revealed an unprecedented determination to remain an important part of the royal apparatus.

It remains a tenable hypothesis in the collective memory today that no King in English history was as revered in his reign as Elizabeth I or Victoria. Queen Mary and the new Queen Mother, then, were seen as guardians of the sacredness, the sanctity of the monarchy. They were like baptized, aristocratic Earth Mothers, carrying the past into a present they nurtured and guaranteed. Matriarchy reigns by the sheer force of *presence,* and woe to those assertive males whose very existence might challenge it (like the Duke of Windsor). In a curious way, Queen Elizabeth The Queen Mother was preparing for the saga of Lady Diana Spencer, who as the Princess of Wales would have just as formidable an ability to project a highly refined sense of herself with a mass of enthusiastic admirers.

The new Queen need not have worried about the strength of her sister, either. At first Margaret was plunged into profound grief. She turned first to her faith, attending classes on prayer and suffering at St. Paul's, Knightsbridge, and she went to a series of lectures on God and eternal life. More than once she donned a black suit and matching beret and slipped quietly into church without a lady-in-waiting for a solitary prayer or a morning service. She was also susceptible to the blandishments of a new friend, the cheerful Reverend Simon Phipps, who held the curious twin posts of Industrial Chaplain for the diocese of Coventry and a member of the Amalgamated Engineering Union. A social gadfly and amateur songwriter, the Reverend Phipps amused Margaret, but he discussed serious matters with her as well.

But as the year passed, Peter Townsend was her constant companion. Finally, one afternoon at Windsor Castle, they spoke alone for hours. According to Townsend,

> It was then that we made the mutual discovery of how much we meant to one another. She listened, without uttering a word, as I told her, very quietly, of my feelings. Then she simply said, "That is exactly how I feel, too." It was, to both of us, an immensely gladdening disclosure, but one which sorely troubled us

—for the obvious reason, no doubt, that he was soon to be divorced. The specter of 1936 hung heavily over the Royal Family. And Margaret's sister was only just on the throne and not yet crowned. As Margaret and her mother prepared to quit Buckingham Palace for Clarence House, thus exchanging residences with Elizabeth and Philip, she remarked sadly, "Nothing seems the same without Papa."

Perhaps none of her friends was surprised that she turned to Townsend, the new comptroller of her mother's household, who accompanied them to Clarence House. He had brought a divorce case against his wife on grounds of adultery, a suit he won at the end of the year. "During 1952," according to Townsend,

> Princess Margaret and I found increasing solace in one another's company. The year began with the Princess's grief, caused by the sudden death of her father; it continued with the change in her own family situation—living alone with her mother (whom she adored)—and the steady deterioration in mine; it ended in the break-up of my family. . . . If on the material plane, as well as temperamentally, the Princess and I were worlds apart, we responded, in our feelings and emotions, as one.

The romance continued throughout the spring of 1953, until the lovers realized there was nothing left for them but to approach the Queen with their wish to marry.

While Townsend was staking an emotional claim on Margaret, and the Queen Mother was laying siege to an unprecedented royal role in the new reign, another person was moving swiftly. The day after the King's burial, Queen Mary learned that Louis Mountbatten had said the throne of Great Britain was now occupied by the House of Mountbatten—the surname Philip had assumed under Louis's influence. "He cared desperately about the name," according to royal biographer Philip Ziegler, "and he always believed that the royal house should not be the House of Windsor but the house of Mountbatten-Windsor. He was defeated on that: he was defeated again and again. But he kept coming back, he kept chipping away."

This, to the surprise of no one on her staff, lifted Queen Mary from grief to angry action. She sent for Churchill's Private Secretary, Sir John Colville, who in turn informed Churchill of Mountbatten's statement. The Prime Minister called a Cabinet meeting, declaring that Mountbatten was trying to take the throne for his family. At the same time, the Lord Chancellor—eager along with everyone else to get the matter right *and* to please grand old Queen Mary quickly— drafted a statement that King George V certainly intended that his descendants and their dynasty be named Windsor. It was just as Field Marshal Jan C. Smuts of South Africa had said to Mary at her granddaughter's wedding: "You are the big potato; the other queens of Europe are small potatoes."

The ambitious Mountbatten swung back, prodding the ailing Prince Philip until he sent a seven-page memorandum of protest on March 5. Philip pointed out to the Cabinet that when Victoria married Albert, the British royal house assumed his name (Saxe-Coburg-Gotha). This rankled Churchill, who saw to it that the Queen received instructions from the Cabinet to retain Windsor as the name of the Royal Family. Of this the Queen was "advised," and it was made official on her birthday, April 21—much to Philip's chagrin. He may have felt his wife was going to be another big potato while he languished— with no constitutional position—in the garden of ineffectual boredom, and his mother-in-law and sister-in-law had more of the Queen's confidence. "He used to say, 'I'm neither one thing nor the other—I'm nothing,' " recalled Eileen Parker. "I think he felt frustration—a lot of it." Her husband agreed: "I think there must have been moments when it would have been pretty heavy for him to take."

It was perhaps not surprising, therefore, that Philip consoled himself with friendships outside the Royal Family—with good and discreet people such as the Parkers. She recalled opening the door of her flat one evening "and there stood Prince Philip —alone. 'Hullo.' He grinned, holding out a bottle of gin. . . . I took a few steps backward, and he stalked into the room with [an] eager walk." It was a stingingly cold late winter evening, and the Parkers had only a two-bar electric heater in their sitting room. "The three of us huddled in front of it, thawing out and mellowing with pink gins and eating my macaroni cheese off our laps. Prince Philip seemed completely at home with what must have been comparatively meagre fare compared to the cuisine of Buckingham Palace. It developed into a most enjoyable evening in every respect"—and one frequently repeated during Philip's early years as the Queen's husband.

The coronation year 1953 could not have begun more grimly. More than fifteen thousand people from Lincolnshire to Kent were killed in winter storms, which also left more than twenty-five thousand homeless. Then, with the arrival of an early spring, the thick, dank London air turned lethal: more than nine thousand men, women and children died of smog-related illnesses and infections, and gas masks, relics from the war, were unpacked and strapped onto frightened school children.

Since the death of King George, Queen Mary had grown frailer, although she enjoyed being honored by her family at luncheon and again at high tea on her eighty-fifth birthday in May 1952. During the first days of February 1953, she braved the cold, asking to be driven twice through Hyde Park to see the stands being built for the coronation. Exhausted for days after, she let it be known that should she somehow be unable to attend the event in June, it must not be postponed on her account. "I am beginning to lose my memory," she told a friend, adding with a sly smile, as if she had misplaced a treasured bibelot, "but I mean to get it back."

Her mental powers were otherwise undimmed and her senses intact. After attending a performance of the play *September Tide,* she was taken backstage to meet the cast, headed by the formidable Gertrude Lawrence (at the time the lover of the novelist Daphne Du Maurier). After expressing her admiration, Queen Mary said she had found some of the words inaudible.

"Do you hear?" Gertrude Lawrence said, turning to her costars. "Now you've all got to speak up."

"Not all of them," Queen Mary corrected. "Just you!"

On February 9 she was taken out for what was to be the last time. Gastric distress and respiratory difficulty required her to stay in bed, but her interest in her family and in art remained undiminished.

On the afternoon of March 23 she asked to have a book about India read to her—the place she first cherished a half-century earlier. By the next afternoon she could not be roused from a coma. The Queen sat briefly by the bedside, and the Duke of Windsor was summoned to London. At twenty minutes past ten on the evening of March 24, Queen Mary stopped breathing.

The world over, there was not a syllable of public criticism of this great old lady, for if single-minded devotion to one's duty is a mark of grandeur, then perhaps no one in this family saga more clearly earned the right to be called honorable. Sometimes inflexible in her standards, rigid in her moral stance and humorless if anyone even remotely compromised royal dignity, Mary was, in the final analysis, a living definition of the genuine Queen. She had seen so much of wars and death and cruelty, and through everything she retained an unshakable honor. It is unlikely that she was ever intentionally unkind to anyone, and surely that in itself is one of the unequivocal signs of true nobility. Her entire character could be summarized in words she spoke to a group of children in wartime: "Remember that life is made up of loyalty. Loyalty to your friends, loyalty to things beautiful and good, loyalty to the country in which you live, loyalty to your King and above all, for this holds all your loyalties together, loyalty to God."

For all her antique ways and ancient protocol, Queen Mary would have much appreciated Elizabeth's decision (made at the suggestion of the Duke of Norfolk, Earl Marshal of England, charged with the preparation of all great royal ceremonies) to allow a televised broadcast of the coronation, for although she never permitted a telephone in her rooms, Mary was fascinated by the new medium. There was only one BBC channel and limited broadcasting in 1953, but the old Queen had followed the programming from month to month and had been impatient with arguments that only edited portions of the ceremony should be seen. Norfolk and Elizabeth prevailed, against the objections of Churchill, the Archbishop of Canterbury and Alan Lascelles, who argued emphatically that the mystery and mystique of the monarchy would be seriously damaged if television cameras gave the world a closeup view of the coronation. The crowning, insisted Her Majesty (quoting the Anglican Service Book), must occur "in the sight of all the people," and she was prepared to take this injunction literally. Trained by her tutor Henry Marten, the Queen may have recalled the injunction of Victoria's eldest son to his mother: "We live in radical times, and the more the people see the Sovereign, the better it is for the people and the country."

Norfolk and the Queen could not have known it that spring, but with this single decision Elizabeth II made herself (and subsequently her family) the world's most glamorous and enduring media celebrities. Twenty million Britons saw the coronation on June 2, and, with filmed versions rushed round the world, another three million saw it within days. Weddings had been private ceremonies in the time of Queen Victoria, celebrated in a chapel royal or quietly at Buckingham Palace. But since the Duke of York's wedding to Lady Elizabeth Bowes-Lyons in 1923, they were increasingly splendid affairs. In 1953 there was a successful royal attempt to use the media to celebrate it, and also in 1981 when the wedding of the Prince and Princess of Wales was seen by half a billion people worldwide.

On May 1 rehearsals began in the White Drawing Room at Buckingham Palace, a vast hall almost as big as the main portion of Westminster Abbey. In addition, the State Ballroom was marked out with tape and chalk as an exact smaller replica of the distances between those participating in the ritual. The Duchess of Norfolk acted as stand-in for the Queen in the first run-through of the actual ceremony at the abbey with the

Archbishop of Canterbury. The Queen herself arrived on May 21 to watch further rehearsals before stepping into her part the next day. Five days later she wore for the first time the five-pound St. Edward's crown. The final dress rehearsal took place on May 29. Philip attended that day, and, feeling like an actor in a fringe play, raced with some chagrin through his public oath of fealty to the Queen. He then threw his wife a kiss and prepared to dash out—until the silence was broken. "Don't be silly, Philip," commanded the Queen. "Come back and do that again, *properly*!" He did.

In the meantime, the Queen prepared privately as well, reading and memorizing long portions of the rite. She walked the length of the palace ballrooms with a book on her head; she moved with a brocade blanket pinned to her dress; she gauged distances and timed herself. Just as crucial, she assumed the necessary dietary restrictions so that from seven o'clock in the morning, when she would be fully dressed and prepared to leave Buckingham Palace, until almost five in the afternoon, when she would return, there would be no necessity for Her Majesty to excuse herself. For four days she lived on hard-cooked eggs (to retard normal intestinal activity) and high doses of salt (to reduce drastically her kidney and bladder function).

There was another kind of discomfort, however. In fact, it was the first crisis of Elizabeth's reign, and it went from a simmer to a boil just as the crown was being lowered onto her head. In late May, Princess Margaret and Peter Townsend lunched with the Queen, Prince Philip and the Queen Mother, all of whom seemed sympathetic to their desire to marry now that Peter was divorced. But the family's feelings were not entirely clear because they were not expressed, although Townsend had the impression the Royals felt the marriage "could not be." And here began the problem; from the outset Margaret and Peter had no guidance from the family, no strong indication of support—merely a wait-and-see attitude that left them alone to deal mostly with hostile courtiers.

There was one major dilemma that the Queen admitted she did not know how to handle. Even as they all sliced into their poached salmon that spring day, the Royal Mint was turning out new coins with "DF"—among her titles was *Defensor Fidei,* Defender of the Faith. And the Church of England was as adamantly opposed to the remarriage of divorced parties in 1953 as it had been in 1936.

The difficulty was plain. How could the young Queen, just when the Royal Family needed to be seen as the continuation of the quaint and stable family of George VI, allow a head-strong, pretty young Princess to marry a divorcé sixteen years her senior? Additionally, there was the fact that Margaret, third in line to the throne, was Regent—not Philip. In the event of her sister's death or incapacity, she would be Acting Queen until Prince Charles's maturity. But on November 11, Parliament approved the Queen's Regency Bill: precisely because of the uncertainty over Margaret's course of action, Philip was named Regent. This was something of a censure for Margaret, too—or at least a vote of no confidence.

Conversely, some thought that the Queen had a double intention: with Margaret removed as potential Regent, an obstacle to her marriage was also removed. That is a generous but unverifiable and unlikely interpretation. Acting Prime Minister R. A. "Rab" Butler, deputy for the ailing Churchill, insisted that the hypothetical marriage had nothing to do with the regency change, which he said had been planned for over a year.

That same week before the coronation, Townsend confided in Alan Lascelles, the guardian of Victorian monarchism who had just objected so strongly to television cameras at the coronation. (Lascelles, whose service went back to George V and Edward VIII, had been King George VI's Private Secretary from 1943 to 1952 and had retained that position with Elizabeth.) When Townsend approached Lascelles with his intentions, the old courtier blurted out, "You must be either mad or bad!"

"I had hoped," Peter said later, "for a more helpful reaction."

But the Group Captain was to be disappointed. Although every member of the Royal Family had only respect and affection for him, "the crucial point," as he said, "was that I was divorced, and the Queen . . . could not, constitutionally, give her consent [to his marriage to Margaret] unless her prime minister saw fit to advise her otherwise." For the moment, any further discussion was delayed by the Queen's coronation. No one outside the family knew about Captain Townsend and Princess Margaret.

*   *   *

At last, with admirable British precision and pluck, everything seemed to go right publicly (except the inglorious and unpredictable London weather, which suddenly turned wet and cold). On June 1, Edmund Hillary and Sherpa Norgay Tenzing reached the summit of Mount Everest. Their timing could not have been better.

June 2, coronation day, had been chosen to ensure fine weather. Alas, it was not to be, and the millions who camped out overnight on the streets of London were soaked by that morning. But there were compensations. That week a surplus in postwar rations had been allowed: everyone was granted an extra pound of sugar and four ounces of margarine or cooking fat.

The spectacle itself was designed to do for the young Queen what an earlier one had done for Victoria when she reentered public life: to recreate the monarchy as a symbol of national identity, a reality to venerate. With the Empire in precipitous decline, the elements of splendor multiplied.

Outside Buckingham Palace, fifty thousand people had waited for two days and nights, and another three million lined the parade route. The first contingent, led by the Lord Mayor of London, departed Buckingham Palace precisely as scheduled, at 7:55 that morning. At 10:35 the Queen and Prince Philip were transported through the gateway of the palace in the splendid gold, four-ton Coach of State, made for Edward VII. Elizabeth was so calm that when an attendant asked if everything was all right, she said yes, thank you: she had just been told that her favorite for the Derby, a horse named Aureole, had behaved sublimely that morning.

At Westminster Abbey, 7,000 had assigned seats; another 110,000 were seated outdoors. It seemed as if they all held their breath when the monarch stepped out of her coach wearing a diamond diadem and crimson velvet robes trimmed with ermine and gold lace. She was soon divested of all this finery and stood in a simple white linen overdress for the consecration. The Archbishop of Canterbury, Geoffrey Fisher, anointed Elizabeth with oil made to a formula devised by Charles I. She was then dressed in layers of ornate golden robes and, for the actual imposition of the crown, was led to the coronation chair, used for that purpose since the fourteenth century. In absolute silence, the Archbishop held the crown of St. Edward high over

her head, then lowered it slowly. The abbey echoed with shouts
of "God save the Queen!" Trumpets blared, bells rang and
guns boomed all over London. Prince Philip then led the peers
of the realm in the well-rehearsed act of homage to the Sovereign: "I, Philip, Duke of Edinburgh, do become your liege
man of life and limb, and of earthly worship; and faith and
truth I will bear unto you, to live and die, against all manner of
folk. So help me God."

By this time the Queen's maids of honor, who had been
standing in the hot television lights for four hours, began to
feel faint and were directed behind a screen by a clergyman.
"The Archbishop of Canterbury produced this little flask of
brandy and said, 'I think one or two of you could do with a
little nip," recalled Lady Glenconner, then twenty. "This was
very welcome—although the Queen didn't have any."

The entire ceremony took four hours and twenty minutes,
and the return procession carried the Queen along Whitehall
and Pall Mall to Piccadilly, then through Hyde Park to Marble
Arch, eastward on Oxford Street, down Regent Street and
Haymarket and along The Mall to Buckingham Palace. The
Queen was not permitted to retire until after midnight, by
which time she had been forced to return to the balcony with
Philip, Charles and Anne more than a dozen times, each time
wearing the Imperial State Crown (less heavy than the crown
of St. Edward), each time smiling and waving in response
to the roars and cheers of a population drunk on pomp and
circumstance.

But the Queen was not permitted to wear only a crown; she
had to wear a halo, too. Gradually, over the next forty years, it
would appear to be very much made of neon, the effect of
publicity and media adulation.

Where monarchies survived in the rest of the world, there
was a modern, commonsense attitude. The Scandinavian countries and the Netherlands, for example, had constitutional fig-
ureheads linking their people to tradition; their presence
reminded the public and politicians that the country had a past,
that at its best it was greater than the prevailing political ethos.
Members of these families were sent to public schools, took
jobs, rode in streetcars and on bicycles, dined at restaurants
and could be easily recognized and greeted by citizens.

Nothing so commonplace occurred in England—not by royal decree but by the collective will of the people. The coronation itself was a sacrament for the people in the age of television—a medium, noted *The Times* in coronation week, that "makes every man and woman in the land a partaker in the mystery of the Queen's anointing." If millions believed this was so, only disaster could follow as television opened up more and more of the Royal Family for the public's estimation. Someone might have said that Bagehot would have turned over in his grave had he seen just how far daylight had spilled in upon the magic.

By a certain curious irony, a process of associating the life of the Royal Family with the life of the ordinary citizen had begun. H. G. Wells's mother, so he recounted, religiously followed everything in Queen Victoria's life with a passionate loyalty, for she saw in the Queen a "compensating personality"—an idealization of the sort of woman she *would like to have been.* More recently, George VI and his Consort had presented the image of one happy little family to the nation— the foursome feeding the ducks in St. James's Park.

Henceforth, the public wanted to know that Royals were just like them, and when they learned this was so, they were outraged. It is a tenable hypothesis that this schizoid attitude could develop only in a post-Enlightenment, rationalist society. If belief in God is unfashionable, there must be someone to serve as the object of humanity's need to adore. Americans had film stars.

The coronation of Elizabeth, therefore, was not at all the spiritual communion the bishops said it was. It was, quite the contrary, a lavish production for a weary people starved for glittery celebration. If the ceremony was to unite the nation, why did everything about it—everything about the monarchy, in fact—support the stratified class system, celebrate wealthy aristocrats? It certainly was impressive, and there is something to be said for ancient liturgies that remind congregations and populations that they have both a history and a unique position among the nations. But the truth is that the crowning was nothing like a democratic (much less a mystical) event that made all one: it was an exclusive, English, Anglican, medieval gesture that confirmed everything in a moribund class structure. There was much talk that year that the monarchy expressed and even effected the aspirations of the collective subconscious. But no one dared ask publicly what precisely were those aspirations. Instead, the young Queen was at the center of an instant cult—and not just in England but around the world, and perhaps preeminently in the United States, which has always seemed to hanker for the monarchy it cast off in 1776. (*A Queen Is Crowned,* a film condensation of the event, narrated by Sir Laurence Olivier using an orotund text by Christopher Fry, was screened to sold-out audiences in a Manhattan theater for months.)

So much was clear to a few, but only a few. Within days of the coronation, *The Times* warned that Britons might be a good people grown careless, whose holiday from reality had now been long enough. "A new Elizabethan Age," warned one journalist, "is in danger of becoming an incantation, a magician's *hey presto,* as if the nation's new stature could be established merely by proclaiming it."

It was perhaps inevitable that in June 1953 the Queen of England began a very long honeymoon with the press and with her people. She was not required to be great, she was merely required to be gracious, and this she accomplished admirably —as film and television cameras documented all that summer when the Queen visited Scotland, Northern Ireland and Wales, and later when she and Philip embarked on a great Commonwealth tour, from November 23, 1953, to May 15, 1954.

But just as Her Majesty left Westminster Abbey, still carrying her orb and scepter, still wearing the Imperial State Crown and ermine robe, the first crisis of her reign was about to break.

It was sparked by a quite casual gesture. As she followed the Queen's entourage departing the abbey, Princess Margaret stopped to chat with Peter Townsend. No trouble there, one might assume; he was, after all, still Master of her mother's Household and a recognizable, highly visible attaché to the Royal Family. Even with photographers swirling about, nothing seemed out of place—until Margaret permitted herself an almost imperceptible gesture. She reached out to brush a loose thread from Peter's jacket. For the first few days the newspapers were full of stories about the coronation, and no editor wanted to upstage or embarrass Her Majesty with the clear implication of Margaret's romantic propriety.

On June 13, Lascelles told Churchill of Margaret's wish to marry Townsend. Lascelles, it may be noted, may have had something of a vested interest in Margaret's future: he was related to the mother of Johnny Dalkeith, one of Margaret's earlier escorts, and some royal chroniclers believe he had a Mountbattenesque ambition about making a vaguely royal connection via marriage. The Prime Minister's reaction to the news of the intended marriage, according to the witness of his Secretary John Colville, was that "the course of true love must always be allowed to run smooth and that nothing must stand in the way of this handsome pair. However, Lady Churchill said that if he followed this line, he would be making the same mistake that he made at the abdication."

This wifely counsel hit its mark, and when the Queen contacted Churchill that weekend, his reply was not what she might have expected. Once a staunch supporter of Edward VIII's right to marry whom he chose, Churchill said he had learned from that debacle. It would be especially disastrous—during Coronation Year of all times—if Her Majesty allowed her sister to marry a divorced man. So also said Lascelles to Her Majesty. It is doubtful that the Queen reminded them that several government ministers—among them Foreign Minister Anthony Eden (soon to replace Churchill)—were divorced and remarried, as was the Prime Minister's own son Randolph. Any inclination Churchill might have had to change his mind was short-circuited by the stroke he suffered on June 23, which effectively began the final phase of his public life and set in motion the wheels of retirement.

And there was, as so often, another force behind the matter. The Queen, according to the Dowager Viscountess Hambleden (a close friend to her and to her mother), "depended a great deal on her mother's help and advice when she first came to the throne, and the fact that the Queen Mother did not positively endorse the affair meant, as far as the Queen was concerned, that it [the marriage] was not on"—that is, it would not happen.

And there the problem remained. Under the terms of the Royal Marriages Act of 1772, Margaret at age twenty-two was required to have her sister's permission to marry, and her sister needed the government's approval to override a religious proscription, which the Prime Minister rightly said would be denied. There was the possibility, however, of a resolution favorable to Margaret. If she and Peter were willing to wait until her twenty-fifth birthday two years later, she could over-ride the Sovereign's veto and marry him. To this postponement Margaret agreed. But the Queen did not inform her sister that even after the delay Margaret would still require Parliament's approval (and, more absurdly, that of the Dominions) to marry Peter and retain her royal status.

Meanwhile, Philip assured his wife and mother-in-law that two years would certainly be enough time for the affair to run its course. And all during this period, Alan Lascelles pleaded with the Queen against her sister. "I shall curse him to the grave," Margaret said years later with uncharacteristic venom. And for the present, the conspiracy of palace silence and noncommunication augured vain hope instead of disappoint-ment, which of course made the eventual outcome all the more crushing.

On June 14, *The People* revealed the rumors of the royal romance and the names of the principals. The Queen's staff, acting with her reluctant approval, then offered Townsend a dignified way out of the camera eye: transfer of work to Bel-gium, South Africa or Singapore. Two weeks later, on July 3, there was a very brief item on page three of *The Times:* "It was learnt in London yesterday that Group Captain P. W. Townsend, Extra Equerry to the Queen, has been appointed Air Attaché at the British Embassy in Brussels and will take up his appointment in about a fortnight."

The tabloids were not so discreet: PRINCESS MARGARET'S FRIEND POSTED ABROAD read the headline in the *Daily Mirror* that same day above a larger banner: A TRUE AND DEEP AF-FECTION:

> For weeks, foreign newspapers have been talking about a romance between the Princess and the dark, handsome, thirty-eight-year-old temporary equerry to her sister, the Queen . . . that she would be prepared to follow the example of her uncle, the Duke of Windsor, and relinquish her royal titles and claims in order to marry a person whom she loves and who has been involved, though innocent, in divorce.

This was nothing so much as 1936 revived with a ven-geance.

"It was obviously my duty to accept [the appointment]," recalled Townsend. "Anyway, there was no alternative. But by precipitately deporting me the Establishment chiefs were, as it turned out, making a serious error. They counted on my exile to break up our relationship. It did not."

Meantime, the London press began to make louder noises. On July 10 the *Daily Mirror* reported on page one that the Cabinet had denied Princess Margaret permission to marry. By this time she and her mother were in South Africa, conveniently unable to reply to questions directed at Margaret's press officer. Sensing a journalistic sensation, the *Daily Mirror* went further on July 13, launching a national poll:

Your Voting Form

 + *Group Captain Peter Townsend, 38 years old, Battle of Britain pilot, was the innocent party in a divorce. He was given the custody of his two children and his former wife has recently remarried.*

 + *If Princess Margaret, now 22, so desires, should she be allowed to marry him?*

 Place a cross in the square opposite YES or NO.

And so began the newspapers' first grand foray into a soap-operatic meddling into the affairs of the Royal Family—although in a sense it was the coronation itself and its intimate documentation of everything relative to the family that day that had already whetted the public's insatiable appetite.

The results were published on page one on July 17, the very day the Princess returned from Rhodesia. Of 70,142 who replied, 67,907 (96.81 percent) said she should marry him. But the government, the Church and the old guard at the palace were not about to be swayed by mere public opinion.

Although the matter would lie dormant for two years and then end with a singular poignancy, the entire business had thus far been mismanaged by the palace—specifically by Her Majesty's Press Secretary Richard Colville (cousin to Churchill's Private Secretary John Colville). For a man appointed to interact politely with journalists, Richard Colville had an inept and inapt dislike for them. His usual response to any question was "No comment" and a cold stare, and far from stanching the flow of ink about Margaret and her lover, he fueled all sorts of wild speculations. Privately, too, he displayed an insultingly high-handed rigidity. On at least one occasion, for example, he telephoned Margaret and asked, "Why did you do this?" She was so shocked, she had no reply.

Elizabeth and Philip left London on November 23, 1953, for the six-month tour of the Commonwealth countries, a journey aimed at consolidating Dominion loyalty, thanking them for wartime support and showing them that "the Crown is a personal and living bond between you and me," as she said in a Christmas Day broadcast from New Zealand. The first reigning British monarch to fly over the Atlantic, she was now the first to go on a round-the-world (fifty-thousand-mile) tour.*

For Philip there was little more to do than escort his wife, and this very quickly wearied him. "I think Philip just got bored with the whole royal business," said one of the Queen's former secretaries. "All those stuffy engagements, all that handshaking. It wasn't his thing at all. He just got fed up with it."

"This is all a waste of time" became something of a ducal antiphon, and in Ceylon he interrupted a discussion about democracy with the startling comment, "I have had very little experience in self-government. I am one of the most governed people in the world." Sometimes perceived as rude and arrogant, he had little patience for those who did not share his viewpoint.

Philip's most genial nature could be seen when, commander-like, he was supervising the running of Buckingham Palace: this was, after all, just about the only job he could assume. Keeping a careful eye out on its 230 servants, 690 rooms and 10,000 pieces of furniture, he also observed with a

---

* The itinerary included Bermuda, Jamaica, Panama, Balboa, Fiji, Tonga, Auckland and Wellington, Sydney, Melbourne, Adelaide and Fremantle, Tasmania, Ceylon, Aden, Uganda and Libya, Malta and Gibraltar. Statistics reveal that this was no holiday: the Queen lost fourteen pounds making 51 journeys by air, 75 by ship, 702 by car or jeep and 44 by rail. She attended 234 receptions, made 157 speeches and shook more than 5,000 hands.

frugal eye the annual inventories. Fond of gadgets, he ordered a dishwasher for the royal kitchen, a primitive telephone recording device for his office and an intercom system that included the royal autos. Otherwise, he was handed schedules of the usual tedious hospital openings, troop inspections, university receptions and garden parties. Asked his opinion about a pressmen's strike when he was visiting a contingent of journalists, Philip did not hesitate. "I really missed the cartoons."

During their parents' long absence, the children were in the care of their nannies. Unlike the fortunate offspring of George V and Mary, who were left with their indulgent and doting grandparents Edward VII and Alexandra, Charles and Anne saw the Queen Mother only rarely. Emerging from mourning, she was supervising the reconstruction at the Castle of Mey (which she planned to use as her country home), and in 1954 she was off to Canada and the United States. As if she were still Queen of England, she toured Virginia and Maryland, visited President and Mrs. Dwight D. Eisenhower, joined in the celebrations of Columbia University's bicentennial and generally made a social splash in New York.

In May 1954 the children were at last shipped out to meet their parents in Libya. "The children were terribly polite," the Queen said later, "but I don't think they really knew who we were." The politeness had to include the usual formalities: Charles had to offer his mother a bow of the head each time he came into her presence, Anne to curtsy. These rituals do not create an atmosphere of casual intimacy.

It is perhaps interesting to note that Elizabeth II was certainly far more formal with her children than her father had been with her and Margaret; not only was the Queen often geographically distant from her children, but in a manner not entirely consistent with her essential common sense, she revived a habit of monarchical aloofness that extended even to her own offspring. The results, alas, would be disastrous for them all—with the apparent exception of her daughter Anne, who had a singularly close rapport with her father. "[The Queen] was rather wistful at times," recalled Eileen Parker, "and often I remember her saying, 'I wish I could be more like you, Eileen, but unfortunately my life is such that I can't.' "

For one thing, the Queen was always busy, hurrying here

and there with men in suits or uniforms, her office forbidden territory to the children. More than once young Charles passed his mother's office when the door was briefly opened: "Please come out and play, Mummy," he called, about to rush in and take her by the hand. "If only I could," sighed Her Majesty as she nodded at an equerry to close the door against her son. Instead, playtime for Charles meant a walk down The Mall with Miss Peebles or a tour of the Tower of London with a detective and a private lecturer or a visit to Windsor with the Queen Mother. Until Charles went to school (and for much of the time thereafter), his was a lonely, sheltered, unnatural childhood, despite the Queen's stated intention of raising her children like others. The problem was that despite the warmth she had known from her own parents, she had not the remotest idea of how normal children were raised. Philip admitted as much: "However hard you try, it's almost impossible to bring them up as ordinary children."

As for other etiquette, an occasional candy was fine at home but not when they rode in a car—someone might see the small royal cheeks puckered, and in any case Princes avoided eating in public. Everything in the children's training emphasized that they were not like other people, that they were a caste apart whose manner must always be carefully calculated for the greatest effect. It may therefore have seemed quite natural when it was explained to young Charles that the tiny spotlights in the Queen Mother's car, just above her face, had the effect of a movie's high key lighting. They had been installed to illuminate her features just so, in order for her to appear cheerful, bright and lineless of face when she waved to crowds.

As a father, Philip's attitude was even thornier. When the boy left a door open and a servant hurried to close it, the Duke barked, "Leave it alone, man. He's got hands. Let him do it himself." That was sensible enough. But because Philip had been denied paternal love and attention, he did not know how to give it—an especially poignant gap since there were so many separations between him and his children.

"Philip tolerated Charles, but I don't think he was a loving father," said Eileen Parker, who often saw them together. "He would pick up Charles, but his manner was cold. He had more fun with Anne, but I think Charles was frightened of him." With good reason, especially after Philip arranged for Stephen

Rutter, an American boy who was also nine years old, to arrive at the palace every Thursday afternoon and challenge Charles to a boxing match. Perhaps the Duke feared that nannies might soften or feminize the child; in any case, he took every step to toughen him. For the young Prince, every Thursday afternoon was to be dreaded, every Thursday night a time of nursing physical and emotional wounds. Nanny too often heard the boy crying himself to sleep, for as humiliating as the round might have been, the fear of displeasing his father was worse. This fear remained with the Prince throughout adulthood; in this regard there was a touch of George V in the Duke of Edinburgh.

This was especially difficult for a sensitive lad like Charles, who could not understand the wide disparities in his life. Disciplined by his father, kept at a respectful distance by his mother, he was still fawned over and served by a full coterie of palace staff. Doors were opened for him, clothes cleaned, meals prepared and elegantly served. Although the Queen instructed the staff not to address the children as ''Your Royal Highness,'' they were certainly treated as such.

As the Townsend affair became a crisis, however, Margaret was not so royally treated. She and Peter had corresponded almost daily during his Belgian exile. During the two years from his departure in July 1953 to her twenty-fifth birthday in August 1955, they met only once. In July 1954 he was quietly whisked to London, visited several hours with Margaret, then saw his children and returned to Brussels the same day. Their intentions were firmer than ever. Marriage was the goal. And for a time it was Alan Lascelles himself who told her to be patient, to obey, that she would be able to marry Townsend. Something would change things. As it turned out, he was being less than forthright with her.

On her twenty-fifth birthday, August 21, 1955, the *Daily Mirror*'s editor, Hugh Cudlipp, again put his tabloid in the press vanguard with an enormous and astonishing headline and front-page story:

COME ON MARGARET!

For two years the world has buzzed with this question:
Will Princess Margaret marry 40-year-old Group Captain Peter Townsend?—OR Won't she?

Five months ago, Group Captain Townsend told the *Daily Mirror:* "The word cannot come from me. You will appreciate it must come from other people."

On Sunday, the Princess will be 25. She could then, if she wished, notify Parliament direct of her desire to marry without first seeking the consent of her sister the Queen.

She could end the hubbub.

Will she please make up her mind?

PLEASE MAKE UP YOUR MIND!

Every newspaper in England picked up the story. *Time* magazine gave it eight full pages. The world watched for another possible constitutional crisis.

The situation quickly became untenable. Margaret was informed that, should she choose to ignore the Privy Council's refusal to sanction the marriage, she would necessarily be stripped of her royal title, status and prerogatives. She would have to forgo her stipend from the Civil List, and she would effectively be divorced from the Royal Family—all in order to marry a divorced man. In fact, as palace lawyers confirmed, a formal Bill of Abdication would have to be drawn up, according to which Margaret would have to sign away her rights to succession and her place as Councillor of State as well. And such a marriage ceremony could not be performed in England. It was, in other words, an altogether intolerable option for a young lovesick lady. She would be taking her place beside King Edward VIII. Yet during September and October, while speculation grew, Margaret for a time seemed ready to abandon everything for love.

And then a very strange thing happened. "The Duke of Edinburgh," according to a London reporter very close to the palace, "urged the Queen and the Queen Mother to oppose the marriage." The reason for this is difficult to fathom, but it may have had to do with the fact that Townsend (who had King George VI's confidence) had initially opposed Philip's marriage to Elizabeth. Now, during the eight years of his marriage, Philip had become more autocratically royal than all of them. ("It is a pleasant change to be in a country that isn't ruled by its people," he said to General Alfredo Stroessner of Paraguay, who was known to protect surviving Nazi refugees. "Your government decides what's to be done and it's done." His staff had quite a time explaining that.)

The Queen Mother was persuaded that a marriage between Margaret and Peter was very ill advised, but at first the Queen was not so certain and tried to find a way to guarantee her sister's desire. Finally, on October 18, Prime Minister Anthony Eden (divorced and remarried) told the Queen that the Cabinet would not approve the marriage. The press then became unimaginably pious. On October 24, *The Times* was the first to run a negative editorial to the effect that if she chose to renounce her royal status and marry, Princess Margaret "must from that moment pass into private life" and that she would bring dishonor on her sister the Queen, who would be "still more lonely in her arduous life of public service." The text gave new meaning to the word unctuous. *The Mirror,* which had backed the romance from day one, hit back: *The Times*'s stand was "the first sinister move in an ugly plan to force Margaret into giving up the man she loves by a bullying, calculated ultimatum. She must presumably spend the rest of her life, like the luckless Windsors [that is, the Duke and Duchess], without roots, without purpose and without hope. . . . *The Times* speaks for a dusty world and a forgotten age."

The Prime Minister and the Queen, in separate meetings, reminded Margaret and Peter that she would have no means of support once her Civil List allowance was rescinded; that she could not be married in an Established Church ceremony; and that she and Townsend would be expected to quit the country for an indeterminate period of time. Made to feel like traitors and felons, Margaret and Peter were finally beaten. The situation had, as the *Manchester Guardian* said, "more than a smack of English hypocrisy about it." Amid the uproar, Margaret attended a performance of Smetana's opera *The Bartered Bride,* sitting expressionless as the heroine sang in English, "I have a lover—I will not forsake him."

On Monday, October 31, the Princess issued the following statement written for her by Townsend himself:

I would like it to be known that I have decided not to marry Group Captain Peter Townsend. I have been aware that, subject to renouncing my rights to succession, it might have been possible for me to contract a civil marriage. But mindful of the Church's teaching that Christian marriage is indissoluble, and conscious of my duty to the Commonwealth, I have resolved to put these considerations before any others.

I have reached this decision entirely alone, and in doing so
I have been strengthened by the unfailing support and devotion of Group Captain Townsend. I am deeply grateful for
the concern of all those who have constantly prayed for my
happiness.

Was it indeed a religious consideration before any other?
Or was it the prospect of poverty, social ostracism and family
dishonor? Probably it was a combination of all these. In the
end, a young woman was forced to give up a man she had
loved for years in order to prove the specious theory that the
monarchy is sacred. And yet in a way she went along with the
very system she tried to bypass. She had always been part rebel
—but only part: the rest is pure princess.

Margaret has always enjoyed being royal, has insisted on
her precedence and her prerogatives, has bristled if she was
addressed improperly. And she did not wish, even if she could,
to escape the fact that she was Her Royal Highness The Princess Margaret, daughter of His Late Majesty King George VI.
And that was the part of her that was not rebellious at all but
rather a loyal monarchist to the core of her being. That conflict
would haunt her for the rest of her life, would free her for
independence, then rein her in with a self-imposed threat of
humiliation. It was true, claimed all those who knew her. She
had made the decision entirely on her own, no matter the
external pressures. Like her sister, she finally wished to remain
a part of a privileged set, a member of an unimpeachable
Royal Family. Peter Townsend returned to Belgium before
Margaret's statement was released. It was impossible to photograph Margaret smiling for the better part of the next two
years.

"We were asked to wait a year," Margaret said years later.

Then there was a muck-up and we were asked to wait another year. If Lascelles hadn't told me that marriage was
possible, I would never have given it another thought. The
relationship would have been out of the question and Peter
could have gone off quite peacefully. Instead, we waited for
ages and then discovered it was quite hopeless. It seems
frightfully stupid to have gone on all that time, and it was
wicked to have given us false hopes.

And when someone asked why they had not gone through with the marriage on their own terms, Margaret replied quietly, "It was Peter who didn't want to." That, many believed, was the true end of the matter: Townsend would not have wanted a marriage in which his suddenly disgraced and impecunious wife was forced to look to her family for support. In the final analysis the affair simply had too many elements of Henry James's novella *Washington Square*. As it sadly unspooled and then tragically ended, this debacle was the first fissure in the meticulously embellished façade created for the House of Windsor.

Many ordinary citizens, then and later, could not understand why the divorced and remarried Anthony Eden could run a government and appoint bishops and archbishops, while a princess with only the remotest chance of succeeding to the throne was denied the right to marry the man of her choice. Furthermore, Margaret and Townsend's renunciation statement—so readily embraced by the Queen, the Prime Minister, the Archbishop of Canterbury and millions of misguided romantics who wanted someone to put duty above all—raised a critical constitutional issue. The right of succession is a matter that Parliament decides with the Prime Minister and the other Commonwealth premiers. It is not in the competence of either the Queen or the Archbishop of Canterbury. Why, therefore, would only a civil ceremony be permitted if Margaret renounced her right of succession?

Finally, sensible people had to inquire what concept of duty required one to forgo a personal life in sacrifice to the monarchy, one that had been confirmed precisely by a royal divorce (Henry VIII's) sanctioned by an Established Church? What the Queen, the government and the Church of England required of Margaret was that she deny herself. Everyone was caught in a web of betrayal, and the truth suffered. As would Princess Margaret, forever after.

And not least of all for the future of the Royal Family, a veritable English media circus had swung into action for the delectation of all the world—the best (or worst) manipulation of private lives since the weeks after the abdication of King Edward VIII.

Princess Margaret and her husband, Lord Snowdon.

12

The First Divorce *1956 to 1965*

This makes no sense.
    A teacher's report on a student essay by Prince Charles

When the monarch does not rule but reigns, the adulation and adoration of the people are transferred from the office to the person. The 1950s saw the flourishing of the modern cult of celebrity, due not only to the proliferation of movies worldwide but also to the instant celebrity provided by television. Therefore, as the endless flow of newsprint about Charles's school grades and his parents' family picnics continued, some astute citizens grew restless. "Is the New Elizabethan Age going to be a flop?" asked an article in the *Daily Mirror* in October 1956. Just what was the Royal Family about? Just how important were they or could they be?

For most people it was perhaps sufficient that the Queen look pretty for the camera and that Prince Philip appear dashing and occasionally say something mildly amusing. But more than one journalist, social critic and loyal citizen saw that the Crown was providing no real inspiration for a complex new postwar world. And some who took the monarchical tradition seriously and with respect became concerned with the essential triviality of life in the Royal Family.

Such concern was well directed. Centuries earlier, Queen Elizabeth I was far more directly connected to her people than her later namesake; she took a more active and intimate part in what affected their lives, moved far more freely among them and spoke their language without any of the formal restraints of upper-class diction in which the Windsors were so carefully trained. What was the point, one might have asked, of trying to prepare Prince Charles for an ordinary life if he was to be forever denied one? Why refine his intelligence if he was never to be permitted to use it professionally? It seemed to many observers that the Windsors were not doing very much that was useful.

"The Royal Family," wrote B. A. Young that year, "have plenty of time on their hands: 30-odd appearances in 90 days is hardly a back-breaking programme for a company whose principal *raison d'être* is the making of public appearances." This was an important point of fact, and anyone who followed the publication of the Court Circular could see that the Royal Family continued to divide each year among their five residences: just as in the days of Edward VII, autumn was spent at Buckingham Palace, Christmas at Windsor and Sandringham, Easter back at Windsor, late spring at Holyroodhouse and August to October at Balmoral. Life had a comforting chronology.

Playwright John Osborne was even blunter than Young: "Nobody can seriously pretend that the royal round of gracious boredom, the protocol of ancient fatuity, is politically useful or morally stimulating."

It was precisely this riot of trivia engulfing royal life that was respectfully questioned by John Grigg, Lord Altrincham, in an important and scholarly essay in *The National and English Review* in the summer of 1957. "Things had not changed at all in the royal household and in the royal routine, despite what was being advertised as a great new age," he said almost forty years later. "The propaganda hype at the time was that this was a great new Elizabethan Age—that sort of thing. But nothing new was happening at all!"

The stuffy immutability had to do with the courtiers—old-fashioned ("tweedy" was Grigg's neat word) and in many ways hopelessly incompetent. Alan Lascelles, a decent and loyal man, was hopelessly mired in protocol and could not accept that the daughter of George VI would choose a married man so soon (almost two decades!) after Edward VIII's abdication. Richard Colville, thrust because of his discretion into the job of the Queen's senior press officer, was a naval commander by profession and preference (hurrah for the spirit of George V); Colville had neither the qualifications nor the talent for his palace post.

How unthinkable it was for Altrincham to write about such matters in 1957 can be gauged by the abuse and misunderstanding to which he was unjustly subjected (he was struck in the face, in public, by a brutish loyalist). Years later most historians hold him in deserved high honor. "Those who care for the Monarchy as an institution," wrote Altrincham,

> should look beyond the hideous coloured photographs of a glamorous young woman in sparkling attire to the more testing realities of twenty years hence. The Monarchy will not survive, let alone thrive, unless its leading figures exert themselves to the full and with all the imagination they and their advisers can command.

Altrincham's point, much misrepresented in the weeks after his summer salvo, was against those who surrounded the Queen—an aging cadre of self-seeking courtiers who wrote her speeches, planned her appearances, chose her friends, shielded her from this and kept her close to that—and generally saw to it that the Sovereign remained remote and irrelevant. "It will not be enough for her to go through the motions," Altrincham continued; "she will have to say things people can remember, and do things on her own initiative which will make people sit up and take notice. As yet there is little sign that such a personality is emerging." In one essay a thoughtful writer thus got to the heart of something crucial. Buckingham Palace lacked the ability to respond creatively to the sociopolitical hand dealt by modern times that demanded an imaginative response and a search for new dynastic meaning that were not forthcoming.

Even some of the Queen's own family recognized and identified the dilemma. "It must be incredibly difficult for someone as hedged in by protocol, by rules, by manners [as is the Queen] to see anything of the real world," said her cousin, the Earl of Harewood.

> You can be told about it, but to watch its view of you changing and to evaluate that, and to know how much you ought to adapt to that—that must be incredibly hard. Then, of course, you need very far-sighted advisers, people of real perception. Not an easy thing to find.

The core of the problem, Altrincham insisted, was that the English monarchy did not transcend race or class. The conventional upbringing of the Queen had prepared her only for an unimaginative Court. "Crawfie," Sir Henry Marten, the London season, the racecourse and grouse moor, the royal tours—all these, as Lord Altrincham rightly reminded, would have bored Queen Elizabeth I to madness. Worse still, the Court of Elizabeth II was composed almost entirely of upper-class white Englishmen. While British society became thoroughly multiracial and multinational (Philip, after all, adopted English citizenship), the Court remained (thus Altrincham) "a tight little enclave of British ladies and gentlemen. This cannot be right." At the least, Altrincham argued, the Court should include Commonwealth citizens. If the Queen is really Head of the Commonwealth, in other words, her household staff (which numbers between four hundred and five hundred) ought to reflect that same diversity. (But as late as 1994 there was not a single nonwhite person on the staff of Buckingham Palace.)

As further indication of the monarch's distance from the people, Altrincham scolded the Queen's "style of speaking, which is frankly 'a pain in the neck.' Like her mother, she appears to be unable to string even a few sentences together without a written text, a defect that is particularly regrettable when she can be seen by her audience" on television. George V's speeches were a natural expression of the man's character, but Elizabeth's are not: "The personality conveyed by the utterances which are put into her mouth is that of a priggish schoolgirl, captain of the hockey team, a prefect, and a recent candidate for Confirmation.

"Those of us who believe that the Monarchy can survive and play an ever more beneficent part in the affairs of the Commonwealth are not content to remain silent while needless errors go uncorrected. . . . There is no limit to what it can achieve if it perfects the change which George V inaugurated." The Royal Family, Altrincham argued, need not live like elegant nomads. The Queen, he concluded, "is a worthwhile institution," and he both admired her "personally and [wished] her well in her infinitely responsible and exciting task."

This was no wild republican sentiment. Nor was Malcolm Muggeridge's subsequent article, "Does England Really Need a Queen?" (in *The Saturday Evening Post* that October 19). Its contents were not so categorical as its title implied. "The circle around the throne," the *Daily Mirror* had declared in October 1956, "is as aristocratic and insular as it has ever been." It was time for a reappraisal of the system. The Queen and her husband "should get off the dreary roundabout of boring and insubstantial [royal activities]."

Neither Altrincham nor Muggeridge called for the abolition of the monarchy, as did the most vocal critics when Queen Victoria withdrew from public life after Albert's death. Yet Altrincham was publicly vilified, undeservedly. He received an astonishing amount of hate mail and his life was threatened. While some in British society were grinning over the fact that their dear Queen was (surprise!) a real human being, people seemed outraged when Altrincham—writing out of the profoundest loyalty—said well, then, she must be treated like a human being and saved from the worst excesses of her own Court and from the encrustations of a mummified Establishment. It would take years before it was clear just how positive a compliment he had paid to the *principle* of monarchy than even the coronation year had done.

As it happened, there was a quiet wave of support for Altrincham's essay and for the unhysterical, measured prose that reflected a thoughtful and intelligent critique of an ineffectual palace system. No less a man than Prince Philip, for one, saw the wisdom: "We ought to take account of this," he told his wife. "It's our job to make this monarchy business work." He was insensitive, however, to the pressures of groups to whom he was himself indifferent. Despite the outcry from animal conservation corps, he stalked endangered tigers in India, Pakistan and Nepal, and regularly potted ducks and partridges all over England. George V would have loved him.

According to Altrincham, "Martin Charteris, assistant private secretary to the Queen, told me that [what I had said] was the best thing that had happened to Buckingham Palace in a long time." In 1963, Altrincham renounced his peerage:

> not because I'm against hereditary titles, which don't matter one way or another, they're like a family heirloom—but simply because I couldn't be a party to inheriting a seat in Parliament. With the title 'Lord' you get a distorting effect and tend to be taken too seriously by silly people and not seriously enough by sensible people. Of course, it would have been very helpful if the outside world had known of [Charteris's] support at the time.

Leading members of the Royal Household realized that he was sincere, that his intentions were honorable and that he was on the side of the institution.

Thirty-six years later, John Grigg's criticisms of the system were more relevant than ever, for his suggestions had, alas, gone mostly unheeded.

> I think what I did was helpful to that minority in the Royal Household who felt that changes were necessary. They are her servants and don't know how to do it themselves. Her prime ministers have been extraordinarily servile and lax in this regard and have not had her best interest at heart.

Inspired by her own public remarks implying a religious motive for her renunciation of Peter Townsend, Princess Margaret had become a supporting player in the application of a strangely pious tone to the drama of the Royal Family, however much her private life seemed sometimes to border on the libertine. ("You look after your Empire and I'll look after my life," she once said when the Queen reprimanded her for flirting with some navy cadets.) The monarchy, thanks to the zeal surrounding the coronation ceremony, was becoming something of a sacred icon. Worse, it was very nearly idolatrous. During World War II a man had not been punished for murdering someone who criticized the Royal Family. Things had scarcely changed in the first years of Elizabeth II, not only in England but also in America, where the monarchy had been booted out only to reach ever more deeply and dearly into the hearts of citizens. If it is true that the French and Germans have a lingering romantic nostalgia for a King, then it is equally true that America was perhaps more bedazzled and smitten with the monarchy than any other country. Elizabeth's first visit to America as Queen, in the autumn of 1957, proved that. The press ransacked its vocabulary for superlatives, and a ticker-tape parade for the Queen and her Prince made the receptions for Charles Lindbergh and King George VI seem like casual nods. Twenty thousand photographers jockeyed for position at every stop of her journey in Washington and New York.

The fact was (and remains) that the British monarchy canonizes the most entrenched system of arbitrary social stratification and class distinction in the developed world. Openly representing rank and privilege in an era committed to democracy and the triumph of classlessness, the Crown stands for the class system, for the right of inherited wealth and status. The monarch embodies not so much the aspirations of a people but the aristocracy itself—all the terms and hierarchies that once defined England instead of the mixed society it aspires to be. In England an untitled gentleman is inferior to a knight, who stands beneath a baronet, who is beneath a baron, who stands beneath a viscount, who is inferior to an earl, who stands beneath a marquess, who is inferior to a duke, who is less than a royal duke, who bows to the King or Queen. One has to go to the Vatican to find a hierarchical structure as quaint.

Even palace employees are subject to a highly defined pecking order. The professional staff that runs the monarchy—the private secretaries and lords chamberlain and masters of the household—are all drawn from the upper classes. Butlers and footmen are subject to a rigorous class distinction: an aristocracy of masters and mistresses who do not speak to a middle class of servants, who in turn do not speak to mere downstairs staff.

But none of this was of concern to the press or general public in the staid year of grace 1956. Rather, new twists appeared in the royal soap opera. That autumn, Philip departed for a four-month tour of the Commonwealth, and in light of the Townsend affair, there was widespread talk that this betokened a rift in the Sovereign's marriage. This was scarcely Philip's first solo journey; there had been many military inspection trips, yachting holidays and naval maneuvers. In addition, he ordinarily tried to avoid the Queen's equestrian events. Asked if the Queen would like to be shown a piece of scientific equipment he was inspecting, Philip replied bluntly, "Certainly not. Unless it farts and eats grass, she's not interested." When reports of such public language reached the Queen, she could only reply, "It's a waste of time trying to change a man's character. You have to accept your husband as he is." Such acceptance meant coping with her husband's remarkably frank statements, as when he told a gathering of British industrialists that they had better wake up, but in saltier terms. "I think it is about time we pulled our fingers out," he said. "I gave up trying to stop him years ago," sighed the Queen when she read that comment.

And so distances in time, space and taste fed the rumors of a widening breach—gossip that grew when Michael Parker was divorced by his wife Eileen; the reason, it was said, was that the Prince and his secretary had been having a wild old time on tour, entertaining ladies and behaving not at all like gentlemen. But when the Queen met Philip at the end of the tour in Lisbon in February 1957, she informed him that he would henceforth be known as a Prince of the United Kingdom. Hitherto he had been known only informally as Prince Philip, for that had been his rank in Greece. With his new status, she effectively dealt with the unpleasant talk of marital discord.

There was much for Elizabeth and Philip to discuss that day of reunion, and included in the topics of conversation must have been the historic event of the previous week: the Queen had taken Prince Charles to school. The idea had in fact been Philip's. "The boy must learn to mix with other kids," he had said, and the Queen had to agree.

As the first heir to the throne ever to go outside the palace for education, he was driven each day to the Hill House School in Knightsbridge, a three-minute limousine ride from the palace. With a roster of 102 boys and a modest fee of £100 per year, the five-year-old school had been chosen for its obscurity. It enrolled the sons of business and professional men, but there was not a noble Lord among them. As for the obscurity, that quickly ended when his mother and a detective delivered Charles to Hill House that chilly February morning and were met by a blinding barrage of popping flashbulbs. He quickly learned just how unique he was. When he and six-year-old Anne once heard a military band outside the palace, she asked, "Is it another coronation?" Charles had a ready reply: "Don't be silly. The next coronation will be mine."

Up to now, eight-year-old Charles had known very little of real life. What minor education he had from Miss Peebles was restricted to the basics of reading and writing, but more worrisome might have been the complete lack of socialization. Men and women bowed to his parents in private, cheered them in public; he saw his parents' pictures in magazines and newspapers—and sometimes his own, too. He had no concept of money other than the fact that his mother's profile was stamped on coins, her face on paper notes. Shopping, standing in a queue, having chores, knowing deprivation—these were as foreign to him as an exotic language.

His five months at Hill House began to redress the imbalance, however slowly and, as it happened, briefly. He shared a double desk with a doctor's son, studied arithmetic and had his first lessons in history, geography and science. He had to obey rules, eat all the food served to him and hang up his uniform jacket on an assigned peg. But there was always a bodyguard nearby, and teachers felt awkward calling him simply "Charles," as they had been told to do. For the most part he was, therefore, called nothing at all; some of his classmates used his first name, and few were in awe of him. But everyone found it difficult to cope with the gauntlet of journalists and gawkers who gathered daily outside Hill House, making Charles's arrival and departure a media circus.

In addition, there was something of a double standard about just how ordinary and companionable Charles could be. His chauffeur recalled one day when eight-year-old Charles asked if a young friend could be given a lift home in the royal limousine. No, his equerry said, no one else was allowed in the car. The driver noted in his diary that this single incident showed how the Prince was being allowed to go out into the real world but without a full chance to benefit from the experience. If anything threatened the rules, he was pulled back to the security of palace protocol. "Charles didn't understand what was happening," noted the chauffeur, "and [I fear] this will lead to difficulties in his life because he [is] neither one thing nor the other."

Still, column after column of newsprint detailed for the public the most banal details. Charles was on the wrestling team. Charles showed a fondness for finger painting and watercolors. Charles ate a lunch of beef stew and carrots. Charles's report card—posted along with the others on a school board—showed he had "made a fair start" or was "good" at some subjects, "not very keen" or frankly "slow" at others. The term's verdict was resoundingly average.

In autumn 1957, Charles was sent as a boarder to Philip's alma mater, Cheam, in Berkshire. In the eighty-eight days of his first term there were no fewer than seventy photo stories about him in the national press, a barrage of publicity that once again (as when he went to Hill House) hardly supported his mother's injunction to the headmaster that the Prince be treated like any other student. Philip, as usual, was more realistic: "There's always this silly idea about treating them exactly like other children. In fact it means they're treated much worse, because they're known by name and association. It's all very well to say they're treated the same as everybody else, but of course it's impossible." Charles would never be treated "the same as everybody else" in his life, and even in childhood he could use this to his advantage. Eager to ride alone in a limousine one day, he asked his father, "Please, can I ride in the back on my own this time? You know, Papa, like a prince." Philip whacked Charles's bottom and put him next to the driver.

The contradictions with the boy's previous experiences were immediately evident at Cheam. Here was a world unlike anything the nine-year-old had known, and Charles, shy and diffident, found it difficult to make friends. Thus, his school terms there, which continued until spring 1962, were neither happy nor reassuring for him. "I hate it—I hate it—I *hate* it!" he cried to a member of the Balmoral house staff. "It's the other boys. They say I'm no good at anything, that my legs are fat, and they make fun of me when I try to do almost anything.

Some of them push me about or bully me and I always have to watch out in case they play tricks on me.''

Years later Charles confided the extent of his childhood misery. ''It was not easy to make large numbers of friends. I'm not a gregarious person, so I've always had a horror of gangs [that is, cliques or groups of buddies]. I have always preferred my own company or just a one-to-one.'' He was, as classmates and masters recalled, painfully insecure.

Charles got into endless scrapes defending his title, but the appellation ''Fatty Prince'' was soon replaced by one more hallowed. In the summer of 1958 his mother announced that at his legal maturity (eleven years hence) he would be formally invested as the Prince of Wales; however, the designation would be his even now. But as Charles found out at Cheam, the announcement did not improve his social standing with schoolmates one iota. He was further embarrassed by the recital of the standard prayers for the Royal Family in chapel, for his name was included after his parents'. ''I wish they prayed for the other boys, too,'' he said wistfully one Sunday.

To please his father, he threw himself onto the cricket and football fields, where he gave as many kicks as he got. But try as he did to excel in sports, Philip and Charles were never close—not only because the Duke considered his son a trifle too sensitive, a bit too vulnerable, but also because Lord Mountbatten, always eager to extend his influence in the Royal Family, was at the ready with his meddlesome good advice for the young Prince.

Where Philip was distant and rather cool, Mountbatten was warm and embracing with the boy. Thus he became by default something of a surrogate father to Charles, and this continued the cycle of distance separating the Prince from the Duke. ''Certainly Lord Mountbatten has had an influence on my life, and I admire him, I think, almost more than anybody else. He's a very great person.'' Such printed comments did not endear Charles to his father. They were sentiments known to the staff, too. When the boy told a palace footman he wanted to join the navy, the servant asked, ''On a ship with your papa as captain?'' The reply was immediate: ''Oh, no! He wants me to do far too much. I don't want to go with him. I want to go by myself and just be with the other sailors. But I shall miss being here with Mummy.'' A few years later Charles scribbled on a photograph of himself and Philip, "I was not meant to follow in my father's footsteps."

The emotional distance was not bridged in 1962 when Charles went on to Gordonstoun, Philip's second alma mater. A few miles from Elgin in Scotland, Gordonstoun was run by Kurt Hahn, a refugee from Nazi persecution who had the odd idea that monastic deprivation would necessarily turn four hundred boys into strong men. To that end, Gordonstoun, unremarkable in matters academic, placed the highest priority on the endurance of a fiercely spartan regime. Charles moved into a large, cheerless dormitory that could have come straight from the pages of Dickens: sixty iron beds lined up on opposite walls, a cold, wooden floor and bare bulbs suspended overhead with all the charm of a lunatic asylum. Any Scottish crofter's stone cottage was a palace by comparison.

"There is more in you," runs the school's motto, although more of what no one could say. Whatever it was, the mysterious element was to be evoked by empty-stomach sprints at seven each morning, followed by the first of the day's two cold showers. Only then were there classes, by which time the boys were ready for a nap. The school was a cross between a Victorian orphanage and a Scottish commando camp; the curriculum emphasized the strenuous life—mountain rescue training, seamanship and yachting, firefighting brigades. These were at least as important as history and mathematics. "My only recollections [of the school] are of complete horror," said Lord Rudolph Russell, son of the Duke of Bedford. "It's absolute hell," Charles said to a friend at the time.

Charles's academic performance at Gordonstoun was unremarkable: he passed French, history and literature but failed mathematics and physics. More to the point, he was miserably lonely. Even two European cousins kept their distance, lest they be accused of social climbing; the other boys were intimidated by his mere presence, and some teachers, finding any form of address awkward, called him "Windsor."

"Do you ever get lonely?" Charles asked his bodyguard, Michael Varney, one day.

"Most people get lonely once in a while," Varney replied.

"But what about you? Do you get lonely?"

"Oh, yes—often." That answer, Varney recalled, "seemed to satisfy him."

Soon word of Charles's unhappiness got back to Buckingham Palace, and when Philip was asked how his son was getting on, he replied with a shrug, "Well, he hasn't run away yet."

For the rest of his life Charles would suffer perhaps the most damaging and diminishing aspect of being a major Royal: no one in his immediate circle, none of his servants or advisors, would ever correct him or indicate that he had acted foolishly. "The older I get, the more alone I become," he said later. Part of that solitude comes from the role, part from his temperament.

> A lot of people are frightened, I think, of what other people would think of *them* if they came up and talked to me. But there are those people, and I can see them coming a mile off, who are rather "pushing" and overenthusiastic and it's usually from some ulterior motive. You know what I mean, they're not the nicest. Unfortunately, the nicest people are those who won't come up and make themselves known. I think, "Good God! What's wrong? Do I smell? Have I changed my shoes? What can be wrong?"

With gleeful malice the press did reprimand Charles when he was once caught, at the age of fourteen, sipping an illegal glass of cherry brandy at a pub. But this was not the first step on the road to perdition, as his subsequent temperance confirmed.

A further moment of embarrassment occurred when a cheeky classmate stole one of Charles's notebooks and sold it to a Scottish newspaper. Intelligence agents were dispatched to get it back, but within days it had been copied and reproduced in November 1964 by *Der Stern,* a German magazine. Charles, the world learned, had a streak of typical royal cynicism. Democracy, he had written, meant "giving equal voting power to people having unequal ability to think." Thornier still was this observation:

> By entrusting the management of affairs chiefly to the upper classes, the country is at least saved from some of the evils that may be produced in the lower classes by corruption, although the upper classes may be lacking in intelligence,

biased by class interest and guilty of great corruption in political appointments. The honor of the class at least secures it from the great corruptions, and its members are permanently connected with the well-being of the country.

On this his teacher had made the written comment, "This makes no sense."

In the spring of 1966 his parents thought it would be a good idea for him to attend a Commonwealth school, and so Charles was enrolled at Timbertop, a Gordonstoun replica in Australia. Cross-country runs and mountain climbing were the sacred events here, but he was much happier than at Cheam or Gordonstoun: "I absolutely adored it. In Australia there is no such thing as aristocracy. The other boys were very, very good and marvelous people, very genuine. They said exactly what they thought. The only person who made me feel unhappy, I think, was an Englishman." But Charles was consoled by the friendship of Dale Harper (later Lady Tryon), an elegant, fine-boned beauty who was later a London girlfriend. He nicknamed her "Kanga," an obvious abbreviation for the indigenous marsupial.

Charles returned from Australia to Gordonstoun and then matriculated to Trinity College, Cambridge, where he studied archaeology and anthropology, interests kindled by having climbed over the rough terrain in Australia and by his visits to New Guinea. "Arch and anth," as the field of study is known, is not nearly so prestigious or difficult as it sounds; in fact, at the university it is considered not much more challenging than sports. Nevertheless, he became the first heir to the throne to stay the course and earn a degree.

At Cambridge he also developed as a good polo player, which pleased his father more than the Prince's predilection for classical music and his earnest cello lessons. Students remembered him as a lanky, likable lad, always a bit embarrassed —and doubtless restricted—because of the constant presence of a detective. "He seemed an easygoing sort of chap, superficially easy to know," said classmate John Molony. "But deep down he's a very private person. I don't think anyone gets to know him really well." One person who did was the dark-eyed beauty Lucia Santa Cruz, daughter of a former Chilean ambassador. They had met in London and she was, by all accounts,

Charles's first romance. According to Lord Butler, Master of Trinity College, the Prince and Lucia spent many nights together in the bedroom of the Master's Lodge, which was given over to them for privacy.

The choice of schools for Charles was the Duke's; in this matter the Queen deferred to her husband's arguments that a tough school life would make for a good future King. This was a major victory for Philip, whose preferences were otherwise ignored by his wife. "When my husband wants something badly," Her Majesty once confided to a friend, "I tell him he shall have it and then make sure he doesn't get it."

Her remark was telling, for Elizabeth II is on balance a woman who believes her position is divinely mandated, inviolable, sacred—an attitude that has somewhat hardened her attitude toward ordinary mortals. "She looks a bit miserable at times," according to another friend, "because she's been trained to resist emotion of any kind, like a Grenadier Guardsman. She throws all her affection into her dogs, but she can't do it with human beings because of her upbringing." She can joke, make a funny face, mock pomposity, show spontaneous pleasure (usually at a horse race). But suddenly the smile vanishes and the face returns to an affectless stare, as if she has suddenly recalled that she is the Queen and must show that she is different from all others.

During Charles's school years—and those of Anne, who went off to boarding school at thirteen—many photographs of the royal children were commissioned by their parents. When blond, mischievous, seven-year-old Anne was brought up from London for a visit with her brother, she thought the rough and tumble of the boys' teams was great fun, and she cheered them on. Unlike Charles, she needed no encouragement to leap on a horse, and from her earliest days she was the heiress of her mother's equestrian talents.

In an effort to include some candid shots among the formal portraits of Charles and Anne, Elizabeth and Philip engaged one of Margaret's friends, a rumpled, jokey, slightly rowdy photographer named Antony Armstrong-Jones. The son of a thrice-married lawyer and a nephew of the famous theatrical designer Oliver Messel, he was Margaret's age, a rising star among the London photographic, bohemian, fashion-and-design set. Together they attended the ballet and a series of hip London parties. But the Princess did not attend her sister's tenth wedding anniversary party in November 1957. "It's all right for you to celebrate ten years of marriage," she told her sister. "But thanks to you I am still unmarried." If there was not a marital rift at Buckingham Palace, there was certainly some chilly air hanging over Clarence House.

By the end of that year Margaret was secretly visiting Tony's apartment in Rotherhithe Street, on the South Bank of the Thames, and the following year he was a regular visitor at Clarence House. One evening after they watched a private screening of the Marlon Brando film *The Wild One,* a footman entered to find the Princess and Armstrong-Jones holding hands. He sold this tidbit of news to the press and was duly fired. Margaret's secretary did not deny the friendship, however, and it blossomed throughout 1958, mostly at a series of fast London parties notorious for a shady clientele given to the casual use of drugs, sex and excessive drinking. It seemed to many of Margaret's oldest friends that with the denial of Peter Townsend, something had hardened in Margaret forever. The gentle humor was sharper, the softness in her nature not so readily apparent. But no one was made unhappier by her compromise than Margaret herself, and when she was aware of having caused real offense she was usually miserable. Even in her most confused moments she tended (to the surprise of many and the disbelief of some) to find real solace in her faith. Perhaps more than any other member of the Royal Family, in fact, Margaret's religious life was never *pro forma;* it always sprang from sincere, quiet devotion.

Before Christmas 1959, she learned that Peter Townsend (then forty-five) was going to marry the Belgian-born Marie-Luce Jamagne (twenty years his junior). "I received a letter from Peter in the morning," she told a friend, "and that evening I decided to marry Tony. It was not a coincidence." Elizabeth had doubts about her sister's choice, not the least of her reasons being that he was known to be just ever so vaguely louche.

Behind the scenes even more powerfully stood the Queen Mother. Eager to see her younger daughter happy at last, she was working on behalf of the Tony-Margaret affair. Ever since she had taken on the Duke of York, Elizabeth Bowes-Lyon had been the single most powerful designer of the fairy-tale monarchy. She had smilingly directed the photographers even during her courageous visits to the East End during the war; she had been a benevolent behind-the-scenes director of many details surrounding the coronation; and her counsel was always sought by Elizabeth and Philip. Now she was extending the family to include a popular, dashing young man. It was she who prevailed on the Queen to withstand some initial Cabinet misgivings because Tony's *father* was much married, divorced and remarried. Here, in other words, was a living argument against those who said the Royal Family mixed only with their own aristocratic set. Shrewd old Eleanor Roosevelt, for one, saw a powerful message in the fact, that same year, that the Queen Mother directed the family games of charades and chose the words everyone else was called to act out.

When she gathered royal support for Tony, the Queen Mother achieved a minor miracle. Princess Marina and her family disliked him, as Noël Coward learned when he lunched with them; their doubts were probably like his own, for he traveled in very knowledgeable social circles. "Whether or not the marriage is entirely suitable remains to be seen," he wrote carefully in his diary. *The Sunday Times* was blunter: Tony was "a most unlikely candidate."

The engagement of Princess Margaret to Antony Armstrong-Jones was announced January 13, 1960, and the wedding took place at Westminster Abbey on May 6, to the accompaniment of flurries of scandals. Jeremy Fry (of the chocolate company family) was dismissed as Tony's prospective best man when it was learned that he was gay. Jeremy Thorpe, later a famous politician, was Tony's second choice; he was dropped for the same reason. (The third choice for best man made the grade: Roger Gilliatt was the son of the Queen's gynecologist.)

From that time and that array of doubtful associations, chronicles of Tony's bisexuality were bruited about for years. "Did you read that story about me rushing up to Rudi Nureyev and kissing him full on the lips?" he asked a partygoer in 1970.

"Yes," was the reply. "Was it true?"

Tony's eyes widened. "Absolutely true. Are they jealous?"

391

Many were convinced that Tony's sexual orientation was not entirely clear. "I'm not prepared to alter my life to fit in with gossip writers," he once said enigmatically. And so he proceeded to be as independent as his wife. More than once, for example, he welcomed reporters to his country home when Margaret was away. Tony's companion was, wrote one newsman, "a delightful house-guest, a young man of exceptional beauty." Which was not much of a circumlocution.

"What Tony had foremost in common with Princess Margaret could be put in three words," according to one of his best friends. "Sex, sex, sex. Theirs was a terribly physical relationship. They couldn't keep their hands off each other, even with other people present." But he was a smiling, buoyant companion for Margaret, and a year after the marriage—just weeks before her sister bore a son in 1961—the Queen created him the Earl of Snowdon. The Snowdons, as they came to be known as long as the marriage lasted, settled into apartment 1A at Kensington Palace, a lavish twenty-one-room flat redecorated at taxpayers' expense. The couple paid a token rent of $2,500 per year.

Lord Mountbatten, for one, was mad about the diminutive groom (at five feet three, he seemed tall only when standing next to his wife, who was three inches shorter)—until Tony showed up at the Imperial War Museum for the preview of the television series on Mountbatten's life. Tony's evening wear, designed by Valentino, was judged by Mountbatten a trifle too fussy: a black velvet mid-thigh-length jacket with watered silk lapels in midnight blue, suede shoes, a pink shirt—and he had arranged one gentle blond curl over his forehead. "He might look divine at a campy Kensington soiree, but this, dammit, is the Imperial War Museum, Lambeth Road, London," wrote one witness to the evening. Tony's reply to his scolders: "They are all Victorian. What is a black tie anyway?"

There were controversial aspects to his photography, too. As a portraitist, Tony was superb; as a documentarist, he could raise an uproar. In his television film *Love of a Kind,* about the British attitude toward animals, he asked Ella Petry, a sixty-year-old housewife, to hatch an egg between her breasts—a remarkable achievement she had managed a dozen years earlier. "I only had the egg in my cleavage for a matter of minutes," Mrs. Petry said later. "I was given a number of eggs at various stages of incubation. I was there for three or four hours, and they were filming all the time. [Armstrong-Jones] insisted that I wear a nylon nightie and went to bed to hatch the egg. God knows why. He seemed very amused by the whole thing.''

If the Sovereign's romantic life was not quite so ardent as her sister's, it apparently was not over, for a month after the announcement of Margaret's engagement, the Queen, having been in seclusion for several months, had her third child. ''We plan to have two more later on,'' the Duke had told the press at the time of Anne's birth in 1950; they were now fulfilling the promise.

The first to be born to a reigning monarch since Victoria had Princess Victoria over a century earlier, the infant was delivered on February 19, 1960, and christened Andrew Albert Christian Edward (his paternal grandfather's name was Andrew). The timing of the birth explains why the Queen was not present for Charles's theatrical debut at Cheam, where he took over the role of Richard III in a Shakespearean compilation drama. His mother's absence was perhaps just as well, although even she may have been amused as Charles recited, without a flicker of irony, ''And soon may I ascend the throne.''

Prince Andrew was, as his brother's valet Stephen Barry recalled, ''no easy task—a boisterous child, into everything, always trying to follow us downstairs where he wasn't allowed, tugging at the footmen's tailcoats, climbing to reach anything that had been put out of his reach,'' and given to hitting the servants. Where Charles was shy and Anne tomboyish, Andrew was almost impossible to control. Far gentler and more presentable was Queen Elizabeth's fourth and last child, Edward Antony Richard Louis, born March 10, 1964, at Buckingham Palace.

Moon-faced and uncontrollably fidgety as a child, Andrew grew up a scamp, constantly laughing, smiling and getting into mischief; Edward, on the other hand, was a towheaded, retiring child, altogether more vulnerable. Both boys had a great deal of privilege and pleasure to make them merry, and even before their first shaves they knew antique advantages: obsequious servants, the gratification of their merest whims, and a life free of duties or responsibilities other than the quest for their own happiness. Nor were they subjected to schools as rigorous as those forced on Charles.

* * *

A boy and a girl, David and Sarah, were born to the Snowdons in 1961 and 1964, but even from that time, pressures
and cracks began to appear in the marriage. Margaret had an
undemanding round of official engagements she found increasingly tedious, while Tony became an ever more popular gadfly
and lionized society photographer. Otherwise, the couple led
an often hectic social life, seeking to find in company what
they lacked in solitude. By 1965 they were spending very
little time together. Bejeweled and breathless, Margaret was
occasionally referred to as Diamond Lil as she swept into a
film premiere or an evening at the ballet—unfair criticism, in
any case, which would never have been leveled against the
Queen or Queen Mother.

In the mid-1960s the Snowdons became media casualties
precisely because they continued to be what the press and
public wanted: a glamorous, high-spirited couple, feuding,
fussing and romancing, not without talent, rich and attractive.
They were rather like a royal version of Elizabeth Taylor and
Richard Burton, which is just what the era wanted of them.
They were therefore both desired and vilified. As royalty, they
were idolized, as celebrities envied. And naughty Margaret, as
she had done since childhood, knew only one way to make an
impression. She had to be rude, had to make bad choices, had
to stand up and be counted. That was her charm, and some of
it even seemed calculated. When good, she could be movingly
good; when bad, unspeakably horrid. She was, in a way, the
dark princess of fairy tales—the angry or wicked, unfortunate
or jealous foil to the golden-haired heroine.

When Margaret gave one of her rare interviews, she was
refreshingly frank. "When my sister and I were growing up,"
Margaret once said,

> it was always, "No, darling, I wouldn't do that. I don't
> think people would understand." . . . My sister was made
> out to be the goody-goody one. That was boring, so the
> press tried to make out I was wicked as hell. It didn't always
> work. Whenever I got a lot of publicity, I used to get a lot
> of letters. Most of the nice ones came from America: "How
> marvellous of you to do that," for they thought we were all
> terribly stuffy and Victorian. Then there were critical letters,
> accusing me of misreported things I hadn't done, mostly

anonymous and mostly from England. I minded that very much. I used to get appallingly upset, with no way of hitting back. I was an absolute wreck after some of the publicity, but luckily that's all over. In the last twenty years there have been enormous changes. Now I could do pretty well anything, apart from tearing [my] clothes off and jumping into the fountains at Trafalgar Square.

She could also, despite her occasional imperiousness, be refreshingly realistic: "My children are not royal," she said. "It just so happens that their aunt is the Queen of England."

But Margaret was perhaps understandably furious in 1967 when her cousin George Lascelles, the Earl of Harewood—Princess Mary's older son—wanted to divorce his wife and marry the divorced woman who had already borne him a son in 1964 and with whom he had since then been living. The matter was thorny for Harewood's cousin, the Queen, for once again the Royal Marriages Act and her position as Defender of the Faith were uncomfortably drawn into what would otherwise have been a private matter. There had been no British divorce in the Royal Family since Henry VIII, but when the Queen tried to impress this fact of history on her cousin and his wife, they were unmoved.

Could the Queen, then, grant her cousin permission to dissolve his marriage—which he and his wife, the former Marion Stein, seemed certain to do in any case—and to marry his mistress, Patricia Tuckwell? This seemed to many the honorable thing to do, for the Earl was clearly in love with Miss Tuckwell and wished to have a life with her and their young son. Elizabeth consulted her Prime Minister, Harold Wilson, who said that the Earl was seventeenth in line to the throne (not third, as Margaret had been at the time of the Townsend affair). Besides, it was now 1967, and public opinion was changing on the matter of divorce and remarriage.

The outcome was quietly historic: "The Cabinet have advised the Queen to give her consent" to the marriage of the Earl and Miss Tuckwell. This bit of legal-governmental legerdemain enabled the Queen simultaneously to preserve her constitutional position, safeguard her dignity in the Church, and not stymie the happiness of her cousin. One proviso had to be honored: the Queen granted permission for the second marriage on condition that the wedding occur outside England, and so George Lascelles and Patricia Tuckwell made their vows before a Connecticut judge on July 31, 1967. And with that there was a precedent for divorce and remarriage within the Royal Family.

Charles and
Diana.

13

Daylight Streams in upon Magic

1965 to 1981

> Well, it beats the changing of the guard,
> doesn't it?
> PRINCE CHARLES, watching bare-breasted
> dancing girls on Fiji

In 1965 the Duke of Windsor, after thirty years of exile from
England, was seventy years old and in swiftly failing health.
Despite the comfort of homes in France and their New York
apartment at the Waldorf-Astoria Hotel, he and the Duchess
had led nomadic lives that left them unfulfilled and increas-

397

ingly testy with each other and the larger social world to which
they had become addicted. Their lives were, as Lord Mountbatten's daughter Lady Pamela Hicks said, "utterly trivial—playing golf and going to the theatre and going on holiday. But
what did that mean, going on holiday? His life was one big
holiday!" Throughout the years, the banishment from the family had remained absolute, as the Windsors had been notably
excluded from the royal weddings of Princess Margaret in
1960, of the Duke of Kent in 1961 and of his sister Princess
Alexandra in 1963.

In February 1965 the Duke of Windsor went to the London
Clinic where he had surgery for a detached retina, only a few
months after a serious operation for an abdominal aneurysm
had been performed in Houston. Contrary to rumors that Wallis
was impatient and indifferent to her husband's illnesses, Hu-
bert de Givenchy insisted that she was "very tender and
thoughtful when the Duke's eyes started to give him trouble.
She [rose] at dinner and moved the candles" if the light was
hurting his eyes. Among many others, Lady Mosley agreed: "I
can't explain enough how courteous the Duchess was to the
Duke."

After consulting her mother, who reluctantly agreed that
some kind of reconciliation was necessary for the sake of public and press relations, the Queen went to the clinic to greet her
uncle for the first time since 1936. "I am so pleased to meet
you at last," she said with an awkward smile to Wallis, who
made a deep curtsy.* Elizabeth sat for about twenty minutes
with the Duke; their conversation mostly concerned the education of Prince Charles and the health of the Duke's brother
Henry Gloucester, who had just suffered the first in a series of
debilitating strokes that would render him incapacitated until
his death nine years later.

Then, a moment before the Queen rose to depart, the former
King said he had a favor to request. When his time came, he
said, he wished there to be services at St. George's Chapel,
Windsor, followed by burial in the family ground at Frogmore.
He would like the same courtesy for his wife. Wallis had no
reason to alter her belief that the Queen Mother was still a

---

* As a ten-year-old, Princess Elizabeth had met Wallis briefly and
informally. This was their first formal introduction.

powerful, controlling force when Elizabeth replied that she could not give an answer to the Duke's request immediately. A few days later, after the Queen again consulted her mother, the request was granted.

Other members of the family went to the clinic, too, among them Princess Marina and her daughter Alexandra, and the Mountbattens. The Queen Mother, though she sent flowers, did not go, and her absence spoke loudly of her perpetual dislike for the Windsors.

On March 17 the Duke was visited by his sister Mary, the Princess Royal, who was nursing her own unhappiness after her son's mistress had given birth. She arrived with a bouquet of flowers and exchanged embraces with both her brother and sister-in-law. Eleven days later, while strolling on the grounds of the family home with George and his two older sons, Mary complained of dizziness and was helped to a lakeside bench. George asked what was wrong. "I really don't know," Mary replied quietly. Moments later, resting against her son's shoulder, she died of a massive cerebral hemorrhage. She was sixty-seven. The Duke of Windsor, who adored her, was speechless with grief; his physicians would not allow him to attend the funeral.

Three years later, in the Court Circular for the funeral of his sister-in-law Marina, the Duke was rudely ranked last of all family mourners. Exquisite, courtly and confident to the end, Princess Marina had lived a life of astonishingly prodigal and fiery sensuality since the death of her husband George in 1942. A devoted mother and grandmother, she was always a welcome addition at any social event. She counted among her lovers Douglas Fairbanks, Jr., Danny Kaye, Robin Fox, David Niven and a small legion of famous and handsome gentlemen who drove down to her country home or were escorted to her apartment at Kensington Palace, where she died quietly at sixty-one, soon after a brain tumor was diagnosed in August 1968.

Very likely because of the Harewood divorce and remarriage, the Queen realized in 1967 that she had to invite the Duke and Duchess of Windsor to a family ceremony honoring the ex-King's mother. The event, held at Marlborough House on June 7, was the unveiling of a plaque dedicated to Queen Mary. The Windsors—who were pointedly omitted from the list of honored and royal guests issued by Buckingham Palace the next day—received the loudest applause and cheers of the day when their car arrived, and Wallis's elegant outfit and manner won over the London press. Here at last, a reunion with the Queen Mother was unavoidable. She and the Duke exchanged the ritual kiss on the cheek, and then she turned to the Duchess and extended her hand. "How nice to see you," she said with perhaps too much silkiness in her voice. Wallis shook her hand but did not curtsy, an omission she later explained to a friend: the Queen Mother had "stopped people from curtsying to me. Why should I curtsy to her?" After the brief ceremony, the Queen Mother said to her, "I hope we meet again," but for Wallis that was unlikely and undesirable. "When?" she asked, and for a reply she saw the Queen Mother smile and move discreetly away.

Princess Margaret was having her own social problems, all of them the result of what Noël Coward knew was her ill-advised marriage to Tony Armstrong-Jones. Bored and lonely when her husband went on a photograph shoot to India in 1966, she invited an old friend to visit. He was the boyishly handsome Anthony Barton, godfather to Margaret's daughter Sarah, and he and his wife had frequently joined the Snowdons for family holidays. Now, Barton and the Princess had a brief, wild affair—"originally encouraged by Tony," said Jocelyn Stevens, one of Snowdon's friends, "for if you yourself are playing around, then your conscience is eased if your partner does the same. Tony has a very complicated character."

The liaison might have been unknown to anyone but for Margaret's astonishing actions. She telephoned Barton's wife to confess and to apologize, actions that she repeated with Tony. If she hoped this would precipitate the end of her marriage—she had no reason to wish ill to Barton's—Margaret miscalculated. Lord Snowdon, perhaps because of his own independent life, was unfazed, and the Bartons lived as happily afterward as such a marital hiccup might have allowed.

The following year, a more tragic friendship ensued. Robin Douglas-Home, a nephew of the former Prime Minister, came from a family that had been close to the Queen Mother's family, the Bowes-Lyons, for generations. In 1967 he was a tall, fair-haired, thirty-five-year-old writer and musician, divorced and a father; his income came mostly from his work as a nightclub pianist. In that capacity he was introduced to Margaret, and soon he was escorting her around London. Contrary to the advice of friends who saw him as not the best companion, Margaret saw more and more of Robin. She shared his love of dance and music, and they both had a quick, devastating humor. They danced at the Travellers Club, they composed light lyrics together, they had private jokes. And they wrote love letters.

That correspondence altered the relationship when excerpts circulated around London and there were rumors of blackmail. "I am in fear of [Tony Armstrong-Jones]," Margaret wrote to Robin on Kensington Palace stationery on March 23, 1967, "and I don't know what lengths he won't go to, jealous as he is, to find out what I am up to and your movements too." This seems not to have been an accurate description of Snowdon's rather casual attitude; indeed, Margaret's purpose in describing her husband as jealous was immediately clear from what followed in the same letter. Explaining why there had to be a temporary separation from Robin, she wrote:

> Our love has the passionate scent of new mown grass and lilies about it. Promise you will never give up, that you will go on encouraging me to make the marriage a success and that given a good and safe chance I will try and come back to you one day. I daren't at the moment.

The collision of commitments was obvious: Margaret wanted to sustain her marriage, and she wanted Robin for her lover. But she was also, however half-consciously, lighting the dangerous fires of jealousy, and her letter proved to be a fatal strategy. Robin, always mercurial and irascible, appeared on a television talk show and, discussing his broken marriage, burst into tears. "I can't even talk nowadays," he said, choking back sobs. In October 1968 he committed suicide.

As if to compensate for a highly unpleasant whispering campaign subsequently leveled against her in London, Margaret at that time became more imperious than ever. She demanded a double motorcycle escort from Kensington Palace to an evening engagement or to a railway station; she tended to apply rather too much makeup; she began to act with a manic girlishness; and she was drinking excessively.

Some of her behavior certainly derived from the unending conflict in her nature. Margaret wanted to be treated as Her Royal Highness, but sometimes she also wanted to be just "Mrs. Armstrong-Jones." But when Richard Burton referred to her once in public as Maggie Jones, her withering glance revealed she was clearly not amused. At private parties she could be annihilatingly funny doing imitations at one moment, but the next she would hop right back on her royal twig, her back would stiffen, and she became the Princess once more.

Thus the differences between Margaret and Elizabeth had never been so dramatic as they became in the 1960s and 1970s, for as the younger became more ornery, more inclined to behavior that alarmed the palace Establishment, just so did the elder become more entrenched in an extension of the personality she had developed as a young princess.

Although Elizabeth had grown up in a happy home, it was also a restricted, repressive and dangerously unimaginative one. She had a father who was honorable but deeply wounded by his childhood, and a mother who was loyal and strong but obsessed with the idea of noblesse oblige. From the age of ten, Princess Elizabeth had been destined for the throne, and everything in her academic, social and recreational life had been geared for queenship; in other words, she knew reality only from the perspective of upper-class manners. Only twenty-five when her beloved father died and she acceded, she had little experience of the modern world and was pitched into an atmosphere of regrettable sycophancy. The coronation had almost made a saint of her in the eyes of the public; certainly the entire ceremony (and the painters chosen to immortalize her during the 1950s) presented Elizabeth as priestess, prophetess and mystic.

The result was that an essentially uncomplicated, decent young woman was somehow lost in an aura of studied queenliness; she was burdened psychologically and restricted emotionally—just as, at the coronation, she was laden with jewels, ermine and cloth of gold. She had to read speeches that were antique in tone and condescending in style. Elizabeth had only to go on her world tours and Commonwealth visits to be hailed as a great lady: as ever, she was required only to *be* and to *appear* at the proper place and time, smiling, waving—an ambassador of what you will. She did not have to do anything significant; indeed, her glory usually consisted in what she did *not* do. She had become a woman who distinguished between "what the Queen can/must do" and "what I think." There was, then, a kind of movie-star split in Elizabeth Alexandra Mary Windsor. She was the observed of all observers (as Shakespeare wrote of Hamlet), but she was also a constant observer of herself and had constantly to present to the world an idealized icon of herself as the Queen. And to see to it that her self-awareness and her education were not broadened one bit, the elder courtiers—Lascelles, Colville and company—guaranteed that little in the protocols of the palace changed.

In light of that, her own personality became somewhat frozen—not necessarily always cold, but predictable, almost immutable. Head of state but denied actual power, she nonetheless refined an influence felt mostly in the sustained idea that the best of Britain was incarnated in an upper-class way of life. In this regard, as Lord Altrincham had boldly and respectfully pointed out in 1957, the new Elizabethan Court utterly failed to represent the growing diversity within the British peoples.

At the root of the entire problem is a simple and utterly poignant fact: Her Majesty the Queen just does not have friends the way other people have friends. Everyone but everyone—her children and oldest pre-coronation acquaintances included—must bow or curtsy on entering her august presence. Presumably there was, at least at the beginning of the marriage and perhaps since, some normal give-and-take with Philip, but there has been nothing in their words or actions to suggest that the dutiful compromises of the marriage have made for a dynamic friendship. Any other possibility has been short-circuited by her role. To summarize the matter, there is no one who can come into her room, sit down, toss aside his or her shoes, and tell Elizabeth she looked silly yesterday afternoon. Nor has she anyone with whom she can kick off her shoes, put up her feet and say, "I need a drink!" Always hailed, always overpraised, she is ever the recipient of uncritical adulation. When alone, as when Philip is abroad, she reads a Dick Francis novella or snaps on the television. "I mean, can you imagine her?" said a woman who has known the Queen for years. "She's often alone in that house, that huge house, Buckingham Palace, with no one to talk to, and she has a meal on a tray in front of the television. It's a very lonely life."

* * *

Lonely or not, carefully edited portions of that private life were revealed to the world on television in 1969. The Queen's perceptive assistant press secretary, the Australian William Heseltine, persuaded her that a documentary on the Royal Family *as family* could be an invaluable help in boosting the national affection for the Windsors. And so from June 1968 to May 1969, cameras were invited to film Elizabeth at work; Philip on tour; Elizabeth, Philip and the children in various (meticulously posed) activities—hiking, feeding the corgis, decorating the family Christmas tree and, most unlikely, grilling meat and tossing salad for a barbecue picnic (just the family, thank you) on the banks of a loch at Balmoral. Cannily timed for broadcast on June 30, just before Charles's formal investiture as Prince of Wales at Caernarvon Castle, *The Royal Family* was a hit in 140 countries. (With so many shots of the royal housepets and their royal mistress, one wag dubbed the film *Corgi and Beth*.)

Although the national effect of *The Royal Family* was a publicist's dream, its main artistic achievement was in showing the monarch to be a pleasant, strong-willed but rather uninteresting upper-class matriarch with few special and no artistic interests. Worse, it seemed in retrospect as if Buckingham Palace was using television—as it had done with the coronation and the Queen's Christmas broadcasts—to popularize the Windsors and so to deflect criticism at a time when the amounts allowed the family in the Civil List were going ever higher. That was certainly part of the motivation; it was better for the Royal Family to make the impression it wanted to make, in evidence of which there was some disingenuousness.

"Sandringham means winter—and a brief holiday," intoned the voice-over narration, but the Queen's winter holiday stretched to almost three months. And the repeated shots of the Sovereign opening the red boxes and reading state papers prepared for her review lamely suggested that this was why she was not out among the people more often. To her credit, the following year the Queen instituted the walkabout, a now familiar custom in which (although they are safely cordoned off from her) she mingles among people on a village street, accepting flowers and, only occasionally, shaking hands.

No one could have foreseen the danger in all this feigned intimacy. Having once allowed cameras backstage, the perpetrators of the situation had opened a Pandora's box. The media machinery could never again be kept out or prevented from becoming ever more intrusive. The Royal Family was slowly but ineluctably becoming the great cast of a never-ending soap opera, and twenty years later, no holds would be barred. They wanted to be seen as normal, and so everyone wanted to know just how normal they were. Bagehot was right: admitting daylight threatens the royal mystique, but it also turns that mystique into an addiction. Thus since 1969, by a curious paradox, the Royal Family has become a willing contributor to the cult of celebrity, cooperating with the media as more and more colorful and glamorous—and, at last, scandalous—images were produced to satisfy the need for romantic figures to adore.

Charles's investiture as Prince of Wales in the summer of 1969, which was preceded by eight weeks of study in the country's language and culture, was also conceived to promote the monarchy at a time of intense criticism over the Civil List and the Windsors' nonpayment of taxes. Although it was an invented modern ritual only as old as Edward VIII's investiture fifty-eight years earlier, the event was brilliantly choreographed with all the trappings of medieval romance. And by an odd concatenation of elements, there was nothing Welsh (and very little English) about the hodgepodge of a ceremony. The Prince's emblem derives from the French fleur-de-lys of African feathers, with a Bohemian phrase (*Ich Dien*—I Serve) as his motto, and under the direction of the Roman Catholic Duke of Norfolk, Charles knelt before his Anglican mother in a nonconformist country.

At twenty-one, Charles was permitted to speak his mind, which was hardly that of a contemporary hippie, much less a revolutionary. Asked if he would like to change his life, he replied,

> No, I don't think so. I don't see how I could now, having been brought up and having the background I do have. It would be very difficult doing anything else. I've been, as it were, trained to do it and I feel part of the job. I have this feeling of duty toward England, towards the United Kingdom, the Commonwealth, and I feel there is a great deal I can do if I am given the chance to do it.

The problem would increasingly be that, like Edward VII as Prince of Wales, Charles would be given the chance to do very little. His mother turned over to him almost nothing at all except ceremonial duties, and of course he was not permitted to take on a job. He was the first Prince of Wales to earn a university degree, and he merrily participated in the college satire that poked fun at him. He joined the Madrigal Society; he played the cello; he contributed to a college magazine; he gave radio and television interviews in which he revealed himself as very much his mother's son ("From my point of view it is pointless to change things purely for the sake of change") —all of it without the brusque, sometimes rude humor of his father.

But also like his mother, Charles has shown little imagination—almost as if that faculty would, if given free rein, bring down the monarchy quicker than armed revolution. "I'm really rather an awkward problem," he said at the time, and his assessment was on the mark. He was the junior member of what his grandfather had called the Family Firm; he had no authority and no constitutional role. And in the most awkward of Oedipal additions to the soap opera, his chance at having a future depended on the death of his mother. "What a rotten boring job you've got," said an astonishingly frank airline attendant. "She was right!" cried Charles when he repeated the remark to several government ministers a week later.

All that remained for him was to act the Prince in private. "He was friendly, he was kind, but he was always Royal," according to his valet, Stephen Barry. "He always expected to receive what he wanted instantly, [and] he is always harboring a sneaking suspicion that someone is ripping him off because he is the Prince of Wales." Charles was, then, more like his father than at first might have seemed.

Philip was certainly blunter, more abrasive than his son, and less concerned with others' reactions—or with an empty formalism about the monarchy. Asking a Brazilian military official where he got his medals, Philip was told, "In the war." With remarkable indiscretion, the Duke countered, "I didn't know Brazil was in the war that long," to which the man replied, "At least, Sir, I didn't get them from marrying my wife."

Similarly, opening a new annex to the Vancouver City Hall

in 1969, Philip momentarily forgot the building's name and settled for: "I declare this thing open—whatever it is." The Canadians were not amused, even when he later explained: "It was raining and I wanted to get on with it, especially as the total audience was about fifteen passing shoppers under umbrellas." Told that Canadian support for the Crown was already compromised and uncertain, he became even more argumentative in an address:

> The monarchy exists in Canada because it was thought to be of benefit to the country. It is a complete misconception to imagine that the monarchy exists in the interest of the monarchy. It does not.... We do not come here for our health, so to speak.... We can think of other ways of enjoying ourselves. Judging by some of the programs we are required to do here and considering how little we get out of it, you can assume that it is done in the interests of the Canadian people and not in our own interest. If at any time people feel that [the monarchy] has no future part to play, then for goodness sake let's end the thing on amicable terms without having a row about it.

Earlier that same year he had grown weary with students at the Scottish university that bears his ducal title. When one of them asked what he considered a dull question about freedom of speech, Philip snapped, "Shut up and grow up!" This evoked hisses and boos from the group, and over the din Philip's voice rose: "Don't assume I am exercising any form of censorship. Neither the [dean of the college] nor I would do that. We may be incompetent, but we are not dishonest. I know about freedom of speech because I get kicked in the teeth often enough for saying things. I am told I damned well ought not to say them. So why should I tell you what to say?"

The Duke, according to one palace courtier, "gets irritated with the Queen's passiveness. You see, she's much better at knowing when it's right to say no, than at taking the initiative and saying yes. So he'll say, 'Come on, Lilibet. Come on. Just do it.' She, in turn, gets cross with his bad temper"—as once, when he was about to quit a lengthy sitting for a portrait, the Queen firmly ordered, "You stay there!" He obeyed.

* * *

No such automatic response would ever have been forthcoming from Margaret, especially amid the chaos that enveloped her life in the 1970s. By that time her marriage was in tatters, not only because she and her husband were spending more and more time apart but because each had intimacies elsewhere. "Worse than anything," Margaret said, "Tony was rude to me in front of the children. It was the last straw."

Her response was action. First, a worldwide scandal occurred beginning in early 1973; Margaret was forty-two and began a complex relationship with Roderick "Roddy" Llewellyn, twenty-five—exactly the age difference between her and Peter Townsend. The problem was that Roddy was a shy, nervous man whose only job had been as a research assistant at the College of Heralds and some time as a male model. Five feet ten inches tall, he was slim, rode well, had an engaging smile and often wore a single silver earring, leather chaps and chains—an outfit of sadomasochistic chic not at all commonplace at the time. Uncertain whether he wanted a stable life with a man or a woman, Roddy had been more or less content for a year with a generous male lover before he twice attempted suicide. Star-struck and emotionally tangled, he was only too glad to submit himself to the strong directives of Her Royal Highness. When photos were finally published of Margaret and Roddy cavorting on the Caribbean island of Mustique (where friends had given Margaret land and a house as a wedding gift), Tony—who had begun keeping company with the woman who would be his second wife—had a tailor-made hatch from which to escape from his marriage.

"It was," wrote one palace chronicler carefully about Margaret and Roddy, "a romance verging on the bizarre." They played bridge with friends, they went out dancing, they entertained at dinner parties. But although the couple went about openly in London, those who accompanied them believed that Roddy was not as enthusiastic a partner as she might have wished. Indeed, he may not have been her lover at all. "I will never marry Princess Margaret," he said, adding significantly that "circumstances—personal reasons—would prevent it. And I have no desire to have children." No code breaker was needed to clarify Roddy's meaning.

The friendship was soon known to the Queen and the Queen Mother, who had been able to cope with the divorce and remarriage of the Earl of Harewood but were not prepared for the threat to the royal image that Margaret obviously posed. No one this close to the throne had cavorted so brazenly since Edward VIII. But no stern conferences could stop the affair, whatever it was, and Margaret and Roddy cantered through five erratic and ambiguous years together, occasionally interrupted by his sudden sprint alone to such exotic spots as Istanbul.

In 1974 some melodramatic suds were added to the soap opera. During one of Roddy's absences, Margaret gulped down a handful of not very potent sleeping pills. "She felt woozy for a while," a friend reported. "It was more a *cri de coeur* than a serious attempt to harm herself. Perhaps she had expected too much of Roddy and he had been unable to cope." In fact, it was Margaret's fear of losing him, and it was her concomitant sexual overtures and demands that had precipitated Roddy's flight: "Not much in the way of bed had been involved," wrote another friend, "and Roddy confessed that he found the physical side of their relationship difficult to cope with." Meantime, the two Elizabeths held their breath and hoped that each separation would mean a finale to the affair.

Amid these somewhat Byronic convulsions, the Duke of Windsor was suffering from terminal cancer of the throat. But his mind was clear and alert, as Wallis's sometimes seemed not to be. In addition to severe arthritis, she had been diagnosed with arteriosclerosis, and the Duke noticed sudden personality changes and memory lapses. Charles visited them at their home in Paris in October 1971. "Uncle David talked about how difficult my family had made it for him for the past 33 years," Charles wrote in his diary. "I asked him frankly if he would like to return to England for the last years of his life . . . [but] he felt no one would recognise him. . . . The whole thing seemed so tragic."

Then, on May 18, 1972, the Queen and Philip, in France for a state visit, went to see the ailing Duke, by then very close to the end and unable to leave his bedroom. Weakened and wasted with disease, the former King struggled to rise from his wheelchair, bowed to his niece and kissed her. "My dear Lilibet, it is lovely to see you again," he said in a faint whisper before falling back into the chair. Decades of rancor and resentment, the virtual exclusion of Edward and Wallis from England, the Royal Family's shameful lack of compassion and large-heartedness—all of this seemed to fade in the spring morning, for imminent death made every other consideration very trivial indeed. For a moment the only sound was his labored breathing and the insistent ticking of an eighteenth-century bedside clock. The Queen, whose role in history had depended on his love for Wallis, was unaccustomed to the sight of morbidity and was stung to silence. She was rescued two minutes later by Philip.

A week later, on the night of May 27, Edward asked his wife if a stewed peach might be prepared for him—it was the favorite supper of his nursery days—but his throat would tolerate nothing. Anxious and gasping for breath, he reached for Wallis, who sat and held his hand for four hours. Shortly after two o'clock on the morning of May 28, 1972, Edward opened his eyes. Wallis, who had been resting in a chair a few feet away, came to his side just as his heart stopped.

By the time she accompanied her husband's body to the funeral at Windsor on June 5, Wallis was in a state of profound shock and confusion. Twice she asked members of the family to find her husband, and to Prime Minister Edward Heath she said, "You must come to Paris to see us. The Duke and I would love to have you." But in that poignant moment just before the coffin was taken away, Wallis said to those around her, "He was my entire life. I can't begin to think what I am going to do without him. He gave up so much for me, and now he has gone." To her surprise and comfort, Prince Charles attended her with real sympathy. "Well, she is family," he said. And she was not unaware of others' sufferings: weeks later she wept at the news that William, the thirty-one-year-old son of Henry and Alice of Gloucester, had been killed in an airplane crash. His father, last of the surviving sons of King George V and Queen Mary, was taken further into the twilight world of paralysis and speechlessness from strokes, lingering two more years until his death in 1974.

Although broken and desolate, Wallis rose brilliantly to meet the unpleasant moment when the rapacious Louis Mountbatten went to Paris, attempting to retrieve as much as he could of the Duke's personal effects, uniforms, robes and decorations. These he spirited away to the Queen. But he was unsuccessful in obtaining Edward's private letters. "It was awful," Wallis told her friend Aline de Romanones. "He wanted me to make out a will right there and then, giving everything to David's family and of course some to himself. He had it all worked out, just where everything should go. Well, I did my best to stick up for my rights. After all, I do want to be fair, and what should go to the Royal Family, should go." With shrewd dignity, Wallis kept their private papers and an estate valued at £3 million (most of which she bequeathed for medical research at the Pasteur Institute).

For the rest, Wallis was mostly secluded after Edward's death. She read, watched television and kept up on world news, but current events depressed her. "It's a bombshell world," she said, "full of violence and horror. I no longer understand or like it very much." Always homesick for America, Wallis had never learned to speak French, and for all her precision in supervising gourmet dinners for guests, her own favorite food in her last years was a juicy rare hamburger. "David loved me," Wallis said frequently in her last years, no matter whether a friend or nurse or servant was in the room. Her gaze would seem blank and uncomprehending, fixed on no one. "He really loved me," she repeated over and over, as if anyone could ever have doubted it. Increasingly frail and disoriented, the Duchess was confined to bed most of the time from 1972 to 1986; she died two months before her ninetieth birthday. She was interred next to her husband at the Frogmore Royal Burial Ground, just south of the Victoria and Albert mausoleum. A plaque notes the final resting place of "Wallis—Duchess of Windsor," but the letters H.R.H. are to be found on her husband's tomb only.

Queen Victoria, Edward VII's Alexandra, George V's Mary, George VI's Elizabeth, Queen Elizabeth II, Princess Margaret: all the women playing major roles in the dynastic saga are remarkable for their strength and independence. Princess Anne, who turned twenty-one in 1971, developed those qualities differently but no less impressively. Impatient of cant, resentful of exaggerated protocol, preferring a life on horseback in the country, she did miserably at school, but this did not seem to bother her at all. "She never worked especially hard," said Cynthia Gee, her housemistress at the Benenden School in Kent. "She wasn't stupid, but economy of effort was her style." Her academic life was over before her eighteenth birthday.

More outspoken and outgoing than Charles, she has always seemed, with her height (five feet seven inches), her somewhat pouty expression and her Hanoverian jaw, more like Philip than the Queen. In young adulthood Anne wanted very much to appear amiable, relaxed and approachable, but she had been trained too well in royal protocol ever to let down her guard. If a schoolmate or friend referred to "your mother," Anne's eyes would flash and she would interrupt sharply, "I take it you are referring to Her Majesty the Queen?"

She seemed most relaxed on horseback, and it was at such a sporting event in 1969 that she met a twenty-two-year-old commodities broker, polo player and son of a lieutenant colonel. Sandy Harper and Anne were seen all over London, he sedately dressed, she wearing orange trouser suits or short mauve skirts with oversized bucket-shaped hats that oddly suited her autocracy. They leaped onstage to join the cast of *Hair* in the final dance—some of the actors were buck naked —but leaving the theater a few moments later, she loudly scolded a tabloid photographer who dared to call "Anne!" in her direction. "She'll go crazy and dance around," said a Duke close to the Royal Family. "And suddenly she'll remember who she is."

Who Anne was *becoming* in the 1970s no one could be quite sure, but one thing was clear: she was carving her own path and was not at all close to her brother. "She was always impatient with him," recalled Charles's valet. " 'Oh, come *on*, Charles,' you'd hear her shouting at him. She was always complaining that he was slow." Whether a general attitude of complaint caused the break with Harper cannot be known, but very suddenly he was engaged to a model. Anne returned to a genteel life of riding, sailing, skiing and occasional ribbon-cuttings at the openings of hospitals and schools.

For all that, she could be surprisingly imperious. She was asked how she liked Australia during a visit in the spring of 1970. "I don't know—I can't see it for this bloody wind." Did she really say *bloody*? "Quite likely," she said, and that was that. "Look this way, love," begged a photographer later. "I am not your love," Anne said icily. "I am Your Royal Highness." Indeed.

Everywhere, she spoke her mind. In Washington that summer, Anne and Charles visited President and Mrs. Nixon and their daughters. She snapped at photographers, whined about having so little time for sightseeing and complained about the torrid weather. "Have you a tape measure?" she asked a shop assistant in the sweater department at Marks & Spencer. One was produced, and Anne unbuttoned her coat. "I wonder if you'd check my bust measurement. Last time I bought a sweater, I found it didn't fit me when I got home." In full view of other shoppers, the royal bosom was measured and the correct size proclaimed.

On his daughter's twenty-second birthday, Philip told a friend he would like to see her "gain some sort of solid achievement—but it is difficult to know in what!" She was, to anyone who stopped to think about it, very like her aunt Margaret—not least in the quick changes of mood, chirpy and giggling one moment, chilly the next if someone addressed her by name instead of saying "Ma'am."

Such formalities were not, of course, Anne's idea. She had been trained in such matters, raised to expect that ladies and gentlemen stood when she entered a room, waited for her to begin before they picked up fork and knife, did not speak to her until she addressed them. Bodyguards always attended her, watching from no more than a few hundred feet.

Even at a party or nightclub, she cared not a whit what detectives thought of her conduct. "Watch her at a dance," suggested a friend. "Five minutes after she arrives, she's surrounded herself with men, the best-looking ones there." After Sandy Harper, Richard Meade and Guy Nevill were among them. An Olympic gold medalist horseman and a property manager in Surrey, Meade was a dashing, nattily dressed socialite thought to be in the running for the role of Anne's husband. So was Nevill, then the wealthy heir to the Marquess of Abergavenny. And Robert Rodwell, with whom she gyrated at the discotheque La Valbonne. "Relax," she told him as they whirled round the floor. "You won't break me, I'm not made of Dresden china." She danced with many, dated some, promised nothing.

Then, on November 14, 1973, Anne, twenty-three, married the handsome twenty-five-year-old Mark Phillips, a captain in the Queen's Dragoon Guards. A country-gentry commoner and noted equestrian, he had first met the Princess in 1968 at a party to celebrate Britain's placing in the Olympics, where Mark was a reserve team member among those on horseback. The wedding was a major news event, televised worldwide.

So were the reports of a bold kidnapping attempt four months later. As Anne and Mark were returning from a benefit film premiere on March 20, 1974, their car was waylaid in The Mall by a lunatic named Ian Ball, who had for months been plotting to kidnap the Princess for a £3 million ransom. Anne's bodyguard, chauffeur, a passing journalist and a police constable were seriously wounded by Ball's gunfire, but she and Mark were unhurt. "Why don't you go away?" Anne shouted at her attacker as he tried to drag her from her car. "What good is this going to do?" Her amazing sangfroid did not desert her for a moment, and two hours later she was at the wheel of her own car and Mark was at his, en route to their country residence as scheduled. "Quite honestly," she said later, "I did not have time to get frightened, so I just got angry with the man. While it was happening I was amazed to see things going on as usual outside our car. Taxis and cars were going by. I felt I was in a time capsule."

In the Phillips's marriage, nothing subsequent to this matched it for drama. Unlike Antony Armstrong-Jones, Mark insisted on maintaining his own identity, and with his wife's approval he refused the Queen's offer of a title. This pleased neither Elizabeth nor Philip, who found Mark somewhat socially limited, unable to converse on anything except horses and the army and afflicted with a schoolboyish humor. Their reservations were accurate, as a reporter discovered when he found Captain Phillips purchasing unusual practical jokes such as teabags that caused severe flatulence and sugar lumps that, when melted, disclosed condoms. "He has a good sense of humor and enjoys a joke like everybody else," said a respondent at Buckingham Palace when asked for an explanation.

As for Anne, she counterpoised royal attitude with submission to her husband, at least for the time being. "I'd like to make all the really big decisions in our life," Mark told her, perhaps overstating the case rather broadly and setting himself up for disappointment. As it turned out, the only really big decisions to make concerned the management of their estate, Gatcombe Park in Gloucestershire, where they moved in 1976:

to this task Phillips devoted himself while his wife tended to her royal engagements. In 1977 the Queen's first grandchild, Peter Phillips, was born; his sister Zara followed in 1981. Anne and Mark preferred that the children have no designation other than Mister and Miss. In 1987, however, Anne did accept the Queen's offer of the title Princess Royal, the highest honor given to a female member of the Royal Family; and several years later she was admitted to the Order of the Garter.

"Sometimes I feel I would like to lead a very different life from the life I'm living now," Anne said on the record. "In great part it is a very public life. But I don't feel I've got any choice. I was born into a kind of life with duties and obligations, and opting out isn't on." Except, as it happened, for opting out of her marriage.

Marriages and divorces once considered out of the question for members of the Royal Family were becoming commonplace in the 1970s. In 1978, thirty-six-year-old Prince Michael of Kent, the youngest of George and Marina's three children, wed the beautiful and intelligent Baroness Marie-Christine von Reibnitz, a divorced Roman Catholic. (Had the Duke of Windsor been alive, he would have been newly infuriated when the new Princess was rightly designated "Her Royal Highness." Nothing, after all, could alter the British common law that the bride takes the style of her husband.)

That same year the Snowdon marriage at last came permanently undone. On May 10, Buckingham Palace announced that Princess Margaret and Antony Armstrong-Jones, who had lived apart for over two years, were taking advantage of the new law that permitted automatic divorce after that interval. He had formed an attachment with the woman who had assisted him while filming in Australia, and whom he later married, and Princess Margaret was still traveling and nightclubbing with the doubtful Roddy Llewellyn, who had suffered a breakdown but now fancied himself a pop singer. Hard-drinking, fast-driving Roddy caused considerable public embarrassment for Margaret, whose sadness over his departure from her life the following year threw her again into excessive tippling and an almost suicidal depression. At the time of the divorce announcement, Margaret was confined to King Edward VII Hospital with alcoholic hepatitis and gastroenteritis. She instructed her solicitors to agree to Tony's request for a six-figure divorce settlement in his favor; she had custody of the children.

Not yet fifty, Margaret bore the worst of the publicity. The press ignored her husband's infidelity and wrote as if Margaret alone was responsible for the divorce: Tony said he was the wounded spouse—"humiliated and in quite an intolerable position." With remarkable frankness, Margaret said later, "Lord Snowdon was devilish cunning." In addition, there was considerable resentment against Margaret's generous share of the Civil List, which rose to an allowance of over £125,000 in 1975. "We are concerned about Princess Margaret's image," said a spokesman at Kensington Palace. "There is little we can do about it, and we can't ask the media to love the Royal Family."

Thenceforth, her life seemed to grind to something of a halt; in any case, she had little to anticipate. In 1974 she had lost part of a lung to cancer, but that did not deter her from chain-smoking, which made her even more nervous and frail; several sojourns in clinics followed, for pneumonia, pleurisy and respiratory infections. The first Royal lady to be sexually enterprising and to act as if free from all restraint, she became something of a tragic figure among the Windsors, lonely and pathetic, alternating an attitude of almost winsome bravado with a remarkably tenacious *folie de grandeur*. Lacking the resources to involve herself in the great causes of the day, she became merely a socialite. It is impossible to theorize how her life might have turned out had she married Peter Townsend, but simple domestic joys are rarely sufficient for those born to the purple.

The Queen's reaction was predictable. She was, according to courtiers, angry and confused, feeling that her sister had betrayed royal values: "What are we going to do with Margaret?" was her refrain that year. The warmth of the coronation had been cooled by the Townsend crisis in 1953; now, as Elizabeth was preparing for her Silver Jubilee, Margaret again was at the center of an embarrassment. She was, in fact, the first member of the immediate Royal Family (the Earl of Harewood and other cousins aside) to be divorced since Henry VIII discarded Anne of Cleves. It was no longer possible to point to the Royal Family as representatives of a higher morality or as models of family stability. With Margaret's divorce, more voices were heard to question the wisdom—the common sense, even—of perpetuating the elaborate fiction and great expense of a monarchy that seemed more and more frivolous.

But Margaret did not approach her senior years as an unsympathetic woman. Her children grew up loyal and close to her, and she earned many friends outside the royal circle. Essentially kindhearted, she learned to soften the edges of her brittle personality with a clear-eyed sense of human failings and foibles and a basic compassion for the benighted. Often lonely, frequently misrepresented by the press and misunderstood by the public, she never found the man she so patently required to leaven and balance her life. In her sixties she could still be seen, as before, slipping into the choir stalls at Westminster Abbey on an ordinary Sunday morning, attended only by one lady-in-waiting. She was there not as a family representative for a special public ceremony; quite the contrary, Margaret was present among common worshipers gathered for the same purpose. She was a wealthy woman acknowledging her poverty of spirit.

As it happened, marriage was very much on the Queen's mind for her heir in 1978: Charles turned thirty that year and showed no inclination to choose a bride and produce an heir. Was the stage being set for a revival of the melodrama of his predecessor, the Wales who had been Edward VIII? Then, because he seemed so slow to show serious, protracted interest in a young lady, there were the inevitable rumors that perhaps the Prince of Wales was gay. To counter such talk and indicate his gravity of purpose, he took to television—as did other celebrities, royal or otherwise—to present his case. "You've got to remember that when you marry, in my position, you are going to marry somebody who perhaps one day is going to become Queen. You've got to choose somebody very carefully," he said to a BBC anchor.

At the same time, the Prince was having serious doubts. "Charles worried terribly about marriage," said a friend, "and he would ask what happened to people who one moment were madly in love with one another and then, six months down the road, parted company forever." The Prince wanted to know if people changed that much, and when his friend replied that change was natural and to be expected, Charles grew troubled "because he knew that he could only have one crack at it. For him there would be no second chance. He had to get it right the first time."

Thus went the life of the Prince of Wales, who demonstrated no rowdiness until after a six-week training course at the Royal Naval College, Dartmouth, in 1971. He was a sublieutenant on the HMS *Norfolk* when the ship docked in Toulon, on the French Riviera. There, he went out drinking one night with petty officers, scouring the red-light districts, ogling prostitutes in side streets, and watching strippers at a notorious café. His father would have been delighted.

During his excursions at sea again in 1973, as at home, women had a place in his life—but nothing like the center. "He was really quite happy being a bachelor," according to his valet Stephen Barry, "[for] after his engagements were completed, he was free to do exactly what he wanted to do—with no woman to interfere with his sporting activities." Dates with young ladies were under his control, of course: he could never be asked, he did the asking. Those invited to share an evening or to attend a royal function included, among others, Georgina Russell (daughter of the British ambassador to Spain); Bettina Lindsay (daughter of a peer); Lord Astor's daughter Elizabeth; Lady Victoria Percy (the Duke of Northumberland's daughter); Lady Henrietta Fitzroy, a childhood chum; Lady Jane Grosvenor (daughter of the immensely wealthy Duke of Westminster); Dale Harper, Lady Tryon; and a glamorous actress or two or ten. "Well, it beats the changing of the guard, doesn't it?" he once said while watching barebreasted girls dancing a fertility rite in Fiji.

In England and abroad, women were routinely brought to him. They flirted, they flattered, they were awed. None of the young ladies spoke, then or later, about their relationships with the Prince of Wales; none ever gave an interview describing their hours or days in Charles's company.

Most of the ladies chosen for special intimacy, for repeated visits to the palace or Balmoral, were soon besieged by media attention; and most soon wearied of that and of Charles's diffidence outside the bedroom. Affairs there were—so exservants confirmed. But it would be overstatement to call them "romances," for they seem to have been liaisons kept firmly in their place. "They never dominated him," said Barry of these relationships. ''The only thing that dominates Prince Charles is his work, and then his sporting activities. Girls come third. Prince Andrew, not having the same future, can show much more interest in girls than his elder brother ever could. Prince Charles is basically shy—and extremely cautious.''

Part of the problem was the awesome nature of the choice he was expected to make—not a romantic choice but a strategic one. He had to select someone suitable to enter the Royal Family and sire the future King of England. She had to have a decent background and breeding and be quite free of scandal; and she had to be firmly Protestant. By the 1970s it was not easy to find a young woman of Victorian virtue willing to assume the role of passive, baby-making Royal Consort, a woman with no personal (much less romantic) expectations, willing to subordinate her entire personal destiny to that of the Windsors. Someone like Queen Mary was not to be readily found.

For his part, Charles was awkward in social situations and utterly lacked his father's easy charm. He had also been raised amid appalling privilege and deference, and every young lady had to address him as ''Sir'' unless instructed otherwise. No matter how royalist or starry-eyed, any modern young lady had to find that a bit much. Most of those Charles fancied were bored rather quickly.

Georgina Russell, for example, removed herself from the royal presence during a week's fishing with Charles in Scotland. He had the servants prepare spartan meals (''he was on one of his economy drives,'' according to Barry) and spent most of each day with a rod and reel, hip-deep in streams. She fled before the week was out.

Just so Lady Sarah Spencer (whose younger sister was named Lady Diana), who had all she could do to handle a tendency to anorexia nervosa, never mind the nervous anxiety caused by a royal date. But after an apparently lovestruck Charles took Sarah on a ski holiday in 1977, she was thought to be a serious contender—an idea she herself scotched when she told a journalist, ''There is no chance of my marrying him. I'm not in love with him, and I wouldn't marry anyone I didn't love, whether it was the dustman or the King of England.'' The Prince, she added, was ''a romantic who falls in love easily.'' Her frankness must have annoyed her grandmother, Lady Fermoy, who was lady-in-waiting to the Queen Mother. Both these women rather hoped that Sarah had a crack at being Princess of Wales.

On the other hand, Lady Jane Wellesley, daughter of the Duke of Wellington, was not keen on Charles's habit of teasing, nor did she like to be hit with melon balls as if they were love notes. Serious women like Lady Jane must have been surprised at such displays of princely immaturity.

Anna Wallace, the daughter of a wealthy landowner, was another case. Tall and blond, she quickly led Charles into a state of sexual obsession in 1979. Self-reliant and confident of her sway over him, she responded to Charles but was not afraid to quarrel with him in public. Anna was also undeterred from dating others, and it was that implication of active attachments to other men that spelled her doom. When palace moles dug up that she had actually *lived* with another, she was history (as was Davina Sheffield, a beautiful blonde who was dismissed for the same reason)—even before she shouted at Charles that she did not appreciate being abandoned while he squired other young ladies onto the floor at a Windsor Castle dance. The American blond socialite Laura Jo Watkins, daughter of an admiral, was also briefly in the running, and there were several quiet meetings in London and Miami. But her nationality removed her from serious consideration.

Until Lady Diana Spencer, no one fared as well as Princess Marie Astrid of Luxembourg.

CHARLES TO MARRY ASTRID—OFFICIAL!

Thus trumpeted the *Daily Express* in huge headlines and a first-page story on June 17, 1977.

The formal engagement will be announced from Buckingham Palace next Monday. The couple's difference of religion—she is a Roman Catholic—will be overcome by a novel constitutional arrangement: any sons of the marriage will be brought up according to the Church of England, while daughters will be raised in the Catholic faith. The Queen and Prince Philip have consented to this procedure, which also has the approval of Church leaders. Prince Charles, who is 28, first met 23-year-old Astrid about a year ago.

Although their association has been kept secret by the Palace—even to the extent of denying they had ever met—a close friend said last night: "They fell for each other at that first meeting." Astrid—who will become Princess of Wales on her marriage and should eventually be Queen, is the daughter of the Grand Duke of Luxemburg. Her mother, the former Princess Josephine Charlotte, is the daughter of the former King Leopold and Queen Astrid of the Belgians.

The entire story turned out to be a pressman's fantasy. Astrid had met Charles two or three times, without any romance flourishing. Fervent denials from Buckingham Palace were interpreted by the press as clear indications that the wedding bells were being polished and tuned. But Charles's deepest, most loving connection was with Camilla Shand, whom he had met through the agency of the ever-present Lord Mountbatten.

The Shands had built half of Belgravia, the most fashionable residential area in London. Plain and unstylish, Camilla (sixteen months Charles's senior) shared the Prince's outdoor interests and earthy humor. "She was a regular tomboy," recalled Broderick Munro-Wilson, a lifelong friend, "always full of beans, laughing and happy and great fun. She always had something to say and was so bright and bubbly." Kevin Burke (a boyfriend when she was eighteen) described her similarly, as "terrific fun . . . and sexy. She was always mentioning Alice Keppel. It was constantly on her mind." The Charles-Camilla romance, according to the Prince's authorized biographer, began in the autumn of 1972: "he lost his heart to her almost at once . . . [and] it seemed to him that these feelings were reciprocated."

Among friends, Charles and Camilla loved to share a number of jokes about her ancestor Alice Keppel, the decorous and discreet mistress of Victoria's heir when he was both Prince of Wales and King Edward VII. They also shared a preference for sport and the outdoor life, and Camilla was even allowed to help arrange Charles's personal matters, advising him on organizing his staff, his wardrobe and his social calendar. Devoted but not possessive, she was very much as Freda Dudley Ward had been for the earlier Prince of Wales. When Camilla married a career officer in the Queen's Household Cavalry, Andrew Parker Bowles (who had once courted Princess Anne) and subsequently had two children, her relationship with Charles was briefly interrupted, but it was resumed later with even greater passion—especially after his surrogate father, Lord Louis Mountbatten, was killed by an IRA bomb in August 1979. That they were lovers was openly admitted by Charles in 1994. He was always so happy in Camilla's company that he went so far as to embarrass his family. Speaking to some schoolboys in 1978, he remarked, "I hope you infants are enjoying your infancy as much as we adults are enjoying our adultery." He was not yet married, but Camilla had been for five years.

Charles's doubts about marrying may have derived, at least in part, from seeing how his parents' union had altered. He had no other context in which to learn how relationships change with time. By 1978, after more than forty years of marriage, a separation existed between Elizabeth and Philip—not rancorous or apparently resentful, but real nonetheless. They did not share the same bedroom, as the investigation surrounding several palace break-ins and the subsequent resecuring of the royal suites revealed. And they quarreled, sometimes loudly. "Voices are raised, acid drops," servants whispered as Elizabeth and Philip glided to their separate rooms after an evening conversation in a drawing room.

Yet it is possible to exaggerate the accommodation the Queen and her husband made in their marriage, and Foreign Secretary Tony Crosland, for one, recalled just how much like a typical couple they could be. During an international crossing in 1976, the royal yacht *Britannia* suffered rough seas after leaving Bermuda. A Force 9 gale was announced; the ship pitched at a forty-five-degree angle, then lurched over a crest and rested once more with its deck pitched at an opposing forty-five degrees. The Queen, however, went to the pre-dinner cocktail hour "looking philosophical, almost merry," as Crosland recalled. "Half a pace behind was her Consort, his face less fresh than usual, ashen and drawn, in fact." When the Queen departed the dining room after dinner, the ship was still rolling badly, and as she gripped a sliding door she slid with it. "Wheeeeeeee!" cried the Queen as the *Britannia* shuddered and her chiffon scarf blew around her head. "Wheeeeeee!" squealed Her Majesty again, like a child on a thrilling ride.

Next day the sea was calmer. As the travelers gathered before luncheon, the Queen spoke of the previous evening: "I have *never* seen so many gray and grim faces round a dinner table." She paused and grinned. "Philip was not at all well." Another pause, and then she added, "I'm glad to say." She laughed quietly, for her husband is, of course, an Admiral of the Fleet.

For all the shifts in their marriage, the Queen continues to rely on Philip as one who provides an unbiased and frank opinion on just about everything. "After all, we're getting on to middle age," he said on television. "Maybe when we're ancient, there'll be a little more reverence, but now is the least interesting period." He pries, asks questions of others, stirs up awkward issues, scolds here and rebukes there—and because he has a natural curiosity and unparalleled access to others, he can express his opinions to Elizabeth without pretense or self-interest.

Charles was thirty-one in 1979 and still single, and like the previous Prince of Wales, he was causing his parents considerable anxiety. His adolescence had been prolonged, his emotional and sexual awakening delayed. As he neared thirty, there was little for him to do except make painfully awkward stabs at the occasional serious social commentary and, more often, accept the blandishments of adoring young women—and in these endeavors he resembled his great-great-grandfather Edward VII. There had been girlfriends aplenty, but he had been serious about none of them except for fiery Anna Wallace, who pleased the Queen only when she withdrew herself from Charles's consideration as a possible mate—not only by her insistence on maintaining a large social circle that included other boyfriends but also because she openly complained of being second in Charles's schedule to his royal duties.

To no one's surprise, then, the Prince sometimes chafed under the system that dominated his life: "You can't understand what it is like to have your whole life mapped out for you a year in advance," he complained. "It's so awful to be programmed. At times I get fed up with the whole idea." But such sensible observations brought him little good, for he could no more escape his destiny than his ancestry. And so as young ladies bored him or he felt depressed by his essentially empty life, Charles became more introspective. After the death of Mountbatten in 1979, there was no one in whom he felt he could confide. He respected his mother, but she had always been the remote, preoccupied Sovereign. His grandmother had been emotionally sustaining in his childhood, but she was now eighty and hardly the best listener for a young man. As for Philip, "the last person Charles would have gone to for advice would have been his father," as one courtier said.

Longing for some kind of occupation, Charles began in 1980 to plan the refurbishing of Highgrove House, the 350-acre Gloucestershire estate purchased for him by the Duchy of Cornwall. Although he had settled on this site to be near Camilla Parker Bowles, Highgrove was to be the place where he would bring his wife; there he would paint, read, welcome visiting scholars and scientists, supervise the gardens and plan an organic farm. But by 1980 the matter of Charles's spouse was no longer an occasional topic of concern at Buckingham Palace: however robust the Queen's health, the Prince's choice was now a dynastic obsession, although he himself was quite happy with bachelorhood, as his valet and friends knew. "You'd better get on with it, Charles," his father said, "or there won't be anyone left."

After World War I, King George V had broadened the list of those who could marry his children by openly encouraging them to consider non-Royals: suitable aristocratic Ladies would do just fine. Now, even that category was thinning, and Elizabeth and Philip found it difficult to arrange meetings with upper-class young ladies of unblemished reputations, acceptable bloodlines and the stamina for both the public eye and royal duties. "The one advantage to marrying a Princess or somebody from a royal family," Charles had said a few years earlier, "is that they do know what happens." But precisely because they *did* know what happens, and because the European royal families were increasingly less royal and more contemporary, that pool was exhausted. To further limit the contestants, Roman Catholics were still unsuitable according to the terms of the Royal Marriages Act.

Amid the flurry of friendships, affairs and romances, one candidate emerged, certainly an unlikely one at first. At a shooting party in November 1977, Charles was introduced to Lady Sarah Spencer's younger sister Lady Diana, whom he had seen now and again since her childhood on the estate of her father, Edward John Spencer. He was the eighth Earl of that name, which was also the name of the family land in Northamptonshire.* Johnnie Spencer had been an equerry to King George VI and then to Queen Elizabeth, a post he resigned in 1954 to marry Frances Roche, daughter of Baron and Lady Fermoy.† In 1956 Lady Ruth Fermoy, a longtime friend of the Queen Mother, became her principal lady-in-waiting, a post she held until her death in 1993.

The Spencers had three daughters: Lady Sarah, once a favorite of Charles; Lady Jane, later the wife of the Queen's private secretary, Robert Fellowes; and Lady Diana. The girls were raised at Park House on the Sandringham estate, where the Spencer marriage, racked by infidelities on both sides, was dissolved in 1969. Both parents were subsequently remarried (Earl Spencer to Raine, Countess of Dartmouth, the daughter of the romantic novelist Barbara Cartland). Young Lady Diana, desolated by the divorce, never again enjoyed the security she felt her mother had taken with her when she left. Her demeanor was rarely carefree or spontaneous, and there was always a hint of sadness to her shyness. This aspect of her temperament led her two older sisters, her younger brother (Charles, born in 1964), and her father—but not her stepmother—to dote on her, which is often the reaction to a certain type of wistful melancholy manifested by pretty, privileged girls.

Diana grew up as the prototypical shy English rose, learning the value of timid reserve not through calculation but experience. "In a way, she was a sad little kid," according to a Norfolk neighbor. "Not morose, but lost and certainly deprived [emotionally]. What Diana lacked and so deeply missed was a real family life. She may have been the daughter of an heir to an earldom, but any little girl with an ordinary mother, father and, if you like, a back-street home in the East End of London

---

* By another odd coincidence, Earl Spencer had also been the actual name of Wallis Simpson's first husband.

† This was the same Lady Fermoy who had been in labor with her daughter Frances when Queen Mary inquired as her husband lay dying in January 1936.

was richer by far.'' In childhood she never went to the theater or even to a zoo or a circus; her life lacked as much constancy and love as it did education.

Nevertheless, Diana was, according to her nanny Mary Clarke, "every bit an actress, astute, devious, nonetheless sympathetic, genuine and sensitive." So much was evident when she attended a boarding school in Kent and a finishing school in Switzerland, though Diana was no academic star. "She was not very sure of herself," reported a classmate. "I remember once, one of us complimented her on a cashmere suit she was wearing and she blushed and said, 'Mummy buys them for me.' God, at that age, we hated anything Mummy suggested!''

But she was a Spencer, quick to recognize a social advantage, and was much taken with the Prince of Wales that brisk November afternoon in 1977. He was thirteen years her senior, slim, with an appearance that conveyed both a slight arrogance and a certain maladroit discomfiture at being the Prince of Wales. Nervous, she giggled; demure, she blushed when he gazed at her. "I remember thinking what a very jolly, amusing and attractive sixteen-year-old she was, bouncy and full of life," Charles said later. Told this years after, Diana had a keen observation: "I suppose it makes a nice little segment of history, but I think he barely noticed me at all."

In a sense the timing was perfect: he had just fought with Anna Wallace and very much needed to console himself with an adoring girl. Two women standing nearby—Queen Elizabeth the Queen Mother and her confidante Ruth Fermoy—began to believe that one day shy Diana might be suitable as a wife for Charles. (Shortly before her death in 1993, Lady Fermoy admitted that she considered the match ill-advised but kept silent at the time.)

Diana, it seemed, would take up the family ambitions where Lady Sarah had left off and would carry to their ultimate fulfillment the dreams of Sarah and Diana's ancestor, the formidable Duchess of Marlborough who two centuries ago had hoped to ally the Spencers with the Hanoverian heir to the throne by marrying that earlier Lady Diana Spencer to the Prince of Wales. And so from the hopes of the Queen Mother and her friend came a carefully orchestrated plan of matchmaking, not least because in 1977 and 1978, Louis Mountbatten, still working on his plan to deepen his family's links with the Sovereign, was pushing his granddaughter Amanda Knatchbull toward Charles. The Queen Mother would have none of that.

"In many ways it was an arranged marriage," was the comment of none other than Harold Brooks-Baker, managing director and editor of *Burke's Peerage.* "Prince Charles needed a lovely wife, and Lady Diana fitted the bill. Diana was an infatuated nineteen-year-old only too eager to marry him. It *was* an arranged marriage." She was in love with him, it seems, and perhaps also with something that might be called her destiny; he, however, was in love with another woman and was entirely unclear about where or when his destiny would be manifest.

For one thing, Diana's pedigree was remarkably impressive, for she was descended from Henry VII and James I. She could also boast among her ancestors four fertile mistresses to Charles II and James II. Another Lady Sarah Spencer had been governess to Queen Victoria's children. George Washington, John Quincy Adams, Grover Cleveland and Franklin D. Roosevelt were distant cousins, as was Winston S. (for Spencer) Churchill, and lighter branches of the family held the names of Humphrey Bogart and Lillian Gish. The recent generation of Spencers, continued Brooks-Baker in *Burke's Peerage,* claimed "nobody of any great importance, but they are nice people who live in beautiful houses and have the good fortune to be related to almost every member of the aristocracy."

It did not hurt Diana's prospects that her paternal grandparents were good friends of Queen Mary. Furthermore, the Queen Mother might have seen remarkable similarities between her younger self and Lady Diana. Both were daughters of old aristocratic families. Johnnie Spencer's service to King George VI made for a sentimental association. And Lady Fermoy's friendship made her granddaughter instantly all the more attractive.

At sixteen, Diana could hardly be pushed at Prince Charles. Her grandmother and the Queen Mother counseled patience, and finally in August 1980 an invitation was arranged for Her Ladyship—by now blond, nineteen and five feet seven inches —onto the *Britannia* for a party that included other young royals. She had, recalled Stephen Barry, a "charming artlessness"—that is, she appealed by not seeming to have much conscious appeal. "But her eyes followed him everywhere." With such concentration it was perhaps inevitable that she finally succeeded in having him notice her. "If I am lucky enough to be the Princess of Wales . . ." she said to the wife of Mountbatten's grandson, her voice trailing off in a romantic reverie worthy of her stepgrandmother's heroines.

Whatever impression Diana made, it was enough to gain her another invitation—to Balmoral for a house party in September. And wherever the eligible bachelor and his new fair Lady went, the press was sure to go. Meanwhile, the Queen, encouraged by her mother, began to see Diana as the perfect Consort—young, with a shyness thought to indicate submissiveness and a girl with no scandalous past. Her inexperience would be her greatest asset, it was reasoned; with no life to be refashioned, she could more successfully be molded into a royal person, the eventual Queen Consort and the mother of yet another King. In this regard she seemed a better-than-average counteroffer to the advancement of the candidacy of Louis Mountbatten's granddaughter.

At the same time the very evident differences between Charles and Diana were blithely ignored. Like his mother, Charles prefers riding to any other sport; Diana is bored by things equestrian. He has neither familiarity with nor interest in fashionable restaurants (much less nightclubs); she finds them exciting. Charles, a country lad at heart, finds fishing soothing; she is a city mouse bored by streams and heather. Diana prefers pop and rock, Charles cello concerti. More seriously, they harbored different expectations concerning love, marriage and family, and regarding public duty there was an abyss between them. She was a member of what has been called the "Me Generation"; he was raised as part of an exclusive "We," the Family Firm that extracted lifelong promises of fidelity to the prestige of the throne.

Conversely, what they shared—a frightening if innocent indolence—denied them both opportunities for emotional growth and a larger view of the world. The Queen was repeating Victoria's worst blunder, for like his ancestor Edward VII, there was for the Prince of Wales no effective role; he was being prepared for eventual kingship in only the most peripheral and shallow ways. And Lady Diana, without a university degree, was a guardian of nursery schoolchildren with no other prospects and no serious interests.

Courtiers, informed by the girl's uncle, then made the astonishing announcement to the Queen that the girl had no romantic past at all—that is, she was a virgin. But quite to the contrary, several of Diana's friends believed that she was not, at eighteen, as she had been born. For almost a year, until autumn 1980, she was known as the constant companion of James Boughey, a handsome army lieutenant who was—thus one knowledgeable reporter—"not known for pursuing platonic relationships." There was also a history of dates with George Plumptre, eight years her senior, the cultured son of a peer; and with Daniel Wiggin, a friend of her brother.

How serious these relationships were cannot be determined, for once Diana Spencer became Princess of Wales the usual curtain of respectable silence was drawn around by those who knew her; to do otherwise was to risk lifelong social ostracism within the serried ranks of the minor aristocracy. All that can be claimed is that during her three years on her own, from sixteen to nineteen, she knew considerable freedom, motoring with friends to weekend house parties, camping out, dating. During this time she lost much of her shyness. But it must also be said that nothing about this time of her life could prompt a biographer to present her as a very interesting young lady.

By New Year's Day 1981, Her Majesty found Charles's hesitations mysterious. If he so enjoyed entertaining her, why not solemnize the friendship? For the sake of the throne, confirmed bachelorhood was unthinkable for him, and since many of his girlfriends were, for one reason or another, unacceptable, why not choose Lady Diana? As Elizabeth, with Philip's support, told Charles, "The idea of this going on for another year is intolerable for everyone concerned." Just why "intolerable" remains unclear, but in the back of everyone's mind were the rumors that Charles's insistent refusal to marry and his intimacies only with married women meant that in the final analysis he found commitment to any woman an unsavory prospect. Finally, his father gave him what amounted to an ultimatum. Continued visits with Diana would compromise her reputation and the image of the Royal Family; he must make a decision.

There were other reasons for royal alarm, for the specter of Edward VIII began slowly to take shape, and in fact the two

Princes of Wales had much in common. Both were among the world's most eligible bachelors; both were emotionally distant from their mothers the Queens; both were attracted to married women who could provide them with the maternal consolation they were denied; both pushed themselves physically to the edge of risk in flying airplanes and on the polo field. Men very much alone and under the relentless spotlight of fame, they could only envision fulfillment on the death of a parent. Edward and Charles both had something of the indecisive, confused, ungrownup boy.

These similarities were apparent to Charles's grandmother, who had a dedication to the Windsor legacy that outbid even that of Queen Mary for sheer, direct control. With the amiable collusion of Lady Fermoy, the Queen Mother swung into action, inviting Diana the following month to her home, adjacent to Balmoral. It may never be known exactly what plans were discussed, but according to Charles's valet, Diana was invited a few days later to the newly purchased Highgrove. Three times that autumn of 1980, Diana was driven to Gloucestershire for a visit and dinner with Charles—eggs, salad and vegetables, the valet remembered, for the Prince was again on a vegetarian binge. And several times they were joined by Camilla Parker Bowles, who the Prince wished to assess the prospective Princess.

Charles and Diana were people of their age, and the idea that they went to the altar ignorant of intimacy with each other is perhaps the single most pathetic of Puritan aspects to this concocted fairy tale. In November 1980 they spent two nights in the same compartment aboard the royal train in western England. When berated for fabricating a slander, Robert Edwards (editor of the *Sunday Mirror*) simply smiled and said, "We take great care to get our facts right." He would not, of course, reveal his sources.

And so the Prince of Wales came to see that since he had to marry, the choice might as well fall on Diana Spencer. She seemed innocent, pliable, nicely subservient, not given to bursts of self-assertion (like Anna Wallace); and she was young, sturdy, and from good stock—thus she would deliver healthy offspring for the Windsor future. Equally to the point, the palace press office had provided journalists with just what they wanted: accounts of a modern young woman who loved children, dressed modishly, cooked pasta for her flatmates, and, even though she was an aristocrat, had enough of an unhappy background to give the story a vague Cinderella quality, although in this case Cinderella was scarcely a banished, besmudged scullery maid. Diana's stepgrandmother, Barbara Cartland, that redoubtable queen of purple prose and pink wardrobes, called her "a perfect Barbara Cartland heroine."

While they were courting, Charles naturally called her Diana; perhaps not quite so naturally, she addressed him as "Sir" and was not instructed to do otherwise. She did have some sartorial influence, however, for Charles accepted her suggestion that casual slip-on shoes, which he had never worn, were very stylish. "She was always buying him little presents," said Stephen Barry. "Shirts and ties were favorites, and I must admit she spruced up his wardrobe." Invariably, after dinner Diana was driven back to the flat she shared with friends. Her job was supervising preschoolers at the Young England kindergarten in Pimlico.

In early 1981, Diana visited Australia with her mother. On February 24, Buckingham Palace announced the engagement of the Prince of Wales to Lady Diana Spencer, and a platoon of the press trampled across the greenswards of the palace gardens to photograph the couple arm in arm, her finger sparkling with a sapphire and diamond ring that cost £28,500 (over $50,000).

Were they in love? asked one reporter.

"Of course!" said Diana, smiling.

"Whatever 'in love' means," countered Charles. Perhaps great romances do not begin with such restraint.

And this was, indeed, nothing like a great romance. "I expect it will be the right thing in the end," Charles confided to a friend at the time. "I do very much want to do the right thing for this country and for my family, but I'm terrified sometimes of making a promise and then perhaps living to regret it." He may well have been thinking of Camilla, still his great love. "I asked Charles if he was still in love with Camilla Parker Bowles," said Francis Cornish, the Prince's assistant private secretary at the time, "and he didn't give me a clear answer."

The questions continued, the cameras clicked mercilessly, and so it went every day thereafter. Diana, beleaguered by the press, tried to leave her flat in Earls Court and drive to Pimlico. "I love working with children," she said on the run one morning, "and I have learned to be very patient with them." And then she smiled: "I simply treat the press as though they were children, too." Had Princess Margaret spoken this way, she would have been reproached by the evening edition, but Diana's riposte made her sound charming, quick-witted, a girl of today. But she was not always so. One day a dozen press cars pursued hers, and when she finally arrived at a friend's house in Mayfair, she broke down in tears on the shoulder of a girlfriend, weeping in Berkeley Square until one less rapacious reporter put a note on the seat of her car: "We didn't mean this to happen. Our full apologies." But the contrition was not backed up by contrary behavior.

"Well, she's going to have to learn to get used to this sort of thing," said the Queen with a sigh as she saw her future daughter-in-law on the television news, surrounded by a crush of photographers as if she were a carcass at the mercy of marauding rooks. It was perhaps surprising to none of Diana's friends that precisely at this time she exhibited the behavior of a bulimic—overeating, then purging herself with laxatives and self-induced vomiting. Longing to shed what she saw as the last ounces of baby fat, Diana became obsessed with thinness. This was certainly not discouraged by dining with Charles, for she saw him eating very little, too: lots of fruits and vegetables, very little protein, no sweets and almost no alcohol. And in the sad conundrum of the time, it was thought that if a man was so abstemious, ought not a woman to be more so?

But to the public Diana was already becoming a kind of compensating personality, the bearer of a youthfulness and color—and, it was presumed, an imminent splendor—that the people's lives lacked. Even now she was expected to supply the missing element of romance, a happy ending to reverse the story of Princess Margaret and Peter Townsend in 1955. Twenty-five years had passed since then. During that time—especially with the production of the *Royal Family* film of 1969—the palace had sought to control the media. But the media were no longer controllable; they were no longer the province of loyal old press barons. Earlier, the British press had been subject to the restrictions of protocol while the press of other nations had not. Now, when this condition was finally lifted, the London media, particularly, went far and quickly, as if to compensate for years of forced deference.

On February 25 the press documented Diana's move from her flat in Colherne Court to Clarence House, and two days later to Buckingham Palace, where a footman and maid were assigned to her and she began a course of instruction under the tutelage of the Queen Mother and a small platoon of courtiers. Diana learned the history of the Windsors, with emphasis on the lives of previous Princesses of Wales; she noted the proper forms of address for various members of the Royal Family; the correct greetings for foreign heads of state; the procedures for state banquets; the unofficial list of topics best avoided in conversation. For the first few days, at least, it was as if Cinderella was in the care of benevolent surrogate parents who had only to raise a hand or ring a bell and every wish was granted. Diana learned quickly. She also took on responsibilities at Highgrove, engaging a designer and poring over paint swatches and upholstery fabrics.

She showed much less interest, however, in learning the family history, and that spring there was a grave omen. Oliver Everett, Charles's assistant private secretary, was asked to act as unofficial tutor, and he casually suggested she read James Pope-Hennessy's monumental and compelling biography of Queen Mary. Diana accepted the book and thanked Everett, but when he departed, she tossed the book aside: "If he thinks I am going to read that boring old stuff, he has another think coming!"

Meantime, Charles was on an official visit to Australia and New Zealand, whence he telephoned Diana frequently. At least one of the calls was monitored, perhaps by British Intelligence.

> *Diana:* "Won't it be nice when we can go out together again?"
>
> *Charles:* "Perhaps we won't know what to talk about."
>
> *Diana:* "Well, you can start by telling me about all those blondes who chase you, and I can laugh because you belong to me."
>
> *Charles:* "Yes. . . . I'm glad to be out of New Zealand. Now I know everything I need to know about the paper industry in New Zealand. But I ask myself all the time about what you were up to."

Diana: "I really miss you, darling. I'm not really alone, but it bothers me that thousands of people can be with you and I can't. I'm really jealous."

Charles: "Yes, I know. It's too bad, but in a couple of years you might be glad to get rid of me for a while."

Diana: "Never."

Charles: "I'll remind you of that in ten years' time."

The Queen and the
Duke of Edinburgh.

14

Breaking into the Palace

1981 to 1994

A bloody awful mistake!
PRINCE CHARLES, on his marriage

From their engagement and marriage in 1981 to the birth of their two sons in 1982 and 1984 to their formal separation in 1992, the saga of Charles and Diana has been chronicled in meticulous, often fanciful detail in an endless orgy of newspaper and magazine articles. In addition, there have appeared more than a dozen books eager to supply a famished readership with scandalous and scurrilous morsels often gleaned from questionable sources or contrived from fervent imaginations. "What do we want?" asked the editor of the *Sunday Mirror* on page one of the issue dated October 26, 1986: "The monarchy or soap opera?" His readers were getting both.

To survey this mountainous mass of words is to have the impression that Queen Elizabeth II's family must be terrifically interesting people of remarkable wit, style and intelligence— and even of social and cultural significance. But this is not so. The plain truth is that in a depressed British society, dependent on American television shows such as "Dynasty" for its concept of melodramatic glamour, the Prince and Princess of Wales and later the Duke and Duchess of York were made to stand in and to supply the missing native ingredients. Even Prince Philip acknowledged the popular source: "What you want is a 'Dynasty' production where everybody can see what we do privately. People want to know about the splashy things or the scandalous things. They're not really interested in anything else." But the sad and ironic truth was that, considering most of the Windsors, there was little else to report. This dynasty acted mostly like a substitute cast of that very series.

No country can rival Britain in its sense of public liturgy and of stage-managed ceremony, and so the Waleses and the Yorks—invested with titles, married in splendor, lionized everywhere—became four of the world's celebrities. They are not bright or talented, they have no special claim to anything but their rank and position, a certain photogenic appeal and mannered charm, and so they were primed for fame. Their quarter-hour in the sun has been marvelously lengthened, mostly because the Royal Family is de facto news and also because it is presumed that Prince Charles may one day be King.

When Charles married Diana at St. Paul's Cathedral on July 29, 1981, it was said that 750 million people worldwide watched the ceremony on television. "A princely marriage is the brilliant edition of a universal fact," wrote Bagehot in 1867, "and as such it rivets mankind." The brightness of the cathedral (specially illuminated by gigantic lights for the sake of television cameras), the cheers of millions thronging the streets of London, the great procession of carriages, the uniforms and stately music, the bride with her *very* long train—it was the fulfillment of the British Tourist Authority's ultimate fantasy. Meanwhile, hundreds of young people were rioting in Liverpool, complaining that the festivities in London occurred against the backdrop of record unemployment (twelve percent of the working population, the worst figure since the Great Depression).

But the press ignored the unpleasantness, for there had been nothing like the royal wedding since the Queen's coronation. The marriages of Margaret and Anne had been duly broadcast, but these Ladies were known commodities. Diana's appeal lay precisely in the fact that at twenty she had very little personality at all. On her, therefore, every imaginable dream, wish and wonder of every observer could be superimposed. Commentators spoke breathlessly about a fairy-tale wedding and the transcendent romance of the new Prince and Princess of Wales, but of course the reality was something very different. For one thing, Charles at thirty-two had been quite content as a bachelor and was forced, with considerable diffidence, into fulfilling his destiny by marriage—in order to provide the Windsors with a guarantee of progeny. And in an ironic twist no one could have anticipated, the extraordinary public adulation offered to his wife made it seem as if Charles's life had reached its fullness, and his career its culmination, in marriage. His young, glamorous bride quickly shone in the center spotlight.

Right up through the separation of Charles and Diana in 1992 and the establishment of their separate lives thereafter, an unprecedented kind of celebrity mania about the Princess of Wales gripped Britain, and it did not take long for America to emulate the behavior. The slightest indications of her feelings were noted, amplified and discussed: laughter, frowns, hesitation, boredom—each glance and manner was plumbed for profundities and interpreted for family ramifications. Traveling the world, Diana was held in the awe once reserved for wandering medieval mystics. Nothing she did was unimportant. Every word was revered, every touch considered sacred. She became the goddess Diana, worshiped and adored. "I would never have believed that the Princess of Wales changing her hair could be front-page news," said her hairstylist, Richard Dalton. "There are so many more important things going on in the world. But whatever she does is always major news."

And so the press went mad for the tiniest details, staking out Diana's favorite restaurants, the homes of her friends and the approaches to her home with long lenses and hypersensitive microphones. The charming, famous Princess, at the same time, had only one reason for being: she was for looking at, for idolizing. Her icon graced every magazine at some time, several of them many times. But until she read a few speeches on behalf of various causes in 1993, few heard her voice, which was tentative, without inflection or warmth. Even after a coach was engaged to assist with her diction, speech rhythms and breath control, Diana made little impression as a public speaker. But she did not have to—she was venerated simply for appearing anywhere. Never mind that privately she had a fund of risqué and even obscene jokes. "She never blushed at my dirty jokes," added Richard Dalton, "but I did at a few of hers!"

Charles was dismayed and disappointed at this wild adulation of his wife; after all, he and his camp reasoned, she would be an unknown nursery-school teacher had he not married her. She showed no special aptitudes, did not even capture something important of her time. When they visited Australia, the Prince was asked why she did not appear at one function. "I'm sorry," Charles said with a rueful, bittersweet half-smile, "you'll just have to put up with me. It's not fair, is it? You'd better ask for your money back." He could not understand the reason for the frenzy, as if her mind and soul were beacons of hope for the world.

"With due respect to Charles," said Bob Hawke, the Australian Prime Minister, "she's a somewhat more attractive personality. She was young, new, vibrant and different. And I could sense at times that that created some sort of tension between them, but there was nothing she could do to help that." Perhaps looking to find flaws in the adored woman accompanying him, Charles complained that he found her lack of sophistication stupefying. When he asked her if in childhood she had enjoyed Kipling's *Just So Stories,* she replied, "Just so *what,* Charles?" She was not joking.

"A bloody awful mistake."

Such was Charles's own description of his marriage to Lady Diana Spencer. The mistake, according to his authorized biographer, was evident as early as the honeymoon cruise aboard the *Britannia* when (it is claimed) the bride's blushing charm turned to erratic melancholia. She was convinced that, far from having broken his liaison with Camilla Parker Bowles, Charles was still committed to it and to her. And by the time they reached Balmoral on the final stretch of the honeymoon, Diana found two love letters from Camilla, documents "so intimate they revealed a long-term commitment between the two," according to one of the Prince's staff. "Diana knew from the tone of the letters that Charles fully intended to continue his relationship with Camilla."

"He was frustrated as hell," said a friend of the Royal Family about the marriage, "and he was beginning to suspect that the court believed in the marriage only to the extent that it served the purpose of the monarchy. Looking back, he was absolutely right, of course."

Her anxiety manifested itself in continuing bouts of anorexia and bulimia; she either unreasonably denied herself meals or manically indulged her appetite. She was also unable to relax when dining with her in-laws, when she only picked nervously at her food and pushed it round the plate. After such occasions, servants later found her in the kitchen, rummaging for tidbits. "I don't know how she'll cope with a state banquet if she can't even cope with a family dinner," the Queen told Charles when he was at Balmoral with his wife later that summer of 1981.

Yet Diana soon shone at state banquets. Tall and slender, she delighted in wearing the most alluring and dramatic evening gowns as well as the prettiest daytime frocks. The Queen and Princess Anne always seemed to look a little ridiculous with their old-fashioned handbags and slightly dowdy hats, while Diana carried sexy little clutch bags and wore colorful, stylish chapeaux. She also photographed more brilliantly than any Windsor, her blue eyes sparkling, her smile radiant. By 1994 she was widely reckoned to be the most photographed woman in history.

Yet she felt she had no proper role in the Royal Family— especially when there were obvious efforts to improve Charles's image at her own expense, as with the authorized biography published in 1994. This was a clear counterstatement to one sympathetic to her, with which she had silently cooperated two years earlier. Unable to find a worthy niche, Diana took refuge in shopping, lunches with friends, visits to designers and couturiers and engagements with ballet dancers, movie stars and rock musicians.

The ultimate failure of the fairy-tale union could have been expressed in the identical words used by Princess Marie Louise, Queen Victoria's granddaughter, who admitted that the collapse of her marriage to Prince Aribert of Anhalt "was not entirely my husband's [fault]. I was impetuous and, I fear, intolerant of the restrictions imposed on me by what I considered the narrow-minded outlook of those with whom I had to live." Royalty is not traditionally known for considering the personal or social needs of inferiors—even of those who marry into the clan.

Yet Diana's value to the Windsors was always evident—perhaps most immediately to the Queen herself. Since her Silver Jubilee in 1977, Elizabeth had been keenly aware of her personal popularity and of the strength the monarchy derived from the public presentation of her family. Energetic and morally irreproachable, she was a focus of national self-admiration. The Queen was as England liked to believe itself. For the moment, so was Diana, particularly in what seemed to be her naturalness and her philanthropy. After she was widely photographed in that most ordinary of activities—shopping—one newspaper editor, invited with several colleagues to a palace conference, bluntly asked the Queen why the Princess did not send servants for such tasks. There was an appalling silence before the Queen's reply evoked laughter from everyone: "What an extremely pompous man you are!" As for Diana's visits to the sick and her alliance with those suffering, they surpassed the Changing of the Guard as an image of Britain beamed round the world.

In her charm and with her empathetic nature, it seemed as if Diana was very like an earlier Princess of Wales, the lovely Alexandra of Denmark. Beautiful, much concerned for her own appearance, intellectually limited, a long-suffering wife devoted to children's charities and, eventually, to her own offspring—the comparisons were not hard to find. But with Diana there was a distinctly contemporary phenomenon, for the public became addicted to her image, her latest local visit, her evenings at gala events or with friends in Kensington. She was an indispensable celebrity, famous for being famous, loved for her title, her looks and her ordinary human empathies—much loved precisely because these qualities seemed in such short supply among the Royal Family.

More to the point, Diana was to Charles as Alix was to Edward—a source of personal disappointment; hence the diversions elsewhere. Patient with children, gentle with adults, kindly but unimaginative, Diana (again, like Alexandra) did not supply the kind of stimulating companionship the Prince of Wales required and which he continued to find with his mistress, Camilla Parker Bowles. When Charles complimented a European hostess on her flawless English, she said, "My father believed in educating the girls," to which he replied, "I wish that had been the philosophy in my wife's family." By 1984, Charles was weary of his wife's social events, and she found him tediously old-fashioned. "I've never been so bored in all my life," she snapped, leaving a supper where her husband was entertaining some polo-playing buddies. And in one critical way, Diana was unlike Alix: the former Princess of Wales and Queen bore her husband's infidelities in silence.

A child of the materialistic 1980s, Diana bought and spent on the grandest scale: from 1981 to 1991, she spent £833,750 on her wardrobe (more than $1.8 million), which goes far toward explaining the attention lavished on her by photographers, fashion designers and the media. But what they celebrated was not accomplished by the Princess on her own. Her sister, Jane Fellowes (wife of the Queen's private secretary), had worked at *Vogue,* and she turned Diana over to its editor, Beatrix Miller, and her staff at the magazine's Hanover Square offices. There, designs and patterns from designers all over the world were gathered, and enormous ensembles were created for her—including cosmetics, colognes and hairstyles. By 1990 she had amassed more than three thousand outfits, a fifty-yard length of ball gowns, six hundred pairs of shoes and four hundred hats. Charles was speechless at such prodigality: he owned two or three dozen suits and several standard uniforms and took little interest in what his valet laid out for him each day.

Nor did parenthood blur the differences in the Waleses' perspectives, for Charles saw no reason why nannies would

not provide his two sons with what they had provided him and
his siblings. But in this regard Diana again resembled Queen
Alexandra (but not Queen Mary). Although there was a full-
time staff to assist her, Diana took a page from Alix's habits,
spending long hours with her babies, bathing and reading to
them. By 1991 the Princes William and Henry were nine and
seven and had passed from nursery to elementary school in
Kensington; boarding at the Ludgrove school followed. But for
all her somewhat dizzy and distracting social life, their mother
was in constant contact with them—too much so, thought their
father.

Windsor family gatherings left Diana cold—sometimes literally. Diana found Sandringham, for example, like a second-
rate hotel, damp, badly heated and inhospitable. Balmoral was
merely the scene of tediously chummy family picnics: ''Boring, raining,'' was her summary of one autumn holiday there,
which evoked a typically pithy response from Princess Anne
(''Diana can be such a bore''), for the sisters-in-law had almost
nothing in common. Diana was at first amused, then irritated,
by the Queen's odd frugalities. She could not understand why
the monarch prowled through unoccupied rooms switching off
lights, or the old custom of ordering bed linens reversed to
save on laundry bills. More than once when someone remarked
that the rooms of Balmoral were chilly, Elizabeth quietly suggested, ''Put on another sweater!''

Such royal economies were passed along from mother to
son, the Princess of Wales soon learned. At Highgrove and in
their apartment at Kensington Palace, Charles ordered that food
never be wasted. Leftovers crammed the refrigerator, and the
Prince regularly asked servants how they might be used in later
meals. Ironically, spoiled remnants often tainted other foods,
resulting in more waste than if the surplus had first been tossed
out. More alarming to Diana, however, was her husband's habit
of inspecting the kitchens to see if his money was not vanishing
too quickly. From her limousine, the Queen was once shocked
to see the price of apples in a market stall, and she ordered a
ban on the fruit for several months. Similarly, Charles's vegetarian sprees were often inspired by an outburst over the cost
of chicken.

To no one's surprise, then, Diana swiftly seized any opportunity for diversion. When a favorite English fashion designer

escorted her to a charity dance while Charles was at a farmers' conference, she remained until four in the morning, dancing with several handsome guests. The Princess of Wales "positively lit up, suddenly aware of everything she was missing."

More formal dancing delighted her even more, and during the early 1980s the Princess of Wales became a good friend of the Royal Ballet dancer Wayne Sleep, whose home she visited, eager to discuss lessons. They sat in his South Kensington studio eating simple suppers he prepared and planning her debut at Covent Garden in a four-minute jazz-dance piece. For months, wearing leotard and leggings, Diana rehearsed with Sleep at Kensington Palace, dancing to the music of Billy Joel. "Secretly the Princess thinks she would have loved the life of a dancer," her instructor recalled. "She has a certain show-business flamboyance about her and she loves to surprise." But courtiers were, perhaps predictably, unamused by the shuffles and kicks of Her Royal Highness, and when she finally appeared onstage as part of a charity benefit, there was some discussion as to whether Diana was really shy at all: "It takes colossal nerve to dance onstage at Covent Garden," Wayne Sleep commented.

Eventually, high-spirited independence became the mark of this modern young Englishwoman, raised in privileged circumstances and now accustomed to curtsies, nods and breathless admiration. But in critical ways Diana was not a free woman at all, and so she could not understand why bodyguards prevented her from shopping alone or from driving on her own to lunch with friends. "She made life very difficult for those whose job it was to protect her," according to one of Charles's most trusted advisors. "She just seemed to refuse to understand that she was now the Princess of Wales and could not do what she wanted anymore."

The reason for the byzantine precautions and the elaborate circumspection was, of course, the demands of security in an era of terrorism and political violence. Still, Diana failed to see how her briefest private excursion should be so rigorously monitored, and although her husband tried to explain the matter to her—using as an example the (blank) shots fired by a young madman at the Queen weeks before their wedding—his wife whined and sulked at the restraints on her freedom. "Diana always gets her own way,'' said her father. ''I think Charles is learning that now.'' Indeed he was, being married to a woman he had not himself chosen; she had been selected for him, and he resented both that fact and her. For his mother's sake, for the good of the monarchy he would one day inherit, he wanted his marriage to work. But the layers of incompatibility were thickening.

More and more, from 1982 to 1992, the unreasonable celebrity attached to his wife ate away at Charles's security. Diana's purpose—although it was only to be the ultimate Princess— seemed to be confirmed daily; his reason for being, as an older man representing the Establishment, was not so apparent. She dashed hither and thither, looking ever more lovely and welcoming public displays of adoration just as she accepted the bouquets constantly thrust into her hands. He seemed frozen in time, his hands tucked nervously behind his back or in the pockets of his conservative double-breasted suits.

Yet he saw the terrible danger of constant media exposure —''a terrible baptism of fire'' for Diana, he called it. The press was insistent on creating a pedestal:

> They put you on top of it, they expect you to balance on the beastly thing without ever losing your footing, and because they have engineered the pedestal, along come the demolition experts amongst them who are of the breed that enjoy breaking things down. And it is all done for a sort of vicarious entertainment. . . . Maybe the wedding, because it was all so well done and because it made such a wonderful, almost Hollywood-style film, has distorted people's view of things. Whatever the case, it frightens me and I know for a fact that it petrifies Diana.

It also made His Royal Highness most unroyally jealous, as the Prince's biographer confirmed. His wife's glamour and fame ''sapped his confidence and made him long to escape.''

Very soon the two were alienated from the public and from each other. At home, Charles undertook ever more dangerous stunts on the polo field and in blithely jumping from helicopters. Very like his great-uncle King Edward VIII, he seemed to be flirting with mortality. ''I want to prove to myself that I can mentally accept things which are perhaps dangerous or which are perhaps slightly frightening,'' Charles said. "I want to prove that I can overcome fear, if I have any. . . . I'm constantly feeling I have to justify myself, my existence.'' Just as Diana could do no wrong, he could do no right. Like Queen Mary, Edward VIII and George VI, he loved everything to do with gardens, but while his forebears were admired for this typically English interest, Charles was mocked.

But when they were seen together, he all but vanished in Diana's long and powerful shadow; his presence faded in the resplendent light of her celebrity. He had been known to the world, his life had been followed for several decades, but she was the new, improved addition to the royal line. What husband, what *man* could withstand the effects of her comeliness? Why, the fact that she spoke but rarely, that it was her *image* that bedazzled made her all the more desirable, more otherworldly. By 1992 when she began to read hesitatingly from prepared speeches before small groups, her status was beatific. She was invulnerable to criticism, despite rumors of affairs with sympathetic men; when at last he revived his affair with Camilla Parker Bowles, all journalistic hell broke loose. With that, Charles came perilously close to a complete nervous breakdown, and with Mountbatten gone, there was no one in whom he could confide. "He'd never have gone to his father'' with his marital problems, one senior courtier said flatly; and his mother would not have known what to say.

Her family was in crisis, but Elizabeth II continued to do what she had done since 1952, visiting the realm and, by her simple presence, bringing hordes of people to the streets to greet her. With every detail of a royal arrival planned to the minute, her activities might well have seemed overrehearsed, but she could surprise people. Stopping in a Norfolk tea shop one summer afternoon, she was approached by a woman: "Excuse me, but you look *awfully* like the Queen!'' Her Majesty's reply was instantaneous and delivered with a broad smile: "How very reassuring!''

Not so amusing was her meeting with a man named Michael Fagan, a thirty-one-year-old unemployed laborer with a passionately high regard for his Sovereign. One morning in July 1982 he easily broke through the lackadaisical security surrounding Buckingham Palace. Wishing to chat with Her Maj-

445

esty about the plight of workers like himself, he found his way in through an unfastened window, strolled through the picture gallery and surveyed the throne room; one servant thought he was a workman. "I wasn't doing anything wrong," he said a decade later. "I was just going up to speak to the Queen. I passed the corgi food on the way, and I knew then I'd find the Queen soon."

He did, and he then proceeded right into the Queen's suite. "I opened the door, and there's a little bundle in the bed," Fagan recalled later.

> I thought, "This isn't the Queen, this is too small." I went to the curtains and lifted them. A shaft of light must have disturbed her. She sat up and looked at me. Her face was a mask of shock and incomprehension. "What are you doing here? Get out! Get out!" she said. Her cut-glass accent really startled me. I just looked at her and replied, "I think you are a really nice woman." She just repeated: "Get out! Get out!" and picked up a white telephone, said a few words, then hopped out of bed, ran across the room and out the door. I was surprised at how nimble she was. She ran like a girl. It was all over in thirty seconds. I really felt sad and disillusioned. It was a complete shock because the Queen wasn't what I had expected. I felt so badly let down. I just sat down on the bed crying my eyes out.

The Queen could not have known that Fagan was not a terrorist or an escaped ax murderer but a simple fellow who wanted to chat with his Sovereign about the state of the nation. "I suppose I picked the wrong place," he admitted, and then added wickedly, "Maybe I should have come at dinnertime?" Later, the Queen told the Reverend Michael Main, Dean of Windsor, "The thing I was really worried about was that Prince Philip was going to come in and all hell was going to break loose!"

Moments later a platoon of policemen leaped up the grand staircase to their monarch's aid. The first to reach her suite recalled seeing her, a robe hastily thrown around her night-gown, standing in an alcove. He automatically stopped to nod and straighten his tie. "Oh, come on," said Her Majesty impatiently, waving him toward Fagan, "get a bloody move on!"

To the embarrassment of palace security, it so happened that Fagan had visited once before, also without invitation. The previous month he had crept in, helped himself to a bottle of Riesling and drank it while sitting on the Queen's throne. He then quietly departed. "Security was so bad I wanted to show as an example that I could get in," he said. As for the wine: "I had done a hard day's work getting in [by climbing] up the drainpipes. I was very thirsty and I could not find a tap. The wine was in a cupboard." Quite rightly, no charges were filed and Fagan was dismissed by police. He had simply trespassed, without criminal intent—an act that is not a crime in England. Security officers at the palace did not escape the consequences of the deed so easily.

Philip, meantime, had no such importunate callers. He continued to escort the Queen on their journeys, vigilant for her safety and making the occasional ghastly remarks. "If you stay here much longer," he warned Scottish students in Beijing, "you will go home with slitty eyes." At a reception before one of his talks, he drank three champagne cocktails, which prompted the Queen to ask, "What kind of speech do you think you are going to make now?"

Comments like this put the press on world alert, and the worst interpretation was attached to his solo holidays—for example when he visited the tropical home of Alexandra Anastasia (always called Sasha), the Duchess of Abercorn, a tall blonde twenty-five years his junior. Her husband James was present, too, but editors conveniently airbrushed him out of photographs showing Philip with them at poolside, clad only in a towel, with his arm round Sasha.

London, of course, soon buzzed with stories of yet another scandal. The Duke of Abercorn, like the Queen, may indeed have been a complaisant spouse, but according to those who know them, the truth—horrors for the tabloids!—was that Sasha and Jim were Philip's *friends*. But the truth must not be permitted to interfere with provocative innuendo.

But for a good story—and a major reason for the devaluation of the monarchy's prestige—it was unnecessary to invent or exaggerate when the life of Prince Andrew was chronicled. "Like all the best families," said the Queen in 1991, "we have our share of eccentricities, of impetuous and wayward

447

youngsters and of family disagreements.'' She might have been thinking of her second son, who left school for a career as a navy pilot at nineteen. There were long furloughs, however, and after the Falklands conflict, he returned to London in the fall of 1982 to resume a life of indulgent indolence.

The press gleefully catalogued his intrigues with, among others, the soft-porn ''actress'' Koo Stark (with whom he dallied at Aunt Margaret's villa on the island of Mustique); the models Vicki Hodge (who was thirteen years his senior and eventually sold her story to the tabloids), Gemma Curry and Kim Deas; Carolyn Seaward, Miss United Kingdom 1980; and a Canadian named Sandi Jones, his hostess at the Montreal Olympics. ''We managed to give them the slip,'' said Miss Jones of Andrew's bodyguards. ''Andrew can be extremely resourceful. He's just an ordinary guy who wants to have a fun time with his girlfriends.'' And so he did.

These affairs, among others, won him the sobriquet ''Randy Andy.'' Not merely mischievous and high-spirited, Andrew's conduct could be downright crude and embarrassingly unroyal: among other pranks, he spray-painted cars, doused journalists with whitewash (''I really enjoyed that'') and pinched young ladies leaving church. When he wore a kilt, he told a reporter who did not ask, ''There's nothing worn under it''—and added with a wink, ''Everything underneath is in good working order.''

Once elegant and subdued, Andrew's suite at Buckingham Palace was decorated, at his bidding, into a wash of purple, orange and green, rather like the rooms of a pot-smoking hippie. The staff, as they had in his childhood, found him ''extremely difficult to deal with,'' for he bullied and even threatened those who waited on him, never mind his mother's injunctions to the contrary. According to Malcolm Barker, who worked at the palace for several years beginning in 1980, there was considerable family tension when Andrew appeared to be welcoming a different woman to his rooms almost every night of the week and when his dinner parties for navy buddies ended up with infantile food fights and the smashing of wineglasses.

But it was his sexual indiscretions that most worried the Queen. Ordinarily she preferred not to interfere in the romances of her children, but the Koo Stark affair (which began in 1981) was beyond the pale. When she learned of the girl's exploits in sex films, Elizabeth had to summon Andrew. "It is one thing for a prince to be seen with a film actress," said a palace spokesman, "but quite another to go away on holiday with a blue movie star. The Queen feels badly let down." So did Andrew when he was ordered to end the affair.

Nor was his mother much amused when the Prince took part in a rowdily sexy drag show in 1984. Satirizing the tradition of sailors' full-dress inspection, Andrew was photographed (appropriately, aboard HMS *Brazen*) surveying navy buddies in various degrees of undress and wearing the flimsiest bustiers, bras and panties. The incident betokened more than British music-hall humor, for it occurred just when there were persistent rumors of bisexual highjinks among Andrew and his friends. Such gossip was not allayed in 1984 when, with thirty shipmates (at least half of whom later admitted to being gay), he submitted his buttocks to a caning from girls costumed as "sexy waitresses" at something called "School Dinners"—a club that imitated Dickensian school dining halls and added a satirical but sadomasochistic twist.

Andrew's disturbing exuberances were to be tamed by settling down with a good wife; such was the expectation of Elizabeth and Philip for him, as it had been for Charles. Among the guests at Diana's twenty-first birthday party in 1982 was an extroverted, fiery, twenty-two-year-old redhead whose social circle had occasionally intersected hers, and with whom Diana had developed a casual friendship. Her name was Sarah Margaret Ferguson, and she was the daughter of Major Ronald Ferguson (once Philip's polo manager and then Charles's) and the society beauty Susan Fitzherbert, who had left Major Ron and their two daughters to marry an Argentine polo player named Hector Barrantes. With Sarah Ferguson—whom friends called "Fergie"—the Windsor melodrama would soon become farcical.

Sarah was, as it happened, very like Andrew but without the arrogance and expectations of deference. Born on October 15, 1959 (and so four months older than Andrew), she was uninhibited, sassy and not exceptionally bright. She had briefly attended secretarial school where a report described her as a "bouncy redhead, a bit slapdash [but with] initiative and personality which she will use to her advantage when she gets older.'' Sarah then went to a public relations company, where a superior complained of her "spending too much time on the telephone.'' She was then engaged by an art gallery and an art-book publisher, where she made no great impression.

Like Diana, Sarah had come from a broken home, and both parents had remarried. The two young women had no clearly defined goals other than eventual marriage; they had no sense of vocation, of direction in their lives, and they had grown up in a time that did not place much value on developing intellectual or aesthetic sensibilities. At twenty, Sarah traveled to South America with a girlfriend for four months, after which she threw herself into a series of more or less protracted love affairs—first, for two years, with Kim Smith-Bingham, a businessman she met in Argentina. He introduced Sarah to Paddy McNally, a wealthy auto-racing driver and manager, twenty-two years her senior and a widowed father of two. Sarah and Paddy lived together (mostly in Switzerland) for three years. She ended this relationship, according to a friend, because "Paddy was constantly unfaithful to her, right in front of her eyes,'' and because he refused to marry her.

By spring 1985, Sarah was twenty-five, single and back in London where friends reintroduced her to Diana, who included Sarah among a small group she invited to the races at Ascot. There Andrew met Sarah, whom he treated to one of his cruder boyish pranks. Learning that she was on a diet, he tried to force-feed her a rich chocolate dessert. Half in jest, she slapped his chin. "It started from there,'' said Andrew, smitten by her feistiness. Theirs would be love as an athletic—sometimes even a boxing—event, and after a passionate year-long affair occasionally interrupted by his sea duties, their engagement was announced in March 1986. They barely knew each other and had dated only three times. "She's either in love with Andrew or in love with the Royal Family,'' said Major Ferguson with astonishing candor, "and I think it's the latter.''

But Elizabeth and Philip were pleased with the match. They believed that an unpretentious, cheerful, aggressive young woman like Sarah, who had already had a somewhat wild life, would quickly settle into a royal routine and tame Randy Andy. Her family tree was also sturdy and respectable. The Major was from a military tradition, and he and his wife could count four dukes among their ancestors.

But there was a moment of caution. Asked about assuming royal duties, Sarah said she was "much looking forward to carrying them out, or whatever I'm supposed to do with them." The press gleefully recorded her whimsical tone; older members of the Royal Family must have felt a flicker of doubt. There was an obvious lack of seriousness in Sarah, whose levity was precisely what the Queen wished was not the impression given by members of the Royal Family. "There isn't a charm school for princesses," said one member of the household. "Sarah will have to learn by example. The most important thing will be to calm her down, as we had to calm Diana down. Everything has to be more discreet." Alas, discretion would never be the strong suit of Andy and Sarah. Plump, pretty and irrepressible, she would soon be the merriest wife of a Windsor.

On the eve of their marriage in July 1986, the Queen named Andrew Duke of York, the title once borne by her father and grandfather. Madcap Sarah was thus Duchess of York; it would be difficult to name one more different from the previous holder of that title, the dynamic and enterprising Queen Elizabeth The Queen Mother. And unlike her predecessor, Sarah had little formative influence on her husband. The new generation of Yorks was a fun-loving and harmless couple, immature and uninterested in anything but themselves and a life of pleasure. They were not to be restrained or restricted by protocols or by the need to sustain a dignified image. Once again it was Philip who saw things rather more acutely: "I'm delighted [Andrew] is getting married, but not because I think it will keep him out of trouble." He was correct. Nothing restrained Andrew, not even the birth of his two daughters, Beatrice and Eugenie, in 1988 and 1990.

And so the Yorks laughed aloud in public, they poked and kissed each other, they made faces, they called out to bystanders, they dined with friends at restaurants and drank at nightclubs, they bantered with the press. They traveled and skied and bought clothes and luggage—just like the "Dynasty" characters—and their lives ultimately became both silly and empty. But part of the responsibility for this belonged to Her Majesty, who still insisted that it was not seemly for children of the Sovereign to hold ordinary jobs—not, it must be added, that they would have done so to any remarkable effect.

Asked to describe life at Buckingham Palace, the Duchess of York described how the toilets worked (by pushing the handles upward, not down). As for her marriage: "Andrew comes home on Friday absolutely tired out," the Duchess told the press, describing her husband's week of naval duties. "On Saturday we have a row. On Sunday we make up, but by then he has to go back to base again." With such inanely chirpy remarks, it was certainly a new age. And if the Yorks were compared with characters from "Dynasty," they had the home to complete the image: the Queen paid £5 million for the construction of a lavish home, Sunninghill Park, five miles from Windsor Castle and a short distance from Sarah's childhood home. In no time it was derisively called South York, after the residence of the "Dallas" television series.

Childish pranks fairly defined much of the young Royals' public conduct. At Ascot in 1987, Sarah and Diana used their parasols to poke male friends in the buttocks. Sarah giggled and tittered and said, "Let's get drunk." Never at ease with the Royal Family's unbending rituals, the endless meals, the changes of clothing, the churchgoing, the planned parlor games, the review of polite family history, Sarah was an outsider, a marginal girl who had landed at the palace by an unimaginable stroke of good luck and royal favor.

But where Diana was sensitive to the point of emotional and physical collapse, Sarah seemed to thrive on scandal. From the start, her marriage to Prince Andrew did not hinder either of them from carrying on extramarital affairs; she, however, had the bad luck to be found out. A journalist's telephoto lens documented her, cavorting first with a Texan named Steve Wyatt and then with another American, financier John Bryan, at a Riviera resort and at a hotel in Thailand.

Any hopes for a reconciliation between the Yorks was perhaps doomed and their separation confirmed by the infamous photographs of the Duchess with John Bryan, published in August 1992. There they were, nuzzling and nestling, as her two small daughters romped innocently around them. And there was Sarah, enjoying the embraces of her lover, who could be seen kissing her from head to foot, paying particular attention to her toes. Soon cast as the faithless tart—a role she seems to have actually practiced for years—she fell from royal grace with astonishing rapidity. Her husband, meanwhile, was widely considered the wronged party, especially when his wife admitted in 1994 to having been tested three times for the AIDS virus. The presumption was that her promiscuous life had perhaps jeopardized her health, but no one publicly suggested that an additional reason may have been her concern for her history with her husband, a man not widely credited with a talent for celibacy.

Nothing could have been more unfair than this unilateral judgment, for Andrew had been busy, too—not only with this girl and that, but (it was rumored) with shipmates he had known since the days of the Falklands skirmish. Once too often, people whispered, Sarah had returned to their home outside London to find Andrew emerging from what seemed to be bedroom antics with a navy buddy. "He preferred the company of navy pals and wasn't man enough or loving enough for Sarah," according to one broadcast report. Servants heard angry arguments at Buckingham Palace and at Sunninghill Park, especially (thus one staff member) when "Sarah discovered that Andrew wasn't coming home on some of his leave. He was going elsewhere, and this just drove her crazy. She didn't like the fact that she was a shore widow, and to discover that she was shore-widowed intentionally really set her off." As for the Duchess: "His life is flying helicopters," she said. "My husband told me he was a prince and a naval officer first and then a husband." Not a good recipe for a stable marriage.

"They tried to put the little redhead in a cage," she added in 1994. And so she flew away—to the Far East, to New York, to exotic ports—after the financial terms of a formal separation were resolved in her favor. "My daughters are my passport to security," she said shrewdly to friends. Indeed, for the next two years she was invariably seen in public dragging her two little passports behind her, the tots looking slightly forlorn and identically dressed. Two years after her separation, she was still seeing John Bryan. She was also in psychotherapy, "and I still have a long way to go." She might be able to sort things out, she said, on a desert island—to which she would take "my children, of course, the Bible—and a man!" Who would read what to whom she did not say.

The publication of her beach tryst with Bryan had been, she said, her "most humiliating experience." But she could not resist self-defense: "For the first six years of our married life together, [Andrew] spent about forty-two days with me every year. And therefore the children didn't see him that much anyway.'' When the Yorks finally separated in March 1992, the Duchess received £500,000 outright, with £1.4 million in trust for her daughters and another half-million for a house. Why did the Royal Family completely abandon her during the difficult early months of her separation and then invite her children but not her to family celebrations and holidays? ''That's a good question,'' she said. ''I think that with a little less hostility and a little more support, things could have been easier, less difficult and traumatic.''

Andrew, in the meantime, bumbled along in the tradition of poor Prince Eddy, that loutish elder son of Edward VII whose pathetic life was aborted by death at the age of twenty-eight. From 1994, the Duke and Duchess of York, inheritors of the title recently borne by the dutiful King George VI and his single-minded consort, began to fade into a certain vagueness. What may be the emotional health of little Beatrice and Eugenie, like that of Princes William and Harry, remains to be seen.

But the Yorks' marriage was not the first to founder. The Queen was ''sad but not surprised'' when Princess Anne and Mark Phillips formally separated in 1989, after sixteen years of what one royal correspondent called ''a phoney marriage, a sham'' defined by extramarital amours, a paternity case brought against Mark by a New Zealander named Heather Tonkin (to whom Phillips paid NZ $80,000 annually for five years), and a fanciful rumor that one of Anne's bodyguards, former policeman Peter Cross, was her lover (and in fact the father of one of her children).

The Phillips divorce followed two years later, and then Anne married Commander Timothy Laurence, one of the Queen's equerries. The situation recalled the relationship between Princess Margaret and Peter Townsend, but with a happy ending.

After years of chilly, mutual criticism, Anne earned considerable respect from the press, politicians and the public. Volatile, plainspoken, often blunt, Anne—who had more of her father's than her mother's personality—had been frequently at odds with the media for years.

But on behalf of Save the Children, an international emergency fund relieving famine, homelessness, and disease, she was traveling as much as fifteen thousand miles a year in the 1980s and 1990s. Enduring the severe reactions she usually suffered after injections against cholera, typhoid and a host of exotic maladies, Anne coped uncomplainingly with all the discomforts in the poorest parts of Africa, the Middle East, India and Russia. Given the honorific title Princess Royal by her mother in 1987, she had become the "Blossoming Princess," as the press called her. But she was a flower with a handy thorn: pestered by a photographer when she was on a train returning to London, she turned on the man with an explosion of anger: "Fuck off!" she cried.

Just as impatient with anything like flattery or praise for her efforts, she put herself at considerable risk, traveling in and out of dangerous and unhealthy areas. Prime Minister Edward Heath understated her heroic work when he praised her as "one of the most active royal patrons of all time, tireless in travel, fearless in facing hazards in countries starved by drought or riddled with disease, and uninhibited in showing understanding of children's problems wherever she finds them." Precisely because of her mature, unselfconscious generosity and the distance she deliberately put between herself and the press, Anne's marriage to Timothy Laurence in December 1992 evoked neither reproach nor pious commentary. And by 1993 it was evident that her commonsensical approach to life had been passed on to her son Peter and daughter Zara, who—without royal titles or honorifics and always shielded by their mother from publicity—were going through adolescence without scandals or haughty attitudes.

Of all the Queen's children, only Princess Anne has made for herself a life admirably down-to-earth. Nor does she share the world's fascination for Diana. "I didn't match up to the public's idea of a fairy princess," she said flatly at the height of her sister-in-law's popularity. "The Princess of Wales has obviously filled a void in the media's life which I had not filled, but I never had any intentions of filling it. I had already made a decision that it wasn't me in any way." Her forthrightness, her fearlessness, her abrasiveness with the press—these qualities won her father's approval; they were, after all, characteristics very much his own.

* * *

As it happened, Anne was the only one of the Queen's four children to have anything like a serious, sustained interest in much of anything, and more than one royal commentator has expressed the impossible wish that Anne be the nation's next sovereign. As the 1990s began, Charles—the most bound to tradition—continued to deliver occasional lectures on architecture and organic farming, but by no means could he convince the press or the public that he was anything but a restless and rootless man whose destiny it was to wait.

Edward, who turned thirty in 1994, was also aimless, and it must be said that like Charles and Andrew, he is neither a particularly bright nor an interesting man, he is merely famous. Over Edward, however, the British press could wink and giggle, for his protracted bachelorhood and friendships with other single young men led to the persistent rumor that he is gay, if not especially happy, for Edward's personality even as he turned thirty seemed boyish, bland and unformed. In support of the rumor was the fact that none of the young ladies he socially escorted indicated that the relationship had been anything other than platonic.

Like his brothers, Edward went to Gordonstoun; he then studied in New Zealand and graduated from Cambridge with a degree in history in June 1986. At his father's insistence, Edward was then shipped off to the Royal Marines, but after fourteen weeks he resigned. "It was an agonizing decision to make," he said. "Four years ago I wanted to be a marine, but having got there I changed my mind and decided that the services generally, not just the Royal Marines, was not the career I wanted."

His father reacted with such explosive anger that poor Edward collapsed in tears. "I've tried to make him see that I'm not cut out for the navy," Edward's great-uncle, George Duke of Kent, had complained decades earlier about an identical contretemps with his father, George V. "But he doesn't understand me. What can I do?" History was, as the saying goes, repeating itself—as well, perhaps, in Edward's sexual life as in George Kent's, for to Philip as to George V, homosexuality was both unimaginable and unacceptable. By spring 1994, there were even some indications that the Queen would bow to her husband's pressure and force their youngest son to marry, for the palace was issuing statements about a tender alliance between Edward and a young public relations consultant named Sophie Rhys-Jones.

After a year of idleness, Prince Edward became the first child of a sovereign to hold a job other than military service. "You're going to do *what*?" shouted Philip when Edward announced his plans to join Andrew Lloyd Webber's production company as an office assistant. Enthusiastic for everything that touched Anne's life (and unfailingly sympathetic to her interests), the Duke of Edinburgh was much less so with his sons, and to Edward most of all, Philip was a chilling martinet. That he wanted to associate with the *theater* was the last straw. In the blunt words of one close to the family, the Duke of Edinburgh was

> an absolute shit to those boys. That's why Charles always went to Mountbatten for advice, rather than to him. Philip was hard and pushing, all the time; he was hell-bent on building their characters and doesn't know the meaning of compassion or kindness. It all came from his own upbringing, and he's been inflicting his bullying tactics, which are a cover for his own insecurities, on everyone around him ever since.

"The whole family looks up to him," said another confidant of Philip, "and they're all frightened."

The issue of Edward's sexual orientation was in the open by 1990 when newspapers reported his "touching friendship" with actor Michael Ball, the star of a Lloyd Webber musical, and also the fact that Edward was called "Mavis" by his workmates. As if protesting too much, Edward then broke royal protocol. In a remarkably homophobic statement that made headlines, he discussed the rumors with a reporter in New York: "It's so unfair to me and my family. How would you feel if someone said you were gay? The rumors are preposterous. I am not gay!" In England and America, this was heard with the same reaction as if a man caught stealing had shouted hysterically "I'm not a thief!" Gay or not, it is perhaps to be hoped that no one will care except those on whom his favor falls. In 1994, as Edward Windsor, he was a joint managing director at Ardent Productions, a television company with special focus in the arts; few cared very much about that.

And perhaps rather unfortunately, Edward began to assume some of the less attractive, grander manners of the young Royal. In 1986, he staged a television farce for charity, a crude, amateurishly embarrassing event into which he dragooned his sister and the Duchess of York, among others. After being forced to stand in the wind and rain for fourteen hours observing the royal fiasco, the press was at last invited to put a few questions to Prince Edward. "I hope you've enjoyed yourselves," he said, and when there was no merry reply, he asked testily, "Well, have you?" More silence. "Well," said Edward with a sneer, "thanks for sounding so bloody enthusiastic! What have you been doing here all day?" And with that His Royal Highness walked off. "He flounced out like a ballerina with a hole in his tights," said journalist Andrew Morton.

But no news of Anne, Andrew or Edward ever displaced Diana and Charles from the first pages of the tabloids, no matter how trivial the tidbits, and when the fairy-tale marriage of 1981 was in certain collapse a decade later, the press was present and accounted for. CHARLES AND DIANA: CAUSE FOR CONCERN trumpeted the *Daily Mail*'s headline for July 2, 1991, seventeen months before the separation was officially announced by the Prime Minister. And when that occurred, on December 9, 1992, when the Royal Family's private life was the stuff of a formal statement in the House of Commons, the thirst for gossip could never again be slaked. As it happened, it was in fact sharpened by the most murderous struggle for increased circulation and new readership in the history of the newspapers. Tabloid journalism was the new literature.

As long as the British monarchy insisted on maintaining an identity that was ancient in form and rigid in its self-driven privileges, Charles and Diana (and Andrew and Sarah) could scarcely hope for something like a normal late-twentieth-century marriage. They were imprisoned within the reality of their birth, separated from one another far more by status than will, temperament or character. As heir to the throne and son of the Queen, Charles was raised to believe in his unique vocation, and no young woman was going to share his innermost thoughts and fears.

Yet Diana rose above her station to become in many ways

a truly Royal Highness, and she could anticipate an ever more active role as mother of two royal Princes. But her husband could look forward to very little, and rumors that Elizabeth, after forty years as Sovereign, would abdicate in his favor were put to rest forever in 1991 when the palace issued a statement that "voluntary renunciation of the Throne strikes at the root of the Monarchy. It has, therefore, always been regarded as a particularly serious threat to the institution itself. Proposals [for abdication], while well meant, do not really fit into the traditions or mystique of the Monarchy as it has evolved in Britain. They would tend to destroy some of the magic of the Monarchy." The ghost of Bagehot was very powerful indeed, it seemed, and the isolated life, true since Victoria, was still the norm of royal existence. "There are very few people I know," said even the outspoken Princess Anne, "whom I would speak to with any degree of freedom about the Family or what one does at home, because that's just the sort of thing people tend to remember most and chat about." The result of this has been, for generations of royals, a certain airless obsession with self.

"Charles was very sad [about the decline of his marriage]," according to a Duke in whom the Prince confided that autumn. "He kept slowly shaking his head, unable to understand where it had all gone wrong. I asked him if he was sure there was no way the marriage could be rekindled, kept alive. No, he believed that events between the two of them had gone too far. There was no going back. There was no way to make it work."

As a matter of fact, neither the Prince nor his Princess had kept the details private. According to several friends, Diana described "how very difficult it was for Charles to say 'I love you.' He seemed to believe that to show emotion, whether privately or publicly, was a weakness. . . . When Diana realized with a shock that Charles couldn't express his love, even when things were going well between them, their relationship only grew worse."

The Prince and Princess had not shared the same bedroom since February 1987, by which time they had both taken lovers: James Hewitt was comforting the Princess, Camilla attended the Prince. The fairy-tale marriage, as Charles told thirteen million television viewers on June 29, 1994, had "irretrievably broken down"—and only then was he unfaithful to his wife. That public admission infuriated his family.

That same winter of 1987, Diana felt the first pangs of the empty-nest syndrome. That year her sons went off to school, a normal event for many mothers but apparently traumatic for the Princess of Wales, who looked more and more to her boys to provide the reason for living denied by her husband and in-laws. By this time, according to Stephen Barry and others, Diana's tantrums were so violent as to leave some rooms at Althorp and Highgrove with smashed furniture, cracked mirrors and dozens of shattered egos, for servants were dismissed or resigned in disgust at her mood swings.

Meanwhile, Charles tried to ignore the melodramatic scenes, perhaps in the hope that time would calm and mature her. But his tactics were counterproductive. He spoke of his role and his future: "My duty," he was overheard to say to his wife, "lies above my loyalty to you." Such a sentiment would scarcely encourage any spouse; but one as emotionally needy as Diana found it chilling. Thus in his distance from his own feelings (not to say his lack of awareness that his diffidence contributed to her dismay), Charles was his mother's son; and in his benign condescension toward women, he was his father's offspring. "He is known as a charming male chauvinist who recognizes women as attractive helpmates but not as intellectual or working equals," said a former aide to the Prince.

But this was not merely an attitude, it was an active posture, realized in persistent infidelity. From 1983 right up to 1992, the Prince had regularly gone off for trysts with Camilla Parker Bowles, departures that left Diana "screaming," according to Charles's friend Ronald Driver, "and accusing him of being selfish, a bastard—and a few four-letter words into the bargain." At the same time her bulimia, with its dangerous cycles of binges and purges, was alarming to everyone around her. This and her other problems led an exasperated Charles to complain to his mother, "Don't you realize she's mad? She's *mad!*"

As her confidence and social importance deepened, Diana found this insupportable, and by 1990 she was openly describing her misery to friends. Then, for the first time in history, a Royal Highness turned to the press to explain her plight, to win sympathy and to court public affection. Diana apparently authorized her friends to speak on the record to Andrew Morton, who prepared a book that presented her unfortunate situation to the world. That he also had access to her family is indicated by the fact that so many of the photographs in the finished book were provided by her father from the family album. Morton's international best-seller, *Diana: Her True Story,* purported to be just that—a brief but shocking account of the reasons for the failure of her marriage to a callous husband.

"She is not a happy person," said her friend Carolyn Bartholomew ominously to Morton, and as witness came accounts of her halfhearted attempts at suicide. Diana threw herself down a flight of stairs; she hurled herself against a glass display cabinet; she slashed her wrists with a lemon slicer. Nothing that antiseptic and small bandages could not easily heal.

Morton's book, combined with the relentless avalanche of colored photographs of Diana in the world's press, increased Diana's popularity a hundredfold. She confirmed the British and the Americans in their obsession with royalty, the ultimate stars to adore in a world where deeper faith was in short supply. But the objects of adoration were indistinguishable from television comedy characters.

As far as the family was concerned, Diana was immediately branded a traitor—but one who, as the mother of the future King, could not be summarily banished. The Queen Mother could not understand that a girl who wanted a monogamous marriage and who was disappointed in its absence could have gone public with her complaint. Diana, present with the family at the 1992 ceremony of Trooping the Colour, was icily ignored. "You could have cut the atmosphere with my sword," according to an eyewitness. Only Princess Margaret offered the Princess of Wales unstinting sympathy, convinced that her nephew had mocked Diana's ideals and indefensibly humiliated her.

Charles followed suit, eventually cooperating in 1994 in an unprecedented manner (to the inclusion of letters and diaries) with writer Jonathan Dimbleby—and, before that, speaking off the record to journalists Penny Junor and Ross Benson, giving his side of the story and implying that any attempt to tarnish his wife's name would be acceptable. Accordingly, Junor's articles in *Today* magazine described the Princess of Wales as a hysteric responsible for the breakdown of her own marriage, a selfish, conniving woman who turned her two sons against

their father. "Charles deserves an awful lot of sympathy," said
Junor. "He saw his friends reaching the pinnacles of their
careers while he was training for a job he still may never get.
He was having a midlife crisis, and Diana wasn't there for him.
He had spent his life as a star, and the loss of status [to Diana]
ate away at him."

And so, whereas previous Royals conducted their battles in
private, here was something new: the Prince and Princess of
Wales, the couple closest to the throne, took the most contemporary but most unreliable means to present themselves—a
childish, mutually mean-spirited engagement of the press to
confirm their popularity. "The Prince and Princess of Wales,"
said Lord Rothermere, who succeeded his father as publisher
of the *Daily Mail* and the *Evening Standard* in 1978, "each
recruited national newspapers to carry their own accounts of
their marital rifts." Even Prime Minister John Major joined
the fray, rebuking Diana for her continued manipulation of the
press.* He did not, of course, go so far in the case of the
Prince.

Ironically, every critic of the Royal Family now had additional ammunition, especially after the publication of tran-
scripts of taped conversations between the Waleses and their
confidants. Queen Victoria's oldest son may have begun to
democratize the Royal Family; now, Queen Elizabeth II's heir
cheapened it.

The matter came to an execrably critical mass with the
publication in 1993 of the telephone conversations recorded
between Charles and Camilla Parker Bowles in December
1989; and of conversations (recorded that same month) between Diana and James Gilbey, a wealthy used-car salesman at
whose flat Diana spent several late evenings. Lord Rees-Mogg,
formerly of the BBC and by now chairman of the Broadcasting
Standards Council, opined that MI5, British Intelligence, had
been keeping surveillance on the Royal Family and was leaking
the tapes as evidence of an incompetent generation of Royals.
Whatever the provenance and however the dissemination occurred, neither the Waleses' press secretaries nor anyone at
Buckingham Palace ever denied that the calls or meetings oc-

---

* Charles was subsequently cleared of leaking anything at all to the
press.

curred; there were no outraged protests over bogus or fabricated conversations; and there were no royal demands for retractions. Obviously, the fairy-tale wedding had become a shabby farce.*

The Queen and Prince Philip were furious. They called family conferences, urging restraint on Charles and Diana, counseling silence, reminding them of the call of duty—all to no avail. Time, of course, mitigated the effect of the conversations, but they indicated clearly that the heir to the throne could talk like a character from a paperback romance. "I want to feel my way along you, all over you, and up and down you, and in and out," whispered the Prince of Wales to Camilla in 1989. She replied with equal ardor: "That's just what I need at the moment. I can't bear a Sunday night without you." She desired him "desperately, desperately, desperately," and this led him to the infamous comment that although he would like to live his life inside her trousers, he felt he might have the ill fortune to be allotted the unfortunate existence of a tampon, only to be rudely flushed away.

Diana ("Squidgy" to her friend Gilbey) was not so stupefyingly vulgar on the telephone. To Gilbey's insistence that he "couldn't face the thought of not speaking to you at every moment," she said, "It's purely mutual." And in the matter of her in-laws she was forthright: "Bloody hell, after all I've done for this fucking family! . . . I can't stand the confines of this marriage. [Charles] makes my life real torture." Most enigmatically, she confided—speaking of her relationship with Gilbey? Charles? or justifying a time of self-imposed chastity?—"I don't want to get pregnant." That Gilbey was her lover was never confirmed absolutely, although their terms of endearment scarcely suggest a platonic relationship. With James Hewitt, Diana was certainly in love, or at least in lust. His affair with her (detailed in a 1994 book with which he cooperated) was never denied by Buckingham Palace.

* * *

* As it happened, the so-called Squidgy tape was recorded by an amateur radio operator named Cyril Reenan from his home in Oxfordshire. Some believe that Mr. Reenan tracked a tape that had already been made and was being transmitted by someone within the palace (or within the government or British Intelligence); in any case, Mr. Reenan was never prosecuted for illegally using his scanner for such purpose.

And so, as the world learned that the Prince of Wales fantasized aloud to Camilla about living forever "inside your trousers—it would be so much easier," it also came to light that his wife had lost her heart to young idlers, that the Yorks were little more than empty loafers, and that Prince Philip wore his xenophobia like a merit badge, warning Englishmen about consorting with foreigners who had "slitty eyes." Staunch monarchists had their greatest challenge since King William IV.

More and more the Royals seemed a crew of tiresome blockheads, good for very little except to provide the public with squalid prattle. The Duchess of York was on a ski holiday with friends while Prince Andrew romped with navy buddies. Princess Anne was busy scribbling love letters to her sweetheart. Viscount Linley (Margaret's son) was cavorting in drag at a Caribbean party. Diana's married brother was tearfully telling the press about his adulterous affair in Paris. Captain Mark Phillips was paying his mistress to keep silent. Amid the horrors available to anyone listening to the evening news, the Royal Family was providing little other than quaint titillation or vacuous entertainment.

There was, in the final analysis, simply no mystique to defend, no mystery in which to believe, no dignity to emulate. In other words, it was no longer possible to justify the Royal Family as living symbols of a great and glorious tradition.

Queen Elizabeth remained formal, powerless to influence the conduct of her children and their families.

Prince Philip, disgusted with the collapse of his children's marriages and weary after almost fifty years of being a royal coat-holder, was spending more time in the tropics, either with friends or a mistress, depending on which rumor one believed. No one seemed to care very much; some cousins and former aides even wished him the comfort, in his seventies, of some tender female companionship.

In April 1994, Princess Margaret—who had seemed out of the picture for so long—was subjected to considerable humiliation in the harsh spotlight of public scrutiny. Her adulterous affair with Robin Douglas-Home, which began at Christmas 1966 and was described in lovers' correspondence, made newspaper headlines. "I think all the time of you," she had written on her own formal stationery to Robin. "Trust me as I trust

you, love me as I love you, know always that I want you. . . .
Thank you for letting me live again.'' The diction was not as
torrid as that of her nephew and his mistress, but there it was.

What good was the Royal Family, many people polled
wanted to know, adding Margaret's name to a list that included
the Waleses, the Yorks and several royal cousins in tattered
marriages, leading rootless and irresponsible lives? What *good*
did they do, with all their millions? What purpose did they
serve?

Even the great 1992 fire that destroyed nine ancient rooms
(including St. George's Hall and the Grand Reception Room)
at Windsor Castle—a conflagration that seemed to many a
living symbol of royal collapse—did not evoke much sentimental concern. If it is the Queen's house, she ought to pay to
restore it—that was the response to a presumptuous government announcement that taxpayers would foot the bill for restoration. Said a palace spokesman: "All of us had relied on the
fact that in such a tragedy there would be nothing but sympathy. We must have got it wrong."

For the most part, however, the Queen did pay—just as she
finally agreed to limit the Civil List to herself, her husband and
her mother. That would not make the monarch short of cash.
In 1992 her personal fortune was estimated at £6.6 billion,
which brought £2 million interest daily. As for taxes, Her
Majesty agreed to pay a personal tax—in what measure, however, may never be known. Queen Victoria and King Edward
VII were scrupulous about paying taxes, but in the early 1930s
King George V made a secret deal with the Chancellor of
the Exchequer not to pay tax on income from the Duchy of
Lancaster. The privilege was extended by his son King
George VI, who decreed that the family would pay no tax on
private income.

The Windsors, it was widely felt, had made themselves
anachronistic, had presented the best reason for their retirement. They were ordinary people with no right to extraordinary
privilege.

For centuries England had been one of history's most vibrant cultures, its language and literature, its music and art.
Now the monarchy's very existence was at stake. Queen Eliza-

beth herself seemed a decent woman, but her fierce sense of duty had at last no realistic point of attachment, for her family was outside her influence and the government beyond her power.

In a way her place as monarch was the most poignant, for the Windsor saga is perhaps above all the epic of strong women much misunderstood—women who overcame terrific obstacles, who were surprised by a destiny they met with remarkable courage and even grace.

Queen Victoria, grandmother of Europe and of the first Windsor monarch, had foreseen a lifetime with her beloved Albert. Sudden widowhood had almost destroyed her and the Crown, but she made her way back to forty years of stern influence and finally showed a touching benevolence that humanized her sublime sense of the realm's destiny.

Her daughter-in-law Queen Alexandra, with a lame leg, a game smile and a quiet faith, kept her family together against all odds. An imported Danish Princess, she had a radiant beauty that was not just skin deep, and her sweetness of spirit finally embodied the best of her adopted country. Deaf, she heard the faintest cries of the poor and the sick; abandoned, she was the soul of equanimity. Who, knowing her or about her, could not love Alix?

Queen Mary, straight of back and stiff of principle, did not evoke the warmth of Alexandra, but she was no less influential with her husband and children—and, indeed, with her granddaughter Queen Elizabeth. For Mary, the country was her life, the King her vocation. She understood none of the mid-twentieth-century's jargon about emotional needs; she saw only her duty, and she lived within it like a cloistered nun in a convent. In one critical way at least, old Queen Mary was right. Giving oneself without reservation conferred on life its only real meaning. When she died, she was offered more deeply felt tributes, and in greater prodigality, than all the trinkets that filled her rooms.

Victoria and Alix had died at eighty-one, and Mary at eighty-six. No one was more aware of her predecessors' longevity than Queen Elizabeth The Queen Mother. Regarded by some as the beloved Granny of all England, she had become a sentimental relic, a sign of a past that, alas, had ceased to influence the present. Even she knew that Charles and Diana would divorce. She did not reach her mid-nineties without surviving a number of shocks, and she was "tough and resourceful," as her old friend Lord Charteris (the Queen's former private secretary) said. She was also "built of stern stuff. Probably because she is a bit of an ostrich, she has learned how to protect herself. What she doesn't want to see, she doesn't look at."

Her daughter the Queen was perhaps the most realistic of them all about the future. "I find that as the years pass my capacity for surprise has lessened," she said at a meeting of Commonwealth heads of government in November 1993. There was serious talk that Australia first, and then perhaps Canada, would entirely sever all allegiance to the Crown, and Elizabeth did not ignore the dissent. "Nowadays I have enough experience, not least in racing, to restrain me from laying any money down on how many countries will be in the Commonwealth in forty years' time, who they will be, and where the meeting will be held. I will certainly not be betting on how many of you will have the Head of the Commonwealth as your Head of State. I suppose the only reasonably safe bet is that there will be three absentees: Prince Philip, the *Britannia* and myself. But you never know."

Or as George Bernard Shaw titled one of his plays, *You Never Can Tell.*

The Windsors at the end of the century are not in any way symbols of a nation struggling to rise from the ashes of a dead Empire to become a social democracy. Quite simply they represent nothing at all except themselves, and what they had become was perhaps too absurd to be taken seriously. Victoria, Alexandra, Mary, the two Elizabeths: they had all believed in something outside themselves, had lived for something beyond themselves.

But the new generation of Windsors—lively, fun-loving, the darlings of the media, the most celebrated faces in English history—seem incapable of living for anything but their own celebrity. Expecting loyalty, deference and undiluted allegiance from their "subjects," they nevertheless communicate to the world the message that the Royal Family is defined by immaturity, irresponsibility, frivolity and irrelevance. They provide the nation with neither a representation of an often noble history nor guidance for a confused present and a dubious future.

In such circumstances, violent revolutionaries are unnecessary in abolishing the monarchy, which will perhaps not be hauled off like unpopular images of Lenin or Stalin. No, all the variations of the British Crown may become mere relics at the Tower of London, the monarchy destroyed by pettiness. The young Windsors cannot be taken seriously, and so sovereignty itself is no longer even a beneficial public relations device.

Right there, in the palaces and royal castles, live those who are causing the fall of the House of Windsor.

Diana, Charles and their sons, William and Harry.

15

The Magic Kingdom 1995

I feel very sorry for them.

PRINCE CHARLES, speaking of his two young sons

In June and September 1995, Charles and Diana's children—
Their Royal Highnesses The Princes William Arthur Philip
Louis and Henry Charles Albert David—marked their thirteenth and eleventh birthdays. After parties and an extended
summer holiday, they returned for the new terms at Eton and
Ludgrove, where the routines were demanding but not spartan.
At Ludgrove, for example, the two hundred students rise at
7:15 each morning, have breakfast in a common dining hall,
attend classes, rush to the playing field, dress for dinner and
turn out their lights promptly at 8:00. They are accorded no
extraordinary privileges, and their classmates call them Wills
and Harry. So described, the boys' lives may seem quite ordi-

469

nary or at least very like those who come from many polite English families that can afford a private country boarding school far from the confusion of city life.

But little is ordinary even in Berkshire, where a crew from the Royal Protection Squad is always nearby. Elsewhere, the boys are rarely out of the public eye. Whether at an amusement park or a ski holiday with their mother, fishing or hiking with their father or riding bicycles in Kensington Gardens, William and Harry are invariably pursued by photographers with tele-photo lenses and reporters with cassette recorders and cellular telephones. One spring day their mother took them for a quick hamburger at a popular casual restaurant; when they departed a half-hour later, three hundred people jammed the street and a movie crew had set up cameras and cables. The lives of these famous boys are more meticulously documented than Shirley Temple's decades ago or Macaulay Culkin's now. Already, before they have done anything at all, they are stars.

Wills, second in line to the throne, is reserved and serious, a cautious and introverted boy who has grown wary of the press and shy of publicity. Conscious of his position and his future, he is becoming a dignified, somewhat stern teenager; his eyes often have a premature, prescient sadness. An uncle has called him "a very self-possessed, intelligent and mature boy, quite formal and stiff, sounding older than his years when he answers the phone." Protective of Diana, to whom he is very close, Wills has more than once said, "I don't want to be a king. I want to be a policeman so I can look after my mother." He often telephones her from school—not to ask for favors or to complain but to assure himself that she is well. This, he seems to feel, is his prime responsibility since his parents' separation. "I hope you both will be happier now," he told them when he received the news.

According to a National Opinion Poll, more than thirty percent of Britons believe Prince William should ascend the throne when the Queen's reign ends; he should supplant his father, at whatever age. This is not likely to happen unless Charles should abdicate, an eventuality for which he shows no inclination.

Harry, on the other hand, is more outgoing and confident—"a mischievous imp," according to Diana's brother. Unlike

Wills, Harry is bold on the ski slopes, fearless on horseback, a terror on the go-cart track and a wicked mimic of his peers and elders. "Harry's the naughty one," according to the Princess of Wales. "Just like me." Also like her, he holds a subordinate place in the dynasty's pecking order, and unless tragedy befalls his brother, he will always be a supporting player.

Both boys will never want for anything, of course. Their great-grandmother has left two-thirds of her £26 million private fortune in trust for them; the rest will go to her other great-grandchildren.

The peculiar situation of the two brothers has not been ignored by certain key government officials. When the Prince and Princess of Wales were arguing about the schooling and custody of their sons, for example, Member of Parliament Frank Field, chairman of the House of Commons Social Services Select Committee, urged Prime Minister John Major to become directly involved in the upbringing and education of the young princes. Their future, Field insists, should be monitored by "wise men," experts with more sensitivity than those at the palace—by which he presumably meant counselors more psychologically astute than the Queen and her courtiers. "The two grandchildren of the Monarch should be able to exercise the same right as all the Queen's other young subjects. Their future should not be settled by the Royal Court and the immediate Royal circle, which has played such a part in their family's unhappiness." A keen observation, perhaps, but also a futile one.

Diana is a doting mother who takes her sons on holidays, is lavish with treats, dresses them as casually as the climate permits and seems to try hard to counteract the formality of life with father: Charles insists his sons dress like perfect little gentlemen, their jackets and ties neat, their manner decorous and subdued. But as in other matters, he is not unaware of conflict. "I feel very sorry for them," he has said wistfully. "I hope they will be all right. Before long they will be taller than me."

Charles likes to take the boys to the misty Scottish hills. Diana prefers to whisk them off with a few friends to Disney World in Florida. There, the youngest Windsors love to race watery rapids, to zoom on a "Star Wars" space ride, to chat with an actor playing "Indiana Jones" or to shake hands with Beauty and the Beast. The boys become, according to Disney's press people, the "pop-up Princes"—they suddenly pop up at the head of queues, after being rushed from their hotel through secure underground tunnels to the park's many attractions.

But when they are at Disney World, the boys do not leave their hotel suite at night. By the Queen's orders, security precautions require isolation after dusk. Dinner is brought to Princess Diana, Prince William and Prince Henry, and from their private dining room they gaze across a lagoon to watch the evening's last explosions of fireworks over the turrets of Cinderella's castle. Disney's fantastic realm has been called "the happiest place on earth." Everyone wants to believe in this tiny parcel of world that is always safe and regulated, efficient and serene. For the next generation of Windsor Royals, this may be the closest they come to a magic kingdom.

Sources

Alice, Princess, Countess of Athlone. *For My Grandchildren.* London: Evans, 1966.

Alice, Princess, Duchess of Gloucester. *Memoirs.* London: Collins, 1983.

————. *Memories of Ninety Years.* London: Collins & Brown, 1991.

Allison, Ronald, and Sarah Riddell, eds. *The Royal Encyclopedia.* London: Macmillan, 1991.

Alsop, Susan Mary. *To Marietta from Paris.* New York: Doubleday, 1975.

Altrincham, Lord (later John Grigg). *Kenya's Opportunity.* London: Faber & Faber, 1955.

————. "The Monarchy Today," *The National & English Review,* Aug. 1957.

Amory, Cleveland. *The Best Cat Ever.* Boston: Little, Brown, 1993.

————. *Who Killed Society?* New York: Harper & Bros., 1960.

Arnold, Harry. "How Those Gay Rumors Started," *Daily Mirror,* Apr. 10, 1990.

Arnstein, Walter L. "Queen Victoria Opens Parliament: The Disinvention of Tradition," *Historical Research,* June 1990.

Aronson, Theo. *Royal Family: Years of Transition.* London: John Murray, 1983.

————. *The Royal Family at War.* London: John Murray, 1993.

Asquith, Lady Cynthia. *The King's Daughters.* London: Hutchinson, 1937.

Sources

Atkinson, A. B. *Unequal Shares.* Harmondsworth: Penguin, 1974.

Austin, Victoria. "Charles, Diana and the Dilemmas of Divorce," *Royalty,* Autumn 1993.

Bagehot, Walter. *The English Constitution.* London: Kegan Paul, 1898; alternately, Oxford: The University Press, 1929 edition.

Bailey, Gilbert. "She Could Charm the Pearl out of an Oyster," *The New York Times Magazine,* Aug. 21, 1949.

Barker, Malcolm J., with T. C. Sobey. *Living with the Queen.* Fort Lee, N.J.: Barricade Books, 1991.

Barry, Stephen. *Royal Service.* New York: Avon, 1983.

Battine, Cecil. "Our Monarchy and Its Alliances," *The Fortnightly Review,* Sept. 1917.

Battiscombe, Georgina. *Queen Alexandra.* London: Constable, 1969.

Baxter, A. B. *Destiny Called to Them.* Oxford: The University Press, 1939.

Beard, Madeleine. *English Landed Society in the 20th Century.* London: Routledge, 1989.

Bedfordshire Times and Independent, Aug. 1921.

Benson, E. F. *Queen Victoria.* London: Longmans, Green, 1935.

Bentley-Cranch, Dana. *Edward VII.* London: HMSO, 1992.

Birkenhead, Lord. *Walter Monckton.* London: Hamish Hamilton, 1969.

Bloch, Michael. *The Reign and Abdication of Edward VIII.* London: Black Swan, 1991.

Bloch, Michael, ed. *Wallis and Edward: Letters 1931–1937.* New York: Summit, 1986.

Blundell, Nigel, and Susan Blackhall. *Fall of the House of Windsor.* London: Blake, 1992.

Boothroyd, Basil. *Philip: An Informal Biography.* London: Longman, 1971.

Botham, Noel. *Margaret: The Untold Story.* London: Blake, 1994.

Bradford, Sarah. *The Reluctant King: The Life & Reign of George VI, 1895–1952.* New York: St. Martin's, 1989.

British Medical Journal, May 1910.

Broad, Lewis. *The Abdication: Twenty-five Years After.* London: Frederick Muller, 1961.

Bryan, J., III, and Charles J. V. Murphy. *The Windsor Story.* New York: William Morrow, 1979.

Buckle, G. E., ed. *The Letters of Queen Victoria: A Selection from Her Majesty's Correspondence Between the Years 1862 and 1885.* London: John Murray, 1926.

Campbell, Lady Colin. *Diana in Private.* London: Smith Gryphon, 1993.

Cannadine, David. *The Decline and Fall of the British Aristocracy.* New Haven: Yale University Press, 1990.

Cannon, John, and Ralph Griffiths. *The Oxford Illustrated History of the British Monarchy.* Oxford and New York: Oxford University Press, 1992.

Carey, M. C. *Princess Mary.* London: Nisbet, 1922.

Cathcart, Helen. *The Queen Herself.* London: W. H. Allen, 1983.

———. *The Queen Mother.* London: W. H. Allen, 1965.

———. *The Queen and Prince Philip: Forty Years of Happiness.* London: Coronet/Hodder and Stoughton, 1987.

———. *The Royal Bedside Book.* London: W. H. Allen, 1969.

"Charles: The Private Man, the Public Role," ITV documentary broadcast (United Kingdom), June 29, 1994.

Chase, Edna Woolman, and Ilka Chase. *Always in Vogue.* London: Victor Gollancz, 1954.

Christopher, Prince of Greece. *Memoirs of HRH Prince Christopher of Greece.* London: Hurst and Blackett, 1938.

Clark, Stanley. *Palace Diary.* London: Harrap, 1958.

Clarke, Mary. *Diana Once upon a Time.* London: Sidgwick & Jackson, 1994.

Colville, John. *The Fringes of Power: Downing Street Diaries,* vol. 2, 1941–April 1955. London: Hodder and Stoughton, 1985.

Corby, Tom. *H.M. Queen Elizabeth the Queen Mother.* London: Award Publications, 1990.

Coughlan, Robert. "Britain's National Deb," *Life,* Oct. 31, 1949.

Crawford, Marion. *The Little Princesses.* London: Cassell, 1950.

———. *Queen Elizabeth II.* London: George Newnes, 1952.

Critchfield, Richard. *An American Looks at Britain.* New York: Doubleday, 1990.

Sources

Crosland, Susan. *Tony Crosland.* London: Jonathan Cape, 1982.

Davenport-Hines, Richard. "Margaret," *Tatler,* June 1992.

Davies, Nicholas. *Diana: A Princess and Her Troubled Marriage.* New York: Carol/Birch Lane, 1992.

De-la-Noy, Michael. *The Queen Behind the Throne.* London: Hutchinson, 1994.

Delderfield, Eric R. *Kings and Queens of England and Great Britain.* Newton Abbot and London: David & Charles, 1990.

Dell, John. "Prince Philip," *Cosmopolitan,* Mar. 1953.

Dempster, Nigel, and Peter Evans. *Behind Palace Doors.* New York: Putnam, 1993.

———. *HRH The Princess Margaret: A Life Unfulfilled.* London: Quartet, 1981.

Dimbleby, Jonathan. *The Prince of Wales: A Biography.* London: Little, Brown, 1994.

Dimbleby, Richard. *Elizabeth Our Queen.* London: University of London Press, 1953.

Donaldson, Frances. *Edward VIII.* London: Weidenfeld and Nicolson, 1974.

———. *King George VI and Queen Elizabeth.* London: Weidenfeld and Nicolson, 1977.

Duff, David. *Queen Mary.* London: Collins, 1985.

Dullea, Georgia. "Mercy, Mischief and a Royal Fiction," *The New York Times,* Feb. 16, 1994.

Duncan, Andrew. *The Reality of Monarchy.* London: Heinemann, 1970.

Edgar, Donald. *The Queen's Children.* Middlesex: Hamlyn Paperbacks, 1979.

Edwards, Anne. *Royal Sisters.* New York: Jove, 1991.

Elliott, Caroline, ed. *The BBC Book of Royal Memories.* Jersey City: Parkwest, 1994.

Ellis, Jennifer, ed. Mabell Countess of Airlie, *Thatched with Gold.* London: Hutchinson, 1962.

Ellison, John. "Wallis Windsor, Duchess in Exile," *Daily Express,* Feb. 13, 1979.

Erlich, Henry. "Anne of the Twenty Years," *Look,* July 28, 1970.

Esher, Reginald Viscount. *Cloud-Capp'd Towers.* London: John Murray, 1927.

———. *The Girlhood of Queen Victoria.* London: John Murray, 1912.

———. *Journals and Letters,* 4 vols. London: Nicholson & Watson, 1934–1938.

Ferguson, Ronald. *The Galloping Major: My Life and Singular Times.* London: Macmillan, 1994.

Fisher, Baron J. A. F. *Memories.* London: Hodder & Stoughton, 1919.

Fisher, Clive. *Noël Coward.* London: Weidenfeld and Nicolson, 1992.

Fisher, Graham and Heather. ''Princess Anne: Britain's Royal Swinger,'' *Good Housekeeping,* July 1970.

Flanner, Janet. *An American in Paris.* New York: Simon & Schuster, 1940.

———. *London Was Yesterday, 1934–1939.* London: Michael Joseph, 1975.

Frankland, Noble. *Prince Henry, Duke of Gloucester.* London: Weidenfeld and Nicolson, 1980.

Friedman, Dennis. *Inheritance.* London: Sidgwick & Jackson, 1993.

Frischauer, Willi. *Margaret: Princess Without a Cause.* London: Michael Joseph, 1977.

Fry, Plantagenet Somerset. *The Kings and Queens of England and Scotland.* New York: Grove Weidenfeld, 1990.

Fulford, Roger, ed. *Dearest Child: Private Correspondence of Queen Victoria and the Princess Royal.* London: Evans, 1964.

———. *Dearest Mama: Letters Between Queen Victoria and the Crown Princess of Prussia.* London: Evans, 1968.

Gilbert, Martin. *Winston S. Churchill,* 5 vols. London: Heinemann, 1976.

Giles, Frank. *Sundry Times.* London: John Murray, 1986.

Golby, J. W., and A. W. Purdue. *The Monarchy and the British People.* London: B. T. Batsford, 1988.

Gore, John. *King George the Fifth: A Personal Memoir.* London: John Murray, 1941.

Graham, Caroline. *Camilla—the King's Mistress: A Love Story.* London: Blake, 1994.

Green, Michelle. ''Royal Watch,'' *People,* Aug. 22, 1994.

Green, Michelle, and Terry Smith. ''Diss and Tell,'' *People,* Oct. 17, 1994.

Greenslade, Roy. "Elizabeth the Last?—Down the Royals! Up the Republic!" *The Guardian,* Mar. 28, 1994.

Grigg, John. "Queen Elizabeth II," *The Listener,* Dec. 24, 1970.

Hall, Phillip. *Royal Fortune: Tax, Money and the Monarchy.* London: Bloomsbury, 1992.

Hall, Unity. *The Private Lives of Britain's Royal Women: Their Passions and Power.* Chicago: Contemporary Books, 1991.

Hall, Unity, and Ingrid Seward. *Royalty Revealed.* New York: St. Martin's Press, 1989.

Hamilton, Ronald. *Now I Remember.* London: Hogarth, 1984.

Hamilton, Willie. *Blood on the Walls.* London: Bloomsbury, 1992.

Hardinge, Helen. *Loyal to Three Kings.* London: William Kimber, 1967.

Harewood (Earl of), George (Lascelles). *The Tongs and the Bones.* London: Weidenfeld and Nicolson, 1981.

Heald, Tim. *Philip: A Portrait of the Duke of Edinburgh.* New York: William Morrow, 1991.

Hibbert, Christopher. *Edward VIII—A Portrait.* London: Penguin, 1982.

Hindley, Geoffrey. *The Guinness Book of British Royalty.* London: Guinness, 1989.

Hoey, Brian. *All the King's Men.* London: HarperCollins, 1992.

———. *Monarchy: Behind the Scenes with the Royal Family.* London: BBC Books, 1987.

Holden, Anthony. *Charles.* London: Weidenfeld and Nicolson, 1988.

———. *A Princely Marriage.* London: Bantam, 1991.

———. *The Tarnished Crown.* New York: Random House, 1993.

———. *Their Royal Highnesses.* London: Weidenfeld and Nicolson, 1981.

Holland, Henrietta. "The Royal Collection," *The Tatler,* Mar. 1994.

Hough, Richard. *Born Royal: The Lives and Loves of the Young Windsors.* New York: Bantam, 1988.

———. *Edward and Alexandra: Their Private and Public Lives.* London: John Curtis/Hodder and Stoughton, 1992.

Hull, Fiona Macdonald. "Diana's Battle Royal," *Ladies' Home Journal,* Apr. 1994.

Hutchins, Chris, and Peter Thompson. *Sarah's Story: The Duchess Who Defied the Royal House of Windsor.* London: Smith Gryphon, 1992.

Inglis, Brian. *Abdication.* London: Hodder & Stoughton, 1966.

James, Paul. *Margaret: A Woman of Conflict.* London: Sidgwick and Jackson, 1990.

————. *Princess Alexandra.* London: Weidenfeld and Nicolson, 1992.

James, Robert Rhodes, ed. *Chips: The Diaries of Sir Henry Channon.* London: Weidenfeld and Nicolson, 1967.

Jay, Antony. *Elizabeth R.* London: BBC Books, 1992.

Jones, Thomas. *Whitehall Diary,* 2 vols. Oxford: The University Press, 1969 and 1971.

Judd, Denis. *The House of Windsor.* London: Macdonald, 1973.

————. *The Life and Times of George V.* London: Weidenfeld and Nicolson, 1993.

————. *Prince Philip.* London: Sphere, 1991.

Jullian, Philippe. *Edward and the Edwardians.* London: Sidgwick & Jackson, 1967.

Kay, Richard. "Anne Wanted Her Freedom," *Daily Mail,* Sept. 1, 1989.

————. "Revealed: Secret Heroism of Prince Philip's Mother," *Daily Mail,* July 26, 1993.

Keay, Douglas. *Royal Pursuit: The Palace, the Press and the People.* London: Severn House Books, 1983.

Kenyon, J. P., ed. *Dictionary of British History.* Ware, England: Wordsworth Editions, 1992.

King, Stella. *Princess Marina, Her Life and Times.* London: Cassell, 1969.

"King's Story, A." A television documentary produced by Jack Le Vien in 1965.

Lacey, Robert. "The King and Mrs. Simpson," *Radio Times,* Dec. 3–10, 1976.

————. *Majesty.* 1977.

————. *Princess.* Toronto: McClelland and Stewart, 1982.

————. *Queen Mother.* Boston: Little, Brown, 1986.

Laguerre, Andre. "Clues to a Princess's Choice," *Life,* Oct. 10, 1955.

Lancet, The, Feb. 18, 1911.

Latham, Caroline, and Jeannie Sakol. *The Royals.* New York: Congdon & Weed, 1987.

Lee, Sydney. *King Edward VII,* 2 vols. London: Macmillan, 1927.

————. *Queen Victoria.* London: John Murray, 1904.

Lees-Milne, James. *The Enigmatic Edwardian: Life of Reginald Brett, Viscount Esher.* London: Sidgwick & Jackson, 1986.

————. *Harold Nicolson.* London: Chatto & Windus, 1981.

Levy, Alan. "Queen Elizabeth and Philip," *Good Housekeeping,* Nov. 1957.

Lewis, Brenda Ralph. "Queen Consort of England," *Royalty,* vol. 12, no. 8 (1993).

Life and Times of Lord Louis Mountbatten, The. A television documentary, 1969.

Litvinoff, Sarah, and Marianne Sinclair, eds. *The Wit and Wisdom of the Royal Family.* London: Plexus, 1990.

Lloyd George, David. *War Memoirs,* 6 vols. London: Nicholson and Watson, 1933–1936.

Lockhart, J. G. *Cosmo Gordon Lang.* London: Hodder & Stoughton, 1949.

Longford, Elizabeth. *Louisa, Lady-in-Waiting.* London: Roxby & Lindsey, 1979.

————. *The Oxford Book of Royal Anecdotes.* Oxford: The University Press, 1991.

————. *The Queen Mother.* London: Weidenfeld and Nicolson, 1981.

————. *The Royal House of Windsor.* London: Book Club Associates, 1974.

————. *Royal Throne.* London: John Curtis/Hodder & Stoughton, 1993.

————. *Victoria, R.I.* London: Weidenfeld and Nicolson, 1964.

Lovell, Mary. *Straight On Till Morning: The Life of Beryl Markham.* London: Century Hutchinson, 1987.

Maclean, Veronica. *Crowned Heads.* London: Hodder & Stoughton, 1993.

Magnus, Philip. *Edward the Seventh.* London: John Murray, 1964.

Manchester, William. *The Last Lion.* Boston: Little, Brown, 1983.

Sources

Marie Louise, Princess. *My Memories of Six Reigns*. London: Evans, 1956.

Martin, Kingsley. "The Evolution of Popular Monarchy," *The Political Quarterly,* Apr. 1936.

————. "Strange Interlude: Edward VIII's Brief Reign," *The Atlantic,* May 1962.

Martin, Theodore. *Queen Victoria as I Knew Her*. Edinburgh, 1908.

Menkes, Suzy. *The Windsor Style*. London: Grafton, 1987.

Mercer, Derek, ed. *Chronicle of the Royal Family*. London: Chronicle Communications, 1991.

Metcalfe, James. *All the Queen's Children*. London: Star/ W. H. Allen, 1981.

Middlemas, Keith. *The Life and Times of George VI*. London: Weidenfeld and Nicolson, 1974.

Middlemas, Keith, and John Barnes. *Baldwin*. London: Weidenfeld and Nicolson, 1969.

Montgomery-Massingberd, Hugh. *Burke's Guide to the British Monarchy*. London: Burke's Peerage, 1977.

————. *Debrett's Great British Families*. Exeter: Webb & Bower, 1988.

Monypenny, W. F., and G. E. Buckle, eds. *The Life of Benjamin Disraeli, Earl of Beaconsfield,* 6 vols. London: 1910–1920.

Morley, Sheridan. *Gertrude Lawrence*. London: Weidenfeld and Nicolson, 1981.

Morrah, Dermot. *Princess Elizabeth*. London: Odhams, 1947.

Morrow, Ann. *Princess*. London: Chapman, 1991.

————. *The Queen*. Suffolk: Book Club Associates/Granada, 1983.

Morton, Andrew. *Diana: Her New Life*. London: Michael O'Mara, 1994.

————. *Diana: Her True Story*. London: Michael O'Mara, 1992.

————. *Inside Buckingham Palace*. London: Michael O'Mara, 1991.

————. *Theirs Is the Kingdom*. London: Michael O'Mara, 1989.

Moye, Hedda. "Hair: By Royal Appointment," *OK!* May 1994.

Munro-Wilson, Broderick. "In Praise of Camilla," *Daily Mail,* Nov. 24, 1994.

Murray-Brown, Jeremy, ed. *The Monarchy and Its Future.* London: Allen and Unwin, 1969.

Nairn, Tom. *The Enchanted Glass.* London: Picador, 1990.

New Idea, Jan. 22, 1993.

Nicolson, Harold. *King George the Fifth.* London: Constable, 1952 (reprint: Pan, 1967).

Nicolson, Nigel, ed. *Harold Nicolson, Diaries and Letters.* London: Collins, 1968.

Parker, Eileen. *Step Aside for Royalty.* Maidstone, England: Bachman and Turner, 1982.

Parker, John. *Prince Philip.* London: Sidgwick & Jackson, 1990.

———. *The Princess Royal.* London: Coronet/Hodder & Stoughton, 1989.

———. *The Queen.* London: Headline, 1992.

Pasternak, Anna. *Princess in Love.* London: Bloomsbury, 1994.

Payn, Graham, and Sheridan Morley, eds. *The Noël Coward Diaries.* Boston: Little, Brown, 1983.

Pearson, John. *The Ultimate Family.* London: Michael Joseph, 1986.

Petrie, Sir Charles. *The Modern British Monarchy.* London: Eyre and Spottiswode, 1961.

Player, Leslie, with William Hall. *My Story: The Duchess of York, Her Father and Me.* London: Grafton/HarperCollins, 1993.

Ponsonby, Arthur. *Henry Ponsonby: His Life from His Letters.* London: Macmillan, 1942.

Ponsonby, Frederick. *Recollections of Three Reigns.* London: Eyre Methuen, 1951.

Pope-Hennessy, James. *Lord Crewe: The Likeness of a Liberal.* London: Constable, 1955.

———. *Queen Mary.* London: George Allen and Unwin, 1959.

"Power of the Royals, The," *The Guardian,* Jan. 9, 1995.

"Prince of Wales, The," *The Spectator,* Oct. 17, 1925.

Pryce-Jones, David. "TV Tale of Two Windsors," *The New York Times Magazine,* Mar. 18, 1979, p. 112.

Quennell, Peter, ed., James Pope-Hennessy, *A Lonely Business.* London: Weidenfeld and Nicolson, 1981.

Rocco, Fiametta. ''A Strange Life: A Profile of Prince Philip,'' *The Independent,* Dec. 13, 1992.

Romanones, Aline de, ''The Dear Romance,'' *Vanity Fair,* June 1986.

Rose, Kenneth. *King George V.* London: Macmillan, 1983.

———. *Kings, Queen and Courtiers.* London: Weidenfeld and Nicolson, 1986.

Royal Family in Wartime, The. London: Odhams, 1945.

Ryan, Ann. ''Prince Charles and the Ladies in Waiting,'' *Harper's Bazaar,* Oct. 1972.

St. Aubyn, Giles. *Edward VII.* London: Collins, 1979.

———. *Queen Victoria.* London: Sinclair-Stevenson, 1991.

Salway, Lance. *Queen Victoria's Grandchildren.* London: Collins and Brown, 1991.

Seward, Ingrid. ''Diana,'' *Majesty,* Oct. 1994.

———. *Royal Children.* London: HarperCollins, 1993.

———. *Sarah, HRH The Duchess of York.* London: Fontana/HarperCollins, 1991.

Shew, Betty Spencer. *Queen Elizabeth, the Queen Mother.* London: Macdonald, 1955.

Shupbach, W. ''The Last Moments of HRH The Prince Consort,'' *Medical History* 26 (1982).

Sinclair, David. *Two Georges: The Making of the Modern Monarchy.* London: Hodder & Stoughton, 1988.

Sinclair, Marianne, and Sarah Litvinoff, eds. *The Wit and Wisdom of the Royal Family: A Book of Quotes.* London: Plexus, 1990.

Small, Collie. ''The Blooming of Margaret,'' *Collier's,* July 17, 1948.

Sondern, Frederic, Jr. ''Royal Matriarch,'' *Life,* May 15, 1939.

Stoeckl, Baroness Agnes de. *Not All Vanity.* London: John Murray, 1952.

Strachey, Lytton. *Queen Victoria.* London: Chatto & Windus, 1921.

Taylor, Noreen. ''Saying What Everyone Thinks,'' *The Spectator,* Jan. 7, 1995.

Thornton, Michael. *Royal Feud.* London: Michael Joseph, 1985.

Tomlinson, Richard. *Divine Right: The Inglorious Survival of British Royalty.* London: Little, Brown, 1994.

Townsend, Peter. *Time and Chance.* London: Collins, 1978.

Trzebinski, Errol. *The Lives of Beryl Markham.* London: Heinemann, 1993.

Van der Kiste, John. *Edward VII's Children.* Phoenix Mill, England: Alan Sutton, 1989.

————. *George V's Children.* Phoenix Mill, England: Alan Sutton, 1991.

Vanderbilt, Gloria, and Thelma Lady Furness. *Double Exposure.* London: Frederick Muller, 1958.

Vansittart, Peter. *Happy and Glorious!* London: Collins, 1988.

Varney, Michael, with Max Marquis. *Bodyguard to Charles.* London: Robert Hale, 1989.

Vickers, Hugo. *Cecil Beaton.* London: Weidenfeld and Nicolson, 1986.

Walker, John. *The Queen Has Been Pleased: The Scandal of the British Honours System.* London: Sphere, 1986.

Wallace, Irving. "Princess Elizabeth," *Collier's,* Mar. 22, 1947.

Warwick, Christopher. *The Abdication.* London: Sidgwick & Jackson, 1986.

————. *George and Marina.* London: Weidenfeld and Nicolson, 1988.

Watson, Francis. "The Death of George V," *History Today,* Dec. 1986.

Weinreb, Ben, and Christopher Hibbert. *The London Encyclopedia.* London: Papermac/Macmillan, 1987.

Weintraub, Stanley. *Victoria.* New York: Dutton, 1988.

Weir, Alison. *Britain's Royal Families.* London: The Bodley Head, 1989.

Wheeler-Bennett, John. *King George VI: His Life and Reign.* London: Macmillan, 1958.

Whitaker, James. *Diana v. Charles.* London: Signet, 1993.

Whiting, Audrey. *The Kents.* London: Futura, 1985.

Who's Who 1992. London: A & C Black, 1992.

Wilson, A. N. *The Rise and Fall of the House of Windsor.* London: Sinclair-Stevenson, 1993.

Wilson, Edgar. *The Myth of British Monarchy.* London: Journeyman/Republic, 1989.

Windsor, The Duchess of. *The Heart Has Its Reasons.* London: Michael Joseph, 1956.

Sources

Windsor, HRH The Duke of. *A Family Album.* London: Cassell, 1960.

————. *A King's Story.* London: Cassell, 1951.

————. "My Garden," *Life,* July 16, 1956.

The Windsors. A four-part ITV television series broadcast in the United Kingdom and the United States in 1994; producers and directors, Kathy O'Neill and Stephen White.

Winter, Gordon, and Wendy Kochman. *Secrets of the Royals.* London: Robson, 1990.

Woman's Own, June 16, 1987.

Woodham-Smith, Cecil. *Queen Victoria: Her Life and Times.* London: Hamish Hamilton, 1972.

Woon, Basil. *The Real Sarah Bernhardt.* New York: Boni and Liveright, 1924.

Wrench, John Evelyn. *Geoffrey Dawson and Our Times.* London: Hutchinson, 1955.

Young, Kenneth, ed. *The Diaries of Sir Robert Bruce-Lockhart 1915–1938.* London: Macmillan, 1973.

Ziegler, Philip. *Diana Cooper.* London: Hamish Hamilton, 1981.

————. *King Edward VIII.* New York: Random House, 1991.

Index

487

Index

Index

Index

Index

Picture Credits

Archive Photos: 397 (inset)

Archive Photos/Popperfoto: 1

The Bettmann Archive: 45 (left), 45 (bottom)

Peter Brooker/Rex Features: xvii (top)

Hulton Deutsch: xxix, 45 (top center), 80, 116, 156

Ian Jones/FSP/Gamma: 435

Julian Parker/Gamma-Liaison: xvii (bottom left)

Popperfoto: 25

Press Association: 268

Reuters: 469

Rex Features: xvii (bottom right)

Sygma: 435 (inset)

Topham: 45 (right), 229

UPI/Bettmann: 195, 334, 375, 397

Dorothy Wilding/Camera Press: 297